CONFRONTING REVOLUTION

CONFRONTING REVOLUTION

SECURITY THROUGH DIPLOMACY IN CENTRAL AMERICA

▲▲▲▲▲ EDITED BY

Morris J. Blachman

William M. LeoGrande

Kenneth E. Sharpe

▲▲ PANTHEON BOOKS

▲▲▲▲▲▲ NEW YORK

All rights reserved under International and Pan-American
Copyright Conventions. Published in the United States by
Pantheon Books, a division of Random House, Inc., New York,
and simultaneously in Canada by Random House
of Canada Limited, Toronto.

Library of Congress Cataloging-in-Publication Data

Main entry under title:
Confronting revolution.
   Includes bibliographies and index.
   1. Central America—Foreign relations—United
States—Addresses, essays, lectures. 2. United States—
Foreign relations—Central America—Addresses, essays,
lectures. I. Blachman, Morris J. II. LeoGrande,
William M. III. Sharpe, Kenneth Evan.
F1436.8.U6C66   1986   327.730728   85-43456
ISBN 0-394-55351-9
ISBN 0-394-74453-5 (pbk.)

Designed by Amy Berniker
Manufactured in the United States of America
First Edition

CONTENTS

Part III: CONFRONTING REVOLUTION:
A NEW U.S. FOREIGN POLICY

The fifteen authors and editors of this book came together in the fall of 1982 out of a deep concern to contribute to intelligent debate about United States foreign policy toward Central America. We believed that a widespread ignorance of the realities of the region, and a certain naïveté about U.S. foreign policy, was fueling a rhetorical debate grounded on dangerous myths and wishful thinking.

We agreed that the essential starting point was understanding the past impact of U.S. policies in the region; only such a careful analysis of our successes and failures would allow us to consider realistic alternatives that serve U.S. interests. We recognized that the hard realities of the region posed certain limits on what the United States could do: the United States did not have the hegemony in the area that many policymakers presumed. We understood that ignorance of reality tempted policymakers to substitute rhetoric for analysis: where historical knowledge ebbs, ideology tends to flow. But just as no good businessman would invest millions simply because he wished that markets were structured to his benefit or that consumers ought to want his products, so too must U.S. policies be shaped by a realistic analysis of what is possible—even though many policymakers would wish the facts were different.

It was also important to our working group that the study be nonpartisan. This flowed quite naturally, not only from our desire to be heard by Democrats as well as Republicans, but by our commitment to analyze objectively the strengths and weaknesses of often well-intentioned policies carried out by both Democratic and Republican administrations since World War II. Further, we took seriously certain enduring interests of the United States as well as of the region and these are certainly nonpartisan in nature. We believed that any U.S. policy must take seriously our strategic interests and promote those interests we have in peace, democracy, and a pattern of economic development whose fruits are broadly shared. We were also concerned that the kind of policy we followed in Central America strengthened democratic values in the United States: a duplicitous and dissembling policy that supports tyranny abroad risks creating cynicism and undermining democracy here at home.

Given our dual goals—objective analysis of the impact of U.S. policy in Central America and the formulation of sound policy alternatives—we were careful to include both country experts and foreign-policy experts in the group. Because the regional and international problems are so complex, we also sought to draw the analysts in the group from a wide range of fields: political science, history, economics, anthropology, and sociology.

But we sought more than an anthology of articles representing a broad range of knowledge. We wanted an active interchange so that the foreign policy analysts would learn more of the regional complexities, and country experts would better understand the importance of U.S. interests in the region and be more realistic about policy options. Further, it was important that the dangers of individual bias be minimized by demanding that everyone submit their work to the scrutiny and criticism of the others.

At over a half dozen full meetings of the working group during the two-year period, the authors presented first an outline and then successive drafts of their pieces. In sharp, challenging discussions, sometimes lasting over the course of two full days, we all demanded that analyses be substantiated by the facts, and policy positions be reasoned, realistic, and carefully argued. At over thirty smaller editorial meetings, the editors joined with group members to pore over drafts, all of which were rewritten several times.

There were three other crucial components to the working process. One was fieldwork. To keep abreast of the rapidly changing events in the region and to answer the specific kinds of questions this project demanded, we sought to ensure that everybody in the working group, even those with extensive recent experience, get into the field and find out what was happening there. Some members of the group have been back two, three, and four times since the project began.

A second component was public outreach. Because we wanted this book to respond to the needs of a democratic citizenry, we encouraged, and helped arrange for, members of the working group to speak at a wide range of public forums around the country. Presenting our evolving ideas, leading discussions, and publicly debating the issues served to educate us about the growing questions and concerns U.S. citizens had regarding their country's role in Central America.

Finally, we understood the importance of sharpening our analyses on the grinding stone of questions and criticism from other experts and officials directly involved in formulating and carrying out policy. We met in smaller meetings with congressional staff people, government officials, and members of the foreign policy community. A number of working-group members have briefed congressmen and candidates for public office; and over half the group have been invited to testify at congressional hearings.

This project would not have been possible without the assistance, advice, and criticism of many people and organizations both here and in Central America.

The dozens of working-group meetings and editorial conferences, the fieldwork, and the administrative costs involved in writing would not have been possible without the support of the Tinker Foundation, the Ford Foundation, the Howard Heinz Endowment, the Plumstock Fund, and the Circle Foundation. Students, faculty, and staff at Swarthmore College, The

American University, and the Institute of International Studies of the University of South Carolina made possible the full working-group sessions and contributed intellectually with their questions and comments during public discussions.

Thanks are also due to members of Congress, Congressional staffers, and current and former State Department officials in Washington and at the embassies in Central America. Their knowledgeable and often critical comments during working-group meetings, in interviews, and at roundtable discussions were invaluable in helping us understand the intricasies of policy formulation and administration. Similarly, we are grateful to the dozens of government officials and citizens of Central America who spent countless hours of their valuable time sharing their knowledge, and often their homes, during our field research.

The diversity of views we encountered spurred us on to separate fact from fantasy and to evaluate past and current policies in terms of their actual (not merely desired or claimed) consequences.

Needless to say, all of the people with whom we spoke share some responsibility for shaping our views, though we accept full responsibility for the formulations in this book.

CONFRONTING REVOLUTION

THE ORIGINS OF CRISIS
Peter H. Smith

On January 10, 1978, newspaper editor Pedro Joaquín Chamorro, a leading voice of opposition to Nicaraguan dictator Anastasio Somoza, was gunned down in the streets of the capital, Managua. The city erupted in a spontaneous paroxysm of violence that lasted three weeks, and over the next twenty months the spark of Chamorro's assassination grew into a firestorm of revolution that swept Somoza from power.

The half-century-old Somoza family dynasty was unique in Central America, but the social inequalities and political grievances that led to its downfall certainly were not. The tinder of revolution had been accumulating in Central America for decades. Its explosion in Nicaragua was merely a sign of things to come elsewhere in the region. In the years since the Sandinista guerrillas rode triumphantly into Managua, El Salvador and Guatemala have both been engulfed in civil war, Nicaragua itself has become embroiled in a new military struggle, and Costa Rica and Honduras have been drawn deeper and deeper into the regional maelstrom.

The rapid spread of political turmoil in Central America has commanded the attention of the United States, but Presidents Jimmy Carter and Ronald Reagan, as different in their approaches to the problems of the Third World as any two U.S. Presidents in history, have both been frustrated in their attempts to contain the crisis.

What started this fire in "our own backyard," and why can't we put it out?

The plain truth is that Central America is no longer a collection of sleepy banana republics—the stereotypical U.S. image of the region that for decades was not so far from the truth. Since World War II, fundamental

changes in the nature of Central American society and politics have transformed the region from a pliant backwater into a complex, polarized, and
much less tractable part of the world. How this happened and what it means
for the United States, both amidst the current crisis and in the future, is
the subject of this book.

We will look first at the common historical roots of the current crises and
then examine the different ways the crisis has emerged in each country and
the role played by outside actors. Why are revolutionary movements emerging now? Why in some countries but not others? How have the United
States, Cuba, the Soviet Union, and other regional actors responded (or
contributed) to the outbreak of turmoil?

Our concluding three chapters concern the role of the United States—
what it has been, and what it might be. Our central argument is that the
approaches exemplified by Presidents Carter and Reagan actually share a
broad common perception about our role in Central America. This perception assumes the United States has both the need and the responsibility to
control events in the region in order to protect its own national interests.
The consistent objective of U.S. policy has been to preserve our ability to
exercise this control, or hegemony, and the foremost corollary of that
imperative has been to prevent any government in the region from falling
into the hands of "the left"—i.e., any political movement determined to
bring about a rapid, fundamental transformation of society.

This hegemonic imperative is increasingly out of touch with the realities
in the region. Policies crafted on the basis of it have become not only costly
but also counterproductive to the national interest that this strategic vision
was originally intended to safeguard.

THE ROOTS OF THE CURRENT CRISIS   ▲

Central America, unlike Mexico and Peru, played a minor role in the
Spanish American empire. The Spanish penetrated the region in stages,
forced to conquer a variety of indigenous communities—the Olmec, the
Nahuatl, the Maya. Each conquest required a new government. The result
was decentralization (or, more precisely, an absence of centralization).
Municipalities assumed day-to-day authority, and town councils became the
most important governing bodies.

The church followed closely on the heels of conquest. The Franciscans
and Dominicans in particular took active part in missionary efforts. By the
late seventeenth century, there were 759 churches throughout the area and
the church had become a powerful source of authority.

Economic activity was modest. The first major export was cacao; after
Venezuela preempted this market, indigo and tobacco took over as the
leading commercial items. The social structure was dominated by a white
elite, itself divided between Spanish-born *peninsulares* and locally born
criollos. At the bottom was the labor force, comprised of indigenous peoples

and some African slaves. There also emerged a stratum known as *ladinos*, people of mixed indigenous and white blood who worked as wage laborers or small farmers in the countryside and as artisans, merchants, peddlers, and skilled laborers in the towns. In the eighteenth century they increased their role as the backbone of an emerging middle sector that would gain political importance over the next two centuries. Near the end of the colonial era approximately 4 percent of the region's population was white (either Spanish or creole), about 65 percent was Indian, and 31 percent was *ladino*. [1]

During the 1820s Central America managed to achieve independence from Spain—and from Mexico, to which it had been long subordinate—in a relatively peaceful fashion. As a result, the colonial order survived almost intact, and the isthmus began the independence period as a single political entity, the United Provinces of Central America: Costa Rica, Nicaragua, El Salvador, Honduras, and Guatemala. Panama was still part of Colombia at this time.

The federation fell apart in 1838, but the ideal of unification remained a goal among many Central Americans. At times countries have tried to impose such unification by force, and there has been a tendency from the 1830s to the 1980s to intervene in one another's internal affairs, with border incursions and support for coups and revolutions. There have been other attempts, reflected in the efforts to build a common market in the 1960s, that have stressed cooperation through negotiation. The United States often played a major role in resolving these intercountry disputes.

After independence and the breakup of the federation, the Central American political elite divided into two factions: liberals and conservatives. The conservatives stood for order and the preservation of existing traditions. They upheld Hispanic institutions, especially the church, and they were suspicious of reform. Led by creole landowners, they first advocated free trade, then reverted to a protectionist stance when they felt the impact of British commercial competition.

The liberals, who tended to draw their support from the middle class, which was excluded from the higher circles of the landed creole aristocracy, were less wedded to the creoles' traditional order. They called for increased restrictions on clerical power, for the abolition of slavery, for the elimination of burdensome taxes, and for the promotion of economic growth through laissez-faire policies.

Decades of struggle finally led to the triumph of the liberals in the late nineteenth century. They stripped the church of power and prestige, confiscating lands and terminating the ecclesiastical monopoly on education. As historian Ralph Lee Woodward would later write, "The major role the clergy had played in rural Central America became minor. This was one of the most important changes ever to take place in Central America."[2] Not until the 1960s and 1970s would the church emerge once again as a major influence on the direction of Central American social and political development, and then the church would play a very different role from what it had historically.

Liberals sought to generate growth, profit, and progress through the promotion of free trade, thus integrating their countries into the world economy. Toward this end they forged alliances with merchants, financiers, and investors from Britain, Germany, and North America. They eliminated the traditional communal land rights that had given the Indians at least some legal protection since colonial times. And by converting this land into "private" property, they made it alienable—and opened the way for forcing the Indians off.

The espousal of free-market economics did not mean a commitment to liberal politics. On the contrary, liberals set up "republican dictatorships" that centralized authority and rigged elections in order to keep themselves in power for extended periods. Participation, when there was any, was limited to the wealthy elites. They modernized their military establishments and police forces, which they freely used to intimidate and suppress the opposition. The militaries they created became forces in their own right, and bickering, personalistic factions often removed governments only to find themselves soon challenged by some other faction.

The liberals' economic program stressed export-led growth: agricultural products would be sold abroad and manufactured goods would be imported. The coffee and banana production the local governments encouraged came to dominate the regional economy. And the way these crops came to be produced in each country shaped their social and political structure as well.

While colonial Central America grew modest amounts of coffee, serious production for export began in Costa Rica in the 1830s, and, after 1870, increasing demand in European markets spurred production elsewhere. While they never accounted for more than 15 percent of the world supply, the exports of relatively high-quality Central American coffee were crucial to local economies. By the outbreak of World War I, coffee accounted for 85.2 percent of exports from Guatemala, 80.4 percent from El Salvador, 63.3 percent from Nicaragua, and 35.2 percent from Costa Rica. Bananas accounted for slightly over half the exports of Honduras and Costa Rica.[3]

The coffee boom had profound social and political consequences. Much of the land in the cool, highland slopes where good coffee could be grown was farmed by Indians tilling communal lands or small peasant producers whose plots had previously not been that valuable to large landowners. In El Salvador, Guatemala, and Nicaragua the traditional elites seeking to cash in on the export opportunities therefore attempted to take over these lands, either through fraud or coercion or state power. The resultant plantations, it is worth noting, remained largely in the hands of Central American nationals.[4]

Though liberal leaders sought to encourage immigration, Central America never received the kind of massive, working-class influx that came from Europe to Argentina, Brazil, and the United States. Labor for coffee cultivation was mostly Indian and *ladino* peasants, often those whose lands had been taken away. In time they fell into two groups: *colonos,* who lived on the plantations and leased small plots of land for subsistence cultivation; and *jornaleros,* day laborers who worked for wages while living at home and retaining control of some land. In either case they had close contact with the earth and kept the outlooks of traditional peasants, rather than forging class consciousness as a rural proletariat. To keep these workers under control, national oligarchs employed force—private armies and, later, national militaries—to create a repressive authoritarian state apparatus.

Precise relationships between the elite, the state, and the peasantry varied from country to country because of differing geographic and social conditions. (*Colonos,* for example, could usually be handled by paramilitary forces on the plantations themselves; hired or migrant labor often required use of the army or the police.) Even so, the political economy of coffee produced one general rule: where strong, recalcitrant oligarchs, backed by hard-line officers, came to dominate, the chances for peaceful reform in later decades were slim.

Banana production was quite different. Cultivation demanded the soils and climate of the tropical lowlands and a modern system of transportation to get the highly perishable crop to markets thousands of miles away. Whereas coffee became the economic base for national elites who sold (initially) to European markets, banana production was controlled by U.S. corporations with the capital to build the railroads and ports and to buy the ships to carry the popular fruit to North American markets. Enormous capitalist plantations, employing thousands of wage laborers, became foreign-owned "enclaves" in Honduras, Costa Rica, and Panama.

United Fruit Company (UFCO) was the first. Established in 1899 out of the merger of two railway and shipping companies already deeply involved in the banana trade, it was followed by other smaller companies, some of which merged into other firms like Standard Fruit. A company with many nicknames—"the octopus" was one—UFCO established extensive vertical control over the production and distribution of bananas. Through government concessions and other means, the company acquired vast tracts of land in the hot, humid, sparsely settled Caribbean lowlands. It controlled a regional railroad network through its subsidiary, International Railways of Central America, and built docks and port facilities. In 1913 UFCO created the Tropical Radio and Telegraph Company. Its ships ("the Great White Fleet") came to dominate shipping between Central America and the United States.

It ran its operations like a private government, with little interference from local rulers. Within its enclaves it controlled transportation, communications, schools, and stores and maintained order. Its supervisors and managers came from the United States, notably from the South, and it often imported black workers from Jamaica and the West Indies, altering the racial composition of the eastern lowland population. Because of natural threats from hurricanes and plant disease, UFCO also sought to keep substantial amounts of land in reserve. These could usually be obtained only by government concession, a fact that drew the company into politics.

While UFCO provided jobs (though often to imported labor) and customs revenues and built infrastructure, it made only a limited contribution to development. Local elites had to ship their goods at its rates on its railroads and shipping lines, buy its electric power, and use its telegraph and telephone lines. Its regional power went largely unchallenged and the taxes were low on the enormous profits it took out of the country—at least until the mid-twentieth century.

Its influence on local politics was tremendous. To ensure a docile, non-unionized labor force, to get land concessions, low taxes, and so on, it bribed officials, made and unmade governments, and often called the U.S. government to its assistance. But there was another side to this: to the extent that government revenue depended on the customs duties from the banana companies rather than on taxes from local elites, the state had somewhat more autonomy from the local oligarchs.[5] Furthermore, the banana companies did not require the strong, repressive military and bureaucratic apparatus created by some of the coffee oligarchies: the companies were not taking land in highly populated areas, forcing peasants to work for them and supressing popular revolt. In comparison to coffee, at least, the political economy of bananas created fewer obstacles to social reform.

Coffee and bananas were the basis for the region's export economy for decades. They accounted for more than 70 percent of Central America's exports from 1913 to 1938 and nearly as much in 1960. The proportion began to decline only during the wave of growth involving agricultural diversification and light industrialization in the 1960s. Although the absolute value of coffee and banana exports increased, they accounted for only about 26 percent and 11 percent, respectively, of total exports in 1972. Cotton (11 percent) and other goods (such as meat, sugar, shrimp, refined petroleum, and light manufactures) accounted for the rest.[6]

Reliance on this agro-export system meant that the economic fortunes of the isthmus would depend almost entirely on the vagaries of the international market, and its political fortunes would depend largely on the constellations and power of interests associated with these two agrarian products. When coffee or banana prices were down, earnings were down and there was little room for flexible response. Land in coffee could not be easily or quickly converted to the production of basic foodstuffs, since it takes three to five years before coffee trees begin to produce, making growers reluctant to cut them down, and the foreign banana corporations were generally content to leave land fallow until the market picked up once again.

These agro-export strategies also led to heavy dependence on trade with a single partner: the United States. Although the coffee trade was initially with Europe, from the 1920s through the 1950s the United States purchased 60 to 90 percent of the region's exports and provided a similar share of imports. The North American predominance in international transactions faded to 30 to 40 percent in the mid-1970s for most countries, which were doing more trade than before with each other and Western Europe. Nonetheless, the United States still had considerable commercial leverage over the nations of the isthmus.

The agro-export system discouraged industrialization: the population was small and income distribution so severely skewed that the vast majority was too poor to provide the purchasing power necessary for an adequate market. The agro-commercial elites could make adequate profits from exports and for many years saw little reason to invest in industry. Society remained predominantly rural. Around 1900 less than 10 percent of the Central American population lived in cities; by 1970 the figure ranged between 20 and 40 percent (compared to 66 percent for Argentina, for example, and 61 percent for Chile). Urbanization came late to Central America.

This delay, in turn, meant that Central America never had a substantial urban working class. There are workers in the cities; there have been sporadic efforts at unionization since the 1920s; there has been migration from the countryside, increasing the number of slum dwellers. But the historical deemphasis on manufacturing and the smallness of the cities did not yield working-class movements comparable to those in Chile or Argentina. When urbanization accelerated in the 1970s, there were few institutions such as trade unions or political parties capable of absorbing the social and political tensions produced by rapid change.

Furthermore, the historical deemphasis on manufacturing meant that agriculture was never supplanted by an industry as the dominant sector of the national economy. Of course there were fledgling business groups, most conspicuously in Nicaragua, but they did not become powerful enough to alter the basic social composition of the nation. The fundamental social antagonism remained that between landlords and peasants. When conflict occurred it would tend to follow class lines, and control of land would be the overriding issue.

By the 1950s, however, some of the more developmentally minded leaders in the region sought to promote agricultural and industrial growth by blending infrastructural investments with progressive fiscal policies and, perhaps most importantly, by combining the small national markets into a larger regional one. In 1960, Nicaragua, Guatemala, El Salvador, Honduras, and (two years later) Costa Rica joined to form the Central American Common Market (CACM). The objective of the CACM was to stimulate industrial growth by promoting free trade among member countries while erecting common tariffs to protect infant industries from the competition of lower-price foreign imports. The CACM seemed to promise a way to expand market size without facing the politically difficult task of internal, redistributive reforms—on, say, land and taxes—that were strongly opposed by traditional elites.

The CACM did help spur industrialization and growth; trade among the five countries went from $32 million in 1960 to $260 million in 1969. Foreign capital (largely U.S.) went in to take advantage of the new possibilities. But among the five member countries, the benefits of the new growth were unevenly distributed. Guatemala and El Salvador seemed to move ahead at the expense of Honduras and Costa Rica. These problems were exacerbated by the 1969 clash between Honduras and El Salvador: the tens of thousands of landless and jobless Salvadorans that had been tempted by deteriorating economic conditions to move into less populated Honduras created a reaction among Hondurans that erupted in the so-called "Soccer War." Honduras withdrew from the CACM. Although it negotiated bilateral agreements with the other countries, the common market lost a good deal of precious momentum.[7]

The efforts of the CACM to bring growth in the 1960s coincided with U.S. aid under the Alliance for Progress. Forged in response to the Cuban revolution, the Alliance program sought to remedy the causes of revolutionary upheaval by promoting long-term economic development, social reform, and political democratization: "a common effort," according to its preamble, "to bring our people accelerated economic progress and broader social justice within the framework of personal dignity and political liberty." President John F. Kennedy hoped to place the United States on the side of reformist and democratic forces in Latin America, mostly from the middle sectors—who would, with U.S. support, move against the intransigent right and push both growth and change. Top priorities included land redistribution to create a more equitable social structure and tax reform to finance the agrarian program and other development projects.

But the Alliance also included a military security component designed to defeat any revolutionary challenge that might preempt or disrupt attempts at reform. Security programs came to dominate the Alliance under the Johnson administration and continued to do so into the 1970s under Nixon and Ford. Military training for "internal security" in the U.S.-run School of the Americas (in Panama's Canal Zone at the time) created an officer corps steeped in counterinsurgency doctrines but not particularly reform-minded.[8]

The U.S. Agency for International Development (AID) provided police forces with training as well as arms, antiriot equipment, and communications and transportation technology. Civic action projects designed to improve the image of the military in the eyes of its people allowed many officers "to expand their personal power (and wealth), militarize former civilian sectors of the economy, and establish police networks that could suppress the peasants."[9] Highly trained and proud of their professionalism, the modern officer corps acquired substantial power and potential autonomy from civilian elites; many grew very wealthy on corruption that was often institutionalized; with few exceptions, however, they tended to side with the oligarchs and other conservative forces to block reform in the name of anticommunism.

The Alliance for Progress did support the efforts of the political and economic elites who sought to spur growth through the Central American Common Market. As Richard Newfarmer points out in Chapter 8, commerce among member countries multiplied and the total value of trade rose by an annual rate of 25 percent in the 1960s and 15 percent in the 1970s.

Some light manufacturing flourished (prepared foods, fertilizers, pulp and paper materials, pharmaceuticals, some electrical equipment) as the isthmus embarked on the path of import-substitution industrialization. But the Alliance and the CACM did not produce much economic or political reform. As the Kissinger Commission later noted (without seeing the critical implications for its own similar proposals) "the other two goals of the Alliance, structural change and political democratization, proved much more difficult to achieve."[10]

By the 1970s, all the countries except Costa Rica still remained under the rule of military governments. The light industrialization created jobs but did not increase overall employment levels, given the rural dislocations and rapid population growth. Newfarmer points out that land concentration actually rose in El Salvador, Guatemala, and Nicaragua, as the spread of commercial agriculture worsened the problem of land scarcity. The number of landless increased dramatically to an average of nearly 40 percent of the rural population by the late 1970s. Wealth remained tightly concentrated and per capita incomes low (by 1980 they were still between $528 and $1,512 U.S.). The root of the problem was the failure to reform the rigid social structure that prevented the benefits of growth from even "trickling down" to the poor.

The failure of the Alliance to produce enduring political and economic reform derived from a fundamental misunderstanding of Central (and Latin) America. U.S. policymakers gravely underestimated the power and resilience of the traditional upper classes and they seriously overestimated the capacities of the middle sectors. And in seeking to promote "democracy," Washington tended to give top priority to the holding of orderly elections. Power, said U.S. officials, should be attained by ballots, not by bullets.

The problem with this emphasis was that historically, elections were not a mechanism for transferring power in Central America. Rather than competitive contests, they were efforts to legitimize de facto power, often held by military officers. Except in Costa Rica, participation was low and margins of victory suspiciously high (from the 1930s to the 1980s many winners claimed more than 80 percent of the votes and some have claimed 100 percent). Consequently, few Central Americans put as much faith in elections as did Washington. By failing to comprehend this legacy, U.S. policymakers ended up focusing on the procedural forms of democracy in settings where it had no social content.[11]

Perhaps the most important U.S. miscalculation concerned the role of the armed forces. It saw them, William LeoGrande has pointed out,

> as "military modernizers" who would serve as allies of the middle sectors rather than as guardians of the status quo. Once the counterinsurgency programs of the Alliance had defeated the guerrillas, who had been inspired by the Cuban revolution, the fear that insurrection would sweep the continent dissipated and the traditional elites of Latin America lost all interest in reform. The growth of their military capability reassured them that pressures

for change could be resisted, and in short order, the guns were turned against
the democratic reformers.[12]

Notwithstanding these failures, the Alliance for Progress and the common
market gave impetus to new social forces in rural and urban areas. Popular
associations and political parties were organized and began pushing for the
kinds of reform that the Alliance had sought.

In rural areas, the successful blocking of land reform by traditional elites
was accompanied by the expansion of export agriculture, which worsened
the inequities in the countryside. Land formerly dedicated to small-scale
production of subsistence crops was taken over and turned into large-scale,
commercial farms to produce new crops like cotton and sugar, and to
expand coffee and banana production. Displaced peasants were forced to
seek scarce work for low wages. Others moved to the towns and cities where
they lived in sprawling slums. The economic downturn of the late 1970s
and early 1980s made their bad situation even worse.

In many areas, urban and rural poor began to be welded into a new social
force by the Catholic church. The revitalization of the church was especially
important in Nicaragua and El Salvador, but affected Guatemala and Honduras as well. Two events marked the shift in the role of the church: the
Second Ecumenical Council of the early 1960s (Vatican II), and the conference of Latin American Bishops at Medellín, Colombia, in 1968. The
Medellín conference, particularly, denounced capitalism and communism as
equal affronts to human dignity and placed the blame for hunger and misery
on the rich and powerful. To redress these inequalities the bishops called
for more education, increased social awareness, and the creation of *comuni-
dades de base*, Christian base communities of not more than a few dozen
people each. The communities became the nucleus for what the church
called its "preferential option for the poor." Layworkers, nuns, priests, and
some members of the hierarchy supported a new catechism, which raised
the social consciousness of thousands of Catholics and was itself spurred
on by the interpretation of the meaning of the scriptures for everyday life
undertaken by the study groups in the local base communities. Convinced
of the importance of social justice—access to jobs and land to live "by the
sweat of their brows" and to educate and feed and clothe their families,
many were spurred to organize local community self-help groups, cooperatives, peasant organizations, Christian-oriented unions, and other popular
organizations. It was often the repression of such popular and reformist
organizations that antagonized their members and helped forge an alliance
between them and more secular, radical, Marxist groups.

While the new social forces stimulated by growth without reform were
being organized by sectors of the Catholic church, important changes were
also taking place among the urban middle and working classes. While
urbanization was modest by Latin American standards, the growing state
bureaucracies, the expansion of business and industry, and the dislocation
in rural areas rapidly enlarged the urban population. The most active

groups in Central America's cities generally consisted of middle-sector merchants and professionals—lawyers, journalists, intellectuals, and students. These groups now sought to organize reformist political movements, center and center-left political parties (eg., Christian Democratic and Social Democratic parties). They expanded their base to include urban workers (who themselves were sometimes able to form unions) in the new industries as well as in more traditional sectors (transportation, utilities, communications). The reform parties frequently propounded improved minimum wages and land reform and produced a considerable number of civilian and political leaders. And in some instances, they sought alliances with popular organizations in rural areas.

The pattern of growth and deprivation thus exerted great pressure on Central American society as new social forces mobilized to push for justice and reform. At times, Cuba, Venezuela, and other countries sought to involve themselves, but the development of insurgency and revolution generally had little to do with such external interference. The new social forces—unleashed by uneven economic growth and rural dislocations, fed on promises of reform, and organized into new associations by the church, by labor and peasant leaders, and by centrist and leftist political parties— demanded change.

THE CURRENT CRISIS   ▲

If the pressures for reform were common, the organization, demands, and strengths of these new social forces were different. So too were the responses: existing elites had to choose whether or not to open the political and economic system or to violently repress those new groups demanding access. Two general patterns emerged. In Honduras, Panama, and Costa Rica, less powerful and less reactionary economic elites, together with less hard-line military officers, were open to at least some social change. Relatively autonomous states have been able to devise and implement meaningful reformist policies. As a result, there have been no serious revolutionary challenges in these countries.

In Costa Rica, its traditional coffee elite was less economically powerful and historically more open to change than the coffee oligarchs of its northern neighbors; it had reformist leaders powerful and wise enough to eliminate the major obstacle to democracy in the region, the military, and it had a military small and weak enough to be disbanded. It had a large agrarian middle class, and a broad, cross-class coalition gradually built legitimate political institutions that were able to respond to demands for reform. While Costa Rica faces serious problems today, it has not had to confront revolutionary upheaval.

To a significant, if lesser, extent, Panama and Honduras—which for different reasons lacked well-organized, entrenched oligarchies and strong, repressive militaries—were also able to leave open channels for reform, at least until the early 1980s. They faced coups, political instability, land seizures, and other turmoil, but not armed revolution.

A second pattern emerged in El Salvador, Guatemala, and Nicaragua. Powerful and recalcitrant elites, backed by increasingly strong militaries, met efforts at reform with brutal repression that ignited the flames of insurgency and revolution. Where the radical movements have been strong and cohesive relative to the right-wing elites, they have either overthrown the old regime (as in Nicaragua where a cross-class coalition united against a common enemy, the Somoza dynasty, leaving it and its national guard isolated both from its own society and from U.S. support); or they have fought to a paralyzing stalemate (as in El Salvador, where a cohesive oligarchy and U.S.-backed military have offered harsh resistance). Where less well-organized insurgents have faced a strong oligarchy and powerful military, as in Guatemala, the result has been cycles of repression, temporary calm, new attempts at reform, followed by repression, renewed insurgency, and ever bloodier repression.

Until the outbreak of open insurrection in Nicaragua following Chamorro's assassination, Washington was oblivious to the gathering storm in Central America. The official violence of the region's governments had produced some criticism in Washington, but—except for the issue of the Panama Canal—Central America was peripheral to the foreign policies of Nixon, Ford, and Carter. It had not always been so peripheral.

As the United States emerged as a global actor at the turn of the nineteenth century, Central America assumed unprecedented importance in Washington. Instability in the border regions of the United States came to be regarded as intolerable—a threat both to the growing U.S. economic interests in the periphery and to the security of the Panama Canal. The doctrines of Gunboat Diplomacy and Dollar Diplomacy symbolized the resolve of the United States to exclude all European economic or political influence from the Caribbean Basin.

The Central American nations were so small and weak that the weight of U.S. power reduced the region to a virtual protectorate. United States ambassadors amounted to proconsuls, and Central American governments rose or fell on the strength of Washington's approval. When this was not sufficient, the marines were sent with dispatch.

As the United States exercised its power in favor of stability, it inevitably came to be identified as an ally of the existing elite—the landed oligarchy. The United States became, in other words, a partisan actor in Central American society. In some cases, such as Guatemala, the partnership was real and profitable. In others, like Nicaragua, it was more a matter of Washington's indifference to the plight of the poor so long as their overseers were friends of the United States.

Franklin D. Roosevelt's Good Neighbor Policy provided a brief respite from direct U.S. intervention in Latin America, but the Cold War brought a revival of Washington's fears about foreign penetration of its border regions and a return to the interventionist predilections of the past. Ironically, the new interventions were prompted by the collapse of regimes that were the legacy of Gunboat Diplomacy. The demise of dictatorships in Guatemala (1944), Cuba (1959), and the Dominican Republic (1961) ushered in populist and nationalist regimes that Washington feared would erode U.S. hegemony in the region and be the prelude to the spread of communism.

In Guatemala and Santo Domingo, U.S. intervention, covert and overt, was able to restore the old order. In Cuba, the effort at the Bay of Pigs failed, however, and Washington's worst nightmare was suddenly realized: an indigenous, nationalist revolution evolved into a communist regime allied with the Soviet Union. In the decades since the Cuban revolution, virtually all of U.S. policy toward Latin America can be traced to Washington's obsession with preventing "another Cuba." Policy toward Central America has certainly been no exception.

As Robert Trudeau and Lars Schoultz indicate in their essay, Guatemala was the first Central American nation to experience the rise of a reformist challenge to the oligarchic order. The revolution of 1944 brought to power a reformist coalition of the center-left. For a time, it seemed as if the new regime might be able to consolidate itself and create a broadly based electoral system responsive to popular demands for change. But in Guatemala, where the local landed elite was in partnership with powerful agribusiness interests in the United States, to attack the established social order meant to engender the wrath of Washington.

The overthrow of the government of Jacobo Arbenz Guzmán by the Central Intelligence Agency (CIA) in 1954 marked the defeat of the first reformist challenge in the region and set the pattern for oligarchic response to demands for change. To a certain extent, it also set the pattern for the United States' reaction to the specter of instability that inevitably accompanied efforts to topple the old order.

The defeat of Arbenz produced a generation of political turmoil in Guatemala. Despite the concerted efforts of the armed forces, demands for change unleashed during the brief interlude of the popular government have never been fully extirpated, though many of the people bold enough to give public voice to such demands have been. Two guerrilla wars and a third (now in temporary remission) have demonstrated the futility of seeking a military solution, not just to the conflict in Guatemala but to the Central America crisis as a whole.

In their chapter on El Salvador, Martin Diskin and Kenneth Sharpe chart the rise of the Christian Democratic and Social Democratic reform movements in the 1960s, culminating in their electoral victory in 1972, and then their decimation during the 1970s at the hands of the armed forces and the rightist death squads.

The short-lived coalition government of October 1979 that combined moderate civilians and reformist military officers was the last hope for avoiding full-scale civil war in El Salvador. Blocked at every turn by the power of the oligarchy and the traditional right in the officer corps, the coalition government collapsed just a few months after coming to power. For the already powerful radical left, the demise of the October regime was the last straw. Joined by many of the moderate politicians who had participated in the October experiment, the left gave up any hope of breaking the oligarchy's stranglehold on Salvadoran society without intensive armed struggle. For its part, the right abandoned all restraint in dealing with its political adversaries; over the next few years, over 40,000 noncombatant civilians suspected of dissidence lost their lives at the hands of the military and its associated death squads.

As the war in El Salvador escalated, so too did the role of the United States. From only marginal involvement in 1979, Washington had become, by 1985, the principal architect, financier, and strategist for the Salvadoran government in general and the armed forces in particular. Paradoxically, though the regime in San Salvador came to rely more and more crucially upon the Washington for its survival, the ability of the United States to control events in El Salvador seemed to improve hardly at all. What Secretary of State Alexander Haig had predicted would be a six months' war was still going strong—and still at a stalemate—fully six years later.

Of all the nations in Central America, none has had a longer or less pleasant association with the United States than Nicaragua. Occupied by the marines almost continuously from 1912 to 1933, Nicaragua was left with the Somoza family dynasty when the United States finally departed. The revolutionaries of the 1970s took their name and inspiration from Augusto César Sandino, a guerrilla hero who resisted the U.S. occupation during the 1920s and 1930s, only to be assassinated by the first Somoza after the marines had withdrawn.

Nicaragua, of course, had the first successful revolution in Central America, and so has become a symbol of hope for revolutionaries throughout the region and a symbol of apocalypse for defenders of the status quo. Dennis Gilbert looks closely at the period since the triumph of the revolution in 1979, a period of conflict and turmoil only slightly less intense than the period of the insurrection against Somoza. The Nicaraguan upper class, part of which joined with the Sandinistas to oust Somoza, has not been willing or able to accommodate itself to a new regime in which it has little or no influence, and that it suspects of harboring plans for the ultimate dissolution of private enterprise. Nor have the Sandinistas had much tolerance for a private sector that shares none of their objectives regarding the radical redistribution of wealth and income in the new Nicaragua.

Washington has not accepted its loss of influence in Nicaragua either. After trying mightily to keep the Sandinistas out of power, the Carter administration resolved to try to find a modus vivendi with the revolutionary government. The Reagan administration, however, proved less tolerant of ideological pluralism, at least on the left, and launched a covert war in the hope of ousting the Sandinistas and restoring a regime more congenial to the interests and influence of the United States.

Next to El Salvador, Honduras has received the lion's share of increased military assistance from the United States and has become a key staging area for U.S. military operations directed toward both El Salvador and Nicaragua. Philip Shepherd's essay addresses these issues but also looks at Honduras itself to see what impact this rapid expansion of U.S. presence is having on the fabric of Honduran society and politics.

Honduras, like Costa Rica, has always been exceptional among the nations of Central America. Though it never developed democratic political institutions like those of Costa Rica, it nevertheless managed to avoid the political polarization and violence that engulfed all its neighbors. Underdeveloped even by Central American standards, Honduran inequality was never so acute nor its social structure so rigid as in El Salvador, Guatemala, or Nicaragua. As political turmoil spread through the region in the late 1970s, Honduras seemed to be the one country in the northern tier that might find a peaceful evolutionary path to democratic political development and socioeconomic reform.

The United States initially tried to promote such changes and had some success. But as the war in El Salvador escalated and the covert war against Nicaragua was launched, these conflicts came to dominate U.S. policy toward Honduras. Strategically located in heart of the region, Honduras was the perfect site for an expanded U.S. military presence, and this objective was given priority over political and economic reforms in Honduras itself.

Costa Rica is the nation in Central America that has always been so different that it seems to belong somewhere else in the hemisphere. Since 1948, Costa Rica has had a functioning democracy that seems to lose none of its legitimacy even in times of intense economic stress. A series of social welfare programs smooth out, to some extent, the extremes of wealth and poverty in Costa Rican society and give the average citizen a sense that government is responsive to his basic needs and demands. In short, Costa Rica embodies all the virtues the United States would like to promote elsewhere in the region.

Morris Blachman and Ronald Hellman offer an explanation for Costa Rica's happy exceptionalism and some cautions about vulnerabilities that threaten to rend the social contract that has insulated Costa Rica from political violence. A key element in the equation is the United States, which in the past few years has sought to draft Costa Rica into the covert war against Nicaragua—against the better judgment of many Costa Rican politicians and the traditions of Costa Rican foreign policy.

Panama is often viewed as part of South America rather than Central America, both because of its origins as a part of Colombia and its level of economic and social development. Thomas Bossert's chapter on Panama belongs in this book for several reasons. The Panama Canal continues to be one of the major factors cited in Washington for U.S. concern over the turmoil in Central America, so the internal condition and international position of Panama has an important bearing on the regional crisis.

Moreover, the Panamanians themselves have played an active role in Central America from the outbreak of the Nicaraguan insurrection right up to the present. It was Panama, more than Cuba, that helped provide the Sandinistas with the arms they used to defeat Somoza's national guard. Since 1983, Panama has been a member of the Contadora group (along with Mexico, Colombia, and Venezuela), which has tried to help negotiate a regional political solution to the Central American conflict.

Part I concludes with Richard Newfarmer's analysis of the economic problems facing all the Central American nations and what needs to be done for them to begin to escape the economic downslide that they have endured since the late 1970s. He begins by examining the links among these economies and between them and the international market. Despite the advances of the Central American Common Market, the region remains deeply dependent for its economic well-being on the export of agricultural goods to the United States. The global recession of the early 1980s, coming on the heels of the second round of petroleum price increases, sent the Central American economies into a tailspin. By the time world trade began to recover, Central America was already engulfed in war, and its economies were suffering both the direct consequences of war damage and the indirect consequences of distortion and militarization. Peace, then, remains the first precondition for real economic recovery in the region.

Reasonable discussion of Central America must pay careful heed to the regional actors and international forces that have affected the crisis. This is the subject of Part II of the book.

Washington has often laid most of the blame for the crisis on Cuba and the Soviet Union. William LeoGrande's essay shows that the Cubans have been intensely interested in the Central American conflict and have consistently supported revolutionary forces there, sometimes with material aid. Nevertheless, the Cubans have shown a conspicuous degree of caution, urging the Sandinistas to moderate their domestic and international policies in order to stay on good terms with the West in general and the United States in particular. In El Salvador, the Cubans have urged the guerrilla opposition to enter negotiations with the regime and to settle for a role in a coalition government, rather than holding out for military victory. Finally, the Cubans have endorsed the Contadora initiative, in effect agreeing to reduce their own presence in the region in pursuit of a regional peace agreement.

Cole Blasier's essay on the Soviet Union traces the history of Soviet involvement in Central America—a region remote from the areas of primary geostrategic concern to Moscow. While there is little doubt that the Soviets would be happy to see the United States embroiled in difficulty in the region and would be even happier to see the emergence of regimes hostile to the United States, the Soviets appear to be unwilling to pay any significant costs to achieve these outcomes. Their refusal to offer the Sandinistas foreign assistance in the form of hard currency shows the limit of their generosity and ambition in the region. If Nicaragua is to become "another Cuba," the Sandinistas will have to finance the experiment on their own; the cost of the first Cuba seems to be as much as the Soviets are willing to bear.

Support for insurgents in the region is much cheaper, of course, but the Soviet Union has taken very little direct role in the provision of such aid. Until 1979–1980, in fact, there was no significant material assistance flowing to Central American revolutionaries from the Eastern bloc, including Cuba. When there has been a significant flow of such assistance, as there apparently was to the Salvadoran rebels in late 1980, it has been channeled through Cuba.

Terry Karl's chapter focuses on other important regional actors: the Latin American nations who flank the Central American region, and who therefore have a great stake in the outcome of the conflicts there. In 1983, Mexico, Venezuela, Colombia, and Panama banded together in the hope that they could help in the search for a regional political solution to the spreading conflict. The Contadora process originated as an effort to avert direct U.S. military intervention in Central America, an eventuality that all the Contadora states agreed would be profoundly destabilizing, not just in the region but beyond it as well. Yet each of these nations has bilateral relations with the United States that are tremendously important to them, dwarfing the significance of Central America. This paradox has kept the Contadora states from asserting themselves against the direct wishes of Washington, and has therefore given the United States effective veto power over any agreement.

Moreover, each of the four member states has different expectations and objectives in the peace process, which leads to complex internal bargaining among them. And, of course, each has a domestic political context that affects the formulation of its Contadora position. Yet despite these difficulties and complications, the Contadora process remains for many observers the best available hope for ending the Central American conflict, short of direct U.S. intervention or regional war.

The chapters in Part III focus on the single most important actor in the Central American drama: the United States. They emphasize the difficulties that have been created by the often unrealistic character of U.S. foreign policy in the region. Evidence shows that the assumed means for protecting U.S. national interests—controlling events in order to keep the left out of power—have not only been growing more costly but also have been counterproductive to the actual ends of U.S. interests.

In order to understand this policy from Washington's perspective, the first chapter of Part III surveys the efforts of both the Carter and Reagan administrations to cope with the escalating regional crisis. These two presidents approached the problem of Third World conflict from perspectives that were diametrically opposed. They sought to solve the problem of Central America with very different strategies and instruments of policy. Yet underlying these deep differences was an element of essential unity: both sought to prevent the radical left from having any significant role in politics, i.e., to prevent "another Cuba." Both began from the presumption that it was within the rights of the United States and within our power to control the outcome of events in the region at least to that extent. And from this essential similarity in objectives came a similarity of effect: both administrations found themselves frustrated in their ability to exercise the degree of control that Washington has typically been able to exert in Central America.

The succeeding chapter takes a step back in time to look more closely at the evolution of U.S. policy in the Caribbean Basin and to identify the source of this hegemonic vision that has been at the root of U.S. policy for over three-quarters of a century. It then explores why traditional methods of control no longer work.

The final chapter looks forward, offering a new policy of principled realism for our relations with the nations of Central America, based not upon the presumptions of Gunboat Diplomacy but upon the realities of our complex interdependent world.

▲ ▲ ▲ ▲ ▲ ▲ INSIDE CENTRAL AMERICA
▲ ▲ THE IMPACT OF U.S. POLICY

2

GUATEMALA
Robert Trudeau
and Lars Schoultz

For decades, reform-minded Guatemalans have sought in vain to use peaceful, constitutional procedures to address the pressing problems of persistent, chronic deprivation. A privileged minority controlling the political system and armed forces has responded with increasing violence and terror. Frustrated in their attempts at peaceful change, and in some cases wishing to protect themselves from repression, many reformers have turned to clandestine movements that aim to change the basic nature of Guatemalan political and economic structures. Decades of conflict—often violent—have severely damaged the Guatemalan political system. Middle-class reformers who might have been a source of moderation have been barred from power, although not necessarily prevented from holding office.

The United States has often supported one faction or another of the oligarchic minority in power, not only worsening the situation for most Guatemalans but also reducing policy options and making the achievement of the stated U.S. goals of reform and democracy less likely. The result today is a political process characterized by extreme polarization, repression, and violence.

A more effective, realistic U.S. policy requires an understanding of the historical background to the current situation in Guatemala.

ORIGINS OF THE CURRENT CRISIS   ▲

From Colonialism to Military-Oligarchic Alliance

Guatemala's history is typical of Latin America: a disruptive conquest, European colonization, independence, and then personalist rule by *caudillos* backed by a politically prominent military. But explaining Guatemala's current crisis demands an understanding of important differences: the specific changes in the uses of natural resources and labor, in the composition and strength of Guatemala's economic elites, and in the impact of international forces on the domestic economy.

The Spanish conquest did not mark the beginning of elite domination in Guatemala. Religious and military elites had dominated the Indian masses for centuries prior to the arrival of the Spanish. Although not idyllic, the life of the majority of inhabitants was not desperate either. The rural subsistence sector of the economy, comprising the vast majority of the people had reasonable access to productive land and adequate nutrition.[1] There was no word for infant malnutrition in the detailed Mayan medical lexicon.[2]

The Spanish conquest established a new elite, one oriented toward using Guatemala's land and labor to produce wealth not only for itself but also for the colonial power, Spain. This new elite used religion and military power to maintain order, expropriate land, and control agricultural labor. Spanish colonization marked the beginning of a systematic and largely uninterrupted decline in the quality of life, especially in nutrition, for most Guatemalans.

Independence in the 1820s removed the political limitations the Spanish crown had imposed on the local elite, opened up new trade opportunities, and generated liberal-conservative conflicts. Until 1871, however, the economic system and class structure changed little from that created by the Spanish authorities.[3] The Great Liberal Reform that began in 1871, one of the two or three most important events in Guatemalan history, reflected the growth in international demand for coffee. Prior to the 1870s, much of the land best suited for coffee was still in Indian communal landholdings, planted in corn, beans, and other staples. The Liberal Reform—a series of laws—eliminated communal holdings and created mechanisms by which the new "private land" of the Indians could be "acquired." In a few short years, Guatemala's coffee oligarchy consolidated its economic power; the army maintained order for the oligarchy.

Although agricultural modernization and increased demand for coffee produced wealth for property owners, the increased poverty of the now landless peasants, most of whom became part of a forced labor system, led to unrest, including many Indian rebellions.[4] The use of a variety of coercive tactics—the dissolution of villages, forced relocation of groups, seizure of land, and systematic violence—was effective in crushing and then discouraging peasant revolts. Vagrancy laws forced workers to provide

cheap or free labor for plantation owners, who relied on government violence to break strikes and quell union activities.

This period, a century ago, set today's internal dynamics in place: an
economy producing wealth for a small minority through dependence on
exports and foreign capital; a political system based on a selective version
of classical liberalism, especially the protection of property rights; and a
continuing reliance on the army to suppress resistance by groups whose
quality of life declined because of these "reforms."

The 1944 Revolution: Unsuccessful Reform

In 1944, first in June and again in October, successful rebellions marked
the end of an era in Guatemala. The groups that led the October Revolution
were urban, mostly middle class, including businesspeople, students, and
intellectuals. They based their movement on the ideas of freedom and
democracy espoused by Franklin D. Roosevelt, and on the example of social
reforms promulgated during the presidency of Lázaro Cárdenas in Mexico
from 1934 to 1940.[5] These "foreign" ideas did not cause the rebellion,
however. Its roots lay in the economic stagnation that had characterized
Guatemala since the collapse of its export economy at the onset of the Great
Depression in 1929. This collapse and continuing stagnation during World
War II led to increasing frustration within the middle class. The goals of
the rebellion were therefore aimed at reforms, political as well as economic,
but not toward any radical departure from the norms of Western development. They were Guatemala's equivalent of the New Deal.

Although some elements of the military resisted the rebellion, younger
officers lent their support. The three-person junta that emerged after the
successful October rebellion included two military officers, one representing
the traditional Army of the pre-1944 period and the other representing the
new, reformist, nationalist movement within the military.[6]

The reforms of Juan José Arévalo, who was elected president in 1945,
were important in dismantling years of dictatorship and in creating structures that would allow for the development of democracy. Arévalo's government eliminated the semifeudal systems of peonage and forced labor, established judicial procedures to ensure protection of workers' rights, and
tamed the violent misuse of power that had marked the Jorge Ubico regime
that preceded the 1944 rebellion. The Law of Forced Rental, for example,
obliged large landowners to lease uncultivated land at low rates to landless
campesinos.

Most important, however, was the government's assistance in creating
structures and institutions that encouraged the mobilization and participation of what are known in Latin America as "popular" groups.[7] For example, legal support was given to cooperatives and labor unions as well as to
organizations of professionals and businesspeople. Rural workers and peasants were given certain legal protections: the rights of working-class people

to vote, unionize, bargain, and strike marked their first participation in national political life. By 1950, the government had established a social security system. But these reforms, mild by U.S. standards, were threatening to elements in the oligarchy and conservative wing of the military. Arévalo faced numerous coup attempts before he turned over the presidency to a second elected administration, that of Jacobo Arbenz Guzmán.

An army colonel from the nationalist reformist wing of the military, Arbenz took office in 1951. He sought to build upon earlier reforms by expanding democracy, specifically by mobilizing the still largely excluded rural working class and Indians into the national political community. As with the Alliance for Progress that was to follow in less than a decade, Arbenz's political reforms were based upon economic reforms. Arbenz knew, as John F. Kennedy knew, that an expanded democracy could work only if economic reforms provided land for destitute rural workers. And also like Kennedy, Arbenz sought to promote economic growth that was primarily capitalist but nationally controlled.[8]

Arbenz's efforts to move Guatemala toward a more nationalist economic development enjoyed the support of the nationalist sector in the military. But he was opposed by the traditional sector, whose members thought of themselves as the guardians of the existing order. Part of the urban business community favored the reforms that would expand domestic markets and diversify the economy, but the traditional coffee oligarchy preferred the export orientation of earlier periods. Not unexpectedly, they particularly opposed any policy that would increase the political or economic power of newly mobilized social groups. The oligarchy thus fought both the increased power of urban labor and the mild land reform—and its historic control over land and labor made it a formidable opposition.

The centerpiece of Arbenz's program was agrarian reform, but it called only for the expropriation of unused land with compensation for landowners —precisely the type of agrarian reform the United States encouraged throughout Latin America in the early 1960s.[9] But this was the early 1950s: land reform seemed radical, and this one touched U.S. corporate interests. Indeed, a major target was the United Fruit Company, *not* because of any ulterior political motive but because it was a major holder of unused land. In 1953, Arbenz announced that his government would redistribute 234,000 acres of the Fruit Company's land, none of which was being cultivated at the time. Indeed, UFCO was using only 139,000 of its more than 3 million acres, which was 42 percent of the nation's land. In Guatemala in 1952, no agrarian reform could have been successful without affecting some of UFCO's land. The government offered $1 million in compensation, based on UFCO's earlier self-assessed valuation of the land for tax purposes: UFCO demanded $16 million.[10]

Other policies that had the effect of reducing UFCO's economic monopoly soon followed: a proposal to build an electrical plant for Guatemala City to supplement the UFCO-owned service; new roads to compete with UFCO's railroad lines; and new port facilities on the Caribbean coast, where UFCO owned the only port. In 1953, the government intervened—that is, assumed managerial control but not ownership in UFCO's electric utility and railroad.

U.S. policymakers came to perceive the Arbenz reforms as steps toward communism rather than toward a Guatemalan "New Deal." United Fruit Company's fierce opposition to the reforms helped create this perception. It put its full weight behind the idea of overthrowing the Arbenz regime. The company received strong backing from Secretary of State John Foster Dulles—who prior to becoming Secretary of State had been a partner in UFCO's law firm, Sullivan and Cromwell—and from his brother, CIA director Allen Dulles.[11] While UFCO's business connections to Dulles may have influenced U.S. policy, a more significant congruence of interest was created by the Cold War ideology through which U.S. policymakers viewed Latin America in general and Guatemala in particular.[12] John Foster Dulles himself remarked that

> if the United Fruit matter were settled, if they gave us a gold piece for every banana, the problem would remain just as it is today as far as the presence of communist infiltration is concerned.[13]

Encouraged by UFCO's crude Red-baiting and by the Cold War McCarthyism of the time, U.S. policymakers perceived Arbenz's land reform as a general attack on private property, and his attacks against UFCO as attacks against the United States. Arbenz's decision to legalize the Communist Party, called the Guatemalan Labor Party (PGT), and to bring some of its leaders into his government had little impact on the reformist character of the regime, but it exacerbated conflicts with opposition groups in Guatemala and reinforced the "Communist" image the State Department and UFCO were creating.[14]

Once Arbenz had been perceived as a communist, the die was cast. The CIA proceeded not only to arm and train (at a UFCO plantation in Honduras) 170 Guatemalan exiles, led by a conservative colonel, Carlos Castillo Armas, but directly supervised their invasion of Guatemala from Honduras.[15] Ironically, the relatively slow pace of Arbenz's reforms meant that rural popular organizations were not yet sufficiently strong to defend democracy. Some of the more rapidly developing urban labor unions might have helped defend the government, but they were not armed or trained for such a task, and Arbenz hesitated to do so for fear of triggering dissent among the military. The unprepared military did not join the coup attempt, but in an extraordinarily confused situation (highlighted by intensive CIA-directed radio propaganda and mock air raids over the capital city) it was unwilling or unable to fight the invasion. The coffee oligarchy and conservative elements of the military, who by themselves had not been strong enough to overthrow Arbenz, welcomed the counterrevolution.

Counterrevolution: Repression and "Modernization"

The invasion of Guatemala by the CIA-organized "Liberation Army" and the Counterrevolution of 1954 ended Guatemala's only serious attempt at reformist democracy. But inside Guatemala, dismantling the previous reforms was no easy task.

The "anti-reforms" of the new Castillo Armas government included the repeal of universal suffrage, the cancellation of the registrations of 533 unions, and the revision of the nation's labor laws to make effective labor organizing impossible.[16] The number of organized workers dropped from over 100,000 in 1954 to fewer than 27,000 in 1955.[17] Land reform was reversed: peasant beneficiaries were dispossessed and their land returned to previous owners. Less than 0.5 percent of the approximately 100,000 beneficiaries under Arbenz remained on their lands by the end of 1956.[18]

Undoing these reforms meant excluding thousands of Guatemalans from politics. But those who had joined labor unions, peasant cooperatives, new political parties, and other such organizations were no more willing to lose their participatory status than American citizens would be willing to be forced to sit in the back of the bus again because of their skin color. These recently enfranchised Guatemalans had gained immensely from the democratic reform period.

Large-scale repression was thus needed not only to undo the reforms but also to destroy the organizations and institutions that had implemented and benefited from the reforms. "Large numbers of executions occurred," writes Walter LaFeber. "How many fell victim to Castillo Armas' firing squads is unclear, although at least several hundred faced the rifles. . . . The leaders of urban and peasant unions became special targets. Those organizations were wiped out for the next decade."[19] Richard Adams also notes that "unions, political parties, agrarian committees, and mass organizations were declared illegal and eliminated. Thousands of the leaders and participants were jailed for varying periods."[20]

Economic Change and the Counterrevolution

Change in the post-1954 period was not limited to the destruction of reform programs and democratic institutions but affected Guatemala's economic system as well.

Prior to 1954, President Arbenz had sought to orient Guatemala's economy away from its almost total dependence on exports and its dominance by foreign companies, specifically the United Fruit Company, toward more diversity. To accomplish this, part of his program called for the creation of a Guatemalan business sector that would, in effect, compete with the traditional oligarchy; in short, Arbenz espoused a program of economic modernization with state assistance. The model was capitalist, but nationalist in orientation, and included socioeconomic reforms as part of the build-ing of a strong economy.

At the time of the counterrevolution, the upper-sector groups were more diverse economically than the coffee-based oligarchy of the pre-1944 era. This diversity increased as governments after Castillo Armas allowed or encouraged industrialization and agricultural diversification (cotton, sugar, cattle), and opened Guatemala to foreign investment (in such industries as banking, mining, food processing, pharmaceuticals, oil refining, paper, and steel tubing). Not surprisingly, among these upper-sector groups, conflicts arose over government policies (tax policy, infrastructure expenditures, and tariff protection), and powerful private associations grew up to protect the economic interests of their members. Despite the conflicts between new and old economic elites, all were willing to agree on one crucial point: land ownership was not to be touched. These attitudes, combined with the ruthless use of repression after 1954, meant that by 1960, the "Guatemalan model" had become "economic modernization *without* social reform."

The performance of this economy was, however, disappointing during the 1954 to 1962 period.[21] But a change in U.S. policy helped spur growth. Prior to 1961, U.S. economic assistance programs in Latin America were extremely modest, an indication of U.S. concern for the region. Then came the explosion of the Cuban Revolution, and shortly thereafter, the inaugura-tion of President Kennedy led directly to the Alliance for Progress, which shifted U.S. policy toward direct governmental assistance for Latin Ameri-can economic growth. The infusion of capital and the support for private investment in Guatemala was used to promote a strong export orientation, to push for economic integration throughout Central America, to stress agricultural and industrial diversification, and to fund the development of infrastructure.[22] And, at various times and with varying degrees of effort, the United States attempted to promote various reforms in Guatemala, including tax and agrarian reforms and support for cooperatives. These reforms, which differed very little from those of the Arbenz period, were central goals of the Alliance for Progress.

U.S. support for Guatemala's economy resulted in improved macroeco-nomic performance. The decade of the 1960s was a period of economic growth: real gross national product (GNP) grew at about twice the rate of population growth until the late 1970s.[23] New export commodities flour-ished. Coffee's share of total agricultural exports declined, while cotton grew to become the second most important crop. Sugar production spurted after Guatemala received part of the U.S. sugar quota that was taken from Cuba. The production of meat for U.S. fast-food chains also grew into a major export activity.[24] Central American integration via the Common Market also encouraged economic prosperity for the business sector in Guatemala.

Reform programs, however, failed to be enacted or implemented. Agrar-ian reform was scarcely mentioned in Guatemala because of its association with the Arbenz regime, despite American suggestions that agrarian reform was necessary. The Alliance for Progress's tax reform proposals initially received wide publicity, but they were abandoned when the Guatemalan elite protested.[25] In spite of the absence of reforms, U.S. assistance was never curtailed, and by the mid-1960s the United States ceased using foreign aid as a lever for social reform.[26]

How much of the new prosperity trickled down to the nonbusiness and nonelite sectors of society?[27] Growth without reform produced growth with misery for large sectors of the Guatemalan population. The increased use of land for export crops caused an increase in land concentration in the hands of the elite. Inequality of land ownership, already one of Latin America's worst, actually increased between 1964 and 1979.[28] Large landowners, producing coffee, cotton, sugar, and cattle for export, not only resisted land reform but actually dispossessed peasants from their existing holdings.[29]

Brockett writes that the "tremendous inequality in land ownership combined with rapid population growth has meant . . . a growing landless population."[30] The loss of peasant landholdings was matched, at least in part, by increased demand for wage labor on cotton and other plantations. By the late 1970s, hundreds of thousands of peasants were migrating annually to find low-paying temporary work under harsh and often dangerous conditions.[31] The wages of those with work were meager, and rural unemployment reached 42 percent by the 1970s.[32] In 1970, an AID-sponsored study concluded that

> all the data that have been reviewed on production, yields, farm size, income and employment indicate that the income position of small farmers has deteriorated considerably since 1950. . . . Over large areas of the central region, per capita production is surely falling, and total production may be falling as well.[33]

In 1980 AID identified the "very low wage rates paid by commercial agriculture and an extremely low minimum wage established by the government" as the principal causes of Guatemalan poverty.[34]

The social consequences of this pattern of development are obvious. With the assistance of the Alliance for Progress, a largely self-sufficient rural peasantry had been converted into a rural proletariat, subject to the vicissitudes of world demand for Guatemala's export commodities and to the vagaries of local elites controlling the plantations.

The concentration on export crops also led to a decline in the production of basic foodstuffs and the need to import rice, beans, and corn. In the process, the price of these basic foodstuffs has risen to levels comparable to those of the urban United States, in a country where three-quarters of the population receives a per capita income of less than $300 per year. In a 1978 study, it was reported that the cost of the *minimum* adequate diet exceeded the per capita income of some 70 percent of the total population of Guatemala.[35] By the late 1970s, over 80 percent of Guatemala's children were suffering from measurable malnutrition, and approximately 6 percent were *severely* malnourished—about twice the proportion for El Salvador.[36]

The worsening situation produced by this "growth without reform" generated popular pressures for change. Economic elites, supported by the military, responded with increasing violence to crush reformers they branded as "communists." In the mid-1960s, one ultraconservative party, the National Liberation Movement (MLN), created its own death squad—the infamous White Hand (Mano Blanca)—to deal with the proponents of reform. Since then, repression organized or condoned by the military has swept in vicious waves over Guatemala.

Changes in the Guatemalan Military

In the decades after the 1954 CIA coup, there were major changes in the unity, efficiency, and politico-economic role of Guatemala's armed forces. The United States played a major role in these changes.

The Guatemalan army was profoundly affected by the success of the CIA-sponsored invasion force in 1954. The overthrow of President Arbenz produced deep divisions in the military, divisions that new leaders were unable to heal. Colonel Carlos Castillo Armas, who ruled for three tumultuous years until he was assassinated by a palace guard in 1957, was succeeded by General Miguel Ydígoras Fuentes, a corrupt and ineffective leader who retained power largely by buying off potential opposition within the army and by pursuing public policies that pleased civilian economic elites.

Already deeply resenting the foreign intervention of 1954, nationalists in the army were further upset by Ydígoras's willingness to let Guatemala be used as a CIA training base for the Bay of Pigs invasion. Frustrated in their attempts to implement needed social reforms, dissident reformist officers staged a coup d'etat in 1960 but failed to take power. These officers, many trained in counterinsurgency techniques by the United States, became the leaders of the guerrilla activity in eastern Guatemala during the mid-1960s.[37]

The United States had been providing military assistance since 1954, but after the attempted coup of 1960, aid increased dramatically. Under the Alliance for Progress such aid was designed to stem other Cuban-type revolutions while reform programs removed the causes of revolution. A major "civic action" program was begun in Guatemala, the first such program in Latin America.[38]

Disunity and inefficiency in the Guatemalan army initially rendered U.S. military assistance relatively ineffective. But in 1963 a coup led by Colonel Enrique Peralta Azurdia brought more "modern" or "professional" sectors of the military to power. Colonel Peralta Azurdia sought to unify the military and make it more efficient at "public administration." U.S. military aid reached its peak levels in the mid-1960s, and another colonel, Carlos Arana Osorio, was placed in charge of the counterinsurgency program, using the aid to turn the Guatemalan army into a formidable fighting force.[39]

At the same time, the United States financed and supervised the "modernization" of Guatemala's police, most of which are directed by the military.

> In 1957 the AID Office of Public Safety began a training program for the Guatemalan National Police. Twenty-four Americans began patrolling with the National Police and the judiciales—the political police—on a daily basis. From 1957 until Congress abolished it in 1974, the program pumped $4.4 million into the Guatemalan police, trained 425 agents in the United States, and provided extensive supplies of arms, antiriot equipment, and communications and transportation technology. . . . Among other services, AID set up the police training center . . . [and] organized and equipped the PMA (the units hired out to landlords and to suppress campesino unrest).[40]

As the Guatemalan military was taking advantage of U.S. military assistance to turn itself into a formidable internal security force, it was also taking advantage of its political control of the government to turn itself into an an economic elite.

The political ascendancy of the military began as early as 1950, during the administration of Colonel Jacobo Arbenz, but control over the political system became institutionalized only after the 1963 coup of Colonel Peralta Azurdia. Closing ranks in 1965, the military produced a new national constitution that

> laid the groundwork for a "limited democracy" with closely circumscribed political party activity and an institutionalized ritual of elections. Any threatening opposition outside an Army-decreed spectrum was constitutionally banned. . . . [It] restricted such "exotic ideologies" as social democracy and Christian Democracy. . . .[41]

Within a decade, the army had institutionalized its direct control over the political system via such time-honored devices as rigged elections and appointments to the public bureaucracy. After the fraudulent election of 1974, in which the Christian Democrats were denied their apparent victory, one party leader admitted that "in Guatemala, it is useless to think of governing, except as the result of a political decision by the army."[42]

Corruption has always been rife in the Guatemalan army, but in the early 1970s military officers began to become entrepreneurs as well. For more than a decade, military policy has melded the state with the economic interests of individual military officers, using the threat (and application) of force to acquire wealth. By the early 1980s, the army controlled forty-six "semiautonomous state institutions," including its own investment and pension fund and a "private" bank, called, appropriately enough, the Bank of the Army (Banco del Ejército).[43] Government appropriations capitalized the bank, and its funds assisted entrepreneurial officers as they invested in various enterprises, including hotels, housing projects, the cement industry, and especially real estate. Officers have been particularly prominent in acquiring land for livestock, agriculture, and forestry in the Northern Transversal Strip. One former president, General Fernando Romeo Lucas García, is reported to own over 100,000 acres in what has come to be known as the "zone of the generals."[44]

The military's new economic power has sometimes created serious conflicts with civilian economic elites, who see their interests challenged by a government whose corruption now favors military officers and bureaucrats. The MLN, for example, has increasingly challenged the military and its political candidates; indeed, intra-elite conflict is behind many of the daily political events in Guatemala—coups, public debates over economic policies, and elections like those in 1978 and 1982, which are frauds within frauds.

The corruption of the military is so deeply institutionalized that they (like their Salvadoran counterparts) have become a "mafia" in uniform. The military has become a new, independent actor with its own political and economic interests, anxious to preserve a corrupt system and its own extraordinarily corrupt position within it. The military has become so deeply involved in killing that the possibility of civilian rule raises the threat that army officers might be brought to justice; thus, civilian rule is unacceptable. The military is so deeply involved in using political power for economic gain that to give up its power would threaten almost every officer's economic position or his hope for future wealth, a hope to which officers have become accustomed.

Consequently, the military must violently oppose any kind of genuine democracy that would give civilians control over the military. In supporting the Guatemalan military, the United States has tied itself to an institution whose record since 1954 demonstrates beyond any doubt an unswerving commitment to blocking social reform—a social force, like the oligarchy, that leaves the opposition no choice but armed insurgency. Once again, the United States finds itself in the uncomfortable position of supporting a group that finds terror a necessary and rational way to maintain order.

MÉNDEZ AND ARANA   ▲

Although the military has held political power in Guatemala since 1954, for the brief period from 1966 to 1970 the civilian government of Julio César Méndez Montenegro held office. Understanding the Méndez Montenegro administration is critical to achieving an understanding of the "centrist civilian alternative" argument in contemporary U.S. policy.

The Méndez election was the fairest election in Guatemala since the 1954 coup. A reformist civilian, Méndez was the candidate of the Revolutionary

Party (PR), a party that sought to identify itself with the Arévalo and Arbenz governments by characterizing itself as the third government of the 1944 revolution. The United States backed Méndez's bid against two military candidates, and once the balloting was over, U.S. policymakers announced that Washington would not support any attempt to annul the election.[45] The Méndez administration offered the possibility of the reformist development strategy envisioned in the Alliance for Progress.

Despite the ability of a civilian reformer to take office after a relatively fair counting of the ballots, electoral conditions reflected the limits of democracy. In the 1966 campaign, the only other parties allowed to participate were the oligarchy's MLN, and the Democratic Institutional Party (PID), the party of the armed forces. The 1965 army-backed constitution had restricted parties with "exotic ideologies"—such as social democracy and Christian Democracy—and outlawed opposition further to the left.[46] Moreover, the PR itself had shifted to the right in the late 1950s, when its leader at the time, Mario Méndez, "purged the entire left wing of the party."[47] Julio César Méndez Montenegro became a presidential candidate only after his brother Mario had been assassinated.

From the beginning, then, the electorate's choices were narrowly constrained and the "reformist" credentials of the PR open to question. Once in office, the Méndez government was severely limited. First, Méndez was not allowed to take office until he agreed to guarantee the military "a free hand in counterinsurgency, autonomy in such matters as selection of the defense minister, chief of staff, budgets, etc." Méndez also had to promise "to exclude 'radicals' from the government, but not to retire too many generals."[48] Second, threats from the oligarchy prevented Méndez from carrying out even relatively mild, U.S.-supported tax reforms, let alone take the initiative on more serious land reforms.[49] Perhaps most seriously, Méndez was powerless to stop a new wave of repression unleashed by an anxious military and the paramilitary death squads controlled by the oligarchy.

A wave of terror swept eastern Guatemala during the Méndez administration. The repression, directed by Colonel Carlos Arana, was presented to the outside world as a counterinsurgency campaign. Supplied and trained by the United States, the army crushed several hundred guerrillas in eastern Guatemala (led by dissident army officers) and also killed between three thousand and ten thousand civilians.[50]

After the guerrillas had been exterminated, the level of violence increased in both the city and the countryside. The army and police were joined in this repression by newly formed private armies or death squads such as the White Hand. MLN leader Mario Sandóval Alarcón explained: "All we are doing is what the Bible suggests: taking an eye for an eye."[51] These death squads, according to a chief presidential adviser

> were organized under the patronage and approval of the government and the Army, because it was the only way to fight guerrillas. They [the death squads]

have the sympathy of most of the Guatemalan people. . . . They have lists
of people that are suspected to be Communists of whatever kind and they kill
them. It's a war, you see. It's a war between the Communists and the
anti-Communists.[52]

The brutal activities of the police were no secret. In May 1962, the U.S.
embassy reported to the State Department that the police *judiciales* were

employed in the investigation and harassment of political opponents and in
the carrying out of this or that unsavory assignment. This body is feared and
despised by virtually everyone in Guatemala except those whom they serve.[53]

A 1971 staff report of the U.S. Senate Foreign Relations Committee noted
that the U.S.-trained police

are widely admitted to be corrupt and are commonly held to be brutal.
. . . They receive their political direction from very hard-line right wingers.
. . . Furthermore the United States is politically identified with police ter-
rorism.[54]

Méndez, the U.S.-backed civilian leader of the only reformist government
able to take office in Guatemala since 1954, stood helplessly by as the
military and death squads terrorized much of the population in a wave of
repression even worse than Castillo Armas's "counterrevolution" after the
1954 coup. Only in 1968, when the military and the MLN kidnapped the
Archbishop of Guatemala and unsuccessfully tried to blame it on the guerrillas, was Méndez able to send Colonel Arana and his supporters in the
MLN into exile.

But Colonel Arana became President Arana in 1970 and the military
consolidated its economic and political power. Arana set the tone of his
administration on inauguration day by declaring a state of siege.

During the next four years, with the guerrilla movement essentially nonexistent, Arana launched the greatest campaign of systematic terror that
Guatemala had yet seen. The Committee of Relatives of Disappeared Persons
estimated that from 1970 to 1975 at least 15,000 Guatemalans disappeared.
In 75 percent of these cases, there was evidence implicating the government.[55]

The targets of this terror were the very people who represented the possibility for nonviolent reform of the political and social system—leaders of the
Christian and Social Democratic parties, major trade unions, and peasant
organizations. Under the Méndez regime, the "reformers" had taken office,
but not power; under Arana, many of the reformers were eliminated.

Regardless of the existence of elections and parties during this period,
political power remained in the hands of the military, whose capabilities
had been enhanced by U.S. military and police assistance. Economic power

remained in the hands of the military and the oligarchy. From the perspective of the deprived sectors of society, the socioeconomic picture worsened, for the export-oriented agribusiness economic growth spurred by U.S. aid and private investment had served primarily to enrich the military and oligarchy while decreasing the supply of food. Using terror as a weapon, the oligarchy and the military stifled dissent, and as a result the political system became *more* closed during the "reformist-centrist" period of Méndez Montenegro. The "centrist alternative" proved to be a great success for the Guatemalan military, but a disaster for the bulk of society.

THE CURRENT CRISIS   ▲

In 1974, General Kjell Eugenio Laugerud García was imposed as president by Arana and the army after the Christian Democratic candidate, former Army Chief of Staff General Efraín Ríos Montt, won the election. In the wake of the economic growth and the repression of the previous eight years, Laugerud's administration relaxed the terror and a small political space opened for reformers. "Unions, student groups, campesino organizations, professional service societies, and moderate political parties sprang up quickly and began to enjoy immense popularity and considerable political force."[56] The reorganization of important sectors of the population to once again seek reform created pressure for change, setting the scene for a cycle of brutal repression and armed insurgency.

The earthquake of February 1976, which killed over twenty thousand people, was the catalyst that led to the resurgence of political mobilization of large numbers of Guatemalans. As international humanitarian aid flowed into the highland areas devastated by the earthquake, reconstruction committees were formed, often with the participation of foreign missionaries. Many of these missionaries were dedicated to the pursuit of social justice along the lines announced by Latin America's Catholic bishops at Medellín, Colombia, in 1968.[57]

The new grassroots organizations that grew up after the earthquake responded not simply to this natural disaster but to the precarious living conditions that have been discussed earlier. Deprived of land and forced to sell labor for low wages on coastal plantations in order to survive, the Indian population decided it would rather fight than remain passive. Unlike the earlier rural mobilization in 1944 to 1954, these "new generation" organizations focused upon local self-improvement and were often connected to private international development agencies. These "popular organizations" included labor unions, rural agricultural and artisan cooperatives, church study groups, and campesino organizations such as the Committee for Campesino Unity (CUC).

It is critically important to note that these new groups were indigenous, grassroots organizations that formed spontaneously to address an urgent need—disaster relief—and continued to function after the immediate needs had been met. These groups were nonideological and, in all probability, few of the members had even heard the term *communism*. They sought bread-and-butter reforms, as for example in the successful CUC-led strike of agricultural laborers in the south coast sugar and cotton plantations in 1980.

In the urban areas, a new generation of urban political leaders had matured by the mid-1970s, and the political process began to show signs of increasing tension as the urban middle-class reformers confronted upper-class sectors, who felt threatened by reform. Although electoral fraud continued (notably the 1974 and 1978 presidential elections), moderately reformist political parties began to organize. From 1976 to 1980 there was marked growth of several political movements.

The army and major sectors of the oligarchy responded to this new surge of popular organizing and reformist pressure with repression. In urban areas, violence against political party and labor union leaders increased dramatically after the fraudulent election of General Romeo Lucas García in 1978.[58] Guatemala's two centrist-reformist political parties, the Social Democrats (PSD) and the United Front of the Revolution (FUR), were crushed following the 1979 assassinations of their leaders, former Foreign Minister Alberto Fuentes Mohr and former Guatemala City Mayor Manuel Colom Argueta, respectively. The grassroots leadership of the center-right Christian Democrats was decimated—150 murders of party organizers in 1980 and 1981 served to silence all but a handful of party activists. Union leaders (Mario Mujía, Pedro Quevedo), university professors (Manuel Andrade Roca, Rita Navarro, Jorge Romero, Guillermo Monzón Paz), and student leaders (Oliverio Castañeda, Ricardo Martínez Solórzano, Alejandro Coti) were among the most prominent targets murdered, and their successors often perceived no alternative except either fleeing the country or joining the armed opposition.

The army and the landowners reacted even more violently in rural areas.[59] The level of repression grew dramatically, especially in the Indian highlands of western Guatemala and in the plantation areas of the southern (Pacific) coast, which were worked by migrant labor from the highlands. Once again, the Guatemalan army justified its military response as a campaign against a communist insurgency inspired by Soviet-Cuban adventurism. But in fact the guerrillas were few in number when the repression began to grow again after 1978 under the General Lucas García regime.

The guerrilla activity that had emerged in 1975—led by some of the survivors of the movement in the 1960s—was at first confined to certain Indian highland areas of Quiché province, notably in the Ixcán and Ixil region. Military repression of reformist efforts and community organization led, however, to widespread defensive mobilization: to protect themselves from the landowners and the military, the Indian communities began to organize for the purposes of self-defense. Victimized by the military and lacking alternatives for economic self-improvement, the Indians became increasingly willing to turn to armed opposition, swelling the ranks of the guerrilla movement. By and large, their resistance was a result of state repression, not its cause.[60]

Who are the guerrillas? Caesar D. Sereseres[61] calls them the "second-generation insurgents" to distinguish them from the military officers-turned-guerrillas who followed the unsuccessful insurrectionist strategy in the 1960s in the northeastern mountains. The second-generation guerrillas have rejected this strategy in favor of a *guerra popular prolongada*, a prolonged popular war.[62]

Three guerrilla groups are particularly important. The Guerrilla Army of the Poor, *Ejército Guerrillero de los Pobres*, (EGP) was formed in 1972, and by 1975 had begun to attract peasant Indian support in the Ixcán region.[63] Within three years the EGP had initiated its armed attacks, supported by local peasants. By 1980 the EGP was operating in a half-dozen departments, able to field fighting units composed, for the first time, of significant numbers of Indians.

Meanwhile, additional guerrilla organizations developed: the *Organización del Pueblo en Armas* (ORPA) first appeared publicly in 1979, followed by the resurgence of one of the groups of the 1960s—The *Fuerzas Armadas Rebeldes* (FAR), which is allied with a faction of the Guatemalan Labor Party (PGT). In the early 1980s, guerrilla units were strong in the northwest, the west, and the plantation lands of the south coast. The EGP and ORPA guerrilla units were largely composed of Indians, nearly all of whom had originally been mobilized into political action during the 1975-to-1980 period as members of the popular organizations who turned to armed resistance in self-defense against state repression.[64]

In 1982, these guerrilla organizations issued a statement under the banner of a new coordinating group, the *Unidad Revolucionaria Nacional Guatemalteca* (URNG), calling for an end to the "economic and political domination of the repressive wealthy, both national and foreign, who rule Guatemala."[65] Each of these groups blends some form of Marxism with demands for ending social discrimination based on race, supporting democratic political structures, and respecting religious preferences. While the Cuban government may have made efforts to unify the guerrilla groups as the State Department has asserted, there is no evidence of any international control over the insurgents. It is a domestic civil war, not an international conflict. To argue otherwise is to seriously misread Guatemala's historical development.

As this scenario of repression was escalating, the formal political system saw changes as well. In the 1982 elections, when General Lucas García tried to impose the candidate of his faction of the army, a coup led by young officers installed retired General Efraín Ríos Montt in power. This former candidate of the Christian Democrats (in 1974) had become an active, born-again evangelist and brought this style to government. Ríos Montt reduced the level of urban terror, but he also established secret summary military trials before the Tribunals of Special Jurisdiction. Executions of suspected "enemies" continued. Repression in the rural areas rose to a fever pitch under his *fusiles y frijoles* ("guns and beans") campaign. There were a number of documented cases of massacres of whole villages. The popular organizations were practically eliminated. Force was used to remove Indians from some villages and reorganize others into "strategic hamlets," where beans were provided by the military at the same time that the Indians were kept in virtual imprisonment, their movements carefully restricted and independent organization forbidden.

In urban areas Ríos Montt announced that no civilians would be allowed to hold executive government positions. He then removed from office all elected mayors (most of whom had been elected in the relatively honest municipal elections of 1980) and replaced them with military appointees. Another decree permitted the president to act as the legislative as well as the executive power, and the major political parties were effectively removed from meaningful political participation.

Parts of the oligarchy opposed the moves aimed at their political parties (like the MLN), creating cleavages within the ruling military-oligarchic alliance. By August of 1983, Ríos Montt's exotic messianism had alienated most sectors of the ruling class and the Catholic church, and he was deposed in yet another military coup, this one led by General Humberto Mejía Víctores. This "change" led to a decrease in "born-again evangelism" as a political style, but had little or no impact on the government's policy of responding to political pressure with brute force.

The repression in rural areas under the Lucas García, Ríos Montt, and Mejía Víctores administrations was truly horrifying. By early 1984, the stories of mass killings in the countryside had become a regular occurrence: fifty-four campesinos in Pacoc, fifteen campesinos in San Martín Jilotepeque, ten campesinos in El Adelanto, about a hundred campesinos in a single village in the department of Quiché—there the army forced the entire population into the courthouse, raped the women, beheaded the men, and battered the children to death against rocks along the riverbank—fifteen campesinos burned alive in Chamaxú, forty-four campesinos (including thirty-three children) killed in Saquixá, eighty-four bodies found in a clandestine cemetery in Chuatalún, twenty campesinos killed in San Marcos, fourteen campesinos in Chijtinimit—the tragic list goes on and on. Although the total number of deaths may never be known, even a study by the Guatemalan government acknowledged a count of over 100,000 Indian children orphaned by the death of at least one parent in the years 1980 to 1984. And thousands have fled to Mexico, to the relative safety of urban areas, or have gone into hiding in the mountains within Guatemala.[66]

It is no secret who is responsible for the carnage.[67] In October 1983, the OAS Inter-American Commission on Human Rights accused the Guatemalan government of "the very gravest human rights violations, including the destruction, burning, and plundering of entire campesino villages."[68] The government of General Mejía Víctores dismissed this and other reports as propaganda designed to undermine Guatemala's international image.[69]

The U.S. State Department has itself tried to shift blame for the carnage onto the insurgents.[70] The guerrillas certainly do engage in violence. But documented allegations of guerrilla violence against the rural population have been extremely few and unsubstantiated by any source other than the military. In 1982, Amnesty International reported:

> In no case known to AI has a campesino who has succeeded in reaching relative safety abroad either in Honduras or Mexico supported claims that opposition forces have been responsible for extra-judicial executions of non-combatant civilians. On the contrary, many who have spoken to foreign journalists outside of Guatemalan territory have indicated that the atrocities which they have witnessed have been perpetrated by government or government-supported groups.[71]

Amnesty International's 1984 report again charged that the Guatemalan government was responsible for most of the violence.[72]

By mid-1983, when General Mejía Víctores ousted General Ríos Montt, "order" had been restored in many of the Guatemalan highlands and southern coast areas that had been in the public eye because of the ferocity and ruthlessness of the counterinsurgency programs. Although widespread massacres appeared to diminish in some areas, in other areas where the guerrillas remained active, Mejía continued to apply the same brutal techniques as his predecessor—burning crops, killing civilians in villages suspected of guerrilla sympathies, and forcing resettlement of the villagers into camps. In 1985 there were still reports by church and refugee workers of killings in the countryside by army units. Urban terror continued.[73]

A good illustration of the Guatemalan government's approach to human rights in 1985 can be found in the case of Guatemala's Mutual Support Group (*Grupo de Apoyo Mutuo*, GAM). Founded by relatives of disappeared individuals, GAM's goal was to investigate disappearances in order either to find individuals being held in prison or to document the deaths of individuals who had disappeared. After initially receiving signals of support from the government, GAM's activities were soon condemned as subversive. Within a period of weeks, four of its six founders had succumbed to death or terror, and the organization, in effect, had been eliminated as anything but a symbol.[74]

And although ample evidence from various monitoring sources indicated continued military violations of basic human rights in the highland areas of Guatemala, specifically in Patzún, Santiago Atitlán, and in Quiché province, the U.S. embassy stressed improvements in "overall human rights conditions," even though its own figures showed an increase in political killings in 1984, compared to 1983.[75]

But like all reports based solely on "body counts" or on the existence of political party debate and "free elections," this evaluation distorted the character of repression in Guatemala by ignoring the institutionalized context undergirding the structure of dominance in Guatemala. In the case of military activities in rural areas, embassy evaluations ignore the cumulative effect of years of killing: a climate of fear and terror exists that makes it difficult for any moderate types of pressure for reform to begin to become organized. Moreover, these evaluations ignore the institutional mechanisms that the military has created in order to cement its dominant position, not only in competition with the deprived sectors seeking justice but also in competition with nonmilitary elites wishing to obtain, or retain, access to wealth-producing resources. Three institutional mechanisms merit scrutiny, for they reduce the need for obvious repression while seeking to ensure reduced levels of popular participation and democracy.

The first of these three institutional mechanisms is the "civil patrols" (*Patrullas de Auto-defensa Civil*, PAC).[76] This structure forcibly recruits males for rudimentary military training, then compels these ill-trained and ill-armed individuals to "patrol" their villages and nearby roadways. Although the public rationale for this is "self-defense" against guerrilla groups, the real intent is to monitor and control the indigenous population in areas under military control. The PAC structure enables the army and its informants to constantly monitor the activities and whereabouts of villagers, making any sort of political activity extremely difficult.[77]

One underreported aspect of the civil patrols is the forced labor involved, that is, the work performed by patrol members in roadbuilding and other infrastructure projects that make land more valuable for, among other things, export agriculture—transforming agricultural land into export production is part of the coordinated development plan for these regions. This process of creating new wealth in previously isolated areas is totally under military control, of course, but frequently ignored by observers concentrating on the counterinsurgency aspects of these activities. Within Guatemala, however, nonmilitary economic elites have complained about the process as yet another example of military use of the state to compete unfairly against private enterprise.

The second mechanism, a counterpoint to the first, is the creation of "model villages" as part of the "Poles of Development" program. This plan is described as one of coordinated development aimed at bringing social progress and basic quality-of-life improvements to highland areas previously marked by isolation and extreme poverty.[78]

In fact, these villages, in addition to offering military officers control over adjacent agricultural lands and individuals desperate for work, appear very similar to the "strategic hamlets" developed by the United States in Vietnam.

As such, although their "development" possibilities dovetail with the quests of military officers for wealth, the basic intent is one of counterinsurgency, of population control. In early 1985, one foreign journalist described the villages:

> . . . people from several villages and sometimes from different Indian language groups are gathered in towns they had no say in designing, guarded

over by soldiers who destroyed their former homes. . . . Asked what the army would do if a resident left the village without permission or refused to join the local [voluntary] civil patrol, one of the men in Tzalbal said matter-of-factly, "They'd kill you."[79]

A third mechanism that aims at establishing a degree of permanent military control over rural Guatemala is the creation of a new structure to regulate civil affairs. This structure is the National Interinstitutional Coordinator (CIN), established in each department and presided over by military zone commanders. Because it will coordinate and regulate all normal civil governmental functions under direct military supervision, the CIN is in essence a parallel government that will allow the military to continue to rule the nation even with Guatemala's return to "civilian rule" with a new constitution in place."[80]

This new corporatist structure is designed, like active repression, to prevent any independent community organization or control over local affairs, to counter the threat the military sees in the creation of self-help organizations, and to ensure that a "democratic opening," including the elections and party campaigns seen in 1985, will not in fact threaten military dominance. These three institutionalized mechanisms for social control led, by 1985, to an environment in which fear, terror, and totalitarian control have replaced (or will replace) murder as the primary mechanism for social domination.

With repression structured and institutionalized, the government turned its attention to Guatemala's tarnished international image, so that foreign assistance and investment might flow more freely into the Guatemalan economy. Although this effort includes international diplomatic efforts in Europe, the centerpiece of the strategy is a series of "demonstration elections" designed to overcome U.S. concerns about Guatemalan politics.[81]

In July 1984, voters elected eighty-eight members of a Constituent Assembly to write a new constitution. In the fall of 1985, presidential and congressional elections were held. The institutionalized repression of the rural population severely limited pre-election electoral activity. No candidate touched on issues like the corruption of the military, punishment for past crimes, and dialogue with the insurgents. All contenders stated they would not actively pursue major socioeconomic reforms and all acknowledged the special status of the military. The military's desire for international legitimacy, however, helped create the least fraudulent national elections in decades.

Christian Democrat Marco Vinicio Cerezo won a landslide victory in the December runoff elections winning 68 percent of the valid vote. Cerezo, an independent-minded reformer, was quick to distance himself from the U.S. covert war against Nicaragua and to call for negotiations to settle regional conflicts. Internally, he claimed he would not press basic land reform but would undertake mild reforms that would be radical departures from the past—like allowing unions to organize, not repressing strikes, and perhaps taxing the oligarchs' unused land. However he also recognized how limited his power would be: the military, he said, had agreed "they are going to give us the office"; but he admitted it would take great skill and effort to exercise political power.

The military had reason to be confident that it could allow a civilian like Cerezo to take office without losing control. They remembered the historical example of the 1966-to-1970 Méndez presidency, characterized by a civilian in office but an autonomous, reorganized military in power. They looked at the example of the administration of José Napoleón Duarte in El Salvador, characterized by a civilian president who was not allowed to organize a stong base of support to push for reforms and whose main importance was as legitimator and conduit for U.S. assistance. As Cerezo explained during the election: "They need a president who can obtain money for the country."[82] And finally, if the terror enforced by institutionalized repression were not to inhibit organized pressures for reform adequately, that is, if serious opposition were to recur because of the current "political opening," the military was willing (and thanks to renewed military assistance, would be even more able) to again resort to active repression.

Although the military was confident that elections would not threaten its power and position, the election of a strong-willed reformer like Cerezo, with great popular backing and international support, may create social forces that are difficult to control. The amount of repression the military is willing to use if reform pressures mount will depend, if only in part, on the kind of policy the United States adopts.

U.S. POLICY FROM CARTER TO REAGAN   ▲

Guatemala became a focus of the Carter human rights policy in early 1977, after the Laugerud government announced that it would forego U.S. military assistance if it were conditioned, as Congress insisted, upon annual publication of a State Department report on the human rights practices of military aid recipients. Congress promptly prohibited military sales credits to Guatemala in the foreign assistance appropriations act for fiscal year 1978, and thereafter the ban continued as a formal understanding (but not a law) between Congress and the executive branch.[83]

Other actions taken by the Carter administration included the decision not to support multilateral development bank loans to Guatemala in October 1979 and May 1980, and an active public diplomacy that included a visit to Guatemala in September 1979 by Assistant Secretary of State William Bowdler. Soon thereafter, the Guatemalan government refused to accept the relatively liberal career foreign service officer George Landau as U.S. ambassador, and the Carter and Lucas García governments could barely be said to be on speaking terms.

The Carter policy did not generate serious reform in Guatemala. Indeed, the human rights situation deteriorated markedly during the Carter administration. The military was still able to meet its armament needs. Despite the ban on new U.S. military assistance to Guatemala, deliveries of previously promised ("pipeline") military aid to Guatemala continued.[84]

Moreover, Guatemala received increased military assistance from other countries, including an important ally of the United States, the government of Israel. Not only did the Israelis sell the Guatemalans large numbers of Galil automatic rifles—the Galil became standard issue to the Guatemalan army—but they assisted Guatemala in the construction of a munitions plant, the first in Central America, to make bullets for the rifle.[85]

But even more significant were the limits put on U.S. leverage by the fact that previous U.S. military training and aid had helped the Guatemalan military become a strong, brutal fighting force imbued with a Cold War national security ideology. It was not immediately dependent on U.S. assistance. The military had eliminated the moderate reformist groups that a Carter-type policy might have strengthened, had they existed. Given these results of *past* U.S. policy, the principal flaw of the well-intentioned Carter initiative was not that it was too little, but that it was far too late.

Despite the continued terror in Guatemala during the first years of his administration, President Reagan sought to improve relations with Guatemala. State Department officials labeled the Carter approach a failure: "They have neither advanced our security interests nor prevented a deterioration in the human rights situation."[86] On May 4, 1981, Acting Assistant Secretary of State John Bushnell announced that the administration would like to establish a more constructive relationship with the Guatemalan government.[87] Within days, the secretary of state's special envoy, retired General Vernon Walters, visited Guatemala. After meeting with officials of the Lucas García government, he told reporters that the United States would help defend "peace and liberty" and "the constitutional institutions of this country against the ideologies that want to finish off those institutions."[88]

This promise was converted into concrete action in early June 1981, when the Department of Commerce approved a $3.1 million cash sale of military vehicles to Guatemala: one hundred Jeeps, fifty 2½-ton cargo trucks, and a variety of vehicle parts. The decision to send these military vehicles provoked a storm of protest from Congress, many of whose members felt they had been tricked by the administration's reclassification of military vehicles and vehicle parts to exclude them from the understanding that prohibited military aid to Guatemala. The administration waited nearly a year before announcing in April 1982 that it had decided to end the freeze on arms *sales*—not aid—and approve the shipment of $4 million in spare parts for helicopters. Six months later, the administration decided to end the U.S. policy of opposing multilateral development bank loans to Guatemala, citing the improved human rights record of the Ríos Montt government.[89] In the face of documented international reports of continuing rural massacres and terror, Reagan concluded after his December 1982 meeting with Ríos Montt that the Guatemalan president was getting a "bum rap" and was "totally dedicated to democracy in Guatemala."[90]

In 1983, however, Congress refused to approve the administration's request for both military and economic aid to Guatemala, and fifty-one members of Congress petitioned the President to cancel the helicopter parts sale, which the Guatemalans had failed to consummate for lack of funds. Earlier, a key House Democrat, Michael Barnes, had warned that "if they do go ahead with this sale, it will be a clear breach of faith with Congress."[91]

Sensing growing Congressional opposition, the Reagan administration's relations with Guatemala turned lukewarm in late 1983. Furthermore, the Guatemalan government's wave of rural killings struck employees of a U.S.-funded AID project designed to teach Spanish to the Indian population. Elliott Abrams, assistant secretary of state for human rights and humanitarian affairs, expressed administration concern: "We're deeply concerned about this pattern of disappearance and murder of AID contract employees" in Guatemala. Citing "an increase in individual acts of murder," Abrams avoided a strong condemnation: "It has not gone from white to black, but the situation has clearly deteriorated."[92] The administration further indicated its displeasure with the human rights situation in Guatemala by recalling U.S. Ambassador Frederic L. Chapin in late 1983 for a lengthy Thanksgiving-through-Christmas stay. Washington also temporarily stopped the flow of economic aid.

Congressional opposition—and to a much more limited extent administration chiding—made it clear to the Guatemalan military that its image as an international pariah would have to be changed if it were to get the economic and military aid its deteriorating economy desperately needed. While foreign assistance needs made such a political opening desirable, the institutionalized control the military exercised in the countryside by 1984 made it possible to move in this direction without great risk. It was in this context that the military agreed to the 1984 Constituent Assembly elections and the 1985 general elections.

In 1984, the flow of aid resumed. The administration allowed the consummation of the previously delayed sale of helicopter parts. For fiscal year 1985, Congress approved $40.1 million in development aid, $12.5 million in economic support funds (cash transfers), and $300,000 for military training—a package about three times as high as FY1984 levels. While Congress continued to make clear that aid would be contingent on a transition to civilian rule and an improvement in human rights, the administration was anxious to increase aid levels—including military aid—before there was any demonstration of marked improvement. Thus, for FY1986, the administration requested $33 million in development aid, $25 million in economic support funds, and $10.3 million in military aid.[93] This eagerness to help the Guatemalan military was only one of many administration signals that its primary concern was not so much with democracy and human rights, but with eliminating the threat to insurgency. Another such signal had been the replacement of Ambassador Chapin in late 1984 (he had apparently become disillusioned with the Guatemalan situation) with

Albert Martínez Piedra, a political appointee identified with an extreme, cold-war version of Guatemalan events.[94]

The inauguration of Marco Vinicio Cerezo as president in January 1986 was thus, at least in part, a result of the unwillingness of the U.S. Congress to reverse the kind of human rights policy begun under Carter. But if future U.S. policy toward the regime is to encourage an expansion of the small political opening created by the elections, it is important that it be guided by lessons of the past.

A reasonable and realistic U.S. policy toward Guatemala must begin by recognizing our consistent misperceptions of Guatemalan reality. Policymakers have misunderstood the sources of turmoil and insurgency in Guatemala, they have failed to grasp the ways in which U.S. economic aid is often misdirected by those who hold power in Guatemala, and they have overestimated the ability of either hard-line or reformist U.S. policies to influence the Guatemalan political system.

Since the time of the Alliance for Progress, policymakers have recognized that poverty and inequality are the sources of turmoil in Guatemala. But they have also perceived this agitation and insurgency as directed by disgruntled urban elites, supplied by outside forces (i.e., Cuba) that have taken advantage of poverty to promote unrest. The oligarchy and military encourage U.S. policymakers to support this perception. Threatened by the turmoil, Guatemala's elites assert that ignorant and gullible Indians have been lured into protest by communists. They know that this characterization of disruption in Cold War terms increases the likelihood of U.S. assistance and, far more important, makes repression seem necessary and therefore more acceptable.

Because they believe this characterization, U.S. conservatives fail to recognize that strikes and demonstrations are relatively moderate attempts by peasants and workers to change an inequitable system through reform, and that armed insurgency is largely a *response* to repression by the military and oligarchy, which has closed moderate avenues to reform. Conservative policymakers have concluded that insurgency must be stopped with military assistance and counterinsurgency programs based upon ambitious development schemes, such as the Poles of Development/Model Villages plan discussed earlier.

U.S. liberals and moderates deplore the poverty and inequality in Guatemala but fail to preceive its cause: the economic system that the military and the oligarchy control. Because of this misunderstanding of the character of social reality in Guatemala, liberal and moderate U.S. policymakers have concluded that they can ameliorate poverty with economic aid aimed at allowing the economic system to operate more justly.

While the goal of U.S. assistance programs is to generate economic development, ameliorate poverty, and encourage equitable, stable growth, U.S. policymakers misunderstand how the Guatemalan context subverts these aims. Aid given to the Guatemalan government is money placed in the hands of the oligarchy and the military, not in the hands of reformers. There is little trickle-down to the poor, for the oligarchy and the military oppose economic changes (such as land reform) that would alter the highly unequal distribution of wealth and allow the benefits of aid to be more fairly distributed. As AID noted in 1981, Guatemala's land-reform program "is a drop in the bucket compared to the size of the problem."[95]

The post-1963 expansion of the army into direct control of economic resources has added a new twist to this process of misappropriation, for it permits the military to use U.S. economic aid to expand its own wealth legally. Meanwhile, the high level of traditional institutionalized corruption continues to divert other aid into the pockets of officials. Thus, for example, U.S. aid intended to increase the commercialization of agriculture promotes land takeovers by military and civilian elites. As these development schemes worsen the lives of the uprooted campesinos, the levels of violence and clandestine mobilization increase. Although this type of modernization means "change" for Guatemala, it does not necessarily mean progress. For beyond the ethical and cultural considerations, such "development" exacerbates social tensions and encourages political instability.[96]

If durable political stability and real economic development depend on ending the repression and instituting major reforms, what can we learn from the past?

One lesson is that a hard-line strategy of controlling political turmoil by aiding the military brings short-term success and long-term problems. When the reformist democracy created between 1944 and 1954 began to threaten the oligarchy's control of Guatemalan society, the counterrevolutionary sectors of the military and the oligarchy, assisted by the CIA, destroyed not only the democratic institutions and popular organizations of the period but also the progressive elites that had started the process. The next generation of moderate reform leaders was eliminated by the military in the late 1970s and early 1980s. In each case, the "order" was temporary, because fundamental problems of inequality were not addressed. Instead, the military and oligarchy have defined reformers as "communists," and Washington has assisted in their destruction. In Guatemala, terror is the political style of governance. It requires continuing attempts to prevent reformers from making demands or becoming organized.[97] It is naïve to believe today that significant reform is possible in such a society. Yet without such reform there will never be long-term stability in Guatemala.[98]

A second lesson to learn is that the United States cannot "reform" Guatemala by using the carrot of economic assistance and military aid. This reform strategy failed during the Kennedy and Carter administrations. The agrarian and other reforms promoted by the Alliance for Progress in Guatemala in the 1960s were resisted by the military and the oligarchy, except when "reform" meant more wealth for the middle and upper sectors. Carter's limits on aid in the face of human rights violations were appropriate policies for limiting U.S. complicity and forcing Guatemala's rulers to bear the economic costs—deficits, disinvestment, recession—of their repressive policies.

But the denial of aid gave the United States little additional leverage. Conditions did not improve in Guatemala because past U.S. policy helped eliminate moderate alternatives while increasing polarization, long before Carter came to office. In fact, the "centrist alternative" as a reform strategy was destroyed in 1954. U.S. influence helped reformists take office in 1966 through 1970, but they had neither the power to carry out mild reforms nor the power to control military repression. The latest manifestation of this destruction is the Guatemalan Christian Democratic Party's promises not to attempt to redistribute wealth nor hold the military responsible for past human rights violations.[99]

The power of the Guatemalan military and oligarchy has grown since 1954 and this antireformist elite is today able to resist pressures for change from within Guatemala more easily than in the past. U.S. policy did not create this dragon, but did help to fuel its fire, thereby making the current situation more difficult for U.S. policymakers to influence.

A third lesson is that the United States should not view events in Guatemala through the lens of the East-West conflict, because to do so means that too little attention is paid to internal dynamics within Guatemala. Because U.S. policymakers confuse domestically produced political turmoil and insurgency with outside (i.e., Soviet or Cuban) intervention, they forget that repression against even moderate reform is the root of the problem.

One product of this misperception is a consistent misunderstanding of Guatemala's formal political system, seen most obviously in the weight placed on elections. Since the overthrow of Arbenz, elections and reformist political parties have meant little in terms of fundamental change.[100] Reformers in Guatemala hope that the 1985 elections will be different, but nobody in that country would call them, as the American embassy did, "the final step in the reestablishment of democracy in Guatemala."[101] The most that can be hoped for with the nonfraudulent election of a moderate civilian like Vinicio Cerezo is that the military and oligarchy will allow at least a limited political space. Cerezo may be able to reduce—at least temporarily —the reign of violence (although precisely the opposite occured after the election of Méndez Montenegro in 1966) and may be able to reestablish a judicial system and protect certain civil liberties. If this were to occur, it would allow moderate opposition elements an alternative to armed resistance.

But such moderate reformers will face the same limitations they faced during other periods of mild openings in the early 1950s and the mid-1970s. The military will seek to remain autonomous, maintaining political control over the rural population with its civil patrols, model villages, and civic affairs units. The military will seek to protect the officer corps from investigations of corruption and try to control all security questions, including dialogue with the insurgents. The military will struggle to block any fundamental land reform or economic redistribution; sectors of the oligarchy allied with the military will profit from this, but sectors opposed to military dominance will lose, thereby increasing the level of polarization and decreasing the likelihood of genuine stability in Guatemala.

Under such conditions, efforts to push for serious reform, to bring the military under democratic civilian control, to end repression, to allow free labor and peasant organization, and, in general, to expand democracy to include truly popular participation would likely trigger renewed repression, right-wing violence, and, once again, an armed insurgent response.

While the United States has tremendous power to help make things worse in Guatemala, its power to create long-term stability based on reform, democracy, and development is severely limited. Although liberal and moderate U.S. policymakers may have the best intentions concerning reform and development in Guatemala, those with economic and military power there do not share these goals. Any group that expresses support for such goals (and many have in the past) risks repression.

Perhaps the most important contribution to Guatemala's future that the United States can make is to cease giving moral and material support to the traditional enemies of democracy and reform. The election of Cerezo should not be viewed as an opportunity to legitimize new military assistance that will be usurped by antireformist elements. But it is an opportunity to show strong support for any attempts to tame the military, carry out redistributive reform, and seek a negotiated solution to the insurgency—all very risky moves for the new government. The United States could strengthen the relatively weak democratic forces by making clear to the military and landholding elites that renewed economic aid is not simply contingent upon elections, but on an end to repression and on a real commitment to democracy and reform.

3

EL SALVADOR

Martin Diskin
and Kenneth E. Sharpe

In October 1979, a reformist coup by junior officers in the Salvadoran military promised an end to five decades of repressive military dictatorship. But the promise of reform was soon dashed as hardline officers and entrenched economic elites instituted a reign of terror which in turn provoked an armed insurgency and widespread civil war.

The somewhat different policies of the Carter and Reagan administrations were grounded on the shared presumption that the left must be kept out of power. As Chapter 12 makes clear, Carter sought to remove the roots of revolution by promoting reform and ending repression; Reagan, viewing the conflict in more stark East-West terms, put primary reliance on military force. These policies blocked both a negotiated solution that would have allowed the left to share power and a military victory by the insurgents. But in thus excluding the left, U.S. policy also weakened the reformers who sought to change the inequality and repression that had spurred the armed insurgency in the first place.

Frequently U.S. policy makers were frustrated in their attempts to control internal events in El Salvador. Their policies, however, did have enormous influence, though sometimes in unintended ways. From 1979 to 1984 United States policy helped undermine the power of moderates, strengthen repressive and often savage right wing forces, and encourage armed insurgency. After the presidential election of Christian Democrat José Napoleón Duarte in 1984, U.S. policy undercut the ability of Duarte to put together a reform coalition that could challenge the military and economic elites, press for democratization and land reform, and negotiate a solution to the bloody and stalemated civil war. The impact of U.S. policy can be fully understood only in the context of the complex internal dynamics that emerged out of El Salvador's turbulent history.

REPRESSION AND THE STRUGGLE FOR DEMOCRACY ▲
AND REFORM: 1931 TO 1979

The Aftermath of the 1932 Massacre

In January 1931, El Salvador had its first relatively open election. Arturo Araujo, a wealthy renegade landowner, ran on a reform program urging the oligarchy to share its wealth with the poor. His ad hoc coalition of labor, peasants, students, professionals, and intellectuals defeated the candidates of the coffee oligarchy that had ruled for decades. But the democratic experiment lasted only until December, when Araujo was overthrown by his defense minister General Maximiliano Hernández Martínez, "El Brujo"— The Warlock.

The coup triggered a peasant insurrection in January 1932. Led by communist leader Augustín Farabundo Martí, it was crushed in a few days by Martínez's troops. After the fighting was over, Martínez decided to teach the peasants a lesson and unleashed a massacre—the *matanza*. The slaughter of ten thousand (some estimate thirty thousand) peasants in the next few weeks seared the memories of the Salvadoran poor for generations.[1]

The *matanza* marked a turning point: the revolt and bloodshed created a fearful oligarchy willing to cede political power to Martínez, thus beginning a period of military rule that has never really ended.

The oligarchy that the military protected comprised families that had expanded their already large landholdings to take advantage of the boom in the world coffee market in the late nineteenth and early twentieth centuries. The land they took had been communally owned by indigenous communities but was then converted to private property through an agrarian "reform." The Indian owners were forced to sell out or were evicted violently.

The new oligarchy spent their money lavishly on imported clothes, cars, and food, but they were astute businessmen who set up their own plants to process and export coffee, and their own banks to finance their plantations.[2] As the oligarchy's economic and political power grew, so did the gap between the rich and the poor.[3] In 1929, newspaper editor Alberto Masferrer warned: "As long as justice is not the same for everyone, none of us is safe."[4]

Economic Growth and Growing Instability

In the 1950s and 1960s a "modernizing" sector of the military and the oligarchy promoted agricultural diversification and light industrialization.

Economic growth, unaccompanied by reform, generated new social forces that challenged the authoritarian order.

The expansion of export agriculture in coffee, sugar, and especially cotton dispossessed small producers, increasing the number of landless peasants from 12 percent of the rural population in 1961 to 41 percent by 1975.[5] The landless joined the tens of thousands more with meager landholdings were insufficient to compete for poorly paid seasonal work at planting and harvest times. The under- and unemployment rate stood at about 50 percent in the mid-1970s.[6] Rural people, often aided by the social-action programs of the Catholic church, began to stir as a political force.

The growth in manufacturing stimulated by the creation of the Central American Common Market in 1961 encouraged the formation of middle-class and urban working-class groups but did not create a modernizing bourgeoisie to challenge the interests of the military-oligarchic alliance. Many in the oligarchy made new investments, broadening their base of economic power; those new entrepreneurs, whose main interests were in industry and commerce, remained dependent on the traditional oligarchy to finance their projects. Thus, despite conflicts among different factions of these ruling groups, industrialization did not create a propertied class willing to join with middle-class, labor, and peasant groups to sponsor the kind of major land reforms that would have redistributed income and expanded the national market.[7]

Attempts at Democratic Reform

The military-oligarchic coalition ensured order with force and ruled through an official party created in 1950 and renamed the Party of National Reconciliation (Partido de Conciliación Nacional—PCN) in 1961. It combined patronage, fraud, and coercion to guarantee victories in the presidential "elections."[8] Reformers among the younger officers made a number of attempts (in 1960 and 1972, for example) to take control of the military and the government, end corruption in the armed forces, and establish moderate reforms and democratic institutions. But hard-line officers crushed each attempt.[9]

The major challenge to the military and the PCN came from parties that drew support from the new social forces created by the post–World War II economic transformations: professionals, teachers, white-collar employees, urban workers, and some peasant activists and rural workers who grew disillusioned with the sham and corruption behind the PCN. Most important was the Christian Democratic Party (PDC) of José Napoleón Duarte, organized in the 1960s. Encouraged by its success in National Assembly and municipal elections (Duarte was mayor of San Salvador from 1964 through 1970), Christian Democrats joined with the smaller Social Democratic Party (Movimiento Nacional Revolucionario—MNR), headed by Guillermo Ungo and the Communist Party (PCS), to challenge the domination of the military-oligarchic alliance. Duarte and Ungo, campaigning for president and vice-president on a platform of land reform and democracy, were branded as communists by the oligarchy, and there was an unsuccessful attempt to assassinate Duarte. When election results showed Duarte and Ungo winning, the military intervened in the vote-counting and then declared PCN candidate Colonel Arturo Armando Molina the victor. A short-lived rebellion by junior officers and civilians, which broke out in response to the fraud, was put down harshly. Duarte was imprisoned, beaten, and exiled.

The 1972 electoral fraud marked the end of reformist optimism about politics in El Salvador. Two new forms of opposition emerged.

The most important was nonviolent direct action. Sit-ins, strikes, demonstrations, occupations, land seizures, and civil disobedience were undertaken by a growing number of labor, peasant, student, and neighborhood organizations. These "popular organizations" had different roots. Some were traditional labor or peasant organizations that had originally been considered safe by the government—the Salvadoran Communal Union (UCS), a moderate anticommunist peasant organization created with the help of the AFL-CIO–backed American Institute for Free Labor Development (AIFLD). Others were federations of labor unions that had grown up in reaction to the government-controlled labor movement. Student organizations often had their roots in Marxist ideology, although many reacted against the orthodoxy of the Communist Party.

Some of the most important organizations—e.g., the Christian Federation of Salvadoran Peasants (FECCAS)—were started by religious activists, usually Catholic clergy and lay people deeply influenced by the "theology of liberation" that took root in the Latin American Catholic church in the mid- and late 1960s. Salvador's archbishop, Oscar Arnulfo Romero, for example, urged the "preferential option for the poor," and many priests, brothers, nuns, catechists, and lay workers focused their work on promoting organization among the poor. Catechism and literacy classes organized in Christian base communities (groups of twenty or thirty in a parish who met regularly for bible study and discussion) taught a message like that given by Father José Inocencio Alas from his pulpit in Suchitoto:

> There is a pyramid of oppression at whose base are the hungry, sick and naked campesinos, intimidated by tendentious phrases like "You'll be accused of Communism! We'll call the National Guard. Seek Eternal Salvation! Give thanks to God if your child dies of hunger—he will go to heaven!" There are too many Christians who go to Communion but avoid community organizations; who are afraid to join the peasant leagues of the workers' movement. To live Christianity dreaming of heaven is to forget this earth, which is also of God.[10]

The second new form of opposition was armed insurgency. The three major groups—Popular Liberation Forces (FPL), People's Revolutionary Army

(ERP), and Armed Forces of National Resistance (FARN)—and the much smaller Central American Revolutionary Workers Party (PRTC) were formed in the early and mid-1970s. Their members included dissidents from the Communist Party who opposed its reformist and electoral strategy, radicalized Christians, and student revolutionaries. The fifth, the Armed Forces of Liberation (FAL), was established in late 1979 by the Communist Party. There were important tactical differences (popular insurrection vs. "protracted war") and some internecine conflicts (which led to the assassination of ERP leader and poet Roque Dalton) that only began to be resolved when the groups became unified in May 1980 as the Farabundo Martí Front for National Liberation (FMLN).[11]

In the 1970s the armed opposition grew slowly and remained confined to occasional raids, bombings, and kidnappings, which brought propaganda and ample funds. The major opposition came from the popular organizations, many of which joined into broad fronts, some associating themselves with a political party or with one of the guerrilla groups, and all of them pressing the government with protests, demonstrations, and occupations.[12]

One response to popular protest was the organization of "paramilitary" forces to supplement the army and three security forces—the treasury police, national guard, and national police. ORDEN, the most famous, was created in the 1960s to counter the rural political organizing of the Christian Democratic Party. It served as an instrument to organize peasant support for the official party (PCN), but freely used coercion against the opposition. Although always "unofficial," it was founded by the chief of the hated National Guard, General José Alberto ("Chele") Medrano, with help from U.S. Special Forces (Green Berets), and it worked closely with ANSESAL, the Salvadoran national security agency founded in 1962 with assistance from the CIA and the U.S. military. In the mid-1970s, ORDEN's 50,000 to 100,000 members became an instrument the right used to counter popular organizations in the countryside, turning peasant against peasant, and making each village a "microcosm of the wider civil war."[13]

A second response to popular protest was the increasing violence by government security forces. The military government of General Carlos Humberto Romero ("elected" in the fraudulent 1977 elections) enacted the Public Order Law, which instituted full press censorship, outlawed strikes, banned public meetings, and suspended normal judicial proceedings. Troops fired at peaceful demonstrations, assassinated priests and political leaders, and the number of "disappeared" doubled.

A third response was the "death squads." Organized by the ultrarightists within the military and financed by the oligarchy, these assassination teams were often composed of members of ORDEN and military men, and worked closely with ANSESAL. To contain the popular protests and the growing strength of the left, they began to wage a campaign of assassinations against priests, students, and trade union leaders.[14]

The increased violence of the Romero regime spurred increased guerrilla activity and greater mobilization by the popular organizations. By late 1978 the Carter administration grew concerned that Romero's human rights violations and opposition to reform would beget revolution.

The United States had not played a major role in El Salvador before this time. Kennedy's Alliance for Progress may have helped promote economic growth during the 1960s, but the failure of the oligarchy to adopt the reforms urged by the Alliance had meant increasing inequity and instability. The military aid and counterinsurgency training that were part of the Alliance's strategy had bolstered the military's capability, but the amounts of aid were relatively small and the United States exercised little influence over the character of the armed forces.

The Carter administration did pressure the Romero regime to end its repression, reducing military aid and exerting diplomatic and some economic pressure.[15] But the signals sent were often ambiguous—the United States maintained its military mission and replaced Ambassador Ignacio E. Lozano, Jr. (who had been openly critical of government repression), with the less critical Frank J. Devine.[16] Economic aid and support for loans was withheld but then resumed after the minor face-lifts Romero rightly reckoned could be used to manipulate the State Department.[17] The State Department was influential in getting Romero to repeal the Public Order Law in February 1979—but repression continued. The overthrow of the Somoza regime in Nicaragua in mid-1979 made the United States anxious, in the words of Ambassador Devine, "to avoid a repetition of the tragic events that had occurred in Nicaragua."[18] Washington's displeasure with the Romero regime lent support to another attempt at reform by junior officers. They, like the Carter administration, were particularly concerned by the overthrow of Somoza and the fate of his national guard—a consequence, they believed, of his repression and failure to bring needed reforms.[19] Many of the officers and civilians who backed the coup by the *juventud militar* (young military) in October 1979 saw it as the last chance to avoid revolution.

A REFORMIST COUP ENDS WITH REPRESSION: ▲
OCTOBER 1979 TO JANUARY 1981

The Armed Forces Declaration of October 15, 1979, proclaimed human rights guarantees that would allow for free elections, free speech, political parties, and labor organizations; a more equitable distribution of national resources through agrarian reform; and an end to the violence and corruption that had infected so much of the military and the government. These measures were seen by the Salvadoran oligarchy as a revolutionary threat.

Although the Carter administration backed the idea of reform, it failed to understand what was needed for reform to succeed: a new military-civilian coalition powerful enough to purge the hard-liners from the military and to break not only the oligarchy's economic power but its control over paramilitary forces and the death squads. Participation of the popular organizations in such a reform coalition was essential. Washington, however, supported the exclusion of these organizations, accepting the oligarchy's portrayal of them as the "extreme left." The Carter administration thus undercut its own efforts to weaken the stranglehold of the right, and inadvertently encouraged a rightward drift.

Colonel Adolfo Majano, representing the most reform-minded junior officers, was joined in the 1979 junta by key civilians, including Román Mayorga, rector of the Central American University, and Guillermo Ungo of the Social Democrats. Both had close ties to the *Foro Popular* (Popular Forum), a moderate coalition of center and left parties, important unions, and popular organizations.[20]

The civilian reformers, backed by Majano and his supporters in the army, succeeded in arranging an uneasy truce between the government and the popular organizations. They also persuaded the junta to issue decrees to disband ORDEN, to investigate the fate of persons who had "disappeared" under Romero's rule, to nationalize the coffee-export trade, and to freeze landholdings in preparation for agrarian reform. They were even able to remove some of the ultrarightist senior officers from power. Despite these successes, however, the nascent reform coalition could not force into retirement the hard-liners who still controlled the high command. These officers included Defense Minister Colonel José Guillermo García; his deputy, Colonel Nicolás Carranza; the heads of the national guard (Colonel Carlos Eugenio Vides Casanova), the national police (Colonel Reynaldo López Nuila), and the treasury police (Colonel Francisco Morán); and the officers in charge of the intelligence agencies, who worked closely with the death squads—and although ANSESAL was disbanded by the junta, it was replaced by the National Intelligence Agency (ANI) and General Staff Departments 2 and 5.[21] These officers had no interest in reform. They blocked the investigations, disbanded ORDEN only in name, and not only refused to participate in a dialogue with the popular organizations but also made no effort to prevent troops from opening fire on them.

Still, the popular organizations renewed their protests. Efforts by reformers to force the resignation of Defense Minister García and to end the repression failed. In early January, Ungo, Mayorga, and the entire cabinet except for García resigned in protest. "The false notion of the neutrality of the military as an institution," they charged, "has generated a rightward turn in the process of democratization and social change."[22] The *derechización* (rightward drift) had begun, but Washington quietly kept its distance.

Of the several reformist groups, only the Christian Democrats were willing to enter the second junta, formed in January 1980. In early March, they nationalized the banks and promulgated a two-phase land-reform program. But they were not able to contain the growing repression. Security forces fired on demonstrations, and death squads killed moderates (even Christian Democrats like Attorney General Mario Zamora). Between January 1 and March 13, 1981, there were 689 political assassinations.[23]

Just days before the land-reform program was announced, Christian Democrat Héctor Dada resigned from the governing junta, stating:

We have not been able to stop the repression, and those committing acts of repression . . . go unpunished; the promised dialogue with the popular organizations fails to materialize; the chances for producing reforms with the support of the people are receding beyond reach.[24]

The day after the land-reform program began, a state of siege was declared. Other moderate Christian Democrats, such as Rubén Zamora (Mario's brother), followed Dada's lead: they resigned from the government, then from the party, and formed the Popular Social Christian Movement (MPSC).

The third junta, formed shortly thereafter, included the reformist Colonel Majano and the conservative Christian Democrats led by Duarte. At U.S. insistence, the junta announced a third phase of land reform, designed in the United States. But the reforms were accompanied by increased repression. Colonel García remained defense minister, and there was no change in the hard-liners' control of the high command.

The junta's decrees legalized the repression. The State of Siege Law issued in March 1980 suspended freedom of movement, the inviolability of communications, and freedom of assembly. The judicial procedures established in December for those charged with sedition, subversion, and treason granted jurisdiction to military tribunals and allowed detention for six months without charge or access to counsel. They also allowed extrajudicial confessions—for example, those coerced through torture—to be used as evidence.

The Carter administration said little about the slow-motion coup that was undermining its reform strategy. It would not admit what moderate Social Democrats and Christian Democrats publicly declared: that the violence was not simply the work of small, uncontrollable bands of ultrarightist death squads but was perpetrated, even actively condoned, by the very military hard-liners in control of the government whom Carter supported and still called "reformist."

The most publicized murder of this period occurred on March 24, when Archbishop Oscar Arnulfo Romero, an outspoken advocate of dialogue with the popular organizations and a critic of military repression, was assassinated while conducting mass. The plot, according to U.S. Ambassador Robert White, was organized by Roberto D'Aubuisson.[25] Formerly active in ORDEN (Medrano referred to him and two other key junior officers as "mis tres asesinos," my three murderers), D'Aubuisson had been an army major assigned to ANSESAL in the late 1970s.[26] After the October 1979 coup, he formally left the army; and ANSESAL, closely linked with assassinations, disappearances, and death-squad activities, was disbanded. But with the assistance of key officers he took the ANSESAL intelligence files and developed a death-squad network, financed by the oligarchy and supported by officers like Deputy Defense Minister Colonel Carranza. He also helped keep ORDEN's structure intact, renaming the organization the Democratic Nationalist Front.[27]

A critical incident occurred in May. Colonel Majano ordered the arrest of D'Aubuisson for conspiring with rightist officers to plan a coup. One week later, Colonel García overrode Majano. With the support of eight of the country's fourteen garrisons, he had D'Aubuisson released. In early September, those officers identified with the young reformist military were shifted out of command positions. Majano was himself forced out of the junta in December. He went into exile, denouncing the repression of the military and the death squads.

Other events that December led to a reorganization that created a fourth junta. National guardsmen murdered four American churchwomen as they drove back from the airport; the United States temporarily suspended all new military aid and sent down a fact-finding mission. Meanwhile, D'Aubuisson and his associates in the military attempted another coup (they had tried earlier, both in February and in May), hoping that the national guard chief, Colonel Vides Casanova, or the vice-minister of defense, Colonel Carranza, would lead their movement. The United States intervened—the presence of the fact-finding commission may have helped—and supported a governmental reorganization. Duarte was given the newly created position of president of the junta. Carranza was transferred to a post at the lucrative (because graft-ridden) government-owned telephone company, ANTEL, and some of D'Aubuisson's closest supporters were also transferred. But with Majano out, and García still defense minister, the consolidation of the hard-liners' power in the military was complete. Although Duarte and the Christian Democrats were in office, they were not in power. Without allies in the military they ended up presiding over the worst terror since the 1932 *matanza.* By the last weeks of the year, the army and security forces were responsible for most of the violence that was claiming the lives of about two hundred civilian noncombatants a week, and these officially sanctioned killings would continue.[28]

Already by April 1980, the groups that could have formed a serious reform coalition but who had been excluded from, or forced out of, the government by the repression had joined to form a center-left opposition coalition, the Democratic Revolutionary Front (FDR). The new coalition included the moderate Christian Democrats (Zamora), the Social Democrats (Ungo), independents, and a wide range of professional, trade union, peasant, and other popular organizations. Its platform, while not unlike that of the moderates in the first junta, insisted that democracy and reform were impossible so long as military hard-liners controlled the government and encouraged the activities of the death squads. The FDR joined with the newly united guerrillas of the FMLN, and the FDR-FMLN became the major political opposition in El Salvador. During the next year it would be recognized as a "representative political force" by the Mexican, French, Dutch, and Spanish governments and important European Social Democratic parties.

During the latter half of 1980, mounting repression by the security forces and death squads severely weakened the trade unions and other popular organizations that belonged to the FDR. Hundreds were killed each month, and many activists fled to the hills to join the guerrillas. The most publicized killings occured in November 1980, when six FDR leaders were dragged out of a meeting in a Jesuit high school (where they were discussing negotiating with the PDC), murdered, and mutilated. Social Democrat Guillermo Ungo was chosen to replace the murdered president of the FDR, and the leadership, convinced that open nonviolent political opposition in El Salvador was suicidal, went underground or into exile.[29] The FDR was reduced to a core of small parties and professional organizations that had traditionally constituted El Salvador's democratic opposition.[30]

The repression created new recruits, and the united guerrilla groups grew rapidly. The coalition was strongly nationalist. Radicalized Christians as well as Marxists exercised important control, and most favored a nonaligned position in international affairs.[31]

With the destruction of the FDR's popular organizations and the elimination of open political activity, the FDR-FMLN focus shifted to organizing guerrilla activity in rural areas. Worried that Reagan's inauguration would mean full U.S. support for the military, the FDR-FMLN planned a "final offensive" in early January. It persuaded Cuba and Nicaragua that the timing was crucial and that the FMLN could bring down the government if they would provide additional arms. But the "final offensive" failed: the hoped-for urban insurrection had been made impossible by the destruction of the popular organizations in the cities.

What impact did United States policy have on these events in El Salvador? Robert White, who had been U.S. ambassador since March 1980, was more vigorous in his efforts to encourage moderation and reform than former Ambassador Frank Devine had been. But in backing the remnants of the reform coalition around Duarte in the third junta, the embassy found itself supporting an increasingly powerless party. The crucial assumption guiding U.S. policy—that the left had to be split, contained, or excluded —further weakened White's power. He could not openly support the junior officers around Majano or the moderates in the FDR for fear of aiding the left. The failure to publicly denounce military excesses and defend the civilian and military reformers who were forced out of the government weakened the potential reform coalition. Washington failed to understand how past electoral frauds and repression had combined with worsening economic conditions for most of the population to spur the creation of powerful, extra-electoral opposition forces—the popular organizations. Their demands for participation in any reform effort could not, as the U.S. embassy hoped, be ignored. By clinging to Duarte and the Christian Democrats as the only acceptable vehicle for reform, the administration was acting in defiance of Salvadoran reality.

Ambassador White was successful in particular instances. He helped thwart D'Aubuisson's May and December coup attempts and promoted a temporary cutoff of U.S. aid after the killing of the four American churchwomen. But his leverage was weakened by continued U.S. claims that the junta was moderate and reformist even as it shifted to the right. This U.S.

posture signaled the hardliners in the military that Washington would not seriously challenge their slow-motion coup and the worsening repression.

White's leverage was undermined still further by the November 1980 election of Ronald Reagan. The night Reagan won, there were feasts and dances by the extreme right in the posh homes of the oligarchy.[32] Here was a president who would no longer restrain them in their fight against communism. Barely a week after Reagan's inauguration in January 1981, White was fired.

DECLINE INTO CIVIL WAR: JANUARY 1981 TO   ▲
MARCH 1984

President Reagan took office just as the insurgents' first major offensive in El Salvador had been turned back. Anxious for a quick, military defeat of the left and convinced that the failure of the January offensive signaled the weakness of a foreign sponsored guerrilla movement, administration policymakers devised a primarily military strategy: aid the Salvadoran armed forces, regardless of their record on reform and human rights, and the left would quickly be defeated. The administration's East-West optic caused it to badly underestimate the indigenous roots and great strength of the insurgency. Its commitment to military defeat of the left led it to spurn a number of opportunities for a negotiated settlement to the conflict that opened up in 1981.

The first opportunity for negotiations came in March and April of 1981. The FDR-FMLN, unable to achieve a quick victory in January, was open to negotiations. The Cubans and Nicaraguans signaled their desire to improve relations with the United States and drastically reduced support for the the guerrillas. The new archbishop, Arturo Rivera y Damas, provided Washington with an opportunity to throw its weight behind a diplomatic alternative. The archbishop got FDR agreement for negotiations, obtained the backing of the International Christian Democrats and the Socialist International and the Pope, and received positive signals from Duarte. In April he met with Vice-President Bush and William Clark (then number two in the State Department). They said they were not interested. This foreclosed any possibilities. The archbishop himself had told Washington that only clear U.S. support could pressure the military into accepting a political solution. Washington ignored other overtures: at the end of May and early June, Ed Broadbent, a Canadian and vice-president of the Socialist International, tried to promote a negotiated settlement; in June the FDR-FMLN signaled its willingness to negotiate without preconditions; in August, Mexico and France recognized the FDR-FMLN as a "representative political force" and promoted a negotiated settlement; in December, all five guerrilla commanders, in one of their first displays of unity, signed an FDR-FMLN letter to President Reagan reiterating "our disposition to undertake them [negotiations] at any time, without preconditions placed on any of the parties in the conflict."³³

The failure to support negotiations, the impossibility of a quick military victory, and the severe repression in El Salvador spurred harsh public, Congressional, and foreign criticism of the administration's military strategy. In mid-1981, the assistant secretary of state for inter-American affairs, Thomas O. Enders, began to develop a policy that still emphasized military defeat of the left but had important political components: one was an effort to build an alliance between the Christian Democrats and the right to hold off the left and legitimize the government (Carter had tried to build a center by holding off both the left and the right); the other was elections. These would serve as a mechanism to bring in and "tame" the right, and would help legitimize the policy in the United States. By the time Congress put conditions on aid (a certification requirement) in December 1981, the administration was denying it had a primarily military strategy and hailing "prompt, free, and open elections" as the "best course for ending civil violence and keeping social peace."³⁴

The administration publically described El Salvador as run by a moderate reformist government battling extremists from the insurgent left and the death-squad right. Land reform and elections, Washington argued, would undercut the appeal of the left. U.S. economic aid would further strengthen the reformist government, which would then be able to draw more moderate Social Democrats and former Christian Democrats away from the FDR-FMLN and into the electoral process, and would exclude the remainder of the left from political power. U.S. military strategy, justified as no more than a "shield" to protect its political strategy, meanwhile would help defeat the armed insurgents.

In a letter to Vice-President Bush in April 1981, Archbishop Rivera y Damas wrote of his surprise that the administration defined the junta as "centrist" and failed to understand that the junta was "greatly influenced by the right wing of the military."

> I think you underestimate the power and resistance of the right wing military to a true political change. . . . Failure to grasp the views of this element of the military, their power in the Junta, and their resistance to change will be a fatal mistake for U.S. policy."³⁵

He was right. Indeed, while the administration was publicly supporting reform and democratization, it was sending clear signals to the Salvadoran military that it would tolerate continued repression and back aid in Congress as long as the left remained a threat. As a result, U.S. policy helped strengthen the right, unify the left, and further marginalize those reformers who had not joined the FDR.

Derechización through Elections

The Reagan administration's political strategy required the backing of a relatively strong reformist government to work. But there were really two governments in El Salvador: a reformist and relatively powerless civilian government led by Duarte, whose primary "popular support" was the U.S. embassy, and a repressive and increasingly powerful military government led by Defense Minister García.

The civilians around Duarte had no control over the military, whose continued repression had made land reform difficult and fair elections impossible.

Phase I of the land-reform program, the expropriation of the largest estates, had been launched quickly and expeditiously in the spring of 1980. But the violence of the state of siege that came with the reform created a repressive context. Three weeks after the reform was promulgated, the under-secretary of the Ministry of Agriculture, Jorge Villacorta, resigned, protesting the "sharp increase in official violence against the very peasants who were supposed 'beneficiaries' of the process."[36] The violence grew during 1980 and throughout 1981: the military and death squads targeted land-reform recipients, leaders of the cooperatives, and the Salvadoran Communal Union (UCS). Most publicized was the murder of UCS head José Rodolfo Viera in January 1981, along with that of two AIFLD American advisers, Michael Hammer and Mark Pearlman.

Phase II of the land-reform program—the most critical in that it would have redistributed a portion of the oligarchy's coffee-growing lands—was blocked by the oligarchy from the beginning.

Phase III, known as the "land to the tiller" program, aimed to give renters and sharecroppers ownership of small plots they had been working. Its implementation was delayed until almost a year after the law was passed. By early 1981, when the Phase III program began to receive applications and to issue titles, land reform no longer had much support from the military, by then purged of the reformers. With continuing pressure from the UCS and the U.S. embassy, the number of applications received, titles issued, and compensation paid slowly increased, but the essence of the land reform was being undermined. The technical assistance and credit needed by those who received Phase III land was severely limited. Further, by December of that year the UCS reported that more than 25,000 sharecroppers or tenant beneficiaries had been forcibly evicted from their farms, "in the majority of cases with the assistance of members of the military forces."

The real power in El Salvador lay in the hands of the military, but within the armed forces important divisions remained even after Majano and the reformers were purged. One faction was closely associated with García. Having moved up through the ranks since graduating together from the military academy (the graduating classes, or tandas, form closely knit cliques), they were ready to enjoy the graft and corruption they felt were their due. But they were uninterested in leading troops against the guerrillas, and they were resistant to U.S.-backed tactics. However, they were willing to give lip service to human rights, land reform, and democratic elections in order to get U.S. aid.

Ever since the October 1979 coup, the García faction was opposed by yet even more reactionary officers closely allied with D'Aubuisson and the extreme right. These ultrarightist officers represented the interests of the most reactionary and recalcitrant members of the oligarcy. The extreme right—deeply entrenched in the oligarchy and business community—resented U.S. support for reform, had carried out a number of demonstrations and attacks against the U.S. embassy, defined the Jesuits as subversives (according to D'Aubuisson, "the worst scum of all"[37]), labeled the Christian Democrats "communists" and wanted them out of office, and complained that U.S. human rights concerns tied their hands in the battle against communist subversion.

Three times these officers had planned coups—in February, May, and December 1980. All were stopped. After the December attempt, the Christian Democrats and the U.S. embassy, then angered by the slaying of the four churchwomen, succeeded in transferring some of D'Aubuisson's closest associates (like Deputy Defense Minister Carranza) to less prominent positions. A fourth attempted coup in March 1981, opposed by the Reagan administration, also failed, but the ultrarightist officers allied with D'Aubuisson and, often in command of intelligence agencies, were still able to use terror to obstruct reform.

After mid-1981 the Reagan administration sought to tame right-wing violence and quell the business sector's harsh criticism of Duarte by promoting collaboration between the right and the Christian Democrats. First, Ambassador Deane R. Hinton failed in an attempt to broker an agreement during 1981: the private-sector organizations—even those "not dominated by the oligarchic element that financed death squads from Miami or Guatemala City"—wanted the military to remove the Christian Democrats and restore their own coalition with the military.[38] Then the embassy hoped that the U.S.-backed elections scheduled for March 1982 might co-opt the right by encouraging them to organize electorally, gain seats in the Constituent Assembly, and join with the Christian Democrats in a governing coalition.

The oligarchy and its allies responded by organizing a new "legitimate" political party of the right, the Nationalist Republican Alliance (Alianza Republicana Nacionalista—ARENA). Three existing organizations joined forces: the Broad National Front, made up of private business associations, antireform groups of coffee growers and cattle ranchers, young executives, a women's association, and a right-wing nationalist youth organization; the old ORDEN network, which D'Aubuisson had kept alive; and the civilian-military death-squad network that D'Aubuisson and the extreme right had organized.[39]

The oligarchy picked D'Aubuisson to head the party. As these Salvadoran rightists, used to living underground and committing acts of terrorism, came out to campaign, they received political support and instruction from conservative public policy groups associated with the Republican Party's new-right movement in the United States.[40]

The major opposition to D'Aubuisson's ARENA party was Duarte's Christian Democratic Party (PDC). The center-left groups in the FDR that might have made a strong showing—and whose support the Christian Democrats would have needed in any post-electoral alliance against the right—boycotted the election. The United States cited FDR opposition to the elections as proof of its antidemocratic character, since FDR had the legal right to participate by registering a petition with three thousand signatures. But from the FDR's perspective, participation would have been dangerous and irrational.

It had abandoned electoral politics in 1980 because of the officially condoned repression against it, which had worsened considerably since then. The FDR leaders killed in November 1980 were only six of thousands of its supporters murdered by the military and the death squads. The names of FDR leaders were on a "traitors list" published by the Armed Forces; in this environment, three thousand signatures on a petition would have amounted to a convenient "death list." Further, the FDR would have been unable to safely organize or campaign. Finally, FDR leaders had no reason to believe that participation in the government would give them any more leverage over the military or the death squads than they had had before many of them (like Ungo and Zamora) resigned from the governing juntas in January and March of 1980.

Because it was irrational for the insurgents to participate, the elections themselves could not end the civil war. Although the presence of hundreds of international observers and reporters in March 1982 minimized irregularities in the actual balloting, the undemocratic conditions of officially sanctioned repression under which the larger electoral process took place excluded the left. Furthermore, the association of the Christian Democrats with the bloodshed that had claimed thousands of lives since 1980 led to a right-wing victory.[41]

The Christian Democrats won 40 percent of the valid vote, a plurality, giving them twenty-four of the sixty seats in the Constituent Assembly. But ARENA (with 29 percent of the vote and nineteen Assembly seats) and the PCN (with 19 percent and fourteen seats) were able to form a majority coalition and thus control the selection of a provisional president.[42] Worried they would pick a rightist like D'Aubuisson, the Reagan administration was thrown back to relying on the military to intervene in politics—despite the image of democracy it was trying to promote. The U.S. embassy successfully pressured García to deny the presidency to D'Aubuisson (which caused García to incur the enmity of the pro-D'Aubuisson faction of the military) and to pick an independent, Alvaro Magaña. In reaction, ARENA and the PCN joined forces to elect D'Aubuisson president of the assembly. By installing Magaña, Washington forced the right to accept a government of national unity and keep the Christian Democrats in. The PDC, however, had little real power.

As a result of the 1982 elections, the most extremist elements of the right gained political power—not only over the new Assembly but, perhaps more important, over crucial government ministries as well. In a bitter irony, ARENA, the party of the traditional enemies of land reform, took control of the Ministry of Agriculture and the Institute of Agrarian Transformation (ISTA), the agency in charge of administering Phase I of the agrarian reform. Through its control of ISTA, ARENA cut training and technical assistance and pressured peasants to replace their cooperative managers with ISTA technicians, who were sometimes relatives of the former land-owners. Through its control of the agrarian bank, it slowed credit delivery, thus squeezing the cooperatives.

D'Aubuisson used his control of the Assembly to legislatively gut Phase II of the land reform (which had never been implemented) and undermine existing reforms. According to a U.S. government audit, for example, about one-third of the applicants for Phase III land "were not working the land because they had been threatened, evicted or had disappeared." The future of the land reform, according to the audit, was "bleak."[43] The U.S. embassy, however, was able to join with the Christian Democrats, García, and a faction of the PCN to block the rollback of other agrarian reform, banking, and trade legislation.

Washington's election-based political strategy thus encouraged a right-ward drift, allowing the antidemocratic right to legitimize its power and to further undermine reform. Perhaps more seriously, it ensured that there would be no effective civilian pressure to stop the *derechización* within the military or end the repression.

Derechización within the Military

In March 1982, the García faction was still in control of the high command. But the willingness of García to do the embassy's bidding by denying D'Aubuisson the provisional presidency and by thwarting his June 1982 attempt to repeal land reform angered D'Aubuisson's allies within the military.[44] In October and November 1982, these ultrarightists again planned a coup. But García, with the strong backing of the U.S. embassy, stood firm. In the aftermath, several top commanders were transferred, including Carranza, who was transferred out of ANTEL.[45]

By mid-1982 other elements within the military had become increasingly concerned about García's lack of military competence. These U.S.-trained officers—*tecnicos* or pragmatists like Colonel Adolfo Blandón, the comman-der of the army's First Infantry Brigade; and Lieutenant Colonel Domingo Monterrosa—believed that the war against the FDR-FMLN was going badly because the older officers of García's generation preferred barracks life and politics to the rigors of antiguerrilla combat.

García's strong U.S. backing in October 1982 made these pragmatists hesitant to back the ultrarightist coup attempt. By January 1983, however, they could no longer afford to remain silent: the guerrilla offensive of the previous months made them worry that the war might be lost because of the military incompetance of García. When García ordered Colonel Sigifredo Ochoa Pérez transferred to Uruguay, a "rebellion" took place. Ochoa had been one of the few Salvadoran commanders to follow the recommendations of U.S. advisers and was considered the most able field commander in the army. This time the United States did not rush to back García and instead adopted a neutral stance. With the support of Blandón and Colonel Juan Raphael Bustillo, commander of the air force, and with some support from the commanders of the three U.S.-trained battalions (like Monterrosa), a deal was struck: Ochoa Pérez agreed to step down and to take a post in Washington; García agreed to resign gracefully within ninety days.

In March, García tried to renege, but the United States, hoping that more competent commanders would be moved into key field positions, seemed more willing to back his ouster. A compromise was struck. García stepped down to allow General Vides Casanova to become defense minister. Vides Casanova represented little change in terms of his military abilities or human rights record (he had headed the national guard whose record of killings included the murders of the American churchwomen and the shootings of UCS chief Viera and the two American labor advisers), but he was an officer acceptable to all factions. As part of the compromise, ultrarightists were given the key positions they had long sought in the security forces by means of coups—positions from which they could better coordinate the official repression of political opposition with death-squad activities. Carranza, for example, was rescued from bureaucratic exile and put in charge of the most secretive and feared of the security forces, the treasury police. The pragmatists got to move into key positions in the army command structure to take charge of fighting the guerrillas. Colonel Blandón became the armed forces chief of staff in November 1983, and he assumed the responsibility for conducting the war that formally resided with the defense minister. Other associates of Blandón and Ochoa Pérez, as well as officers in the D'Aubuisson faction, took up important army posts.

The Deepening Repression

The rightists' control of the government and the consolidation of ultrarightist control in the security forces further institutionalized the repression that was the primary reason most moderates and leftists had gone underground in the first place.

But it is clear that the administration's description of a "moderate government" bravely battling the "violence of the extreme right and the extreme left" was distorted in at least three ways.[46]

First, the preponderance of the human rights violations in El Salvador were committed not by the left but by the right. While guerrilla groups kidnapped and attacked soldiers, government officials, trade union leaders, members of ORDEN, oligarchs, and businessmen, the vast majority of El Salvador's victims were killed by the armed forces or paramilitary groups. The statistics are numbing. Between October 1979 and late 1983, the internationally recognized human rights office of the Roman Catholic Archdiocese of San Salvador, now known as Tutela Legal, tabulated more than 38,000 murders of civilian noncombatants by government security forces and paramilitary groups associated with them. When the violence peaked, as in early 1981, 300 to 500 people were killed each week; during times of relative "quiet," as in the last three months of 1983, the murders continued at a rate of 120 a week (the proportionate figure in the United States would be 5,700 a week).[47]

Second, the administration wrongly depicted the death squads as extreme rightist groups independent of the government. But senior officers in the government security forces (particularly intelligence chiefs) helped to inform, direct, and protect these hired killers. "If the web of complicity tying the armed forces to the death-squad violence ever did unravel," asked one analyst, "who would be left to fight the war?"[48]

The third and most troubling distortion was the administration's misrepresentation of the U.S.-supported military and security forces. These armed forces were the real government in El Salvador. They, and not the death squads, were responsible for most of the killings of noncombatants. According to Tutela Legal, an average of 76 percent of the civilians killed each month by government forces are killed by the army alone. Some of the killings by regular security forces were more or less selective, as when civilians were pulled from their houses and summarily executed. Others were indiscriminate, as when the armed forces engaged in free-fire against civilians in conflict zones and in guerrilla-controlled areas of the country.[49] Certain massacres, such as those at Rio Sumpul, El Mozote, Las Hojas, and Copapaya, became landmarks of military brutality. No military officer was ever brought to trial—not surprising since the involvement with the terror went right to the high command. There was evidence, for example, that both García and Vides Casanova were involved in the cover-up of the murder of the four American churchwomen, possibly to protect high-ranking officers, including Vides's cousin. One of the defense lawyers for the guardsman accused in the slaying later admitted that he had been forced to take part in a "conspiracy" aimed at preventing higher-ranking officers from being implicated.[50]

The repression carried out by the military and security forces was institutionalized, not random. It was not a problem of poor training, not the result of faulty command and control. Americas Watch concluded in 1984:

> Such gross abuses of human rights are not incidental to the way the armed forces conduct their war against the guerrillas . . . Terror is the means whereby the armed forces maintain their authority. Accordingly, there can be

no let-up in the political murders, as far as the armed forces are concerned, because this would cause their authority to slip away.[51]

New York Times reporter Raymond Bonner later summarized administration policy toward the repression:

> Each time the administration issued another certification, it was a message to the ruthless Salvadoran military officers that they really didn't have to change their ways. Each time the administration insisted that officers were being punished when in fact, they weren't, it reinforced the military's belief that it did not have to punish officers. Each time the administration covered up atrocities and torture, it encouraged more. Each time the administration blamed the "extreme right" and the death squads, it was exonerating the military and the government. "Quiet diplomacy" didn't work.[52]

It was not until shortly before the 1984 Salvadoran presidential elections that the Reagan administration reacted with forceful language. In late 1983 there was an upsurge of death-squad assassinations of moderate, U.S.-supported labor and political leaders. For the first time, the administration strongly condemned the "extremist terror" of the death squads, which both U.S. Ambassador Thomas R. Pickering and Undersecretary of Defense Fred C. Iklé branded as "fascist" and ultimately serving the interests of the guerrillas.[53] In December 1983 Vice-President Bush, while in El Salvador, demanded action against the death squads, including the exiling of about twenty-five military officers and civilians suspected of involvement in their activities. He warned the government that failure to act would cost it the administration's support. The military responded by transferring some of the officers to other command posts or attaché posts overseas.

On the eve of the 1984 presidential elections over 38,000 civilian non-combatants had been killed or disappeared; the war had displaced hundreds of thousands from their homes, disrupted the economy, and severely worsened conditions of everyday life for the majority of the population.[54] The administration's political strategy had failed to promote reform or democracy and end repression or bring peace. The White House rhetoric about elections and reform served in Washington as a "shield" for the real strategy: military defeat of the FDR-FMLN. But in early 1984 the embassy in El Salvador did not have good news about the military situation to send back to Washington.

The Deteriorating Military Situation

After early 1981, both the armed forces and the insurgents grew in number and military strength, but the armed forces gained neither the will to fight nor the support of the civilian population.

The army's tactics of big sweeps designed to chase guerrillas out of an area were not working: the guerrillas, warned in advance by supporters in the local population, would simply leave and then return when the troops withdrew. Faced with growing military obstacles in 1982 and early 1983, the military adopted a U.S.-sponsored "National Plan." The new strategy was to send troops into an area and keep them there until it was guerrilla-free. Civic action programs would be used to win support of the population, and local militias would be trained to defend villages. Small battalions would be trained to hunt down and ambush guerrilla units. The new strategy was first tested in San Vicente province.

When five thousand government troops entered the area in the summer of 1983, the FMLN retreated. The summer months—the rainy season—were relatively calm militarily. As in the two previous summers, United States and Salvadoran officers expressed "cautious optimism." But the calm turned out to be no more than a rainy-season lull. In the fall, the fighting escalated quickly in San Vicente and throughout the country.

In September and October alone, more than eight hundred Salvadoran soldiers were killed and four hundred were captured. At the end of December the FMLN overran a major army base at El Paraíso in Chalatenango, a modern counterinsurgency base designed by the United States, capturing large amounts of weapons and ammunition. Shortly thereafter, it drove several hundred government troops from Salvador's militarily crucial bridge at Cuscatlán, the largest in the country, and destroyed it. U.S. Ambassador Thomas Pickering admitted, "The plan is at a stage where it needs reinvigoration after the guerrilla counteroffensive. The army has not shown the capacity to deal with the counteroffensive in the area of the plan. We had said that was a key test."[55] By mid-1984 the plan was no longer mentioned.

Many officers and enlisted men were simply not committed to fight against the highly motivated insurgents. Although the more professional, U.S.-trained officers (like Monterrosa, Blandón, and Bustillo) had taken key command positions, corruption was still endemic to the officer corps. Indeed the armed forces traditionally were more like a mafia in uniform than a military. The Armed Forces Security Council, the ruling body of the military, was composed of seven to ten top-ranking officers representing the most powerful *tandas*:

> For five prosperous years, the council members and their allies within the armed forces will become fabulously wealthy through systematic corruption, fraud and kickbacks. At the end of five years, the Council members retire, and the next class of *tanda* leaders move in to take their place. . . . The Army's relationship with the country's economic elite is a mutually benefi cial one. The oligarchy needs the Army to keep a starved and restless peasant workforce on the job for $133 a year. But the Army needs the oligarchy as well, to keep the economy going. Immense profits go to top officers from kickbacks from government contracts with large businesses and industries.[56]

The particularly lucrative posts include ANTEL, the state's telecommunications agency, and the national light and power company. Once U.S. aid began to flow, this provided a new opportunity to rake off dollars.

If corruption weakened the officer corps, forced draft recruiting—many "enlisted men" were picked up by the army and compelled to serve—weakened the ranks. Many soldiers lacked the will to fight. In early 1984, U.S. advisers admitted that the army was still plagued by low morale. The reenlistment figures were telling. About half of the seven thousand troops and officers trained by the United States between 1981 and 1983 left the army after their two-year tours.

By the March 1984 presidential elections, even the pessimistic conclusion of a June 1983 classified report prepared for the National Security Council still held true: the Salvadoran military, although bolstered by some short-term gains during its spring 1983 offensive, faced at best a stalemate in the long run. Senior officials began drawing up contingency plans for the possible use of U.S. combat troops, if the current strategy for defeating leftist forces in the region failed,[57] and the administration pressured Congress for more aid to increase the firepower and mobility of the military.

The administration understood the importance of a Duarte victory in 1984. For those in the embassy and State Department truly committed to a middle way, a Duarte victory over D'Aubuisson was a necessary condition for any nonextremist alternative to survive. For the more hardline strategists in the Pentagon, CIA, and National Security Council, Duarte was essential to sell an increasingly reluctant Congress on more military aid to support their primary strategy of defeating the left militarily. Not only did the administration spend $10 million to finance electoral technology and administration and pay air fares of international observers, but it also funneled almost $1 million through the CIA to support Duarte's campaign.[58]

THE CHRISTIAN DEMOCRATS TAKE OFFICE: 1984 ▲

In May of 1984 Duarte won the presidential elections in a runoff against D'Aubuisson. Then in March 1985 his Christian Democrats took control of the Legislative Assembly from the right-wing ARENA-PCN alliance. The Christian Democratic victories appeared to vindicate the Reagan administration's political strategy: despite the war's tremendous cost in lives and destruction, elections had put a centrist party in office. In Washington, the Duarte victory all but eliminated the reluctance of Congress to finance the administration's massive aid requests. Internationally, Duarte gained important recognition from Mexico, Venezuela, and Western European governments.

But in El Salvador, the reality was sobering. Duarte held office but still had very limited power to reverse the *derechización* that had begun shortly after the 1979 reformist coup. Two strategies were open to Duarte.

One was to build a reform coalition, organizing and mobilizing those who backed Christian Democratic electoral victories in 1984 and 1985. These voters hoped that Duarte could fulfill his campaign promises embodied in the *pacto social* he signed with labor in February 1984: to reactivate agrarian reform, to protect labor organizations and give them a voice in government, to reverse the deteriorating economic conditions plaguing the everyday life of the majority, and above all to end the repression and seek a political solution to the civil war. Such a strategy would demand (as the failure of the first and second reformist juntas in 1979 and 1980 showed) some incorporation of the left if it were to overcome the power and recalcitrance of the right.

The political space opened by the electoral victories allowed the slow reemergence of unions and other popular organizations, and these groups pressured Duarte to create a reform coalition, but he had very limited room to maneuver. The right was determined to use its economic power, death squads, and connections with influential officers in the military to block reform. While the military showed some independence from the oligarchy on questions of reform, the high command had no intention of submitting to civilian control or punishing officers guilty of murder or corruption and was reluctant to have an open confrontation with the death squads, given the involvement of many ultrarightist officers. And Duarte knew it would be dangerous to break with the military.

Adding to the difficulties of this reform strategy, the Reagan administration frequently undermined Duarte by its less than full support for reform and its strong support for the private sector (encouraging pro-business policies, urging the PDC to bring this sector into the ruling coalition) despite its antidemocratic and antireformist politics. Washington's insistence on defeat of the insurgents, and its opposition to a political settlement of the war further strengthened the far right.

The right, the military, and the United States thus pushed Duarte toward another strategy: a reconstitution of the conservative PDC-military coalition he presided over during the fierce repression of the 1980–82 period. While he may have been committed to fostering reform, ending the repression, and negotiating a political settlement to the war, he was led to act against the goals of the potential pro-reform coalition. Duarte often moved against his former supporters when they actively demanded democratization and reform; he was able to moderate death-squad activity but not other forms of repression; and he tolerated the pursuit of a primarily military solution to the civil war.

The Obstacles to Reform

Duarte's major internal support came from what some Salvadorans dubbed "the silenced majority."[59] It included many middle-class professionals as well as small- and medium-scale private entrepreneurs hard hit by the war, abandoned by the government, and mistrustful of the FDR-FMLN. But the potentially most important political forces were those who were members of the popular groups in the 1970s, whose organizations were destroyed by the systematic terror directed against them after early 1980. Before the 1984 and 1985 elections, they did not constitute a "center" or a "third way" because fear of repression left them fragmented and weakly organized. Although many had withdrawn completely from organized opposition, some were still members of Christian base communities; others were members of peasant and labor organizations—moderate unions like the peasant UCS and others affiliated with the UPD, and the more left-leaning Coordination of Solidarity with the Workers (CST), a new labor federation that brought together remnants of unions previously affiliated to the FDR but decimated by repression.[60]

The economic condition of these lower- and middle-income groups had declined dramatically as a result of four years of war. Real income had plummeted in the face of rising prices, declining real wages, and unemployment; economic production had fallen; a stringent credit squeeze and war-fueled uncertainty reduced private and public investment.[61] Exhausted by the war and continually in fear of the terror and killing, many in the silenced majority rejected the repression of the right, generally supported the reforms advocated by the FDR-FMLN, but were unwilling to openly support armed insurgency.

Duarte's election opened some political space, allowing these groups to begin reorganizing and pressing their pent-up demands. Unions and other popular organizations began to re-emerge and strike activity increased. While the security forces could still control labor activity with selective repression, massive repression was ruled out. Labor and peasant organizers frequently tested and tried to expand the limits placed upon them. Furthermore, by early 1986, even representatives of the FDR were cautiously testing the waters to see the extent to which they could come back to the country and operate openly. While U.S. newspapers reported strains between the FDR and FMLN, much more significant was the understanding shared by both groups that the new political opening had to be quietly explored. While the military assumed it could control the political opening, the economic demands of these groups, and their broad sympathy for the wider political demands of the FDR (a negotiated settlement, changes in economic policy, guaranteed rights of association and other freedoms) creates pressure to expand the opening far more than the right is prepared to accept.

Although Duarte's election allowed the Christian Democrats to take control of the bureaucracy from the rightists who had captured key positions after the 1982 election, he still faced serious obstacles in meeting these growing demands for economic relief and reform.

Until March 1985 he faced a National Assembly controlled by the right and committed to thwarting his efforts. It voted, for example, to end transfers of land under Phase III, made it impossible to reactivate the crucial

Phase II (which touched the coffee lands at the heart of the oligarchy's power), and reduced Duarte's requests for funds for land-reform agencies.[62] Christian Democratic control over the Assembly after March 1985 helped remove legislative obstacles, but Duarte's supporters still waited for signs that he would seriously pursue reform.[63] But even with a legislative majority, there were still three serious constraints on Duarte's ability to build a reform coalition.

One was the strong opposition of the private sector to any serious reform effort. While Duarte's control over banking and foreign commerce gave him some leverage,[64] the private sector's ability to withhold needed investment, its high level of organization (for example the National Association of Private Enterprise—ANEP), and its links with the death squads, influential military officers, and the U.S. embassy put serious limits on government power.

A second constraint was the nature of the nonmilitary U.S. aid. The administration was continually worried that the right would defect from the regime, bringing further economic deterioration and a resurgence of death-squad violence and thus difficulties in getting aid from Congress. In its efforts to bring in the right, Washington's policies often ended up hindering reform while strengthening the rightists in the private sector. While the Reagan administration labeled the bulk of the aid "economic," less than 16 percent of the FY1984 and FY1985 totals actually went to finance the agrarian reform and AID development projects Duarte needed to build a reform coalition. The bulk of the so-called economic aid—just over 40 percent of the total—was targeted to redress the damage done by the civil war, and most of this was in the form of cash transfers (mostly through U.S. AID's Economic Support Funds Program) to sustain the government and economy in the face of the economic collapse brought on by the war.[65] Such funds did nothing to support needed reforms but did strengthen those who could draw on these funds in the private sector and the military. So long as the oligarchs and officers had Washington to bail them out, they had neither the incentive to stop blocking reform nor the the incentive to negotiate a solution to the war, which was soaking up the "economic aid" in the first place.

The right was further strengthened by the "Reaganomics" that often informed U.S. economic objectives; for instance, AID's emphasis on such things as a reduction in government spending, allowing private banks to operate alongside nationalized banks, "privatizing basic grains marketing" (likely to return grain-selling to monopolistic businesses), a "reorientation of the agrarian reform program consistent with the free enterprise approach of the Government of El Salvador," and "increased privatization of the economy" supported policies that favored those groups most opposed to reform.[66] Moreover, the U.S.-backed austerity program that Duarte announced in early 1986 could put a particularly heavy burden on labor and peasant groups, further undermining the support of important Christian Democratic constituents.

The third constraint on Duarte's ability to build a reform coalition was the continued repression. There would be little real reform without organized pressure from peasants, workers, professionals, and others. Only by establishing the rule of law; preventing kidnappings, disappearances, killings, and arbitrary arrests; gaining control over the military and security forces; and punishing those guilty of murder could Duarte create the political space for his supporters to push for reform and for the left to have a rational alternative to armed insurgency. In 1985, Americas Watch still concluded there had been "no significant movement . . . towards democratization."

> That is, there is no indication that a left-wing opposition newspaper could function, as such newspapers did function until they were violently closed by the armed forces in 1980 and 1981; there is no indication that left-wing unions could function, as they did until their leaders were murdered, disappeared, imprisoned and tortured in 1980, 1981 and 1982; there is no indication that left-wing political parties could function, as they did until their leaders were murdered or disappeared in 1980, 1981 and 1982. The political space that exists in El Salvador permits Salvadorans a choice between the Christian Democrats and the parties of the right. Unless and until the political space widens so as also to permit peaceful opposition by newspapers, labor unions and political parties to the left of the Christian Democrats, it will not be possible to say that democratization is underway.[67]

For Duarte to establish a reform coalition and move toward democratization he first had to end the repression.

The Difficulties of Ending the Repression

Although the 1983 constitution made the president general commander of the armed forces, Duarte had very little control over the high command. By mid-1984, however, there was an important coincidence of interests between Duarte and the more professional, U.S.-trained officers like Armed Forces Chief of Staff Adolfo Blandón. "We knew that public opinion in the United States and the view of many Senators and Congressmen opposed to military aid for El Salvador were largely due to our bad image because of the squads," Blandón later explained.[68] These powerful *tecnicos* or pragmatists thus realized that a resurgence of death-squad activity or a military coup would threaten congressional funding. The military was willing to uphold the 1984 election of Duarte and the 1985 victory of the Christian Democrats in the National Assembly; and it was willing to shift officers with well-known ties to the death squads.

Even before Duarte's inauguration, these pragmatists moved to downplay the institutional link between the armed forces and the death squads. Four officers linked to D'Aubuisson—including the commander of the treasury police, Nicolas Carranza—were transferred to foreign posts.[69] Shortly after Duarte took office, there was some restructuring of the treasury police, national guard, and national police. These security forces were put under the control of Colonel Carlos Reynaldo López Nuila, former head of the national police, who was given the newly created post of deputy minister of defense for security. The new commander of the treasury police, Colonel Rinaldo Golcher, disbanded the S-2 intelligence unit, notorious for its excesses, and closely linked with the death squads. Defense Minister Vides Casanova explained: "We know that improving our image is worth millions of dollars of aid for the country."[70]

After Duarte's inauguration there was a marked improvement in the treatment of those arrested by the security forces. The acknowledgment of arrests and permission for families and lawyers to see those arrested accounted for this decline in torture. The number of death-squad killings and disappearances declined.[71] Increased labor and peasant organization, while still severely restricted, was tolerated. In sharp contrast to previous years, some strikes and demonstrations by unions were handled relatively peacefully by the security forces.[72]

But while the pragmatists in the armed forces allowed Duarte some political space, the whole of the military remained autonomous. Duarte could thus neither control the conduct of armed forces, nor eliminate the right-wing terror.

The armed forces were still responsible for killing or displacing thousands of civilian noncombatants, mostly in indiscriminate attacks during military operations.[73] Such attacks not only occurred during ground operations—the massacres in Los Llanitos, in Cabañas, and around the Gualsinga River in Chalatenango in the summer of 1984 were two that were particularly well documented[74]—but after early 1984 were mounted from the air. As early as April the *National Catholic Reporter* noted that "the shadow of a little noted air war is falling over this country's rural population, emptying towns and terrorizing civilians."[75] This expanded air war was supported by U.S. helicopters, planes, bombs, training, and sometimes even U.S. reconnaissance flights out of Honduras and Panama.[76] While the State Department officially denied indiscriminate bombing, U.S. journalists and independent human rights observers presented evidence to the contrary. In September 1984 Duarte himself issued guidelines to the air force to reduce civilian casualties from air strikes, but subsequent evidence showed the president's directives had been disregarded.[77] The bombing drove tens of thousands of civilians from their homes, while others were forcibly removed by ground forces.[78]

The indiscriminate killing and forced displacement was neither accidental nor the result of lack of training but part of the very strategy the military employed to terrorize civilians in guerrilla-held zones, forcing them to flee and thus depriving the guerrillas of food. The *Dallas Morning News* reported:

To help cut out civilian contact with the rebels, the program in Chalatenango prohibits civilian movement or residence in 12 free-fire zones. Air strikes and artillery bombardments now are being carried out indiscriminately in these areas, the military leaders said.

"Our first goal (said Col. Sigifredo Ochoa) is to clean up the province militarily. . . . This means we cannot permit civilian contact with the rebel army. We must separate the people from the guerrillas and then crush the guerrillas. The civilians can return when we have searched the area.

"Without a civilian base of support, the guerrillas are nothing but out-laws," Ochoa said leaning over a map in his command headquarters. "Without civilians the rebels have no food and cannot maintain their army."[79]

Americas Watch concluded: "While it is possible that this is an effective way for the Salvadoran armed forces to prevail in their struggle with the guerrillas, the cost in civilian suffering and civilian lives is both incalculable and appalling."[80] The failure of officers to distinguish between civilians and guerrillas in zones of conflict was reflected in the comment of a major in the U.S.-trained Atlacatl battalion after its involvement in the Los Llanitos massacre, where at least forty-two peasants died: "There are no people living in those hamlets—only terrorists."[81]

Duarte's inability to bring the army and air force under enough control to end the indiscriminate killing—the air war against the civilian population and the massacres by ground troops—meant he could not end the repression and create the conditions for democratization, reform, or a political settlement.

Duarte was further constrained by the continued existence of right-wing death-squad organizations inside and outside the military. Although the decision by the high command to rein in these groups brought a decline in the number of death-squad killings, these terrorist organizations continued to operate, selectively targeting their victims. Thus despite the lower body counts, death squads still had a chilling effect. As one labor leader explained in late 1985: "They do not need to kill too many to remind those of us who are leaders that if we continue our activities, it may be us next time. People remember repression." So long as these organizations were in place and the officers and civilians who led them went unpunished, the threat remained. The reassignment of Carranza and three other officers to foreign posts did not send a message that murder was a serious abuse of authority. Nor did the reorganization of the S-2 intelligence unit: these officers were transferred to command positions, sometimes with U.S.-trained battalions.[82] The officer corps knew that when the political climate changed, those transferred would be brought back—like Carranza, who was brought back in 1983 to head the treasury police, and Ochoa, who was twice brought back from diplomatic exile. President Magaña, on the eve of Duarte's inauguration, even explained to a reporter how the government tried to persuade military officials suspected of participating in death squads that their proposed transfers were not to be considered punishments.[83]

The core of the problem is that the high command and officer corps are deeply involved in the killings—and the institutionalized corruption.[84] Informed sources, including a high-ranking Salvadoran officer with strong links to intelligence circles, have explained that the Armed Forces Security Council approved major death-squad actions. The council,

> composed of seven to ten top-rank officers representing the most powerful *tandas* . . . decides who lives and who dies; Army troops and police carry out its will. It is not an accident that these people have been systematically eliminated by uniformed soldiers or plainclothes policeman. . . . It is not surprising that not a single massacre has been investigated and not a single officer disciplined for carrying out that policy. The Security Council must cover its own complicity in these crimes, as well as protect the younger officers behind them who are also implicated.[85]

Duarte's majority in the assembly removed some of the legislative obstacles to getting funding for such investigations.[86] It also allowed him to remove the conservative and obstructionist attorney general appointed by the previously rightist-dominated assembly. But the central problem was not legislative control or technical ability but rather the unwillingness of the armed forces to support criminal punishment of its members, and Duarte's continued lack of control over the high command.[87]

For example, Duarte promised an investigation of the Los Llanitos massacre but asked the army high command to carry it out, and then failed to release any report, stating publicly only that it did not show that the armed forces had intentionally or negligently used violence against civilians. He refused to order an investigation of the massacre at the Gualsinga River, instead denouncing the guerrillas for using civilians as a shield against army attacks.[88] Duarte was unable to forcefully investigate a number of notorious crimes involving the military and the death squads that he had publically promised to prosecute. He did not lift the state of siege, in effect since 1980, which officially sanctions restrictions on civil liberties like freedom of movement and freedom of the press. The increase in strike activity by labor unions was met with an increase in repressive measures against trade unionists.[89] In March 1985, Duarte even denounced Tutela Legal, the human rights office of the Roman Catholic church. In response to Tutela Legal's contention that the government had killed a number of citizens in indiscriminate air attacks, Duarte charged the organization with being unreliable and "trying to help subversive groups."[90] This "shooting the messenger" was ominous: it signaled the military that Duarte was prepared to participate in cover-ups, and it signaled the thousands of people who had given testimony to Tutela Legal that the Duarte government was not serious about ending repression.

The United States continued to play a crucial but contradictory role in controlling repression after the 1984 elections. Congress made clear that continued death-squad activity would threaten aid, and that support for massive aid would only continue so long as Duarte was not removed and elections were respected.[91] It was this pressure from the United States, and only secondarily Duarte's influence, that convinced the pragmatists in the military to promote even the limited steps they took.[92] But Congress did not press the government to end the other forms of repression.

The hard-liners in the Reagan administration took actions signaling that the White House was willing to ally itself with the extreme right, if that were necessary to achieve a military victory over the insurgents. One signal was the response to the discovery of a right-wing assassination plot against U.S. Ambassador Thomas Pickering in early October 1984—the second in five months—organized by close associates of D'Aubuisson.[93] The embassy not only granted D'Aubuisson a visa to visit the United States, but announced that Pickering would be removed as ambassador. The visa, the visit (and warm reception by conservative Republicans in Washington), and the announced transfer were interpreted by the right in El Salvador as great victories and signs of administration support.[94] In the weeks preceding the March 1985 election, some embassy officials even let it be known that they favored a rightist victory in the National Assembly elections: if the Christian Democrats won, diplomats feared the right would return to terrorism to block reform.[95] The perception among the pragmatic faction in the officer corps was that the United States would not strongly support the pragmatists if they confronted the extreme right.

The Challenge of the Civil War

Bringing an end to the civil war was the most important challenge Duarte faced. Until the conflict was resolved there would be no economic recovery, let alone reform. The choice between a military defeat of the FDR-FMLN or a political settlement was deeply influenced by U.S. policy. The hard-liners in the Reagan administration continued to push for a military "solution." U.S. aid ruled out an insurgent victory, but did not end the costly stalemate.

To back its military strategy, the administration was able to use Duarte's electoral victories to push through Congress massive increases in U.S. military aid. In August 1984, the approval of $70 million in supplemental aid brought the FY1984 total to $195.5 million, a figure equal to U.S. military aid provided over the past three fiscal years combined. The 1984 Congress also approved $128.25 million in military aid for FY1985.

By 1985, U.S. aid had financed the expansion of the Salvadoran army and security forces from 12,000 in 1980 to over 42,000.[96] The number of U.S. military personnel had doubled to over a hundred; there were several hundred members of a U.S. intelligence battalion based in Honduras regularly flying missions over El Salvador to gather battlefield intelligence; and despite "standing orders" to avoid areas of combat, U.S. advisers accompanied air-mobile assaults, U.S. pilots regularly flew aerial reconnaissance over rebel territory, and Operational Planning and Assistance Teams (OPATs) of two to three "trainers" were stationed in each of El Salvador's six army brigade headquarters throughout the country, assisting commanders in management and planning and moving with the headquarters during field operations.[97]

U.S. military strategy broadened and deepened from what was originally presented by the administration as an attempt to expand and upgrade the Salvadoran army to get them out of the barracks and fighting in small mobile units, to a sophisticated, technological, "counterinsurgency strategy, reminiscent of Vietnam, of aerial bombardment and air-mobile assault."[98]

The new air tactics became increasingly important after the pacification, and civic-action projects of the National Plan had clearly failed by early 1984. The aerial bombardment was not simply aimed at preventing guerrillas from massing for attacks but at terrorizing civilian supporters and forcing them to flee conflict zones. The air-mobile assaults, modeled on the air cavalry techniques used widely in Vietnam, were "designed to keep the rebels on the run through unexpected helicopter assaults in rebel zones, and eventually to wear them down to a small number of rural 'bandits' who pose no substantial military threat."[99] The *New York Times* explained the theory:

> To catch the guerrillas, the army is developing long-range reconnaissance patrols of 10 to 20 men. The patrols are trained to enter guerrilla areas to gather intelligence and carry out ambushes at night. With a fleet of 40 to 50 helicopters, the army is expected to be able to send small patrols to make contact with the guerrillas and immediately reinforce them by air with a 500- to 800-man battalion.[100]

The air-mobile tactics required an augmentation of airborne firepower, such as the introduction of modified C-47 rapid-firing gunships. While useful in a purely tactical sense, firing 3,600 rounds per minute in dense population areas where insurgents and the civilian population are mingled inevitably increased civilian casualties.[101]

The bombing and air-mobile tactics killed and displaced thousands of noncombatants. These tactics made it more difficult—but not impossible—for the guerrillas to mass for large-scale attacks; and they avoided direct engagement during major military offensives.[102] These tactics also stopped what had seemed by early 1984 to be a deteriorating situation for the government forces. But they did not end the military stalemate.

The FMLN adapted its units and tactics by breaking its attack columns into small groups that stayed highly foot-mobile and assembled quickly for offensive column strikes. They then rapidly dispersed to present a difficult target and moved back into stronghold areas before the army could pin them down with its air mobility. The guerrillas were still able to strike throughout the country at times and places of their own choosing. Some of the new methods they adopted continued to take a high toll on the military: almost 70 percent of the 2,337 soldiers killed or wounded between June

1984 and April 1985 were hit by land mines. Further, the insurgents had enough weapons to at least maintain the stalemate.[103]

While the White House insisted on the importance of external arms flows from Nicaragua, interviews conducted in El Salvador and Washington— some with officials with access to classified materials—indicated that the administration was grossly distorting the amount of arms coming in from outside of the country and misrepresenting the Sandinistas as the major source of such supply. While the Sandinistas (and the Cubans) did assist the FDR-FMLN with some supplies and other support (refuge, meeting places, communications assistance, and, until early 1983, facilities for an operational command center in Managua), it was not this assistance that sustained the armed insurgency. The bulk of FMLN weapons were captured (and some were even bought) from the military. Of the arms and supplies that did come from outside, many were bought on the open market by the FMLN and transshipped through Honduras, Guatemala, and Nicaragua. The military strength of the guerrillas—and thus the continued stalemate —did not depend primarily on the Sandinistas.[104]

The new air tactics encouraged other shifts in guerrilla tactics, such as movement into urban areas and an increased resort to kidnapping. Militarily the move to the cities meant creating urban organizations that could attack soldiers (including U.S. personnel), officials, and installations—a kind of combat that made air warfare useless but was likely to escalate the intensity of violence and counterviolence in the major cities.[105] In June 1985, for example, guerrillas raided an outdoor café, killing four marines from the U.S. embassy, two American businessmen, and seven Latin American civilians. The most dramatic kidnapping was of President Duarte's daughter in September 1985. The insurgents exchanged the president's daughter and twenty-three kidnapped Christian Democratic mayors for rebel prisoners—including a number of important leaders—that had been captured by the military.[106]

The character of the military and insurgent forces was another important element in the stalemate. Although by 1985 the army greatly improved its top-level command and control, as well as its organization for battle, it continued to be short of trained small-unit combat leaders. There was evidence of weariness among fighting personnel on both sides. Morale was somewhat higher than it had been but many of the enlisted personnel were still press-ganged into service from the poorest and least-educated segment of Salvadoran society.

> There is little incentive for a low-ranking, teenage soldier to do more than serve his time and try to survive to return to poverty. . . . It is not difficult for anyone who has experienced infantry combat to understand why these young soldiers, who are paid less than fifty cents a day, and have little to look forward to after their service but to return to the same exploitation, are not particularly anxious to aggressively risk their lives in combat. And they know

that the guerrillas generally release prisoners to the Red Cross and the army then discharges them because they are no longer considered reliable.[107]

The morale of the insurgent fighters may also have suffered somewhat from the army's new tactics, and there were indications of recruitment problems.[108] But observers said morale in general remained satisfactory.[109] The dedication of the guerrillas was reinforced by the army practice of not taking prisoners, and they were sustained "by their belief that if they can win, they look forward to . . . something better from life."[110]

Despite continued optimistic reports from administration spokesmen, by early 1986 the U.S.-backed military strategy was faring little better than the political and economic policies it had come to overshadow. A 1985 report by congressional critics accurately concluded:

> In spite of increased U.S. financial aid and increased U.S. involvement of personnel, conditions within El Salvador continue to deteriorate. The number of displaced people grows daily. The number of civilian casualties increases, and threatens to worsen under increased aerial assaults. And finally, official estimates of the number of rebels have climbed steadily. . . . [111]

The military defeat of the FDR-FMLN that the White House continued to seek created a logic for the the kind of war that the ultraright in El Salvador supported: the creation of free-fire zones with no restrictions on killing civilians, an increase in the level of aerial strafing and bombing, and a blind eye to large-scale massacres in the countryside. Such tactics denied military victory to the left, but they did not assure defeat of the insurgents or an end to the military stalemate.

La Palma and After

While the "bottom line" for the Reagan administration was to defeat the FDR-FMLN (or so weaken it that it could not hope to gain a significant share of power), the military stalemate created forces in El Salvador that supported a political settlement to the civil war. Duarte publically committed himself to this route, and the 1984 and 1985 elections made him a central actor in forging such a possibility.

The most important force pushing for negotiations was the political and military leadership of the FDR-FMLN. By 1982 its analysis was that a military victory would be too costly: it would not only mean more years of bloodshed but also inheriting a devastated economy and facing vehement opposition from the United States, whose support they saw as crucial for reconstruction.[112] But the FDR-FMLN was only willing to negotiate a solution in which it shared enough power to ensure that there would be no repetition of the slaughter that occurred after many of them tried to participate in the reform juntas that followed the October 1979 coup. And they understood that it was their military strength that made them, in the words of one FMLN commander, a "veto force": the civil war could not be ended without their agreement.[113]

A second major force for a political settlement was the somewhat less silenced majority that began to emerge after 1984 elections. The *pacto social* that Duarte signed with the UPD in February 1984 to gain electoral support from these moderate peasant and labor organizations had as its first point a political solution to the war. Professionals, small- and medium-sized businessmen, and even some of the less-reactionary larger businessmen also understood that the violent stalemate made normal life and business impossible. The votes for Duarte and the Christian Democrats were clear indications of a desire for a negotiated settlement: the economic hardships, the daily possibility of violence and death created strong pressures among Duarte's supporters for dialogue with the FDR-FMLN.

There was also strong support for dialogue among many Christian Democrats who understood that a necessary condition for creating a "reform coalition" was ending the civil war and bringing the left in.

> There is no military solution to our conflict now, unless it is a military victory by the guerrillas. . . . If we continue to resolve the conflict militarily, we will lose. Only a dialogue and eventual incorporation of democratic elements of the left into our ranks offer any exit for us now.[114]

Some even recognized that without the insurgency they would not have been allowed by the military to take power and that a military defeat of the FDR-FMLN would quickly make them dispensable. But all the Christian Democrats understood the electoral logic: if they were to gain a legislative majority in the March 1985 elections, Duarte had to prove to his constituents that he was willing to make good on his electoral promise to seek peace through dialogue.

While Duarte understood the logic of a negotiated solution, powerful right-wing forces in the oligarchy and within the military, who already saw him as too leftist, opposed any form of dialogue on the grounds that it would legitimize the opposition. But while the first choice of the officer corps was a military victory, many of the more pragmatic, professional, U.S.-trained officers were concerned about the weariness of their combat officers and the tenuous morale of their forced-draft recruits. They questioned whether they could overcome the stalemate without destroying the country economically and suffering great military costs. They were therefore willing to consider some form of dialogue with the FDR-FMLN, but remained extremely cautious. They knew there was strong opposition to dialogue within the officer corps and that demands by the left for restructuring the military were unacceptable. They knew that any move toward dialogue would generate fierce opposition by the ultraright, and its allies in the military might provoke a confrontation—a challenge to the unity of the armed forces that historically had always led reformers to cave in to hard-liners when reform risked serious rifts. And they knew the Reagan administration was opposed to any negotiations that would give the FDR-FMLN a significant share of power, and that it was determined to defeat the left militarily.

Duarte's options were thus seriously limited, but he gambled that neither the military nor Washington could afford to abandon him. In early October 1984, Duarte decided to use a previously scheduled U.N. address to invite the FDR-FMLN to talks one week later at La Palma.

The White House, surprised by the move, had no choice but to offer support, although Secretary of State George Shultz made it a point to visit San Salvador and publically reiterate U.S. opposition to any power-sharing arrangements. Duarte gained cautious support from some of the less reactionary business community. But most important was the public support of key officers in the high command, particularly the pragmatists around the armed forces chief of staff, Colonel Adolfo Blandón. Duarte's indispensability in getting Congressional aid was one crucial factor in gaining their backing. But also important to some key officers was their perception that the stalemated war was not going well and that there was strong support for dialogue among Congressional moderates who were important in future conflicts over aid.[115]

The content of such negotiations was a critical issue. One model was graceful surrender: the FDR-FMLN participation in the March 1985 elections in return for laying down their arms. This was the model supported by the United States and the pragmatists in the military. The other model was some kind of power-sharing in which the death squads would be dismantled and the military would be restructured (to include, for example, some of the FMLN forces) so that the insurgents would be guaranteed there would be no repetition of the slaughter of 1980 and 1981. This is what the FDR-FMLN demanded. Whatever Duarte's real intentions, he was put in a box: he could not publicly support power-sharing without bringing the military, the ultraright, and the United States down on him. But the left would not seriously contemplate surrender, however graceful. The best that could be hoped for was to set a process in motion that would open new possibilities—allow his supporters to mobilize, expand political space, bring the right under enough real control that the FDR-FMLN could have the security it demanded to begin a process of cease-fire and to participate in nonarmed politics, and to corner Washington, anxious not to publicly oppose Duarte, into supporting the process.

The La Palma meeting appeared to be a good first step. Agreements were made to set up a joint commission to "develop appropriate means to incorporate all sectors of the nation in the search for peace" and to "discuss measures to humanize the armed conflict," an oblique reference to the air war.[116] Both sides agreed to meet again. The symbolic impact was enormous: the FDR-FMLN was officially recognized as a legitimate party in any solution. Perhaps most importantly, the meeting temporarily opened political space and encouraged popular mobilization. The thousands of people that thronged to La Palma to support a political solution to the war found that they could, for the first time in over four years, publicly advocate dialogue and negotiations without risking death.

The second meeting at Ayagualo on November 30 was less fruitful. The government reiterated its offer of graceful surrender, asking the guerrillas to accept a general amnesty, lay down their arms, and join the democratic political process by taking part in elections. The FDR-FMLN for the first time formally offered their phased peace plan: gradual de-escalation-followed by a cease-fire, and then a new government, a new constitution, and a reorganization of the armed forces before elections were held.[117] There was no movement on either proposal and both sides described the twelve-hour talks as tense, hard, and inflexible. Pressure from Archbishop Rivera y Damas did produce an agreement on a very limited Christmas truce, and there was agreement on ground rules for future meetings.

But Duarte's ability to meet again was restricted by right-wing forces. ANEP grew vocal in its opposition.[118] Army commanders had placed severe limits on Duarte's freedom to maneuver: they opposed efforts to "humanize the war" that were intended to limit bombing and, according to one source, told Duarte that they would not accept a cease-fire or any other arrangements that might limit military action, unless such measures were explicitly approved by the army itself.[119] Death-squad threats against Archbishop Rivera y Damas (for his support of the talks) forced the government to assign him bodyguards. Most importantly, by January, influential officers in the high command, including the armed forces chief of staff, Colonel Blandón, had backed away from support for the talks. In part this was because of signals from the United States that they interpreted as an unwillingness to protect them from the right wing in their support for the negotiating process.[120] Further, the massive military and economic aid Congress had approved in the second half of 1984 began to create a certain "triumphalism"—an optimism about a military solution.

The next serious negotiations did not occur until the fall of 1985. Then, however, the issue was not peace but the exchange of Duarte's daughter and the Christian Democratic mayors for political prisoners and safe conduct of wounded insurgents out of the country. The negotiations involved a complex set of interlocking agreements demanding good faith and trust on the part of the high command, the government, and the FMLN. They were made possible by the active mediation of the Catholic church, the International Red Cross, and representatives of the Contadora countries, as well as France and West Germany. The United States neither participated nor interfered.

The success of these negotiations indicates the possibilities for moving the peace process forward if all sides proceeded by taking small but decisive steps: negotiating prisoner exchanges, de-escalating the air war, securing temporary truces, allowing popular mobilization in support of the dialogue process, integrating groups from the UCS and UPD, as well as from professional and business organizations, into the talks, and eventually perhaps achieving a cease-fire.

But such progress will be foreclosed without strong support from the pragmatists in the military. But these officers will only accept this second-best solution if their first choice—military victory—is impossible and if they are assured strong U.S. backing for a negotiated solution. So long as the White House, backed by Congress, supports massive military and economic aid and opposes all negotiations except insurgent surrender, support for negotiations within the military will be limited. This, in turn, will continue to weaken Duarte's ability to build a reform coalition and negotiate a political settlement to the war.

Since 1979, Washington has assumed that it was necessary to keep the left out of power in El Salvador in order to promote U.S. interests, but the Carter and Reagan administrations followed somewhat different policies.

The Carter administration saw the revolutionary potential of the internal conditions in El Salvador and sought to promote socioeconomic reform and an end to repression; it was only when the recalcitrance and brutality of Salvadoran officers and landed elites spurred widespread armed insurgency that the Carter administration moved toward military force to keep the left out of power. The Reagan administration, viewing the conflict through an East-West prism, overinflated the role of outside interference and relied primarily on military force to destroy the insurgents. It was only when a reluctant Congress balked at funding a repressive, authoritarian government that the Reagan administration began to formulate a political strategy as well.

The Carter and Reagan policies did succeed in keeping the left out of power: they prevented both a political settlement that would have allowed the left to share power and a military victory by rebel forces. But in doing so, they also undermined the power of those moderates who sought to change the conditions of repression and inequality that fueled the insurgency.

From the reformist coup in October 1979 until early 1984, the White House supported each succeeding government despite clear evidence of a shift back to harsh authoritarianism. The Carter administration sought to promote a reform coalition as an alternative to the right and the left. But such a reform coalition would only have been strong enough to wrest power from officers and oligarchs if it were supported by popular sector organizations and parties on the left. The Carter administration, however, was unwilling to give strong political and diplomatic backing to such a broad, center-left coalition: rather it sought to exclude the popular organizations which it defined as the radical left. The State Department used its political leverage and economic aid to support centrist politicians who alone were too isolated and powerless to either carry out reforms or stop the repression that fueled a widening armed insurgency.

After the Reagan administration came to office in 1981, the increasing military aid it sent to defeat the armed insurgency strengthened the right and undermined Washington's declared policy of modernizing the oligarchy, taming the military, and building a center-right political coalition. Most seriously, U.S. policy ruled out the negotiated settlement sought not only by the insurgents, but by the remaining moderates, the Church, and the Contadora countries. The civil war that ravaged the country made growth, let alone development, impossible and brought a dramatic decline in the standard of living for the middle and lower classes.

The 1984 and 1985 elections in El Salvador were important victories for the Reagan administration and changed the internal dynamics in El Salvador. Having President Duarte and his Christian Democratic Party in office enabled the administration to convince Congress—previously reluctant to back an obviously rightist and authoritarian regime—to increase economic and military aid. This U.S. aid and training was crucial for the Salvadoran armed forces. By moving to a counterinsurgency strategy that relied increasingly on air power, the creation of "free fire" zones, and the relocation of the civilian population in contested zones through indiscriminate bombing and forcible roundups, the military was able to stem the growing offensive strength of the insurgents.

But the Reagan administration's success in getting the military aid necessary to contain the insurgency has not served the core interests the U.S. has in peace, development, democracy, and security.

While Duarte and the Christian Democrats held office, their power was severely constrained. U.S. policy did not encourage Duarte to build the kind of reform coalition that would be necessary to challenge the power of the military hard-liners and right-wing oligarchs. As such, the Christian Democrats were not able to bring about the more equitable development and meaningful democratization needed to garner popular support and discourage armed insurgency: they were blocked in their efforts to sustain, let alone carry forward, the crucial land reform programs; they have not been able to dismantle the death-squad organizations, bring to justice those in the military responsible for murder, control the air war against the civilian population, restore civil liberties or the rule of law, or stop the jailing, disappearance, and murder of peasant and labor leaders. The military was willing to tolerate Duarte as long as he kept open the spigot of U.S. aid, and did not challenge their power.

Without such fundamental reforms, the conditions of inequality and repression that first promoted the insurgency were still in place and discouraged any long term peace in El Salvador. The civil war itself dragged on. While increased U.S. military aid allowed the Salvadoran army to fight the guerrillas to a bloody stalemate, the insurgents were still strong militarily and there were few signs that such a military strategy would soon end the conflict. By 1985, this conflict had already taken a tragic toll: "more than 40,000 civilian noncombatants killed—murdered by government forces and 'death squads' allied to them; another 3,000 disappeared; 750,000 or so (15 percent of the population) refugees beyond its borders; 500,000 or so (another 10 percent of the population) homeless or 'displaced' within its borders."[120] Further, by unquestioningly assuming that leftists would likely pose a security threat to the United States, Washington helped sustain a conflict that was actually detrimental to U.S. security: civil war in El Salvador destabilized the entire region, threatened to encourage ever increasing U.S. military involvement, and encouraged the insurgents to look at us as their enemies, and our enemies as their friends.

The alternative strategy for settling the conflict—one that Duarte received much support for in his campaign—was a negotiated solution of the conflict. Since 1981, such a solution also had strong backing from the Catholic church, regional actors like Mexico and Venezuela, as well as the insurgents themselves. The FDR-FMLN, concerned that current conditions still made unarmed opposition dangerous, insisted on protection against repression through some restructuring of the military and some arrangement for power-sharing. But when openings occurred for negotiations—for example, in March and April of 1981; in La Palma in October 1984; and after the March 1985 elections—the right, backed by the United States, blocked any significant progress.

No group in El Salvador can put together a coalition strong enough to press for either reform or a negotiated political solution to the civil war without support from key elements inside the military and the private sector. As long as Washington demonstrates its willingness to sustain the economy and provide unconditional military assistance in order to exclude the left from power, these forces will have little incentive to support land reform, democratization, or negotiations. The result will be either increased U.S. military involvement or a prolonged civil war.

4

NICARAGUA
Dennis Gilbert

As Nicaraguans prepared to observe the sixth anniversary of the Sandinista revolution on July 19, 1985, they were also preparing for an invasion by the United States. Such efforts could scarcely be dismissed as irrational. Since 1981, the United States had been conducting an almost continuous series of military exercises in which thousands of American troops joined Honduran forces in maneuvers on Nicaragua's northern frontier, while carrier battle groups conducted large scale naval and air exercises off Nicaragua's Pacific and Caribbean coasts. Simultaneously, the United States was supporting a major buildup of the Honduran armed forces, led by officers openly hostile to Nicaragua's Sandinista government, and backing covert armies of anti-Sandinista contras (counterrevolutionaries) waging war against Nicaragua from sanctuaries in Honduras and Costa Rica. In Washington, President Ronald Reagan and other top officials made little secret of their desire to see a new government in Nicaragua.

The object of this intense American concern is a small, poor country in the midst of an immense social and political upheaval. Nicaragua is no bigger than Iowa. In a good year its GNP ranges a little over $2 billion, not quite enough to buy one of the American aircraft carriers sent to patrol its coasts. Statistics gathered during the late 1970s showed low per-capita income, exceptionally high levels of malnutrition, and the highest rate of infant mortality in Central America.[1] A visitor to Nicaragua would find a country that, even by Latin American standards, is underdeveloped—a country whose capital is still in ruins more than a decade after it was leveled by an earthquake, where most enterprises still employ traditional methods of production, and where running water is an uncommon household luxury.

There is, of course, more to underdevelopment than archaic technology and an anemic GNP. The majority of Nicaraguans are poor not only because their country is poor but also because the benefits of national production have been distributed inequitably.

American involvement in Nicaragua reaches back to the last century. In 1855, an American adventurer named William Walker led a privately financed invasion of Nicaragua. Before he was driven out two years later, Walker set up a puppet regime that was recognized by the United States, "elected" himself president, legalized slavery, and declared English the official language. In 1909, U.S. forces intervened in a civil conflict to depose Nicaraguan President José Santos Zelaya, who had shown insufficient deference to American investors and had attempted to interest the Germans and the Japanese in building an interoceanic canal through his country. From an engineering point of view, Nicaragua offered an attractive alternative to the Panama route, where the Americans were already at work.

U.S. marines occupied Nicaragua almost continuously from 1912 to 1933, propping up governments whose affairs were guided by a succession of American diplomats. One such government negotiated the Chamorro-Bryant treaty, infamous to subsequent generations of Nicaraguan nationalists, under which Nicaragua renounced its rights to build a competing canal for a one-time payment of $3 million. During the last five years of U.S. occupation, the marines fought a bloody guerrilla war against a peasant army led by nationalist Augusto César Sandino. The war proved indecisive on the ground and unpopular in the United States, forcing American withdrawal in 1933.

The principal legacy of the U.S. occupation was the national guard, a military force trained by the marines and commanded by an ambitious American-educated politician, Anastasio Somoza García. One of Somoza's earliest acts as guard commander was to order the assassination of Sandino. Somoza inaugurated a dynasty that dominated Nicaragua for over four decades, accumulating a fortune worth hundreds of millions of dollars and developing a reputation not only for systematic corruption but also for gross violations of human rights. The power of the dynasty rested upon two essential bases of support: the national guard, always kept under the command of a member of the Somoza family, and the United States, with which the Somozas maintained the closest relations.

THE CRISIS OF THE OLD ORDER ▲

The insurrection that toppled Anastasio Somoza Debayle, the last of his clan to rule Nicaragua, was precipitated by the political events of the 1970s but was more fundamentally rooted in the pattern of economic development of preceding decades. Toward the end of the nineteenth century, a gradual process of economic change began that transformed Nicaragua's subsistence agricultural economy into a agro-export economy, producing coffee, cotton, sugar, and beef for the world market.[2] This process created new wealth but it was also socially disruptive. Peasants were forced off land needed for export production. Many became wage workers in export agriculture, contending with sharp seasonal swings in labor demand typical of such crops, and all Nicaraguan workers became subject to the capricious fluctuations of international commodity prices. Inevitably, long periods of unemployment or underemployment became part of the typical experience of lower-class Nicaraguans.

Agro-export development tended to create poles of affluence and misery: at one extreme, export producers and other capitalists associated with them, at the other, landless peasants and urban shantytown dwellers. The flawed character of Nicaraguan development was especially evident in the last two decades of Somoza's rule, which brought a new wave of agro-export expansion and the beginnings of a national industrial sector. But while the GNP grew rapidly, the rate of childhood malnutrition doubled.[3] Somehow lower-class Nicaraguans were getting poorer as their country grew richer.

Repressive force was required to hold this system together and the Somozas' national guard functioned to maintain the control over the land and labor that the agro-export economy required. The use of such force contributed to deep popular resentment of the existing order. Even the Nicaraguan upper class, although it depended upon the dictatorship, resented being shut out of political power and feared the voracious expansion of Somoza's economic empire. Periodically, small groups of upper-class political activists attempted armed coups against the regime—always unsuccessfully. Others made cynical electoral pacts with the Somozas, gaining private advantage in exchange for providing token opposition in fraudulent contests.

The political crisis that finally unleashed the tensions in Nicaraguan society began to unfold after a massive earthquake leveled the greater part of the national capital Managua in 1972. Tens of thousands of Nicaraguans lost relatives, homes, and jobs in the disaster. The Somoza government and the national guard responded by systematically looting millions of dollars in international relief aid that was rushed to the country. When reconstruction began, the Somozas made sure that a large share of the resulting business was steered to enterprises associated with the dictatorship. In this manner the regime managed to offend Niaraguans of all classes.

The anti-Somoza movement that developed in the years after the quake consisted of two distinct oppositions: the moderate opposition led by members of the upper class whose primary goal was to remove Somoza, and the radical opposition led by the Sandinista National Liberation Front (Frente Sandinista de Liberación Nacional—FSLN), which sought major social and economic change as well. The decade of Nicaraguan political history that began in 1972 is the story of how these two currents drew together to overthrow the dictatorship, formed a national unity government under the leadership of the FSLN, and finally came into conflict over their different conceptions of the new Nicaragua. U.S. policy helped shape this course of events—first by contributing to the circumstances that pushed the two oppositions together, later by supporting (albeit briefly) the unity government, and finally by mounting a broad campaign to destroy the Sandinista revolution, thereby exacerbating and hardening the conflict between the upper class and the FSLN.

The driving force behind the moderate opposition was the "middle bourgeoisie"—owners of the modern enterprises that lie between the multitude of traditional peasant farms, artisan shops and neighborhood stores at the bottom of the Nicaraguan economy, and the three large financial conglomerates (one dominated by the Somozas) at the top. By American economic standards many of these businessmen and their families would be considered upper middle class. But their comfortable homes, automobiles, and Miami vacations represented a life of unimaginable affluence by the standards of the great majority of Nicaraguans.[4]

The growing dissatisfaction of this class in the 1960s and 1970s was frequently expressed in public positions taken by the Superior Council of Private Enterprise (Consejo Superior de la Empresa Privada—COSEP), an umbrella organization formed by the country's major private-sector associations, including the national chambers of agriculture, industry, and commerce. COSEP's members were unhappy about the way the Somozas were monopolizing reconstruction opportunities after 1972, but they were also disturbed by indications of growing popular unrest.

Many urban workers lost their jobs when workplaces were destroyed in the earthquake. Both urban and rural wageworkers lost purchasing power in the inflationary economy of the 1970s. The decade saw increasingly left-wing political agitation and growing labor protest. Nicaraguan unions were not only becoming more militant, they were also broadening the scope of their demands to encompass national political issues. At the same time both lower- and middle-class Nicaraguans were responding to the radical social ideas of the "liberation theology" then developing in the Latin American Catholic church. Priests, nuns, and Catholic lay activists working among urban slum dwellers, peasants and rural wageworkers were instilling a new social awareness among members of these long quiescent groups and helping them to organize to press for change. The regime's generally brutal response to these activities further radicalized the participants and evoked increasing criticism of the government from the traditionally conservative Catholic hierarchy. COSEP leaders hoped to undercut the revolutionary potential in these developments by encouraging liberal reform programs.

In the 1970s, the moderate opposition coalesced in two broad alliances of business, labor, and political organizations opposed to the dictatorship: the Democratic Liberation Union (UDEL) and its successor, the Broad Opposition Front (FAO). Both coalitions included left-wing organizations whose programs ranged beyond the reformist intentions of the coalitions' upper-class leadership. But UDEL and FAO avoided taking explicit ideological positions and concentrated on mobilizing nonviolent opposition to the government.

While UDEL and FAO fought Somoza with declarations, petitions, negotiations, demonstrations, and strikes, the Sandinistas prepared for armed struggle. Founded in 1961 and named for the national hero who had resisted the U.S. marines, the FSLN was highly nationalistic, anti-Somoza, and dedicated to fundamental change favoring the poor. Because of the intimate connection between the United States and the Somoza regime, Sandinista nationalism was distinctly anti-Yankee. FSLN leader Daniel Ortega confessed years later, "As young people we were all involved against Somoza and we didn't differentiate between the North Americans who supported him and those who knew nothing about his politics. We saw all of them as evil."[5]

The Sandinistas shared the Marxism that was common in the anti-regime student-political milieu from which most FSLN leaders came, and they were inspired by the young Cuban revolution. Some were connected with the Moscow-oriented Nicaraguan Socialist Party (Partido Socialista Nicaragüense—PSN). However, Sandinista ideology was and remains ill-defined, heterodox and pragmatic. From the beginning, party programs spoke of preserving a place for private enterprise within a planned economy. Catholic radicals gained positions of prominence among the leadership, a situation unimaginable in an orthodox Marxist-Leninist party. Ties with the Socialist Party were soon ruptured because the Socialists (loyal to the current Moscow line) regarded armed revolt against the Somoza regime as historically premature.

The FSLN was still a small political movement in the mid-1970s. Although it gained strength in the aftermath of the earthquate, the FSLN was forced onto the defensive by the national guard's brutal counterinsurgency campaigns of 1975 and 1976. During this period the movement split into three factions, or "tendencies," each with a different conception of how to defeat Somoza. The Prolonged People's War Tendency (Guerra Prolongada Popular—GPP) led by Tomás Borge and Henry Ruiz favored a continuation of the FSLN's original plan of gradually developing a guerrilla army and peasant political support in the mountains. The Proletarian Tendency (Tendencia Proletario—TP), led by Jaime Wheelock, urged a shift in tactics, focusing on political organizing among the urban poor.

A third faction, the Insurrectional Tendency (Tendencia Insurrecional, known popularly as the *Terceristas*), led by Daniel and Humberto Ortega, was the most pragmatic. It argued that the Somoza regime was so widely hated that it was possible to unite the entire nation against the dictatorship. Politically, the Terceristas favored opening channels to the anti-Somoza bourgeoisie in order to build a common front against the regime. Militarily, they favored bold actions—a kind of "propaganda of the deed"—to spark a national insurrection.

The Terceristas' assessment ultimately proved to be the most accurate. Their strategy opened the way for the creation of the broad multiclass revolutionary coalition that finally destroyed the Somoza dynasty. As the insurrection predicted by the Terceristas actually began to unfold, people who had become politicized through the church, trade unions, peasant groups, and student organizations looked to the FSLN for leadership in deposing the dynasty. The Terceristas, having proven in practice the accuracy of their political judgement, were able to unite the other two factions of the FSLN behind their leadership, and lead the revolutionary movement to victory.[6]

For both the bourgeois opposition and the Sandinistas, 1978 was the year that changed everything. It began with the assassination of Pedro Joaquín Chamorro, head of UDEL and editor of *La Prensa,* Managua's most prestigious daily and principal organ of the moderate opposition. Few doubted that the Somozas were responsible for his death, which galvanized popular opinion against the regime.[7] After an enormous popular demonstration at Chamorro's funeral, COSEP called for a national work stoppage to support demands for both the prosecution of the assassins and the resignation of Somoza. The strike, which was widely observed and produced frequent demonstrations and violent confrontations between authorities and strikers, lasted three weeks without attaining its objectives.

In late August a second strike called by the FAO turned into the massive September insurrection led by the FSLN. The revolt was defeated at a cost of five thousand lives (mostly noncombatants) and extensive bombing of several provincial cities.[8] In the aftermath of the revolt, it was obvious that Somoza had managed to unite virtually the entire country against him and that the political initiative had shifted away from the bourgeois-led opposition to the FSLN. At the same time the Frente Sandinista and the anti-Somoza bourgeoisie were moving closer together. The efforts of the Terceristas to reach out to the bourgeois opposition in the late 1970s had allayed some of the bourgeoisie's suspicions about the FSLN's radicalism. By the end of 1978, the FSLN was receiving extensive aid from the upper class. The prevailing logic in these circles was that nothing could be worse than Somoza.

As Somoza's position deteriorated, the United States struggled to manage the crisis—first by urging Somoza to moderate his behavior, then by promoting dialogue between him and his opponents, and finally by trying to arrange his departure and replacement by moderates. Ironically, Washington's efforts actually aggravated the internal situation in ways that proved contrary to American objectives.

When the FSLN had first stepped up its guerrilla activities in the early 1970s, the United States had increased military aid to Somoza substantially. In 1977, however, the Carter administration (backed by human rights advocates in Congress) suspended military aid in response to the brutal and indiscriminate campaign of repression unleashed by Somoza's national guard in 1975 and 1976. Since, as Somoza himself observed, most Nicaraguans believed that "the decision about the survival or disappearance of Somocismo" would be made in Washington, the significance of the cutoff was as much symbolic as material.[9] It encouraged all opponents of the regime, including the politically moderate but increasingly aggressive FAO:

Perhaps American support for the dictatorship was not boundless after all.

In mid-1978, however, the United States appeared to shift ground again. Under pressure from Somoza's powerful supporters in Congress and fearful of political instability in Managua, Carter released $12 million in economic aid.[10] In August, the president wrote Somoza, congratulating him on the regime's improved observance of human rights, although there was scant evidence of real change. Again, American moves were laden with symbolic significance for Nicaraguans. By appearing to re-endorse Somoza, Carter inadvertantly undermined the moderate opposition and increased support for the FSLN.

Throughout the prolonged crisis of the Somoza regime, Washington was slow to grasp the meaning of events in Nicaragua. Only in the wake of the popular insurrection of September 1978 did the Carter administration recognize that Somoza could not be sustained. From that point on, the United States pursued a series of initiatives designed to ease Somoza out of office through an understanding with the moderate opposition that would preserve as much of the regime as possible (in particular, the national guard) and keep the FSLN far from power. All failed. Few Nicaraguans were interested in preserving the national guard, and Somoza, encouraged by his allies in Washington and Carter's inconsistency, could not be budged. While the United States toyed with Somoza, the Sandinistas gained strength and support. The moderate opposition in the FAO counted upon the United States to remove Somoza for them through mediation, and when Washington failed, the moderates looked to the FSLN, which had already become the leadership of the more militant and increasingly radical lower-class anti-Somoza movement.

In early June 1979, the FSLN launched its final offensive and rapidly gained control of every major city outside the capital. As the Sandinista forces advanced, the United States convened a special meeting of the Organization of American States, where Secretary of State Cyrus Vance issued Washington's first public call for Somoza's resignation and outlined a plan involving a cease-fire supervised by an OAS peacekeeping force and transitional rule by a broad-based government that would encompass key elements of the existing regime. Ironically, only the Somoza government supported the American plan, which was widely regarded as a facade for armed intervention to forestall a Sandinista victory and maintain *Somocismo sin Somoza*—the regime without the dictator.[11]

The final American effort to contain the FSLN came in early July when the country was largely under Sandinista control and the national guard was collapsing before Sandinista forces. The United States offered to obtain Somoza's resignation (which had already been tendered to the American ambassador) in exchange for the preservation of the national guard and the dilution of FSLN representation in the recently formed provisional government. Since most Nicaraguans felt that the FSLN had won the moral right to lead the new government and Somoza's defeat was, in any event, imminent, the offer was rejected outright. At that point the United States relented and asked Somoza to leave.

With the initiatives of June and July, U.S. policy toward the Nicaraguan crisis completed its record of failure: having inadvertantly undermined Somoza and his moderate opponents, the United States had finally confirmed the Sandinistas' historic suspicion of the United States without blocking their ascension to power. The Carter administration was the victim of its consistent misreading of events in Nicaragua and its own divided motives, but these shortcomings reflected larger flaws in the way Americans have traditionally approached Central America. For years Washington had been interested only in stability in Nicaragua. Somoza's friendship with the United States blinded U.S. policymakers to the cost of "stability" inside the country, and left them unable to grasp readily the deep animosity the Nicaraguan people had for the dictator and his praetorian national guard. Similarly, Washington's instinctive anticommunism and its desire to avoid "another Cuba" produced a reflexive hostility toward radical leftists of any variety. Policymakers were unable to understand how the FSLN could gain such wide popular support and, in particular, how the moderates could join an alliance with the guerrillas. Finally, Washington was so used to exercising control over events in Central America that policymakers were stunned when a besieged Somoza refused to make the quiet exit scripted for him by Washington.

In short, Carter's policy during the insurrection failed mainly because it was based on the core presumptions that had guided U.S. policy in the Caribbean Basin for decades—a preference for stability over social justice, a deep suspicion of and opposition to radicalism, and a dictum of ultimate control. These presumptions failed policymakers in the case of Nicaragua not because Nicaragua was somehow unique but rather because the Central America of the 1960s and 1980s was no longer the Central America of the 1910s and 1920s.

A GOVERNMENT OF NATIONAL UNITY: SEEDS OF CONFLICT ▲

On July 19, 1979, the last remnants of the Somoza government were evacuated from Managua on board a plane provided by Guatemalan dictator General Romeo Lucas García. The triumph of the revolutionary forces led by the FSLN was complete. In the years that followed, the Nicaraguan revolution was shaped by two new and related conflicts: a domestic struggle between the upper class and the FSLN over redistributive socioeconomic policies and political power; and a confrontation with the United States.

The Sandinistas came to power at the head of a broad anti-Somoza coalition in which the private sector organized around COSEP was a leading element. In the process of forming a provisional national unity government, the FSLN repeatedly pledged to maintain "political pluralism" and a "mixed economy" (i.e., part private, part socialized). But the FSLN also had a long-standing commitment to build a new society guided by what some Sandinistas called "the logic of the majority"—a system whose first priority would be to satisfy the basic needs of the poor majority of the population. Herein lay the seeds of conflict. The new societal logic implied a fundamental reorientation of Nicaragua's agro-export economy. It meant redistributive policies in such areas as agrarian reform, education, health, and nutrition. As such, the logic of the majority amounted to an attack on the privileges of the upper class, since their share of national income would have to fall in order to pay for these policies. Moreover, the Sandinistas were determined to retain the political control they felt necessary to carry out their program. This set the stage for political conflict, since the Sandinistas' bourgeois partners in the anti-Somoza coalition expected to play a strong role in national decision making.

The initial composition of the new government reflected the varied political forces that had opposed Somoza. The private sector received key cabinet posts and representation on the governing Junta of National Reconstruction, which held ultimate executive and legislative authority. In addition, private-sector organizations and several upper-class-led political parties were all allocated seats in the Council of State, a legislative assembly to be inaugurated later.

By early 1980, however, the bourgeoisie felt its interests threatened by the consolidation of institutional power in the hands of the FSLN, and by a series of concurrent political and economic developments. Businessmen were being confronted by aggressive expansion of the labor movement (which had been sharply restricted under Somoza), new state regulation of private enterprise, increasing taxation, and rapid growth of the state sector of the economy (sometimes through worker-initiated expropriations). COSEP and other private-sector voices began urging the government to clarify its attitude toward private enterprise.

At the same time it was clear that most significant lines of state authority were converging on the nine comandantes of the FSLN's National Directorate. Three of the five members of the government Junta were Sandinista party members, a fact not generally recognized when the Junta was formed. They considered themselves subject to the authority of the Directorate, thereby making the two representatives of the upper class (industrialist Alfonso Robelo and Violeta de Chamorro, widow of the slain editor Pedro Joaquín) a permanent minority. A reorganization of the cabinet in December 1979 placed most important portfolios (planning, agriculture and agrarian reform, defense, and interior) in the hands of National Directorate members.

In April, the Sandinistas announced a reorganization of the Council of State on the eve of its inauguration. Seats were added for representatives from the FSLN-affiliated mass organizations that had grown up during the insurrection against Somoza and in the months after the triumph. Although the new composition of the Council was probably a more accurate reflection of relative political support among the populace, the added seats gave the FSLN a working majority in the Council. Since this had been the one government body that the upper class hoped would play a moderating role on the FSLN-dominated executive branch, the reorganization of the Council precipitated a political crisis between the FSLN and its increasingly skeptical private-sector partners.

The crisis began when Robelo resigned from the Junta on April 23 (a few days after Violeta Chamorro's quieter departure) in protest over the alteration of the Council of State. Other elements of the private sector used the resignation as an opportunity to press their demands; they threatened to boycott the Council unless the FSLN provided guarantees about the future of private enterprise in Nicaragua and a timetable for elections. With U.S. Ambassador Lawrence Pezzullo mediating, the FSLN and representatives of the private sector reached a settlement that included reassurances of respect for private enterprise embodied in a new law providing for judicial review of arbitrary administrative actions against persons or property. The National Directorate also agreed to announce a date for national elections and to protect democratic rights generally. With these concessions COSEP and representatives of bourgeois political parties took their seats in the Council of State when it was inaugurated on May 4, in an atmosphere of reconciliation and harmony. Later that month new upper-class representatives were added to the Junta.

The resolution of the Council of State crisis proved to be merely a pause between skirmishes in a developing political war which broke into the open again in November. That month opened with the election of a new American president who promised an aggressive foreign policy—a development that may well have bolstered the bourgeoisie's determination to confront the FSLN. In Nicaragua there were sharp exchanges between the government and Alfonso Robelo's party, the National Democratic Movement (Movimiento Demócrata Nicaragüense—MDN), over the Interior Ministry's denial of permission to hold an outdoor rally, and the sacking of MDN headquarters in Managua by Sandinista militants. On the tail of these events, COSEP issued a report sharply critical of the government's political behavior and economic policies that accused "the most radical sectors of the FSLN Party, with open Marxist-Leninist tendencies," of working to implant a "Communist" system in Nicaragua.[12] Whatever attention the COSEP report might have attracted was cut short by the news that Jorge Salazar, a vice-president of COSEP, had died in a confrontation with state security agents. The government subsequently charged that Salazar and several lesser private-sector figures had been involved in a conspiracy to overthrow the government; in upper-class circles the government was accused of entrapping Salazar and killing him. His death hardened attitudes on all sides.

By the end of 1980, a loose coalition of anti-Sandinista interests had emerged, which—by virtue of its middle- to upper-class composition and leadership—can be labeled the bourgeois coalition. At its center was the middle bourgeoisie represented by COSEP. Other key members were the editors of *La Prensa,* which had become the principal organ of the new opposition, several middle- and upper-class political parties, and most of the hierarchy of the Catholic church. These elements were drawn together by a sense that the Sandinistas were opposed to liberal democracy and capitalism, and, more vaguely, represented a threat to their way of life.

The bourgeois coalition has never been the sole opposition to the FSLN. Especially in the early months of the revolution, ultraleft groups unhappy with the deliberate pace and pragmatic tenor of the Sandinista program, challenged the FSLN among urban workers. In the 1984 elections, boycotted by the bourgeois coalition, the FSLN was most effectively opposed by three centrist parties, which subsequently became the parliamentary opposition to the government. These two oppositions have important bases of working-class and middle-class support, but they lack the resources, links to the press and church, and external support from the United States (or others) which have focused attention on the bourgeois-led opposition.

FROM CARTER TO REAGAN: THE LINES ARE DRAWN   ▲

With the departure of Somoza, the United States began to build a new policy toward Nicaragua on the ruins of the old. Conscious of the fact that American hostility had helped drive the young Cuban revolution into the Soviet orbit, the Carter administration sought a constructive relationship with the Sandinista government. In Nicaragua, the United States was willing to accept a sweeping transformation of the old order in the hope of strengthening moderate elements in the new regime and holding the government to its self-proclaimed goals of a pluralist polity, a mixed economy, and an independent foreign policy. The Sandinistas had their own reasons for seeking friendly relations with the United States. They knew that it would be difficult to obtain the international financing and domestic private-sector cooperation that were critical to the reconstruction effort without American support.

Until the final weeks of Carter's presidency, the new relationship worked relatively well. The United States committed about $100 million, largely in soft credits, in support of relief and reconstruction efforts through the end of 1980.[13] American influence was used to stabilize and moderate the new order, as when Ambassador Pezzullo mediated the April 1980 Council of State crisis. Pezzullo consistently urged representatives of the bourgeoisie to develop a cooperative relationship with the government. Although the conflict between the FSLN and the opposition was growing in intensity, the Sandinistas were generally tolerant of the political opposition, allowed a free press to operate, and built economic policy around the private sector. The Sandinistas also refrained, for the most part, from shipping arms to the guerrillas in El Salvador, at least until after Ronald Reagan was elected president in November 1980.

Nonetheless, there were tensions in the new relationship between Nicaragua and the United States. Washington was unhappy with the dilution of the political power of non-Sandinista sectors in the new government, Nicaragua's warm relations with Cuba, its rhetorical attacks on "Yankee imperialism," and its foreign policy positions, which included support for the Palestine Liberation Organization and abstention on the United Nations resolutions condemning the Soviet invasion of Afghanistan.[14] For Managua, the long, acrimonious congressional debate surrounding aid to Nicaragua and the restrictive provisions imposed on the final legislation were both insulting and threatening. Each side retained deep suspicions about the other. The United States feared that the Sandinistas would carry their country into the Soviet camp. The Nicaraguans feared that the United States would, sooner or later, intervene against their revolution, an anxiety fed by their own national history and American covert action against revolutions in Guatemala (1954), Cuba (1961), and Chile (1973).

Ronald Reagan's election to the presidency in November 1980 shifted the focus of U.S.-Nicaraguan relations. Reagan had run on a party platform that, in thinly veiled language, urged support for efforts to depose the Sandinistas. While the Carter approach had been predicated on the notion that American support for progressive change in Nicaragua could hold the Sandinista revolution to a moderate course, Reagan, his right-wing supporters, and his aggressive Secretary of State Alexander Haig viewed Nicaragua and the rest of Central America as part of the East-West conflict. Naïvely, the new administration regarded the civil war in El Salvador as an easy opportunity for the United States to demonstrate its capacity to control "Soviet-Cuban aggression." In this context, Nicaragua was—initially at least—of little significance in its own right. The Reagan administration could only see the Sandinista revolution through the double prism of U.S.-Soviet relations and the civil war in El Salvador.

Surprisingly, the change in administrations did not produce an immediate reorientation of U.S. policy toward Nicaragua, although official rhetoric became menacing. Ambassador Pezzullo, closely identified with Carter's policy, was retained in his post until August 1981 (unlike Robert White, his counterpart in El Salvador, who was sacked immediately), and the covert war was not launched until the end of 1981. The immediate issue facing the new administration was whether to resume aid to Nicaragua, which had been suspended by the outgoing Carter administration because Nicaragua had begun supplying arms to the Salvadoran rebels.

When Reagan administration officials raised the matter with the Sandinista government, the Nicaraguans denied supplying the Salvadorans, but agreed to control arms movements through their territory. In mid-February, the administration gave Nicaragua thirty days to halt all arms shipments to El Salvador or face a definitive cut-off of assistance. Reports emanating from the State Department in February and March, including comments

from Secretary of State Haig, consistently indicated that the flow of munitions from Nicaragua to El Salvador had been halted or drastically reduced.[15]

In spite of the positive response from Nicaragua, the United States
announced on April 1 that aid would not be resumed. Concessionary wheat
sales were also cut off—a very unpopular gesture in Nicaragua. These
decisions represented a triumph for Reagan's right-wing supporters in
Congress and hard-liners within his administration over Latin American
experts in the State Department, who contended that ending assistance
would sacrifice remaining American leverage with the Sandinistas. The
effect of the decision in Managua was to reinforce the notion—encouraged
by the Republican platform and foreign policy documents produced by the
Reagan transition team—that friendly relations with the United States were
impossible in the long run.

During the brief period from mid-1981 to early 1982 Nicaragua's relations with the United States and the FSLN's relations with its domestic
opponents were decisively redefined. Because decision makers in each
capital were reacting to developments in the other, the two processes were
closely intertwined.

The domestic reorientation grew out of the Sandinistas' preoccupation
with the economic performance of the private sector. Private investment
had plunged to anemic levels. In fact, the government and its supporters
were convinced the private sector was disinvesting—they called it "decapitalization"—through such illegal devices as allowing plants and machinery
to run down while profits were pocketed, or taking out low-interest investment loans and banking the money abroad. A government economist complained to an American visitor that the problem was endemic: "It's not as
if there are just four or five of the big guys. If there were, you could round
up one or two and make an example of them." The bourgeoisie was subject-
ing the country to "death by a million cuts."[16] The FSLN's attitudes toward
the private sector were also being influenced indirectly by growing evidence
of American hostility. The Sandinistas began asking themselves whose side
COSEP and its allies would be on if the United States invaded.

At the July 19 celebration of the revolution's second anniversary, the
government announced a stunning package of new measures designed to
control private-sector behavior. Included were a stringent new decapitalization law, a broad agrarian reform law, and a decree expropriating thirteen
major private firms accused of decapitalization. Speeches by Sandinista
leaders placed the new legislation in a rhetorical context that was decidedly
hostile to business, despite an evenhanded promise from Junta Chairman
Daniel Ortega to fight "lockouts, strikes, seizures, all of the ways which the
rank and file can deplete capital."[17]

The July decrees and the speeches accompanying them were interpreted
by both domestic and international audiences as indications of a radical new
departure in the revolution. In August, however, the Sandinistas simultaneously opened new contacts aimed at reconciliation with representatives of

the private sector and the United States. Talks with the United States were initiated by a quiet trip to Managua by Assistant Secretary of State Thomas Enders. For several weeks thereafter, American and Nicaraguan officials met periodically to consider ways to improve bilateral relations. The Americans proposed that Nicaragua cut off its support of the Salvadoran rebels and accept limits on its military expansion in exchange for a nonaggression pact with the United States, efforts to close the paramilitary training camps being operated by anti-Sandinista exiles in the United States, and an administration request to Congress for a renewal of economic aid.

These terms might have provided a basis for reaching an understanding, but in the atmosphere of mutual distrust that had developed, little was achieved beyond a mutually accepted cease-fire in the rhetorical war between the two governments. The assistant secretary's personality may have contributed to the failure. "Enders," says a Sandinista official who participated in the talks, "didn't come to negotiate, but to tell us what we had to do to achieve the grace of the United States." "The personal chemistry," admits one American diplomat, "wasn't very good." But another notes that there was division in the Reagan administration over the Enders initiative and administration hard-liners forced Enders to phrase the American proposals in a way that inevitably offended the nationalistic sensitivities of the Sandinistas. The process died in early October when the United States and Honduras conducted joint amphibious-assault exercises that Nicaragua denounced as a threat to its security. The United States chose to interpret the Nicaraguan outburst as a violation of the rhetorical truce and cut off the talks even though Nicaragua was interested in continuing them.

The FSLN's discussions with private-sector representatives were neither as formal nor as sustained as those with the United States. The Sandinistas were reluctant to deal with COSEP, which they regarded as an essentially political organization representing a reactionary minority. The bourgeoisie for its part was repelled by two extravagant speeches delivered in late August by Defense Minister and National Directorate member Humberto Ortega. One speech threatened to hang traitors in the event of an invasion and the other equated Sandinismo with Marxism-Leninism. The speeches obliterated the effects of conciliatory statements from other members of the leadership during the same period. Unable to discern which speeches represented the policy of the National Directorate and which represented only the views of the orator, the opposition was predisposed to think the worst. The tendency of the Directorate to speak with multiple voices made dialogue between the Sandinistas and the opposition especially difficult and misunderstanding commonplace.

COSEP's response to the July decrees and the rhetorical excesses of July and August came shortly after the U.S.-Nicaraguan talks were broken off. In a sharply worded letter dated October 19 to Junta Chairman Daniel Ortega, the officers of COSEP accused the FSLN of advancing "a Marxist-Leninist project behind the backs of the people," of preparing "a new genocide" (this in response to Humberto Ortega's "hanging" speech), and of leading the nation to the "doors of destruction." The COSEP letter, which was printed the next day in *La Prensa* and widely disseminated abroad, came at a time when the Sandinistas felt their revolution under increasing international attack. To the Sandinistas, COSEP appeared to be taking its cue from the United States. The letter was interpreted by the FSLN's leadership as part of a coordinated campaign to destroy the revolution—in the words of an official statement, "a frank and open destabilizing effort."[18] The letter writers were quickly arrested, tried, and sentenced to seven-month prison terms. Three months later, however, all were released in response to intense international pressure, especially from Mexico, an important supporter of the revolution.

In early November, as if to confirm Sandinista fears, Secretary of State Haig refused to rule out American efforts to overthrow the Nicaraguan government. After hearing him testify before the House Foreign Affairs Committee, Representative Michael Barnes commented, "Based on your responses, if I were a Nicaraguan, I'd be building my bomb shelter."[19]

The administration attributed its hardening attitude to the political situation inside Nicaragua, but Washington was still reading Nicaraguan developments through its preoccupation with El Salvador. Shortly before the Enders initiative was abandoned, Salvadoran insurgents had launched a new national offensive that demonstrated they were much stronger than Washington had thought. The deteriorating military situation in El Salvador set off a panicked review of Central America policy, strengthening those who favored a more aggressive policy in the region. The decision to launch a covert war against Nicaragua was taken during this period.

The first fruits of the new policy were borne a few months later in March when anti-Sandinista commandos, trained by the CIA and operating from base camps in Honduras, blew up two bridges in northern Nicaragua. From reports in the American press, the Sandinistas knew the bridge attack was part of a wider U.S. paramilitary operation.[20] The Nicaraguan government immediately declared a "state of emergency" that suspended most civil liberties for the first time since Somoza's departure. The decree imposed stringent new constraints on the opposition, including prior censorship of the press (an earlier law made certain types of stories punishable, but did not required government approval before publication).

Although the FSLN did not yet regard the internal opposition as a fifth column aligned with the externally based contras, neither did they trust the private sector to remain a loyal opposition. The emergency law was clearly aimed at limiting the opposition's ability to mount an internal political challenge, lest such a challenge become a vehicle for counterrevolution. In this sense, the covert war crippled the internal opposition, dashing any hopes it retained about achieving a significant share of political power. Bourgeois political leaders interviewed in early 1982 complained that the Reagan administration's hostile rhetoric and policies toward Nicaragua were constricting the political space available to the moderate opposition.

A POLICY OF HOSTILITY   ▲

U.S. policy toward Nicaragua from the end of 1981 onward was one of intense hostility on all fronts: economic, political, and military. Although elements of this program were in place earlier, the key decisions were made in the course of the late-1981 policy review.[21]

The most significant outcome of that review was the decision to have the CIA begin giving financial and logistical support to the paramilitary forces already operating against Nicaragua from Honduras. Authorized by the president in November, the force was originally small (only a few hundred men) and ostensibly designed to interdict arms bound for El Salvador. By 1983, the Nicaraguan Democratic Force (Fuerza Democrática Nicaragüense—FDN), the major beneficiary of the aggregate $100 million spent on the covert war, had grown to fifteen thousand well-equipped fighters engaged in attacks on both military and civilian targets.[22] While the FDN was not the only counterrevolutionary force active against the Sandinistas, it eclipsed all others in size and level of activity, including the Costa Rican-based forces led by former Sandinista hero Edén Pastora (who also received some CIA funding), and two smaller groups of Miskito Indian fighters on the Atlantic coast.[23]

The FDN was built on an existing band of former national guardsmen commanded by Colonel Enrique Bermudez and backed by Argentina's right-wing military regime. It began conducting raids against Nicaragua in 1980. Although the members of the FDN's political front, recruited and paid by the CIA, were generally free of such Somocista ties, the civilians appeared to have little control over their military partners. The rank and file of the FDN was composed largely of small farmers and rural workers from the rugged and thinly populated northern reaches of Nicaragua, the FDN's principal zone of operations. While some were former guardsmen or members of families with national guard ties (the north was an important recruiting area for the guard), most claimed objections to Sandinista rural policies as their reason for joining the contras. Many resented being required to sell their crops at the low prices imposed by the government during a period of rapid inflation (a policy adopted in the case of basic grains to hold food costs down) or being pressured to join cooperatives organized under the agrarian reform program.[24]

The immediate objective of the FDN appeared to be social and economic disruption rather than military engagment. It launched frequent attacks on such targets as farms and schools, and it employed brutal tactics against civilians—a practice reminiscent of Somoza's national guard, where most FDN commanders, including Bermudez, began their military careers. A 1985 report by Americas Watch, an independent human rights organization with extensive experience in Nicaragua, found that the FDN made "deliberate use of terrorist tactics," and accused it of murdering unarmed civilians, kidnappings, and indiscriminate attacks on civilian targets.[25] The FDN's CIA handlers bear some responsibility for its performance. Agency employees produced a manual on psychological warfare for distribution to FDN personnel that advised such tactics as "neutralizing" public officials and hiring "professional criminals" to foment violent confrontations that would create civilian "martyrs" for the contra cause.[26]

The Americas Watch report also covered abuses by other contra groups and the forces of the Nicaraguan government. It concluded that the FDN has the worst human rights record among the contra groups and that government abuses were infrequent after the first year of the war. The most serious human rights offenses committed by Sandinista forces grew out of a series of bloody contra attacks on the Atlantic coast beginning in December 1981. In 1982, some twenty-one to twenty-four Miskito Indians from the region were killed by government troops and another seventy disappeared and remain unaccounted for.[27]

The Atlantic region is geographically isolated from the rest of the country and the people of the region are divided from most Nicaraguans by race, language, culture, religion, and long-standing conflicts over local autonomy. As the Sandinistas now concede, their insensitive early administration of the region aggravated these differences, which were subsequently exploited by the contras for their own purposes. Recent government policy on the east coast has eliminated the worst abuses of the past and substantially reduced the tension between the Sandinistas and the people of the region.[28]

Even before press accounts made the covert war a matter of public debate in the United States, U.S. funding of the contras engendered concern in Congress. Fearful that the operation would expand beyond its stated aim of arms interdiction, Congressional intelligence committees imposed a secret prohibition (later adopted publicly) against U.S. funding of paramilitary groups for the purpose of overthrowing the Nicaraguan government or provoking war between Nicaragua and Honduras. It was for this reason that the Reagan administration repeatedly insisted that it was not trying to depose the Sandinistas.

Within months of launching the covert war, the administration had to back away from the arms interdiction rationale since no munitions were being captured or destroyed by contra patrols. The new goal, according to one administration official, was "to raise the cost to the Sandinistas of meddling in El Salvador."[29] During this same time, though, CIA operatives on the ground were telling the contras that the purpose of the operation was to overthrow the Nicaraguan government.[30] The contras themselves were unambiguous about their objective; it was, in the words of Col. Bermudez, "to overthrow the communists. . . ."[31]

In Washington, the administration continued to contend that its aid to the contras was within the law so long as the United States did not share the contras' aim of ousting the FSLN.[32] However, once the prohibition lapsed, as at the end of fiscal year 1983, administration officials became less circumspect about expressing their intentions. President Reagan, who described the contras as "freedom fighters," suggested at a press conference that peace in Central America could be attained only if the Sandinistas were removed. Referring to the contra forces and the Managua government, Secretary of State Shultz commented, "Their goal is one that, given our opinion of that government, we can hardly back away from."[33]

The CIA's covert funding of the Sandinistas' opponents was not limited to the exile army of contras. Beginning under the Carter administration, the CIA provided funds to opposition political parties, labor unions, private-sector organizations, and the press.[34] The United States also provided open funding to organizations independent of the Sandinista government through AID. In August 1982, the Nicaraguan government blocked the transfer of $5 million in AID funds to COSEP and the Catholic church, after the funding had been promoted in Congress as a means of strengthening opposition to the Sandinistas.

The policy of hostility had an economic dimension as well, which began in April 1981 with the definitive cutoff of U.S. bilateral assistance to Nicaragua. It escalated in 1982 into an open effort to block Nicaragua's access to vitally needed hard currency credits, particularly the long-term, low interest loans available through multilateral agencies like the World Bank and the Inter-American Development Bank. From 1981 to 1984, the United States blocked an estimated $200 million in noncommercial development credits to Nicaragua and pressured private banks to withhold new loans as well.[35]

In May 1985, the Reagan administration imposed an embargo on trade with Nicaragua. Since no other country joined the embargo, and Nicaragua had diversified its trading partners in anticipation of such a move, the effects of the embargo were limited.[36] Nevertheless, some Nicaraguan firms highly dependent on U.S. supplies—ironically, most of them privately owned—were likely to be driven out of business, and Nicaraguan trade dependency on the Soviet bloc was likely to increase.

THE SANDINISTAS AND THE DOMESTIC OPPOSITION ▲

As the contra war expanded, relations between the opposition and the FSLN became increasingly hostile. Initially a loyal opposition to the revolutionary government, the members of the bourgeois coalition ultimately became identified with the contras. By 1983, most had given up any real effort at rapprochement with the Sandinistas, preferring instead to wait for either the contras or the United States marines to depose the government or impose a radical restructuring of the regime.

In part because Nicaragua never had a strong reformist political party like El Salvador's Christian Democrats, COSEP activists played a key role in organizing the middle- and upper-class opposition to Somoza during the late 1970s. Under the Sandinistas, however, COSEP's effectiveness has been limited by its essentially middle- and upper-class constituency; neither the economic issues (defense of private property) nor the political issues (formal democratic rights) raised by the organized private sector drew much popular interest. Nonetheless, in 1980 and 1981, COSEP was the focus of opposition to the government. By 1983, that role appeared to have shifted to the hierarchy of the Catholic church.

As an institution that cuts across social classes in a devoutly Catholic country, the church can exercise enormous political influence. The conflict that has developed between the Sandinistas and a large sector of the church led by Cardinal Miguel Obando y Bravo reflects not only competing efforts to appropriate this potential, but also a profound division within the church itself. Many nuns and priests support the revolution, and several priests continue to hold high government posts over the objections of the cardinal and the Vatican.

The tensions within the church are rooted in the 1970s, when Nicaraguan Catholics began to respond to the liberalizing tendencies then sweeping the Latin American church. That decade saw an explosion of Catholic lay activity, especially among the poor, encouraged by socially conscious priests and nuns. Although initially liturgical in focus, such activity proved to be fertile ground for a radical Christian critique of Nicaraguan society, emphasizing Christ's commitment to the poor and the worldly obligations of Christians. A large sector of the FSLN's support and some of its top leaders emerged from this radical Christian milieu. The bishops, however, were never drawn to the FSLN, and when they finally did turn against Somoza, they did so hesitantly and from a more moderate ideological perspective than the Christian radicals. Thus, the fall of the old regime left a latent division in the church, which paralleled the tension between the FSLN and its former allies in the private sector. The bishops came to regard the laity and clergy who supported the FSLN (often referred to collectively as "the popular church") as a direct challenge to their own ecclesiastical authority. It is this perceived threat, as much as any other factor, that has driven most of the bishops into the opposition.[37]

Although a few well publicized incidents, such as the noisy confrontation between the Pope and Sandinista militants at an outdoor mass in March 1983, have created the impression of a persecuted church, the government has generally been quite cautious in dealing with the church. The bishops have enjoyed more freedom to oppose the revolution than any other elite. They have moved systematically and effectively against the popular church —for example, by transferring clergy associated with it away from their followers, often over the protests of parishioners. In pastoral letters read out in church and published in *La Prensa*, the bishops have taken overtly political positions, often echoing other members of the opposition coalition: they opposed the 1983 military draft law, questioned the 1984 elections, and insisted that the government negotiate with the contras (a position the Sandinistas reject, since they identify the contras with Somoza's national guard). The bishops have never condemned U.S. support of the contras or contra human rights abuses but have allowed some religious observances to become anti-Sandinist political rallies.[38]

The activities of the church and of other members of the opposition coalition are enthusiastically covered in *La Prensa*, Managua's largest-circulation daily and even under censorship, a crucial opposition platform. The paper retains much of the prestige won through years of opposition to the Somozas under the paper's martyred editor, Pedro Joaquín Chamorro. It is not quite the same paper, however. In 1980, most of the staff, including editor Xavier Chamorro (Pedro Joaquín's brother) left *La Prensa* after losing a bitter internal dispute over editorial policy, to found an independent pro-Sandinista paper, *El Nuevo Diario*. *La Prensa* was taken over by the more conservative wing of the Chamorro family and since that time has been staunchly anti-Sandinista. (A third daily, *Barricada*, is the official organ of the FSLN.) Like its Sandinista competitors, *La Prensa* presents a very selective version of the news. The paper is often guilty of manipulating its readers. For example, in late 1981 and early 1982, *La Prensa* attempted to persuade Nicaraguans that a certain plaster-of-paris statue of the Virgin Mary, which exuded moisture through its "pores" was "crying" for Nicaragua because of the country's turn toward "communism."

Prior to the 1982 Emergency Decree, there were few papers in Latin America as consistently and aggresively critical of their governments as *La Prensa*. Under the decree, censorship has varied from quite stringent to relatively light (especially during the campaign period preceding national elections in November 1984). At no point did *La Prensa* cease to be a forum for anti-Sandinista opinion. But censorship allowed the government to withhold inconvenient news or material like the sweating-Virgin story which the censor regarded as politically manipulative. The Sandinistas' inconsistent behavior toward *La Prensa* has been influenced by their awareness, on the one hand, that treatment of the press is a standard by which foreign audiences will judge the revolution, and, on the other, that the Chilean paper *El Mercurio*—subsidized in the early 1970s by the CIA—helped destabilize the democratic, left-wing government of Salvador Allende. The FSLN was determined that *La Prensa* would not become another *El Mercurio*. [39]

Political parties are the weakest element in the opposition. Somoza's monopoly of power and his unwillingness to tolerate any significant organized opposition left a legacy of anemic party organizations. A Western ambassador interviewed in Managua gave this assessment of the opposition parties in 1983: "They have no leaders, no program, and so few members that they would have a hard time coming up with poll watchers in an election." Under the 1982 emergency law, the opposition parties have been permitted to maintain offices, receive foreign visitors, issue newsletters, and conduct indoor meetings. Except during the electoral campaign of 1984, however, they have not been allowed to organize outdoor rallies, and their activities have occasionally been disrupted by Sandinista militants.

In an effort to fill the organizational vacuum left by the weakness of the parties, the opposition coalition created the Democratic Coordinating Committee (Coordinadora Democrática) to map and carry out a joint strategy against the regime. The Coordinadora included COSEP, four moderate to conservative political parties, and two trade union federations (one with Christian Democratic connections, the other organized with the help of the AFL-CIO's American Institute for Free Labor Development).

The openness and continuing vitality of the bourgeois coalition's opposition to the FSLN belie the effort of the Reagan administration to brand the Sandinista regime "totalitarian." Judging by the reports of independent human rights organizations such as Amnesty International and Americas Watch, the human rights record of the Sandinista government has been better than could be expected, given wartime conditions and the level of domestic political tension.[40] The revolutionary government has never permitted the death-squad activity that remains common in neighboring El Salvador and Guatemala. Since the 1982 incidents on the Atlantic coast, life-threatening human rights abuses have been infrequent in spite of the expanding scale of the war. There remains, however, a systematic pattern of lesser violations permitted under the emergency law, such as frequent short-term detentions for security-related matters, and trials of defendants suspected of violent subversive activities in special courts that do not offer the procedural guarantees available in ordinary courts. Prominent members of the bourgeois opposition (whose loyalty is naturally suspect) are often called in for questioning by security officials. Some have had property expropriated for what appear to be political reasons. But by their own accounts, bourgeois activists do not feel physically threatened by the government.

In 1985, the issues dividing the Sandinistas and the opposition were the same as they had been five years before: the opposition sought to regain enough political power to guarantee the future of private enterprise in Nicaragua, while the Sandinistas sought to use their control of the state to force the private sector to accept a new social order based on the logic of the majority.

What had changed in the intervening years were the terms and venue of battle. In 1979 and 1980, the conflict was played out politically inside Nicaragua, and people on both sides of the issue were seeking an accommodation that all could live with. Even the United States was lending its weight to such a compromise. By 1985, few people seemed to believe that a modus vivendi was still possible, and the main arena of conflict between the Sandinistas and their opponents was no longer inside the country. The 1984 elections offered a major opportunity for reducing the polarization of politics, but it was wasted in large part because neither the internal opposition nor the United States wanted elections to divert attention from the main effort to secure their interests in Nicaragua—the war.

THE 1984 ELECTIONS   ▲

In early 1984, the government announced that the national elections to which it had committed itself in 1980 would be held on November 4, 1984. Electors would be voting for a president, vice president, and members of a national assembly that would serve as an interim legislature and draft a national constitution. In the ensuing debate over who would participate in the elections, and under what terms, both the Sandinistas and the bourgeoisie were playing largely to foreign audiences.

The FSLN, confident that it could sweep any popular contest, viewed the elections as an opportunity to legitimize and institutionalize its power. The need to do so was imposed more by international than domestic considerations—in particular, by U.S. hostility and growing international criticism of the curtailment of pluralism under the emergency law. Especially in the wake of the October 1983 Grenada invasion (which carried an implicit threat that a similar operation might be mounted against Nicaragua), the FSLN's leadership felt the need to shore up sagging support in Latin America and Western Europe as a way of deterring a direct U.S. attack.[41]

Working through the Democratic Coordinator, the bourgeois opposition developed its approach to national elections from the same starting point as the Sandinistas—the assumption that the FSLN was unbeatable. Why, then, participate? A minority within the Coordinator argued that the campaign offered the opposition an opportunity to make its case to the Nicaraguan people and perhaps strengthen democratic institutions that might be used in the future to challenge the FSLN's power. Others doubted the FSLN's long-term commitment to liberal democracy and argued that participating in the election would only help legitimize Sandinista rule, both at home and abroad. The abstentionist argument was made particularly by the COSEP representatives, who proved to be the dominant force within the Coordinator. Thus, even before the government had set the date for elections, the bourgeois opposition had decided not to participate.[42]

The electoral strategy of the Coordinator was designed to delegitimize the elections, especially among foreign audiences. "We have to play on two fields," explained a ranking Coordinator official interviewed in mid-1984. "We cannot forget the internal, but much of the game is on the international field." Most opposition leaders had concluded that their only hope of influencing the course of events in Nicaragua lay with the United States and the contras. American pressure might force a broad restructuring of the regime or escalate into the removal of the Sandinistas by invading U.S. forces—a prospect some opposition leaders welcomed. Internationally recognized elections in Nicaragua would certainly undercut these possibilities.

Throughout the preelectoral period, the Coordinator insisted that it could not participate in the campaign because the government was not creating the necessary conditions for fair elections. Its sweeping list of prerequisites included opening direct negotiations between the government and the contras. In late July, the Coordinator named a standard-bearer—Arturo Cruz, a well-known banker who had served in the national unity government before breaking with the Sandinistas in 1981—but refused to register him as a candidate. Cruz flew to Managua from his home in Washington, but after a few campaign appearances left the country for a political tour of Europe, where he was accompanied by contra leader Edén Pastora. About the same time, the American-backed FDN endorsed the activities of the Coordinator, which, in effect, had become the political wing of the contras.[43]

The preelection maneuvering of 1984 completed the political transformation of the bourgeoisie: from wartime collaborators of the Sandinistas to partners in a unity government and then to loyal opponents of the regime; finally, the bourgeoisie had become—in both word and deed—the internal ally of the armed opposition. Each of these shifts paralleled changes in U.S. policy. While the dynamics of the domestic situation were at least as important for the evolution of bourgeois-Sandinista relations as external influences, the refusal of the bourgeoisie to collaborate with the new order was clearly based on the assumption that the United States would not allow the revolution to survive. The intransigent attitude of the bourgeoisie, in turn, limited the options of the Sandinistas as they formulated domestic and foreign policy.

By deflecting international attention to its own activities, the bourgeois opposition succeeded in delegitimizing the Nicaraguan elections in the United States. Since that was where key decisions would be made about the covert war and any use of U.S. forces, the opposition's achievement was substantial. Yet the electoral process was hardly the "Soviet-style" sham that the Sandinistas' enemies charged. By making significant concessions (including twenty-two hours of free prime-time television for each party and forty-four hours of radio time), the government persuaded six opposition parties to participate, including three to the right of the FSLN and three to the left. During the campaign, censorship under the state of emergency was eased significantly. Disruption of opposition activities by Sandinista militants, which marred the early part of the campaign, was subsequently brought under control. Visiting in October, a *Wall Street Journal* reporter found that moderate and leftist parties had "succeeded in mobilizing campaigns that are highly critical of the revolutionary process."[44] On election day, 75 percent of the electorate turned out, and according to independent accounts, the balloting and canvassing of votes was carried out in an orderly and scrupulous fashion.[45]

The strongest electoral challenges to the FSLN came from three moderate parties: the Independent Liberal Party (PLI), the Popular Social Christian Party (PPSC), and the Democratic Conservative Party (PCD). The PLI is a center-left party founded in 1944 by anti-Somoza dissidents within the ruling Liberal Party. The Independent Liberals participated in the national unity government (party head Viligio Godoy was labor minister from 1979 until elections were announced in 1984). The party, which has a significant middle class base, argued for a more moderate, more democratic social revolution. Both the PPSC and the PCD are factions of parties also represented in the Coordinator. The PPSC is a left-leaning Christian democratic party that abandoned the larger Social Christian Party in 1975. The Popular Social Christians were critical of the Sandinista government's acrimonious relations with the church hierarchy and expanding ties to the Soviet Union, but supported the FSLN's social and economic programs. The Conservatives, one of the two traditional upper-class parties, split several months before the elections when a faction with close ties to the government gained control of the party machinary. The defeated faction associated itself with the Coordinator. The PCD's campaign supported the private sector, called for lifting the 1982 emergency decree, and favored negotiations with the contras.

In the November 4 contest the Sandinistas won 67 percent of the valid vote (6 percent of all ballots were spoiled, some obviously in protest). The Democratic Conservatives carried 14 percent, the Independent Liberals (who had tried unsuccessfully to remove their party from the ballot days before the election) 10 percent, and the Popular Social Christians 6 percent. Three leftist parties collectively received about 3 percent of the vote. The moderate parties would hold 30 percent of seats in the new assembly, enough to give them an important voice, but little power in the Sandinista-dominated body.[46]

If the November 4 election was not a fully convincing test of the popularity of the FSLN, it was because the parties of the Democratic Coordinator, which had the most compelling anti-Sandinista credentials, refused to participate. The United States was both indirectly and directly responsible for their abstention—indirectly, because calculations about ultimate American intentions reinforced bourgeois reluctance to face the electorate, and directly, because the Reagan administration actively lobbied against participation. Late in the campaign, U.S. embassy representatives visited leaders of the registered moderate parties and pressured them to withdraw. Some party leaders charged that American officials bribed or attempted to bribe Nicaraguan politicians. A senior administration official told the *New York Times*, "The administration never contemplated letting Cruz stay in the race because then the Sandinistas could justifiably claim that the elections were legitimate. . . ."[47]

THE LOGIC OF THE MAJORITY   ▲

The FSLN was able to turn out hundreds of thousands of Sandinista voters in 1984 both because it had a superior political organization and because the party had built a popular following unrivaled in Nicaraguan history with policies designed for the country's impoverished majority. From the very beginning of the revolution, this "logic of the majority" was embodied in agrarian reform, expansion of health and education, and a program to maximize production and equalize distribution of the basic food commodities on which lower-class diets depend. A key objective was the achievement of food self-sufficiency, a capacity that has steadily slipped away from the agro-export economies of Central America.

Agrarian reform began in Nicaragua before the triumph of the insurrection when the Sandinistas started redistributing land belonging to the Somoza family and its close political associates in areas under rebel control. During their long years in power, the Somozas and their friends had accumulated over 20 percent of the country's agricultural land, all of which was nationalized with the fall of the old regime. For the next two years, however, the FSLN resisted launching a comprehensive agrarian reform program for fear of losing the support of the bourgeoisie and disrupting production. By the time they announced the agrarian reform law in July 1981, relations with the bourgeoisie had soured and FSLN had come under considerable popular pressure to distribute more land.[48]

Agrarian policy has had two objectives: to improve the welfare of rural people and to maintain the production of the food and export crops on which the national economy depends. With the second objective in mind, the 1981 law placed no limit on the size of private landholdings, as long as they were exploited efficiently. Ultimately the Sandinistas anticipated redistributing about 60 percent of the arable land, mostly to peasant cooperatives, and leaving the rest in private ownership.[49]

Although agrarian reform was seen by most large- and many small- and medium-sized farm owners as a threat to the traditional social and economic order in the countryside, the net political effect of the reform was positive since the rural poor, who benefited most from the redistribution of land, far outnumbered the reform's opponents. When the contra war in the north escalated in 1983, one of the government's political responses was to step up the pace of land distribution in that area.

Some of the revolution's most impressive accomplishments in social policy have involved finding ways to attack major problems with limited resources. For example, the Health Ministry developed a highly successful program to combat childhood diarrhea, the major killer of infants in Latin America. A network of Oral Rehydration Centers was set up to administer a lifesaving solution of salts and sugar to affected children. The ministry has also organized neighborhood committees and other mass organizations associated with the Sandinista movement to carry out immunization and sanitation campaigns. In 1980, the Education Ministry launched a national literacy campaign, mobilizing the energies of thousands of college and high-school students who served as volunteer teachers. By the end of the year, the national illiteracy rate had been cut from 50 to 13 percent.[50] As a follow-up effort, the ministry helps adults in rural areas and urban slums conduct Popular Education Cooperatives, small self-education groups that meet evenings to work on basic reading and mathematical skills.

Given the magnitude of the tasks facing the revolution and the dilemmas of competing priorities (e.g., how can food prices be kept low without

discouraging peasant production?), implementing the "logic of the majority" has presented difficulties from the beginning. But the strain of the war
has made the social goals of the revolution even more elusive. The FDN
contras have singled out health facilities, schools, and agrarian reform
farms—along with the health workers, educators, and peasants associated
with them—as prime targets for their attacks.[51] In 1984, defense absorbed
40 percent of the national budget, cutting into the social programs and basic
food subsidies that had been the major budget items. A wartime austerity
budget imposed in 1985 eliminated food subsidies and halted most construction of new schools, hospitals, housing, and utilities. Dozens of schools
and health centers have been abandoned in conflict zones. The retreat of
health care threatens previous gains in the control of epidemic diseases.
Polio, eliminated by vaccination campaigns, began to reappear in 1984.[52]
"We are seeing," comments an Argentine doctor working close to the
northern war zone, "the epidemiology of aggression."

CAPITALISTS AND COMANDANTES IN A ▲
MIXED ECONOMY

The very programs that help build support for the FSLN among the populace at large are a source of tension between the Sandinistas and the
bourgeoisie, whose power and privileges are threatened by the "logic of the
majority." The fact that the economy remains dependent on private producers does little to relieve this tension. Although precise figures are not
available, government and private-sector economists agree that private enterprise still accounts for about half the gross national product.

Sandinista leaders continue to insist that they are committed to a mixed
economy and point to policies such as liberal investment credit terms and
stringent wage controls that benefit the private sector. As businessmen
concede, many firms have enjoyed healthy profits under Sandinista rule.
Nonetheless, government–private-sector relations could hardly be worse.[53]

The most common private-sector complaint concerns the failure of the
government to establish consistent "rules of the game" that clearly define
the mixed economy and prevent arbitrary confiscations. The Sandinistas
have, in fact, made some progress in defining "rules" in legislation such
as the 1981 agrarian reform law which formally protects efficiently exploited landholdings of any size from expropriation. However, periodic
seizures of enterprises on dubious legal grounds, and inflammatory an-
tibusiness rhetoric from certain leaders, undercut private-sector confidence
in the future of the mixed economy. Many businessmen are convinced that
the Sandinistas intend to eliminate all private enterprise in the long run.

The Sandinista counterpoint to "rules of the game" is, of course, "decapitalization," the injurious process of disinvestment that the government was
trying to control with the July decrees in 1981. The FSLN regards private-
sector insistence on "rules of the game" as an implicit demand for a share

of national power and evidence of the refusal of a wealthy minority to accept an economy built on the "logic of the majority." It is, in fact, difficult to imagine a restoration of business confidence without some concession of political power to the bourgeoisie—precisely the sort of concession the FSLN is least willing to make. Jaime Wheelock, Minister of Agriculture and the National Directorate member who has most consistently defended the idea of a mixed economy, says the FSLN seeks a "bourgeoisie that just produces, without power; that limits itself to exploiting its means of production and that utilizes these means of production to live, not as instruments of power, of imposition."[54]

The National Directorate, according to businessmen and foreign advisors who have dealt with them, is divided over how to deal with the private sector. A pragmatic faction, led by Wheelock and Daniel Ortega, favors a government-guided mixed economy. Henry Ruiz, Bayardo Arce, and Tomás Borge (all associated with the Prolonged Popular War faction of the late 1970s) are characterized as "ideologues," committed to imposing a Soviet-style command economy. The pragmatists have generally controlled policy. Their hand would probably be strengthened by a negotiated understanding between the United States and Nicaragua, and weakened by continued mutual hostility and the attendant expanding dependence on the Soviet Union.

Of course, the mutual hostility of the government and the private sector is only one of the problems afflicting the national economy. Nicaragua faces the external economic imbalance that is common to the entire region. Even before the war began to affect export production, Nicaragua's buying power in international markets had eroded as a result of a 35 percent decline in its terms of trade from 1977 to 1982.[55] Foreign exchange earnings in the early 1980s were barely enough to cover the costs of petroleum imports and debt service. These trends were choking the economy and forcing difficult choices on Sandinista policymakers, who had to allocate scarce dollars among competing import needs, ranging from industrial inputs and agricultural chemicals to medical supplies and foodstuffs.

The war imposed a new set of strains. Beginning in 1983, the FDN made the disruption of the economy one of its principal objectives.[56] The Nicaraguan government estimates the war's foreign exchange costs in damaged capital goods, lost export production, and increased food imports due to domestic crop losses at nearly $300 million for 1983 and 1984, the equivalent of 35 percent of export earnings for the period. Macroeconomic calculations suggest that the production losses for the entire economy during the same years amounted to about 5 percent of actual GNP.[57]

Under current circumstances decisive resolution of the conflict between the private sector and the Sandinista government seems unlikely. The bourgeoisie has been stripped of power over the economy and of the support of a right-wing military that traditionally allow upper classes to control workers and bring down bothersome governments in Latin America. The FSLN is in no position to eliminate the private sector, which—as Sandinista

leaders have repeatedly acknowledged—possesses administrative and technical skills that are essential to the functioning of the economy.

Moreover, the Nicaraguan bourgeoisie has the backing of West European
and Latin American governments whose support is crucial to a regime
besieged by the United States and presiding over an economy tightly linked
to the Western economic system. High-ranking visitors from Mexico, Spain,
Germany, Venezuela, and other countries, which have given the Sandinistas
economic or political support, do not leave Managua without a well-publi-
cized meeting with COSEP officials. These governments would be pleased to
see the Sandinistas reach an accommodation with the private sector, but such
an understanding would have to form part of a larger settlement of the issues
dividing the bourgeois coalition and the United States from the FSLN.

NICARAGUA AND THE UNITED STATES: ▲
THE DIMENSIONS OF CONFLICT

In the wake of the 1984 Nicaraguan elections, it was clear that there was
no hope of reconciliation inside Nicaragua unless and until there was some
resolution of the conflict between Nicaragua and the United States. So long
as the internal opposition had the hope that Washington would remove the
FSLN, they had little incentive to seek any sort of accommodation with the
regime. And so long as the FSLN saw the internal opposition as the disloyal
ally of the contras and the Yankees, it had little incentive to offer any
concessions toward accommodation.

Yet, as the covert war escalated, the prospects of Nicaragua and the
United States reaching some accord seemed to grow dimmer. In fact, the
war had the perverse effect of exacerbating two of the major grievances
Washington expressed about Sandinista behavior—their military buildup
and their deepening relations with Soviet bloc countries.

Since 1982, Nicaragua has substantially expanded its military capabilities. It has a regular army of about forty thousand troops (close in size to
the armies of El Salvador and Guatemala, but larger than that of neighboring Honduras), in addition to a militia of seventy thousand people of whom
twenty thousand are on active duty. The Nicaraguan armed forces are
equipped with over one hundred Soviet T-54 and T-55 tanks, a large fleet
of trucks and armored personnel carriers, ten Soviet MI-24 helicopter
gunships, and a considerable number of modern anti-aircraft weapons.[58]

The administration publicly interprets the Nicaraguan military buildup
as a direct threat to the security of other nations in the region. President
Reagan speaks of the Sandinista "war machine," while Secretary of State
Shultz has asserted that "the Nicaraguans are contemplating using massive
force outside their borders." However, a classified CIA intelligence report
obtained by the *Wall Street Journal* described the recent Nicaraguan
buildup as "primarily defense-oriented" and aimed at "improving counterinsurgency capabilities."[59]

The defensive intent of the Nicaraguan military establishment is suggested by both its history and character. The Sandinista government did not begin to obtain heavy weapons, such as the Soviet tanks, or create its militia until 1981, when it was confronted with an openly hostile administration in Washington, paramilitary training camps preparing anti-Sandinista exiles at several locations in the United States, and attacks by Argentine-backed contras, already operating from Honduras.[60] It did not obtain the more sophisticated weapons in its arsenal, such as advanced antiaircraft missiles or the MI-24 helicopter (designed for counterinsurgency use) until 1983 or 1984, by which time the American-supported contra forces had caused thousands of deaths and millions of dollars in physical damage.[61]

Four years after Nicaragua began building up its military, the country had accumulated little capacity to fight outside its own borders. The army's major offensive weapon, the T-54 or T-55 tank, is of 1950s vintage and would have a difficult time negotiating the rugged terrain that separates Nicaragua from its neighbors.[62] Nicaragua has nothing worthy of being called an air force—a few light planes, but no combat jets or bombers. Lacking air cover, Nicaraguan ground forces (tanks included) would be extremely vulnerable in an international conflict. Honduras, Nicaragua's most likely opponent, possesses a modern air force built up with years of American advice and assistance. El Salvador has a smaller, but relatively sophisticated air arm, also developed with the help of the United States. Since 1982 the Reagan administration has been charging that Nicaragua is about to acquire Soviet MIG fighters and has suggested that it would act to remove them if Nicaragua did so. In March of 1985, Nicaragua announced a unilateral moratorium on the acquisition of any new weapons system, including high performance aircraft, but the moratorium was lifted in June when the U.S. Congress voted to resume funding of the contras.[63]

One key to the strategic situation in Central America is the recognition by all parties that any offensive move by Sandinista forces against a neighboring state would provide an opening for the Reagan administration to move directly against Nicaragua. To suppose that Nicaragua would take such a risk is, in the words of Foreign Minister Miguel D'Escoto, "to believe that in addition to being evil, we are also insane." A senior U.S. defense official concedes, "That would be the solution." The United States would "most certainly attack."[64]

A second consequence of the covert war in the realm of foreign policy has been to push Nicaragua into a closer relationship with the Soviet bloc. In the past few years, the Soviet Union and its allies have become the main source of arms for Nicaragua to fight the contra war, and an important source of economic assistance to help Nicaragua endure U.S. efforts to impose a trade and credit embargo.

The Soviet Union and Eastern Europe have become Nicaragua's principal munitions suppliers, in part because the United States pressured Western Europeans not to sell weapons to the Sandinistas. Pentagon data indicate that Soviet-bloc military supplies were relatively small through 1981, but surged as the covert war escalated in 1982 and thereafter. In 1984, the Soviet bloc supplied $250 million in military aid to Nicaragua, up from only $5 million in 1979 and $7 million in 1980.[65]

By U.S. estimates, there were approximately 7,500 Cubans in Nicaragua in early 1985, a reduction from an earlier peak of 9,000. Of these, the U.S. believed that some 3,000 were military or security advisers.[66] In March Nicaraguan President Ortega disputed these figures, claiming that there were 786 Cuban military advisers in the country.[67] The majority of Cubans working in Nicaragua are civilian professionals, especially teachers and doctors, assigned to remote areas. There are also several hundred Soviet and other East European development technicians and security specialists. In May 1985, Nicaragua sent 100 Cuban military advisers home as a good-will gesture to the United States.[68]

But if the Cubans and Soviets are providing vital economic and military support to Nicaragua, there are apparent limits to their willingness to back the Sandinistas and thereby confront the United States in its own sphere of influence. The Soviets have given no indication that they intend to provide the economic support that would free Nicaragua from dependence on the West: Soviet-bloc financing has been running under $150 million annually and is limited to bilateral trade credits, rather than the hard currency loans Nicaragua requires. Soviet-bloc purchases are absorbing only 6 percent of Nicaragua's exports and have not expanded since 1980.[69] The USSR has never given the Sandinistas sophisticated offensive weapons of the sort they have supplied to their closest allies—for example, the Syrians, whom the Soviets have recently armed with advanced MIGs and M-72 tanks.[70]

To the extent that Nicaragua's military buildup and its growing ties with the Soviet bloc are a reaction to covert war, a change in U.S. policy might be able to bring about a reversal of these negative trends. But these issues have never been the Reagan administration's main complaint against Nicaragua. From the outset, the administration has charged the Sandinistas with exporting violence and subversion to their neighbors and justified its policy of hostility on the grounds that it was acting to counter this aggression.

While there is no doubt that the Sandinistas did give significant material aid to the Salvadoran guerrillas in preparation for their ill-fated "final offensive" in January 1980, evidence of Nicaraguan arms trafficking since that time has been sparse. The public evidence that has been presented has been undercut by news dispatches from the region based on interviews with unnamed U.S. military and intelligence officials who report that outside supplies are no longer extensive or vital for the Salvadoran guerrillas. Instead, the rebels rely largely on munitions captured or purchased from government sources.[71]

PEACE INITIATIVES   ▲

As the conflict between Nicaragua and the United States deepened, the search for a peaceful resolution to their differences quickened. In 1982 and 1983, Nicaragua made repeated private and public attempts to open negotiations with the United States.[72] Parallel to these overtures, a series of mediation proposals were put forward by Latin American powers concerned with the growing violence and the broadening scale of American involvement in Central America. In February 1982, Mexican President José López-Portillo publicly warned that American intervention in Central America would be "a gigantic historic error" and outlined a comprehensive peace plan for the region. In September, as tensions built on the Nicaraguan-Honduran border, Venezuela joined Mexico in calling on the United States, Honduras, and Nicaragua to find diplomatic means to avoid an imminent regional war. Mexico and Venezuela urged the United States to initiate talks with Nicaragua and implicitly offered themselves as mediators. The following year the Mexican-Venezuelan initiative was broadened to include Panama and Colombia. The four states, collectively known as the Contadora Group, after the site of their first meeting on Contadora Island, Panama, embarked on a sustained diplomatic effort to build a workable consensus among the five Central American nations and the United States.

American responses to the overtures from Nicaragua and the initiatives of the regional powers soon fell into a predictable pattern: All proposals required "study" or were "constructive" but failed to address some critical concern; there the matter rested. Off the record, the Reagan administration was more candid. The United States was stalling on negotiations, admitted "senior administration officials" because they did not believe that Nicaragua was "sincere" and wanted to wait until its negotiating position was undermined by domestic unrest.[73] As the diplomatic process nurtured by the Contadora group began to gain momentum in 1983, President Reagan was described as "privately impatient" with the group's efforts because they might lend "world respectability" to the Sandinistas, who were cooperating with Contadora.[74] The administration had no immediate interest in a negotiated settlement and regarded any pressure in that direction as a public relations problem.[75]

In April 1982, under pressure from Mexican President José López-Portillo to negotiate its differences with Nicaragua, the United States presented Nicaraguan authorities with an eight-point "proposal for improving U.S.-Nicaraguan relations." The eight points were essentially a reiteration of the 1981 Enders proposals with the addition of one new element, a requirement that Nicaragua hold free elections.[76]

A second change in the American position, not reflected in the eight points, was an insistence that any peace accord between the United States and Nicaragua would have to form part of a multilateral settlement encompassing all the major issues and actors in Central America. Nicaragua was seeking bilateral negotiations, especially with the United States and Honduras. This new requirement simply complicated matters and provided the United States a shield behind which it could hide its own unwillingness to carry on substantive negotiations.

Nicaragua replied to the United States with a thirteen-point counter-proposal stating that it was willing to sever its connections with the Salvadoran rebels, limit its arms and armed forces, and accept international verification of compliance as part of a negotiated settlement. However, the Nicaraguans were still unwilling to discuss domestic matters. "It is," a ranking Sandinista official later explained, "the only point on which we are intransigent."[77] The exchanges, which never got beyond the ambassadorial level, soon died out.

In mid-1983, Nicaragua launched a diplomatic offensive designed to identify itself with the emerging Contadora Group initiatives, and to appeal to American policymakers and opinion leaders. In a conciliatory speech delivered at the annual July 19 ceremonies commemorating the triumph over Somoza, Daniel Ortega indicated that Nicaragua was willing to negotiate an agreement that would prohibit it from supporting the Salvadoran insurgents or allowing foreign military bases on its territory in exchange for guarantees of its own security. In keeping with Contadora principles, Ortega emphasized the need to free each country from interference in its internal affairs and free the region from military involvement by foreign powers. He also expressed, for the first time, Nicaragua's willingness to enter into multilateral peace negotiations—a concession to both Contadora and the United States. Compliance with any accords, Ortega suggested, could be verified by the United Nations.

In the months that followed, the Sandinistas elaborated an increasingly explicit and conciliatory negotiating position. In September, Nicaragua joined the other Central American nations in endorsing the Contadora Group's twenty-one-point negotiating framework, designed to provide a basis for a regional peace agreement. Among the twenty-one points were the phased removal of foreign military advisers, the elimination of regional arms traffic, a prohibition on foreign military bases, and a commitment to honest and regular elections.[78] The following month, Nicaragua proposed a package of four draft treaties to the Central American governments and the United States. The package encompassed an agreement with the United States that would prohibit foreign military bases in Nicaragua, plus regional accords that would bar arms shipments or any other form of support for subversive movements in neighboring countries. Compliance would be monitored by the Contadora states. In November, Ortega publicly stated what Nicaraguan officials had been saying privately for several months: Nicaragua would stop buying arms and ask all foreign military advisers to leave if other Central American governments would do the same.[79] (This proposal would, of course, require the United States to curtail its military support of right-wing regimes in the region.)

As they defined their diplomatic position, the Sandinistas announced a series of new policies designed to counter growing domestic and international criticism of their regime. Between Ortega's July 19 speech and the end of the year the government eased censorship of the press, loosened restrictions on the political opposition, began preparations for the promised elections, and announced amnesties for Miskito Indian prisoners and for Nicaraguans in exile (including those who had joined the contras, but excluding their leaders). The government also asked some Salvadoran rebel leaders and one thousand Cubans (both teachers and military advisers) to leave the country.

The 1983 proposals from Managua addressed the principal stated security concerns of the United States: Soviet and Cuban penetration of Central America and the arms flow to the Salvadoran rebels. They should therefore have stirred American interest. Publicly, they evoked the administration's habitual perfunctory response. Behind the scene, the administration was divided between conservatives like Secretary of State Shultz, who were skeptical of the Sandinistas but willing to test their new attitude, and hard-liners such as CIA Director William Casey and United Nations Ambassador Jeane Kirkpatrick, who had no interest in negotiations with Nicaragua. Any agreement that might emerge would require the United States to accept the existence of the Sandinista revolution—something the hard-liners were not ready to do.

The hard-liners prevailed. The United States offered no counterproposals and made no serious effort to probe the sincerity or flexibility of the new Nicaraguan proposals. If anything, Nicaragua's conciliatory stance appeared to evoke negative responses from the United States. A few days after Ortega's July 19 speech, the United States announced the massive and lengthy Big Pine II joint maneuvers with Honduras. At the same time, the FDN was expanding its operations, and the CIA was deepening its involvement in the war.

In the fall, the United States launched a sabotage campaign against strategic targets in Nicaragua such as ports and oil storage facilities. Some of the raids were carried out by the FDN, but others—such as the demolition of the oil storage facilities at Corinto—were conducted by CIA personnel or contract agents known as UCLAs (Unilaterally Controlled Latin Assets) and simply attributed to the FDN. The campaign culminated in the mining of three Nicaraguan harbors by CIA commandos in January and February 1984.[80]

The decision to mine the harbors had been taken at the highest levels of the administration, but no one appears to have anticipated the consequences of an act so overt and warlike. Although the mines were of relatively low explosive power, several small Nicaraguan boats were sunk and at least five international ships damaged, two of them seriously.[81] The United States was widely condemned for the mining, even by some close allies in Europe. When Nicaragua sought legal redress in the World Court, the United States refused to recognize the Court's juristriction. From the administration's point of view, the mines did their worst damage on Capitol Hill. Already uneasy about the direction of American policy, the Congress was stunned by what the administration had done and, as a direct result, allowed contra funding to lapse in May 1984. It was not restored for over a year.

In the interim, the FDN managed to sustain itself by shifting to more economical small-unit tactics and finding alternative sources of aid, including private corporations, individuals, and several foreign governments, among them El Salvador, Honduras, and Israel. Administration officials helped FDN fundraisers with introductions to wealthy conservatives. It is probable that the governments mentioned—all recipients of substantial U.S. military aid—proceeded with explicit American approval.[82]

Not until June 1984, in the aftermath of Congressional suspension of contra aid, did the administration yield to intense diplomatic and domestic political pressures—made more persuasive by looming national elections—and reopen serious contacts with Nicaragua. Secretary of State Shultz traveled to Managua where he met briefly with Daniel Ortega and they inaugurated a series of meetings between ranking American and Nicaraguan diplomats. The talks, which were held in Manzanillo, Mexico, lasted until the end of the year and were conducted in an atmosphere characterized as positive by diplomats on both sides. But administration hard-liners were able to hobble the proceedings by shaping the negotiating position of the United States. The Americans insisted that Nicaragua commit itself to provisions for the implementation of democracy. Nicaraguan negotiators again insisted that they were unwilling to discuss domestic matters. Progress was blocked because negotiating instructions given to Special Envoy Harry W. Schlauderman, the chief American negotiator, did not permit him to explore ways to narrow the gap between the two positions. "No one will tell Schlauderman what the endgame is, what the road map to a final agreement is," an administration official told the *New York Times*. "The reason is that the administration doesn't want a settlement with the Sandinistas."[83]

As the Manzanillo talks bogged down, the Contadora process moved forward. On September 7, after twenty months of negotiations among the Contadora countries and the nations of the region, a draft treaty was completed. Two weeks later, Nicaragua announced that it was willing to sign the treaty, which already had the nominal approval of American allies in the region. The administration was stunned by what it viewed as a propaganda victory for the Sandinistas. A secret National Security Council background paper later explained how the United States, "effectively blocked" the treaty by persuading El Salvador, Honduras, and Costa Rica to withdraw earlier support and raise new objections to its provisions.[84] In early 1986, the Contadora nations were still trying to salvage the draft treaty.

The Manzanillo talks barely survived the U.S. elections. The last meeting was held on December 8 and one month later the United States announced that it was breaking off the discussions. The decision, resisted by the State Department, reflected the continuing power of administration hard-liners.[85] In the weeks that followed, the administration's campaign for renewed funding of the contras featured some of the most extravagant anti-Sandinista rhetoric of the long struggle between the two governments. The people of Nicaragua, Secretary Shultz told a congressional committee, had fallen "behind the Iron Curtain" and the United States had a "moral duty" to help them escape that condition. The contra fighters, said President Reagan, were the "moral equivalent of our founding fathers." The goal of American policy, the President acknowledged in a press conference, is to "remove" the Sandinista government "in the sense of its present structure. . . ."[86]

THE SANDINISTA REVOLUTION AT HOME AND ABROAD ▲

From the earliest days after the triumph of the Nicaraguan revolution it was clear that the political dynamics of the revolutionary process would produce a series of conflicts, both in domestic and in international realms. There was no way to avoid conflict between the FSLN and the bourgeoisie over the socioeconomic policies of the revolutionary government, given the Sandinistas' commitment to the "logic of the majority." Once the Sandinista revolution turned fundamental economic questions into issues of public policy, it became inevitable that the conflict over economic policy between the Sandinistas and the private sector would evolve into a conflict over political power.

The history of U.S.-Nicaraguan relations and the evolution of the Sandinista movement combined to make it inevitable that the revolutionary government would seek some distance from the United States—that the close relationship Washington had so long enjoyed with Somoza was not to be replicated with the Sandinistas. Since the Cuban revolution was one of the initial inspirations for the Sandinista movement, and Cuba was willing and able to provide aid to the new Nicaraguan government, the emergence of a close friendship between the two revolutionary regimes was predictable, thereby further aggravating relations with the United States.

But while the Sandinistas' commitment to radical social transformation at home and radical nationalism abroad made these domestic and international conflicts unavoidable, the outcomes were certainly not preordained. The Carter administration set out in July 1979 to moderate the revolutionary process in Nicaragua—to keep the domestic conflict over economic issues from producing a command economy on the Cuban model, to keep the political conflict between the FSLN and the bourgeoisie from producing a one-party authoritarian state, and to keep the Sandinistas' suspicions of the United States and their affinity for Cuba from taking them into the Soviet orbit.

The Reagan administration came to office largely convinced that the outcome of the revolutionary dynamic in Nicaragua was, in fact, preordained to lead to "another Cuba" unless the revolutionary process itself could be aborted. This is why the administration has been only marginally concerned with the fact that its policy of hostility has exacerbated the very elements of the revolutionary process that Washington purports to despise —the restrictions on pluralism, the military buildup, and the reliance on the Soviet bloc.

Whereas the Carter administration's efforts to moderate the revolutionary process seemed to have some positive effect, at least until they were undercut by Carter's lame duck status after November 1980, Reagan's policy of hostility has failed to achieve its counterrevolutionary objective. The more extravagant hopes that attended the launching of the covert war have been disappointed: the externally orchestrated attack has not split the National Directorate or the army, much less produced an internal uprising. Fighting since 1982 with American backing, the contras have inflicted enormous suffering (ten thousand Nicaraguans had died in the war by early 1985)[87] and considerable physical damage, but they have failed to gain control of any significant territory, population, or town within Nicaragua. Although contra groups clearly had some supporters in the far north and on the east coast, there was no indication that they had won a following in the central Pacific region where most Nicaraguans live, even among those who have grown disenchanted with Sandinista policies. General Paul F. Gorman, the retiring commander of American forces in Latin America, told a congressional committee in 1985 that there was no prospect that the contras could overthrow the Sandinistas "in the foreseeable future"—with or without American aid.[88] It is this widely shared recognition of failure that encourages speculation that the United States might deploy its own forces against Nicaragua.

Given the domestic political resistance to military involvement in Central America, and the legal limitations imposed on the president by the War Powers Act, it is unlikely that an invasion of Nicaragua would be planned unless it was assumed that a quick victory would be possible. With a preponderance of military might, it would not be difficult for U.S. forces to quickly gain control of major strategic objectives. But this would simply mark the initial phase of the conflict. Sandinista strategy is openly based on the assumption that American opinion cannot sustain a bloody war of attrition. The Sandinistas are experienced guerrilla fighters and they are preparing for a new guerrilla war. They have, for example, established arms caches around the country. It is widely recognized that the revolution has found its strongest support among the poor and the young, the key sources of potential guerrilla fighters. An American invasion would surely stimulate the nationalist instincts of Nicaraguans in a way that the contras have not. The Sandinistas have a well-trained and ideologically motivated army. They have established a large territorial militia, organized on a neighborhood-by-neighborhood basis, and have armed tens of thousands of civilian supporters. Thus, they are in a position to inflict many deaths on the invading army as they retreat from populated areas to the remote regions where guerrilla forces could establish themselves. Without doubt, the United States and its

Nicaraguan allies (ideologically burdened by their imperial support) would find themselves entrapped in a deadly guerrilla war against a tenacious enemy, with little support from the American electorate.

Some supporters of the administration point to the apparent softening of Nicaragua's diplomatic stance since 1983 as an indication that military pressure is producing results. But even before small-scale attacks had broadened into full-scale war, Nicaragua was insistently signaling its willingness to talk. The war may have made the Sandinistas more intent upon negotiations, but there is scant evidence that the administration is, in fact, prepared to negotiate with Nicaragua.

The Reagan administration's policy of hostility has contributed to the political polarization of Nicaragua—in effect, recruiting much of the internal opposition into ranks of the contras, figuratively if not literally. Yet despite the hardening of views on both sides, the outcome of the domestic conflict remains in doubt. The Sandinistas have not eliminated the private sector or the political opposition. They continue to profess a willingness to try to make the mixed economy work and to try to find grounds for internal reconciliation.

Similarly, in the realm of foreign policy, the Sandinistas have not responded to attacks from the United States by throwing themselves into the Soviet camp. They continue to look as much to Spain and Mexico as to the Soviet Union and Cuba for leverage in their conflict with the United States. And they continue to participate in the Contadora process, where they have pledged themselves to the elimination of all foreign military advisers and bases, to a prohibition on aiding insurgent movements against their neighbors, and to hold their armed forces below a mutually agreed upon ceiling if their neighbors will do the same and if Washington stops trying to overthrow them.

For some time it has not been within the capacity of the United States to control domestic developments in Nicaragua. It is certainly not in this country's national interest to attempt to do so. But through the Contadora process, combined with bilateral negotiations, the United States could achieve the elimination of the Cuban and Soviet military presence in Nicaragua, cut the military ties between the Salvadoran rebels and the Sandinistas, and reduce the current danger of regional war in Central America. In the process, the United States would help create an international climate in which the Nicaraguan parties will be encouraged to settle their differences in a reasonable fashion.

But thus far, the Reagan administration has shown little interest in settling its conflict with Nicaragua at the bargaining table. Unless that attitude changes, there seem to be only two policy alternatives: a continued policy of hostility that is ineffectual for deposing the FSLN but polarizes the country while bleeding it, or an invasion.

5

HONDURAS
Philip L. Shepherd

Although Honduras has long shared serious problems of poverty, under-development, and political instability with its Central American neighbors, until relatively recently these problems had not led to widespread political violence as in Guatemala, El Salvador, and Nicaragua. Moreover, these troubles had their roots in a peculiar history that, among other things, has been remarkably free of direct U.S. military intervention.

Yet U. S. foreign policy has always had a great influence on Honduras. It certainly has had a large effect in recent years. These policies, often designed with more attention to Honduras's geopolitical position than to Honduras's interests, have had a severe negative impact on the government, economy, and people of Honduras. To put it bluntly, Honduras is doing Reagan's dirty work in Central America.

THE POLITICAL ECONOMY ▲
IN BRIEF HISTORICAL PERSPECTIVE

Before 1950: The Creation of a Banana Republic

In a region itself known mostly for its poverty and underdevelopment, Honduras has been the poorest and least-developed nation. The Spanish conquest left Honduras as a colonial backwater, a third-rate mining and cattle-producing region, wholly dependent on colonial Guatemala. Indepen-dence altered little in Honduras (as Hondurans say, it came "by mail," as a result of Mexican success). By the 1840s, the nation had settled into the inauspicious pattern of precapitalist patrimonial landholding and subsistence agriculture that still characterizes much of rural Honduras today.

Importantly, Honduras did not develop an agrarian capitalist coffee export oligarchy as did Costa Rica, Guatemala, and El Salvador. With a low man-to-land ratio, and little pressure on land from coffee, there were much greater possibilities for subsistence crop production. Peasants were not forced off their plots by land-hungry oligarchs seeking to transform the peasants' land from subsistence farming into their own commercial coffee production. Thus communal forms of land tenure endured and even state lands were not pressed into service for coffee. The land struggles and "enclosure" movements that created a coffee oligarchy in the 1880s in El Salvador and forced peasants to work for it were not significant in Honduras. As late as 1950 only 48 percent of the land was private. Land tenure was unequal but much less so than elsewhere in the region until the arrival of commercialized agriculture after World War II. Even the widespread production of bananas by U.S. firms after 1900 had little direct adverse impact on Honduran peasants, since these lands had been uncultivated and the companies originally imported the labor to work them.[1]

As the nation entered the twentieth century, it did so lacking an agrarian capitalist class, an intransigent landed oligarchy, or an allied commercial and industrial bourgeoisie. Honduran elites, concerned with their country's backwardness, invited U.S. banana firms to build railroads and to "develop" the nation. But lacking a solid coffee bourgeoisie, Honduran elites proved "unable to organize an adequate state and were incapable of negotiating favorably with foreign capital."[2] These events led to the transfer of political and economic control to U.S. banana producers and the U.S. government. The function of Honduran elites in the banana republic became a bureaucratic one: providing the politico-administrative and legal conditions for foreign capital and doing local chores for the fruit companies. So as long as this continued, direct U.S. military intervention—so prominent in Nicaragua—was unnecessary.[3]

By 1950 the dynamics of underdevelopment had left Honduras exceptionally poor. By almost any measure of socioeconomic or political well-being, Honduras was ranked lower than any other country in the hemisphere save Haiti. The banana enclave did not spread development but rather constrained it. Honduras had virtually no nationalist leadership, economic or political. Instead, dominant groups were content to live off meager rents from subsistence-farming peasants or to hustle a dependent, parasitic existence from the government, always in the shadow of the banana firms and the U.S. embassy. Showing remarkably little economic initiative, Honduran elites concentrated their sights on government jobs and patronage, leaving the few dynamic economic activities to foreigners. The commercial sector went to Arabs and Chinese, while export agriculture and mining went to Americans.[4]

Politics (as Hondurans only half-jokingly admit) also remained undeveloped. Liberal-conservative struggles of the nineteenth century were muted in Honduras, but the major parties still follow those divisions. Traditional left-right distinctions and clear ideological differences do not apply. Other factors tend to dominate, making Honduran politics a veritable "witch's brew" of strange bedfellows, personal ambition, friendship and family ties, patronage, and half-baked ideology.

On the other hand, Honduras was different from its neighbors in certain positive ways. There was no entrenched economic oligarchy dependent on maximum exploitation. Land scarcity before 1950 was rarely a problem and subsistence agriculture provided most peasants with a meager but relatively secure existence. Moreover, when commercialized agriculture disrupted traditional land tenure after 1950, it gave rise "to the most militant and, before long, best organized peasant movement in Central America."[5] With little local oligarchy to protect, Honduras did not develop a professional military tied to concentrated economic interests, and the military did not view its function as making more or less permanent war on its own people. Only in the banana plantations was there much clear class conflict and, regardless of class, Honduras enjoyed relatively tolerant political attitudes, derived at least partially from a certain sense of community.

After 1950: The Erosion of "Honduran Exceptionalism"

Honduran society changed considerably after 1950. Three changes—in the economy, in political institutions, and in the military—were particularly important.

The economic changes centered on the commercialization of agriculture and some incipient industrialization. Capitalist forms spread beyond the banana plantations and the tiny urban commercial sector as the government stimulated growth with credits and infrastructure, including a vastly expanded array of state agencies for agriculture, banking, labor, and the like. Much of the push for change came from outside: U.S. and international aid institutions pressured for "modernization," and international demand for primary products began to change the precapitalist productive profile. An important agrarian capitalist sector began to form around cattle, cotton, and coffee, while bananas began to decline in relative terms. Agrarian capitalism and population growth began to put pressure on traditional forms of peasant land tenure.

These economic transformations helped stimulate a second change as pressures to reform the system of political domination built up. A restructured Liberal Party (PL) became the vehicle for emerging groups like organized labor and peasants, as well as the new urban middle class. The Liberals won the election of 1954 but did not actually take power until 1957.[6] This reformist regime broadened participation and opened the state to the nascent progressive sectors of the urban and industrial bourgeoisie. Organized labor and peasants also obtained some concessions (the first agrarian reform law, a labor code, state social assistance in health and education). When increasing popular mobilzation and threats to the military as an institution surfaced in 1963, a conservative reaction by landowners and banana firms put an end to it with a coup. In cahoots with these conservative sectors represented by the National Party, this military government headed by Colonel Oswaldo López Arellano ruled for the rest of the decade. Corrupt, venal, repressive, and unpopular, this government tried to put the lid on change and mobilization.

Capitalist development continued to advance in the 1960s. The Central American Common Market increasingly turned Honduras into a captive market for goods from El Salvador, although Honduras benefited somewhat as well. This, and increasing migration of Salvadoran peasants into Honduras, eventually led to the 1969 war—a disaster for both sides. The war exposed the bankruptcy of the conservative regime and the inability of the armed forces to carry out their avowed mission of protecting the nation.[7] In a climate of "national unity," a Colombian-style national-front government briefly ruled until 1972 when it collapsed under organized pressure from land-hungry peasants.

Honduras in the 1970s increasingly resembled a "living museum" of political and economic actors; new forces were added to the arena while old ones refused to leave.[8] Coalition building among the civilian-military leadership became progressively more complex and difficult. Building on the nonideological character of Honduran politics and the ever-greater autonomy of the military, a populist military government took over in 1972. Doing a 180-degree ideological flipflop, this government was also headed by López Arellano. It included the more progressive but weak bourgeoisie, reformist officers, technocrats, peasants, and labor. This second reformist attempt from 1972 to 1975 instituted a brief but effective agrarian reform, expanded state aid to the modernizing bourgeois groups, and increased the scope of the government in the economy. All these measures provoked widespread suspicion and opposition, both in and out of Honduras. By 1975, conservatives were able to split the military and López was accused of having taken a bribe from United Fruit, causing an internal coup. The military governments of Juan Alberto Melgar Castro and Policarpo Paz García that ruled for the rest of the decade increased the level of repression and turned sharply to the right. Both were known chiefly for their outlandish corruption.

The third important change was the increasing autonomy and political strength of the military. Traditionally the instrument of various *caudillos* and personalistic interests, the military first began to emerge as an independent actor in the growing pluralism of the 1950s. Weak initially, its first modern, overt intervention (1956) was carried out under the rationale of its role as "guardian" or "protector," making it the supposed "arbiter" of political stability. It then negotiated considerable autonomy from civilian control in the 1957 constitution as a prize for handing over power to Ramón Villeda Morales, a Liberal Party reformist. When the military seemed threatened by the popular mobilization and the civil guard of Villeda, however, it quickly allied itself with the Nationalist Party and ruled throughout the 1960s in rough equality with the conservatives.

The military, however, has not identified itself exclusively or even mainly with the Honduran oligarchy, such as it is. This obviously contrasts with the Salvadoran military. The military's abrupt about-face in 1972, when it allied itself with progressive and popular sectors, demonstrated both the autonomy of the institution and its lack of identification with traditional conservative coalition partners. And even when it joined the nationalists in excluding the progressive sectors in the late 1970s, it never completely closed off avenues of political communication. By 1980, the Honduran military had still not defined its role and mission. This would come to depend heavily not only on the military's particular leadership but on the growing regional crisis and the influence of the United States.

THE EMERGENCE OF FRAGILE DEMOCRACY: ▲
CARTER POLICIES AND THE 1980 AND 1981 ELECTIONS

By 1979 the stage was set for another cycle of change, attempted reform, and reaction. Nearly everyone in Honduras had come to agree that a return to at least nominal civilian control was desirable. The mismanagement, incompetence, and corruption of the Paz García military regime was unequaled, even in Honduras's tragic history. The prospects for holding elections and a return to civilian government were improved by growing public rejection of almost twenty years of nearly continuous military rule and calls by conservatives for elections as a way to give a democratic façade to a conservative regime.

Moreover, by 1978 and 1979 the situation in Central America had already begun to deteriorate from Washington's point of view. But Honduras looked as if it could be an "island of stability" in a sea of turmoil. Carter policymakers sought to encourage mild reform and elections to create alternatives to insurgency, but at the same time sought to strengthen Honduran military forces with aid and advisers to ensure that order could be maintained.

Honduras appeared to be a country where militarization-cum-reform strategies might work. Despite the increasing repression of the military government and its attempt to close off political space after Paz García took the reins of power in 1978, Honduras was clearly much less prone to revolutionary violence and turmoil than its neighbors. Honduras, heretofore virtually ignored by Washington, began to acquire geopolitical significance among top-level policymakers.

Carter's policymakers used diplomatic pressure and U.S. largesse to encourage those who backed elections, and the electoral timetable was maintained after the Reagan administration took office. Thus in 1980 and 1981, relatively free and open elections (by Central American standards) were held, first to elect a constituent assembly, and then to elect a new government. The Liberal Party, mildly reformist in orientation, won both elections. But elections, however fair and honest, do not in themselves produce democracy, and the return to civilian government proved to be more illusory than real.

Before the second elections, for example, the military met with the principal leaders of the National and Liberal Parties in October 1981 to lay down their conditions for elections: no post hoc investigations of military corruption, a veto over all cabinet appointments, dominance in foreign policy making, and absolute authority over all matters pertaining to the military itself. Further, Liberal Party presidential candidate Robert Suazo Córdova, anxious to defeat the National Party, which had been symbioti-cally close to the military, allied himself with then- Colonel Gustavo Alvarez Martínez. Alvarez, then head of the national police, was an ambitious and important, but younger and less-known figure in the military hierarchy.

This alliance was a brilliant stroke, in terms of breaking the traditional Nationalist-military alliance, but it would force Suazo Córdova to exchange the mildly antimilitary reformist tradition of the Liberal Party for the continued support of Alvarez and his military allies. Suazo Córdova may have used Alvarez at first, but the deal eventually became the undoing of Suazo and the Liberals.

THE USS HONDURAS: ▲
REAGAN ADMINISTRATION POLICIES, 1981 TO 1983

During early 1981 there was considerable continuity between Carter and Reagan policies in Honduras. Both were willing to increase U.S. military aid and advisers to Honduras as long as there seemed to be movement toward elections, and both visualized Honduras as geopolitically crucial in the region. Thus, the Carter democracy-cum-militarization policies con-tinued after Reagan took office.

But after the Honduran elections in November 1981, it became apparent that Reagan had a much more ambitious strategy. Not content with the containment of either the Salvadoran guerrillas or the Nicaraguan revolu-tion, the Reagan policymakers sought a military victory in El Salvador and a "rollback" of the Nicaraguan revolution. Moving from containment to counterrevolution, the Reagan administration sought to recruit Honduras into the effort to intimidate and destabilize Nicaragua, eventually overturn-ing the Nicaraguan revolution, and (by extension in the administration's logic) checking Cuban and Soviet power. They also drafted Honduras into the support of the Salvadoran government's struggle against its insurgents, many of whom were based in regions along the Honduran-Salvadoran border. Finally, Reagan policymakers viewed Honduras as a perfect staging base between El Salvador and Nicaragua, and they began the forward deployment of U.S. troops and equipment to assist possible direct U.S. military intervention in the region's troubles.

Although it has always taken a backseat to the administration's political-military strategy, the Reagan policymakers also sought to transform Honduras into a Central American paragon of free market capitalism. Through the aggressive promotion of an export-led private-sector development strategy heavily dependent on foreign investment, the administration hoped to vindicate its claims that unbridled free enterprise and foreign investment are the way to economic development in the Third World.[9]

GROOMING HONDURAS FOR A   ▲
COUNTERREVOLUTIONARY ROLE

Specific tasks were assigned to Honduras for carrying out U.S. military strategy: providing a base and cover for the CIA-backed contra operations against Nicaragua, what the *Sunday Times* (London) called "the most ambitious paramilitary and political action operation mounted by the CIA in nearly a decade;"[10] training Salvadoran (and other nations') military forces in Honduras for U.S. fiscal or political reasons, thus becoming another Panama for counterinsurgency training; providing key military support for the Salvadoran army along the border to prevent guerrillas from using Honduran territory and to control the refugees; providing strategically placed bases from which U.S. sea, land, and air forces could operate to intimidate and pressure Nicaragua and the Salvadoran guerrillas; a rapid Honduran military buildup to support these operations; and providing training bases and a scene for U.S. rapid-deployment airborne missions in a regional war that seems more and more probable to all. Honduras has become, in a word, the USS *Honduras*, a permanent aircraft carrier providing a platform for U.S. military intervention in the region.

In pursuit of these objectives, U.S. military sales and assistance to Honduras have skyrocketed under the Reagan administration. More U.S. military assistance and sales were provided to Honduras in either 1982 or 1983 than during the entire period from 1946 to 1980. U.S. military aid increased more than tenfold from 1979 to 1984. The Reagan administration either gave or sold over $68 million in military equipment and supplies to Honduras in 1982 and 1983, and provided military grants of $77.5 million for 1984.[11] The United States has tripled the number of U.S. advisers in Honduras, set up two sophisticated radar stations operated by U.S. military and CIA personnel, and sent over a hundred Green Beret "trainers" to the base at Puerto Castilla where the Regional Military Training Center has been set up to train Salvadoran and Honduran soldiers.[12]

These "official figures" obscure rather than reveal the dimensions of the military buildup in Honduras. One of the primary goals of the series of joint U.S.-Honduran military exercises since 1981 has been to provide the Honduran army with much larger amounts of military assistance than would otherwise be possible given congressional constraints. The "end-run" mechanism here is really very simple: hardware, supplies, and other mili-

TABLE 1
U.S. MILITARY AND ECONOMIC ASSISTANCE TO HONDURAS, 1946–1984
(U.S. Fiscal Years—Millions of Dollars)

	1946–1979	1980	1981	1982	1983	1984	Supplemental 1984*	Proposed 1985*
Military								
Military Assistance Program	5.6	0	0	11.0	27.5	40.0	37.5	61.3
Credit Financing	12.5	3.5	8.4	19.0	9.0	0	0	0
International Military Education Training	8.5	0.4	0.5	1.3	0.8	1.0	0	1.2
Economic								
Security Support Funds	2.4	0	0	36.8	53.0	40.0	72.5	75.0
Economic								
Agency for International Development	213.8	45.8	25.7	31.2	35.1	32.0	7.3	45.0
TOTALS	271.8	49.7	34.6	99.3	125.4	113.0	118.0	182.5

*These figures represent Reagan administration requests as of April 1984.

SOURCE: Central American Historical Institute, Georgetown University, "U.S.-Honduran Relations: A Background Briefing Packet," Washington, D.C., May 1984, from U.S. Agency for International Development, *Congressional Presentation: Latin America and Caribbean, 1985/86, 1984/85, 1983/84,* Annex III.

tary necessities are sent to Honduras for the maneuvers and are never withdrawn.

The "exercises" also provide an excuse for essential infrastructure construction that would otherwise be difficult to finance. The United States has spent over $100 million in military construction in Honduras. Eight different airfields have been built, expanded, or improved; hundreds of miles of roads have been constructed (to aid the CIA-backed contras); tank traps built; several base camps and training facilities set up; a large-scale command and logistics center built; and radar installed.[13] In addition, some unknown portion of the covert action budget for the contras' operation against Nicaragua (estimated to be as high as $100 million) is also destined to help the Honduran military buildup. After a fact finding mission to Honduras, Senator James Sasser (D-Tenn.) termed these activities "nothing less than a backdoor military buildup in Honduras, a military buildup which far exceeds what is necessary for the successful completion of military exercises."[14]

Perhaps even more serious, the exercises have provided a way for U.S. military forces to intervene in Central America. These joint exercises—the brainchild of General Paul Gorman, then head of U.S. Southern Command[15]—have allowed the development of a permanent U.S. military presence in Honduras with little publicity or congressional debate.

There have been three stages in the development of the excercises. The first set of relatively brief joint U.S.-Honduran military exercises took place in the Caribbean coastal areas near the Nicaraguan border intermittently from October 1981 to February 1983. These excercises allowed the Reagan administration to skirt congressional limits on military aid to Honduras and the contras, not only by leaving behind equipment but by covering the building of the infrastructure necessary to supply, train, and organize the CIA-backed operation against Nicaragua.

The second stage began in August 1983. These "Big Pine II" exercises ran for six months—the longest set of U.S. military exercises ever held. Involving at their height over five thousand U.S. troops in Honduras and over sixteen thousand on nearby naval ships and planes, these war games allowed the United States to develop a relatively sophisticated permanent combat infrastructure and presence in Central America.

The third stage, beginning in early 1984, has been less clear-cut in orientation, largely because of the downfall of General Alvarez in Honduras and the apparent resistance of some of the Honduran military leadership to some of the aims of these exercises, which call for ever closer cooperation with El Salvador. The original idea was seemingly to "tighten the screws" even further on both Nicaragua and the Salvadoran guerrillas during an election year by poising U.S. forces on the very brink of the battlefield. Granadero I, an obvious invocation of the "post-Vietnam syndrome" the administration thinks it created after Grenada, began in April with construction and exercises close to both the Salvadoran and Nicaraguan borders. The third stage has also featured provocative unannounced war games in conflict-ridden border areas such as the Gulf of Fonseca. The United States also originally planned to make the maneuvers multilateral by including troops from El Salvador, Guatemala, and Panama, but the latter two nations decided against participation.

In sum, the exercises serve as a pretext, a politico-military camouflage, for U.S. military intervention and war preparations. With increasing numbers of troops rotating in and out of Honduras, U.S. military planners have managed to establish a permanent military capability in the heart of Central America. Each successive exercise has enlarged the presence of the U.S. military and expanded its role. By 1984, U.S. military activities in Honduras had become a centerpiece of its military strategy in Central America. The Pentagon has announced that it plans to continue excercises through 1988! No wonder Hondurans increasingly view their land as an occupied country.

THE CONSEQUENCES OF THE MILITARIZATION ▲
OF HONDURAS

U.S.-sponsored militarization of Honduras has had five major negative effects, reviewed below in highly summarized fashion: the militarization of Honduras has undermined its fragile process of democratization; the economic policies foisted on Honduras are wholly at odds with U.S.-inspired politico-strategic policies, aggravating the serious economic decline in Honduras; accelerating militarization has prevented Honduras from coming to grips with deeply rooted socioeconomic problems; regional instability has increased as Honduras has been drawn into the conflicts in El Salvador and Nicaragua, threatening regional war; and taken together, all these effects of militarization threaten to undermine the stability of Honduran society. In each of these areas, not only have Reagan policies failed to accomplish their avowed objectives of peace, democracy, reform, and stability, but they have been overwhelmingly counterproductive, leading to the very opposite of their declared aims.

Undermining Democracy

The strategy of combining a strong Honduran military with a stable, civilian democratic government, an idea dating from the late Carter years, embodies a contradiction based on a misunderstanding of Honduran reality: given the military's growing political dominance over the years, strengthening the military would almost inevitably result in the erosion of democratic processes. And considering the conditions of turmoil and unrest prevalent in the region, Honduran democracy had only a slim chance at best.

The Reagan administration neither understands the social reality of Honduras nor cares about the nation, except as it can be used as a counterrevolutionary trampoline. As a result, the Reagan team played directly into the hands of the most reactionary, antidemocratic sectors in Honduras, those centered around General Alvarez Martínez.

This was made possible, in part, by the position of the Honduran governing class. Historically relatively weak, with no real political-economic vision of its own, it has traditionally followed the U.S. embassy's political line in foreign policy in exchange for U.S. aid and support. Reagan's ambassador, John Negroponte, was simply the last of a long line of U.S. ambassadors who have served as proconsuls. But Honduras's nearly absolute submission to the Reagan line was unusual even by Honduran standards. The explanation lies in the power of certain political and military factions inside Honduras, whose interests and agendas were at least temporarily consistent (if not wholly coterminous) with U.S. policies, most notably those following President Suazo Córdova and General Alvarez Martínez.

After Suazo took power in early 1982, he carried through on his promises to Alvarez, elevating him to head of the military and bestowing various honors on him (including the rank of general in violation of established military procedures for rank) in exchange for military support. Like so many of their predecessors, Suazo and Alvarez struck a deal with Reagan and Negroponte. In this Faustian bargain, Honduran geopolitical, military, and economic obedience to the United States would be exchanged for American economic largesse and military "protection." By the end of 1983, this attempt to "sell Honduras" (as the influential Facussé family argued) had become a central question in Honduran politics. Having mortgaged their future to the United States, the Honduran leadership became increasingly anxious about the economy and U.S. intentions to carry through on its part of the bargain.

The Suazo-Alvarez leadership gained its position in exactly this fashion and maintained itself this way into the early months of 1984. The militarization that resulted from this bargain allowed the military to reestablish and restructure itself after public repudiation of ten years of military rule that was climaxed before the 1980 and 1981 elections by revulsion against the orgy of corruption under Paz García. The U.S. military assistance, increase in salaries, training, joint exercises, and so on, allowed the military to expand, bolstering its political autonomy with minimal obligation to the civilian political leadership. Indeed, under the civilian "democracy," the military came to enjoy even greater power than under past military governments—without having to share the responsibility for its exercise. As one observer noted, "The military has all the power and the civilians have all the problems."[16]

U.S.-sponsored militarization was particularly important to Alvarez, who parlayed his relationships with Suazo and Negroponte in 1982 and 1983 into a position of virtually unquestioned authority. He exercised control in all matters pertaining to the military and its role, major foreign policy issues, internal security through his control of the police, and any major political or economic question before the government. Moreover, the long arm of Alvarez reached into the internal policies of the two traditional parties, his Machiavellian tactics and Napoleonic ambitions having been the cause of major internal splits in both parties. Finally, his power even extended to important, supposedly independent, pluralist organizations such as unions, cooperatives, the National University, and peasant and business groups, which he sought to influence, divide, and conquer by a variety of means. Encouraged, or at least unopposed by the United States, Alvarez was calling the shots, while Suazo was docilely minding the shop.

For the first months of the Suazo regime, Suazo was Dr. Jekyll to Alvarez's Mr. Hyde. Suazo declared a diplomatic initiative for the "internationalization of peace" that emphasized Honduran neutrality in regional conflict; Alvarez was busy violating such neutrality by closely cooperating with the Salvadoran army, supporting the contras, and provoking border clashes with Nicaragua. As Suazo extolled the virtues of civilian government and democracy, Alvarez was repressing and dividing pluralistic, democratic groups. As in the story, Mr. Hyde slowly came to dominate Dr. Jekyll. Thus the real power in Honduras became Alvarez, not Suazo. By the end of 1983, this schizophrenia had taken on alarming dimensions. Alvarez and his radically anticommunist civilian elite allies were virtually running the government through the Association for the Progress of Honduras (APROH), a neofascist corporatist body espousing the "national security state" doctrine popular among the military regimes of the Southern cone (Argentina, Uruguay, and Chile).[17]

These developments undermined the whole purpose of the 1980 and 1981 elections in which hundreds of thousands of Hondurans had duly gone to the polls to overwhelmingly reject ten years of military misrule and corruption. The Liberal Party, with a long heritage of antimilitarism and reformism, turned out to be neither. What both the United States and the official Liberal Party did was to ally themselves with the least popular sector in the Honduran political system and then allow it effectively to assume power, i.e., Alvarez, his right-wing cronies, and the military. As one knowledgeable observer of the Honduran political scene put it, civilians became "spectators in their own political game."[18]

The results for Honduras's political future were even more devastating because the ascendancy of Alvarez and the military took place within a fanatically anticommunist "national security" ideological plan. Alvarez had studied in Argentina, and Argentine and Chilean military advisers were brought to Honduras in 1982 to train and advise Hondurans in the techniques of anticommunist "dirty war." For the first time in its history Honduras began to witness systematic state terrorism: disappearances, political assassinations, secret cemeteries, and clandestine detention centers.[19]

THE TRAMPLING OF HUMAN RIGHTS. The violation of elemental human rights was, for the most part, historically off-limits in Honduras. Although the human rights abuses under the Suazo-Alvarez regime pale by comparison to those in El Salvador and Guatemala, they signified a dangerous process of escalating repression and political violence. In 1983 alone, the toll was 24 political assassinations, 20 disappeared, 43 political prisoners, and 28 tortured.[20] By 1984, there had been approximately 105 disappearances, 88 political assassinations, and 57 political prisoners. Another 138 persons were "saved," including those who had disappeared or were tortured and later released or turned over to the courts and charged as subversives. Honduras has an active Committee for the Defense of Human Rights and a Committee of Families of the Detained and Disappeared.

After stonewalling the issue for a year and a half, the Suazo government was finally forced to admit official disappearances in June 1983. So, too, have Reagan officials. Ambassador Negroponte admitted that, "If there is a soft spot in Honduras's otherwise positive political record it is in human rights."[21] Nevertheless, a report on human rights by three U.S. groups entitled "Honduras on the Brink" concluded that at best the United States had remained silent and at worst defended the abuses committed in Honduras."[22]

ATTACKS ON POLITICAL FREEDOM AND POPULAR ORGANIZATIONS. Just as disturbing were the tactics employed to repress, divide, and destroy pluralist, nongovernmental "popular organizations." Labor unions, peasant organizations, and professional and student associations have all been under increasing attack since the Suazo government came to power. Leaders of these groups have been assassinated, persecuted, and simply removed from office by force or threat of force. Where this has not proved successful, alternative "parallel organizations" have been set up to sap strength from the groups. Rump assemblies have taken over leadership of these institutions by bribery and force. Using huge infusions of money and influence, as well as rigging internal elections, others have been co-opted.

Not in recent Honduran history has any government been so divisive, so repressive, on such a scale as has this one. Bolstered by a 1982 Anti-Terrorist Law, Alvarez and the government set out to systematically split or destroy the very institutions and pluralism that have helped save Honduras from widespread political and economic violence in the past. While these sectors very rarely ever got all (or even very much) of what they wanted in the past, at least they were allowed to organize. Even in the most repressive previous military governments they were heard. This systematic campaign to suppress and root out legitimate dissent and organization squandered the (always fragile) political tolerance and dialogue that Honduras has justly and proudly celebrated in the past. Such actions destroy the trust and organizations, indeed the very "building blocks," necessary for a functioning democracy. As de Tocqueville noted long ago in the United States, these groups are the "training ground" of democracy.

The systematic division and destruction of pluralist organizations in Honduras is causing the same polarization and violence that has taken place in Nicaragua, El Salvador, and Guatemala. What we are seeing in Honduras are the early stages of the "Salvadorization" of Honduran politics, as one analyst called it, the radicalization and polarization of all sectors.[23] It is a closing off of political space that weakens and destroys reformist groups in the center that have the most to gain from democratic institutions and processes. These policies of confrontation obstruct and finally eliminate the institutional mechanisms for peaceful discussion, participation, and decision making until the only alternative is violence and political murder on a large scale. As a rightist-sponsored rally entitled "Re-Encounter with Honduras" in August 1983 had it, implying some Hondurans had strayed from the path of "patriotism," one is either "for" or "against" Honduras. Once political and economic issues become defined in these terms, democracy is obviously in more than a little danger.

Although it can only be briefly mentioned here, there is much other evidence suggesting that, despite the 1980 and 1981 elections, Honduras is not even minimally democratic. Although these general elections were relatively honest (largely because of U.S. pressure), internal primary elections and processes in the traditional parties have been characterized by the massive fraud and manipulation known to everyone in Honduras as "elections Honduran-style." To take just one example, the primary elections in the ruling Liberal Party in August 1983 were doubly fraudulent, a fraud within a fraud, as it were. The left wing of the party, the Popular Liberal Alliance (ALIPO), was first taken over in June 1983 by a minority faction through a series of questionable procedures. Then, when the primary elections were held in August, the "official" Suazo wing of the party rigged the elections against ALIPO in a series of moves so blatantly fraudulent they would have made a Chicago machine politician blush. When the president of the party, José Azcono Hoyo, denounced the elections he was forced to resign and lost his post in the cabinet as Minister of Communications and Transportation.

Similarly, election-related scandals, frauds, manipulation, and resignations have occurred in both parties as they geared up for the 1985 elections and have attempted to rig national electoral machinery such as the National Population Register and the National Tribunal of Elections. In March and April 1985, President Suazo's persistent and Machiavellian attempts to play the role of "king-maker" among the candidates of both major political parties led to a full-fledged constitutional crisis. When dissident members of the National Congress called for honest primary elections and challenged Suazo's manipulation of the electoral system (exercised through his appointees to the Supreme Court) by replacing the justices, Suazo threw the new chief justice in jail and ordered the others arrested. The crisis was only resolved in late May 1985 by a compromise mediated by the military in which there will be no primaries but virtually anyone is free to run for office. Obviously enough, this antidemocratic behavior undermines the faith of people that electoral processes are a feasible way to socioeconomic and political progress.

Perhaps even worse than electoral fraud in this regard have been both the performance and treatment of the National Congress since the Suazo government began. Until the March 1985 crisis, the Congress had been a legislative farce in important matters of policy. It has been dealt with accordingly by the real powers. Completely cowed and marginalized, the National Congress has been a rubber-stamp body incapable of defending its most basic authority under the 1981 constitution. The same is true of the Honduran judicial system, which meekly acquiesces in the grossest violations of human rights and constitutional strictures.

The only bright spot in an otherwise grim and worsening situation is the continued vitality of the press in Honduras. Although there is only one real opposition newspaper in Honduras, *El Tiempo*, the others being conservative organs of groups basically sympathetic to government and U. S. policies, all papers (as well as the radio and television) have been relatively free of direct government pressures and controls. *El Tiempo* admits it practices self-censorship to avoid problems with the authorities; even so, it is under a commercial advertising boycott from conservative business groups and has had several skirmishes with the government.

Contrary to its stated intention, the Reagan administration was neither "promoting" Honduran democracy nor "protecting" it with a "military shield." It was undermining it. It is clear that Reagan's policies have been extraordinarily counterproductive in the Honduran case if its aims were to foster democracy.

Economic Decline, the Garrison State, and "Reaganomics for Honduras"

The Honduran economy is in very poor shape, indeed. Even the most optimistic assessments are grim, and the short-run forecast is for more of the same. In fact, as is widely recognized in Honduras, economic decline threatens the stability of Honduras at least as much as any other factor, including the conflicts in Nicaragua and El Salvador.

But one must be careful to distinguish between the *current* crisis and the *chronic* crisis.[24] While the chronic crisis in Honduras has meant that 80 to 85 percent of the population is "normally" poverty-stricken, the current crisis has made them even worse off and now threatens at least part of the other 15 to 20 percent as well. The chronic crisis stems from a model of "development" that is, even in the best of times, incapable of providing for the barest necessities of the majority but able to provide the levels of earnings, salaries, and investment the minority require. The current crisis is defined by the fact that this model finds itself in "crisis," not only from the viewpoint of the majority, but also from the viewpoint of the minority.

Much of the current crisis, as Richard Newfarmer points out in this volume, is shared by other Central American countries suffering from the world economic recession and regional instability. These factors in turn have led to diminishing investment, both public and private; increased debt; a decline in exports and imports; large numbers of business failures; a high rate of unemployment; decreasing civilian public spending and a reduction in private consumption; a severe reduction in international credit flows; massive capital flight; and large balance-of-payment deficits.

What is much less widely recognized, however, is the adverse impact Reagan administration policies—both politico-military and economic— have had on the Honduran economic situation. Reagan economic policies are especially significant in Honduras because, in addition to its influence in politico-military affairs, the United States has dominated the formation of economic policy in Honduras. In fact, the Suazo government's economic program consisted largely of Reagan administration "recommendations." These ideas simply *became* policies of the government. Acceptance of U.S. guidance in economic matters was an important part of the deal struck between the Reagan policymakers and the Suazo regime. The latter has, in effect, traded a considerable portion of its authority in economic decision-making for Reagan promises of a massive economic bailout. This, too, is part of the Faustian bargain between the United States and Honduras.

One of the most striking characteristics of U.S. economic policies for Honduras has been their starkly prominent promotion of U.S. economic interests over any consideration of their effects on Honduras. Taking advantage of Honduras at its weakest, when it can least afford the loss of taxes and duties, Reagan policymakers have forced an even closer and more dependent relationship with U.S. firms. For example, under the rubric of a "revitalization plan" emphasizing the private sector, Honduras has had to "liberalize" its treatment of U.S. petroleum, banking, banana, tourist, agribusiness, and mining firms, ostensibly to attract new investment.

More important, however, the Reagan administration's emphasis on private-sector, export-led growth in Honduras has collided head-on with its politico-military policies of confrontation and militarization. The required investment, both foreign and domestic, has not been forthcoming in the face of declining investor confidence in the region. And, paradoxically enough, the administration itself has turned Honduras into a garrison state, economically as well as politically, undermining and contradicting its emphasis on the private sector. As more and more economic activity revolves around the militarization of Honduras, the vision of a free-market, export-led economy becomes less and less viable. The "Reaganomics for Honduras" private-sector strategy is practically all but dead, and economic garrison-statism has begun to replace it.

This, in turn, has led to yet another contradiction. The administration's free-market rhetoric about turning Honduras into another Hong Kong, Singapore, or Taiwan fits oddly with its program of a huge economic bailout. As the private-sector strategy failed, it had to be replaced with U.S. economic assistance simply to keep Honduras afloat. Honduras has become an international welfare case not entirely but at least partly because of Reagan policies. The Reagan politico-military strategy has, in effect, torpedoed its economic strategy.

Nor will the economic bailout solve Honduran economic problems. In the

current war economy, even huge injections of U.S. aid become economic
"relief," not development-generating aid. Without an end to the military
conflict and preparations for war, such assistance will simply prop up the
economy, stemming the tide of economic erosion caused by militarization.
In the absence of real peace, the economy will continue to decline and the
amount of aid will only determine the pace of that decline.

At the same time that U.S.-inspired militarization prevents any real
improvement in the current crisis, it is also at loggerheads with longer-term
structural reforms needed to solve the chronic crisis in Honduras. U.S.-
sponsored military expansion has meant that sorely-needed social and economic reforms have been put on the back burner. For example, despite the
fact that earlier Honduran efforts in agrarian reform from 1972 to 1975
are widely conceded to have had a positive impact on improving the lot of
the rural poor and ameliorating rural unrest, the Suazo government's record
in land reform is very poor.[25] In essence, U.S. foreign policy has subordinated economic recovery and necessary reforms to the military buildup.
The Honduran government cannot get on with either reform or recovery
while it is busily engaged in creating a garrison state in Honduras. Moreover, the Reagan policymakers have cautioned the Suazo regime to go slow
on structural reform, emphasizing instead a trickle-down private-sector
strategy. The "Reaganomics for Honduras" approach is inherently nonreformist, yet fundamental reforms are precisely what are needed for both
socioeconomic equity and recovery.

If reform is not begun and militarization reversed, major economic aid
programs will either be wasted or may actually prove to be counterproductive and destabilizing. Economic aid will become an extension of the war
effort, freeing up government resources for further militarization and attacks on the shreds of democracy (such as a remarkably free press). Aid
will legitimize war preparations and the garrison state. The Reagan administration in Honduras confronts a real dilemma, the economic equivalent of its dilemma in El Salvador with death-squad activity. The problem
is how to ensure efficient use of aid when that aid is going to be channeled
through the same old, generally corrupt and incompetent gang of political
and military cronies and elites that were partly responsible for economic
mismanagement and decline in the first place. On the other hand, if the
United States attempts to go outside of the established power structure to
seek real, broadly shared growth, it will surely jeopardize its politico-
military strategy, which is supported by the structure.

Thus, within the current structure, massive aid will not do much good.
The Reagan "trickle-down" nonreformist policies and resources may prop
up the circle of banking, military, and party hacks. But corruption, capital
flight, mismanagement, and patronage will not result in either immediate
help or long-term structural reform, so desperately needed by the great
majority of Hondurans. Until overall U.S. policy changes and structural
reforms are begun, large-scale U.S. economic aid, however favored by U.S.

congressional moderates, will do little to make things better, and might make things worse, in Honduras.

By mid-1985, even the Suazo regime had become sensitive to U.S. heavyhandedness in the realm of economic policymaking, leading to increasing Honduran resistance to U.S. Reaganomics demands. Although a host of questions were at issue—including privatization of state-run enterprises, food distribution systems, price controls, interest rate subsidies on housing—the key issue eventually became the devaluation of the *Lempira*, pegged at two to one to the dollar since 1927 and especially tough to swallow in an election year.

A minicrisis developed in the first three months of 1985 when the United States refused to disperse $147.5 million in AID funds to Honduras unless it accepted a series of measures, including devaluation. Eventually an accord was reached in March, but U.S. insistence on devaluation will likely mean it will be the very first problem the incoming government will have to face after the November 1985 elections.

Increasing Regional Instability and the Threat of War

By drafting Honduras into its role as counterrevolutionary springboard, the United States has drawn Honduras into the civil and class wars of its neighbors. Instead of attempting to isolate Honduras from these conflicts, U.S. policies have widened them by involving Honduras; indeed, pushing Honduras into a broader regional role is what U.S. policies are all about. In doing this the United States has stirred up longstanding nationalistic hostilities and produced new sources of conflict in the region, even among its own allies.

Honduras's relations with El Salvador have been traditionally antagonistic, and especially bitter since the disastrous four-day "Soccer War" of 1969. Almost a decade later, the Carter State Department and Pentagon managed to work out an accord that formally ended the war and reestablished diplomatic and commercial relations but still left important border issues unresolved. The agreement enabled the United States to enlist Honduras in the role of backstop for "hammer and anvil" operations against the Salvadoran guerrillas as far back as 1980; and in 1983, Washington got General Alvarez to support U.S. training camps for Salvadoran troops on Honduran soil.

Also in 1983, the training of Salvadoran troops in Honduras became a source of deep nationalistic discontent in Honduras, the U.S. equivalent of having Vietcong and North Vietnamese train at Fort Bragg, North Carolina! The training center also deeply offended most Hondurans because of the manner in which it was presented by Alvarez and the Pentagon as a fait accompli. Because the Honduran constitution requires Honduras congressional approval for foreign troops on Honduran territory, the secretly negotiated Alvarez-Pentagon plan had to be shoved through a reticent Congress a week after a hundred Green Berets joined twenty U.S. advisers who were already building the facility. Adding insult to injury, Honduran eligibility for U.S. Caribbean Basin Initiative funds was later blocked in the United States when a U.S. citizen claimed the facility was built on his land (although the Honduran constitution also prohibits foreigners from owning land in such coastal or border areas).

Thus, four years of U.S.-enforced cooperation between El Salvador and Honduras has only served to increase their mutual antagonism, fanning the dying embers of distrust and resentment that linger from the 1969 fiasco. Honduras has gained little from El Salvador in return for its assistance. El Salvador has been intransigent in resolving unsettled border issues. To make matters worse, Honduran participation in U.S.-sponsored military operations along the border has embroiled Honduras in a series of messy international conflicts over the some twenty thousand Salvadoran refugees that have crossed into Honduras. The most tragic outcome of these joint military pincer movements, however, has been the cold-blooded massacres of the refugees, mostly old men, women, and children: six hundred were killed while fleeing across the Río Sumpul in 1980, three hundred while crossing the Río Lempa in 1982.[26]

Moreover, joint border operations and the training of Salvadoran forces has made Honduras the target of Salvadoran terrorist attacks. There was a period during 1982 and 1983 when every joint border operation was met in tit-for-tat fashion with a terrorist strike in Honduras. The offices of Air Florida, IBM, and other U.S. firms were bombed, banks robbed, the Tegucigalpa power supply destroyed, and President Suazo's daughter kidnapped, among other incidents.

Of course the major point of conflict has been with Nicaragua, with scores of border incidents since 1980. Although a Honduran-Nicaraguan border war has so far been avoided, a regional conflagration has become a real possibility. Some unknown portion of the Honduran military, especially the Alvarez faction, is known to think that a Honduran-Nicaraguan armed conflict is virtually inevitable and the sooner the better. Honduran plans for some sort of "preemptive strike" against Nicaragua have had to be vetoed by the United States since at least as far back as the spring of 1981. The infiltration of a small Honduran guerrilla force from Nicaragua in late 1983 was eagerly used by the Honduran right to heighten jingoistic fears. It was easily rounded up with the help of U.S. advisers.[27] In the wake of the U.S. invasion of Grenada, and amidst growing economic and political instability, there were insistent calls from the Honduran right in 1983 for a direct U.S. "military solution" against Nicaragua. A regional war of this sort could only have disastrous consequences for Honduras, particularly, and incalculable implications for the future of the region as a whole.

As in the Salvadoran case, Honduran relations with its supposed "allies," the contras, have also been tense. Nicaraguan contras operating out of Honduras have terrorized Hondurans in border areas, especially in the south where reports of rapes, robberies, extortion, and vandalism have become common. More important, Hondurans of all persuasions have become increasingly worried about what will become of the contras if their offensive fails or if U.S. aid to them is cut off. As Hondurans have become increasingly uneasy about the adverse consequences of the contras' presence, the Honduran military has tried to exercise greater control over their activities in Honduras, beginning shortly after the coup against Alvarez, when it was rumored that Alvarez might try to return via a countercoup abetted by the contras. Thus while continuing to allow them to operate out of Honduras, the Honduran military have nonetheless forcibly relocated contra camps, deported several contra leaders and their U.S. "free-lance" military advisers, publicly blamed them for abusing the human rights of Hondurans, and blocked the shipments of U.S. "humanitarian" aid to the contras.[28]

Finally, Honduras's role as the U.S. "point man" in Central America has led it to a hard-line, ineffective, and inflexible foreign policy, following the United States to retain the lead. For example, the Honduran position in the Contadora process is one that insists on multilateral negotiations, profound structural changes in the Nicaraguan political system, and Nicaraguan concessions on foreign relations (aping the Reagan demands on elections, talks with the contras, aid to Salvadoran insurgents, border tensions, etc.). The Honduran negotiating position has been basically a position of non-negotiation. As Honduran diplomats and others have become the butt of jokes throughout Latin America and Europe, Honduras has felt more and more diplomatically isolated. Diplomatic failure has had more than simply symbolic consequences: although U.S. economic aid has increased, other donors in Europe and elsewhere have pulled out, leaving Honduras with a net loss in economic assistance at a time when it needs it the most. Hence there is growing pressure to realign Honduran foreign policies along less slavish lines.[29]

Destabilizing Honduran Society

By early 1984, the cumulative impact of all these developments—increased regional instability, economic decline, political polarization, growing state terrorism and deterioration in democratic practices—had been to threaten Honduran stability, the very thing U.S. policies were supposed to avoid.

As things began to unravel in late 1983, Hondurans of all political stripes recognized that the economy was in very poor shape, that uncertainty and fear reigned, and that Honduras was on the edge of political and economic turmoil not seen at least since the 1954 banana strike.

Hence in late 1983 and early 1984, there was a pervasive sense of gloom and foreboding in Honduras, a bizarre atmosphere of uncertainty, crisis, polarization, insecurity, and impending doom. Even the likely beneficiaries of the government's economic strategies doubted they would work. The

private sector was scared, doubtful, and suspicious. Perhaps they understood, as Suazo, Alvarez, Reagan, and Negroponte do not, that the principal
defense of Honduras cannot be military, much less military hardware. It
must be real socioeconomic reform, justice, democracy, respect for human
rights, and peace.

Desperate for a last-ditch effort to save the situation before something
dreadful took place and the existing structure was threatened, the Honduran right called for some dramatic action, such as the invasion of Nicaragua,
that might simultaneously justify the woes and solve them. What they would
not admit, of course, was that the deteriorating conditions were the result
of both their own and U.S. policies: militarization, the lack of reform,
repression, increasing corruption, and poor economic policies. It was much
easier to blame it all on the war in El Salvador, the Sandinistas, Cuba, and
the Soviet Union. Like a cat chasing his own tail, Alvarez made the consequences of his own policies into the cause of them. In an inversion of real
causality, the results of his acts were made into the causes of those acts.

If there is any lesson to be drawn from the history of civil conflict in
Central America it must be that poverty alone is only a necessary not a
sufficient cause for revolt. Honduras, by far the poorest and yet still fairly
tranquil country, should demonstrate that. However, when one adds grinding poverty and large-scale repression together (a closing off of political
space), along with U.S. intervention, this can be a powerful, heady stimulus
to revolt. Unfortunately, that is precisely the mixture being brewed in
Honduras.

The minor guerrilla incursion of late 1983 should have been a red alert
that something very basic was going wrong. Instead, it became the justification for more of the same. Reagan policies, paradoxically enough, are
proving that the only chance for social justice and genuine national independence is through adherence to an uncompromising radically leftist faith
in a conflict that more likely than not will have to be decided by armed
struggle. While there may always be, theoretically speaking, the chance of
a profound reformist path carried out through democratic and largely peaceful processes, in practical terms this is becoming nearly impossible. The
reformists and the democrats simply get wiped out.

The United States mistakenly allied itself with Alvarez and Suazo, leaders who literally pawned their nation for personal political ambition and
greed. These are exactly the kind of ruling cliques that have supported the
United States at any cost to their own people, and have led to insurgency
and violence elsewhere in the region. These cliques have been willing to
turn over their nation's sovereignty, economic policy, and democratic institutions to make war on their own people and generally mortgage Honduras's soul. This Faustian bargain will have nightmarish consequences for
both the United States and Honduras, not the least of which is an eventual
backlash against excessive dependence on the United States.

With leaders like this, Honduras hardly needs enemies. Perhaps it is not
surprising that if its own leadership is willing to sacrifice or ignore Hondu-

ran interests, the United States will also. After all, one does not normally look to foreigners to defend such basic national interests as sovereignty, peace, and prosperity. Still, the United States might have treated Honduras differently out of both self-interest and a decent respect for a small, poor nation so obliging to it.

The Reagan administration regards U.S.-Honduran involvement of this sort (the maneuvers, the military buildup, and the contras) as "signs of stability," a demonstration of U.S. support and commitment to defend Honduras. What seems much more likely—especially when we consider the impact of U.S. policies on internal events—is that Reagan policies will destabilize and perhaps even destroy much of Honduras as we know it today. As an opposition politician told me, "It will not be possible to destabilize Nicaragua without also destabilizing Honduras." Thus, as in Vietnam, we will "destroy the village in order to save it."

In sum, in Honduras, militarization has become an end in itself, unrelated to any sensible U.S. foreign policy objectives. In so doing, it has become a means not to peace, stability, and development but to the very conditions militarization was presumably designed to avoid: uncertainty, insecurity, instability, violence, repression, and loss of freedom and well-being.

BACK FROM THE BRINK IN 1984: DISASTER AVOIDED?   ▲

The Fall of Alvarez: The General Goes Too Far

In the early morning hours of March 31, 1984, as he was returning from a meeting with APROH supporters, Alvarez was arrested by his own military, deposed, and put on a plane for Costa Rica. His closest military supporters were also relieved of their commands and spirited out of the country, many of them to diplomatic exile as military attachés abroad. Both the number and high rank of those removed suggested significant change, not simply a routine barracks revolt.

The coup caught everyone outside the military by surprise, including the U.S. embassy and the Suazo government. But the pressures had been building for some time. Alvarez's belligerence toward Nicaragua and his willingness to cooperate ever more closely with El Salvador upset some of the more nationalistic officers, who felt Honduras was being led into a potentially disastrous war not of its own choosing. Growing state terrorism was another concern: popular protest, growing domestic tensions, and several disappearances just prior to the coup worried a variety of middle-ranking military officials, who were concerned with the image of the military, with investigations like those President Raúl Alfonsín was carrying out in Argentina, and with the possibility of violent military purges by Alvarez. Evidence of widespread corruption (rumored to involve as much as $30 million) by Alvarez and his military clique, at a time when Honduras was undergoing exceptional economic and political difficulties, led to further internal military dissatisfaction. Finally, Alvarez's personal political schemes with APROH, the Liberals, and the Nationalists annoyed some officers who were not upset about the military's political predominance as an institution but did resent Alvarez's personalistic ambitions and wished to keep the civil and military sectors formally separate.

These particular pressures, however, were all secondary to the threat that Alvarez's personalistic rule posed to the military as an institution. The diverse group within the military that carried out the coup all shared opposition to Alvarez's arrogantly authoritarian rule and his personal concentration of power.[30] Alvarez had in a sense *deinstitutionalized* the military. Since the early 1950s, successive generations of military rulers had fought to liberate the military from confining ties and alliances with other sectors; that is, to make the military as an institution progressively more autonomous externally and more collective internally. But by 1984, Alvarez had abolished collegial decision-making procedures and returned the military to its former position as an instrument of personal political ambition, not unlike its role before 1954 in the classic era of *caudillo* politics. At the same time, Alvarez had become a "loose cannon" on the decks of Honduran civil-military politics in the Central American conflict. It was time for someone to either tie him down or throw him overboard. Since neither the Suazo regime nor the United States would or could step forward, the military did.

Plans for the coup had been in the works since December 1983 among younger, middle-ranking reformist officers. They were spurred to act in March 1984, earlier than planned, because Alvarez's plan to restructure the military was nearing rubber-stamp approval by the National Congress. Such restructuring would have enabled Alvarez to further consolidate his power, root out dissension and block any coup attempt. Conflicts in late March between Alvarez and the Superior Council of the Armed Forces (CONSUFA), the collective decision making body of the military, enabled coup supporters to incorporate both more senior officers and more conservative ones. They struck at a time when Alvarez had broken his old alliance with certain senior officers but had not yet organized a new one. Like a trapeze artist caught momentarily between trapezes, Alvarez was cut down at precisely the time when he had no support.

Although this allowed the coup leaders to carry off the ouster without a hitch, the diverse alliance inside the military meant a dilution of the coup's original reformist objectives. Thus, Suazo was not forced out (although when he was told of the coup the following morning, he was bluntly advised not to oppose it or he would go, too). And Alvarez's closest supporters were treated to diplomatic exile, while other followers were allowed to remain at their posts in exchange for their support and acquiescence.

Although both Suazo and the U.S. embassy hurriedly tried to portray the coup as a sign of the vitality of Honduran "democracy," there is much evidence that it was nothing of the sort. It was simply a fait accompli.

Neither the civilians nor the United States was involved or even aware of it, at least not until the very last minute. In fact, the coup took everyone by surprise precisely because of the *undemocratic* nature of the military-dominated Honduran political system. The internal politics of the military are shrouded in secrecy and lack democratic accountability and representation. This explains how the ouster of Alvarez—the most significant political event in the past four years—could take place so unexpectedly and without the participation of civilian leaders. Thus, while it was surely a positive development, it cannot be reviewed as an affirmation of democratic practice. On the contrary, it shows just how far Honduras has yet to go toward real civilian democratic rule.

After the Fall: Whither Honduras?

The forced departure of Alvarez caused most Hondurans to breathe a huge sigh of relief. The general feeling has been that now that Alvarez is gone, things can hardly get worse and they might get better. The coup dealt a severe blow to the most reactionary elements that had coalesced into APROH, since they are now deprived of the power and direct connection to the military that Alvarez supplied.

While the Honduran far right is now on the defensive, the coup has changed the form but not the substance of the direction of the developments in Honduras. At least two important influences, U.S. policies and military dominance of the political system, remain largely unchanged. In fact, in some ways, Alvarez's removal has made it easier for U.S. policies to continue unimpeded. It is still impossible to say what the precise meaning of the coup is or its implications for the future. Thus the short answer to the question "Whither Honduras?" is simply that it is still too early to tell. The long answer, based on developments both before and after the coup, suggests that there are at least four things to watch closely.

POPULAR DISCONTENT: THE OPPOSITION EMERGES. Protest demonstrations and strikes had begun in early 1984 even before the fall of Alvarez. In mid-March, for example, the layoffs of four hundred workers triggered a take-over of the Ministry of Communications, Public Workers and Transportation by unionized workers. The disappearance of a popular union leader who headed the state-run power company spurred strikes, arrests (over three hundred), and a large demonstration of some fifteen thousand workers in the leftist United Federation of Honduran Workers (FUTH) on March 22. When the electric company was militarized, almost forty thousand workers protested, leading to further (almost one thousand) detentions. On March 26, the Chinchonero Liberation Front, a far-leftist group responsible for several hijackings and bombings since 1979, exploded five bombs throughout Honduras—at the Supreme Court, two police stations, the Salvadoran consulate, and a military officers' training school.

With the fall of Alvarez, demonstrations became larger, more organized, more broadly based politically, and encompassed a wider set of demands: organizations demanded respect for human rights, the release of political prisoners, stepped-up land reform, Honduran neutrality, and the withdrawal of U.S. troops. Suazo's May austerity measures, pressed by the IMF, included a package of new taxes and forced government bond deductions from government workers' paychecks. These spurred other sectors to join union protests and demonstrations of up to fifty thousand people, including the National Party, factions of the Liberals, the leading business organizations, smaller political parties, and all three union federations.

Such popular protest is not surprising, given the deteriorating political and economic situation in Honduras. The serious question for Honduras's future is whether such political activity can be effectively organized for reform, or whether it will be met with more repression.

THE MILITARY AFTER ALVAREZ. Part of the answer will depend on the role of the military. After the coup it was thoroughly restructured to reverse the concentration of power of the Alvarez era. The new head of the military, Air Force General Walter López Reyes, had only a fraction of the authority wielded by Alvarez.

Moreover, with Alvarez gone, there is no longer any single, clear-cut military plan or project (such as Alvarez's "national security" doctrine) nor any single individual with the power to guide or impose it.[31] The military and its new leadership is divided by a complex set of cross-cutting cleavages that have rent the fabric of the military. The only thing the military could all agree on was their opposition to Alvarez and that this opposition was based on various differences. All this seems to add up to a highly factionalized system that will have to be mediated by the quasiparliamentary organs of the military such as CONSUFA. If centrifugal tendencies continue, it will be hard for the military to avoid spinning off in various directions and to control its own organization. CONSUFA rule in the late 1970s was not distinguished by high standards of honesty, ideological clarity, or military professionalism.

The military proved less repressive under López than under Alvarez, less willing to unquestioningly bend to U.S. contra policy, and less explicitly tied to any right-wing cabal like APROH, but it remained the center of political power. Moreover, many of the officers who supported continued state repression remained at their posts, and despite promises to investigate past crimes, little was done. As one observer commented, "The machinery of repression has yet to be dismantled."[32] In February 1986, some of these more recalcitrant officers (with the blessing of the U.S. embassy) were able to oust López.

Whatever the objections of the United States, which needs the image of a civilian, "democratic" Honduras, the military will stay in the background only as long as a civilian government does not challenge its power, or plunge the country into a severe economic or political crisis. And if economic decline continues to make reform difficult, it will make a return to military repression more likely.

RAISING THE RENT: RENEGOTIATING THE FAUSTIAN BARGAIN.[33] The one area where military intentions appeared clear is its interest in renegotiating the terms of the U.S.-Honduran alliance. Many in the military had come to feel that they were doing Reagan's dirty work in Central America, and very cheaply at that. These changes have also been based on a general feeling prevalent in Honduras for some time that the United States has not really kept its part of the bargain and may be setting up Honduras for a fall. As an opposition newspaper editorialized in July 1983: "We have lost everything, even our honor."[34]

Major Honduran dissatisfactions have centered specifically on: inadequate U.S. military and economic aid; the training of Salvadorans in Honduras; the future of the Nicaraguan contras; the economic as well as political impact of soaring military expenses; Honduran subservience to the U.S. line in international diplomacy; the refusal of the United States to pressure El Salvador into concessions on border issues; in sum, a host of "national interest" issues, most of which have been reviewed above. In spite of its internal divisions, the new military leadership has been intent on driving a harder bargain with the United States in the direction of a less submissive, more self-consciously independent role.[35] The military know Honduras is considered crucial to the United States, and they may be able to use their bargaining power to bring changes at the margin: greater benefits from the U.S. military presence, less gratuitous hostility toward Nicaragua, more training for Honduran troops, increased economic assistance. For the first time in many years, bargaining power has begun to shift toward Honduras.

It is, nonetheless, important to emphasize that the coup has *not* fundamentally altered the U.S.-Honduran relationship outlined here. The military leadership is committed to maintaining the overall thrust of the status quo in U.S.-Honduran relations. There are unlikely to be great changes in the current Honduran politico-military role in the region. The U.S. military presence will continue; "maneuvers" will be carried out; the contras will remain; the military buildup will continue; and limited operations with Salvadoran troops will take place.[36] Therefore, what is being renegotiated are the *terms* of its bargain with the Reagan team, *not* the bargain itself.

The coup, by removing Alvarez, has proved to be a blessing in disguise for the Reagan administration. Having largely served his function, Alvarez had increasingly become an embarrassment to the administration. With Alvarez out of the way, the Reagan team inherited an equally anticommunist leadership that has tried to clean up the "democratic" image of Honduras and has been easier to work with than the feisty, often unpredictable Alvarez. The administration has thus been spared the excesses of Alvarez and avoided the backlash against the military that might jeopardize U.S. plans.

Elections and the New Azcona Government

On November 24, 1985, Honduras held presidential, congressional and municipal elections. José Azcona Hoyo, a civil engineer and center-right dissident member of the Liberal Party, won the presidential contest. His inauguration on January 27, 1986, marked the first time in Honduras in over fifty years that one civilian government peacefully succeeded another.

This peaceful transition was a positive development, especially in light of the relatively high voter interest and turnout (80 percent) and the fairly honest and orderly conduct of the elections. But evidence from the period before and after the elections indicated a wide gap between these elections and real democratization.

The electoral campaign was marked by unusual slander and intrigue while the actual substantive issues contested were quite limited. The major contenders avoided addressing the most serious problems facing Honduras: the economic crisis, human rights violations, the presence of the contras, U.S. troops stationed in Honduras, and relations with El Salvador and Nicaragua. Their reluctance to tackle such issues indicated that the influence of the real centers of power in the country—the army high command and the U.S. embassy—were not being contested in the elections.[37]

Throughout the electoral process there was pervasive uncertainty about the democratic "rules of the game" and intense political manipulation. Much of the maneuvering came around a complex new electoral law adopted in May 1985. The new law sought to resolve a constitutional crisis unleashed by then-President Suazo's attempts to use control of the electoral machinery to impose his candidate. Under the new law (which in effect combined primary and general elections), nearly any candidate could run but the winner was to be determined by summing up all the votes for a particular political party. The front runner would thus receive all the votes of all the candidates who campaigned under a given party label. This system favored the two main traditional parties, but undercut the 1981 Constitution which states that the president shall be elected by a simple plurality of all the votes cast.

The new law led to varying interpretations and uncertainty, exacerbated by the continuing behind-the-scenes attempts of President Suazo to remain in office, or at least to get his candidate elected. Suazo did everything in his power to encourage ambiguity and uncertainty about the procedures in order to create a situation in which his interests might prevail.

The main candidates shuttled back and forth between the military and the U.S. embassy, thus revealing the real seats of political power in Honduras. Both the military and the U.S. embassy steadfastly refused to postpone the elections and rejected Suazo's high pressure tactics, for both the United States and the military desperately needed the appearance of democratic rule in Honduras to extract aid and public support in the United States.[38] The day before the election, the military finally forced the National Electoral Tribunal to issue a definitive ruling that the new electoral law would prevail over the 1981 Constitution.

Nonetheless, even after Azcona had won, the possibility remained that he might be prevented from taking power because, while he clearly won under the new law, he just as clearly lost under the constitutional rules. Azcona received 49 percent of the nearly 1.6 million votes cast (counting all the Liberal Party candidates' votes), while his main rival, Nationalist Party candidate Rafael Leonardo Callejas, received 44 percent (counting all the National Party candidates' votes). However, individually, Azcona received only 27 percent of the vote while Callejas clearly won with 41 percent. While behind-the-scenes mediation by the military prevented an opposition challenge to the validity of the elections, the minority vote seriously compromised Azcona's mandate to govern.

Azcona's difficulties were compounded by similar problems surrounding congressional elections. Indeed, the results here were hardly more conducive to democratic stability than those for president. In July 1985, Congress itself increased its total number of seats from 82 to 132. The new formula was passed by a coalition of various party factions, including PINU (Innovation and Unity Party) and the Christian Democratic Party (fearful that elections might eliminate representation for their small parties), despite cries of unconstitutionality and fiscal irresponsibility. In the elections themselves, the Liberals eked out a razor-thin plurality of 66 seats while the National Party got 62. The PINU and Christian Democrats got two seats apiece. The problems Azcona faced putting together a coherent legislative program with this slim Liberal majority were compounded by the deep factionalism in both parties. With his own representatives actually holding only a small minority of seats, the probabilities of a political impasse were great.

The 1985 Honduran elections thus provided a mechanism for transition which preserved a certain façade of civilian rule. But these elections, like those of 1981, did not serve the functions outlined in democratic theory: they neither resolved important conflicts, imposed a degree of accountability, provided a mandate to govern, nor encouraged political stability. That is partly because Honduras is not accustomed to having elections fulfill these functions but mostly because elections are largely irrelevant, even beside the point. So long as the most important decisions and policies continue to be made in the U.S. embassy and in military barracks and clubs, elections cannot serve these functions. Indeed, under the conditions that exist in Honduras, such elections contribute to, rather than resolve, conflict and instability. These problems will continue until the basic problem of politics and democracy in Honduras—who is to rule, the United States, the military, or civilians?—is addressed and resolved.

Recent U.S. foreign policy in Honduras has threatened to turn a difficult situation into disaster. The poverty that long plagued Honduras was tragic, but in the early 1980s reform was possible and revolution avoidable.

Unfortunately, U.S. political and military policies have helped strengthened some of the most reactionary, repressive forces in Honduras, encouraged economic decline to become economic crisis, and helped close off channels for reform. Preaching peace, democracy, stability, and anticommunism, U.S. policymakers encouraged war, repression, revolt, and radicalization.

In allying itself with Alvarez and Suazo, the Reagan administration befriended leaders who literally pawned their nation for personal political ambition and greed. They were willing to turn over their nation's sovereignty, economic policy, and emerging democratic institutions and to make war on their own people. They mortgaged Honduras's soul in a Faustian bargain that threatens to have nightmarish consequences for Honduras.

For its part of the bargain, the United States got a springboard for its geopolitical strategy of military pressure on El Salvador's insurgents and Nicaragua's Sandinista regime. But in destabilizing Nicaragua, the United States is also destabilizing Honduras. The Reagan administration seems willing to risk a Honduran-Nicaraguan war, the involvement of Honduras in Salvadoran and Nicaraguan internal conflicts, the collapse of civilian government, and the undermining of Honduran internal stability in pursuit of these counterrevolutionary objectives. Undermining the political legitimacy of the Honduran government at home and abroad, the United States has sacrificed Honduran national interests to U.S. strategy. Such stark, hegemonic dominance and dependence is the stuff of which nationalist revolutions are born. If it continues in Honduras, it will have this kind of reaction there too.

The overthrow of Alvarez in 1984 temporarily halted the worst political abuses and stopped the destruction of those political institutions and popular organizations that could, possibly, forge a constructive alternative for Honduras. The mistakes of past U.S. administrations, greatly extended and aggravated by the Reagan team, might still be reversed. But that will not happen without a truly extraordinary about-face in the current U.S. approach to Honduras and the region as a whole.

The recent history of U.S. foreign policy in Honduras illustrates the enormous destructive influence the United States can have on the internal affairs of another country. But in turning U.S. power toward more constructive purposes, it is important to realize that the power of the United States to impose "a solution" on Honduras is very limited. It is much more difficult to do good than to do harm. The United States has resembled the proverbial bull in a china shop: not much good can come from its overwhelming presence but a lot of damage is almost certain.

There is no way, for example, that even the best-intentioned U.S. policy could create a moderate, reformist democracy or an honest, decent civilian regime that exercised control over the military. The powerful, autonomous military is resistant to civilian control, and both civilian and military leadership are apprehensive about political mobilization and reluctant to allow unbridled freedom of expression, rapid structural reform, or full democracy. Not only is the Reagan administration ignorant of the limits of U.S. power in Honduras, it is blithely unaware of, or indifferent to, its negative impact on Honduras and frequently exaggerates its positive influence. This might best be termed "hegemonic ignorance,"—a willingness to rush in and try to run things with very little understanding of the situation at hand.

But there are still more possibilities in Honduras than in its northern neighbors. The oligarchy is not as strong or reactionary; the military is not as venal, brutal, or repressive—and its movement in that direction has been at least temporarily averted with the overthrow of Alvarez. There are still vestiges of respect for certain important political traditions—a respect for human rights, freedom of speech and the press, and freedom to organize that Alvarez sought to abolish. Further, elements of a reform coalition still exist in Honduras: honest, courageous, and competent individuals from the smaller Christian Democratic and the Innovation and Unity Party, from the left and center of the Liberals, trade unionists, peasant organizers, schoolteachers and doctors, progressive businessmen and women, even nationalist-progressive leaders of the National Party. Nor is it, as the administration might have us believe, that these elements are a "lunatic fringe," lacking support and incapable of governing. Quite the contrary, many of these same sectors and people actively participated in the 1972 to 1975 populist government and are even (however begrudgingly) credited by the Reagan team with having "saved" Honduras from socioeconomic and political unrest and violence.

While U.S. policymakers cannot impose a reformist solution, a wise policy would remove the obstacles the United States poses to the reformers and the support it gives to their enemies. First and foremost, the United States must stop using Honduras as a proxy for its essentially military strategies in Central America. Such a policy strengthens those who, like Alvarez, are most opposed to fundamental reform and democracy. It encourages all actors in Honduras to play on U.S. anticommunist heartstrings in order to survive. It creates regional tensions that make further militarization seem rational but will be disastrous. It creates a climate of distrust and uncertainty that encourages disinvestment, the flight of capital, economic decline, and the repression of any reform opposition.

Any reform coalition would surely demand as a condition for its participation a profound change in the regional role Honduras currently occupies, but current U.S. policy makes such demands impossible and thus helps destroy the possibilities of reform it rhetorically claims to support. If the United States stopped treating Honduras like a geopolitical pawn, withdrew its military presence, and offered aid and support to civilians seriously interested in reform, the hand of these reformers would be strengthened. They would have a greater possibility than they currently do to reverse the economic decline, halt the repression, bring the military under at least some civilian control, and increase the political space available for reform activities.

A Honduras characterized by these kinds of efforts would have little to fear from its neighbors and, like Costa Rica, would find most of the Western democratic world solidly on its side.

Because the Reagan administration's policies toward Honduras have been so interwoven with its policies elsewhere in Central America—especially in Nicaragua and El Salvador—changing U.S. policy toward Honduras is more than usually dependent on changing U.S. policy toward the region as a whole. This makes a change in the direction of U.S. policy in Honduras at once more difficult and more easy than it would be in a strictly bilateral case.

It is more difficult because real changes in Honduras policy depend on a whole "package" of policy modifications elsewhere in the area. For example, changing Honduras's role as a counterrevolutionary springboard would not only require removing U.S. troops on "exercises" and reducing U.S. military aid to Honduras, but also ending the CIA-backed contra operation and the Salvadoran-Honduran military cooperation and training. This, in turn, would require the United States to abandon its military-centered strategy in favor of diplomatic means and solutions.

At the same time, changing the direction of policy in Honduras could prove remarkably easy if the United States adopted a different approach to the entire region. The need for the militarization of Honduras would disappear: there would be no more cause for military construction, large-scale military aid and training, "maneuvers," and U.S. military forces stationed in Honduras; there would be no rationale for the contras, for enforced Honduran-Salvadoran military cooperation, for the economic "garrison state" in Honduras, and for Honduran state terrorism. In one stroke, such changes would eliminate many of the sources of regional tension and Honduran internal instability and uncertainty.

One cannot simply rewind the historical clock in Honduras and start all over. But with appropriately designed and executed U.S. policy, some of the damage of the last years could be undone and much of the rest at least forgotten. Honduras is not yet El Salvador or Guatemala, where too many bridges may have been burned to make a relatively peaceful and easy return to a more sane and humane political order. But the clock is running out in Honduras.

6

COSTA RICA
Morris J. Blachman
and Ronald G. Hellman

CONFRONTING MYTHS AND MYTHOLOGIES ▲

According to *Readers Digest*, "Costa Rica is almost too good to be true. Unlike many other Latin American republics, it has no appalling social problems, no military dictator. Instead, it is an oasis of democracy.... Costa Rica remains a nation of farmers who till their own fields and live in trim stucco houses along a network of first-class paved roads." In the midst of the maelstrom in Central America, the "Ticos," as they are affectionately known, live in the grace of a democratic society resting on a broad base of social reform legislation. Since its first truly democratic election in 1889, Costa Rica has regularly transferred power from one administration to another by the ballot, not the bullet, with the exception of two brief periods —1917 to 1919 and 1948 to 1949.

"We are proud of the fact that there are more schoolteachers in our country than soldiers, more schools than cannons, more books than guns, more libraries than guardhouses. This civility is not a recent product, but the work of generations and it is an intrinsic part of every Costa Rican."[2] Indeed, its highly literate population enjoys the most advanced system of education and health care in the region and has taken the remarkable step of abolishing its military. The human rights of its citizens are not habitually violated, executive power is checked by a strong legislature, and the legal system is well-developed and internationally respected. Costa Rica never developed powerful oligarchies with large, landed estates to the degree found in the northern tier of Central America. As a territory without great mineral wealth and no large population for the Spaniards to exploit, Costa

Rica was left out of the mainstream of Spanish colonial activity. Although coffee elites dominated the political institutions from the mid-nineteenth century to the 1948 revolution, the backbone of society was the "yeoman" farmer.

Relative to the other Central American countries, Costa Rica experienced little political violence in the twentieth century. In election after election the population freely chose its president, and the transfer of power from one administration to the next was made peacefully. The presidential election of February 1986 marked the ninth consecutive such transfer following the 1948 revolution. Thus Costa Rica has been seen as the exception in Central America, the "democratic oasis" in a desert of authoritarian and underdeveloped societies, the "Switzerland" of Central America.

While there is much truth in this image, there is another Costa Rica that must also be understood. Costa Rica harbors a highly skewed, inequitable distribution of land and income with enormous differences in opportunities and the quality of life among the population. Despite the openness of the political system and the high degree of participation in voting by the electorate, there has not been a "greater degree of participation of individuals from the middle and lower classes in the higher levels of the political system." Nor has there been much upward social mobility, especially from the lower classes.[3] The political institutions that have emerged during the past four decades are fragile and limited. Democratic resiliency in Costa Rica rests on a weak social and economic foundation endangered by intense economic and political international pressures. As President Monge pointed out in March 1984,

> ... unless we resolve the inequities and imbalances of the social crisis, unless we increase production, unless we increase exports, every advance that we have made in combatting our current period of adversity could fall apart, with catastrophic results for Costa Rica. . . . The most serious aspect of this is that we would be unable to preserve peace and our democratic institutional system.[4]

The present crisis in Central America is severely straining Costa Rica. Historical developments in Costa Rica have cast the direction of the society, but its ability to continue on its current trajectory as a social democratic society will be significantly affected by U.S. foreign policy and other developments in the Central American region.

THE 1948 CIVIL WAR AND ITS LEGACY   ▲

The election of Rafael Angel Calderón Guardia as president of Costa Rica in 1940 marks a turning point in Costa Rica's modern history. After receiving electoral support from the traditional coffee-growing elite, Calderón, inspired in part by the social doctrine expressed in the encyclical

"Rerum Novarum," embarked on a controversial, though popularly backed, course of social reform. The traditional elites opposed his expansion of social welfare and reform, including an advanced social security system, national health care, and a labor code. Many resented Calderón's confiscation of German properties in sugar, coffee, and banking, properties belonging to many friends of the oligarchy.[5]

Responding to growing internal opposition from traditional political forces, Calderón took several initiatives. He pursued a pro-Allies policy to garner support from U.S. President Franklin D. Roosevelt. He gained the support of the Catholic church, led by Archbishop Victor Manuel Sanabria y Martínez, and also to the Popular Vanguard (Costa Rica's Communist Party). Further, he drew important support from large segments of rural workers (especially in the banana plantations in the south that were controlled by United Fruit), the landless peasantry, and the emerging industrial workers. Particularly important among this group was the Vanguardia Popular, which was formed by the Communist Party (legal and active in electoral politics) when it dissolved in 1943 to expand its bases of support. Led by Manuel Mora, the Popular Vanguard had a strong base among the banana workers, and its defense of the social legislation passed by the Legislative Assembly with Calderón's backing became increasingly critical over time.

Calderón was succeeded by President Teodoro Picado in 1944, who continued to pursue similar reformist policies with Mora's backing. Though Mora was influential in these two administrations, both Calderón and Picado limited the power of the Popular Vanguard in their governments. In the meantime, Calderón's alliance—especially his support from Mora— was tolerated for several years by the United States, itself allied with Stalin's Russia during the war against the Axis powers. But U.S. support for Calderón's alliance would crumble as World War II drew to an end.

Within Costa Rica, two important opposition movements emerged. The more moderate conservatives under Otilio Ulate Blanco organized into the strongly anticommunist National Union Party (PUN). A Social Democratic party (that eventually became the National Liberation Party, PLN) was organized by a small, but influential group of middle-class professionals and intellectuals led by the economist and social democrat Rodrigo Facio, and a previously conservative politician, José "Pepe" Figueres Ferrer. "An aggressive and somewhat demogogic planter,"[6] Figueres was outspokenly critical of Calderón during World War II, thereby earning himself deportation to Mexico. For all their differences, both factions of the opposition seized on the Calderón-Picado alliance with the Popular Vanguard and increasingly played on Washington's growing preoccupation with communist influence in Latin America.

The crisis came in early 1948. In February, Otilio Ulate had been elected president with 54 percent of the vote after a hotly contested and sometimes violent campaign against Calderón. But Calderón's supporters contested the election and used their control over Congress to annul the elections and arrest Ulate and other opposition leaders. This became the precipitating incident for armed insurgency by the opposition. "Pepe" Figueres, supported by exiles from Nicaragua and Honduras, launched an attack to overthrow the government.

U.S. actions helped shape the outcome of the conflict. In Washington, Truman had set forth his Cold War approach to foreign affairs, and U.S. policy toward the region became defined by East-West considerations. The reliance of Picado and Calderón on the Popular Vanguard caused serious concern at the U.S. embassy in San José. Ambassador Nathaniel Davis made it clear to Picado that the United States would not help his government combat the mounting insurrection. Picado was repeatedly denied his requests for military assistance from the United States, which closed its eyes to the support Figueres was getting from Guatemalan President Juan José Arévalo and took efforts to block aid that the Somoza regime in Nicaragua (Somoza and Figueres were outspoken enemies) was offering.[7] The United States, with British assistance, stationed five ships off the Limon coast as a deterrent to the Picado government's ability to take military control of Costa Rica's southern zone.

In six weeks it was all over; two thousand lost their lives. Picado stepped down in favor of a junta led by Figueres.[8] The junta ruled for eighteen months, until mounting pressure at home and from Washington led Figueres, in November 1949, to turn power over to Ulate (who had his own claim to the presidency as a result of having won the 1948 election). The actions Figueres took during this period would have an enduring effect on Costa Rica.

Although an ally of the oligarchy against Picado and Calderón, Figueres had his own agenda when he marched into power. He had no intention of restoring the status quo ante; he moved swiftly to bring about a new economic and political order that would constrain the old landed oligarchy as well as diminish, if not eliminate, the popularly backed left.

Figueres purged the left from the government and state bureaucracy and, in 1949, outlawed the Popular Vanguard from participating in the political system—moves continued by Ulate, who suppressed all communist efforts to organize labor. These actions against the left, strongly urged by the United States, would have a number of lasting effects. They seriously weakened organized labor.[9] They encouraged the exclusion of popular urban and rural working-class groups from the political party system that developed over the next thirty-five years and, relatedly, encouraged an elite-style political leadership with little real popular participation. Finally, they seriously damaged future relations between moderate social democrats (the future party Figueres would organize) and Costa Rica's left. Had U.S. policy at that time encouraged a coming to terms between these two political forces, a future national consensus might have been more attainable.

Although Figueres moved against organized labor, the junta he led retained many of the legislative reforms initiated by Calderón and Mora (e.g., the labor code, collective bargaining reforms, and legislation on social security) and pushed forward on a few others, such as nationalizing the Costa Rican banks and raising taxes.[10] Other reforms that Figueres proposed to modernize Costa Rica's social and economic system were defeated by the Congress, which was under the control of the old guard. But perhaps Figueres's most important move was to eliminate in Costa Rica what elsewhere in Central America was the major impediment to democracy: the army.

Figueres was well-positioned to make this move. Having taken power by force, Figueres held the only military card during the interregnum between the Picado and Ulate administrations. He was distrustful of the oligarchy and understood the potential internal threat the military posed for a civilian democratic order. Also, Don "Pepe" did not wish to leave any government with the military capability to prevent his own eventual return to power via the electoral route. As a result, Figueres announced in December 1948, that the armed forces would be abolished, an action that was formalized in the 1949 constitution. With this action, Costa Rica became the only country in Latin America to rid itself of an institution that has so often been anathema to democracy and a cause of rampant political instability throughout the Western Hemisphere. Figueres's action changed the course of his country for the next thirty-five years. Neither he nor any subsequent leader in Costa Rica has taken any action that gained such broad popular support. Unfortunately, present trends threaten to undermine Figueres's most important legacy.

THE SOCIAL DEMOCRATIC MODEL OF REFORMIST ▲
CAPITALISM: 1953 TO 1982

Growth and Reform

Drawing on the small social democratic party and the growing number of middle-class professionals and intellectuals influenced by Rodrigo Facio, Figueres formed the National Liberation Party (PLN). Elected president in 1953, Figueres embarked on a transformation of Costa Rica's economy. The PLN's goal was to create a "society attentive to the well-being of all its members, under a capitalist economic system within a framework of state regulation and selective state involvement."[11] Figueres and subsequent PLN and opposition administrations have all followed one version or another of this social democratic model of reformist capitalism: state-sponsored, private-sector growth along with a substantial social welfare orientation. The growing power of the state and its social basis in an expanded middle class weakened the disproportionate political power the traditional coffee-growing elite had once exercised. Meanwhile the social welfare programs were particularly important in mitigating the costs to those lower classes who did not benefit from the overall strategy.

With the development model in place, and no corrupt and powerful military waiting in the wings, the basis was laid for over three decades of relative political stability: honest elections, in an atmosphere of tolerance and political freedom, took place every four years. The social democratic PLN maintained its dominance in Congress, but presidential office rotated between it and the somewhat more conservative National Union Party, which controlled the executive branch about half the time. From time to time there was turmoil (for example in his second term, 1970 to 1974, Figueres faced violence from impatient students and labor), but the generally healthy political process enjoyed great legitimacy and Costa Rican citizens proudly contrasted their democracy to the dictatorships to the north.[12]

Both parties recognized the overdependence of the economy on the export earnings of coffee and bananas and sought to diversify the economy by stimulating industrial development and modernizing agriculture, especially to spur the growth of exportable cash crops.

The state invested heavily in human and material infrastructure: its road network, electric generating capacity, and educational opportunities soon exceeded those in the rest of Central America.[13] Relying on an import substitution industrialization model and membership in the Central American Common Market (CACM), policies were designed to stimulate and protect the emergence of national industries. The state established incentives, including subsidies and favorable tariff regulations, and encouraged foreign investment.

Significantly, the state also vastly increased its own direct involvement in the economy through its government-controlled agencies and autonomous institutions: the state entered banking and finance, industry, trade, and agriculture. Twenty autonomous institutions were established in the decade of the fifties and an additional seventy-six in the period from 1960 to 1978.[14] As a consequence, the public sector grew dramatically; and a new powerful middle-class constituency, dependent on the public sector, arose. Employment in these institutions kept pace with their growth, rising from 3,000 in 1950 to about 36,000 in 1975.[15] Overall government employment increased fourfold in that same quarter century.[16] By the early 1980s, one out of every five employed Costa Ricans was working for the public sector.[17] Perhaps, more importantly, public-sector employment included 74 percent of all professionals and over 82 percent of all technicians.[18]

For many years the model appeared to be working economically. From 1960 to 1975, for example, inflation was low and the gross domestic product (GDP) was growing at a rate near 3 percent.[19] Industry increased its share of exports from 4 percent to 30 percent between 1960 and 1978;[20] direct foreign investment increased 3,500 percent from 1960 to 1970, 75 percent of which was from the United States;[21] and manufacturing became the largest productive sector in the economy.[22] And the work force in the industrial sector nearly tripled.[23]

There were also important social gains. Great strides were made in public health care (hospitals dominate San José's urban setting). Infant mortality dropped drastically (69 percent from 1970 to 1980); malnutrition of children under five was reduced (the only Central American country in which that occurred in the mid-1960s to mid-1970s); and life expectancy is now in the seventies. Education has been a high priority for all post-1948 governments. A symbol of its significance was Figueres's decision to convert the building housing the Ministry of Defense into the Ministry of Education. By the mid-1960s, 95 percent of all eligible children actually entered the first grade and better than one in six of those who had entered primary school stayed to complete high school.[24]

Beneath the Surface: The Structural Problems

On the surface Costa Rica's future appeared steady and positive. But in 1981, Costa Rica was struck by an economic crisis. The immediate causes were ones that plagued nearly all of its Latin American neighbors: Costa Rica had financed much of its growth by borrowing abroad, but it lost its ability to pay back when prices for its major export, coffee, plummeted at the same time that OPEC oil price increases forced up its import bill. However, there were much deeper structural problems in the economy and these were compounded increasingly by troubling social problems created by the social democratic model of reformist capitalism.

One structural economic problem was the economy's continued dependence on the export of its two traditional crops, bananas and coffee, as the major source for foreign exchange. Despite successful efforts at agricultural diversification, these crops still constituted 55 percent of all merchandise exports between 1981 and 1983.[25] This left the whole economy particularly vulnerable even to slight fluctuations in the prices of bananas and coffee. Although the rise in coffee prices in 1976 and 1977 had helped offset the oil price hikes of 1973 and 1974, the sharp drop after 1978 left Costa Rica even more vunerable to the oil price increases in 1979 and 1980.[26]

Yet another structural problem was created by the import substitution industrialization model. While it succeeded in spurring light industrialization and eliminated the import of some goods now produced in the country, it had the effect of increasing demand for new imports. Some of these were consumer and luxury goods demanded by the new urban middle class, but more serious was the growth of imports needed as inputs for industrial production. By 1975, 40 percent of all raw materials and intermediate goods used by industry were imported, up from 27 percent in 1963, increasing, rather than reducing, Costa Rica's import bills.[27] By 1981, these imports accounted for 60 percent of all imports.[28] This situation was compounded further as Costa Rica had to rely more and more on financing these imports by agricultural exports, yet government policies favoring industry over agriculture were hurting agricultural production. In addition, from

1973 to 1980, food production stagnated and a rising proportion of scarce foreign exchange had to be used on agricultural imports.[29]

A third structural problem was the

> mushrooming of autonomous institutions . . . traditionally, financially, and administratively independent of the Central Government, and [characterized] by the absence of adequate information and administrative machinery for monitoring public expenditures.[30]

These institutions "beyond the control of the central bank . . . could dip into the public treasury. Public firms in oil, electricity, and water began to generate large losses that the central government had to cover."[31]

While spending by these autonomous institutions was insufficiently controlled, the actual revenues available were limited by a fourth serious problem: the existing tax system was inadequate to provide needed revenues. About half of the taxes were already

> earmarked for specific outlays. Legally mandated and incompressible expenses . . . reached such proportions that the Central Government . . . had to borrow to pay wages and salaries.[32]

Reform had been strongly and successfully resisted by the privileged economic and political elites as well as by many in the middle class who did not want to sacrifice the standard of living to which they had become accustomed. The lack of tax revenue and growing government expenses led to rising public-sector deficits to cover the increasing wage bills of state employees and the losses of public-sector enterprises. Policymakers turned to internal and external borrowing.[33]

These structural problems set the context for the immediate short-term crisis that hit full force in 1981. The trade deficit rose from $97 million in 1977 to $185 million in 1978 to $315 million in 1979 and peaked at $366 million in 1980—reaching over a quarter of all exports.[34] Costa Rica borrowed more and more, and in doing so was forced to rely heavily on private sources, which meant higher interest rates and shorter payback periods, thus accelerating the crush of the debt burden. The combination of continued borrowing, the drop in coffee prices, the big jump in the price of oil, a contraction of export markets, and the internal conditions discussed above led to an astronomical increase in the debt.[35] Gold reserves were depleted and international commercial banks refused to lend any more money. Costa Rica could no longer meet its financial obligations, and in August 1981, having failed to fulfill the International Monetary Fund (IMF) agreements of March 1980 and June 1981, the government of President Rodrigo Carazo (1978 to 1982) suspended its payments.

The external financial crisis wreaked havoc on the economy. During 1981 and 1982, inflation soared fivefold before being brought down in 1983. "Investment went down to zero."[36] The national currency was devalued officially by almost 500 percent from 1980 to 1983 and unofficial speculation was considerably higher. Costa Rica's internal productive capacity virtually collapsed. From a growth rate of 6.3 percent in 1978, GDP dropped to 0.6 percent in 1980 [37] and then fell even further in 1981 and 1982 (4.6 percent and 6.1 percent).[38] While the agricultural sector had held its own, manufacturing declined, as did most other sectors of the economy. Construction, a labor-intensive sector, "declined by 40 percent [in 1982] following a fall of 11.6 percent in 1981. Likewise, commercial activity fell by 17.8 percent following a decrease of 18.5 percent in 1981."[39] Unemployment more than doubled to almost 10 percent.

By the time the economic crisis hit, the deepening structural problems in the economy were compounded by growing social structural problems: the rapid growth of the last decades had worsened conditions for many Costa Ricans and their needs put an increasing strain on Costa Rica's social democracy.

In the countryside, the expansion of agribusiness focused on export agriculture had brought nearly 41 percent of cultivated land into planting for export crops—and these exports constituted over 80 percent of agriculture's income.[40] But this expansion came at a cost. The acquisition of land by agribusiness, whether for crop production or for grazing, had two major effects on the sector. First, it reduced the number of landowners; and second, it reduced the size of the work force as labor was replaced by capital, thus contributing to unemployment.

By 1973, the subsistence sector had virtually disappeared. The introduction of modern farming techniques pushed out the marginal yeoman freehold farmers of which Costa Rica was justifiably proud. Unable to compete economically with the larger plantations, unable to afford expensive grain, fertilizers, or farm machinery, they were forced to sell out to the larger landowners seeking to expand. Also, the campesino laborers were no longer so important or needed in rural areas as labor on the plantations became more mechanized.[41]

Commenting on this issue in 1982, ex-Labor Minister Rafael Angel Rojas stated:

Today we have in proportional terms less property owners and more proletariat than in 1950. . . . The small agricultural proprietors are disappearing as such, to emigrate to the population centers and are enlarging the urban proletariat.[42]

Between two-thirds and three-fourths of all those who are economically active in agriculture are landless.[43] Forced to abandon their traditional life in the country, the rural poor moved in increasing numbers to the country's urban centers, primarily San José. The vast majority of these people had only limited education and vocational skills; in most instances they added to the growing numbers of urban unemployed or underemployed.

Although the government did promote agrarian reform and some land redistribution, the consequences of the development model in agriculture was to create a greater, not a lesser, inequity in the distribution of land. According to a study published by U.S. AID in 1979, the GINI index measuring farmland ownership actually rose slightly from 1950 to 1973.[44] Less than 1 percent of farm owners owned over 41 percent of the land; while 68 percent of the farmers owned only 3.2 percent of the land.[45] More telling still is the fact that 75 percent of all Costa Rica's poor (30 percent of the total population are classified as poor) live in the rural areas and about two-thirds of them are landless.[46]

The social problems created in agriculture were compounded by problems in the industrial sector. Costa Rica's growth in nonagricultural exports, especially to CACM, was impressive, but the import substitution strategy created problems. Many Costa Rican businessmen were concerned because the emphasis on large-scale and capital-intensive development led to the "heavy displacement of local producers by foreign investors and considerable concentration of industry accompanied by a tendency towards inappropriate capital-intensity."[47] While the foreign investors brought needed capital, attracting the foreign investment required the state to offer incentives that cost it needed revenues.[48] And some Costa Ricans feared it was creating an incentive to keep wage scales low—which would hurt labor—in order to attract the corporations. But the most serious problems involved the failure of the new industrialization—domestic and foreign—to generate much-needed jobs to absorb the growing population and displaced people from the countryside.

In industry, as in agriculture, emphasis on capital-intensive development meant that even with expanding production the absorbtion of entrants into the labor force was weak. Despite the strides in growth from 1960 to 1975, the economy was unable to keep pace with the demand for jobs, which grew at a rate of 4 percent per year. The economic model was beginning to wind down. In fact, jobs absorbed the new entrants at a rate of only 2.7 percent, meaning that each year an additional 1.3 percent were added to the ranks of the unemployed. The 1981 crisis accelerated the problem. Whereas the economy had generated 39,400 new jobs in 1977, it was only able to provide 3,900 in 1981. For the public sector, the figures were 14,000 new jobs in 1978, but only 100 in 1981.[49]

The social structural problems created by Costa Rica's growth strategy were summed up in 1973 by Oscar Arias Sanchez, a leading politican who was to become the PLN's 1986 presidential standard-bearer:

> We have learned that a modern economy, growing urbanization and industrialization, and increased education and health benefits do not reduce socioeconomic inequality. On the contrary, the inequality today is more marked than it was twenty-five years ago.[50]

Income distribution had not improved since 1961.[51] While the top 5 percent garnered 25 percent of the income, the bottom 20 percent received less than 5 percent,[52] a figure that had deteriorated somewhat since 1961.[53] Strategies designed to help the poor had actually benefited those in the middle groups.[54] The widespread emiseration was reflected upon by ex-Minister of Labor Rafael Angel Rojas, as he pointed out that, in 1970, two-thirds of the heads of families were able to meet the minimal cost-of-living standard, but by 1982, only about one-third of them could do so.[55] The disparities between urban and rural dwellers was also great. In a 1973 survey, peasant incomes were found to equal only 15 percent of urban ones, and peasants, on average, had only about one-fourth as many years of education.[56] The education system was seen by many as slipping due to the difficulty the government was having in generating sufficient funds to support it. Of those who had entered the first grade, only about 8 percent were completing high school, down considerably from 17 percent nineteen years earlier.[57]

By the time the financial crisis came to a head in 1981, Costa Rica's genuine accomplishments could no longer obfuscate the negative consequences of three decades of the development model that had moved Costa Rica closer to being a dualistic society—those who benefited and those who did not. The primary beneficiaries were the new urban upper and upper middle class—managers of domestic and foreign firms, skilled and highly educated bureaucrats in positions created by the expanding state bureaucracy and autonomous or semi-autonomous government enterprises and agencies.[58] Meanwhile, those who lost—the peasants, marginal farmers, and urban poor—took less. This growing contrast threatened to strain Costa Rica's democratic order.

The PLN, with its long commitment to social democracy, was restricted in its ability and will to deal with these problems: much of its base was in exactly this new privileged urban class, who had a stake in maintaining the size and organization of the state bureaucracy—with its inefficiencies and lack of central control—and was unwilling to sacrifice the comfortable standard of living the development model had created for it.

Indeed the development model of social democratic reformist-capitalism that had been supported by both parties created a politico-economic bind for whichever party took office. There seemed to be two basic policy responses to deal with the problem. One was to initiate a series of structural reforms that would give a larger segment of the population the incentive and material capacity to participate directly in the system. The other was to continue to provide social welfare benefits for what was becoming a larger and larger segment of the society.

Each of these responses would be difficult for any government. In the case of the former, the reforms required political support from precisely those social classes who benefited from the present model and saw the reforms as threatening their continued enjoyment of those benefits. Given their key institutional positions, they could make significant structural reforms difficult. In the case of the latter, the state would be forced to come up with greater amounts of revenue to support the increasing flow of benefits required to meet the needs of increasing numbers of benefit recipients. Because this path was politically easier in the short term, it was the one followed. When the economic crisis hit in the early 1980s, President Rodrigo Carazo, from the National Unity Party, could not lower wages and government spending fast enough to balance Costa Rica's accounts. The administrative and tax measures he did propose "were delayed in a parliament afraid to alienate their constituents, who were not psychologically prepared for deep cuts in living standards."[59] Yet the economy was not generating sufficient funds to make such a largesse, from which the state could dole out benefits, possible.

When Luis Alberto Monge of the PLN took his oath of office on May 8, 1982, he had to face deep structural problems in the economy that had created serious social structural problems as well—and do so in the context of an economic crisis that needed immediate resolution.

COSTA RICA AND THE U.S. GEOPOLITICAL STRATEGY ▲

Monge and the Economic Crisis

Monge moved quickly to alleviate the economic crisis he inherited. He knew that he would need help from the United States and international financial agencies. Assistance from the IMF was crucial in meeting Costa Rica's immediate trade and deficit problems. But IMF policy required Costa Rica agree to a stabilization program that was very difficult politically. The IMF demanded that Costa Rica

> reduce sharply its external and internal deficits by increasing taxes, cutting some public sector expenditures, raising the prices charged by autonomous agencies, reducing real wages and regaining some control over credit creation. The external accounts [were to be] improved by maintaining the real colon near its devalued rate of about fifty to the dollar and by limiting the magnitude of external borrowing from commercial lenders.[60]

The inability of the previous Carazo government to implement such severe austerity measures in a preelectoral period had led to two breakdowns in arrangements with the IMF. But Monge reopened talks and proceeded with the austerity program, pointing out to the country: "To deal with the IMF is bad, but not to deal with it is catastrophic."[61] The result was that agreement was reached and the resources were disbursed in 1983.

The austerity program Monge adopted did impose difficult measures on Costa Rica. Taxes were increased, public utility rates were increased, and the colon was devalued. In an effort to get agriculture going, a greater portion of total credit was shifted to that sector, squeezing imports. Real wages had dropped; although by 1983 salaries had increased by 30 percent in real terms, recovering part of what had been lost previously.[62] In early

1984 additional measures were adopted in the Economic Emergency Law the Legislative Assembly was forced to pass to satisfy IMF conditions. These included: a 20 percent across-the-board budget cut, a public-sector employment cut, and a 25 percent price hike in gasoline.[63]

External assistance from the IMF and the United States helped Monge weather the short-term economic crisis. Initially preoccupied with the hot spots of Central America, the Reagan administration did not pay much attention to Costa Rica. An apparent stable democracy, Costa Rica seemed to be largely unaffected by what the United States saw as the playing out of the Cold War in El Salvador and Nicaragua. As the administration began to turn to Costa Rica as a bastion of democracy in the region and a desirable ally in its fight against the spreading cancerous sores of Communism, it had still hesitated to come forward with much in the way of economic assistance until Costa Rica had satisfied the conditions of the IMF.

U.S. aid began to flow, slowly at first, and then more rapidly by the end of Reagan's first term—from a total of only $15.8 million in FY1981 to $53.8 million in FY1982 to a high of $220.2 million in FY1984. The character of the aid changed dramatically. Economic Support Funds (ESF) went from zero in FY1981 to 37.2 percent of the package in FY1982 to about 72 percent in the next three years, with a request for FY1986 in which ESF constituted over 77 percent of the aid. Equally important for Costa Rica, the proportion of grants increased and that of loans decreased: 25 percent of the ESF was in grants in 1982 and 1983, rising to almost 75 percent in 1984 and hitting 100 percent for 1985 and 1986.[64] Referring to the impact of U.S. aid, President Monge, during an interview in May 1985, said, "This aid has been significant and decisive."[65]

The economic decline bottomed out and there were some signs of recovery. Inflation dropped from 90 percent in 1982 to 33 percent in 1983 and to about 15 percent in 1984.[66] Economic growth improved, reaching around 6.5 percent in 1984, clearly outpacing the population growth rate of 2.5 percent, but leaving the economy far below what it had been a few years earlier. The exchange rate was more stabilized, and unemployment figures improved.[67]

Despite the progress achieved thus far (November 1985) by the Monge administration, especially in stabilizing the debt payment process, Costa Rica faces a total debt of a bit greater magnitude than it did when he first took office. According to Ennio Rodríguez Cespedes, minister counselor for foreign debt, Costa Rica's public debt stood at $3.45 billion in July 1985. With an additional $750 million owed by the private sector, the total debt amounted to $4.2 billion. Given that the debt service alone for 1985 was estimated to reach $380 million and that Costa Rica will earn no more than $1 billion from its exports, it is not surprizing that Eduardo Lizano, chairman of the Central Bank, pointed out that interest payments were choking off the refueling of the economy. They are "excessively heavy" and tend to consume almost all of the loans and grants the country receives.

The Monge administration thus still faced serious internal problems. The external aid and austerity programs were, at best, stopgap measures. Not only did they leave Costa Rica still facing an enormous debt, but they also left Costa Rica facing essentially the same long-term structural problems— social and economic—that Monge had inherited. And the pressure to use the gains of growth to repay the debt severely limited the possibilities of tackling these important long-term problems. As Lizano explained, Costa Rica is hindered from "liberating important amounts of foreign aid to devote them to increased export production" and for addressing underlying structural problems in the economy. Unless the more serious underlying problems are given attention, he suggested that the current stability "will be short-lived." The issue is sufficiently serious to warrant the suggestion that Costa Rica's "sources of foreign financing keep contributing capital . . . [but] at the same time accept the cancellation of half of what we must now honor." This would allow the government some $150 to $200 million dollars "every year to devote to development programs."[68]

While U.S. economic assistance did little to help resolve the long-term social and economic problems, it was crucial in helping Costa Rica ride out its immediate crisis. But U.S. assistance came at a price. A number of public and private officials, as well as the press, resented measures or comments they felt were undue direct interference by the United States in its internal affairs. For example, AID had insisted that certain of its loans go directly to the private sector, bypassing the Costa Rican Central Bank (this reflected the new emphasis in AID under the Reagan administration to favor strongly the private sector). Such channeling of funds, however, was not possible under existing laws, and the Costa Rican Congress was told that it had either to change the legislation or the money would not be disbursed.

By mid-1984, the changes were still held up in the U.S. Congress; AID responded by freezing $58 million until the laws were changed. The result was a cash-flow crisis. President Monge, visiting Rome at that time, was forced to put in a personal call to President Reagan to get the badly needed aid flowing again.[69] National Assembly member Julio Jurado saw the action as "a direct attack on our sovereignty. . . . The United States wants to change laws in effect for 30 years through force, through pressure, through intimidation, by suspending our credit."[70] The Costa Rican legislature did adopt the change in August 1984 and the "crisis" was resolved, but it left a residue. One cabinet member criticized that the U.S. "prescription for our economic crisis is a conflict between development and underdevelopment."[71]

Costa Rican officials have also rankled at many of the statements made by the U.S. ambassador, Curtin Winsor. For example, in commenting on Costa Rica's efforts to come forth with its own development program, he said that "*due to their democratic and therefore inefficient* government, they have been unable to put together that program" (emphasis added).[72] Or, in discussing Costa Rica's reforms to stimulate exports, he remarked, "In the case of the customs service and the ports, as well as the banking system, everything there is now scandalous." In an unusual public response, the directorate of the ruling National Liberation Party accused Ambassador Winsor of "unheard of" interference in domestic affairs. They went on to say,

> it is not right that we should receive indications from outside on how to manage our economy, no matter how respectable the position of the foreign ambassador who does it.[73]

An editorial in *El Debate*, a newspaper whose private ownership includes members of the PLN, criticized Winsor's statements as "absolutely unacceptable to Costa Rica as a sovereign nation" and added that "the declarations of [this] . . . representative of a foreign nation look like orders from a Roman proconsul saying how the province he is in charge of should be governed."[74]

The sense that U.S. interference is a problem is not limited to officials or particular elites. In a public opinion poll in which respondents were asked to name a country that interferes too much in Costa Rica's internal affairs, "some 43 percent of those with a high school education named the United States."[75] In what has often been called the "most pro–North American country in Latin America," there has been an "uncharacteristic irritation about U.S. meddling in their financial and political affairs." As acting Foreign Minister Jorge Urbina had put it, "The United States has been touching some very sensitive nerves."[76]

The Impact of Regional Turmoil and U.S. Policy

In fact, the feelings regarding U.S. interference were only a small piece of a larger problem. Costa Rica could not avoid being caught up in the deepening regional crisis; nor could it avoid being defined as a part of a regional strategy by policymakers in Washington. Costa Rica's ability to cope with its own internal economic and social problems—indeed its very ability to maintain its social democracy—was adversely affected by the growing regional turmoil, a turmoil contributed to by the policies of the Reagan administration. Such heavy dependence on the United States for economic assistance gave government officials great pause in opposing U.S. regional foreign policy. Former President "Pepe" Figueres made clear Costa Rica's vulnerability and its sense of being squeezed by the regional crisis. "Costa Rica . . . badly needs U.S. economic help, and this weakens our position."[77] "We're like the meat in the sandwich caught between the U.S. and Nicaragua."[78]

At the same time that the United States and international financial agencies were pushing Costa Rica to expand its exports, turmoil in the region was restricting Costa Rica's market access with its trading partners in the Central American Common Market. (See Chapter 8.) The economic problems in Nicaragua, the largest of its regional trading partners, had had a dual effect: Costa Rica lost an important source of raw material inputs, which it imported for its own industry, and it lost a major source for the sale of its exports. One such item, the sale of electricity, had dropped from $1 million a month in 1984 to only $350,000 a month by mid-1985.[79]

Costa Rica's problem, in part, was that the other countries were not able to pay their bills. Obviously, given Costa Rica's precarious financial situation and the size of its external debt, it could not afford to continue the free, or extended-payment, ride. By mid-1985, Costa Rica was owed over $300 million by its regional trading partners.[80] The lack of foreign exchange in these nations to pay their debts to Costa Rica led the president of Costa Rica's Central Bank to consider refusing "to authorize more exports . . . until Costa Rica had imported from them enough to even out that particular bilateral trade balance," a measure that, if followed through, he admitted would cause exporters to lose even more sales.[81]

Ironically, U.S. pressure for Costa Rica to join it in the economic embargo against Nicaragua would, from the Costa Rican perspective, have the effect of even greater damage on the Costa Rican economy. President Monge believed it

> would provoke a collapse within the CACM: that would be the equivalent to liquidating the organization. Costa Rica would not be able to compensate its losses through other means. Twenty percent of our exports are still being sent to Central America. We do not see how we could recover from that loss in the short term.[82]

Given Costa Rica's position in the overall geopolitical strategy of the United States (Costa Rica is to be a bastion of democracy to provide support internationally to legitimize U.S. actions in the region; a base out of which contra exiles could operate against Nicaragua; and a country with a military-type force sufficient to put further pressure on the Sandinistas), the Reagan administration often expected Costa Rican support for policies that San José saw as detrimental to its own interests in easing domestic and regional tensions. Further, the particular policies aimed at undermining or overthrowing the Sandinista regime in Nicaragua—the economic squeeze, and the organization of the exile contra army—created or intensified internal problems inside Costa Rica. Given Costa Rica's "indebtedness" to the United States, it was often difficult, but not always impossible, for Costa Rica to take an independent stand.

The Costa Ricans well understood how they were enmeshed in this dynamic. President Monge expressed it as follows:

> I am deeply concerned about the Central American problem. We are not part of the crisis in the isthmus, but it is part of our problem and we cannot ignore it, just as we cannot isolate ourselves, because the negative reflections are also felt here. It is a terrible truth: We cannot leave here. We have a 320-km

border with Nicaragua and, without trying to offend anyone, we would prefer having the Swiss or Austrians as neighbors, but that is impossible.[83]

In a further reference to the impact of the U.S. embargo on Nicaragua he pointed out, "The economic embargo . . . threatens to increase even more the immigration bomb within our country, and we are already at the limit of our capacity to take care of these refugees."[84]

While the number of refugees from Nicaragua by early 1985—8,100 registered refugees and about the same number unregistered[85]—was nowhere near the over 100,000 who had fled into Costa Rica during the insurgency against Somoza, the Costa Ricans were understandably concerned about what they feared would be a massive flow, as economic deterioration grows in Nicaragua.[86] Costa Rica could ill afford the additional economic burden, given its already strained social welfare system and the stringency of its austerity program. Furthermore, officials worried that refugee camps would become anti-Sandinista centers with close links to the contra exiles operating in the border areas, thus increasing border tensions with Nicaragua.[87]

To the extent that U.S. policy in the region exacerbated, rather than helped resolve, the domestic and regional conflicts in Central America (as the other country studies in this book demonstrate), such a policy had indirect consequences on Costa Rica that were quite negative—in spite of Washington's stated goal of strengthening democracy and economic development in Costa Rica.

But far more serious for Costa Rica than U.S. economic strategy were the problems created by U.S. encouragement of the contra exile forces, some of which operated out of Costa Rica against Nicaragua's southern borders. Three problems merit special attention: the tensions created between Nicaragua and Costa Rica; the difficulties Costa Rica faced in sustaining its policy of neutrality; and the internal conflict generated within Costa Rica that threatens to tear at the delicate social democratic fabric of the society, particularly in regard to the issue of militarization.

NICARAGUA AND COSTA RICA: BORDER CLASHES AND TENSE RELATIONS. The current tensions between Nicaragua and Costa Rica take place in the context of a long history of conflict. That history includes the seizure of territory, disputes over boundaries, and, particularly in the past forty years, a number of efforts by some from one of the countries to topple the government in the other one. For example, Somoza had sent five hundred troops in 1948 to support Calderón against Figueres's ultimately successful insurgency, and he then supported another attempt against Figueres in 1949. In late 1953 Costa Rica participated in a plot against Somoza; in January 1955 Nicaraguan planes bombed utilities in Costa Rica; in 1960 Figueres supported efforts of Nicaraguan exiles to get arms in Costa Rica; and the Sandinistas themselves found safe haven and support in Costa Rica in the late 1970s as they successfully struggled to overthrow the Somoza regime.

The historical conflicts between Nicaragua and Costa Rica are so commonplace that a local refrain proclaims that there are three seasons in Costa Rica: the rainy season, the dry season, and the season of fighting with the Nicaraguans. That history is also overlaid with a strong sense of nationalist superiority tinged with racism. " 'We consider ourselves somewhat cultured here,' said an engineering student who reflected widely held opinion. 'The Nicaraguans are thick-headed Indians.' "[88] Yet a further complication in the relationship is the presence of a strong anticommunist sentiment in Costa Rica, which gained strength following the Figueres overthrow of Calderón and the outlawing of the Vanguardia Popular in 1948. While there was much sympathy for the Sandinistas in their struggle to overthrow the Somoza dictatorship, the failure of the Sandinistas to institute a constitutional democracy and its clear leftist orientation have ignited strong anti-Sandinista feelings among much of the population.

Thus it is not surprising that a number of Costa Ricans have been willing to support the anti-Sandinista exiles—particularly those groups led by Edén Pastora and Fernando Chamorro—who sought to use Costa Rican territory as a base of operations against Managua after 1981, in spite of official government opposition to such activities. Between 1981 and 1983 these two leaders were estimated to have trained about one thousand and three to four hundred exiles, respectively, in camps along the border.[89] While the Costa Rican government (unlike the Honduran government) did not actively support such activities, Costa Rica's small and poorly equipped rural guard and civil guard (a total of less than ten thousand men) could not adequately patrol the 220 miles of often sparsely populated border, much of which passes through jungle along the San Juan River.

The operations of the contras out of Costa Rica, or from camps within a few hundred yards of the Costa Rican border, inevitably created incidents along the border area. Nicaragua accused Costa Rica of harboring and supporting contras, and as Nicaraguan troops skirmished with the contra bands near and on the border, Costa Rica accused Nicaragua of violating its borders—firing across the border, shelling Costa Rican territory, and shooting at Costa Rican guardsman on the border.[90] By May 1985 the Costa Ricans had issued sixty-eight notes to Nicaragua regarding acts of aggression by Nicaragua against Costa Rican sovereignty, and thirty-six such notes had been issued to Costa Rica by the Nicaraguans.[91] The situation included movielike intrigue as a number of apparent incursions by Sandinistas, or apparent attacks by Sandinistas on Costa Rican civil or rural guardsmen, turned out to be contra exiles attempting to pose or pass as Sandinistas.[92]

Perhaps, the most serious incident occured in mid-1985 at Las Crucitas, when the Costa Ricans accused a Sandinista army patrol of attacking and killing two Costa Rican civil guardsmen. A subsequent investigation by an OAS commission did find that the shots had been fired from the Nicaraguan side of the border, though they were unable to say who had actually fired the shots. Although few of the border incidents would have been likely to have occurred had the contras not been operating from or near Costa Rican territory, each incident added to the fury—fueling tensions between the two countries and increasing the growing sentiment in Costa Rica that the Sandinistas are bellicose, expansionist, and dangerous communists.

Tensions were heightened even further by a series of about ten terrorist incidents in 1982 and 1983—few by Central American standards but highly unusual and thus very disturbing in Costa Rica. While the Sandinistas were not implicated in most of these incidents (which involved Costa Rican middle-class youths or exiles from elsewhere carrying on their struggles within Costa Rica), in cases where there was evidence of links to Sandinistas, it clearly upset the Costa Ricans.[93] And the very fact that any such action could occur in Costa Rica increased speculation that, in the future, the Sandinistas might be involved in such acts and might have an interest in destabilizing Costa Rica.[94]

Not surprisingly, the border tensions between Nicaragua and Costa Rica often resulted in strong public rhetoric on both sides. Nicaraguan accusations of Costa Rican involvement with the contras, of U.S. use of Costa Rica as a political reserve center to attack Nicaragua and as a training ground for CIA-backed exiles, and other such attacks were perceived as a disinformation campaign by the Costa Ricans and contributed to a national mood that made conflict difficult to resolve.

NEUTRALITY. The new border conflicts and increased tensions with Nicaragua have created serious difficulties for Costa Rica. To control contra activity within its borders effectively, or to seal its borders more tightly against Sandinista incursions, would have demanded expanding the rural and civil guards in ways that risked exactly the kind of militarization Costa Rican democrats sought to avoid. And as there were some Costa Ricans, particularly along the border, who aided and helped harbor the contras, military solutions raised the spectre of a kind of military conflict among Costa Rica's own citizenry that would endanger internal peace even more. To support the overall policy goals of the Reagan administration in the region would have meant active support for the destabilization and overthrow of Nicaragua, support for policies that were militarizing Honduras and undermining its fragile democracy, and support for a military solution in El Salvador. These actions would not only be antithetical to Costa Rica's traditional values and foreign policy, but would embroil it as a militant actor in Central American conflicts and would create yet further pressures for militarization. Yet on the other hand, openly opposing the United States, upon which it depended for economic assistance, was difficult. It was within these constraints that Costa Rica attempted to articulate a policy of neutrality that would help insulate it somewhat from the regional turmoil, from militarization, and would not alienate the United States.

Costa Rica has been able to exert some independence from the United States. Even before the policy of neutrality was announced, for example, Costa Rica had refused to give the kind of support to the contras that

Honduras had been providing and did take some limited steps to control
their activities. At times the government has temporarily deported some of
the contra leaders.[95] In mid-1983 Costa Rica supported the establishment
of a Contadora observation force on its borders and since that time has
participated in a number of bilateral and multilateral efforts to reduce
border tensions through observation teams and direct discussions with
Managua. In other moves the Monge government publicly criticized the
presence of U.S. ships off the Nicaraguan coast; supported a UN resolution
against the U.S. invasion of Grenada; turned down U.S. invitations to
participate in war games and to train guardsmen in Honduras; denied
permission for U.S. navy maneuvers off the Costa Rican coast near Nicaragua, and rejected an invitation to send observers to the Central American
Defense Council (CONDECA).[96]

Monge had presided over a somewhat divided cabinet on the neutrality
issue. He had to contend as well with resistance from some strong voices
within the PLN leadership to the formal adoption of a neutrality position.
The policy emerged only after a difficult internal debate. Foreign Minister
Volio, leader of the anti-neutrality forces, had strongly favored bringing
Costa Rica's policy into direct synchronization with that of the United
States. He supported CONDECA, did not trust the Contadora process, and
opposed the policy of neutrality. Other members of the cabinet disagreed
sharply with Volio's direction. They managed to isolate him and eventually
were able to institute neutrality as official policy. The combination of a
disagreement with President Monge over a vote in the UN—he did not want
to condemn the U.S. invasion of Grenada—and the Monge decision to go
ahead with the neutrality policy led Volio to resign in November.[97]

Though politically opposed to what in his judgment the Sandinistas stand
for, Monge held Costa Rica to neutral ground in the fight between pro- and
anti-Sandinistas. On November 17, 1983, Monge formally proclaimed the
unarmed, perpetual, active neutrality of Costa Rica. While the United
States refrained from public attacks on the policy, the embassy made clear
its dissatisfaction and appeared to be trying to discredit it. A source in
Monge's party, the PLN, spoke of cabinet discussions about reports that
Ambassador Winsor, in private conversations with fellow diplomats, had
dismissed the neutrality declaration in November 1983 as "bull——," a
charge the embassy later denied.[98] A few months later U.S. diplomats had
warned that a demonstration that drew over twenty thousand people in
support of the neutrality policy was being controlled by the communists.
This warning was given despite the fact that Monge's party, the PLN, had
called on all Costa Ricans to participate "in this important national civic
act"; public offices and schools were closed so that people could take part;
top government officials endorsed it; Costa Rica's archbishop endorsed it;
"two ex-Presidents, four members of Parliament and the rector of the
university spoke at the rally"; and it was backed by representatives from
the major political parties.[99]

The declaration of the policy of neutrality did, in fact, provide an even stronger public framework, which gave Costa Rica some leverage in its relations with the United States. This was especially important in regard to Costa Rica's policy toward Nicaragua. Costa Rica had been able to resist being recruited as an outright adversary against Nicaragua. Monge, though critical of the Sandinistas and staunchly anticommunist, had deliberately and successfully avoided being part of a military effort to bring down the Nicaraguan government. When the U.S. mined Nicaraguan harbors in early 1984, Costa Rica allowed goods to be unloaded at its ports and shipped overland to Nicaragua. Despite great U.S. pressure, the Monge government criticized the nonlethal military aid that Reagan pressured Congress to ship to the contras in mid-1985 and he also criticized the trade embargo.

Two years after the neutrality policy had been initiated, President Monge succinctly summarized the country's intentions with respect to Nicaragua:

1. Although Costa Rica does not agree with that country's Marxist-Leninist regime, it respects it and demands reciprocity from Nicaragua.

2. Costa Rica will maintain its neutrality in Nicaragua's domestic conflict.

3. Costa Rica cordially urges Nicaragua to strive to maintain total control over its territory, which is currently not the case.

4. Costa Rica will not allow its territory to be used to attack Nicaragua.

5. Costa Rica will appeal to the OAS if Nicaragua attacks it and the Costa Rican people will defend themselves.[100]

Within Costa Rica, Monge's policy of neutrality enjoyed strong support— 79 percent from the population.[101] Yet the policy has continuously been undermined by Costa Rica's inability to deal with the tensions created at its borders. Almost independently of where any fault may lie, each border incident tends to inflame Costa Rican public opinion and gives encouragement to those, like Volio, who would support an explicitly anti-Nicaraguan policy. Rafael Angel Calderón Fournier, the Social Christian Unity Party's candidate for the 1986 presidential elections, and major opposition to the PLN's Oscar Arias Sanchez, campaigned on the need for a tougher policy, one that would abolish "neutrality." Such a tougher policy would also create pressures for increased militarization, a route publicly advocated only by right-wing groups. The latest U.S. efforts, in 1984 and 1985, to get exiles in Costa Rica to link up with those in Honduras, who have received strong CIA backing, simply complicated matters further. It not only pulled Costa Rica more into the regional fray but also made it clear that U.S. and Costa Rican interests were, at times, antithetical. Monge, himself, had previously nixed a CIA scheme proposed to him in the interim between his election and taking office in the spring of 1982. The United States had wanted him to approve the setting up of secret camps to train Nicaraguan exiles, arguing that it would be a short-term action as the contras in Costa Rica, along with the ones in Honduras, would be successful in six months. As Robert Tomasek reports, Monge "refused adamantly, realizing that this foolish request not only would be a domestic bombshell if publicized but also could worsen relations with Nicaragua to an extremely risky level."[102]

Costa Rica is in a bind. While it can oppose the United States on its contra policy, it does not have the capability to contain contra activities on its borders without U.S. support. A change in U.S. policy could virtually eliminate such pressures, not simply by no longer providing support for contra activity against Nicaragua but by actively discouraging it. Thus far, this has not been in the cards. Rather, as an adviser to President Monge stated in May 1984, the pressures on Monge to abandon his policy of neutrality had been "increased tenfold" in the past two months. "What Reagan needs is the moral support for an invasion of Nicaragua."[103]

MILITARIZATION. The exile activity on Costa Rican borders and tense relations with Nicaragua have spurred a sometimes tense domestic debate within Costa Rica about foreign policy, with opposition politicians and conservative business groups criticizing what they see as the Monge government's "bland and complacent policy toward the Sandinista communist regime" and demanding "forceful, clearly defined actions against the aggressors" (the Social Christian Unity Party)[104] or requesting a "rupture of diplomatic relations as a matter of honor" (the Chamber of Commerce).[105] The policy toward the contras even spurred serious conflict within the Monge government. Equally serious were reports in 1985 that some high government officials and members of the civil guard were actively helping the contras.[106] While debates over foreign policy are a healthy element of Costa Rican democracy, the raising of foreign policy toward Nicaragua to the level of a major public policy issue was, in large part, the indirect result of U.S. geopolitical strategy in the region, and it created splits and tensions within Costa Rica that diverted attention and resources from dealing with the pressing and serious problems of structural reform in the economy and polity.

The tensions with Nicaragua also encouraged the formation and strengthening of right-wing groups in Costa Rica, which do more than simply use legitimate democratic channels to criticize government foreign policy. The right-wing Movement for a Free Costa Rica (MCRL), for example, openly advertises paramilitary training programs in Costa Rican newspapers. In June 1985, its members were responsible for a violent demonstration in front of the Nicaraguan embassy, breaking windows and causing other damage. President Monge quickly and forcefully condemned that action and apologized to the Nicaraguans. Even more serious was the sabotage of an electricity tower carrying power to Nicaragua by a previously unknown right-wing terrorist organization calling itself *Patria y Libertad* (Homeland and Freedom), reportedly comprised of middle-class Costa Rican youth.[107] Such activities indicate the depth of the potential for internal polarization. Given the presence of armed contras in the border areas, and the additional presence of foreigners from international right-wing paramilitary organizations (like members of the Alabama-based group Civilian Military Assistance) who are assisting the Nicaraguan exiles,[108] there is the danger that right-wing organizations in Costa Rica might get the assistance and training they need to expand, indirectly increasing militarization.

Perhaps the most serious internal problem, however, is the pressure, largely generated by border tensions, for militarization within Costa Rica. Militarization is publicly eschewed by all major political parties: lack of an army in Costa Rica is a source of national pride and publicly credited as a key element in the creation and maintenance of Costa Rica's unusual democracy. Fully 83 percent of the population have indicated they are opposed to the creation of an army.[109] This has made the Costa Ricans particularly sensitive to signals from the United States that could be interpreted as pressure to militarize. In 1981, when Jeane Kirkpatrick, U.S. ambassador to the UN, remarked that Costa Rica might need U.S. military aid, President Carazo was so angry that he demanded two official letters of apology.[110] Similarly, many Costa Ricans reacted strongly when U.S. Ambassador Winsor and the U.S. Army Southern Command chief, General Paul F. Gorman, suggested Costa Rica might use U.S. national guardsmen to help construct roads and airports in remote areas of the country (close to the Nicaraguan border) and in the process, as Ambassador Winsor put it, give "these guys of ours a realistic opportunity to train on terrain that would be quite typical of what they might encounter should they get into a problem in a third-world country in this latitude."[111] Former Costa Rican President Daniel Oduber's comments reflect the sentiment of many of his countrymen: "If the guard plan were approved, it would be the beginning of the militarization which we have historically rejected."[112] The plan was eventually dropped because of public pressure.

Many Costa Rican officials believe that the policies of the Reagan administration have been designed to create a military capability in their country. This point was stated quite clearly by a top Costa Rican security official in May 1984:

> There are certain sectors of the North American government that want Costa Rica to militarize. They want Costa Rica to have a powerful army, military bases, and to participate in regional training. And there are insinuations. But we will keep resisting them.[113]

But despite resistance to what are interpreted as U.S. pressures to militarize, the very structure of the situation to which the U.S. has contributed —the contra activity and border tensions—created its own irresistible pressure to move in that direction. The poor equipment and training of the rural and civil guard made it unable to patrol the borders adequately, and the mounting tension with Nicaragua and terrorist incidents created a further "logic" to expand the size, training, and equipment of the guard. In 1981, U.S. security assistance was renewed after a thirteen-year lapse. Between then and mid-1985 the United States provided about $26 million to equip and train Costa Rican forces. The aid program aims to arm civil guardsmen with the same kind of equipment as a U.S. infantryman. Each soldier would have an M-16 automatic rifle, and border units would have grenade launchers, 80-millimeter mortars, M-60 machine guns, and other combat weapons.[114] Since 1983, five hundred civil guards have been trained by the U.S. in Panama and in Fort Benning, Georgia.[115] In May 1985, twenty-four U.S. Army Special Forces (Green Beret) advisers began training four companies of Costa Rican civil guards in Costa Rica.

In addition to the expansion of the guard, the Monge government also created a national emergency force in May 1982, the Organization for National Emergencies (OPEN). This civilian militia had about ten thousand members by 1985.[116] The volunteers are being trained in the use of light weapons and in emergency techniques to be employed during special events and natural disasters.[117] OPEN was used for crowd control during the visit of the Pope in March 1983, and was later used to help break a hospital workers' strike.[118] Government officials deny that OPEN constitutes the beginning of an army under another guise. But critics worry about even the unintended consequences of organizing such a force.

Former Costa Rican Security Minister Juan José Echevarría argued that establishing a permanent paramilitary organization was potentially danger-ous and suggested that the government should instead rely on reserve forces. Other critics fear that OPEN could be taken over by right-wingers "especially since members of the official recognized Costa Rican Communist Party are barred from the organization"; whereas members of the far right are not.[119]

The increases in military assistance and training and the organization of OPEN are routinely accompanied by public assurances that such moves do not represent the creation of an army (which would be a violation of the constitution) but are simply a necessary measure to defend against possible subversion, terrorism, and foreign attacks. Security Minister Benjamin Piza Carrenza explained: "The police [Green Berets] are here to protect our lives and neutrality."[120] And other officials deny that an army is being created, "noting that the standard accouterments of an army, such as a justice system, a corps of general officers and a body of strategic doctrine, do not exist in the civil or rural guard."[121]

But a pattern has emerged. As contra activity continues and tensions on the border grow, U.S. offers of aid are first criticized, and then cautiously accepted. In 1981 President Carazo had reacted angrily when Ambassador Jeane Kirkpatrick even suggested Costa Rica needed such aid, but Costa Rica then accepted it; Costa Rica initially declined invitations to have its police train in Honduras, but then later sent them there, to Panama, and the United States; Costa Rica declined offers to accept U.S. national guard engineers for road and airport construction, but by May 1985 was willing to accept Green Berets to give its guard counterinsurgency training. U.S. pressure to take military-type aid is clearly an element in these decisions. A senior Costa Rican government official spoke of President Monge's seri-ous misgivings about the Green Berets, but when his minister of public security requested they be sent, Monge, fearful of straining American good will, did not rescind the order: "Monge can only say no to a generous friend so many times."[122] However, the more important element is the border situation itself—a situation U.S. policy affects but more indirectly so. The protests within Costa Rica were much more restrained when the Green Berets arrived in mid-1985 than they would have been earlier in the Monge administration.

That the Monge administration was continuously forced to defend moves or concessions that added to Costa Rica's "military" capability demonstrates the significance of the issue. The buildup has also included the development of an intelligence capability, which again is of great concern for Costa Ricans. As Don "Pepe" and others understood so well in 1948 and 1949, the mere existence of a military force—regardless of the nomenclature—poses a potential threat of great magnitude in a country like Costa Rica. The more the regional situation deteriorates, especially with Nicaragua, the more rational it becomes to develop the military capability. Costa Ricans understand from their own history and that of their neighbors that the presence of an army will lead to great influence, directly or indirectly, on the affairs of state. Sooner or later, they fear, such a military would begin to restrict political liberty and divert economic resources. Yet, the bind remains: their reality is that they must deal with the implications of conflict generated on their border with Nicaragua. To do so means to rely on the United States and that inevitably means to be entangled in the web of U.S. geopolitical strategy.

With an oligarchy much weaker than its northern neighbors and a distribution of land and wealth far less unequal than those countries, Costa Rica's often wise and moderate rulers were able to eliminate the army as an institution and create a social democracy that is a model for all of Latin America. But the reformist capitalist development strategy Costa Rica adopted in the early 1950s generated serious economic and social problems that were heightened further by the economic crisis of the early 1980s. The United States, rightly interested in strengthening the economy of such a bastion of democracy, poured in economic assistance, which helped alleviate the short-term economic crisis faced by the Monge administration. But the Costa Ricans' ability to tackle the serious long-term structural problems were compounded not only by the large foreign debt that remained even after the immediate economic crisis bottomed out but by the growing regional turmoil that threatened to engulf the country.

Costa Rica's new president faces a challenge that is fundamentally more political than economic. It requires that the entire political establishment come to terms with its own past—readdressing policies that sometimes helped alleviate immediate hardship for less well-off Costa Ricans but did little to provide them with real economic and social opportunities. The social costs of austerity and structural adjustment packages of recent years have been disproportionately borne by the less powerful sectors of the

society. The nation's leadership, which has presided over the emergence of
a dual society, will face the challenge of incorporating its disenfranchised,
of achieving what Oscar Arias Sanchez, the PLN's successful presidential
candidate, once referred to as a "greater participation of the population in
the process of adopting decisions" and creating a "society capable of
producing the basic necessities for its population under a basically democratic political and economic control system."[123]

In facing this challenge, Costa Rica's political order still suffers from the
truncated base of support created following the overthrow of the Calderón-
Picado regime and the subsequent purge of the Costa Rican left from the
nation's political family. In recent years, the political bases of both the PLN
and the Social Christian Unity Party have been narrowing rather than
expanding. This has heightened the strains caused by the structural, economic, and social problems. But fortunately, Costa Rica, unlike the rest of
Central America, possesses forty years of civil tradition upon which a more
broad-based political community can be constructed. The primary challenge
facing the country's political establishment is to open further its political
system. In Arias's words: "the deficiencies of democracy can only be solved
by a better and more genuine democracy."[124]

Resisting national and international pressures toward greater ideological
rigidity, Costa Rica's leaders know that political space must be available
to the fullest array of ideological persuasions—right, center, and left. This
entails assuring a significant role for both the democratic right and left, the
former having grown impatient with sectarian policies of both major political parties, while the latter has been kept marginal to national decisions and
governmental participation. The PLN especially needs to develop its ability
to work with forces on the left side of the political spectrum, which it has
resisted since the purges of the Figueres junta.

U.S. policy under the Reagan administration, however, has encouraged
a narrowing, not a broadening, of political and economic space in the region
as well as in Costa Rica. Costa Rica has been more seriously affected by
the overall U.S. policy in the region, especially toward Nicaragua, than it
has by its direct bilateral relations with the United States. U.S. attempts
to weaken the Nicaraguan economy contribute to a deterioration that undermines Costa Rica's bilateral trade with Nicaragua, as well as creates pressures pushing more refugees into Costa Rica, adding to economic and social
burdens. The contra activity in the border areas, encouraged by U.S. policy,
inflames border tensions and actually prevents the peaceful border relations
desired by both Managua and San José. Border conflicts and tense, often
acrimonious, relations between Costa Rica and Nicaragua undermine Costa
Rican efforts to remain neutral, encourage internal polarization, and create
pressures for a militarization, which actually threatens a major pillar of
Costa Rican democracy—the nonexistence of an army. U.S. policy thus
ends up exacerbating the kinds of pressures that are antithetical to the very
kind of democracy Washington praises and the Costa Ricans cherish.

What is needed is a U.S. policy that reflects the common interests of the

United States and Costa Rica. That policy would seek to reduce political and military tensions in the region, encourage the opening of the political community to include the broadest segments of the society, and contribute to the reinvigoration of the Costa Rican economy. In short, it would contribute to the fulfillment of the promise of the social democratic revolution of 1948. The United States cannot "control" the destiny of Costa Rica, but it most assuredly does have a significant impact on its direction. A U.S. policy that, in fact, treats the Costa Ricans with the dignity and support they deserve is also the policy that will most contribute to the stabilization of the region, the enrichment of democracy in Costa Rica, and the promotion of the true national and security interests of the United States.

7

PANAMA
Thomas John Bossert

Panama appears to be the one calm country in Central America. The region's conflicts have not yet ruffled the surface tranquility of Panama's politics. Panama's economy is facing serious strains but is far short of the level of crisis experienced in all the other countries. While Panama's transition toward democracy after 16 years of overt military rule was marred in September 1985 by the forced removal of the elected president, Nicolas Ardito-Barletta, the underlying continuity of the military-dominated regime has yet to be seriously challenged. The exploding nationalism that has emerged throughout Panama's history as violent calls for Panamanian control of the Canal seems to have been defused by the Torrijos-Carter treaties. These agreements, signed in 1977, established the process by which full operational control of the Canal would pass to Panama by the year 2000. Although the implementation of the treaties has not been without tension and conflict, the treaties appear to have weakened anti-U.S. nationalism. Even in intense political campaigning for the 1984 elections, the issue of the Canal never became a central theme.

This stability is the legacy of a carefully constructed populist coalition built during the first years of the military government of Omar Torrijos Herrera (1968 to 1981). Prior to the enactment of the Canal treaties, Torrijos made strong nationalist appeals for unity during the negotiations, while at the same time creating a strengthened state that implemented significant social reforms. The Torrijos coalition was built on lower-class support in both rural and urban areas that joined the growing middle class in opposition to the political rule of the traditionally dominant business elites. The United States, through its structural importance in Panama—

the Canal, military presence, and economic interests—directly and indirectly played a decisive role in creating conditions for this coalition. Responding to Torrijos's skillful control of Panamanian nationalism, U.S. policies toward the treaty negotiations demonstrated some sensitivity to the Panamanian political process and a respect for those conditions which would maintain stability of the populist coalition's reformist and nationalist orientation. Washington understood that the security of the Canal depended on retaining stability in Panama and avoiding violent expressions of nationalist discontent.

In the 1980s, however, the military-populist coalition has been under increasing stress. Continuing economic stagnation and rising problems in financing the large foreign debt have forced Panama to adopt austerity programs, resulting in the withdrawal of vital reforms that had been crucial to maintaining lower-class and middle-class support for the regime. Center-right opposition, dominated by the business elites and strongly hostile to both the earlier populist reforms and a continuation of the military role in politics, has mounted a broad attack—including sometimes violent street demonstrations as well as a vituperative media campaign—against the current government, further undermining its already weakened legitimacy and restricting its policy options.

This weakened regime is also facing increasingly restrictive external constraints and pressures. Rather than granting sufficient room for government maneuverability, the International Monetary Fund (IMF), private banks, and U.S. aid policies have forced Panama to adopt restrictive austerity programs, without offering significant new investment for an alternative pattern of economic growth. Nor is there hope for significant new job opportunities to mitigate growing social pressures from the high levels of unemployment. In addition, growing pressures from the United States encouraged a shift in Panama's neutral and nationalist foreign policy toward closer association with the U.S. military approach to the regional crisis. This shift, and its accompanying growth in the size of Panama's military, has undermined the stable foreign policy consensus in Panama and brought forth new issues for domestic conflict.

Finally, while the Canal treaties appear to have weakened Panama's explosive nationalism, they continue to present constant irritants, some of which—particularily issues related to the U.S. military presence—could mobilize nationalist resentment again. U.S. attempts to retain this presence, such as the unsuccessful pressure to continue U.S. control of the School of the Americas military training center, have so far been resisted by Panama's governments, despite the large economic losses that will have to be absorbed by Panama when U.S. spending at these installations ceases. Nonetheless, such U.S. pressure in the face of nationalist resistance does little to enhance the stability of the weakened regime.

NATIONALISM AND EMERGING CLASS CONFLICT   ▲

The overwhelming presence of the Canal has been the determining factor
in Panama's history, economy, and politics. The only Central American
country with such obvious, enduring, and important U.S. strategic and
economic interest, Panama's political life has been punctuated by periodic
incidents in the struggle of Panamanians to regain ownership and sovereignty over the Canal. Furthermore, constant U.S. interference in
Panamanian politics inhibited the development of a strong and autonomous
national political process, leaving national dominant classes with tenuous
political control and authority. They had to balance their economic, and
sometimes military, dependence on the United States with popular nationalist pressures to remove the U.S. presence. It was a precarious balancing act,
with success often hinging on U.S. willingness to grant treaty concessions.
However, stability also rested on the elites' ability to create domestic unity
by mobilizing lower-class and middle-class support with reformist, as well
as nationalist, appeals.

The early efforts by dominant elites to manage nationalism were often
failures, both because the elites were weak and divided along personal and
economic lines and because no major reforms were initiated to defuse
inter-class conflict. Later populist efforts under Arnulfo Arías Madrid to
create a successful nationalist-reformist coalition in the 1940s were halted
by military coups that restored the traditionally dominant elites to power.
Again these elites appeared unable to regain internal unity, force concessions from the U.S., and co-opt lower-class support through reforms. It was
not until the 1970s that the military emerged as a central, relatively autonomous force under Omar Torrijos. Torrijos was able to cement a successful
nationalist and reformist political coalition, achieving both the promise of
Panamanian control of the Canal and establishing the reformist basis for
social peace. To understand this historical process we must briefly examine
the role of nationalism and class conflict since Panama was founded early
in this century.

While not the cause of the long-brewing independence movement, the
U.S. interest in building a canal in Panama provided the support necessary
to guarantee Panama's separation from Colombia in 1903.[1] U.S. support
for Panama's independence, along with the threatened possibility that the
United States might choose an alternate canal route through Nicaragua,
helped ensure the negotiation of a treaty on highly favorable terms for the
United States.[2] Having assisted the Panamanians in their quest for independence, Philippe Bunau-Varilla, a self-interested French entrepreneur, was
authorized to negotiate a treaty with the United States regarding the building of a canal. Eager for an easy settlement, Bunau-Varilla offered a draft
treaty that established full U.S. control over Panama's most important
economic asset. Secretary of State John Hay quickly accepted the draft and,
once the treaty was signed, Bunau-Varilla convinced the new Panamanian
government that reopening negotiations and changing treaty provisions

would probably cost them U.S. support and lead the United States to seek to build a canal at an alternative site in Nicaragua. This treaty, formally accepted but with sections that elicited deep resentment, would form the central focus for Panamanian nationalism throughout the century. For Panamanians, the most disturbing and enduring aspects of the treaty granted the United States the right "in perpetuity" to control the Canal and a watershed zone, which created a ten-mile band in which the United States exercised power and authority as "if it were the sovereign of the territory."

The United States buttressed its control over the Canal with broad interpretations of the treaty, claiming rights for arbitrary U.S. acquisition of watershed land and bases. Beyond these actions, U.S. troops intervened from 1903 to 1933 to end election-related violence and rent riots. Also, in flagrant support for U.S. business interests, U.S. troops occupied Chiriquí province for two years to protect United Fruit Company's banana plantations.

The Canal had a profound effect on the economy and class structure of the new republic. While Panama's role as a crucial interoceanic transit point had distinguished Panama's economy from that of its neighbors for centuries, the Canal assured and strengthened the importance of commerce and the service sector in the national economy. The Canal and its commercial opportunities became the central base for the economy. Commerce greatly eclipsed the traditional agricultural base that in the rest of Central America continues to dominate the national economies. One consequence of this economic structure was that the traditional oligarchic hegemony so apparent in most of the other countries was never as important in Panama. The dominant economic elite, a small group of families called *rabiblancos*, while continuing to control much of the local agriculture—including exports like coffee and sugar—derived its major economic power from commerce dependent upon the Canal, and from related real-estate and financial interests. Even in agriculture this elite did not fully control the economy since it was forced to share the export sector with the U.S.-owned United Fruit Company.[3]

As a consequence of this urban-based economy near the Canal, rural class divisions did not become the most important class relations, as they did in the rest of Central America. A remnant rural upper class of cattle ranchers continued to challenge the hegemony of the commercial business elite. However, the dynamic that dominated Panamanian politics was the urban conflict in Panamá City and Colón, initially confined to squabbling within the elite itself but later widening to the emerging middle classes as they grew rapidly after the 1940s. While Panama's political and economic elite reached an uneasy accommodation with the United States, the broader population resented the heavy-handed U.S. presence and its series of arbitrary military interventions and land grabbing. The Panamanian elite, however, worked carefully to manage this nationalism so as to maximize concessions from the United States while at the same time not losing the crucial stability that was necessary to the security of the Canal. Panama's stability always depended on how well the elite was able to cope with, manipulate, and pressure the United States so as to change the initial terms of the first Canal treaty. Nevertheless, at various periods in Panama's history, explosive and violent nationalist incidents have demonstrated how tenuous elite control of nationalism has been.

The business elite first focused its attention on wresting concessions from the United States in order to restrict U.S. rights of intervention, to limit land acquisitions, and to gain greater access to Canal markets for their commercial enterprises. However, in crucial periods there were others who were more adept at mobilizing this discontent and were able to mold it into a broad coalition of political support for more radical demands of nationalist control of the Canal. U.S. policy during the first half of this century was quite blind to the growing dynamic of populist politics that, by direct appeals to anti-U.S. nationalism, successfully challenged the urban elite's control of the political system.[4]

The most effective and enduring populist movement began in the 1920s and later swept its charismatic leader, Arnulfo Arías, to the presidency on three separate occasions from 1940 to 1968. The military overthrew him all three times, twice restoring the traditional elite to power. While Arías's movement was unable to consolidate power at any time in its history, it was able to mobilize and gain the loyalty of a broad range of middle- and lower-class supporters, as well as the rural cattle ranchers. His movement formed the core of populism: emphasizing strong anti-Yankee nationalism and promises of moderate economic and social reforms (such as requiring that Panamanian citizens control commercial establishments and creating a social security system). His major appeal came from his charismatic nationalism and his challenge to the traditional political elite. Since the 1940s this elite and the increasingly important and increasingly autonomous national guard have attempted to co-opt and weaken this populist support base by their own appeals to nationalism and their own modest reform efforts.

The initial attempts to undermine Arías were quite clumsy. Arías had been elected to the presidency in 1940 and was overthrown the next year when he resisted U.S. pressure for more military bases during World War II.[5] Arías was followed by a series of weak presidents from the traditionally dominant Liberal Party who ruled throughout World War II. During this period, Panamanian nationalism flared in repeated riots as the United States imposed new demands for bases to defend the Canal. The business elite, divided by internal bickering in part arising from competition emerging with the new wave of "easy" import-substituting industrialization, was unable to contain the nationalist pressures in the immediate postwar period and was forced to rebuff U.S. demands for concessions to continue the wartime bases indefinitely.[6] Riding a wave of nationalism back to power in 1949, Arías began to implement some populist reforms before he was again removed by a coup in 1951. In the following elections National Guard Commandant José Antonio Remón, taking advantage of continuing divisions within the elite and the growing autonomy of the national guard, won the presidency. Unable to obtain the personal popularity of other populists, Remón nevertheless instituted several important reform measures in health, education, and commercial agriculture. At the same time, he gained some nationalist support when he began negotiating a new treaty with Eisenhower. The Remón-Eisenhower treaty contained several economic benefits, most notably opening greater commercial opportunities for Panamanian business in the Canal Zone, but did nothing significant to resolve the nationalist desire to establish Panamanian control of the Canal.[7]

Returning to power after the assassination of Remón in 1955, Liberal Party governments presided over the worst outbreak of nationalist violence —the Flag Incident in 1964 in which twenty-eight people were killed and almost three hundred wounded in confrontations with U.S. troops from the Canal Zone. In the wake of this breakdown in control of nationalist pressures, the governing Liberals were anxious to conclude a more favorable treaty with the United States. Their efforts met with the Johnson administration's refusal to reformulate the treaty on terms that would remove the crucial "in perpetuity" clause of the 1903 treaty.[8] The weak treaty negotiated by Liberal President Marcos Aurelio Robles failed to satisfy even minimal nationalist demands and was rejected by the National Assembly —a failure that contributed to the breakup of the Liberal coalition and set the stage for the military coup in 1968, which brought Omar Torrijos to power.

Nationalism was not the only force promoting populism in Panama. Economic changes after World War II contributed to the development of growing middle- and lower-class forces that would later support a resurgence of populism. These class forces were supplemented by an increasingly active role for the state that not only challenged the economic control of the urban business elite but also provided growing employment for the middle class in the service sector. Encouraged in the 1950s by a steady boom economy averaging 6.83 percent growth per year, the elite at first discouraged any attempts to enhance the public role in the economy until the late 1950s and early 1960s, when Panama entered a rapid stage of growth in industrialization. This growth was stimulated by commercial concessions from the United States that enhanced the Canal Zone as a market for Panamanian goods and services. In addition, Panama took initial steps to attract international banks with liberal banking laws designed to make Panama the financial Switzerland of Latin America.[9]

While the traditional, old-family, *rabiblanco* commercial elite extended its economic role into these new industrial and commercial sectors, it was also able to co-opt an emerging class of small-scale and immigrant-dominated mercantile and financial entrepreneurs, often of Jewish, Lebanese, and Spanish origin. Less sure, however, was their control over the growing middle class and urban lower classes, drawn to the cities by new industry and commerce and by growing state employment opportunities. Middle-class student groups—particularly in secondary schools—began to form a locus of radical nationalism and antimilitarism that on a number of occasions led to confrontations with the national guard and the U.S. military of the Canal Zone in the 1950s and 1960s. Urban lower classes grew through the process of urbanization and began organizing into divided and weak traditional trade unions. Lower and middle classes also began participating in a wide range of unstable political parties.[10] In rural areas, reforms of the Remón period and the early 1960s Alliance for Progress programs brought schools, credit and technical assistance, and protection for union organizing. On the major export plantations of United Fruit in Chiriquí province, the communist Partido del Pueblo, historically active in these areas, was particularly effective in combining demands for reform with nationalist appeals, building a small but enduring union base in the region.

In the mid-1960s, these growing but disparate economic and social groups were separate centers of discontent that no single political movement was able to capture. They were up for grabs. The traditional elite had lost its capacity to manage the explosive nationalism when it failed to achieve a satisfactory Canal treaty. Again rent by internal divisions, the elite also failed to introduce effective co-opting reforms. Minor reform efforts sponsored by the Alliance for Progress had produced meager results and engendered hostile obstruction from traditionally dominant economic elites.[11] Arnulfo Arías, still extremely popular, especially in rural areas, had tempered his nationalist opposition to the United States and was increasingly accommodating to the traditional elite in his 1968 campaign for president. Running primarily on his charismatic appeal, Arías was clearly gaining increasing support from the emerging urban middle and lower classes.

At the same time, there was no viable alternative on the left to unite and mobilize these emerging sectors. High school and university students espoused a vague leftist and nationalist ideology but did not attempt to build alliances with unions or strengthen the established leftist political parties, such as the Partido del Pueblo. In addition, a guerrilla-based challenge to the regime never really emerged. Only two small groups briefly appeared in early 1959, apparently following the excitement of the recently successful Cuban revolution. They were quickly controlled by the national guard.[12]

In the mid-1960s, Panama was experiencing a stressful crisis in which the established political parties had lost legitimacy both within the elite itself and in the rest of the population. Arías could mount an effective challenge to this divided elite but his hold on the broader population was uncertain. New middle-class and urban lower-class economic groups from the emerging industrial and service economy and the growing government bureaucracy were increasing in political importance but were fragmented and unable to mobilize around any single candidate or program. It was a crisis of politics that would require strong action by the state to resolve. The national guard, increasingly acting as arbiter in the political system, was the likely candidate for imposing strong state action in the face of a political crisis. Arías, coming to power after winning the 1968 election, provided the spark for guard intervention by attempting to force the retirement or reassignment of senior officers in order to gain control of it. The attempt led the threatened officers to remove him once more from power, this time after only eleven days in office. This incident marked the failure of both the traditional elites and Arnulfo Arías to build a successful coalition that could manage nationalism and class conflict through successful negotiation with the United States and through reforms to co-opt lower-class support. It was left to a relatively autonomous military under a populist reformer to restore stability.

THE TORRIJOS MILITARY–POPULIST STATE   ▲

When the guard overthrew Arías in 1968, it was responding to his immediate threats to its established internal command structure. However, as it consolidated power and as Colonel Omar Torrijos emerged as the leading force within it, a major new role for the guard was forged. Torrijos's political achievement was to make the national guard the centerpiece in a renewed populist coalition that then combined elements of Arías's old lower- and middle-class support (especially students, professionals, and rural workers), the leftist labor movement, and the new group of technocrats employed by the growing state. The traditional business elite was excluded from the governing coalition, and the state itself, whose central element was now the national guard, arose as the major, relatively autonomous center of political power. The cement binding this disparate and tenuous coalition was solidified through a series of moderate reforms initiated early in the regime, the skillful use of co-optive government patronage, and the enduring nationalist appeals gained through the successful negotiations of a new treaty to end U.S. control of the Canal by the year 2000.

The core of the Torrijos regime was the national guard. It was the national guard that formed the institutional base for state power and for Torrijos's broad personal coalition. The guard had evolved from a weak police force into a more unified and professionalized armed force by the 1950s.[13] The officer corps was trained in Somoza's Nicaragua and in Peru and participated increasingly in U.S.-sponsored military courses at the U.S. Army School of the Americas in the Canal Zone. In the 1960s their training often encouraged a more active military role in national development.

Unlike the military forces of Guatemala, El Salvador, and Nicaragua, Panama's national guard was only rarely called on to control the lower classes and hence did not gain a history of large-scale repression of popular groups. In addition, although often willing to defend and promote the economic interests of the business elite in the pre-Torrijos era, the guard was considerably more nationalistic than the traditional elite and maintained a distance from the U.S. military, in spite of the training and equipment that the United States supplied. The guard avoided open confrontation in the nationalist riots of 1964, refusing to quell the riots and forcing U.S. troops to confront the disorders directly.

The one experience of guard involvement in counterinsurgency activities, the brief and successful effort to eliminate the small bands of guerrillas in 1959, appears to have had the effect of persuading some young officers involved in the operation—including Torrijos—that socioeconomic reforms were a more appropriate response to such challenges.[14] Taking advantage of the military's response to Arías's attempt to replace the high command, this reformist wing of young officers rapidly gained control of the guard. In the shift from support for the business elite to the assertion of the guard's own political dominance in a strengthened and autonomous state, Omar Torrijos played a crucial role. Although a strong nationalist and a member of the reformist wing, Torrijos was unwilling to adopt the more radical nationalist stance of the initial leadership of the coup. Torrijos maneuvered the removal of the more nationalist Colonel Boris Martínez within a year of the initial coup and emerged as the central, charismatic, *caudillo*-like leader of both guard and nation.[15]

With the guard as its core, the rest of the state also expanded its role in society and the economy, and in the process it gained broader populist support. A key to this popularity was a series of moderate reforms: a highly visible agrarian reform, labor legislation favorable to collective bargaining, enhanced social security benefits, and health and education reforms. Torrijos, frequently making highly publicized visits to reform sites, capitalized on these reforms to build his charismatic image. Torrijos also restructured the political system, banning the traditional political parties and creating a larger National Assembly, giving disproportionate power to rural and lower-class representatives. An initial period of repression aimed at political opponents on both the far left and the right discouraged early challenges to Torrijos's rule. While government control of the media and constraints on civil liberties (including the exiling of opposition leaders) remained in force throughout Torrijos's rule, physical repression appeared to decline quickly in the early 1970s as Torrijos came to depend more on populist reforms and also demonstrated willingness to accommodate some of the economic interests of the business elites. Emulating Mexico's PRI, Torrijos also began to build a populist political party the Partido Revolucionario Democrático (PRD)—which mobilized popular support largely through patronage. In an attempt to strengthen the economy and gain more leverage against the business elite, Torrijos also sponsored a rapid expansion in international banking, enacting one of the most liberal banking laws on the continent. While excluding the traditional elite from political power, Torrijos nevertheless made sure that they received economic benefits associated with the new international banking sector and growing state contracts for supplies and construction.

Crucial to Torrijos's success was his ability to manipulate the nationalist sentiment that held his broad coalition together. Coming to power on the heels of the failure of the Johnson-Robles treaty negotiations, Torrijos soon made the renegotiation of the treaty his central task. This process began with the skillful heightening of international awareness of the Canal issue and mobilization of Latin American and other Third World, as well as European, support in a series of international arenas—including the highly publicized meeting of the UN Security Council in Panama in 1973. Once U.S. President Richard Nixon responded to this renewed pressure by initiating the Kissinger-Torrijos negotiations, Torrijos was able to maintain the pressure for concessions by demonstrating that the stability of his control over Panama in part depended on significant gains in treaty negotiations. Unlike his predecessors, Torrijos was not bound by an election schedule, so he had some room for maneuver. However, his ability to maintain social peace and, in the economically troubled mid-1970s, reestablish austerity programs depended on his sustaining strong nationalist support.

The negotiations were not easy. Torrijos refused to consider proposals that did not remove the "in perpetuity" clause and replace it with a timetable in which Panama would regain full control of the Zone before the end of the century. The U.S. position was more complex, as different groups in the Pentagon, State Department, and Congress battled out the negotiating stances for the United States. The initial agreement with Kissinger in 1974 marked the central outline for the final settlement that Carter negotiated in 1977 and made one of the centerpieces of his Latin American policy.[16]

The political effect in Panama of the Torrijos-Carter treaties was to initiate a lengthy period of tranquility, defusing the hostility of nationalist sentiments regarding the Canal and U.S. presence in Panama. The agreement scheduled a transition in which the most glaring issue of nationalism —control of the Canal—will be resolved in Panama's favor once and for all. This process, with its foreseeable series of successful progressive gains for Panama, may provide the basis for a prolonged period of less strident nationalism.

However, the treaties were only a qualified success even in 1977 when they were ratified. Many political observers questioned the validity of the initial referendum, which showed that two-thirds of the Panamanian voters approved the negotiated treaties. Aside from their charge that the antitreaty campaign was hampered by Torrijos until late in the game, these observers suggested that the referendum was rigged to reach the level of approval that the government arbitrarily had projected months before the actual voting. Extremely high levels of voting and inconsistent and conflicting "official" vote counts for some provinces suggested fraud.[17] Nevertheless, public support was probably considerable. A public opinion poll taken one week before the plebiscite found that only 13 percent thought the treaties were bad for Panama, while 29 percent were strongly in favor and 42 percent thought the treaties were acceptable.[18]

Subsequent to the plebiscite, however, the DeConcini Condition and the detailed enabling legislation (the Murphy Bill, Law 96–70) were passed by the U.S. Congress. During the negotiations to gain U.S. Senate approval of the treaties, Torrijos was forced publicly to accept the DeConcini Condition, which asserted—somewhat ambivalently—the right of the United States to defend the Canal and gain preferential access in times of emergency, rights that went a long way to undermine the apparent recognition of Panamanian sovereignty in its own territory. These rights are the most recent formal statement of the hegemonic vision of U.S. power in Latin America. They were followed two years later with the Murphy Bill that, among other conditions, imposed a modified salary scale that discriminated against Panamanians newly hired by the Canal Commission.[19] Perceived as humiliating and embarrassing to Panamanians, these legislative acts planted the seeds of future conflict.

These conditions undermined Torrijos's nationalist appeal and weakened his support, despite the gains embodied in the treaty. University students, professors, and lawyers mobilized in opposition to the treaties, and riots occurred in response to the DeConcini Condition.[20] Even at the height of his success with the treaties, Torrijos faced a dilution of the nationalist cement that held his coalition together.

The second element essential to his early success in building the populist coalition was the reform effort that gained lower-class and middle-class support and strengthened the state's autonomy from the business elite. The state, however, would face serious constraints on its ability to continue the reform efforts. Among the most significant was the dependence of the economy on the external sector. The oil crisis of 1973 led to a serious economic decline. Private investment, both domestic and foreign, began to fall off in the face of the weakening economy and the uncertainty of the treaty negotiations. State enterprises were often poorly managed and failed to provide an alternative source of dynamic growth. As in the rest of Latin America, the state attempted to fill the gap in private investment by extensive public borrowing from international sources. This debt financing, however, did not strengthen state control of the economy and would ultimately lead to severe limits on state flexibility. The public debt soon grew out of proportion to Panama's reasonable ability to repay, rising to over 60 percent of total exports.

By 1976 Torrijos began to reach out for an accommodation with the business elite and began a slow process of withdrawing many of the earlier social and labor benefits. These moves were justified as temporary efforts to maintain national unity during the crucial treaty negotiations, but they were met with considerable resistance. Discontent began to accumulate and finally emerged in a series of labor conflicts, once the treaties had been approved.[21] During this later period, Torrijos and the guard appear to have relied more and more on selective patronage and corruption to maintain the loyalty of important lower- and middle-class leaders.

In response to the weakening of his populist coalition, Torrijos began in 1978 to lay the basis for a transition back to formal democracy. Some observers attribute this move in part to Torrijos's desire to establish a new basis of legitimacy for his own personal rule. He appears to have been stung by the public attacks on his "dictatorship" that were often voiced in U.S. Senate treaty debates and were simultaneously broadcast in Panama. Other observers argue that Torrijos had a genuine desire to return to the barracks with his historic treaties achieved and restore civilian rule before his popularity eroded even further. In any case, he began opening up some legislative posts for party competition, allowed the establishment of other political parties, and set in motion a calendar for the return to full national elections by 1984. In the midst of this process, he was killed in a plane crash in 1981.

During the 1970s, Panama's stability depended on the successful maintenance of Torrijos's populist coalition, despite the stresses of dissent against compromises of the 1977 treaties and the erosion of the initial moderate labor and social reforms. Economic constraints, however, increasingly limited the ability of the state to pursue reforms and to promote economic growth. In particular after 1980, deteriorating international conditions, both economic and diplomatic, severely restricted the ability of Torrijos's successors to maintain his broad populist coalition.

DEMOCRATIZATION AND THE DECLINE OF POPULISM   ▲

Since the death of Torrijos, the national guard has attempted to draw the excluded business elite back into the process of constructing the transition toward democracy, while at the same time not losing the at least tacit support of the remnants of the Torrijos populist coalition.[22] Willingness to turn toward the elite has been facilitated by the general movement toward the right within the guard. The crucial question will be how long the popular elements of the coalition can be retained as their early acquired benefits continue to erode.

Several dramatic shifts in policy occurred in the period following Torrijos's death. These shifts occurred after a new leadership had emerged in the guard, when in a blatant display of power General Florenzo Flores was placed under house arrest for five days until he agreed to resign in favor of Colonel Rubén Darío Paredes. Paredes, despite his association with Torrijos reforms when he was minister of agriculture, was long indentified with the right wing in the guard. As Torrijos's representative to business conventions, he had been able to develop strong personal ties with some members of the business community. However, Paredes was only able to consolidate his position in the guard with the support of the enigmatic chief of intelligence, Colonel Manuel Antonio Noriega. The more progressive but less powerful Colonel Roberto Díaz Herrera, a cousin of Torrijos, appeared to have lost some influence in this shift.

With his position relatively secure in the guard, Paredes next sought to remove the symbolic head of the progressive wing of the Torrijos coalition by forcing President Aristides Royo to resign in favor of his vice-president, Ricardo de la Espriella, a respected member of the banking community in

Panama. To retain an appearance of ideological balance in the government, the more progressive foreign minister, Jorge Illueca, was made vice-president. Paredes then pronounced a series of public "suggestions" that were to become general guides for a more conservative policy.

The new policies of the post-Torrijos period marked an accelerated turn toward a free-market economic policy. Strict government austerity was imposed, several government-controlled enterprises were turned over to the private sector. Social welfare programs were trimmed. Renewed efforts were made to attract foreign investment in export-oriented, nontraditional enterprises. The private sector was lauded as the new "engine of growth" that needed to be freed from the previous decade's government intervention.

Associated with this domestic shift was the growing concern in the guard with the Central American regional crisis. While the Foreign Ministry continued to support diplomatic efforts to resolve the crisis, the guard became the center for more militaristic responses, which increasingly targeted Sandinista Nicaragua as a threat to the Canal. The result was a bifurcated foreign policy, a growing emphasis on strengthening the military capacity of the guard and a breakdown of the neutralist foreign policy consensus forged by Torrijos.

To support these shifts in policy, Paredes accelerated the process of including the traditional elite in the political process. He convened representatives of the traditional parties and independents to revise the Torrijos-imposed constitution and electoral code. The sixteen-member commission reported out a reform that changed almost half of the articles in the constitution, modestly strengthening the independence of the legislature and judiciary, formally weakening the role of the national guard, assuring greater civil liberties, and constructing a new electoral system. The reforms gained the official support of almost all political parties. In the referendum that followed, over 85 percent of the voters approved the reforms. With perhaps less evident success, similar processes of carefully constructed commissions with representatives from various pertinent interest groups were formed to revise the electoral code, the labor code, and the agrarian reform.

These efforts to bring the previously excluded business elite back into the political process were, however, not sufficient to overcome its hostility toward the military-populist coalition. Members of the traditional political parties, business associations, and the independent press had long expressed vehement opposition to the Torrijos government and his successors. They criticized the populist reforms, in particular the labor code and state enterprises, as undermining private initiative and discouraging foreign investment. They chafed under the restrictions on civil liberties and denounced the growing corruption within the military regime. As the regime began to respond to their economic and political demands, the traditional elite only sought more concessions in a drive to regain power and push the military back to the barracks.

At the same time as the traditional elites mounted their center-right opposition to the regime, the lower- and middle-class members of the military-populist coalition were also growing restless. As noted above, the Torrijos coalition was built on the leadership of Torrijos and his masterful ability to combine nationalist appeals with moderate socioeconomic reforms benefiting the lower classes. With Torrijos's death and the steady erosion of these reforms, the bases for this coalition had decidedly weakened. Furthermore the state's independent force had been weakened by the international debt crisis and by the restoration of the private sector as the preferred engine of growth—effectively strengthening the business elite's leverage over the political leadership and reducing the regime's capacity to give benefits to lower-class members of its coalition.

Until recently, the government and the guard successfully retained the open support of unions, students, and other professional groups. While somewhat discontent with the loss of reforms, these groups still saw the guard as more likely than the center-right opposition political coalition to respond to their reformist and progressive demands. However, as the guard and government shifted increasingly toward the right, these groups began to search for alternative political expression. In July 1983, a moderately successful general strike was called—it was only the second general strike since the formation of the military government. Several small leftist political parties were able to gain the required thirty thousand registrants to become legal, and some formed an electoral coalition behind a popular physician, Dr. José Renán Esquivel, who was responsible for the most active stage of the Torrijos health reforms. Once a staunch supporter of the government, the communist Partido del Pueblo ran its own presidential candidate rather than promote the government candidate. However, the fragmented left was still quite weak and did not pose a major challenge in the 1984 elections.

The 1984 presidential elections were to mark the culmination of the long process of transition toward formal democracy that Torrijos initiated in 1978. They were a test of the ability of the military-populist regime to transform itself into a new stable democratic regime. The governing coalition attempted to retain power and extend its legitimacy by gaining a clear electoral mandate. Despite the fragmentation of its own support and the growing center-right opposition, the government still had considerable support through its legacy of reform, its patronage, and the implied stability of guard support. Its presidential candidate, Nicolás Ardito-Barletta, a former minister of planning under Torrijos and a vice-president of the World Bank, was chosen as a respectable moderate, similar in many ways to the former president Ricardo de la Espriella. He was, however, a political unknown who had to rely primarily on the governing party machine and the guard.

The government faced a serious challenge by Arnulfo Arías, now in his eighties and running again with the combined support of his own Panamanista party, the popular moderate Christian Democrats, and the remnants of the traditional parties. Arías, now a friend of Ronald Reagan and a strong supporter of the United States, retained his populist charisma largely as a national hero and a strong opponent of the national guard. His economic program was vague but clearly in favor of continuing the free market orientation of the current government. His major policy differences with the military regime had to do with the military itself. Rather than following the government's policy of expanding the military force, he would have reduced it, and—ironically for a past anti-Yankee nationalist—he proposed that the defense of the Canal remain in the hands of the U.S. military.

There were seven presidential candidates in the elections, including General Paredes who ran as a "Third Force" candidate after being frustrated in his attempt to maintain support of the governing party and the guard. However, the real contest was between the government candidate, Barletta, and the opposition candidate, Arías. The campaign was relatively peaceful but quite vituperative. The opposition was particularly strident in its charges of "treason" and "fraud" even before the elections were held. In a long process of vote-counting and validation, the contest was finally decided narrowly in favor of Barletta. However, the opposition did not accept the results and, finding that even the head of the Electoral Tribunal questioned the tally, was able credibly to charge that the elections were fraudulent and illegitimate. Some riots and one death followed the elections but the guard soon restored the peace.

Winning a very close and hotly contested election amid broad and credible charges of electoral fraud, Barletta was not able to provide new dynamic leadership necessary to replace the decaying military-populist coalition with a more enduring democratic-reformist model. In one of his first acts as president, he imposed new and widely unpopular austerity measures, reinforcing the right-leaning drift begun under the military government and contributing further to the gradual deterioration of populist support. Furthermore, Barletta's dependence on the guard and the Torrijista party machine made him a continuing target for the center-right opposition. Protest marches and demonstrations, which included professional associations, high-school and university students, and business associations, thwarted Barletta's new tax proposals—proposals designed to spread the burden of austerity to the middle and upper classes. Their continuing campaign against Barletta's fraudulent election and against government and guard corruption further weakened the regime.[23]

In September 1985, the opposition went further, accusing the military of engineering the assassination of a colorful revolutionary, Dr. Hugo Spadafora, whose decapitated body was found after he had been seen with Panamanian border guards. This charge was particularly serious since, unlike other Latin American militaries, the Panamanian military had a reputation for maintaining its rule without resort to torture or assassination.[24]

In the wake of this crisis and the growing opposition to his unsuccessful economic austerity policies, President Barletta was forced to resign after less than one year in office. In a move reminiscent of the removal of the two recent presidents who had been installed by the military, Barletta was summarily called home from a visit to the UN and closeted with Noriega until he issued his resignation. He claimed that, having lost the confidence of the military, he could no longer stay in office.[25] As before, the appearance of constitutionality was retained when the vice-president, Eric Arturo Del Valle, another businessman with no independent political base, assumed the presidency. However, the resignation only underlined the failure of the regime to achieve a transition toward an alternative form of rule. Panama was left with a regime that was increasingly alienated from its earlier popular bases of support, facing a growing opposition, with no new solutions in sight.

ROCKING THE BOAT: CONSTRAINTS ON   ▲
PANAMA'S STABILITY

Economy

Although generally more healthy than the rest of Central America, Panama's economy has also been extremely dependent on its external sector and quite responsive to changes in the international economy. Reflecting this dependence, the booming economy during World War II soon gave way to severe depression as wartime demand for the Canal dropped precipitously. Following world trends in the 1950s and 1960s, Panama profited from steady growth in maritime trade and import-substitution industrialization. Reaching peak growth rates of 11 percent in the early 1960s, this period of growth was marred only briefly in 1964 in response to the political violence of the Flag Incident in January that year.[26] World-wide recession accompanying the oil crisis in 1973 marked an end to Panama's broad prosperity. In the aftermath of the treaties, Panama recovered a 7 percent annual growth rate for 1978 and 1979, but by 1980 its growth slowed with the continuing world slump. In 1983 and 1984 the growth rate was near zero and no relief was anticipated in the near future.[27]

The combination of a narrow domestic market and a large export sector —approximately 40 percent of the gross national product (GNP), one of the highest in Latin America—have made Panama particularly vulnerable to changes in the international economy. The Canal and U.S. military bases account directly for 15 percent of the GNP and have a multiplier effect that brings their contribution to at least 26 percent of the GNP.[28] Canal traffic reached a peak in 1982, but suffered a 20 percent decline in response to the slump in world maritime trade and competition from Panama's own recently completed oil pipeline.[29] Once a major contributor to the growth in export earnings in the 1970s, the Colón Free Zone, a duty-free transport and commercial center that rivaled Hong Kong, experienced severe setbacks in recent years. Growth dropped from an average annual rate of 24 percent in the 1970s to 8.8 percent in 1981, and from 1982 to 1983 suffered a precipitious decline of almost 30 percent.[30] The Free Zone depended directly and indirectly on Venezuelan and Mexican markets, which collapsed in the wake of the dip in petroleum prices in 1982. While this loss in export earnings has had a national impact, it also seriously eroded the already troubled regional economy in Colón, Panama's second city.

The third major external sector was international banking. Banking directly accounted for 13 percent of the GDP, and its multiplier effect, through demand for construction and through employment of middle-class professionals, made its contribution to the economy even more significant. While banking contributed to the growth of the economy in the 1970s, this sector appears to have reached its peak in the 1980s. Recently, major banks began to move some of their regional offices from Panama.[31]

A central influence in the economy has been the IMF, which imposed a severe austerity policy on Panama's debt-ridden government. Panama has one of the highest per capita public international debts in the world and therefore is particularly vulnerable to IMF conditions. The public sector's external debt in 1983 was $2.8 billion, up 20 percent from 1981, and equal to over 60 percent of total export of goods and services. Total national debt of $4 billion was the equivalent of 93 percent of the GDP, and debt service in the public sector equaled 40 percent of the central government budget, contributing to a 1982 fiscal deficit of $340 million.[32] IMF conditions forced the state to withdraw from its previously active role in state enterprises, halt housing projects, reduce public health efforts, and trim government jobs. While in the past the IMF has shown some flexibility in its conditions, in recent years this tolerance appears to have faded.[33] This externally imposed burden on the state has continued to erode the reforms so important for populist support and has weakened the state's capacity to direct the economy in ways that challenge the desires and interests of the traditional elites.

The economic policy of the Barletta government conformed to the IMF austerity program but was also inspired by a new team of Chicago-trained economists, including the president, who sought a "liberalization" of the economy. They promoted the private sector as the central "engine of growth" in the economy and continued to reduce the state role in the ownership and management of economic enterprises. They relied on President Reagan's Caribbean Basin Initiative to provide incentives to attract foreign private investment as the only source of growth that could bring Panama out of its enduring stagnation. There have been, however, no clear indicators that major new investments are forthcoming. Furthermore, these economists admitted that such investment had little chance of reducing the growing unemployment that posed a threat to Panama's stability. Estimates of unemployment showed a steady rise in the early 1980s to 17 percent, nearly double the historic standards of structural unemployment.[34] In 1984 several urban areas were experiencing considerably higher and growing rates of unemployment. Colón had an estimated 28 percent rate and San

Miguelito, an urban slum near Panamá City, was also experiencing high unemployment and housing problems.

The economy, extremely vulnerable to external perceptions of a stable Panamanian business climate and on general economic conditions of other recession-plagued Latin American economies, was entering a dangerous transition period. Growing unemployment, severe shocks to the weak regional economy in Colón, and no clear engine of growth to lead the economy out of its stagnation—all suggested the need for active government efforts to soften the social impact of unemployment and to promote economic activities that might provide for growth. It was, however, precisely at this period that the government's austerity program severely restricted Panama's public-sector flexibility and forced the government to reduce efforts in social reforms that could ameliorate the social effects of a declining economy.

Slumbering Nationalism

Panamanians generally are cautious when they discuss their own explosive nationalism. They describe it as "irrational," "cyclical," and "unpredictable." They suggest that Panamanians can be remarkably unconcerned about the Canal one day and the next explode in anti-Yankee rage. Most observers agree that the Canal has not been a salient political issue since the ratification of the Torrijos-Carter treaties, but even the most optimistic argue that a new cycle of nationalism could easily emerge. The treaties appear to have "put nationalism to sleep," but they suggest that they would not be surprised to see it "awaken at any moment." Some see growing nationalism among students—including one incident of a student immolating himself in front the U.S. embassy in January 1984—as foreshadowing a rise in nationalist violence.[35]

The Canal treaties hold provisions that have potential for enflaming the nationalist issue once again. The dual salary scale that was mandated by the enabling legislation is particularly humiliating to Panamanians. The dual scale was to hold down Canal costs in the future and to bring Canal salaries more in line with the lower national salary levels in the rest of Panama. The effect, however, has been a de facto discrimination against the newly hired Panamanians workers. Efforts in the Canal Commission to change this scale have resulted in movement toward greater equality; however, the dual scale will remain an issue until it is completely removed in the next five years. Related to this salary issue was a debate over the award of cost-of-living adjustments given to U.S. citizens to make up for the loss of PX, commissary, and mail privileges. These increases came out of Canal revenues at a time when the revenues are shrinking and when there was a threat of layoffs of Panamanians.[36] A second irritant was the structure of voting in the Canal Commission. Until 1990, the U.S. delegation to the commission is, by treaty arrangement, always in a majority and the U.S.

head of the commission can mandate how the whole U.S. delegation will vote, thus making it impossible for the Panamanian position to prevail whenever it conflicts with the U.S. director's position.

While the progressive turning over of Canal Zone lands and buildings to Panama has proceeded generally on schedule—in some cases ahead of schedule—the major transfers are yet to be made, and more ominously, yet to be negotiated. The negotiations over the future of the symbolically charged U.S. Army School of the Americas suggested the seriousness of this issue for the Panamanian government. The School of the Americas, long denounced by Panamanian nationalists as a training ground for dictators, was scheduled to be transferred to Panama by October 1984, subject to agreement between Panama and the United States. The U.S. Department of Defense expressed considerable interest in retaining the school as the major training facility for Latin American officers.

The United States entered negotiations with Panama with an extremely strong position. Other sites were being actively considered. The school provided direct economic benefits of $12 million to Panama and made a particularily important contribution to the already precarious economy of nearby Colón. Furthermore, the national guard saw the need for continued training to prepare for its responsibility to defend the Canal beginning in the year 2000.

Initial negotiations produced an agreement in which the School was to be renamed the Panama-American Institute of Military Science and National Development. The institute would have been headed by a U.S. commandant but divided into a U.S.-run school for military science—basically the current School of the Americas—and a Panamanian school for civic-action programs, which would also have U.S. military administrators under a Panamanian school director. This thinly veiled compromise clearly retained a dominant U.S. role and was met with strong nationalist resistance, both within and outside the Panamanian government. While the national guard appeared to accept the compromise, it was not willing to test the response of more vehement nationalists, including outgoing President Jorge Illueca. In a highly nationalistic speech on the third anniversary of Torrijos's death, Illueca finally announced that the school would revert to Panama as planned by the treaties, on October 1, 1984. It appeared that the Panamanian government was willing to forgo the great economic benefits of the school, even in a time of economic duress, rather than test the potential nationalist response to a continuing U.S. presence.[37]

In the coming years negotiations for other elements of the U.S. presence in Panama, in particular the major military bases, may also hold potential for future nationalist reaction. The U.S. military presence has long been an issue of nationalist concern. U.S. military interventions in the 1910s and 1920s, followed by attempts by the United States to retain its wartime bases in 1947, were met with violent nationalistic protests. The U.S. military presence is a potential time bomb that has exploded in the past, undermining the very elites who negotiated the compromise in the first place.

So far the implementation of the Torrijos-Carter treaties has been handled with considerable care by both U.S. and Panamanian negotiators and has not provoked wide nationalist outrage. However, areas of tension exist and they suggest the possibility that, if Panamanian nationalism is "asleep," it could be a "fitful sleep" from which it might awaken again in the future.

Panama's Regional Role

Torrijos initiated a period of particularly open neutrality in Panama's foreign policy, in sharp contrast to previous governments' more passive support for the United States. His support for Cuba and for Third-World positions in international organizations marked a general independence from U.S. positions. This stance in turn gained wide Third-World support for Panama during the treaty negotiations. For ardent nationalists, it was an important aspect of Torrijos's populist appeal. While it was never a consistent policy and often could result in anomalies such as Torrijos's role in protecting the shah of Iran, it nevertheless gained for Panama sufficient reputation in the international arena to allow Panama to play important roles on issues beyond the Canal.

During the insurrectionary period of the Sandinista struggle against Somoza, Torrijos displayed his independence by directly supporting the Sandinistas with arms, munitions, and transportation. In this effort he coordinated activities with Venezuela, Costa Rica, Colombia, Mexico, and the Social Democratic European states—nations who had been old allies in the international support for the Canal treaties. More recently, this tradition was continued by Panama's participation in the Contadora Group: Panama hosted the initial meetings with Mexico, Venezuela, and Colombia in efforts to find a peaceful negotiated solution to the Central American conflicts. (See Chapter 10.)

Since Torrijos's death, however, this policy of neutrality and independence from the United States has increasingly been threatened by an apparent and growing fear of the Sandinista government. During a visit to Costa Rica in 1983, while still head of the national guard, General Rubén Darío Paredes asserted that Panama's defense began at Costa Rica's border with Nicaragua and that Panama would break diplomatic relations with Nicaragua and Cuba if they would not "moderate their activities in the region." Observers in Panama saw this shift in policy as undermining Panama's "honest broker" role in the Contadora Group.

Since Paredes's retirement, his successor, General Manuel Atonio Noriega, continued this policy and encouraged Panama's cooperation with renewed efforts by U.S. General Paul F. Gorman, to build a strengthened regional military capability through the revival of an earlier alliance—CONDECA. This alliance was an attempt to coordinate military activities of Guatemala, Honduras, El Salvador, and Panama against the perceived threat from Nicaragua. Panama, like the United States, remained officially only an "observer" in CONDECA, but Noriega's public statements suggested a more active role.[30]

This shift in Panama's foreign policy independence reflected the general trend within the government, and especially the national guard, to respond to and embrace U.S.-defined economic and political positions. It may be part of a strategy to gain U.S. economic and military support during the current economic difficulties. By moving more firmly into the U.S. foreign policy camp at a time when other patrons—such as Venezuela and Mexico—were losing their capacity to support independent foreign policies, Panama may be in a position to gain considerable U.S. assistance. Already Panama is benefiting from larger AID packages, and it stands to gain more from current Reagan aid proposals and the Caribbean Basin Initiative. More significant, however, is Panama's success in gaining greater military assistance. Under the treaties, Panama is to receive $50 million in foreign military sales credits over a ten-year period. The first installments of the credits have only recently been allocated by the United States, and requests for additional military assistance are being processed in Washington.

The implications of this shift from neutrality and diplomacy to greater military interest in the region is likely to have profound effects within Panama. For the first time since the treaties were approved, the guard is beginning to take serious steps toward assuming responsibility for the defense of the Canal in the year 2000. Rather than orienting this defense on the social peace established by the early Torrijos reforms and efforts in Third-World diplomacy, the guard is turning toward increased militarization and a more aggresively pro-U.S. regional policy.

Recently the guard was reorganized into a "Defense Force," which separates the military defense organization from the police force (both defense and police functions were previously integrated within the guard). This separate defense force was organized initially into a single light infantry battalion, but there were plans for three more to be in operation by the year 2000. There is also an ongoing and growing cooperation with the U.S. military in combined training, supplies, and maneuvers. Some Panamanians fear that this growing militarization and aggressive regional military stance will foretell a greater drain on the national budget, decreases in the capacity to provide reform benefits to the lower classes, and increasing reliance on military response to social protests. Furthermore, the editor of *La Prensa*, a right-to-moderate opposition newspaper, feared that Panama could be led into Central America's version of the Spanish Civil War: Small Power armies carrying out a proxy war for the Great Powers.

It appears that U.S. pressures to draw Panama into the regional crisis and to build up its military have raised new conflicts within Panama. These conflicts appear openly in the contradictions between the Foreign Ministry's promotion of the diplomatic Contadora process and the guard's cooperation with CONDECA. There have also been strong nationalist objections to the enhanced coordination between the guard and the U.S. military and to the growing use of U.S. bases in Panama as transport centers for U.S. military activities in the region. Perhaps as important, however, is the fear on the part of the center-right that this policy implies further growth in Panama's own military—a consequence of U.S. policy that many see as undermining efforts to reduce the military's political dominance. While most of the differing factions in Panamanian politics had been supportive of the neutralist independent stance of the Torrijos foreign policy, the new shift toward U.S. policy has broken this consensus, adding yet another element to the tensions that threaten regime stability.

DANGEROUS WATERS   ▲

The populist legacy that has been responsible for Panama's apparent stability is being undermined with no clear alternative emerging to replace it. The military-dominated populist regime is an exhausted model of governance, still limping along but unable to resolve the economic and political crises it faces. Economic stagnation is likely to continue to erode regime support at a time when the state's capacity to respond with co-optive reforms is severely restricted. Broad opposition from the right has further undermined regime legitimacy. In addition, increasing pressures to become actively involved in the Central American military crisis threaten to break the neutral foreign policy concensus established by Torrijos. While the military coalition managed to mobilize its supporters enough to assure victory in the 1984 elections, the closeness of the elections and the charges of fraud weakened the emerging new democratic regime. Barletta's forced resignation exposed the inability of the military-populist regime to transform itself into a real democracy. This weakened regime has no new answers to the growing challenges in the economy and in the regional crisis. Without explosive incident, the present weakened regime may be able to continue indefinitely. However, it seems unlikely that the new government will be given the luxury of continued tranquility. The stagnant economy will be a source of growing frustration among the unemployed and organized labor. Right-wing opposition will also be seeking means to discredit the government it claims stole the elections. Growing militarism, the continuing regional crisis, and the sources of nationalist tension in the implementation of the Canal treaties each hold potential for a severe regime crisis.

In this context, U.S. policies have done little to facilitate the growth of an appropriate democratic alternative to the decaying military-populist regime. U.S. support for continued austerity, emphasis on the private sector as the engine of future growth, growing militarization, greater military involvement in the regional crisis, and pressures aimed toward continuing U.S. military presence in the Canal Zone could be policies that combine in an explosive brew.

It is not clear what type of regime could best replace the exhausted military-populist regime of the Torrijos era. Probably some kind of democratic reformist regime could hold the promise of development while also granting co-optive reforms to the increasingly marginalized lower classes. In any case, the United States can do little directly to shape the new regime, which must emerge through domestic processes in order to gain significant legitimacy. However, U.S. policy influences the context in which a new regime might flourish and be able to maintain stability. A shift in U.S. policy so that it encourages reform, supports neutrality, reduces emphasis on militarism in both Panama and the region is likely to provide a more conducive environment for maintaining stability in this fragile period of transition toward democracy. Just as the United States can take some pride in its ability to enhance stability in Panama by having passed the Torrijos-Carter treaties, it must now take some responsibility for maintaining the conditions for that stability. Its current policy stance appears to assume that the apparent tranquility will be enduring, while in fact it engages in actions that actually undermine that tranquility. It does so only at the peril of finding a serious threat to the Canal emerging in the future.

8

THE ECONOMICS OF STRIFE
Richard S. Newfarmer

The United States has committed more than $3 billion in economic aid to Central America since 1980, but growth rates there continue to plummet. Growth in average per capita consumption has been negative in four of the last five years (Table 2). By 1983, the average Central American had less to consume than in 1978. In El Salvador, the decline has been so precipitous that per capita consumption is now less than it was a decade earlier.

Few would deny that the United States is uniquely positioned to make a major contribution to the region's recovery. One-third to one-half of the region's exports go to the United States, and a slightly greater proportion of its imports come from there. More than three-quarters of the region's foreign direct investment and private debt is held by U.S. corporations. The economic relationship is predictably asymmetrical: Central America accounts for a small proportion—less than 2 percent—of U.S. trade, investment, and debt; but American economic policies resonate with loud echoes through the mountains of this small region. For example, a strong economic recovery in the United States—from, say, no growth to 5 percent annually—increases the demand for Central America's exports and hence its foreign exchange earnings by about 6.5 percent, more than four times the effects of the free trade provisions of the Caribbean Basin Initiative.[1] This means that sound macroeconomic policies in the United States combined with a well-crafted economic aid program can make a major contribution to the region's recovery.

But the outcome of the first $3 billion in aid shows, if nothing else, that positive results are not automatic. Only if programs are designed with a

TABLE 2

ANNUAL CHANGE IN AVERAGE REAL PRIVATE CONSUMPTION PER CAPITA

(Percent)

	1978	1979	1980	1981	1982	1983	Per capita private consumption 1983 as percent of 1978
Guatemala	2.6	1.3	0.5	−1.3	−6.2	−4.7	89.8
El Salvador	−1.8	−5.7	−8.7	−10.6	−8.1	−8.9	64.4
Honduras	8.9	5.0	2.0	−2.9	−8.8	−7.7	87.5
Nicaragua	−9.0	−28.7	23.0	−9.8	−12.9	−4.4	65.8
Costa Rica	5.6	−0.3	−4.1	−15.3	−7.1	−7.2*	69.9
CENTRAL AMERICA WITHOUT PANAMA	1.3	−5.7	2.5	−8.0	−8.6	−6.6	75.5
Panama	2.6	15.6	6.8	0.8	5.2	2.0	108.2
CENTRAL AMERICA WITH PANAMA	1.5	−2.1	3.3	−6.5	−6.3	−5.2	80.9

*Projected on basis of 1983 reported total consumption.
†Unweighted average.
‡Includes changes in national accounting due to the transfer of the Canal to Panamanian sovereignty.

SOURCE: Inter-American Development Bank (IDB) *Economic Report* various countries, 1983, and IDB *Economic and Social Progress Report in Latin America*, 1983, for population data.

thorough understanding of the long-term political and economic nature of the current crisis can they avoid the distortions of good intentions that led to the demise of previous efforts to aid Latin America.

Recall the experience of the Alliance for Progress, heralded in 1961 as capable of closing gaps in income levels in the hemisphere by the 1980s. The program withered as it confronted recalcitrant domestic political elites who were seen as good friends of the United States but who stubbornly opposed the reform measures needed to ensure that the benefits of growth trickled down to the poor. The Alliance also contained an expanded military aid program that strengthened domestic militaries as a "shield" against revolution inspired by Cuba. Ultimately, as development assistance efforts became frustrated, the military program came to overshadow the economic component of the Alliance, and the militaries, which the United States had intended to train as professionals, too often became authoritarian, antidemocratic forces preventing the very reforms the Alliance advocated.[2]

Avoiding these mistakes for the billions of dollars of future U.S. aid to Central America requires an understanding of the underlying long-term problems of the region—increasing poverty, inequality, landlessness, and unemployment—as well as the short-term crisis brought on after 1979 by an unfavorable international climate and war. An analysis of the intersection of these trends suggests new cornerstones for U.S. economic policies toward the region.

THREE DECADES OF GROWTH WITH POVERTY   ▲

Ironically, after three decades of rapid growth, Central America now confronts problems of poverty and inequality that are more severe and socially explosive than ever before. The explanation for this dilemma lies in the nature of the growth itself: commercial agriculture and a relatively capital-intensive industrial development took place in a context of rapid population growth and highly unequal distribution of wealth and political power.

The region's per capita income of about $900 is only 57 percent of the Latin American average.[3] Most of the absolute poor live in Guatemala, El Salvador, and Honduras, where per capita incomes are particularly low. Infant mortality—an indicator of the general health of the population since it often reflects the health of the mother and the available diet—is nearly 30 percent higher for Central America (excluding Costa Rica and Panama) than for Latin America as a whole (see Table 3). Nearly one-third of the children in Honduras and Guatemala are undernourished; the situation is perhaps most desperate in El Salvador, where, according to researchers at the Central American University, more than 80 percent of children under the age of five are undernourished and more than 200,000 are in danger of losing their sight because of a lack of Vitamin A.[4] Costa Rica and Panama have been able to minimize these problems and provide a standard of living comparable to the rest of Latin America.

The question remains: Why has poverty continued to be so acute in the face of three decades of growth?

Agricultural Development

Agricultural exports have historically constituted the economic engine of Central America and have accorded landowners a privileged place in the power structure of the country.[5] Exports of commercially grown crops— cotton, coffee, sugar, and bananas—ranged from 16 to 37 percent of the GDP (in 1982 for Guatemala and Costa Rica, respectively). These crops, together with beef sales abroad, account for about 70 percent of the region's export earnings, most of the government tax revenues, and a large share of national income. This dependence on a narrow economic base left the region vulnerable to sharp swings in commodity prices and sustained periods of falling export prices relative to import prices. So long as export prices remained buoyant relative to the cost of imports, the regional economy prospered.

But prosperity in the 1950s and 1960s did not alter the face of poverty in the region. This failure can be traced in part to the institutions and organization of the rural sector. Land ownership is highly concentrated. In Guatemala, 10 percent of the landowners with the largest farms control 81 percent of the arable land; in El Salvador, prior to the reforms, the comparable figure was 78 percent; in Honduras, the richest group owned 73 percent (see Table 3). In these countries, the growth of commercial agriculture in the 1950s and 1960s was superimposed upon a land-tenure system that has been highly concentrated since colonial times.

Commercial agriculture, always important in the twentieth century, grew explosively in the 1950s. The spread of cotton production in Guatemala, extensive coffee, cotton, and sugar cultivation in El Salvador, banana production in Honduras, and sugar and cotton cultivation in Nicaragua aggravated already concentrated patterns of land-holdings. Large landholders bought or otherwise obtained new land for export crops that were made profitable by the sustained postwar demand of the industrialized countries. The spread of cotton production in Guatemala and El Salvador displaced thousands of small landholders, many of whom were Indians. The post–World War II wave of land concentration in El Salvador was part of a much longer historical process, but at the margin it induced a yet more painful squeeze on the mainly Indian peasantry. Cotton cultivation was the most devastating to small-farm production because it displaced many from the land, reduced rural employment opportunities with its progressively more mechanized technology, and simultaneously reduced the amount of land devoted to food production (Table 4). A

TABLE 3

CENTRAL AMERICA: QUALITY OF LIFE INDICATORS, 1970s AND 1980s
(Percent unless otherwise indicated)

	Health and nutrition			Income distribution		Literacy rate	Land distribution		
	Infant mortality*	Caloric intake†	Children below 75% weight for age‡	Highest 20%	Lowest 20%		Share of land owned by: Largest 10%	Smallest 10%	Landless as percent of rural population
Guatemala	70	92	31	66.5	6.7	47	81	0.5	30
El Salvador	60	90	23	61.4	5.5	63	78	0.4	32
Honduras	118	94	31	65.0	3.0	57	73	0.5	47
Nicaragua	94	109	15	60.0		87			48
Costa Rica	18	114	9	60.0	6.0	90			36
CENTRAL AMERICA WITHOUT PANAMA	72	100	22			69			39
Panama	22	103		52.7	2.1	85			
CENTRAL AMERICA WITH PANAMA	64	100				71			
LATIN AMERICA	64					79			

*Death before first birthday per 1,000 live births.
†Average percent of minimum daily requirement for caloric intake for adults. The calorie deficiency in a population is significant if average calories available do not exceed 120 percent.
‡Percent of children whose weight is 75% below average for age group. Based on surveys for various years: Honduras and Nicaragua for 1966; El Salvador and Guatemala for 1977; Costa Rica 1978. Given the deterioration since 1978, these figures are probably overstated.

SOURCE: Inter-American Development Bank, World Bank, U.S. Agency for International Development, Overseas Development Council, Adelman and Morris, *Society, Politics and Economic Development*.

TABLE 4

ALLOCATION OF LAND TO EXPORT AND FOOD CROPS, 1950 AND 1979
(1,000 hectares unless otherwise indicated)

| | Arable land | Export cropland | | | Food cropland (residual) | Food cropland —hectare per capita |
		Coffee	Sugar	Cotton		
Costa Rica						
1950	353	51	23	0	279	.33
1979	490	83	48	12	347	.16
El Salvador						
1950	546	0	103	19	424	.22
1979	710	37	180	102	391	.08
Guatemala						
1950	1,438	111	0	2	1,325	.45
1979	1,810	248	74	122	1,366	.19
Honduras						
1950	810	63	14	0	733	.52
1979	1,757	130	75	13	1,539	.42
Nicaragua						
1950	769	56	0	17	696	.63
1979	1,511	85	41	174	1,211	.44

SOURCE: UN Food and Agricultural Organization as presented in U.S. Department of State, "Central American Agriculture, Technology, and Unrest," Bureau of Intelligence and Research, Report 839–AZ, May 15, 1984 (unclassified).

State Department intelligence report summarized the situation candidly: "No other factor in Central America, however, seems to be correlated so strongly with the destabilization of governments as the expansion of cotton."[6]

Honduras, Costa Rica, and Panama, while undergoing increased concentration, avoided the worst aspects of rural displacement. In Honduras, the expansion of banana production had a similar effect in some areas, though it was much less widespread; also, the relatively late development of Honduran coffee cultivation, combined with the rugged mountains that permitted only intensive coffee cultivation on small farms, produced a less concentrated coffee economy than in El Salvador and Nicaragua. Costa Rica escaped from the old colonial pattern, in large measure because its mountainous terrain and sparse population led to the prevalence of medium-size, family-owned farms throughout much of the nineteenth and early twentieth centuries. This permitted the evolution of a social structure based more or less upon egalitarian principles; without an indigenous Indian population to exploit with subminimum wages and without the population density characteristic of the other countries, the country could more easily absorb population growth and release rural workers to the city as commercial agriculture and industrialization gained momentum later. The Panamanian economy was oriented mainly around the Canal Zone and the agricultural population was small; population pressure was vented through colonization of new lands.

Until the recent land reforms in El Salvador and Nicaragua, the degree of land concentration rose in El Salvador, Guatemala, and Nicaragua during the 1950s and 1960s.[7] Parallel to this increase, the number of landless grew dramatically, reaching an average of nearly 40 percent of the rural population by the late 1970s. The number of families on plots too small to produce a living grew as a percentage of the rural population.[8] The amount of land devoted to food production per capita dropped throughout the region. In El Salvador, the drop was particularly severe because per capita food acreage fell by two-thirds, to the lowest level in the region, and it coincided with the rapid expansion of capital-intensive cotton production. The situation was only slightly less devastating in Guatemala and Nicaragua.

This explosive situation in the countryside remained for the most part dormant so long as industry-led growth rates were high. To be sure, rural conflict over land and water rights frequently flared up in Guatemala and El Salvador, accelerating to include several peasant land invasions in the late 1970s. But these efforts were sporadic, regionally confined, and with infrequent mass mobilizations. Violence against the social order was contained with repressive military force. The creation of a small but significant number of new industrial jobs in the cities provided the most aggressive of the disenfranchised with opportunities for social mobility that were foreclosed in the countryside.

Industrial Growth

The formation of the Central American Common Market in 1960 provided the stimulus to new job-creating industrial growth. Besides creating a common external tariff, the CACM created a Central American economic identity based upon a network of businessmen, administrators, and technicians. The results were impressive. The total value of intraregional trade rose at an annual rate of 25 percent in the 1960s and 15 percent in the 1970s. Even in 1980, trade grew by 26 percent, fueled primarily by the demand for reconstruction in Nicaragua. By 1980 nearly 15 percent of the labor force in the region was employed in manufacturing, nearly three times the level of three decades earlier.

The import-substitution policies of the CACM were not without problems.[9] Many of the industries built in this period had limited potential for becoming internationally competitive. Although the levels of effective protection were relatively low (an average of less than 15 percent, according to William R. Cline), the system of tariffs created distortions that in effect subsidized imports and penalized exports. Petroleum-based chemical products, pesticides, plastic products, and electrical appliances proved to be especially costly industries after the sharp price hikes in raw materials— notably oil—in the 1970s. Since the incentive structure in the foreign trade regime heavily favored the use of capital instead of labor, these industries created far less employment than a less distorted tariff structure would have.

Another problem was that regional growth tended to benefit the richer countries more than the poorer ones, especially Honduras.[10] After the border tensions between El Salvador and Honduras erupted in the so-called Soccer War of 1969, Honduras effectively pulled out of the CACM. Nonetheless, for all its faults, the integration experience was on the whole positive and the distortions relatively small, in comparison to the import-substitution programs of the large Latin American countries. The CACM effectively promoted regional integration and economic diversification and provided an important source of new jobs in the cities.

Integral to the economic strategy of the region was foreign investment, especially American investment. Direct investment by the United States quadrupled from $254 million in 1950 to over $1 billion in 1980; these amounts were paltry when compared to total direct investments in the hemisphere by the United States of nearly $40 billion but constituted an important economic and political force in the small markets of the region. Most of the old investment had been directed into export agriculture, notably bananas, where it was a foundation of the rural political economy. This investment forged the historical ties between U.S. investors and conservative elites in many countries.[11] The creation of the Common Market provided an opportunity for investment in manufacturing, especially processed foods, light manufactures, pharmaceuticals, and some chemical products. New investment came from the families of the old oligarchs, and from new venture capitalists who were without the attitudes of the traditional agricultural elites. But often even these new industrialists became inadvertent partners with the old military-oligarchy alliance.

Increasing Inequality and Joblessness

New growth opportunities created primarily in industry during the 1960s and 1970s were insufficient to absorb the rapid increases in the labor force due to population growth. Years of population increases in excess of 3 percent produced a flood of labor that could not be handled in existing employment channels. Clark Reynolds estimates that new growth in the labor supply exceeded new employment opportunities by nearly 13 percent in the region between 1960 and 1971. Most of the hard-core unemployment was concentrated in Guatemala and El Salvador. This employment gap rose to more than 19 percent between 1971 and 1975.[12] As a consequence, unemployment rose and held the growth in real wages in the region below rates of growth in productivity throughout the 1960s. Labor's share in national income declined.

During this period, however, additional inequities within the wage component compounded the overall distributional effects of economic change. As industrial growth in the cities took root, urban workers were able to claim a greater portion of the national wage bill—as a consequence of their higher skill level, the greater productivity gains in industry compared with agriculture,[13] and the monopolistic product markets that allowed employers to pass on a portion of their monopolistic profits to labor groups sufficiently organized to make effective demands for higher wages.[14] Government tax and tariff policies accentuated the widening distribution of wages. After the first oil shocks, the effects of world inflation further undermined the real wage of workers.[15] Thus, even while economic growth rates were respectably high, labor's share of the national income declined and income distribution worsened.

The effects of these phenomena differed from country to country. Those countries with a history of repression of labor unions and subsistence wage policies—Guatemala, El Salvador, and Nicaragua—experienced greater decreases in labor's share of national income. Costa Rica, on the other hand, had for decades had a strong union movement, a liberal wage and social policy, and a more slowly growing population; as a result, labor's share in national income grew. Yet even those countries with policies relatively intolerant to rural and urban labor unions were able to withstand the building pressure of inequality as long as economic growth was strong. The brightest and hardest-working could usually find jobs in the city or at least eke out a living in the informal commercial sectors. But when the regional economy began to stagnate, this social safety valve was shut off, creating new pressures on already severely strained societies.

AFTER 1979: SPIRALING DETERIORATION   ▲

Economic decline engulfed the region beginning in 1979. Although the international recession swamped all economies in the region, the declines have been most heavily concentrated in the war-torn countries. Nicaragua, devastated by its civil war, suffered a 20 percent drop in gross domestic product (GDP) in 1979, yet rebounded well in 1980 and 1981, primarily through recouping production in agricultural exports and increasing utilization of existing industrial capacity. But this minirecovery was cut short by a hostile international environment and unsuccessful economic policies. El Salvador's civil war escalated after 1979 and the economy suffered successive declines in every year after 1978. Stagnation soon overcame Guatemala, Honduras, and Costa Rica as well.

Some economists in the Reagan administration and elsewhere contend that a principal cause of the decline after 1979 was the inward-oriented import-substitution policies of the 1960s and the 1970s; import substitution had effectively become exhausted by 1979.[16] To be sure, the system of regional protection had created a few heavily subsidized, uncompetetive industries. More important, the governments of the region failed to recognize the depth of the crisis soon enough and adjust trade policies (especially exchange rates) to promote exports and efficient import-substitution activities.

No set of government policies, however, could have insulated the economies of the region from three causes of the region's decline that were outside the control of economic policymakers: shocks from the international economy, internal military conflicts, and regional disintegration. If appropriate policies of the Central American governments are a prerequisite for adjustment to external shocks and eventual recovery, appropriate U.S. policy is equally essential to reversing all three "nonpolicy" causes of the region's woes.

External Shocks

The economies of Central America are extremely open and vulnerable to changes in the international economy. Trade accounts for one-quarter to one-third of the national income and export revenues depend on a handful of export crops. The 1970s witnessed a series of international shocks unknown since the 1930s: a sharp deterioration in the terms of trade, declines in export volumes, and suddenly rising interest rates on international debt.

TERMS OF TRADE LOSSES. The region had been fortunate for most of the 1970s in that the prices it received for its exports increased more rapidly than the prices it paid for its imports. Such was not the case after 1978. The quadrupling of oil prices in late 1978 seriously increased average import

prices, which rose by 38 percent between 1976 and 1982. Imported industrial inputs became more costly as the wave of inflation in the Organization
for Economic Cooperation and Development (OECD) countries following
the first oil-price increases began to be incorporated into the price of
industrial goods. Meanwhile, export prices rose at a less rapid rate than
import prices after 1977, and actually fell after 1980. By 1982 one dollar
of the region's exports at 1976 values was worth only seventy-eight cents.
Said differently, the region had to produce 28 percent more in export
volume just to buy the same amount of imports.

In resource terms, the implications were severe. The 1982 trade deficit
was $1,259 million. Without the shift in terms of trade the region would
have had a trade *surplus* of $334 million. Even though output per capita
rose by 7 percent in volume terms—24 percent absolutely—between 1976
and 1982, income per capita was actually much lower because exports had
lost their purchasing power.

DECLINE IN EXPORT VOLUME. Despite the weak prices for the region's exports
after 1977, increases in export volume kept total earnings rising through
1979. However, the recession in the industrialized countries after 1979 cut
deeply into the volume of Central American exports as well as their price.
The region's total exports began to decline, falling to 90 percent of their
1979 peak by 1982. The countries of the region had no choice but to
compress their imports—and their standard of living.

RISING INTEREST RATES. A final external shock was the rise in world interest
rates. Expansionary fiscal policy in the United States, together with a
relatively tight monetary policy, drove up the U.S. prime interest rate
dramatically; it peaked in the third quarter of 1981 at 21 percent in
nominal terms. Central America's debt service as a percent of export earnings rose—roughly doubling between 1980 and 1982, from 11.4 percent
in 1980 to 27.6 percent in 1982. In contrast to the large debtors of the
hemisphere, the problem in the region's rising ratio of debt-service to
export earnings stemmed not so much from the rise in the debt-service
numerator but from the fall in the export-earnings denominator, which fell
much more sharply in Central America than in the other debtor countries
of Latin America.[17]

The debt problem assumed different dimensions in each country. Because Nicaragua had led the region in contracting debt under Somoza,
maturities came due sooner, leaving an unfortunate legacy for the Sandinistas. Ironically, much of this debt had been incurred for nonproductive
military expenditures to fight the civil war. Debt service reached 66 percent
of export earnings in 1982, forcing rescheduling of amortization payments
due. Costa Rica had contracted large amounts of private debt and exhibited
high debt-service ratios before the reschedulings in 1982. Panama too
relied excessively on foreign borrowing and soon experienced severe problems. The other countries have fared somewhat better.

Military Conflict

The civil wars in Nicaragua and El Salvador and the subsequent increase in military violence constituted a second blow to the regional economy and explain the concentrated economic decline in those countries. Five related effects can be distinguished.

The most obvious effect of military conflicts is *the destruction of economic plant and infrastructure.* The devastation in Nicaragua's civil war between 1978 and 1979 was immense: plants were bombed, bridges blown up, electrical power lines downed. Investment required simply to replace destroyed capital stock was estimated to be well over $1 billion. Several plants in Managua that had been bombed in the final days of the civil war were still inoperative in 1983.[18] The Honduran-based counterrevolutionaries (the contras), while thus far scoring only limited success in undermining the political base of the government, have destroyed several important, costly economic targets in Nicaragua. In a shift in strategy, the insurgents apparently decided in 1983 to move strongly against economic targets and postpone the fight to capture territory. In El Salvador the destruction has probably been greater; an estimate done by AID put the total loss due to civil war at roughly $600 million between January 1, 1979, and March 1, 1982. Damage since then, as well as unrecorded destruction, indicates the figure has probably surpassed $1 billion. Violence has affected Guatemala far less and, aside from a few isolated incidents, has not touched Honduras and Costa Rica. Panama, in the wake of the Canal treaty, has remained relatively free of internal political violence.

A second economic consequence of the military conflict is *the enormous rise in nonproductive debt.* In contrast to the other high-debt countries of Latin America, such as Brazil and Mexico, a large share of the debt accumulated in the conflict-ridden Central American countries has gone directly or indirectly into purchases that yield no future earnings (much less foreign exchange) to pay back the debt. The United States alone has lent the region several million dollars under its military-sales program. Of late, Israel has also been extending cheap credits for military purchases. To this must be added debt that has been rendered unproductive by military destruction. If an electric power station financed through debt is destroyed, the country must still pay back the debt, even though the power station makes no contribution to national income. Finally, most of the new economic aid is in the form of Economic Support Funds (ESF), aid used to finance balance-of-payments deficits and not strictly tied to development projects; these loans have limited productive return because they in effect subsidize consumption or capital flight. All this is creating an immense burden of nonproductive debt. The dead hand of accumulated debt used to fund current consumption and military operations will weigh with increasing heaviness on the future income of the region, and aid levels will have to grow to maintain even the shrunken present levels of consumption and investment.

A third consequence of the on-going military conflicts in El Salvador, Nicaragua, and to a far lesser extent Honduras is *the reorganization of their economies toward military production.* Ironically, this militarization has resulted in a new "inward-oriented" industrialization at the expense of export-led development—at precisely the time when all international agencies, including AID, are advising policymakers to adopt an outward orientation. For example, factories in El Salvador that formerly produced printed cloth for export have been converted to the production of camouflage cloth for the military. Factories producing ladies' shoes for export were converted to boot production for soldiers. A large segment of light manufacturing—processed foods, soaps, matches—is purchased by the military. Meanwhile, normal rural and urban commerce has been disrupted in many areas, and the economic base of city and countryside is changing: large segments of the countryside have become more oriented toward subsistence agriculture, while the cities have become enclaves dependent for support on foreign finance and war-related commerce. The war itself becomes a chief source of profit for the few growing businesses, and these groups develop a political interest in perpetuating the inflow of foreign aid, a pattern hauntingly reminiscent of Vietnam in the 1960s.

In Nicaragua, military and defense-related activities have become the single most important source of new demand for employment and domestic producers. Although enclave economies have not emerged in Nicaragua because the counterrevolutionaries do not hold territory, many of the same factors are at work.

Related to both of the above two mechanisms, the conflicts cause national resources that would otherwise be used for investment to be channeled into *military consumption.* Between 1972 and 1980, the share of government expenditures on national defense doubled as a percent of GDP in all countries except Costa Rica (which has no armed forces, although even here expenditures for the national police force have risen dramatically).[19] Since 1980, expenditures on national defense have undoubtedly risen further.[20]

Finally, the escalation of military tensions in the region has precipitated *a massive crisis of investor confidence.* This is not limited to the conflict-ridden countries of El Salvador, Nicaragua, and, to a lesser extent, Guatemala and Honduras. Rather, the perception that the violence might spread, combined with the deteriorating economic climate itself, have provoked a capital flight unprecedented in the modern history of all the countries in the region. Private investment in gross fixed capital formation has turned substantially negative in all five countries. Moveover, private capital flows have been overwhelmingly negative throughout the post-1980 period. The net private capital outflows have amounted to $1.2 billion in 1980 to 1983—an amount roughly equal to U.S. economic aid to the region. Foreign investment has dropped to a virtual trickle in all countries except for Panama; in the five Central American countries foreign investment actually declined from $1 billion to less than $800 million. New private commercial loans have been extended to the region only as part of debt reschedulings. Finally, private firms in all countries were reported to be investing heavily outside the region.

The high levels of private capital outflow and reduced investor confidence were not solely attributable to the military conflicts. The lack of demand for the region's products; the high real interest rates in the United States, which attract private capital from an unsettled Central America to Miami and New York; and the hostile policy environment in Nicaragua also contributed to the region's lack of appeal. But changing any one of the other causes of the region's decline without bringing about a peace with stability will probably not rekindle economic growth in the region. Peace and stability are prerequisites for future regional growth.

Regional Disintegration

The external shocks and military conflicts ended the process of regional integration that had propelled industrialization and growth in the 1970s. In 1981, regional trade suddenly became a drag on growth rather than its propellant. In nominal terms intraregional exports fell by 18 percent in 1981 and 32 percent in 1982.[21] The fall continued through 1983. Since a notable share of the region's manufactured exports is destined for regional markets, regional disintegration implied the loss of manufacturing jobs connected with exports.

The integration process of the preceding two decades actually worked to the disadvantage of the region after 1980. Since they were each other's principal trading partners, the decline of one country's exports reduced its capacity to buy from the others, and income losses multiplied throughout the region. Gabriel Siri estimates that a fall in 1 percent of the exports of any one country precipitates a 0.4 to 1.0 percent fall for the other Central American countries, and a 1.6 to 2.5 percent fall in the product for the region as a whole.[22] If one or two countries had gone into a recession, regional demand in the others might have buoyed their sagging economies, but since all countries simultaneously entered the recession, cutbacks in regional demand compounded the general contraction.

The problem was accentuated by abrupt shifts in relative prices brought on by reluctant devaluations. This suddenly gave some countries new cost advantages over others and interrupted traditional trade patterns. As currencies assumed new values relative to each other, some countries, such as Nicaragua, began to run large trade deficits with other countries; the surplus countries became increasingly wary of financing growing deficits of their neighbors and halted trade credits. This heightened political tensions within the Common Market.

THE POLICY RESPONSE: ▲
NEW ADJUSTMENT MECHANISMS

The international shocks, the endemic political violence, and the disintegration of the Central American Common Market created a new set of economic problems of an entirely different magnitude for governments than the management of adjustment to business cycles in the 1950-to-1979 period. Although each country experienced slightly different problems and responded with different policies and lags, the similarities are sufficient to permit generalizations. During most of the postwar period, if export prices and volumes fell, the economies of these countries adjusted automatically. Currencies were pegged to the dollar and domestic monetary growth anchored to the influx of dollars, so a fall in export revenues or capital inflows was compensated by a fall in imports and monetary contraction, inducing domestic contraction. The growth in real wages would fall as unemployed workers competed for jobs. Any labor unrest could be dealt with by co-optive, selective wage concessions or quick repression, tools that became less effective as workers gained in organization and militancy.

Financing Deficits and Capital Flight

When commodity prices and export volumes collapsed after 1979, however, governments were faced with a difficult choice: imposing extraordinary declines in real wages and consumption to meet the inflated cost of manufactured imports and oil *or* effectively breaking the link with the dollar and expanding domestic credit to cover the fiscal gaps of the state. (Panama was an exception to this problem because it uses the U.S. dollar as its currency.)

Governments chose to finance the gap and attempted to fend off the drop in real income. To cope with the terms of trade losses and finance deficits, countries at first borrowed wherever they could. The public-sector deficits more than doubled as a share of GDP in Guatemala and El Salvador between 1979 and 1981, and they increased by more than one-third in Nicaragua and Costa Rica.[23] The expansion of domestic credit quickly translated into increased demand for imports, aggravating the trade imbalance or demand for dollars to ship capital abroad. As reserves fell, central banks rationed dollars at the official rate, and soon parallel markets for dollars blossomed. As the economy crumbled and uncertainty spread, investors lost confidence and moved their resources abroad. Governments after 1980 found themselves increasingly borrowing abroad to finance this capital flight as well as the trade deficits.

By 1980, net private capital outflows had already reached $600 million, which, together with deficits for trade and services of another $1.5 billion, left a $2.1 billion gap in required resources. Official capital inflows provided only $1.2 billion of this, and the overall deficit drained the region of remaining international reserves.

The crisis was complicated by the internal consequences of domestic policy responses. Although each country adopted slightly different policies, most involved initially strict controls on foreign-exchange markets, the emergence of black markets at considerably lower values for the domestic currencies, and the eventual adoption of dual exchange rates. (Costa Rica was the only country other than Panama to have adopted a fully unified exchange rate by the end of 1983.) Similarly, to fight the inflation caused by shortages of imports or devaluations, governments often subsidized state enterprises and social services. By 1982, it was not uncommon for governments to be subsidizing—through the exchange rate, the treasury, or the financial system—electricity, oil consumption, some imported capital goods, the cost of borrowed domestic capital, and some food. Since tax revenues were falling and the central banks were unable to capture foreign-exchange surpluses, it was only a matter of time before governments began to run out of money.

Subsidizing the Rich?

These policy responses probably had immense redistributive consequences in the various countries. Although no comprehensive studies of changes in personal-income distribution exist for the region, it is probable that the bulk of the internal subsidies—although at times adopted in the name of the poor—were captured by the relatively wealthy. The wealthy consumed most of the subsidized petroleum and electricity, not only because they have a large share of the total income but also they usually consume far more energy and energy-intensive products per unit of income than the poor; subsidized (often negative) interest rates benefited the users of capital, who are most frequently the well-to-do; as the costs of some imports were made artificially cheap and others expensive through the dual exchange rate, it is a safe assumption that those with political power captured the greatest benefit.[24] Subsidies for food consumption had mixed effects: on the one hand, urban consumers could buy food at a lower rate, but these prices hurt rural producers, most of whom are small farmers. The subsidies implicit in these policies clearly benefited importers at the expense of exporters, urban consumers at the expense of rural producers, those with political access to subsidized credit and foreign exchange, and users of cheap energy. In addition, the inflation that followed in the wake of these policies also taxed the poor more than the rich. Those who were least able to defend themselves—workers who sell their labor or wares in competitive markets (or monopsonistic markets, in the case of the landless peasantry working on large estates or selling as contract farmers)—were undoubtedly penalized.

The Sandinista government, with its political base in the poor, attempted to target its subsidies to the poor and probably mitigated the regressive effects of many of the price distortions during this period. But even here, the case is not clear; Forest Colburn reports that the internal terms of trade turned dramatically against smallholders producing food in Nicaragua in 1981 and 1982, much as it did in the other countries.[25] On the other hand, the government also expanded public services in education and health that directly benefited the poor, and it redistributed wealth through its land reform.

The cost of the subsidies eventually became too great, and by 1981 and 1982, all countries were virtually bankrupt. All except Nicaragua turned to the International Monetary Fund (IMF) for emergency financing.

Enter the IMF

The IMF, as a condition of its lending, sought a package of policy changes to end the financial drain on government coffers by restoring balance to international and governmental accounts. In exchange for refinancing illiquid central banks, the IMF sought a sharp cut in imports and an expansion of exports. This entailed effective devaluation of the local currencies to raise the price of imports and provide greater profitability to exports. This, together with cuts in the budget deficits commonly achieved through reducing government expenditures, was designed to reduce import demand through slower growth, and thus reinforce the stabilization effort. Because of the magnitude of the income losses imposed upon the region by international and military events, there was no economic alternative to a reduction in consumption, growth, and employment.

The ability to carry out stabilization programs and the distribution of its burden were different in each country. Costa Rica and Guatemala eventually entered into IMF-sponsored programs and deflated their economies. In El Salvador, the one-year standby arrangement did not lead to a longer-term arrangement and the situation continued to worsen. Honduras's three-year program was suspended in late 1983 over the country's failure to meet agreed-upon performance targets. Both countries continued to be sustained primarily by U.S. aid. However one judges the policy prescriptions for stabilization, it appeared doubtful that the stabilization programs could be successful in the countries where violence continued to scare away investment capital.

Stabilization Attempts in Nicaragua

Nicaragua tried to follow a different package of adjustment measures, which would throw the burden onto the relatively wealthy. To cope with a deteriorating balance-of-payments situation, the Sandinistas maintained the official exchange rate and rationed imports while offering subsidies to exports. The government attempted to limit the purchase of luxury goods with foreign exchange (thereby driving up their internal price), though it continued to subsidize imported food. To expand exports, the government offered subsidies to exporters to offset the penalties of the overvalued cordoba. Nonetheless, these measures were insufficient to balance the trade accounts and offset the capital flight that has occurred since the Sandinistas assumed power.

The government has financed the huge trade deficits and capital flight through an increasing reliance on bilateral arrangements with other Latin American countries and the Eastern bloc. The Reagan administration cut U.S. aid and exhorted allies to do the same. The French and other Western European governments declined to follow the U.S. lead but did not increase aid. Because the international financial institutions did not believe that the program would stabilize the economy or lead to renewed growth, the share of finance from the international financial institutions reportedly dropped to 17 percent in 1982, down from a peak of 79 percent in 1979. The share of Eastern-bloc countries had reportedly grown to 45 percent by 1982, and Latin American countries accounted for 38 percent, mainly through oil credits offered by Mexico and Venezuela.[26]

Simultaneously, the government also sought to redistribute income toward the poor by keeping food prices low to consumers and expanding social services. This created the unintended distributional consequences discussed above: small food producers in the countryside were compelled to subsidize urban consumers, who were on average better paid; and most subsidies through the exchange market and utilities have been captured by urban groups. Penalties to food producers were reduced by the introduction of further countervailing subsidies in fertilizers and by some price increases in late 1983.

Perhaps of greater importance was the economic viability of the strategy itself. The massive subsidies, together with the rise in expenditures to support military activities, were not accompanied by increases in domestic tax revenues, so the public-sector deficit continued to grow. Moreover, the contraction in imports that occurred as the foreign-exchange shortage became more acute caused many firms to go out of business and prompted the government to take over others to maintain employment and production. Most were subsequently operated at a loss, which increased the deficit yet further. Because of the hostile international financial and trade situation, these policies appeared to make it nearly impossible to bring the balance of payments or the fiscal accounts into equilibrium. The strategy did not appear likely to foster growth without major changes in policy or continual large-scale transfusions of capital from abroad.

Limits to Stabilization in Wartime

External and internal factors left the region stagnant, bankrupt, and with few options other than economic retrenchment. In an unfavorable international environment, policy responses generally were inadequate, too late, and—with the possible exception of Nicaragua—probably highly regressive. Stabilization programs in the countries with insurgencies seemed particularly tenuous: economic policies by themselves would not be sufficient to stem the capital flight from the war. Restructuring and reforming the economies, after a political solution to the military disputes had been found, offered the only hope of eventual economic recovery and broadly based development. The grim prediction of the Kissinger Commission seemed to be slowly coming true:

> Without a considerable reduction in the levels of violence, efforts to revive the regional economy will fail. Economic and financial incentives to invest or even to produce would be overwhelmed by the direct and indirect effects of political turmoil. Capital flight would continue, draining the new financial resources which we propose be made available.[27]

POLICIES FOR THE FUTURE   ▲

The interaction of inegalitarian social structures with the post-1979 deterioration has created an economic crisis of unusual proportions. U.S. security interests in the region are inseparably linked to social reform and economic growth as foundations for a new political stability. This is a difficult challenge. The regional deterioration is so extensive and the economic fabric upon which past progress was based is so raveled that it may not be possible to regain living standards known in the mid-1970s until the mid-1990s. In order to be successful, U.S. economic policy toward the region should be based on six cornerstones.

The first is a recognition that development can occur only with peace. A military shield cannot insulate the peaceful or pacified areas from the war-torn parts of the economies; military activity tends to distort the whole economy, while continued violence scares away private investment. In the small countries of the region fighting guerrilla insurgencies, investors realize that no investment can be completely shielded. Peace is, therefore, a precondition to renewed and sustained private investment and productive public investment. Unless one assumes that an essentially military strategy will produce a complete victory over the insurgents in a short period, such a military strategy is antithetical to recovery.

Peace is also a prerequisite for successful stabilization. To be sure, the emphasis on economic aid to stabilize the countries of the region is well-founded; financial stability is a prerequisite to growth. But in the absence of peace, stabilization programs may actually undermine long-term development because if stabilization fails, the cutbacks in social programs affecting the poor will not rekindle offsetting future growth but merely push the health and nutritional levels of the poor to new lows.

Third, reform—in land-tenure patterns, foreign-exchange regimes, regressive tax structures, and delivery of social services—has become a prerequisite of broadly shared development.[28] Social reform offers the only hope of reversing long-term trends toward increasing absolute poverty and inequality and of recreating the social stability necessary for development. But reform often conflicts with the domestic political agenda of the conservative economic and military elites who are the main U.S. allies in the region. As long as U.S. policy is unwilling to seek a broader alliance with social groups advocating reform, conservative elites who oppose reforms will hold them hostage to U.S. fears of insurgencies. U.S. policy must therefore welcome political allies among the progressive center and left to help create a constituency for the reforms that will eventually lead to social stability.

Fourth, the economies of the five CACM countries are so interdependent that the Sandinista regime cannot be isolated without undermining the objective of revitalizing the Central American Common Market. As shown above, to wage war against one economy reduces the growth prospects of the others. Based on relationships prevailing in 1966 to 1975, if the contras succeeded in reducing Nicaraguan exports by 10 percent, they would effectively reduce the GDP of the entire region by a cumulative 2.9 percent. The income of Guatemala would be cut 1.8 percent, El Salvador 1.7 percent, Honduras 2.7 percent, and Costa Rica 2.8 percent.[29] Therefore, economic policies to promote growth based on regional integration cannot be constructed upon foreign policies aimed at political and military partition.

A fifth cornerstone of policy is true economic multilateralism. The Kissinger Commission recognized that the amounts required for the region— $18 billion in official aid, according to the commission—are simply too large for the United States by itself to provide without a quantum increase in the overall U.S. aid program.[30] The commission envisioned the multilateral and non-U.S. bilateral contribution to be $10 billion to $12 billion, but current levels of disbursement are less than one-quarter of this amount. U.S. allies in Europe and in the Caribbean Basin remain profoundly skeptical of U.S. policy goals because of their uncompromising reluctance to accord legitimacy to any leftist insurgents in El Salvador and Guatemala and to the Sandinista regime in Nicaragua; they read the failure to pursue diplomatic efforts to end the strife as an attempt to secure an essentially military solution to the region's problems. For their part, the international financial institutions also recognize the constraints on recovery. Thus, the United States finds itself with the unfortunate choice of either abandoning its policy or becoming the principal financier of economically vulnerable regimes. The United States can help mobilize funds from these other sources—but only if it seeks a consensus approach to the region's problems which creates some reasonable prospect that stabilization and development efforts would succeed. A policy of economic multilateralism would therefore require a nonhegemonic political approach to the region and a serious diplomatic effort to end the civil strife. A strong multilateral consensus that united development and diplomacy would then position the United States to lead the stabilization, reform, and recovery efforts.

Finally, greater access to the U.S. market as recovery continued could be the strongest stimulus to development that the United States can offer.[31]

Two changes in U.S. trade policy would complement aid. The Caribbean Basin Initiative should be expanded to incorporate products that were excluded from coverage, especially textiles and leather products, and to include countries that will not qualify under the exclusionary principles of the legislation, particularly Nicaragua.[32] Second, given the primacy of coffee as a stimulus to growth, the United States should explore with the Central American countries an enhanced program to stabilize commodity prices and export volumes. This need not be expensive but could achieve substantial income gains.[33]

PART II

▲ ▲ ▲ THE OTHER ACTORS IN THE REGION

9

CUBA
William M. LeoGrande

From the outset, Ronald Reagan justified his policy in Central America as part of the wider struggle between East and West. The Soviet Union, acting primarily through "proxies" in Cuba and Nicaragua, was held to blame for the turmoil in El Salvador, Guatemala, and elsewhere in the region. From this vantage point, the security of the United States was very much at stake in these small countries, and major commitments of resources were called for in order to secure the region against Soviet penetration. Cuba served as a touchstone for Reagan's policy. The Cubans were the flesh and blood embodiment of the East-West dimension of the conflict in Central America; their presence gave credence to the administration's conception of the crisis.

Cuba has an intense interest in Central American events, as do the other Latin American states on the periphery of the area, such as Mexico, Venezuela, Panama, and Colombia. The Cuban presence in Nicaragua has grown tremendously since the crisis erupted there in 1978, and Cuba's longstanding support for the revolutionary movements in El Salvador and Guatemala has expanded as well. Moreover, Cuba's longstanding antagonism with Washington and friendship with the Soviet Union makes its presence disconcerting for the United States. The Reagan administration's response to this challenge has been to try to drive the Cubans out of the region, at times threatening and even actively considering direct military action against Cuba, with all the attendant dangers for world peace that such action would imply.

The nature of Cuba's role in Central America is more complex than Washington's rhetoric suggests. While the Cubans have an interest in promoting revolution, they also have an interest in averting a regional war. While they are close friends and partners with Moscow, they have interests and policies in the region that are not identical to, and at times conflict with, those of the Soviet Union. And while the Cubans are always interested in weakening Washington's influence in Latin America, they also recognize that geographic fate has put them next door to the United States and they must eventually find a way to coexist with the colossus to the north. Though the antagonism between Cuba and the United States is intense, there is nevertheless some common ground between the interests of the United States in Central America and those of Cuba.

CUBA'S RELATIONS WITH LATIN AMERICA   ▲

The ideology of the Cuban revolution has always had a strong internationalist dimension, and Cuba's leaders have felt a special affinity for national liberation struggles. Even before Cuba adopted a socialist path of development, the new government offered the island as a haven for revolutionaries from around the hemisphere, and in some instances supported their conspiratorial activities. Cuba's support for other revolutions was not limited to Latin America; assistance to anticolonial movements in Algeria and Portuguese Africa also dates to the earliest years of the revolutionary government.[1]

The example of the Cuban revolution spawned guerrilla movements in many Latin American countries in the 1960s. Cuba's early policy toward these movements was romantic and relatively unsophisticated—it endorsed virtually all of them and provided material assistance to most, regardless of how weak or miniscule they were. These attempts to "export" revolution increased markedly in the latter half of the decade, after the Organization of American States, at the behest of the United States, imposed an economic and diplomatic embargo on Cuba. The promotion of revolution became partly retaliation against those Latin American governments that joined the sanctions (everyone but Mexico), and partly an effort to break the U.S.-imposed isolation by helping to create other revolutionary governments to stand with Cuba against the United States.[2]

Cuba's support for Latin American guerrillas brought it into conflict with the hemisphere's traditional communist parties, most of which were following united-front or popular front strategies emphasizing electoral competition. Cuba denounced the parties as soft on capitalism and pledged to help any true revolutionaries, whether they called themselves communists or not. When Cuba sponsored the Tricontinental Conference in 1966, it invited few Latin American communist parties to this unprecedented international assembly of the world's revolutionaries. This unyielding support for armed struggle, combined with Cuba's hostility to the Soviet doctrine of peaceful coexistence, strained Cuban-Soviet relations in the late 1960s, though never to the point of causing an open break between them.[3]

By 1968 it was clear that the guerrillas supported by Cuba were no match for the counterinsurgency forces deployed against them under the security assistance programs of the Alliance for Progress. Repeated defeats, particularly Che Guevara's death in Bolivia in 1967 while trying to create a focal point for continental guerrilla war, prompted the Cubans to reevaluate the strategy of armed struggle. Based upon a new assessment that conditions in Latin America were not ripe for revolution, the Cubans abandoned the policy of indiscriminate support for guerrilla movements. By 1969, material aid to such movements had virtually ceased.[4]

For several years, no replacement for the defunct strategy of exporting revolution appeared. From 1968 to 1972, Cuba turned inward, preoccupied with the drive to produce ten million tons of sugar in 1970, and the task of economic recovery in the aftermath of its disastrous failure. This retreat from foreign involvement was so startling and so complete that it led at least one observer to describe Cuba's domestic preoccupation as "socialism in one island."[5] When Cuba reemerged on the world scene in 1972, the international situation was very different from what it had been in 1968.

The guerrilla movements that Cuba supported in the late 1960s had failed to achieve any success through armed struggle, but in several Latin American countries, the left had made gains through methods the Cubans had always disparaged. In Chile, the Popular Unity coalition of Communists and Socialists had won the 1970 election and were trying to pursue a peaceful road to socialism; in Peru, a military government appeared to be enacting a revolution from above; and in Argentina, the left wing of the Peronist movement had returned from the political wilderness with the election of Héctor Campora.

All three countries broke the 1964 OAS sanctions against Cuba by reestablishing diplomatic and economic ties. In the new international climate of detente, even conservative Latin American regimes showed a willingness to normalize relations with Cuba. The Latins were joined by the newly independent nations of the English-speaking Caribbean, who also promoted Cuba's reintegration into the hemisphere. Not having been targets of Cuba's earlier efforts to export revolution, these states were less fearful of Cuban subversion. Indeed, several Caribbean nations were ruled by left-leaning populist governments with some ideological affinity for Havana.

Such favorable developments led Cuba to adopt a hemispheric policy more conciliatory and tolerant of ideological diversity than Havana's past posture. Rather than seeking to end its isolation by promoting revolution, Cuba sought to achieve the same result by diplomacy—establishing normal state-to-state relations whenever it found willing neighbors. This conciliatory approach had considerable success; the OAS sanctions were undermined by a continuous stream of defections during the early 1970s, until they were finally abandoned in 1975.[6]

Inevitably, Cuba's diplomatic strategy was incompatible with significant aid to guerrilla movements trying to overthrow the governments with which

Havana was trying to resume relations. Cuba continued to be a haven for exiled revolutionaries, but its program of arms assistance was not resumed.[7]

By the late 1970s, however, progress on the diplomatic front had halted. Cuba's military involvement in Angola and Ethiopia, both carried out in coordination with the Soviet Union, demolished prospects for the normalization of relations with the United States. Moreover, the African wars contributed to the resurgence of the Cold War, with Cuba again at the focal point of the antagonism between East and West.[8]

In Latin America, the sight of Cuban soldiers trooping off to Africa rekindled the fears of the late 1960s. Once again, Cuba seemed intent upon promoting revolution abroad, but this time using regular Cuban troops rather than merely aiding indigenous rebels. Although no Latin American government broke relations with Cuba over the deployment of Cuban troops to Angola and Ethiopia, the process of reintegrating Cuba into the inter-American community slowed considerably.[9] It was in this context that the outbreak of the revolution in Nicaragua brought Cuba's attention back to Latin America.

THE NICARAGUAN REVOLUTION   ▲

The Sandinista National Liberation Front (FSLN) was founded in 1961 by a group of Nicaraguans long active in the revolutionary opposition to the Somoza dynasty. Throughout the 1960s, the FSLN received arms and training from Cuba, though the amount of Cuban assistance was circumscribed by the FSLN's small size—fewer than fifty members—and its inability to establish a guerrilla base against the well-trained and well-equipped Nicaraguan national guard.[10]

When Cuba reduced its support for Latin American guerrillas in the 1970s, arms aid to the FSLN was halted and the training of cadres was greatly reduced. Diminishing material assistance did not, however, signify diminishing solidarity. Cuba remained a refuge for Nicaraguan exiles and Sandinistas freed as a result of the FSLN's military actions. In 1970, when four Sandinistas (including FSLN founder Carlos Fonseca Amador) were released from prison in Costa Rica in exchange for a hijacked airliner, they were given refuge in Cuba. Again in 1974, when fourteen Sandinistas were freed by Somoza in exchange for the hostages taken in the FSLN's famous Christmas party raid, they sought asylum in Cuba before making their way back to Nicaragua.[11] Cuba's sympathy for the Sandinistas was never in doubt, but it was not until the insurrection against Somoza was far advanced that Cuba would again offer the FSLN more than moral support.

As the opposition to Somoza intensified in the late 1970s, Cuba's policy of refraining from the provision of material aid remained unchanged. Even the eruption of political turmoil following the assassination of opposition newspaper editor Pedro Joaquín Chamorro in January 1978 did not prompt an increase in Cuban involvement; Cuban officials still did not believe a revolutionary situation existed in Nicaragua. During this period, the bulk of the FSLN's weapons were bought on the international arms market and shipped through Costa Rica, which allowed the Sandinistas to maintain supply routes and base camps along the Nicaraguan border.[12]

The massive uprisings in Nicaraguan cities in September 1978 demonstrated the depth of the anti-Somoza sentiment and the fragility of the dynasty's hold on power. Though the insurrection was unsuccessful, it persuaded the Cubans that they had underestimated the strength of the revolutionary movement in Nicaragua and perhaps in Central America generally. Shortly thereafter, Cuba resumed material assistance not just to the Sandinistas but to the guerrilla movement in El Salvador and perhaps in Guatemala as well.[13]

As the dimensions of the Nicaraguan political crisis became apparent, the cast of foreign powers entering the fray increased rapidly. Between October 1978 and July 1979, Costa Rica, Venezuela, Panama, and Cuba undertook a partially coordinated effort to provide the Sandinistas with the arms necessary to defeat the National Guard. Mexico, Peru, Ecuador, and Bolivia added their diplomatic support for the insurgents. On the other side of the battlements, Israel, Argentina, Spain, Brazil, Honduras, Guatemala, and El Salvador came to Somoza's aid, replenishing his depleted military stocks.[14] The United States increased its political involvement, trying vainly to replace a recalcitrant Somoza with a moderate politician popular enough to stem the growth of mass support for the revolutionaries.[15]

Until the last few weeks of the war, the Cuban role in all this was relatively minor. After September 1978, the Cubans increased the training of FSLN combatants, provided some arms shipments, and helped the Sandinistas establish contact with other international arms sources. The Cubans also encouraged Central American communist parties to provide whatever assistance they could to the Nicaraguan revolution. Perhaps the most important Cuban contribution was its mediation of the differences between the FSLN's three factions. As a result of this effort the FSLN concluded a pact in March 1979 that reunified the movement and set the stage for the final offensive against the dynasty.[16] Most of the arms for the final phase of the war were provided by Venezuela and Panama, which transshipped them to Nicaragua through Costa Rica. Cuban arms shipments did not become significant until the last few weeks of the war when military aid to the FSLN from Venezuela declined after the electoral victory of the Venezuelan Christian Democrats.

There were good reasons for what the Central Intelligence Agency described as Cuba's "low-key" approach to aiding the FSLN.[17] Foremost among them was the fear that a significant Cuban involvement would trigger a resumption of U.S. military aid to Somoza, thereby doing the revolutionary cause more harm than good. Although the United States did not abandon the Somoza regime until the very end of the war, neither did it provide Somoza with military aid to continue fighting. Had the Cubans been more deeply involved in arming the Sandinistas, the chances of active U.S.

military support for Somoza would have been much greater. In fact, when the Cuban role expanded in June 1979, the United States cited it as an argument in favor of intervention by an OAS peacekeeping force that would have halted the war just as the Sandinistas were on the verge of victory. Latin Americans reacted skeptically to the U.S. proposal, since the FSLN was receiving as much assistance from others in the hemisphere as from the Cubans.

Cuba's caution can also be traced to the worry that a major effort on behalf of the Sandinistas would rekindle fears of Cuban intervention among other Latin American governments, thereby undoing much of the diplomatic progress Cuba had achieved over the preceding decade. Venezuelan President Carlos Andres Pérez, for example, traveled to Cuba in June 1979 seeking assurances that Cuba would not intervene massively in Nicaragua. And so long as others were providing the required supplies, there was no pressing need for massive aid from Cuba.

Cuba greeted the victory of the FSLN on July 19, 1979, with great fanfare and immediately pledged to help in the massive task of rebuilding Nicaragua's war-torn economy. Less than a week after the Nicaraguan Government of National Reconstruction came to power, a Cuban plane arrived in Managua carrying ninety tons of food and a Cuban medical team of sixty people.[18] It returned to Cuba with a high-level Nicaraguan delegation, including two members of the ruling junta (Moisés Hassán and Alfonso Robelo) and twenty-six FSLN commanders. The Nicaraguans were the guests of honor at Cuba's national celebration on July 26, at which Castro called upon all nations to aid Nicaragua in its time of need. Castro even challenged the United States to a peaceful competition to see which nation would give more to Nicaragua; Cuba, he promised, would begin sending food, teachers, and medical personnel immediately.[19]

The Nicaraguans requested aid in the fields of health and education because, as Robelo put it, "That is where the Cuban revolution has shown the greatest gains."[20] More than one hundred Cuban doctors and nurses arrived in Nicaragua in the final months of 1979 and were dispatched to outlying towns and villages to establish emergency clinics. By 1983, some five hundred Cuban medical personnel were in Nicaragua helping to staff the growing health-care system.[21]

In late August 1979, Cuba and Nicaragua signed an educational exchange agreement in which Cuba pledged to provide 1,000 elementary school teachers and 40 university professors to teach in Nicaragua. The agreement also included seven hundred scholarships for Nicaraguan students to study in Cuba.[22] The Nicaraguan literacy crusade of 1980 was modeled in part on the Cuban literacy campaign of 1961. Cubans helped plan the crusade, and Cuban volunteers joined the thousands of Nicaraguans who went into the countryside to carry it out. After the completion of the crusade, Cuban educational aid to Nicaragua continued to expand;

by 1982, there were 2,200 Cuban teachers serving in Nicaragua, a figure that remained more or less constant over the next several years.[23]

Cuba provided technical and economic assistance in other fields as well. In 1981, Cuban construction workers helped to complete the first all-weather road between Nicaragua's Pacific and Atlantic coasts and worked on a variety of public construction projects throughout the country. Cuban advisers assisted the Sandinistas in the task of building a new administrative bureaucracy to replace Somoza's apparatus.[24] In April 1982, Cuba and Nicaragua signed a major economic cooperation agreement in which Cuba pledged to provide 3,800 technicians, doctors, and teachers along with $130 million worth of agricultural and industrial machinery, food, medicine, and construction equipment.[25]

Some Cuban advisers also worked with the armed forces and security ministries, although their exact number is unclear. The Cuban military presence expanded with the escalation of hostilities between Nicaragua and the United States, and particularly with the growth of the covert war being waged against Nicaragua by CIA-backed exiles operating from base camps in Honduras. By 1985, Washington was claiming that there were 2,500 to 3,000 Cuban military advisers in Nicaragua; the Nicaraguans acknowledged the presence of only 786.[26]

Cuban aid to Nicaragua, substantial as it has been, does not convey the depth of the relationship between the two countries. The FSLN was founded by revolutionaries who were inspired by the example of the Cuban revolution. For almost twenty years, Cuba was the one nation that supported the Sandinistas, and after 1979 it was the one whose good will they could rely upon without reservation. The Cubans, for their part, had been waiting two and a half decades for another Latin American revolution. They had witnessed setbacks and defeats of every description—Guevara's death in Bolivia, Allende's murder in Chile, Manley's defeat in Jamaica. The victory of the FSLN was a long-delayed dream finally fulfilled.

It is not surprising that under these circumstances, Fidel Castro became a key adviser to the Sandinista leadership. Ironically, his advice tended toward pragmatism rather than militancy. He warned the Sandinistas not to follow the Cuban model of a rapid transition to socialism, which had led to the exodus of the middle class, profound economic dislocation, dependency upon the Soviet Union, and enduring hostility from the United States. Instead, he advised them to maintain a mixed economy with a role for the middle class so that its economic and managerial talents would not be lost. He advised against a break with the United States, lest Nicaragua be forced to devote vast resources to defense and throw itself upon the Soviet Union for both economic and military security—a burden that the Soviet Union might not be willing to shoulder and a dependency that the Nicaraguans should avoid in any case.[27]

In short, Castro warned the Sandinistas to avoid becoming the focal point of a new cold war, entangling themselves in the same dilemmas of international politics that Cuba had been struggling with for two decades. Washington was not accustomed to sharing foreign policy objectives with Cuba, but in fact, the advice Castro gave to the Sandinistas was fully consistent with what the Carter administration hoped to achieve with its policy of openness toward the new Nicaraguan government.[28]

As the multiclass coalition that made the revolution against Somoza began to break down in 1979 and 1980, the extent of Cuban influence in Nicaragua became an issue in the internal political debate. The private sector and much of the middle class feared that the Sandinistas would eventually take Nicaragua down the road of Cuban-style socialism. The Sandinistas' close friendship with Cuba exacerbated these fears, and the issue of the Cuban presence became a kind of political shorthand for this deeper conflict over Nicaragua's future.[29]

CUBA AND THE CENTRAL AMERICAN REVOLUTIONS ▲

The Sandinista victory in Nicaragua renewed Cuba's faith in the revolutionary potential of Central America—particularly El Salvador, where a revolutionary movement had already reached maturity, and Guatemala, where the episodic guerrilla struggle against military dictatorship was once again on the rise.[30] Optimism led Cuba to resume material assistance to these movements, although it was limited by a variety of circumstances.

In El Salvador in 1980, it was difficult for the Cubans to maintain a low profile as they had in Nicaragua. Whereas Somoza had faced virtually universal opposition in Latin America, the civilian-military junta that ruled El Salvador was able to maintain some legitimacy because of the participation of the Christian Democrats. Beside Cuba, only Mexico and Nicaragua supported the revolutionary opposition. Nevertheless, during 1979 and early 1980, Cuba followed the precedent of cautiousness established during the Nicaraguan revolution by providing only limited material support for the Salvadoran guerrillas.

Cuba's most significant contribution was probably political. As in Nicaragua, Cuban mediation helped the disparate factions of the Salvadoran left to set aside their ideological differences and unite in a broad opposition coalition—the Revolutionary Democratic Front–Farabundo Martí Front for National Liberation (FDR-FMLN).[31]

The logic behind Cuba's restraint was similar to what it had been in the Nicaraguan case. The Carter administration, although it was supporting the Salvadoran government politically, was not providing large-scale military assistance lest it strengthen the hand of the right-wing military at the expense of the Christian Democrats. A significant influx of weapons from Cuba would certainly have brought forth a counter escalation by the United States—as it eventually did in early 1981.

But the new element in Cuba's calculus was the existence of the revolutionary government in Nicaragua. From the moment Somoza fled, the consolidation of the Sandinista regime became a top priority in Cuba's policy toward Central America.[32] Under Carter, the United States was willing to maintain normal relations with the Sandinistas, so long as they did not become deeply involved in the Salvadoran civil war. For the Cubans, a policy of restraint toward El Salvador was intended not only to avoid an escalation of the U.S. military role there, but also to avoid disrupting Nicaragua's relations with the United States. A major Cuban involvement in El Salvador would have risked placing the whole Central American conflict squarely onto center stage in the new cold war. Nicaragua's revolutionary politics and friendship with Cuba would then have been a serious liability in its relations with Washington.

Cuba's policy of cautious support for the Salvadoran opposition changed in late 1980 with the election of Ronald Reagan as president of the United States. Based upon Reagan's staunch anticommunism, the Republican Party platform's hostility toward "Marxist Nicaragua," and the ultraconservatism of Reagan's advisers on Latin America, the Cubans concluded that a Reagan administration would enter much more directly into the military conflicts of Central America, and would do so as an ally of the traditional right.[33] To the extent that Cuban restraint in providing military assistance to the Salvadoran guerrillas (and to the Nicaraguan government) was premised on a desire not to provoke the United States into a more active military posture in the region, that incentive disappeared with Reagan's election.

Anticipating Reagan's victory, the Salvadoran guerrillas began in mid-1980 to prepare for a massive "final offensive" that would sweep them to power before Reagan's inauguration in January 1981. Cuba, in cooperation with Nicaragua, apparently agreed to expand assistance to the guerrillas in preparation for this offensive. According to U.S. intelligence reports, arms shipments began arriving in Nicaragua from Cuba during the late summer and early fall of 1980, and began moving into El Salvador after the November election.[34] Although the Reagan administration exaggerated the amount of equipment provided to the Salvadoran guerrillas between late 1980 and January 1981 when the abortive final offensive was launched, Cuban officials subsequently acknowledged Cuba's "material assistance" to the Salvadorans during this period.[35]

Cuba's aid for the Sandinistas and the Salvadoran rebels did not signal a return to the romantic and ineffective policies of the 1960s, when Cuba sought to catalyze revolutions even in the absence of any significant internal base. Guatemala was the only other Central American country with a large and growing revolutionary movement in 1980 and 1981, but even there Cuba's role was surprisingly limited. As in Nicaragua and El Salvador, Cuba urged the disparate political and military organizations of the left to join together. The Guatemalans, however, seemed less amenable to Cuba's good offices; despite several efforts to unify, most organizations continued to operate independently. Whether because the Guatemalans have been unable to forge a unified movement, or because they have not been near enough to victory, Cuba has provided them with few arms.[36]

There was even less evidence of Cuban involvement in Costa Rica or Honduras, neither of which had any significant armed opposition. Virtually all the Reagan administration's charges of Cuban activity in Costa Rica relate to the smuggling of arms into Nicaragua during the war against Somoza and into El Salvador in 1980. Even the 1984 terrorist incidents that Washington blamed on Cuba were directed at foreigners (i.e., Nicaraguan contras, Guatemalans, North Americans, and so forth) rather than at Costa Ricans or the Costa Rican government.[37]

In Honduras, the Cubans have allegedly increased their support for efforts by the radical left to begin a guerrilla war, despite the absence of any broadly based radical opposition movement. Although this would be out of character for contemporary Cuban policy, it is possible that Cuba, along with Nicaragua, is supporting such activities in retaliation for the Hondurans' harboring the contra movement. Even if Washington's accusations are true, however, the Cuban effort in Honduras has not been very substantial.[38]

REAGAN RESPONDS TO CUBA   ▲

In the aftermath of failure of the Salvadoran guerrillas' "final offensive," the newly inaugurated Reagan administration declared El Salvador to be a "test case" in the struggle against international communism. In February, the State Department released its White Paper, *Communist Interference in El Salvador*, charging that the war there had been transformed from a domestic conflict into "a textbook case of indirect armed aggression by Communist powers. . . ." At the center of this alleged aggression were Cuba and Nicaragua, both accused of serving as arms conduits for the Salvadoran guerrillas and turning El Salvador into a Cold War battleground.[39]

Almost immediately, senior administration officials, especially Secretary of State Alexander Haig, began to talk of "going to the source" in order to resolve the war in El Salvador. In a meeting with European diplomats in February, Haig promised that the United States would not become involved in "another bloody conflict" like Vietnam, but this time would direct its response against the real instigators of the problem, Moscow and Havana.[40] A few days later, Presidential Counselor Edwin Meese said that a naval blockade of Cuba to punish it for its misbehavior in Central America was "entirely possible."[41]

The often-repeated threat to "go to the source" was no mere bluff. Haig was articulating one of the central lessons that the U.S. military learned in Vietnam—a guerrilla insurgency cannot be beaten if its external logistical supply continues without interruption.[42] Going to the source—i.e., halting external aid from Cuba and Nicaragua—was seen by Haig as essential to winning the war in El Salvador, even though the evidence of sustained Cuban and Nicaraguan aid to the FMLN was spotty.

The idea of some military action against Cuba appealed to President

Reagan as well; on the campaign trail, he had called repeatedly for a blockade of Cuba in retaliation for the Soviet invasion of Afghanistan.[43] When Reagan first assumed office, he had to be dissuaded by his top advisers from launching an invasion of Cuba to rid the island of Castro. The decisive argument against the attack was that the Cubans were so well armed and organized that Cuba would become another Vietnam, only this time on our doorstep.[44]

On three separate occasions—in June 1981, November 1981, and early 1982—Haig recommended that the United States establish a naval blockade of Cuba. Each time, he was successfully opposed by the Joint Chiefs of Staff, who felt that a blockade would be politically unpopular, ineffective as a means of stopping arms smuggling, and too great a diversion of forces from other more vital theaters of operations. Moreover, the Joint Chiefs also worried that a blockade of Cuba would provoke a confrontation with the Soviet Union. Haig, on the other hand, was convinced that the Soviets would not fight over Cuba unless the United States launched a direct military assault on the island.[45]

The most intense and immediate threat of U.S. military action against Cuba came in October and November of 1981, just after the Salvadoran military suffered a series of setbacks at the hands of the FMLN, dashing the administration's hopes that the war there could be won quickly and easily. The Cubans were so convinced by the administration's public threats that action against Nicaragua and Cuba was forthcoming that Castro placed the Cuban military on full alert for the first time since the 1962 missile crisis. But he did not offer any concession on Cuban policy in Central America.[46]

Instead of direct military action, Reagan settled for launching the covert war against Nicaragua and ordering the Pentagon to prepare contingency plans for "unacceptable" military actions by Cuba, particularly any effort to deploy troops to Central America. The responses devised included a petroleum blockade and punitive air strikes against Cuban installations.[47]

Both these options had been rejected by President Kennedy during the 1962 Cuban missile crisis because they posed too great a risk of war with the Soviet Union. By seriously considering an invasion, a blockade, or air strikes against Cuba, the Reagan administration reflected its willingness to abrogate the accord that brought the missile crisis to an end. In that accord, the Soviet Union agreed to withdraw its missiles and not reintroduce strategic weapons into Cuba; the United States agreed to lift its naval blockade and pledged not to attack the island.

Some on the Republican right have long argued that this agreement was a mistake, that the United States should have eliminated the Castro regime by force in 1962. As Ronald Reagan put it a decade after the confrontation, "We have seen an American President walk all the way to the barricade in the Cuban missile crisis, and lack the will to take the final step to make it successful."[48]

More recently, the Republican right has argued that the missile crisis agreement either does not really exist or that it has been violated by Cuba and the Soviet Union so that it no longer holds force—thus, the United States is no longer bound by its pledge not to attack Cuba. When President Reagan was asked in 1983 whether he believed that the missile crisis agreement was still binding, he replied, "As far as I'm concerned, the agreement that ended the Cuban missile crisis has been abrogated many times by the Soviet Union and Cuba. . . ."[49]

The Kissinger report on Central America echoes this idea. The report, which was drafted in close consultation with administration officials and generally reflects the administration's view, implies that Cuban involvement in the Third World constitutes a violation of the 1962 accord, even though that issue was never discussed during the missile crisis. The report states that Cuban subversion in Latin America has become "arguably more dangerous to the stability of the region than the IRBMs of the 1960s."[50] This, of course, invites the conclusion that the United States should itself abrogate the 1962 agreement, for if subversion is arguably more dangerous than the IRBMs that Kennedy went to the brink of nuclear war to eliminate, then a contemporary president would be justified in going to the brink again to eliminate the source of subversion—i.e., the Castro regime itself. Political rhetoric like this emanating from Washington convinced both Cuba and the Soviet Union that an attack upon Cuba by the United States was more likely under Reagan than it had been for two decades.

CUBA RESPONDS TO REAGAN   ▲

Since Ronald Reagan became president, Cuban policy toward Central America has had two fundamental objectives: to avert a U.S. military attack against Cuba growing out of the Central American conflict; and to consolidate the Nicaraguan revolution. To achieve these objectives, Cuba has pursued a two-track policy of strengthening its own armed forces and those of Nicaragua, while at the same time trying to build a diplomatic firebreak against direct U.S. intervention. A third objective, achieving victory for the guerrilla forces in El Salvador, was a priority during the last few months of 1980, but since that time seems to have been downgraded significantly.

To bolster its own security, Cuba has resorted to the same formula that it relied upon in the 1960s and 1970s—a combination of military strength and friendship with the Soviet Union. Cuba's strategy is simple enough— to deter the United States from attacking the island by making certain that the direct cost of any attack and the risk of confrontation with the Soviet Union are so high that policymakers in Washington will be unwilling to pay the price.

Even before Reagan was inaugurated, Cuba began drawing closer to Moscow to assure that the Soviets would defend Cuba against U.S. attack. In his major address to the Cuban Communist Party's Second Congress in December 1980, Castro offered the first explicit endorsement of the Soviet invasion of Afghanistan nearly a year after the fact, and also gave what amounted to justification in advance for Soviet intervention in Poland.[51] The quid pro quo was not long in coming. In an address to the Czech Communist Party Congress in April 1981, Soviet President Leonid Brezhnev singled out Cuba as "an inseparable part of the socialist camp"—a clear warning to the United States that military action against Cuba would provoke a confrontation with Moscow.[52]

The direct threats of military action against Cuba that emanated from the Reagan administration during its first year in office seemed to confirm the Cubans' worst expectations. To strengthen their deterrent, they sought and received massive increases in military assistance from the Soviet Union. In 1980, for instance, Cuba received about 20,200 metric tons of military equipment from the Soviets, an amount 50 percent below the peak year of 1978. In 1981, however, Soviet military shipments to Cuba shot up by over 200 percent to 66,300 tons and have remained at about the same annual level since.[53] In addition, the Cubans reorganized their armed forces to make them more capable of deploying as small guerrilla units in the event of invasion, and they organized a new militia of some 500,000 people to supplement the regular military.[54]

These efforts appear to have been successful. No senior administration official since Secretary Haig resigned in 1982 has seriously advocated direct military action against Cuba. Instead, the Reagan administration has fallen back on a series of relatively small sanctions that are intended, according to U.S. officials, to "raise the cost" of Cuba's meddling in Central America.[55] The sanctions imposed, however, constitute more of an annoyance than an injury to Cuba.

One of the first sanctions was Washington's initially successful efforts to reimpose hemispheric isolation on Cuba. In 1981, Cuba's relations with a number of Latin American nations deteriorated significantly: Costa Rica broke relations over the aftermath of the 1980 Mariel exodus; Colombia broke relations charging Cuba with responsibility for arming the M-19 guerrilla movement; and relations with Venezuela became more difficult, continuing a downward trend begun when the Christian Democrats came to power in 1979. Only Mexico was willing to extend its relationship with Cuba despite the opposition of the United States.[56]

This new isolation of Cuba did not last; it was broken in the spring of 1982 when Argentina and the United Kingdom went to war over the Falklands-Malvinas islands. The United States supported Britain, whereas Cuba joined the rest of Latin America in support of Argentina. Since that time, U.S. efforts to isolate Cuba from the hemisphere have been largely futile. The South Atlantic war, combined with the worsening Latin American debt crisis, produced a certain solidarity among Latin Americans—including Cuba—that was directed at least in part against the United States.[57]

Among the other sanctions against Cuba undertaken by the Reagan administration were a series of measures designed to tighten the economic embargo, which had grown a bit slack in the 1970s. The travel ban prevent-ing U.S. citizens from going to Cuba was reimposed in 1982, although the exemption for Cuban-Americans made the ban economically insignificant since they constituted the vast majority of U.S. travelers to Cuba. The United States warned a number of its trade partners, including Japan, Italy, and the Soviet Union, that they would have to certify that their products being sold in the United States contained no Cuban nickel. The United States also allowed a fishing treaty signed with Cuba during the era of detente to lapse in 1982.

In what appeared to be an effort to close off even communication between Cuba and the United States, the administration initially tried to stop the importation of Cuban books and magazines into the United States, and repeatedly denied visas to Cuban officials seeking to visit the United States for academic conferences and public gatherings.

The administration's most touted sanction against Cuba was the creation of Radio Martí—a radio station named for the father of Cuban indepen-dence—which would broadcast anti-Castro propaganda into Cuba. The station had a difficult time in Congress and was ultimately placed under the authority of the Voice of America to keep it from being dominated by strident anti-Castro exiles. It also encountered such a welter of bureaucratic problems that it did not begin broadcasting until mid-1985, two years after its approval by Congress.

Despite the harsh rhetoric of the Reagan administration, the real sanc-tions available for use against Cuba were extremely limited. So long as the United States was unwilling to risk global war by launching a military attack against the island, Washington's leverage with Havana was marginal at best.

Nicaragua, however, was much more exposed to attack, both direct and indirect. In an effort to help bolster the Sandinistas' security, the Cubans took on a major role as military trainers and advisers for the Sandinista army, particularly as it expanded to meet the threat from the exile army of contras funded by the CIA. Here, however, the success of Cuba's policy was less clear. While the Nicaraguan military was strengthened to the point that the contras were unable to make any progress on the battlefield, the United States did not abandon its efforts to depose the Sandinista regime. Although the size of the Nicaraguan military was such that a U.S. invasion would be immensely costly, the Reagan administration explicitly refused to rule out direct military action as an eventual option if the Sandinistas refused to say "uncle."[58] Moreover, the very Cuban presence that enhanced the military capability of the Sandinistas also aggravated Nicaragua's rela-tions with Washington and with other nations in the region.

The main objective of Cuba's diplomatic effort was to defuse regional tension in order to make direct U.S. intervention less likely. This led the Cubans to support a variety of regional peace initiatives by Mexico, Venezuela, and the Contadora nations, to urge the Sandinistas to be flexible in negotiations with their neighbors and with the United States, and to press the FDR-FMLN to accept a negotiated solution to the Salvadoran civil war. It also led them to try to reduce bilateral tensions in their own relations with Washington.

The Cubans were not optimistic about the prospects for a revolutionary victory in El Salvador after the failure of the FDR-FMLN's "final offensive" in January 1981. The defeat demonstrated that the guerrillas had grievously overestimated their strength and were still far from having the military capacity or political infrastructure necessary to win the war. In light of the Reagan administration's determination to provide massive infusions of military aid to prevent the FMLN from defeating the Salvadoran army, an early victory in El Salvador seemed very unlikely.

Almost immediately after the failure of the "final offensive," Cuba began counseling the Salvadoran opposition to seek a negotiated solution to the war.[59] It continued to urge this position despite strong resistance from hard-liners in the FMLN—particularly from Cayetano Carpio's Popular Liberation Forces (FPL), the oldest and most militant of the guerrilla groups, and, ironically, the one most closely identified with Cuba.

Pessimism, however, was not the only reason for Cuba's support of negotiations in El Salvador. By early 1982, the pessimism of the previous year had disappeared; the guerrillas had scored several major victories and seemed to have taken the initiative on the battlefield. As Constituent Assembly elections approached, the FMLN promised heightened military action, and many observers, including the Cubans, believed a guerrilla offensive might push the Salvadoran army to the point of collapse. Both the Cubans and Nicaraguans urged the FDR-FMLN *not* to launch a full-scale offensive, lest it provoke direct U.S. intervention and possibly attacks on Cuba and Nicaragua as well.[60] The Salvadorans refused to accept the Cubans' advice, but their military actions around the elections proved to be less formidable than anticipated and the pessimism of the previous year returned.

As the covert war against Nicaragua expanded, a new danger developed —that a border incident might spark fighting between Nicaragua and either Honduras or Costa Rica, thus giving the United States a rationale for intervening against Nicaragua. The fear that the United States might attack Nicaragua if given even the flimsiest pretext was heightened by the invasion of Grenada in 1983. The invasion's basis in international law was extremely tenuous. But more ominous still was the administration's justification for intervention, the charge that the Grenadan government was acting as a Soviet proxy and threatening the security of the hemisphere—exactly the same accusations that were being leveled against Nicaragua.

Grenada was a sobering experience for the Cubans because it demonstrated that they could offer no real military assistance to a revolution under attack if the United States was prepared, as the Reagan administration clearly was, to use direct military force to prevent it. Prior to Grenada, there was much speculation as to whether Cuba would follow the precedents of Angola and Ethiopia by sending troops to aid Nicaragua in the event of a conflict between Nicaragua and its neighbors. After Grenada, there was no such speculation. The Cubans themselves acknowledged their inability to act militarily in Central America in the face of the overwhelming military might of the United States.

Cuba's fear that the Central American conflict would escalate to the point of prompting direct U.S. intervention was shared by most of the other Latin American nations on the periphery of the region, making it possible for Havana to join its diplomatic efforts with theirs. The Cubans consistently backed diplomatic initiatives launched by these other countries, while at the same time trying to open a bilateral dialogue with the United States.

The first diplomatic signal came from Havana just after the failure of the FMLN's January 1981 offensive. The Cubans reduced their arms shipments to the Salvadoran guerrillas and indicated to Washington that they favored a political solution to the Salvadoran conflict and an improvement in bilateral relations. The United States did not reply.[61]

A few months later, when Nicaragua was meeting with Honduras and Costa Rica concerning border problems, the Cubans communicated to Washington their concern about increasing regional tension and indicated that they would favor mutual security guarantees among the Central American states. They suggested that Mexico be brought into the process of trying to reach such an accord and said they would help achieve it as well. The Reagan administration informed the Cubans that it had no interest in such a process.[62]

After the war scare of November 1981, Mexico began to play a more active role in the search for peace in Central America. One of Mexico's first efforts was to sponsor a secret meeting in Mexico City between Haig and Cuban Vice-President Carlos Raphael Rodríguez. The meeting amounted to little more than a restatement of positions on each side, producing nothing positive.[63] Nevertheless, in the wake of the meeting the Cubans called again for bilateral discussions with the United States to reduce regional tension. The State Department again rejected the call.[64]

A second meeting occurred in early March 1982 when Ambassador Vernon Walters traveled to Cuba to meet with Castro. He inquired as to whether the Cubans were willing to discuss U.S. concerns in Central America. Castro replied that anything was open for discussion, but Cuba would make no unilateral concessions. Walters returned to Washington, and the administration began claiming, publicly and privately, that the Cubans were unwilling to talk.[65]

In February 1982, Mexican President José López-Portillo unveiled a plan to reduce the danger of regional war in Central America by opening negotiations around "three knots of tension" in the area: between the Salvadoran government and the FDR-FMLN; between Nicaragua and the United States; and between the United States and Cuba. Mexico was prepared to use its good offices to facilitate these negotiations. Cuba, Nicaragua, and the FDR-FMLN all accepted the López-Portillo plan, but Washington was cool toward it. Although discussions were eventually opened with Nicaragua, the

United States was not prepared to undertake a dialogue with Cuba or to support an internal dialogue in El Salvador.[66]

In April, a senior Cuban official met with a group of U.S. scholars and journalists who were in Cuba for an academic conference. He told them that Cuba was willing to play a constructive role in resolving the conflict in Central America, and that Cuba was willing to begin discussions on this issue with the United States without preconditions. A few days later, this offer was repeated to the head of the U.S. diplomatic mission in Havana, Wayne Smith. The Cubans told Smith, "We want a peaceful solution in Central America. We understand your security concerns and are willing to address them. If you are willing to meet us halfway and to deal with us on the basis of mutual respect, there is no reason we cannot at long last begin to put aside this unproductive animosity between us."[67]

Washington responded by allowing the fishing treaty between the two nations to lapse, and by reimposing the ban on travel to Cuba by U.S. citizens. The rationale presented for Washington's unwillingness to even talk with the Cubans was disarmingly simple: the administration asserted that the Cuban offers were not sincere. By not replying to the offers, of course, there was no way that Washington could test the Cubans' sincerity. The real reason for the administration's resistance to talks was the belief that any negotiations with the Cubans were worthless, and that the opening of talks would encourage critics of the administration and generate the impression that the United States was willing to abandon El Salvador.[68]

From 1983 onward, the search for a political solution to the Central American crisis was carried on mainly by the Contadora nations (Mexico, Venezuela, Colombia, and Panama). The first major step forward in the process came in July 1983 when Nicaragua agreed to accept multilateral rather than bilateral negotiations among the Central American states. The Nicaraguans also called for an immediate end to arms shipments to both sides in the Salvadoran civil war and an end to foreign sponsorship of insurgent movements in the region. Cuba immediately endorsed the Nicaraguan position and communicated to the Contadora nations its willingness to cooperate in the search for peace.[69]

In an impromptu news conference with foreign journalists on July 28, 1983, Castro discussed the issue of Central America at length:

> If a policy is adopted whereby everyone stops supporting . . . the revolution-aries as well as those who are oppressing the country or repressing the country, we would be willing to accept such a formula. If it's agreed that advisers be withdrawn, we would accept that formula. . . . If it is agreed that no one sends weapons, we would be willing to accept the compromise of not sending weapons to Central America. . . .
>
> We are willing to make compromises similar to those made by all the other countries, including the United States, to find a solution, and we would be seriously willing to support such a solution. Because the alternative to such

a solution is the aggravation of the conflicts, the intervention of the United
States.[70]

At each juncture of the Contadora process, Cuba continued to voice its
support for the initiative. But Contadora by no means represented a perfect
solution from the Cubans' point of view. Contadora focused almost exclusively on the danger of conflict among the nations of Central America; the
participants were reluctant to engage the issue of internal conflicts lest they
be accused of interfering in the internal affairs of Central American nations.
In practical terms, this meant that a Contadora solution would probably
obligate Nicaragua and Cuba to halt all material assistance for the Salvadoran guerrillas without achieving a negotiated solution to that conflict. The
Salvadorans, sensitive to Cuba's earlier efforts to restrict their military
activity lest they provoke U.S. attacks against Cuba or Nicaragua, were
justifiably suspicious that their interests might be sacrificed in a Contadora
accord.

Castro tried to link El Salvador to Contadora in his July press conference,
warning, "There can be no negotiated political solution in Central America
if there is no negotiated solution in El Salvador. The other position would
be asking the friends of the Salvadorans to forget about them, to betray
them. No one can make a compromise on that basis."[71] But the Cubans
were in no position to realistically enforce such linkage. They were not a
participant in the Contadora negotiations, and having endorsed the process
repeatedly, they could not afford politically to refuse to accept its outcome,
whatever that might be. Nor was Nicaragua in a position to block an
agreement over the issue of El Salvador; to do so would allow the Reagan
administration to blame Managua for Contadora's failure, thereby justifying
an escalation of military pressures against Nicaragua.

The upshot of these various imperatives was not salutary for the FDR-
FMLN, but they were as powerless to change the situation as were the
Cubans and the Nicaraguans. It seemed clear that if a Contadora accord
were actually achieved, it would not include a mandate for negotiations in
El Salvador and would certainly not be tied to the successful conclusion of
such negotiations. Thus, after the accord was signed, the FDR-FMLN would
be thrown almost entirely upon its own resources.

The extent to which the FDR-FMLN was operating on its own resources
or receiving aid from Nicaragua and Cuba was a hotly contested issue in
the United States. The Reagan administration consistently claimed both
Cuba and Nicaragua were deeply involved in the shipment of arms to the
FMLN, and in providing all sorts of logistical support (e.g., medical supplies, food, training, military advice, and command and control). This
assertion formed the basis for the administration's own deepening military
involvement in the region since, according to the administration, the Salvadoran military was not merely fighting internal opponents, but an externally armed and organized insurgency. Thus it needed help, and help was
justified. The claim of arms shipments to El Salvador also formed the

foundation of the administration's policy of hostility toward Nicaragua. So convenient was this allegation for justifying the whole edifice of Reagan's policy in Central America that it was hard to see how the policy would have been defended without it.

For instance, the intensity of the administration's anti-Cuban rhetoric and its claims of new arms shipments from Cuba and Nicaragua bore an uncanny relation to the fortunes of the Salvadoran armed forces and the Congressional budget cycle. Whenever the floundering Salvadoran army needed a new infusion of military aid, the administration would report an increase in Cuban and Nicaraguan arms shipments to the guerrillas, citing this as a rationale for why Congress should approve a major increase in military aid to the army. The evidence behind these claims was spotty at best.

Untangling the truth about Cuban and Nicaraguan aid to the FMLN is no easy matter since most of the relevant information is classified. There is general agreement that Cuba and Nicaragua did not provide significant aid to the Salvadoran guerrillas prior to the fall of 1980.[72] In September, the Carter administration certified to Congress that Nicaragua was not exporting violence to its neighbors. The finding was controversial within the intelligence community because there was some evidence of an arms flow from Nicaragua to El Salvador, albeit a limited one.[73] Carter decided to give the Sandinistas the benefit of the doubt, believing their assertion that such smuggling was contrary to government policy. This was not entirely implausible, since arms were being smuggled through Costa Rica, Honduras, and Guatemala without the cooperation of those governments.

As intelligence reports revealed an increasing flow of arms leading up to the guerrillas' January 1980 offensive, the Carter administration felt compelled to suspend economic assistance to Nicaragua as required by law. Shortly after taking office, the Reagan administration released its White Paper, *Communist Interference in El Salvador,* alleging a global campaign to arm the FMLN conducted by Cuba, Nicaragua, the Soviet Union, Vietnam, and Eastern Europe. The White Paper charged, inter alia, that communist countries had promised eight hundred tons of arms to the Salvadoran guerrillas and delivered two hundred tons in late 1980.[74]

Upon close examination, the White Paper proved to be grossly exaggerated and, in places, intentionally misleading. The captured documents upon which it was based did not support most of its conclusions. The two hundred-ton figure, for instance, was constructed not from any evidence in the documents, but from the amount of equipment that *could* have been sent from Cuba to Nicaragua based on the volume of air traffic between the two nations, and then *could* have been smuggled into El Salvador. The only actual delivery of arms is reported in a document dated September 26, 1980, which says that only four tons of arms had arrived. The eight hundred-ton figure was also an extrapolation rather than a figure actually reported in the documents themselves.[75]

In several instances, the documents were mistranslated in ways that distorted their meaning, and portions of the documents that were not supportive of the administration's case were either ignored or not publicly released. When read in their entirety, the documents showed a guerrilla movement desperate for arms and having a very difficult time acquiring them. Both the Nicaraguans and the Soviets, in particular, were extremely reluctant to provide supplies or, in the Nicaraguan case, to allow their national territory to be used as a smuggling route. Even the State Department's principal analyst of the documents admitted that parts of the White Paper were "misleading" and "overembellished."[76]

After the failure of the FMLN's January offensive, the Cubans and Nicaraguans halted their arms assistance at least temporarily. The Nicaraguans were responding to a U.S. warning that the maintenance of constructive relations and the resumption of U.S. economic assistance depended upon terminating aid to the FMLN. By mid-March, both Cuba and Nicaragua were giving the United States assurances that they had halted their aid to the FMLN, and intelligence indicated that the flow of arms was, in fact, much reduced.[77]

On April 1, 1980, however, the Reagan administration cut off economic assistance to Nicaragua anyway. Since that time, the extent of Cuban and Nicaraguan aid to the Salvadoran insurgents has been a matter of intense controversy. The administration has insisted that the arms flow resumed in May 1981, eventually reaching a volume equivalent to the flow just prior to the final offensive. But very little evidence has been provided to support this claim. The administration argues that to release the evidence it has would jeopardize sensitive sources and methods of intelligence collection. Skeptics doubt that the administration has any persuasive evidence to release.

Among those people who have access to classified information, judgments seem to depend upon whether the observer is predisposed to believe the worst about the Cubans and Nicaraguans or insists upon proof beyond a reasonable doubt. Congressman Michael Barnes, chairman of the House Subcommittee on Western Hemisphere Affairs, said in 1983 that he had seen all the evidence the administration had and it was not persuasive. Wayne Smith, former head of the U.S. diplomatic mission in Cuba, also had access to the classified evidence before his retirement in 1982, and he concluded that the evidence "has never been solid. . . . While some arms have been sent from Cuba to El Salvador, the quantities are almost certainly far less than alleged." He added that he had spoken with analysts in the intelligence community about this issue and that they agreed with his assessment.[78]

In 1984, David MacMichael, a CIA analyst responsible for assessing the arms flow from Nicaragua to El Salvador (as he had been responsible for assessing the arms flow from North to South Vietnam during the Indochina War), went public to say that there was no credible evidence of any arms flow into El Salvador from Nicaragua.[79]

On the other side of the ledger, the House Intelligence Committee concluded in 1983 that the Nicaraguans and Cubans were involved in smuggling arms to El Salvador, although the report was silent on the quantities involved, thereby papering over differences within the committee on that key issue.[80] The administration also produced several defectors from Nicaragua and the Salvadoran guerrilla movement to testify about Cuban and Nicaraguan arms smuggling.[81]

The administration had some difficulty explaining its inability to intercept a single arms shipment after early 1981, given that the U.S. had surrounded Nicaragua and El Salvador with a vast network of intelligence-gathering resources. Even the "night flights" that were allegedly the main means of transporting arms never seemed to crash—an unusual run of luck for low-flying small planes engaged in smuggling.[82]

Assembling all the bits and pieces of evidence, it seemed reasonably certain that there had on occasion been a flow of arms from Cuba and Nicaragua to El Salvador; that the Salvadorans used Nicaragua as safe haven with the consent, albeit sometimes reluctant, of the Sandinistas; and that the dimensions of outside aid were substantially smaller and less consequential for the course of the Salvadoran conflict than the Reagan administration portrayed them. This had important implications for Cuban and Nicaraguan support for Contadora, since it meant they would probably be prepared to accept and abide by an agreement requiring a halt in their aid to the FMLN. Although the FMLN would obviously not be pleased by such a development, neither would it be crippled by it.

Overall, the results of Cuba's strategy for coping with the Reagan administration have been mixed. Cuba's military buildup appeared to have reduced the danger of a direct U.S. attack on Cuba, although that remained a possibility if the crisis in Central America were to flare into wider war. Not that U.S. military activity was declining; on the contrary. The United States continued to conduct large-scale military exercises in the Caribbean, both to intimidate Cuba and to practice for the eventuality of an actual attack. The invasion of Grenada, for example, was practiced during the Ocean Venture 1981 exercises when U.S. forces assaulted "Amber in the Amberdines"—a clear reference to Grenada in the Grenadines. The Ocean Venture 1982 exercises included mock saturation bombings of the ports and airfields of an island nation, "Brown," which, according to the forces attributed to it, could only have been Cuba. In the exercise, the purpose of the bombings was to punish "Brown" for supporting insurgency in Central America.

On the diplomatic front, Cuba had much less to show for its efforts. The Reagan administration steadfastly refused to enter into bilateral discussions with Cuba about Central America. The Contadora nations remained frustrated by the unwillingness of the United States to allow a regional solution that would require a significant reduction of the U.S. military presence. Regarding Nicaragua, the Reagan administration seemed to grow increasingly adamant about overthrowing the Sandinistas, and no diplomatic initiative by Nicaragua or the Contadora nations seemed able to dissuade it.

CUBA AND THE SOVIET UNION   ▲

Washington's concerns about Cuban involvement in Central America have in reality been concerns about the Soviet Union. Even though the Soviets themselves had a surprisingly limited presence in the region, as Chapter 10 demonstrates, Cubans have always and everywhere been seen as the vanguard of Soviet interests.

Cuba's partnership with the Soviet Union and the potential danger it holds for U.S. interests are real, although the relationship has not always been realistically portrayed. Cuba has never been the Soviet satellite so often depicted in polemics from Washington. Though its connection with the Soviet Union has been Cuba's most important bilateral relationship since 1961, it has been a complex and often tense one. The economic, military, and political facets of Cuban-Soviet relations have varied tremendously over the years, and not always in harmony with one another.

The Soviet Union did not rush to the aid of the Cuban revolution in 1959.[83] Instead it remained cautious in its relations with Havana until the deterioration of relations between Cuba and the United States was well advanced. Washington and Havana shared responsibility for the spiral of mutual hostility, but once Washington undertook to strangle the Cuban revolution economically and subvert it militarily, Havana was forced to find a patron willing and able to defend it. Moscow simply stepped in to fill the void. Without Soviet assistance, the Cuban economy could not have survived the severing of ties with the United States; without Soviet arms, Cuba's revolution could not have survived U.S. efforts to overthrow it.[84]

The Cuban missile crisis nearly shattered Moscow's relationship with Havana. For Cuba, the missiles were a deterrent against a U.S. invasion; when they were withdrawn, the Cubans felt betrayed because they were stripped of their newly acquired weapons and insulted because they were left out of the negotiations that ended the crisis. But Cuba had nowhere else to go. When preliminary feelers about a possible rapprochement with the United States produced no results in 1963 and early 1964, Cuba repaired and deepened its relations with the Soviet Union.

Still, the animosity produced by the missile crisis did not dissipate quickly or easily. Cuban-Soviet relations during the late 1960s were marked by major political and ideological conflicts on both foreign and domestic issues. Cuba's economic strategy emphasized central planning and an almost exclusive reliance on moral incentives at a time when the Soviets were criticizing such policies as inefficient and were themselves moving away from them. Internationally, Cuba was supporting guerrilla movements in Latin America and attacking the Soviet policy of peaceful coexistence.

Cuba denounced the Soviet Union's pursuit of detente as an abdication of proletarian internationalism, an abandonment of anti-imperialist struggles in the Third World. To Cuba, peaceful coexistence was a fraud in which the interests of the Third World would be sacrificed on the altar of superpower accord. The Cubans vocally demanded that the Soviets increase their support for national liberation struggles, but to no avail.[85]

The Soviet Union viewed the Cuban approach as adventurist and ineffective. Moscow held firm to the policy of caution and restraint in the Third World that had been adopted by the new Brezhnev leadership following the disappointments of Khrushchev's more aggressive strategy in the late 1950s and early 1960s. In Latin America in particular, Cuban and Soviet interests were divergent. Moscow was interested in establishing diplomatic and economic relations in the region, even with regimes participating in the OAS embargo against Cuba. Havana was only interested in overthrowing those regimes and deeply resented Moscow's efforts to court them.

Despite Cuba's rhetorical attacks on Soviet domestic and foreign policy, the bedrock of the Cuban-Soviet relationship was largely unaffected by the polemics. The Soviets continued to provide large-scale economic and military assistance to Cuba, in effect financing its "ultraleft" experiments. In its dealings with a recalcitrant Cuba, the post-Khrushchev leadership in Moscow seemed determined not to "lose" Cuba the way Khrushchev had "lost" China.

Cuban-Soviet relations improved markedly after 1968 when Castro endorsed the Soviet invasion of Czechoslovakia. At about the same time, Cuba abandoned its policy of exporting revolution because of its ineffectiveness, and for the first time officially endorsed the doctrine of peaceful coexistence.[86] On the domestic side, increased Soviet economic aid in the early 1970s played an essential role in Cuba's recovery from the economic disaster of the 1970 sugar harvest. Economic and political reforms following the harvest brought the Cuban system into much closer accord with Soviet practice, thereby eliminating another major source of discord.

In 1975 and 1976, Cuban-Soviet collaboration rose to new heights when Cuba dispatched some 36,000 combat troops to Angola. The initiative for involvement came from Cuba rather than the Soviet Union, and the Soviets were somewhat reluctant participants, but the success of the venture improved Cuban-Soviet relations significantly.[87] In 1978, the two allies mounted another joint operation, this time to help Ethiopia's leftist government defend the Ogaden region against Somalia. By the late 1970s, Cuba and the Soviet Union were cooperating in several African and Middle Eastern countries, despite some policy differences over Angola and Ethiopia.[88] These ventures, combined with Cuba's role as chief spokesman for the socialist camp in the Nonaligned Movement, provided the Soviet Union with the first really tangible benefits from its two decades of aid to Cuba.[89]

Since the early 1960s, the Soviet Union has supplied all of Cuba's military equipment without charge. Several thousand Soviet military advisers assist the Cuban armed forces in areas ranging from technical assistance to combat training.[90] The Soviet Union has also provided economic assistance to Cuba since 1961.[91] As the Cuban economy encountered difficulties at the end of the 1970s, the level of Soviet economic assistance climbed from approximately $600 million per year between 1971 and 1974 to $2 billion per year between 1975 and 1977, $3 billion in 1978 and 1979, and over $4 billion by 1984.[92]

How much influence does Soviet foreign aid buy in Havana? Even though Cuba's relationship with the Soviet Union has been as close in the 1980s as at any time since 1959, it would still be a mistake to view Cuban policy as merely derivative of Soviet policy. The Cubans have long had their own views on what a correct revolutionary foreign policy is, and they have pursued it with or without Soviet support.

Historically, these differences have been clearest in policy toward Latin America—an area of major concern to Cuba, but of only marginal geopolitical interest to Moscow. For this reason, Cuba has enjoyed considerable freedom in setting its policy toward Latin America, so long as that policy did not disrupt Soviet state-to-state relations either in Latin America or with the United States. The Soviet Union has generally conceded that Latin America is part of the sphere of influence of the United States just as Eastern Europe is in the Soviet sphere. With the sole exception of Cuba, it has not been willing to defy the United States in its "own backyard," by making a major investment of resources or prestige in a "second Cuba." Moscow is always ready, of course, to cause political problems for the United States so long as the cost is low.

Nicaragua is a perfect example of how Cuban and Soviet policies can and do conflict. Political turmoil in Central America is generally beneficial to the Soviet Union. It distracts U.S. attention from issues that are of more interest to Moscow, it corrodes U.S. relations with Latin America, and it exacerbates political debate within the United States, making it all the more difficult to achieve a foreign policy consensus. In fact, one could imagine that a direct U.S. intervention in Central America might be welcome in Moscow, for it would benefit the Soviet Union in the same way that the Soviet invasion of Afghanistan has benefited the United States. An intervention would weaken NATO and could destroy the OAS. It would divert U.S. military forces from other theaters around the world and keep them tied down indefinitely, and it would almost certainly create domestic opposition reminiscent of the Vietnam era. So long as Moscow has made no great investment of material or prestige in Central America—which it thus far has refrained from doing—U.S. intervention holds a certain attraction.

Although the Soviets are pleased to watch the United States become increasingly entangled in Central America, they have so far been unwilling to take on the economic burden of another Cuba. The overwhelming power of the United States in the region makes any Soviet political gain extremely tenuous, and Moscow does not have much to gain over what their partnership with Cuba already provides. Thus the Soviets have been unwilling to give the besieged Sandinistas what they need in order to guarantee their survival: large-scale military assistance to build a credible deterrent and, even more importantly, hard currency to cover their growing balance of payments deficit. Thus far, the Sandinistas have tried to piece together aid packages from a variety of sources, but the reality is that if the United States persists in its policy of unmitigated hostility, only the Soviet Union is in a position to make the long-term commitment of resources that would guarantee the Sandinistas' survival. Despite Cuba's advice to the Nicaraguans to avoid such a situation, the United States has placed Nicaragua in almost identically the same situation Cuba faced two and a half decades ago.

Nicaragua is far more important to Cuba. The Cubans are deeply committed to the survival of the Nicaraguan revolution, a commitment that takes second place only to their own survival. The Cubans themselves lack the resources to make a decisive difference in the ability of the Sandinistas to survive, but the Cubans have considerable leverage with the Soviet Union. Fidel Castro will go to great lengths to secure as much Soviet support for the Sandinistas as possible. His refusal to attend the funeral of Konstantin Chernenko because of the Soviets' apparent timidity in the face of U.S. military exercises in the Caribbean was a signal to Moscow that there would be costs involved in its relations with Havana if it remained unwilling to give greater support to Nicaragua.[93]

A Soviet response was forthcoming almost immediately; after succeeding Chernenko, Mikhail Gorbachev publicly suggested that the role of Pakistan in Afghanistan was parallel to what Washington alleged Nicaragua was doing in El Salvador, and therefore if Washington insisted on taking military measures against Nicaragua, it could hardly expect that the Soviet Union might not take parallel action in an area vital to its national interests.[94]

If the Soviets were serious about such symmetry, it meant that the events in Central America and relations between the superpowers would be directly linked as never before. But the Soviets' earnestness was perhaps belied by the fact that they remained unwilling to provide economic assistance on a scale sufficient to really improve Nicaragua's deteriorating economic situation. President Daniel Ortega's May 1985 trip to Moscow produced a grand furor in Washington, coming as it did only days after the Congress rejected President Reagan's request for military aid for the contras, but it did not produce a qualitative increase in Soviet assistance.[95] It remains to be seen how far Cuba can push the Soviet Union into a commitment to the Nicaraguan revolution that Moscow is obviously reluctant to make.

A BASIS FOR ACCORD?   ▲

The renewal of Cuba's interest in the revolutionary potential of Central America, and its willingness to once again provide significant amounts of material support for Latin American guerrillas are not simply a return to the romantic policies of the 1960s. Cuban aid in recent years has been much more selectively targeted, flowing almost exclusively to movements that have a strong political base of support and a reasonable chance of overthrowing the incumbent regime. Only a handful of Latin American movements, most of them in Central America, have met these criteria.

Even then, Cuba's policy has been a cautious one, following the precedent set in 1979 with the Nicaraguan revolution. Only when it appeared that increased Cuban aid might make the pivotal difference in the Salvadoran guerrillas' final offensive of January 1981 were the Cubans willing to become more involved, as they did at the end of the Nicaraguan revolution. But with the failure of that offensive, the Cubans became increasing skeptical of the Salvadorans' chances for military victory. They claim to have halted arms shipments to the guerrillas in early 1981, and the United States has not been able to produce persuasive evidence to the contrary. In Guatemala, Honduras, and Costa Rica, Cuba's role has been surprisingly limited, and in the latter two, the Cubans appear to doubt that objective conditions for armed struggle exist.

Despite the general assumption in Washington that Cuba seeks to create political instability and conflict in Central America, there are strong incentives for the Cubans to favor a reduction of tension in the area and negotiated political solutions to the region's conflicts. The Cubans are clearly fearful, as are the Contadora nations, that the continued escalation of those conflicts will eventually result in direct U.S. intervention. Such intervention, whether it came in Nicaragua or El Salvador, would be a disaster for Central Americans, including Cuba's allies, and would quickly produce regionwide conflict that could ultimately endanger the security of Cuba itself.

While the Cubans have been building their military strength in order to raise the cost of a possible U.S. attack, they have also vigorously pursued the diplomatic option by encouraging efforts at regional peacemaking and trying, albeit unsuccessfully, to reduce the level of bilateral tensions with the United States. From bilateral initiatives almost every year since 1981, to support for every initiative by Mexico, Venezuela, and the Contadora nations, the Cubans have made it clear that they are willing to contribute positively to diplomatic solutions of the region's conflicts.

Cuba's stated willingness to cooperate in the achievement of a regional agreement and to abide by its terms may well be sincere, for it follows the pattern of Cuban policy in Africa. After victory of the Cuban-supported forces in Angola, the Cubans were surprisingly amenable to Western diplomatic initiatives aimed at reducing conflicts in southern Africa. When cross-border raids by the Katangan gendarmes became a point of serious friction between Angola and Zaire in 1981 and 1982, Cuba urged the Angolan government to negotiate an accord with Mobutu, and then helped disarm the Katangans and relocate them away from the border. Cuba was also helpful to the Carter administration's efforts to achieve an agreement providing for the independence of Namibia and endorsed the Lancaster House Accords that brought Zimbabwe's civil war to a peaceful conclusion.[96]

The motivation behind Cuba's reasonableness was not magnanimity, but self-interest. The Cubans wanted to stabilize the regional political situation in order to consolidate the government in Angola. The defense of this newly successful revolution was accorded much higher priority than bringing about new revolutionary victories in neighboring countries. In the case of Zimbabwe in particular, the Cubans were extremely sensitive to the policies of the "front-line states," and were not willing to pursue a regional policy that was illegitimate in the eyes of that key constituency.

It appears that the same logic is guiding Cuba's Central American policy; the survival of Nicaragua is Cuba's top priority in the region, and any political agreement that advances the prospects of the Sandinistas' survival is probably capable of garnering Cuba's endorsement and support. The Contadora nations are the Central American equivalent of the "front-line" states, and Cuba will almost certainly follow their lead on any political initiative aimed at achieving a political settlement. Since a Contadora agreement based on the objectives agreed to in 1983, and spelled out more precisely in the 1984 draft treaty, would result in an end to U.S. and Honduran support for the contras, it would go a long way toward guaranteeing Nicaragua's security. Here, then, is a potential point where U.S. and Cuban interests in Central America may coincide. Many policy analysts in the United States have argued that Contadora represents the best hope for a peaceful solution to the regional crisis and hence for averting an intervention that would be disastrous for long-term U.S. relations with the hemisphere. Even the Reagan administration has been forced to give at least rhetorical support for Contadora, although Washington's actions have often belied its rhetoric.

But in Washington, there is no apparent recognition of this coincidence of U.S. and Cuban interests. Cuba remains a totem for U.S. policy in Central America, the Evil Empire's outpost in "our own backyard," and the rationale for returning to a Latin America policy that harks back to the days of the first Cold War. Everything the Cubans do is still seen as inimical to the United States, and this myopia prevents Washington from taking seriously Cuba's offers to discuss a settlement in the region or taking advantage of the fissures in the Cuban-Soviet partnership that are appearing over the Central America issue.

10

THE SOVIET UNION

Cole Blasier

Ever since the eruption of the Nicaraguan revolution in 1978, the policy of the United States toward Central America has been shaped by Washington's concern that the Soviet Union and Cuba might exploit the regional crisis to gain some strategic advantage over the United States. Under President Reagan, U.S. officials have gone so far as to blame the very existence of the regional crisis on external subversion by America's global adversaries. As President Reagan put it, "The trouble that is going on down there . . . is revolution exported from the Soviet Union and from Cuba," actions he characterized as "the first real communist aggression on the American mainland."[1]

U.S. officials have spoken so often and so alarmingly about Soviet actions in the Caribbean Basin that one might think the region is at the center of Soviet policy. In fact, Central America and the entire western hemisphere (with the notable exception of Cuba) has never been a high priority for the Soviet Union. Diplomatic and economic ties with the area have been few, largely because the region has been so closely tied to the United States, and because Latin America is geostrategically marginal to the traditional focus of Soviet foreign policy—its immediate border areas. In the one place where the Soviets made a major commitment of resources—Cuba—the cost has been so high that Soviet leaders have been cautious about acquiring new clients elsewhere in the hemisphere.

This, of course, does not mean that Moscow has been uninterested in developments in Central America. On the contrary, the growth of radical revolutionary movements with a Marxist or "anti-imperialist" ideological bent is welcomed in the Soviet Union. Even though such movements have not been led by local Communist Parties aligned with Moscow, their radical nationalism challenges U.S. hegemony. To the extent that the Soviets can encourage and support such movements without incurring any major cost to foreign policy objectives that have higher priority, they will undoubtedly do so, acting directly through local communists, and—so long as their interests coincide—through Cuba.

The Soviet Union's role in Central America is of critical concern in Washington because, in and of itself, the regional conflict can pose no significant threat to the security interests of the United States. It is only the Soviet presence that holds the potential for endangering U.S. security. But how involved in Central America has the Soviet Union actually been? To what extent are the region's revolutionary movements beholden, either materially or ideologically, to Moscow?

SANDINO, MARTÍ, AND THE COMMUNIST   ▲
INTERNATIONAL

Today's revolutionaries in Central America are the successors of Augusto César Sandino in Nicaragua and Agustín Farabundo Martí in El Salvador, the revolutionary martyrs of the 1930s for whom the contemporary revolutionary movements in these two countries are named. Then, as now, armed rebels from the left sought to unseat right-wing governments and eliminate U.S. influence from their countries. Then, as now, the United States feared that local rebellions were backed by extra-hemispheric powers—especially the Soviet Union—acting through proxies within the hemisphere (in the 1920s and 1930s it was the new revolutionary government in Mexico rather than Cuba that Washington regarded as Moscow's proxy). Then, as now, Washington worried that its inability to defeat the rebellions would open the hemisphere to foreign penetration, thereby endangering vital U.S. interests.

When the U.S. marines landed in Nicaragua in 1927 to resolve a conflict between Nicaraguan liberals and conservatives by installing a conservative president, one liberal general, Augusto Sandino, refused to accept the U.S.-imposed settlement. Instead, he withdrew his forces to the interior and launched a guerrilla war against the marines that lasted for nearly six years. In his first manifesto on July 1, 1927, Sandino spoke as one of the "oppressed" who opposed the Yankees who had come "to murder us in our own land."[2] The general's romantic guerrilla operations and his defiance of the Colossus of the North aroused sympathy in Latin America and elsewhere in the world.

Sandino's rebellion took place amidst a complex political rivalry over Central America involving the United States, Mexico, and the Soviet Union. The United States was intent upon maintaining its naval supremacy in the Caribbean, preserving its control over the only canal across the isthmus, and protecting the vested business interests of U.S. citizens in various countries of the region. In the aftermath of the Mexican revolution, Mexico

considered Central America a zone of special interest and an area of potential conflict with the United States. The Soviet Union was interested both
in advancing the world revolution and stirring up difficulties for the United
States in its "own backyard" as part of its long-term campaign against U.S.
imperialism.

The Mexican government supported Sandino's guerrilla war against U.S.
occupation forces in Nicaragua, giving the general a headquarters in Mexico
City and 2,000 pesos a month.[3] The executive committee of the Communist
International, attracted by the political turmoil in Central America, urged
anti-imperialists everywhere to help Sandino in his fight against "American
imperialism," and established the Hands Off Nicaragua committees to
oppose U.S. policy.[4]

Agustín Farabundo Martí, a Salvadoran Communist, was detached from
the International Red Aid, a Comintern-affiliated legal aid society, to serve
on Sandino's general staff as his personal secretary. Martí appears to have
tried to pressure Sandino in the direction of a more radical social revolution
but the latter insisted that "neither the extreme right, nor the extreme left
but a united front is our slogan."[5]

Before 1929, Soviet relations with the Mexican government were cordial.
At the end of that year, however, General Ortiz Rubio was chosen president
of Mexico. A staunch anticommunist, he immediately launched a wave of
repression against the Mexican Communist Party and in 1930 broke relations with the Soviet Union. Torn between his Mexican patrons and Communist International supporters, Sandino opted to maintain his close ties
with Mexico. He dismissed Farabundo Martí from his staff and shortly
thereafter the Comintern denounced him as a traitor.[6]

Martí said Sandino had "betrayed the world anti-imperialist movement
and converted himself into a petit bourgeois liberal caudillo." Sandino
maintained that "an effort was made to twist a movement for national
defense . . . into a struggle of a social character. I opposed that."[7] A
1972 Soviet book on Central America reaffirmed Martí's charge that Sandino had refused to accept a communist program, arguing that Sandino's
coming to terms with internal "reaction" was a profound mistake leading
to the defeat of his movement and his own assassination by Somoza.[8]
After the Sandinistas' victory, however, an authoritative Soviet study characterized Sandino as a "revolutionary democrat" and "patriot," an obviously positive assessment of someone with a noncommunist position.[9]

After Martí failed to win Sandino to communism, he returned to El
Salvador as the Salvadoran representative of the International Red Aid.
With a few followers, Martí traveled the country organizing the peasants.
In 1930 and 1931, the Communists were committed to electoral participation as a means of gaining political power. They supported the successful
campaign of Labor Party candidate Arturo Araujo in 1931, only to have
him jail several of the Party's top leaders, including Farabundo Martí.
When Araujo was ousted by General Maximiliano Hernández Martínez in
1931, the Communists at first sought to resume electoral activity. They

participated in the municipal and congressional elections of January 1932, but subsequently denounced the results as fraudulent. This led the Party to abandon its electoral strategy for one of armed insurrection. Led by Martí, the Central Committee decided on January 7, 1932, to organize an insurrection.[10]

Before the uprising could be mounted, Martí and two of his followers were captured and shot. When the insurrection was finally launched, the Communists, whose experience was primarily in political rather than paramilitary mobilization, proved no match for the army. Some soviets were established briefly in a few communities, but soon the insurrection was brutally suppressed, with deaths estimated at between twenty thousand and thirty thousand persons.[11] The insurrection was a disaster for the Salvadoran Communist Party. Most of its leaders were liquidated and its political base, the Indian peasants, was decimated and dispersed. The Party was not reorganized until 1936, and even then it took more than thirty years for it to really recover.

The role of the Communist International in Sandino's guerrilla resistance to the United States and in mounting the Salvadoran insurrection illustrates the historic willingness of the Soviet Union to take advantage of political turmoil, especially if it weakens a Soviet adversary. But it also demonstrates the difficulties that Moscow has encountered trying to affect events in a distant and unfamiliar area.

Washington's view that outsiders meddling in Central America constitute a challenge to U.S. hegemony has changed little from the early decades of the century, and the Soviet Union's readiness to try to take advantage of political instability there has not changed much either.

LATIN AMERICAN COMMUNISTS AND   ▲
THE "PEACEFUL ROAD"

After the suppression of popular revolts in Nicaragua and El Salvador in the early 1930s, Moscow had little contact with Central America. The Soviet government had no formal diplomatic ties with any governments in the region until after World War II when Guatemala and Costa Rica, along with many other Latin American countries, recognized the Soviet Union. The first exchange of diplomatic representatives with the region did not take place until 1970, when Moscow exchanged envoys with Costa Rica. The next formal tie did not come until 1979 when the Soviet Union promptly recognized the Sandinistas in Nicaragua after Somoza's fall. The Soviet Union has never had official relations with El Salvador, Honduras, or Guatemala and does not appear to want them.[12]

Consequently, for most of the postwar period, the Soviet Union's primary contact with regional events was through the Communist Party in each country.[13] In general, these parties have not been very large or influential. By 1983, after a period of some growth in party membership, estimates of the membership in the national parties ranged from a few hundred in El Salvador to some 3,500 in Costa Rica.[14] But despite their small size and precarious political situation, the Central American Communist Parties were caught up—as were the larger Communist Parties of South America —in the debate over revolutionary strategy that followed the victory of the Cuban revolution in 1959.

In the 1950s, Soviet policy stressed the peaceful road to political change in Latin America. In part this reflected Moscow's view that Latin America was not socially advanced enough to be ripe for socialist revolution, and in part it reflected doubts—based upon the experience of the Guatemalan revolution—that the United States would allow the survival of a revolutionary regime in its sphere of influence.[15]

Fidel Castro's armed overthrow of Batista in Cuba, however, gave fresh impetus to armed struggle as the path to revolutionary victory. Throughout Latin America, guerrilla movements arose trying to emulate the Cuban formula. Castro encouraged these efforts and made scathing attacks on the Communist Parties of Latin America, which, for the most part, rejected this upsurge of armed struggle as ill-founded and dangerous.

Castro's brash leadership and great influence among Latin American revolutionaries placed the USSR in an awkward position. Soviet leaders had no objection to the use of force per se, but favored it only if it would lead to durable revolutionary regimes. They winced at seeing hard-won communist and other radical networks decimated by local armed forces bolstered by U.S. counterinsurgency specialists. At the same time, they were loath to openly oppose Castro's guerrilla strategies, for fear the Chinese Communists would gain influence with Castro and come to dominate the Latin American revolutionary movements.

The Soviets' reservations about the Cubans' guerrilla *foco* theory proved correct as the guerrilla movements of the 1960s were wiped out in one country after another, setting back the cause of revolution in Latin America nearly a generation. Throughout this period and into the 1970s, the Communist Parties of Latin America held to the strategy of nonviolent political organizing and electoral competition as the best way to build a mass following.

The Communist Parties in Central America generally followed a similar strategy, preferring peaceful political competition to armed struggle wherever possible. Even in countries where the Communist Party was outlawed, such as in Nicaragua and El Salvador, it continued to seek whatever marginal political gains it could from quasilegal activity. As a result, dissident members in several countries left the Communist Party to form more aggressive armed movements of their own. It proved to be these movements that grasped the opportunity provided by the social and economic changes that had swept the region after World War II. The 1970s witnessed the rapid growth of guerrilla organizations and radicalized mass political movements in Nicaragua, El Salvador, and Guatemala. By the end of the decade, the military regimes of all three nations seemed on the brink of collapse. But as in Cuba twenty years earlier, it was not communists but "petty bourgeois adventurers" leading the revolutionary wave, with the orthodox Communist Parties in their wake, paddling frantically trying to catch up.

MOSCOW AND THE SANDINISTAS   ▲

The Sandinista National Liberation Front, founded in 1961 by Carlos Fonseca Amador, led the Nicaraguan revolution. Born in 1936, Fonseca grew up as a radical youth, tutored in Marxism by a friend who was familiar with the Guatemalan revolution of 1944 to 1954.[16] Fonseca became a Communist in 1955, joining the youth movement of the Nicaraguan Socialist Party (PSN), the Moscow-aligned Communist Party in Nicaragua.[17]

Founded in 1937, the PSN was outlawed almost immediately and remained illegal throughout the Somoza period. Although the PSN never ruled out the possibility of insurrection, the party's leadership did not believe conditions in Nicaragua were suitable for the use of violence. Instead, they sought to build a mass base of popular support through peaceful political organizing, despite the party's illegal status.

In 1957, Fonseca went as a delegate from the PSN to the Sixth World Youth and Student Festival in Moscow. He was greatly impressed by the USSR and wrote a paean to Soviet Communism entitled *A Nicaraguan in Moscow*—an uncritical account of Soviet life and a refutation of western criticisms of Soviet Communism. On returning to Nicaragua, Fonseca was arrested, jailed, tortured, and eventually exiled. In June 1959, he joined a guerrilla column of some fifty Nicaraguans and Cubans who planned to invade Nicaragua from Honduras. The Honduran army surprised the group, however, wiping it out. Wounded, Fonseca escaped to Havana.

After this experience, Fonseca split definitively with the PSN, rejecting its adherence to the line of peaceful political work. He believed that the Communists showed "insufficient interest in integrating the tactic of armed struggle in the context of the struggle against the dictatorship."[18] Only "armed popular insurrection" could remove the Somoza dictatorship.[19]

The PSN, which in December 1959 reiterated its view that military action against Somoza was premature, was not tolerant of Fonseca's heresy. When he tried to return to Nicaragua clandestinely in July 1960, the PSN publicly announced his arrival, which in turn led to his arrest and deportation.[20] The following year, Fonseca, Tomás Borge, and Silvio Mayorga founded the Sandinista National Liberation Front, dedicated to overthrowing the Somoza dynasty by force.

The PSN's adherence to the peaceful road did not change even when popular opposition to Somoza grew rapidly in the late 1970s. The gulf dividing the Sandinistas from the PSN was clearly evident in an interview with PSN First Secretary Luis Sánchez Sancho published in Moscow in

1976. There were "deep strategic and tactical divergences" between the two parties, he said, and the masses did not support the Sandinistas. He expressed willingness to collaborate with the Sandinistas but rejected their "messianic avant-gardism."[21]

As a result of such analyses, the PSN played almost no role in the Nicaraguan revolution. Moscow, which presumably got most of its information about the Nicaraguan political situation from the PSN, paid little attention to Nicaragua even after the insurrection broke out in 1978. As one Soviet analyst later observed, "The small Nicaraguan Socialist Party which was largely cut off from the masses, and which was weakened by a factional struggle, was unable to lead the antidictatorial popular movement."[22] Shafik Jorge Handal, leader of the Salvadoran Communists, was more blunt: "Latin America has had two great revolutions, that of Cuba and Nicaragua, in neither of which cases were Communists at their head. In the case of Nicaragua the experience of our brother party was disastrous, except for the part which joined the armed struggle after 1978."[23]

Neither the Soviet Union nor its local allies, the Nicaraguan Socialist Party, played any significant role in the Nicaraguan revolution. The insurrection was led by others whose ideology was radical and nationalistic, and who stood at the front of a broad and ideologically heterogeneous coalition of anti-Somoza political and economic groups.[24] The Soviets and the local Communists were certainly happy to see Somoza's demise, but they made no real contribution to attaining it.[25] After Somoza fell, the Sandinistas, not the Communists, took over the leading governmental and political positions in Nicaragua.

MOSCOW AND THE CENTRAL AMERICAN REVOLUTION   ▲

The triumph of the Nicaraguan revolution led Soviet analysts to reassess the prospects for revolution in the rest of Central America. In a series of articles published in the Soviet journal *Latinskaia Amerika* in 1980, armed struggle was endorsed as the appropriate strategy for the region's revolutionary movements. Che Guevara's theories of guerrilla warfare, severely attacked by Moscow when he originally devised them, were rehabilitated. Editor S. A. Mikoyan wrote, "As yet only the armed path has led to the victory of revolutions in Latin America. And the Nicaraguan experience affirms what had been considered refuted by some after the death of Che Guevara and the defeat of a number of other guerrilla movements."[26]

The Nicaraguan experience of a broad politico-military front leading the revolutionary struggle was endorsed by the Soviets as a correct model for other nations in Central America.[27] El Salvador and Guatemala were singled out as countries in which armed struggle based on revolutionary unity was the proper strategy. This meant, in effect, that the Communist parties of the region would subordinate themselves to these broad politico-military fronts and would have to be resigned to playing a relatively minor role. It was the price the parties paid for their long history of tailing after events.[28]

Like their Nicaraguan comrades, the Salvadoran Communists also joined the revolutionary armed opposition late. The historical burden of the repression of the Communist-led insurrection of 1932 was so severe, and its effects on the party so crippling, that it appeared to sap the spirit of armed resistance for many decades. In fact, the Communists did not become fully involved in the armed opposition until 1979, when they founded the Armed Forces of Liberation (FAL). In the previous decade, the main armed forces of the Salvadoran revolution had already been assembled.

One of the strongest revolutionary organizations established in El Salvador was the Popular Forces of Liberation (FPL), founded by the late Salvador Cayetano Carpio, former secretary general of the Salvadoran Communist Party. Carpio broke with the party in 1970 to form the FPL because the party refused to abandon its electoral strategy. "I did it when it was evident that it was not possible under the circumstances to make the party understand the necessity of a politico-military strategy, of an integral revolutionary strategy, and it was necessary to demonstrate it in practice to our people."[29] Fighting under the nom de guerre of Marcial, Carpio continued to consider himself a Marxist-Leninist, directing the struggle against U.S. imperialism and the Salvadoran oligarchy. He began with only a few close comrades, mostly from the Communist Party, lacking arms, training, and money. By 1980, the FPL had become the largest of the politico-military organizations.

In 1972, the Revolutionary Army of the People (ERP) was formed by young members of the Communist and Christian Democratic parties, and radicalized members of the middle class. Two factions developed within the ERP, one a Maoist group that insisted on a heavy military emphasis, and a second group that called for mixing military and political methods. Roque Dalton, the Salvadoran Communist and well-known poet, was a leader of the latter group.[30] The promilitary faction of the ERP charged him with betrayal, condemned him to death, and executed him. Dalton's group broke off from the ERP and formed its own organization, called the National Resistance (RN), and its own armed wing, the Armed Forces of National Resistance (FARN).

A fourth armed group, composed mainly of trade union members, was formed as the Revolutionary Workers Party of Central America (PRTC), which was organized selectively on a regional basis in 1976. The Communist Party of El Salvador (PCES) was the last group to take up arms, forming the FAL in 1979. Of the five politico-military organizations fighting against the Salvadoran armed forces in the early 1980s, the PCES was one of the smallest, having at most a few hundred combatants in the field, compared to thousands fighting with the FPL, ERP, and FARN.

The armed organizations included ex-members of the Communist Party, Castroites, Maoists, socialists, and radicals from various parties. Carpio and others, especially in the FPL, considered themselves Marxist-Leninists. But they rebelled from or rejected Moscow-sponsored strategies. While the members of these armed revolutionary movements were risking their lives, the Communist Party spent the 1970s taking part in local and national elections and working closely with reformist parties.

During most of the 1970s, the Communist Party functioned quasilegally in the National Opposition Union (UNO), collaborating with Christian and Social Democrats. As one Soviet scholar commented, the UNO recognized "the possibilities of the peaceful road of revolution, tried to achieve the unity of the people and the army by means of propaganda. With the aim of mobilizing the masses, these opposition forces developed a broad parliamentary struggle."[31] When the army rigged the results of the 1977 elections (as it had in 1972), the Communist Party concluded that another route to power would have to be found. The decision to give up the peaceful road was taken in 1977, but was not formalized until the party's Seventh Congress in 1979. General Secretary Handal explained why it took two years to implement the decision: "Our Party never had gotten to the point of condemning armed struggle . . . but other ideas and styles . . . influenced us against the development of military work."[32] The party, he concluded in another article, had "suffered more in those forty years from reformist than from leftist illnesses."[33]

By early 1981, the various revolutionary political and military organizations, including the Communists, were edging toward unity. The five politico-military organizations joined together in the Farabundo Martí Front for National Liberation (FMLN), named for the Communist Party leader of the 1920s and 1930s. Meanwhile, the popular organizations, including the Communist Party, created a political body, the Democratic Revolutionary Front (FDR). Finally, these two groups joined together to form one broad revolutionary coalition (FDR-FMLN) including everyone from dissident Christian Democrats to Maoists. The Communists joined the FDR-FMLN as a minority, and not a large minority at that.[34]

Since the Salvadoran Communists' decision to take up arms, Soviet spokesmen have never concealed their strong political and moral support for the armed opposition in El Salvador. Nor is there any reason to believe that they would hesitate to provide material support if they deemed it in their interest to do so. But whether the Soviet Union has actually provided material support to the FMLN is another question. In early 1981 the Department of State published a much criticized White Paper describing Salvadoran Communist Shafik Jorge Handal's travels to various Communist countries in search of arms. The Soviet Union was prominently featured in the report, but the documents upon which the White Paper was based actually showed Soviet reluctance to become involved in aiding the Salvadorans. In one, Handal expressed frustration at his inability to get the Soviets to finally agree to ship weapons provided by other Eastern bloc countries. None of the documents indicate that Moscow finally did agree to help, and there was no other indication in the documents of a Soviet role in providing material support for the FDR-FMLN.[35] No additional evidence has been uncovered since, suggesting that there was probably little or no direct assistance from the Soviet Union.[36]

The other Central American nation that the Soviets came to see as ripe for armed revolution was Guatemala. Guatemala has intermittently been the scene of fierce civil conflict and guerrilla war since the fall of the Arbenz regime in 1954. The Communist Party, known as the Guatemalan Labor Party (PGT), has been illegal, active, and vocal during much of this time. In fact, however, the main guerrilla and revolutionary forces have been composed of other groups, many of whose members were ex-Communists. The PGT, like its fraternal parties in Nicaragua and El Salvador, tended to focus on political rather than guerrilla activities. Over the years, many members left the party to take up arms in the mountains. Although the PGT came out for the use of force in 1969, it did not actually commit itself fully to armed struggle until 1981.[37]

Many of the revolutionary organizations in Guatemala are now united in the Guatemala National Revolutionary Unity (URNG), which includes the Rebel Armed Forces (FAR), the Guerrilla Army of the Poor (EGP), and the Revolutionary Organizations of the People in Arms (ORPA). These are all anti-imperialist, Marxist organizations that are nevertheless independent of the PGT. The Communists, still not in the front in 1984, spoke positively about it adding, however, that it should be made "complete, without any exceptions," that is, the PGT should be admitted to it as well.[38]

MOSCOW'S RELATIONS WITH NICARAGUA'S REVOLUTIONARY GOVERNMENT ▲

In one sense, the overthrow of Somoza and the seizure of power by the Sandinistas in July 1979 was a political defeat for the Soviet Union. The Sandinistas were the principal rival of the Communists for leadership of the anti-Somoza movement. But experience had taught Moscow to swallow its pride and collaborate with leftist parties it could not defeat. A strategy designed to influence the Sandinistas required, at a minimum, prompt and continuing political support and the possibility of some material support as well.

More aware than they used to be about political opportunities in Latin America, Soviet leaders moved more rapidly to establish ties with the Sandinistas than they had with Cuba. Within hours of the Sandinista victory, General Secretary Leonid Brezhnev's message congratulating the Nicaraguan people on their victory was broadcast in Managua. *Kommunist* quoted Brezhnev as reaffirming the "sacred rights of each nation and of each country to select its own development path," and expressed the Soviet Union's readiness to normalize relations with Nicaragua.[39]

In March 1980, Moscow warmly welcomed a delegation of Sandinista

leaders and concluded a wide range of agreements on economic and technical cooperation with them.[40] Several aspects of the talks appeared significant. In the first place, although Nicaragua was not a socialist country and
the Nicaraguan Communists were not influential in the government, the
talks were conducted through Party as well as government channels. This
suggested that the Soviets hoped the FSLN might eventually evolve into a
Marxist-Leninist party as did the July 26 Movement in Cuba and the
Movement for the Popular Liberation of Angola in that former Portuguese
colony. A second interesting aspect of the talks was the wide agreement that
the two sides reached on a broad range of issues in Africa, the Middle East,
and Asia (including Afghanistan). Finally, the two nations signed an agreement on economic planning that opened up the possibility for closer economic relations than is typically the case between the Soviet Union and a
non-Communist country.

Over the next few years, a fairly large number of high level Sandinista
delegations traveled to Moscow. Sandinista leader Daniel Ortega seemed to
make at least one major visit annually, meeting with Brezhnev in May 1982,
Andropov in March 1983, Chernenko in February 1984, and Gorbachev
in May 1985.[41] By 1985, Soviet relations with Nicaragua were closer than
with most other nonsocialist countries. There was a conformity of views on
many international issues, and economic cooperation was greater, too. Yet
Sandinista leaders have not hesitated in private conversations to criticize
the Soviet Communists for being unresponsive to popular needs and shack-
led by dogma.[42]

Most of these trips have been capped by new economic agreements in the
areas of trade and technical cooperation. Soviet trade statistics show that
trade began slowly but increased rapidly in 1983 and 1984. Even so, it was
still a tiny fraction of Soviet trade and not a very large fraction of Nicaragua's. In 1981 Soviet imports from Nicaragua were far greater than exports,
but in 1982 the trade balance was sharply reversed. Soviet exports were
nearly 37 million rubles for 1982 (about $37 million, or somewhat more
at the Soviet official rate), and Soviet imports from Nicaragua were less than
6 million rubles. The figures rose to 42 and 10 million rubles in 1983.[43]
In the first six months of 1984 Soviet exports were running at nearly twice
the rate of 1983. Even more interesting was the fact that Soviet imports
during this short period were less than 1 million rubles.[44] Most of Soviet
exports to Nicaragua in 1980 to 1984 were machinery, equipment, and
transport. In 1984, the Soviets began supplying oil to Nicaragua, and
during Ortega's May 1985 visit to Moscow, agreed to supply about 90
percent of Nicaragua's petroleum needs. (Venezuela and Mexico, Nicaragua's previous suppliers, had halted shipments for a combination of political and economic reasons.) Nicaraguan exports to the Soviet Union are
mainly coffee, cotton fiber, and sugarcane.

In the first half of 1984 Soviet exports to Nicaragua were running at an
annual rate of about 100 million rubles, and it appeared that the annual
trade deficit might be nearly that much. The USSR finances machinery and

equipment at concessionary rates for export promotion; the deficit could therefore be considered a crude indicator of Soviet "assistance," less services. It may well be that certain categories of Soviet deliveries, including but not limited to arms transfers, are not reflected here.

The pattern of increased trade between Nicaragua and other members of the Council for Mutual Economic Assistance (COMECON) was similar, with Bulgaria and the German Democratic Republic the two most important East European suppliers. The importance of trade with COMECON (including the USSR) should not be exaggerated; in 1981 and 1982 (first six months) it was only from 4 to 7 percent of all Nicaragua's trade. Even though it increased significantly in 1983 and 1984, trade between Nicaragua and the COMECON nations was still only about 10 percent of all trade—less than Nicaraguan trade with the United States (before the imposition of the embargo), the European Economic Community, the other Central American countries, or the rest of Latin America.[45]

Virtually all economic aid from the Soviet Union and the rest of the COMECON countries has been in the form of either technical assistance, development project aid, or trade credits. The Soviet foreign aid program almost never includes hard currency grants since Moscow itself faces a hard currency shortage, and since such grants would only be needed to purchase goods outside the bloc. The data on Soviet economic aid clearly indicate the limits of Soviet largess. From 1979 to 1981, economic aid totaled about $125 million. It jumped sharply in 1982 to a peak of about $253 million and subsequently fell to about $146 million in 1983 and $170 million in 1984, even though Nicaragua's economic situation has deteriorated substantially, making its need all the greater.[46]

A significant portion of aid from socialist countries was given through technical cooperation. In early 1983, Soviet technicians and advisers in the country, including members of their families, numbered about 150. The East Germans had about 100 and the Bulgarians 50. All Eastern Europeans were estimated at something less than 500, although there were reportedly about 6,000 Cubans engaged in technical cooperation.[47]

In September 1983, Nicaragua was granted observer status in the COMECON. Whether it is admitted to full membership at some future date will depend on a variety of factors, not the least of which are the efforts of the United States to cut the Nicaraguan economy off from the West. So far the Sandinistas do not appear to want such close ties to the Soviet bloc, but Nicaragua's economy remains underdeveloped and deeply dependent upon foreign trade. If linkages with the West are severed as a result of U.S. policy, Nicaragua will have no choice but to fully reorient its economy toward the East—just as Cuba did twenty-five years ago.

It is not at all clear, however, that the Soviet Union is interested in paying the price necessary to acquire another client state in Latin America. Soviet burdens in Vietnam, Afghanistan, Poland, and elsewhere, not to mention a weak economy at home, do not encourage it. Moreover, Nicaragua's security situation is particularly tenuous. Surrounded by hostile neighbors, facing an army of some fifteen thousand contras, and the target of a concerted destabilization effort by the United States, Nicaragua does not appear a particularly attractive place for the Soviet Union to invest large amounts of resources.

As the war between the Nicaraguan government and the counterrevolutionary forces aided by the United States escalated, the Sandinistas undertook a major military buildup. Pressure from the United States blocked Nicaragua's efforts to purchase arms in the West, except for one agreement with France, so most of the Sandinistas' military supplies have come from either the Eastern bloc or other Third-World countries. Although the Sandinistas have acquired arms that are mostly of Soviet manufacture, until 1983 they avoided obtaining arms directly from the Soviet Union. Algeria was a primary supplier.[48]

However, as the war has intensified and the Nicaraguans' ability to purchase arms has decreased because of the shortage of hard currency, Nicaragua has relied increasingly upon direct military aid from the USSR and other Eastern bloc nations. Equipment provided thus far includes tanks, armed transport vehicles, rocket launchers, and armed helicopters.[49] Although the United States has repeatedly charged that Nicaragua is preparing to receive advanced MIG fighter aircraft from the Soviet Union by way of Cuba, no such planes have as yet appeared. According to data from the Department of Defense, Eastern bloc military aid to Nicaragua grew from very limited amounts in the years just after the fall of Somoza ($5 million in 1979 and $7 million in 1980) to ever greater quantities as relations between Nicaragua and the United States deteriorated. In 1981, President Reagan's first year in office, Soviet military aid jumped to $45 million. The following year, when the United States launched the covert war, Soviet military aid doubled to approximately $100 million. It totaled $110 million in 1983 and doubled again to $250 million in 1984.[50]

Nevertheless, Moscow has been very careful not to offer any security guarantees to the Sandinistas.[51] When Yuri Fokin, General Secretary of the Soviet Foreign Ministry, was asked how the Soviet Union would react to a U.S. invasion of Nicaragua, he replied, "We will support Nicaragua politically in every way." In general, Soviet media coverage of Nicaragua's war with the contras has stressed the Sandinistas' ability to defend themselves.[52]

UNDERSTANDING THE SOVIET ROLE ▲

The Soviet role in Central America has been more limited than the Reagan administration's rhetoric would suggest. Moscow has never had much of a direct presence in the region, and still did not in mid-1985, except in Nicaragua. The Soviet role in Nicaragua has only recently become significant, a development that has been largely a product of U.S. hostility, which forces Managua to seek a patron and protector against Washington. Even

then, Moscow seems reluctant to take on the economic or security burden
of "another Cuba" in the western hemisphere.

Certainly, the Soviet Union did not create the revolutions in Central
America. Evidence of direct aid from the Soviet Union to the revolutionary
movements was sparse; what evidence existed seemed to indicate that the
Cubans were playing the leading role, but even they had not become active
in the region until after the outbreak of the Nicaraguan revolution.

In both Nicaragua and El Salvador, the pro-Soviet Communist Parties
participated little and late in the insurrections. In fact, the revolutionary
movements in those nations developed in opposition to the strategy and
tactics of the Communists. While the Communists in Guatemala have had
a longer history of armed struggle against the military dictatorship, there
too they have been but one revolutionary group among many contending
for leadership of the popular movement.

The Nicaraguan revolution made the pro-Soviet Communists in Central
America face up to two unpleasant facts: their strategy of peaceful political
organizing was a failure, and, as a result of that failure, other revolutionary
movements willing to engage in armed struggle had taken over leadership
of the left. In order to play any role whatever in the revolutionary process,
the Communists were forced to seek unity with the broad and ideologically
heterogeneous radical movements that had taken over the role of political
vanguard. In Nicaragua, this meant supporting the Sandinista regime,
despite the fact that PSN members had virtually no role in it. In El
Salvador, it meant subordinating the PCES to the joint command of the
FDR-FMLN, led in the political domain by Christian and Social Democrats
and led on the battlefield by a renegade Communist.

The Cubans, of course, have had a much greater role in Central America.
The Sandinistas, several of the revolutionary organizations in El Salvador,
and several in Guatemala have had Cuban support for a decade or more.
But Cuba's role and its influence in the region are not equivalent to Soviet
influence. Certainly the Cubans and Soviets share many interests and objectives—including a desire to weaken the position of the United States in
Latin America. But as the controversies of the 1960s demonstrated, Latin
America is a much higher priority for Cuba than it is for the USSR, and
that difference can lead to sharp disagreements on practical policy. In recent
years, Moscow seems more inclined to follow Havana's lead in Central
America, but even then with more cautiousness than Havana is happy with.

The Soviet Union's limited involvement in Central America does not
mean that Moscow has no interest in the region. On the contrary, the Soviets
would like nothing better than to see the deterioration of U.S. influence in
an area traditionally under U.S. hegemony. Moscow would certainly like to
see the emergence of Marxist-Leninist regimes in Central America, so long
as it is not called upon to keep their economies solvent with large infusions
of aid. While the United States doesn't want "another Cuba" for strategic
reasons, the Soviet Union doesn't want to have to pay for one.

In any event, the Soviets are not confident that Marxist-Leninist regimes could survive in Central America in the short term, given the overwhelming power of the United States and its reluctance to tolerate such regimes in its sphere of influence. Cuba is regarded as an exceptional case because of the accord reached with Washington at the time of the 1962 missile crisis. The Soviets would probably settle for revolutions in Central America that produced radical nationalist regimes independent of, and perhaps hostile to, the United States. Since such regimes would not be Marxist-Leninist, they could not make strong economic or security claims on Moscow.

Soviet objectives in Central America are, therefore, more political than they are strategic or military. While military planners in the United States worry about the possibility that some Caribbean Basin regime might allow the creation of a Soviet military outpost that could endanger vital sea lanes of communication and supply, the Soviets do not have great need of such an outpost. The Soviet navy can send ships out on the high seas just about wherever it wishes, including the Caribbean, but it remains at a tremendous conventional military disadvantage in the area, compared to the United States. It is unlikely that the Soviets would deploy any significant forces into such a vulnerable area far from their home bases. The acquisition of basing facilities in the Caribbean would not alter this unfavorable balance.

Some policymakers in Washington have argued that President Reagan's policy has had the effect of intimidating the Soviets and Cubans, causing them to be more cautious and to be more open to political solutions to the regional crisis. This may be true of Nicaragua's policy of aiding the Salvadoran guerrillas, and it may even be true of Cuba's policy as well. But the Soviets have not been intimidated. They tripled their military assistance to Cuba in the face of U.S. threats, and expanded both their military and their economic assistance to Nicaragua in almost direct response to the escalation of U.S. hostility. Rather than driving the Soviet presence out of the region, Washington's recent policies have given the Soviets a wider opportunity for increasing their presence and influence at relatively low cost—exactly the sort of circumstance under which the Soviets are most likely to become more active.

Ultimately, Soviet leaders have little to fear from U.S. military intervention in Central America. They have made no commitment to the security of any Central American regime, so the survival of the Sandinistas, let alone the fate of Central American revolutionaries who have not yet come to power, threatens no vital Soviet interest. In fact, an interventionist U.S. policy plays into Moscow's hands. Not only has such a policy radicalized Central American politics, driving the revolutionaries toward Moscow, but it has also antagonized the rest of Latin America, damaging U.S. relations with countries of much greater importance, such as Mexico, Brazil, and Argentina.

11

MEXICO, VENEZUELA, AND THE CONTADORA INITIATIVE

Terry Karl

In his address to a joint session of the U.S. Congress on May 16, 1984, President Miguel de la Madrid of Mexico said, "We . . . reject, without exception, all military plans that would seriously endanger the security and development of the region. This continent must not be a scenario for generalized violence that becomes increasingly difficult to control, as has occurred in other parts of the world."

President de la Madrid's strong and open disagreement with U.S. policy toward Central America—in the very heart of Washington—symbolizes a striking break from past foreign policy behavior by Latin American regional powers. In the midst of a major U.S. military buildup in Central America and a commitment by the Reagan administration to undermine the Nicaraguan government, neighboring countries have warned against foreign military intervention from any source and have insisted upon respect for the fundamental principles of international law: the peaceful resolution of conflict, the sovereign equality of states, and the right of self-determination. These actions of the so-called Contadora countries of Mexico, Venezuela, Colombia, and Panama in Central America also represent a qualitative change in U.S.–Latin American relations.

The debate between the United States and the countries of the region over the meaning of security is one measure of this change. For the first time in the postwar era, Latin American nations have put forward their own definitions of collective security, thereby challenging some of the basic assumptions underlying the Inter-American System established after World War II. They argue that conceptions of hemispheric peace must be linked to social reform as well as to the more traditional balance of military power between the United States and the Soviet Union. Thus they have proposed a series of negotiated trade-offs between U.S. security interests and Latin American sovereignty to cope with revolutionary conflict in a setting of sharpened global competition. They have given meaning to these suggested trade-offs through the formation of Contadora and the development of a comprehensive peace treaty for Central America.

The new level of political engagement and will on the part of regional actors is a second measure of change. Their perseverance in the Central American conflict has come as a surprise to many politicians and academics accustomed to understanding Latin American foreign policies within frameworks of dependency or pragmatic realism. Specialists predicted that the effect of a massive U.S. military commitment to the region, combined with the heightened economic vulnerability of Latin American countries to debt crunches and falling oil prices, would force a tactical retreat on the issue of Central America, particularly by Mexico and Venezuela. Independent positions would eventually be curtailed in the face of an aggressive Republican administration determined to restore unquestioned U.S. supremacy on the continent. Given the obvious differences in power, neighboring countries ultimately would follow the general policies of a United States willing to resort to military force or would remain somewhat remote from the crisis. Events since 1981 have only partially born out these predictions. Despite powerful pressures to reduce their activities, regional actors have continued to maintain a presence in the Central American entanglement.

The successful utilization of collective action in the international arena, aimed in part at the United States, is a third indicator of this shift in U.S.–Latin American relations. Although multilateral activity has been a traditional Latin American strategy for dealing with power asymmetries, its impact has been particularly important in Central America. Mexico, Venezuela, Colombia, and Panama have critically affected the consolidation of various political and military forces inside Nicaragua and El Salvador, the level of tension in moments of acute crisis, and above all, the parameters for a political solution to the Central American conflict. This has not been an easy task. To the dismay of Latin American governments, their actions have often placed them in direct conflict with both the Reagan administration and significant sectors of their domestic constituencies. In addition, contrary to Bolivarian images of Latin American unity, they have frequently had strong disagreements with each other. Yet rather than remain aloof from Central America, they have unexpectedly done the reverse: As the danger of a full-blown conflict increases and U.S. military pressure on the region mounts, they have united their foreign policies through the Contadora initiative and become the major international symbol of a nonmilitary solution for Central America.

How can the autonomy and initiative of these nations be explained, particularly in light of U.S. displeasure with much of their activity? What accounts for their initial decision to get involved in the problems of their neighbors? Why have they persisted in these activities despite internal and external opposition as well as self-doubt? How have they managed to unite as a group in Contadora despite strong policy differences? Most important, what are the possibilities and limitations of their future action, either multilaterally or individually, to influence U.S. policy and resolve the Central American crisis?

This chapter examines the foreign policy of Mexico and Venezuela in Central America, especially in Nicaragua and El Salvador. It seeks to illuminate the opportunities and constraints upon regional activity as well as the roots of the Contadora initiative. Although a full treatment would include Panama and the critical role of Colombia under President Belisario Betancur, Mexico and Venezuela have been chosen due to their greater individual involvement before the formation of Contadora.[1]

MEXICAN POLICY IN CENTRAL AMERICA: 1979 TO 1982 ▲

On May 20, 1979, during a luncheon in honor of visiting Costa Rican President Rodrigo Carazo, President López-Portillo suddenly attacked "the horrendous genocide in Nicaragua" and announced that Mexico would sever relations with the government of Anastasio Somoza. His actions stunned observers of Mexican foreign policy. Although Mexico had refused to recognize the violent seizure of power from a legitimately constituted regime by authoritarian rulers in Spain and Chile, there was no precedent for breaking established relations with any country. To the contrary, a firm principle of nonintervention in the internal affairs of other countries had always reigned in the past, regardless of the nasty twists and turns of existing governments. López-Portillo's remarks signaled the beginning of a new role for Mexico in Central America.

In retrospect, the president's actions were not so unusual. Mexico's foreign policy has been based upon and consistent with its own definition of state interests since the Revolution of 1910: the security of its borders and the stability of the regime depend upon preventing foreign military interventions by political means rather than the use of force, as well as a development strategy of limited reform. These interests rest upon two immutable realities that set Mexico apart from the rest of the continent: its own revolutionary history and its proximity to the United States.

The Mexican revolution formed the basis for toleration of a wide variety of political forms in other countries as well as a relatively low fear of the outcomes of violent social change. Mexico has never shared the Cold War preoccupation with the Soviet Union or other external sources of instability that colors U.S. perceptions toward Central America. Given its own revolutionary heritage, it has consistently identified political stability, both internally and regionally, with the ability to come to terms with what are seen as inevitable forces for change. Indeed, regime survival is intrinsically linked to the country's ability to cope with economic deficiencies and political backwardness through timely limited reform. This understanding,

which permeates the Mexican state, has been applied with a vengeance to
the crisis on its borders. Mexico favors structural change within Central
American countries because the resulting stability will ultimately contribute
to the maintenance of Mexico's own regime. Already threatened by flows
of refugees into its territory and Guatemalan soldiers along its southern
flank, Mexican officials feel that their country's institutional arrangements
would be badly shaken by a regional war. At minimum, neighboring turmoil
would require the expansion of Mexico's armed forces and their concentration along the southern border. This in turn would entail an increase in
military spending at the expense of development, thus creating a change
in the current balance of civil-military relations and the possibility of
domestic radical activity.[2]

The preservation of territorial integrity and national sovereignty form the
basis of another central preoccupation of the regime. The overwhelming
hegemony of the United States, which seized over half of Mexican national
territory by force in the last century and threatened to invade during the
1938 Mexican oil nationalization, created a long-term requirement to support international norms of nonintervention and peaceful resolution of
conflict as an important means of self-preservation. Although observers
often consider Mexico's firm defense of international law and the sovereignty of nations to be motivated by the need to appease the nation's
radicals, this pillar of foreign policy is far more than the rhetorical sop to
placate the left. The reliance upon negotiated settlements and the renunciation of force between parties in conflict as a principle has enabled the
Mexican regime to survive in the midst of neighbors as politically incompatible as Guatemala, the United States, and Cuba.

The militarization of Central America has deeply exacerbated the Mexican regime's sense of threat to its own sovereignty. In part this is due to
conflicts with the Guatemalan military, one of the most dangerous and
unpredictable forces in the area. But Mexico is also worried about the
actions of the U.S. government, including a possible decision to rearm the
Guatemalan military. Feelings of vulnerability are heightened by the existence of important oil fields located in the south. While few policymakers
openly discuss the possibility of a U.S. intervention in Mexico itself, the
thought of U.S. troops on the country's southern flank and close to the oil
fields—for whatever purpose—is hardly comforting. As one high official of
the Institutional Revolutionary Party (PRI) explained: "We already share
one border with the United States. We do not want to share two."[3]

Mexico's dramatic oil-propelled change in the mid-1970s intensified
differences with the United States that had surfaced during the administration of Luis Echeverría (1970 to 1976). Oil altered Mexico's world role by
generating enormous export revenues that could be used to support foreign
policy commitments in Central America. In addition, it permitted planners
and entrepreneurs to expand Mexico's markets in the region. Finally, oil
fueled a burst of policy confidence that led state officials boldly into arenas
that they had previously not dared to enter.

Nicaragua was the first of these new arenas. In 1979, President López-Portillo initiated an international diplomatic offensive against Somoza that was joined by other Latin American countries. This international ostracism laid the groundwork for blocking the Carter administration's proposal to the OAS for a "peacekeeping force" to intervene in Nicaragua in order to prevent a FSLN victory. Mexico's initiative marked a historic moment in U.S.–Latin American relations—the first diplomatic rebuff from the OAS to a U.S. request for the use of force on the continent. Once military action was effectively circumscribed, Mexico continued to give political support as well as quiet financial assistance to the resistance against Somoza until the dynasty was defeated. Due to its firm position on the renunciation of the use of force in international relations, there was one limit to its support: when other Latin American countries airlifted arms to the anti-Somoza forces, Mexico did not participate.

As soon as the FSLN took power, López-Portillo promptly emerged as an outspoken defender and a strategic ally of the new government, implementing a Mexican definition of "containment." Fearing that intense hostility from the United States would ultimately force the Sandinistas into an undesirable radicalization process under Cuban tutelage, his administration attempted to create a third path by granting a virtual blank check to Nicaragua. Mexico guaranteed Nicaragua's external debt, became a major aid donor, and was its major source of much-needed petroleum.[4] For three years Nicaragua received all of its oil under long-term credits, with almost no cash down, as part of the 1980 San José Accord sponsored jointly with Venezuela. Unlike Venezuela, which cut off oil to the Sandinista regime in 1981, Mexico remained a reliable supplier through 1983. By 1984, however, U.S. pressure, military threats from the contra forces in Central America, and opposition from PEMEX and Treasury officials as well as the private sector forced some disruption of supplies.[5]

Economic aid was coupled with staunch political support. The López-Portillo administration formed close personal ties with the Sandinistas.[6] When the contra war against the Nicaraguan government began on the Nicaraguan-Honduran border under the auspices of the Reagan administration, the Mexican president sought to build a broad Latin American united front against a possible future U.S. intervention. In May 1981, he personally mediated a cross-border dispute between Honduras and Nicaragua, thus preventing the initiation of a dangerous spiral of conflict. This pattern of mediation, later adopted by Contadora, remains a substantial part of Mexico's contribution to peace in the region.[7]

Mexican involvement in El Salvador after the October 1979 military coup also demonstrated a new pattern in foreign policy. Although the strong personal ties that characterized relations with Nicaragua were absent, Mexico lent a base of operations to the political front of the FDR-FMLN during the height of right-wing repression, withdrew its ambassador at one point, and repeatedly issued statements supporting the right of the Salvadoran people to decide their own destiny just "as the people of Nicaragua were able to do a year ago."[8] As U.S. hostility to the opposition grew and El Salvador was declared a "test case" for the defeat of communism in Latin America, the Mexican government took stronger action in order to avoid a possible military confrontation between the rebels and the Reagan administration. On August 28, 1981, López-Portillo presented a joint communiqué with the Mitterrand government of France to the UN Security Council that recognized the FDR-FMLN as "representative political forces" and called upon the international community to "facilitate an understanding among the representatives of the opposing political forces in El Salvador with the aim of reestablishing peace in the nation and avoiding all outside interference in Salvadoran affairs."[9] This French-Mexican communiqué had an instant impact: It granted important diplomatic and political legitimacy to the Salvadoran opposition while promoting the idea of a political settlement. To the outrage of the Reagan administration, it elevated national reconciliation and "power-sharing" to an important agenda item in regional diplomacy.

By the end of 1981, the López-Portillo government directly opposed the United States in both Nicaragua and El Salvador. It initiated high-level talks between Secretary of State Alexander Haig and Foreign Minister Jorge Castañeda to seek ways of mitigating conflict with its powerful neighbor. These talks marked a shift from Mexico's previous role of advocate to a new stance of mediator between the United States, Cuba, and Nicaragua. As the foreign minister explained: "Mexico is prepared to serve as a bridge, as a communicator, between its friends and neighbors."[10] In February 1982, during a state visit to Managua, President López-Portillo announced a specific formula for political negotiations that involved a three-part dialogue between the United States and Cuba, the contending parties in El Salvador, and Nicaragua and its neighbors. The so-called Declaration of Managua led to new momentum for broadly linked negotiations throughout the region. Haig and Castañeda met again and Mexico announced that it had received the "go ahead" from the United States to carry ideas to both Cuba and Nicaragua with the understanding that talks could begin in April.

But the Reagan administration blocked efforts for a political solution. Firmly committed to the newly announced Caribbean Basin Initiative and to its newly designed electoral strategy in place of negotiations in El Salvador, it put a quick brake upon any buildup in momentum for talks. On March 15, Secretary Haig killed the diplomatic effort. The international success of the Salvadoran elections later that month reinforced the U.S. decision to avoid negotiations. Although Mexico persisted in its efforts to arrange some form of dialogue throughout 1982, the Reagan administration blocked all overtures. As one official noted, the Reagan administration made "no secret of its desire to eliminate Mexico as an intermediary in the region." Regional communicators were simply not welcome in the traditional backyard of the United States.[11]

The collapse of Mexico's oil boom in 1982 suddenly changed the foreign policy context. The sense of independence and confidence, originally engendered by petroleum revenues and sustained in the face of U.S. opposition, began to drop in tandem with falling oil prices. All foreign policy issues, including Central America, necessarily took a back seat as government attention focused upon such emergency economic measures as monetary controls and the nationalization of the banks. Given Mexico's intensified bargaining with the United States, international banks, and the IMF to rearrange its finances, there was a general perception that confrontation over Central America could be quite costly.[12] For the first time since Mexico made its initial regional commitment, both the salience and the content of its foreign policy came into question.

Economic problems brought domestic opposition to Mexico's foreign policy into the open. Although there had been some quiet grumbling about López-Portillo's activist role, the downturn provoked the private sector, particularly the bankers, into public criticism of continued aid to the Sandinistas in light of Mexico's own financial troubles. State bureaucracies echoed their concern. PEMEX and the Ministry of Finance, searching for every possible peso to resolve the country's immediate crisis, fought with the Ministry of Foreign Affairs over whether to demand a settling of petroleum accounts with Nicaragua.[13] As economic fears grew, the Ministry of the Interior and the military also began to dispute refugee policy on the Guatemalan border with the Ministry of Foreign Affairs, arguing that Mexico could not take care of another country's poor and should attempt to prevent the entry of Guatemalans. Disagreements, although hidden, were deeply felt and cut into the traditional policy realm of the foreign ministry, a professional service unused to the presence of so many state officials in its own sphere.[14]

By 1983, Mexico stood at a crossroads. The heady days of oil-fueled activism had been replaced by caution and pressures for a foreign policy retreat. The strength of external and internal opposition to Central America policy was reflected in the subdued positions of President-elect Miguel de la Madrid during the 1982 campaign. Reportedly unhappy with ties to Central American revolutionaries, disinterested in international relations, and wishing to distance himself from the policies of his predecessor, de la Madrid sought to shift the emphasis in foreign policy. While Mexico would not retreat from its past goals of nonintervention and the insulation of its own polity from regional turmoil, the country was under siege and could no longer afford to stand alone against the United States. Fortuitously, Venezuela, Colombia, and Panama were waiting in the wings.

VENEZUELAN POLICY IN CENTRAL AMERICA: ▲
1978 TO 1982

The Venezuelan regime, like that of Mexico, has had twin foreign policy preoccupations—the defense of its sovereignty and the protection of its political stability. Separated from the events in Central America by land and

water—a luxury not afforded Mexico—threats to Venezuela's statehood
from that region have seemed more remote. Given this lower level of threat,
individual party interests have been able to dominate the making of foreign
policy. Thus the interpretation of national security has shifted with the
political winds. This has produced abrupt policy twists. In 1978, President
Carlos Andrés Pérez—of Acción Democrática (AD)—coordinated an unprecedented arms operation that involved at least three countries in the
Sandinista effort to overthrow the U.S.-backed Somoza dictatorship. A mere
two years later, the Christian Democratic (COPEI) administration of Luis
Herrera Campíns threatened to withhold aid to the Sandinistas, while
generously supporting the U.S.-backed government in El Salvador. By the
election year of 1983, Venezuela switched again—this time working
through Contadora to prevent a U.S. military intervention in the region.

Yet traditionally there has been an underlying continuity in Venezuela's
international behavior. Like other Latin American regimes, concern for
sovereignty and territorial integrity has produced a long-term emphasis
upon nonintervention and the peaceful resolution of conflict. Since the
discovery of petroleum and iron ore deposits in the early twentieth century,
the crux of Venezuela's preoccupation has been the establishment of control
over its own natural resources. Unable to protect its patrimony through
force, Venezuela relied upon bargaining and multilateral activity through
international organizations like OPEC. It became adept at consensus building among nations of differing regimes, a talent that later proved invaluable
in Central America. Although Venezuela's commitment to nonintervention
was not as visceral as that of Mexico, the principles of self-determination
and political bargaining have been seen as an important means for protecting its petroleum, resolving border disputes with Colombia and Guyana,
and keeping the United States at bay.[15]

In Venezuela, the promotion of democracy in the hemisphere, a foreign
policy goal not found in the Mexican case, has competed with the principle
of nonintervention. The linkage between security and democracy originated
with Rómulo Betancourt, the major architect of the country's party system.
He believed that the survival of existing political arrangements was intri-
cately tied to the capacity to weave between the twin dangers of revolution
and military takeover. The Betancourt Doctrine extrapolated Venezuela's
democratization experience to the international arena by arguing that the
durability of a fragile party system in one country is dependent upon the
strength of democracy throughout the continent. Unlike Mexico with its
collective fears of a U.S. military presence, the Venezuelan regime was
haunted by the memory of its now-defeated guerrilla movement, once aided
by nearby Cuba. This prompted a strong anticommunism, a decision to
"export" democracy to the rest of Latin America, and a commitment to
prevent "more Cubas"—goals that often coincide with the concerns of the
United States.

These twin concerns of regime survival and sovereignty, characterized by
a special tension between the promotion of democracy and the principle of

nonintervention, meshed in a particular way in the Caribbean Basin. Venezuelan officials have viewed a politically disruptive Central America or Caribbean as a security threat that could eventually endanger the stability of petroleum shipping lanes to the United States or even the country's democratic arrangements. This security emphasis, founded on fears of Cuban-inspired communism, has meant a strong presence of the armed forces in Caribbean policy and programs in the past. In this sense, the general coincidence of U.S. and Venezuelan policies was not incidental.

The 1973 oil price increase and the election of Carlos Andrés Pérez of Acción Democrática dramatically changed the context of Venezuelan foreign policy. The oil-fed expansion of the country's foreign policy horizons solidified the emphasis on the Caribbean Basin while adding a new economic dimension. Convinced that this area represented Venezuela's natural sphere of influence and a trade outlet for domestic production, Pérez established formal diplomatic relations with Cuba, worked with Omar Torrijos and Jimmy Carter for the approval of the Panama Canal treaties, promoted Belize in its claims against Guatemala, and helped to prevent a military coup against the incipient democracy in the Dominican Republic. In a creative display of oil diplomacy in 1974, he initiated the first program of subsidized oil for Central America and the Caribbean, later joined by Mexico in the San José Accord of 1980. Pérez's economic generosity and intense political involvement won the gratitude of President Carter who, in his own pursuit of regional stability and human rights, referred to Pérez as "my best friend in Latin America."[16]

Events in Nicaragua were to test that friendship. Based upon Venezuela's own experience in defeating its former dictator Pérez Jiménez, the Pérez administration believed that Somoza's demise ought to be encouraged, since a long and brutal struggle could only produce radicalization and the defeat of democracy in Nicaragua. Strong personal ties between AD government party officials and the Nicaraguan opposition to Somoza added a sense of urgency to this desire.[17] The Carter administration, while rapidly losing sympathy for Somoza, had a different interpretation. Although most U.S. officials agreed that Somoza should be forced to resign, they refused to take decisive action and engaged in policy vacillations that gave implicit aid and the appearance of support to Somoza almost until his defeat in July 1979.[18]

Venezuelan policy toward Nicaragua began to diverge significantly from that of the United States as Caracas sought to do its utmost to get rid of Somoza. In the summer of 1978, on his own initiative, President Pérez held a secret meeting with Somoza on the island of La Orchila to persuade the dictator to leave power:

> I told him that he didn't have more than a year left. I told him that he could ease a transition to democracy if he would leave now. But he was certain that he could maintain his position, particularly since he thought he still had the

tacit support of the United States. He even produced a letter from President
Carter which congratulated him on his progress in human rights.[19]

When Somoza refused to consider the Venezuelan president's advice to
resign in the face of an imminent Sandinista victory, Pérez—supported by
his party, the government of Panama, and a network of Socialist International contacts—committed his administration to substantial aid to the
opposition.

By 1979, Venezuela was coordinating an unprecedented arms operation
between three countries to overthrow Central America's most despised
dictator. Without the knowledge of the Carter administration, the governments of Presidents Pérez and Torrijos mounted a campaign to supply the
Sandinistas, using Costa Rican territory as a base. When Somoza threatened
to bomb unarmed Costa Rica, Venezuela offered to send in its own air force
as a counterweight.[20] In a quiet but all-out effort, Pérez, Torrijos, and Costa
Rican President Carazo organized massive arms shipments to the rebels,
eventually becoming their principal source of weapons in the crucial period
before their victory. Venezuelan petrodollars covered much of the cost of
this unprecedented endeavor. Cuba also sent weapons and continued to
supply the FSLN once Pérez stepped down from the presidency in March
1979. The United States was to discover the extent of these shipments only
after the fact, and subsequently place all responsibility upon the Cubans.
Privately, however, the actions of the AD government created strong tensions with Washington in the final months of the Somoza dynasty as U.S.
officials became aware of Venezuelan activity.[21]

Venezuela's 1979 elections, held in the midst of rapidly spiraling events
in Nicaragua, produced a victory for the Christian Democratic Party's Luis
Herrera Campíns and abrupt foreign policy changes. Although COPEI
shared AD's concern for democratization, the new administration had distinctly partisan views about foreign policy. The promotion of democracy
became closely intertwined with the party's attempt to construct a Latin
American Christian Democratic community. In the process, President Herrera often circumvented the foreign ministry, a traditionally weak bureaucracy that had already suffered from the concentration of power in the
presidency that had occurred during the Pérez years, in order to rely upon
informally placed COPEI party regulars. The new president gave free rein
to the party through former Foreign Minister Arístides Calvani, a virulent
anticommunist and guardian of Christian Democratic ideology at the Institute for Christian Democratic Formation (IFEDEC), the party's ideological
center. Under COPEI, Venezuela would begin to promote democratization
—Christian Democratic style—with a vengeance, echoing the sentiments of
President Herrera: "Either we bring in democracy today or there'll be a
revolution tomorrow."[22]

The change was felt immediately in Nicaragua. Upon taking office in
March 1979, the new Venezuelan government attempted to construct a
non-Sandinista opposition by specifically tying aid to the fate of its Christian

Democratic counterparts. When Mexico, the Andean countries, Costa Rica, Panama, and the Dominican Republic sent ebullient congratulations to the Sandinista victors, Herrera Campíns greeted the revolutionary government with suspicion. Venezuela pressured for early elections, reportedly delayed aid payments as a means of obliging the Nicaraguans to bring a moderate Christian Democrat into the governing junta, conditioned oil grants upon the political behavior of the Managua regime, and finally stopped supplying petroleum altogether.[23] The pressure was necessary, a former Venezuelan ambassador to Nicaragua explained: "We should make them democrats. We should nail the democratic masks to their faces."[24]

The Herrera Campíns government adopted a twofold strategy to achieve its own version of democratization. On the one hand, it sought to use economic aid to maintain its influence and prevent the isolation that had previously pushed Cuba into the Soviet camp, generously providing approximately $150 million in credits and donations in the first two years of the junta's existence. On the other hand, it attempted to support the forces inside Nicaragua that it considered to be the "institutionalization of liberty" —the Catholic church, the private-sector association (COSEP), certain political parties, and the La Prensa press group. As one architect of the policy explained:

> We considered our government to be a neutral force between two groups: the Sandinista government and the Nicaraguan opposition. As long as there was a tiny bit of political space, we would stay and help our friends inside. President Herrera did everything he could to show his support for the opposition, always within certain boundaries. Our relationship with the church, particularly Archbishop Obando y Bravo, was very close. The president visited La Prensa during his visit to Managua. We channeled our aid through Robelo when he was in the government because we thought he was the most democratic. We let our embassy be used for "encuentros" of opposition politicians. We tried to balance between the government and the opposition, but we always helped the opposition.[25]

This policy drew Venezuela deeply into the internal affairs of Nicaragua, eventually involving embassy personnel in armed plots against the Managua government. By 1983, relations had deteriorated badly.[26]

Policy toward El Salvador demonstrated still greater tensions between the principle of nonintervention and Christian Democratic concepts of exporting democracy. In 1980, when the Christian Democratic Party of El Salvador was widely criticized for breaking with other opposition parties to form a shaky alliance with the military, the Venezuelan government rapidly came to the aid of its fellow Christian Democratic Party. The strong personal tie between President Herrera Campíns and José Napoleón Duarte was fundamental. "I would do anything for him," Duarte once explained. "If he had asked me to meet with the guerrillas I would have done it."[27] The Venezuelan administration linked its foreign policy directly to the fortunes of the

Salvadoran party leader. Venezuelan aid to El Salvador was substantial. The Herrera government gave generous grants, a hydroelectric plant, and outright cash payments. Caracas was also forthcoming in its diplomatic support. In the tense days following the death of four U.S. religious workers, Arístides Calvani helped to negotiate a political compromise between the armed forces and Duarte's wing of the Christian Democratic Party in El Salvador that could satisfy U.S. requirements for continued aid. In mid-1981, the Herrera Campíns administration took the lead in denouncing the French-Mexican agreement by refusing to buy French Mirage jets, threatening to suspend all commercial links with France, and mounting a Latin American campaign largely aimed at Mexico to defeat the endeavor.

The Christian Democrats, using both direct governmental relations and indirect party links, also became involved in covert military and intelligence activities in El Salvador—often working in tandem with the United States. These covert activities in the name of democratic promotion pulled Venezuela deeply into Salvadoran affairs, just as they had in Nicaragua. Venezuela trained Salvadoran soldiers in counterinsurgency, an activity which the Herrera government officially denied.[28] It helped to improve the Salvadoran intelligence system, whenever possible channeling its aid through Duarte in an attempt to enhance his precarious position vis-à-vis the armed forces. Under the direction of Aristides Calvani, the Christian Democrats established the Venezuelan Institute for Popular Education (IVEPO), an organization which was officially tied to COPEI and claimed to be nongovernmental. Ostensibly a publicity agency in San Salvador which did campaign work for Napoleon Duarte without charge, produced television and radio advertisements on his behalf, and conducted political polls, IVEPO was actually a more ambitious operation. Venezuelan in origin, staffed by Chilean Christian Democrats, funded in part by the Konrad Adenauer Foundation, and closely associated with the political section of the U.S. embassy in San Salvador, IVEPO was adept at political engineering. It sought to unite the Christian Democrats with the ultraright and the military in order to "design a game that everyone can play."[29] IVEPO became deeply involved in the 1984 elections, serving as a conduit for cash flows from external agencies. Due to activities of this sort, Venezuela was eventually accused of interference in internal Salvadoran affairs by both the ultraright and the FDR-FMLN.

Venezuela's immersion in Salvadoran politics was largely welcomed by the United States, since it coincided with the views of the Reagan administration, but there was a moment of policy divergence in early 1981. When the Reagan administration first took office, it appeared to abandon the partnership that Carter officials had carefully constructed with Salvadoran Christian Democrats for a flirtation with Roberto D'Aubuisson and the forces of ARENA. In February, as the Reagan team talked openly of war and an alliance with the ultraright, the Venezuelan government took an abrupt foreign policy U-turn and made its first policy approach to Mexico. Mexico and Venezuela mutually agreed to support nonintervention in

Nicaragua and a political settlement in El Salvador, the compromise that formed the eventual basis of the Contadora agreement.[30] But upon receiving a U.S. sweetener in the form of permission to buy F-16 fighter jets and the assurance that elections would take place in El Salvador, the Herrera government abruptly abandoned its efforts at regional diplomacy and, in a second U-turn, was soon leading the Latin American opposition to Mexico's policies in Central America.[31]

The strong identification with U.S. policy and the equation of Christian Democratic party interests with Venezuelan national interests had a domestic price tag. As preparations for the 1983 elections began, an emerging foreign policy debate revealed the lack of internal consensus about Central America. This was fueled by Venezuela's growing economic troubles brought on by the collapse of strong oil markets. Opposition parties criticized the government's overemphasis upon Central America to the neglect of economic issues, the mishandling of simmering border disputes with Colombia and Guyana, and the failure to win entry into the Non-Aligned Movement due to its actions in Central America and Guyana.[32] Although AD now opposed the Sandinistas in international forums, the party, like the smaller organizations on the left, criticized COPEI's overt interventionism in Nicaragua.[33] In their view, support for covert activities and political engineering in the name of Christian Democracy could only hurt Venezuela's international reputation and destroy a valuable domestic consensus among the leading political parties. More problematic, these operations could not be controlled; they fomented a new and different type of covert military activity, and ultimately threatened to upset the balance between Venezuela's own military and its political parties. Party leaders contended that involvement in covert operations was a dangerous practice for a young and struggling democracy that constantly worried about its own civilian control over the armed forces. Destabilization of others could always rebound back to the internal polity.[34]

By 1982, these criticisms found a powerful echo within the president's own party. The hard-line policies of Calvani and other *Copeyanos* associated with him had become an important internal party issue, merging with other deep preelectoral divisions, exemplified by the split between former President Rafael Caldera and Luis Herrera Campíns. Party members generally associated with former President Caldera, now seeking the 1983 presidency, quietly denounced the emphasis upon conspiratorial activity and military involvement in Central America. Caldera himself called for regional detente and the return to a modus vivendi with Cuba.[35] When Duarte failed to win a majority in the March 1982 elections, COPEI members viewed this as a failure of Venezuelan policy as well, and added their voices to demands for a policy shift.

It took a perceived threat to Venezuela's sovereignty and dignity, however, to provoke a change. The source was unexpected. In April, the Falklands-Malvinas war broke out, ringing a death knell to any possibility of close U.S.-Venezuelan collaboration in Central America. Thinking of the

British roots of its own territorial dispute with Guyana, Caracas reacted more strongly to the war than virtually any other Latin American country.[36] In the COPEI administration's view, U.S. support for England had demonstrated its scorn of the Inter-American system precisely when Venezuela had been willing to share the U.S. policy burden in Central America. In addition, by refusing to help Argentina, a country which had been a military ally to the United States in Central America, Washington had shown that it would not necessarily reward cooperation. The Falklands-Malvinas war, combined with highly publicized revelations of the CIA's role in the efforts to overthrow the Sandinista government, marked a new turning point in foreign policy. Faced with demonstrations of thousands in Caracas protesting external aggression in the hemisphere, declining oil revenues, Duarte's electoral disappointment in El Salvador, an increasingly aggressive U.S. administration, growing party divisions, and its own approaching elections, the Herrera Campíns administration quickly sought to distance itself from its Central America policy of the past two years. As it looked around for allies, Venezuela focused upon a beleaguered Mexico.

THE CONTADORA PROCESS: 1983 TO 1985   ▲

The slow convergence of the foreign policies of Mexico and Venezuela came to fruition on the island of Contadora in January 1983. Definitions of national security differing from that of the United States, the growing U.S. military presence, and the difficulties of their past practice led them to join with Panama and Colombia, other neighbors concerned about the growing threat that regional war seemed to pose to their polities. Colombia's newly elected president, Belisario Betancur, had an additional incentive. He saw in Contadora a means of facilitating his own cease-fire initiative with a strong internal guerrilla movement as well as an opportunity for overcoming the foreign policy isolation that had resulted from Colombia's failure to support Argentina in the Falklands-Malvinas war. Panama, angry at U.S. political involvement in their national guard and preoccupied by the Reagan administration's distaste for the Carter-Torrijos treaties, believed that multilateral action could help to protect the orderly transfer of the Canal. Arguing that the United States was too much of a protagonist to play a mediating role in Central America and that the OAS had been discredited during the war between Argentina and England, these four countries formed the Contadora group and offered their collective "good offices" to help bring peace to Central America. In their view, their task was "to intensify dialogue on the Latin American level" in order to "reduce tensions and establish the bases for a lasting climate of peaceful coexistence and mutual respect between countries." They contended that an independent all–Latin American diplomatic initiative could provide an impartial forum for conflict resolution.[37]

The threat of a widespread regional war and direct military intervention by the United States, having brought the Contadora group together, became the glue that cemented their cooperation. The increase in the U.S. military buildup throughout 1983, which culminated in the October invasion of Grenada, exacerbated concern about the Reagan administration's apparent willingness to resolve the Central American crisis by force. The majority of the membership of the OAS, fearful of a similar action on the isthmus, censured the United States for its actions in Grenada.[38] The subsequent mining of Nicaragua's harbors in early 1984, the U.S. defiance of the World Court, and public Pentagon boasts about its capacity to assume a combat role in Central America transformed multilateral action from a desirable option to a virtual imperative in the perceptions of regional governments.[39] Although the initial involvement of regional actors had stemmed from a mixed bag of regime interests and political choices, their range of foreign policy options had narrowed perceptibly, in tandem with the growing probability of war.

The increase in U.S. military pressure, having pushed Mexico into a new pattern of multilateral activity, reinvigorated that country's declining activist role. Upon entering the presidency, de la Madrid had demonstrated a willingness to lower Mexico's foreign policy profile in order to defuse tensions with the United States. Determined to moderate the support his predecessor had given to Nicaragua and to the FDR-FMLN, the new administration had curtailed public manifestations of support for the Salvadoran opposition, cut back on visa privileges for rebel groups, and reduced the level of communications between Mexico and its Central American allies. Supporting PEMEX and the Ministry of Finance against its Ministry of Foreign Relations, it requested payment on oil shipments to the Sandinista regime. By the fall of 1983, the Nicaraguans had to recognize an official debt to Mexico, pay interest on loans, and deliver some cash up front for petroleum received.[40] Yet the persistent bellicosity of the Reagan administration toward Nicaragua made any meaningful effort at distancing Mexico from the Sandinistas an impossibility, since de la Madrid could not hope to maintain Mexican influence in the region or his own domestic prestige if he gave the appearance of buckling under U.S. pressure. But if Mexico were to be pushed to the wall on its commitment to the peaceful resolution of conflict, participation in Contadora could at least help to spread the risk.

Fears of U.S. intervention in Central America motivated Venezuela, Colombia, and Panama as well. The Contadora initiative provided a graceful exit from policies that had become too controversial in the context of U.S. militarization. For Venezuela, Contadora promised to re-create domestic bipartisan support for foreign policy. Although initiated by COPEI President Herrera Campíns, its program could be supported by the newly elected Acción Democrática government of Jaime Lusinchi, thus putting to rest the policy swings of the past. More important, it could assuage new tensions between the Venezuelan military and the leadership of the political parties that had surfaced when the government condemned the U.S. invasion of

Grenada, much to the dismay of the Venezuelan armed forces.[41] Further-more, Venezuela would be able to turn its attention to its own border disputes and repair its reputation in Latin America and in the Non-Aligned Movement.

The Reagan administration, seemingly unaware that its own actions did more to promote collective action than any other single factor, greeted the development of regional diplomacy with quiet hostility. Angry at the Con-tadora countries' exclusion of the United States, the administration unsuc-cessfully sought to prevent any form of independent multilateral activity on the part of regional actors by launching its own Forum for Peace and Democracy. Ostensibly promoted by Honduras and Costa Rica to unite the democratically elected governments in the area, this so-called Enders Forum was widely viewed as a U.S. ploy to isolate Nicaragua and block the first successful united efforts of Mexico and Venezuela. When it received little regional support, it was ultimately abandoned.[42] After the announce-ment of the formation of Contadora, the Reagan administration insisted that all discussion regarding Central America take place in the Organization of American States where it could influence outcomes directly, but this effort also ultimately failed.[43]

The U.S. government consistently undermined the intent of regional diplomacy despite public statements to the contrary.[44] The overall thrust of U.S. policy promoted militarization, which ran counter to the Contadora proposals. Immediately following the formation of Contadora in January 1983, with its publicly proclaimed platform of nonintervention and disar-mament, the United States initiated the Big Pine I exercises in Honduras, which brought the first mass landing of U.S. troops to the area. In July, when the presidents of Mexico, Venezuela, Panama, and Colombia met in Cancún to call for a prohibition on the installation of foreign bases in the region, the Reagan administration began the construction of eight bases in Honduras and launched five thousand new U.S. troops into that country through Big Pine II. In September 1983, when the twenty-one-point Con-tadora peace plan was unveiled, explicitly calling for a policy of nonaggres-sion in the Caribbean Basin and the rejection of force in international relations, the Reagan administration attempted to revitalize CONDECA, a Central American military alliance. In October, it invaded Grenada.

By 1984, the subversion of the regional peace effort by the Reagan administration was even more direct. The United States strongly pressured Mexico to lower its profile. A National Security Council memo warned Mexico that future economic aid from the United States could be contingent upon that country's support of U.S. policies in Central America. In a speech that deeply disturbed Mexican policymakers, U.S. General Paul Gorman declared that Mexico itself, with its unacceptable foreign policy position, was perhaps the greatest single threat to U.S. security interests. While Mexico received the brunt of U.S. displeasure, Panama, Costa Rica, Spain, and even Honduras also reported pressures.[45]

Finally, the Reagan administration tried to scuttle the Contadora effort at the very moment when successful peace negotiations seemed imminent. In September 1984, the Nicaraguan government unexpectedly announced its unconditional acceptance of a Contadora draft treaty. The treaty included provisions for amnesty for political dissidents, impartial elections under international auspices, and the termination of support for groups fighting to overthrow Central American governments—the key demands raised by the Reagan administration to justify its efforts to dislodge the Sandinista regime.[46] The Reagan administration, stunned by Nicaragua's actions and unwilling to negotiate, encouraged its Central American allies to block progress on accommodation. Although a consensus to accept the treaty previously had been reached among all five Central American countries, U.S. pressure led to new objections from Honduras, El Salvador, and Costa Rica regarding the timing for the withdrawal of foreign military advisers, the closing of military bases, arms and troop reductions, the verification process, and the signing of a protocol.[47] This ended the diplomatic momentum until April 1985. A background paper to the National Security Council later boasted: "We have effectively blocked Contadora group efforts to impose a second draft of a revised Contadora Act."[48]

Despite U.S. opposition, the results of collective regional action to date have been impressive, even if they fall short of a peace. The Contadora countries have succeeded in capturing the moral high ground by becoming the symbol of a negotiated settlement to the Central American conflict. Their stance for peace, neutrality, and the rule of law has enabled them to win widespread international support for nonintervention and negotiations.[49] International support highlights the advantages of collective action. Mexico and Venezuela, working with Panama and Colombia, have been able to bring together two strong transnational networks that had previously been deeply divided in Central America: the Socialist International and the international Christian Democratic movement. Through their links with these different party forces, deeply at odds in Central America, they have encouraged consensus building as well as a greater level of European pressure on the United States for a political solution than might otherwise have existed among NATO allies.[50] International support has spread the risk of confrontation with the U.S., thus helping regional actors to sustain a consistent long-term presence while dedicating considerable resources to peace.

Perhaps most important, Contadora has succeeded in influencing the U.S. congressional debate over foreign policy in Central America. This is especially evident in the controversial votes in the House of Representatives over U.S. aid to the contras. In 1985, one of the compromise bills presented by House Democrats in an attempt to block the President's request for $14 million for the contras proposed that these same monies be allocated to the Contadora group instead. By 1986, Contadora had become the only viable congressional alternative to administration policy in Central America. The new surge of interest in the regional peace initiative was not surprising. In late 1985, four Latin American countries—Peru, Argentina, Brazil, and

Uruguay—formed a "support group" for their four original counterparts, giving the multilateral peace effort a badly needed shot in the arm. For the first time, these eight countries took a tough *public* stand: they explicitly stated their opposition to U.S. aid to the contras, asked the administration to set aside its militaristic emphasis, and called for the resumption of bilateral talks between Nicaragua and the United States. Thus, by the spring 1986 congressional vote over aid to the contras, the debate had been framed by two sharply opposing alternatives: the contras or Contadora.[51]

Contadora has also been successful in crisis management. Regional actors have been able to mediate in an isthmus where sudden flare-ups can lead to an unwelcome spiral of conflict. For example, the Contadora group, working in conjunction with the Socialist International, is credited with improving relations between Costa Rica and Nicaragua in mid-1983, then again in May 1984. When battles broke out along their common border due to the operations of the contras, the Contadora countries and their European allies were able to soften Nicaragua's reaction while simultaneously encouraging a strict interpretation of Costa Rican neutrality on the part of the Monge government. Their combined clout counteracted pressures from the U.S. embassy in San José and diminished tensions.

Most important, collective regional action has produced a viable, if imperfect, peace treaty. The Contadora draft treaty, put forward in September 1984, has specific provisions for regional security, disarmament, and democratization—the underlying issues of the Central American conflict. In the elaboration of this treaty, the disparate and sometimes conflicting interests of neighboring countries that proved to be a disadvantage when acting alone have become an advantage in multilateral activity.[51] Intense negotiations have succeeded in defining the inevitable trade-offs necessary for conflict resolution. Carrying domestic practices of bargaining and pact-making to the international arena, each nation has been able to deliver a different trusted constituency to the bargaining table—i.e., Mexico with Nicaragua and Venezuela with El Salvador—and therefore forge some form of compromise, while guaranteeing the compliance of their "special" ally.

Negotiated trade-offs have come in stages.[52] The first successful breakthrough, an implicit agreement to defend the sovereignty of Nicaragua, was adopted during the July 1983 meeting in Cancún. This took the form of a commitment to nonintervention and the sovereign equality of states, in exchange for an agreement to keep the Soviet Union out of the isthmus while stopping armed subversion against existing governments. In principle, all Central American countries agreed to the following program: the creation of demilitarized zones, the elimination of foreign advisers, arms control, the proscription from using the territory of one state to destabilize another, the eradication of arms trafficking, and the prohibition of any interference in the affairs of another country. The compromise was clear: These treaty obligations would guarantee the survival of the Sandinista regime through provisions that would terminate contra activity and lead to the withdrawal of U.S. bases in Honduras. In return, Nicaragua's ability to aid the FDR-FMLN against El Salvador's government or to forge military alliances with the Socialist bloc would be clearly circumscribed.

The second major breakthrough, accepted in the September 1983 Declaration of Objectives, involved the recognition of democracy as a preferential type of political regime for Central America. Although Mexico, Nicaragua, and Guatemala considered a democracy clause, or any stated regime type, to be interference in internal matters and therefore contrary to the Contadora mandate of nonintervention, the insistence of Venezuela, Colombia, and Costa Rica and persistent pressure from the United States led them to concede ground—a diplomatic victory for the United States. Yet the democracy clause, while directed against Nicaragua, was a two-edged sword. In the future it could be used to pressure Guatemala's notoriously repressive military establishment as well as the governments of El Salvador and Honduras. The insistence on pluralism also broke an invisible barrier against pronouncements over internal matters, thus preparing Central Americans and their various allies to support internal negotiations in El Salvador.

This third breakthrough came in July 1984. In a departure from the past, Contadora announced that it would address "national reconciliation" within countries suffering from internal strife as well as government-to-government relations in Central America. Previously the group's initiative had been directed at Nicaragua and had ignored El Salvador, in recognition of the overwhelming role of the United States. Realizing that a settlement in El Salvador was a requirement for any viable regional peace, it abandoned its "hands-off" policy and publicly offered to help the new Duarte government begin negotiations with Salvadoran rebels. Since this had been the position of Mexico and the FDR-FMLN prior to the French-Mexican accord, later to be joined by Acción Democrática and other parties of the Socialist International, the pro-negotiations statement represented a diplomatic victory for these forces. Duarte, pushed by strong domestic forces as well as his neighbors, initiated talks with the FDR-FMLN in October 1984, which soon broke down.

The final package of agreements, then, presented an important set of trade-offs: In exchange for accommodating U.S. and Latin American fears of Soviet bases or external armed subversion by circumscribing the traditional sovereignty of Central American states to choose their own foreign alliances, the United States and its allies would agree to refrain from destabilizing the Nicaraguan (or any other) Central American regime and to withdraw its military presence. The provisions to implement this trade-off would be subject to verification by neutral parties that, although imperfect, could ensure fundamental long-term compliance.

Regional actors have played a qualitatively new role in Central America. They have demonstrated a surprising degree of political initiative, an ability to define a new agenda for the region, and a capacity to work together in a forum of their own creation. Their definition of their national security,

different to varying degrees from that of the United States, underlies this
level of commitment. While Mexico, Venezuela, Colombia, and Panama
initially became involved in Central America for different reasons, ranging
from personal friendships, economic interest, oil exuberance, party loyal-
ties, or fears about their own internal peace, they have each sustained their
efforts due to a common concern: They believe that peace in Central America is vital to their national interests. They must help bring about a political
solution because the alternative, a potentially uncontrolled and uncontrollable regional war, threatens their influence in the area as well as the very
viability of their regimes and states. Given these considerations, these
actors can be expected to persist in their regional role, albeit with distinct
concerns, degrees of compellingness, and intensity of involvement—even
if the Contadora effort itself should collapse under the persistent weight of
U.S. pressure.

Ironically, to this point, the pressure has merely served to sustain Latin
American countries in the regional role. The convergence of the foreign
policies of four countries into the Contadora initiative is largely the unintended consequence of the threatening behavior of the Reagan administration in Central America. As the experiences of Mexico and Venezuela
demonstrate, the United States created the overall incentive to engage in
multilateral activity—even among countries with different foreign policies
—as a means of containing the continent's dominant power. While the
wisdom of international relations generally dismisses the ability of small
states to "contain" larger powers through united action, Contadora's actions
are part of a long, Latin American tradition of overcoming relative asymmetries in bilateral relations by joining forces and seeking to tie the United
States (or other dominant powers) into juridical obligations and treaties.[53]

But do the actions of regional powers matter in the long run? After all,
as the Contadora countries themselves point out, they have not yet managed
to bring peace to Central America or even win over the United States. Yet
Mexico, Venezuela, Colombia, and Panama have succeeded in developing
a set of regional norms and a concrete peace proposal. Their treaty agreements have backed the Reagan administration into a diplomatic corner by
sharply framing the choices available to the United States in Central America: The administration can continue along the same path by slowly (or
rapidly) escalating its involvement and the war or it can decide to negotiate
a political solution to the Central American imbroglio. Indeed, the Contadora countries have constructed a tight and intricate web of political
relations that maintains and legitimates the choice of a peaceful resolution
of conflict while also raising the political costs of direct military intervention
to the United States. Whether the threads of the web—in conjunction with
domestic opposition to Reagan's policies, pressure from European allies,
and most important, the events in Central America—can actually deter a
U.S.-sponsored war in the region is still unknown. What is clear, however,
is that a new structure of options has been consciously woven around the
continental giant.

The choice between war and peace ultimately resides with the Reagan administration and the U.S. Congress. If the United States should escalate its military activity or merely continue to pursue an overall politico-military strategy that undercuts serious efforts at diplomacy, then it can tip the balance toward widespread regional war. It will have to pursue this path alone. Latin American support for Contadora has demonstrated that the Reagan administration will be unable to win the backing of the continent's major powers through the OAS, justify military escalation in the face of a Contadora "road not taken," or ultimately count on regional allies in a long military struggle on the isthmus. In addition to the consequences noted elsewhere in this volume, the path of escalation in Central America would hasten the deterioration of the Inter-American system by flaunting the wishes of Latin American countries. More important, military escalation could seriously destabilize the larger countries of the Caribbean Basin and perhaps threaten the polities of some of Central America's neighbors.

But what would happen if the Reagan administration were suddenly to embrace the Contadora initiative? What would occur if the United States were to abandon its past efforts at undercutting regional involvement, overcome its objections to the draft treaty, and, like Nicaragua, agree to the unconditional acceptance of the Contadora provisions? At the very least, a treaty that would stop the arms buildup in Central America, terminate external support for insurgent movements in both countries, send Cuban and Soviet advisers out of Nicaragua and U.S. advisers out of El Salvador and Honduras, check the growth of the region's armed forces, limit U.S. military involvement, close down all foreign military bases in the region, and encourage more pluralistic regimes could be expected to diminish the external sources of conflict in Central America and reduce the prospect of regional war. In addition, active U.S. support for Contadora would strengthen significantly the efforts of regional countries for peace while constraining and eventually isolating internal actors intent upon using violence. This external pressure would increase the likelihood of achieving a durable peace.

Yet Contadora promises still more. In its essence, the proposed peace initiative represents a new political vision for U.S.–Latin American relations: In exchange for limiting its military options in Central America, the United States would receive the formal assurance of Central American countries, backed by international law and multilateral guarantees, that external powers or their allies, Soviet or otherwise, would not establish a strong military presence in the isthmus. Thus the security interests of the United States could be guaranteed through multilateral accords. At the same time, by agreeing to permit the existence of revolutionary regimes on the continent with their own models of development, the United States would acknowledge that necessary social change can be expressed through a variety of governmental forms. Contadora presents the United States with the opportunity to endorse norms of greater independence, shared responsibilities, and international pluralism that might replace the now-deteriorating "rules of the game" for inter-American collective security. Indeed, if the United States should accept Contadora, the actions of regional powers in Central America could prove to be the embryonic form of a new international regime based on the recognition that peace in the Americas is related to ending hunger and injustice rather than the blind support of reactionary regimes.

▲ ▲ ▲ ▲ CONFRONTING REVOLUTION
▲ ▲ ▲ A NEW U.S. FOREIGN POLICY

12

GRAPPLING WITH CENTRAL AMERICA: FROM CARTER TO REAGAN

William M. LeoGrande, Douglas C. Bennett, Morris J. Blachman, and Kenneth E. Sharpe

The crisis in Central America has dominated United States policy toward Latin America since the outbreak of the Nicaraguan revolution in 1978. President Jimmy Carter approached the crisis as a liberal Democrat: in assessing the causes of the crisis, he gave greater weight to local conditions and complaints than to Soviet subversion. In seeking a solution, he was willing to tolerate, and in some cases even promote, change in the region.

Ronald Reagan approached the crisis differently, seeing it primarily as a Soviet-Cuban geostrategic thrust requiring a primarily military response. Whereas Carter sought stability through progress, Reagan focused on the maintenance of order.

Yet despite obvious differences in conception and practical application, the policies of both Carter and Reagan derived from the same basic premise: that to protect the national interest of the United States it was necessary to control the character of Central American governments so as to keep the radical left (i.e., any mass movement seeking rapid and fundamental social transformation) from any share in political power. The corollary to this imperative was the assumption that the power of the United States made the exercise of such control feasible.

CARTER'S LATIN AMERICA POLICY: FROM EAST-WEST TO NORTH-SOUTH ▲

President Carter made a conscious if not always successful effort to break with the traditional tendency of U.S. policymakers to view Third World conflicts through the prism of the Cold War. With the East-West conflict dampened by detente, Carter sought a policy more sensitive to North-South issues, and more cognizant of the "regional" political forces shaping the Third World independently of superpower machinations. This new approach promised to be a more rational—and hence more effective—response to the nationalist impulses sweeping the increasingly multi-polar international system.

The Carter administration did not propose to ignore the implications that regional issues might have for the rivalry between the United States and the Soviet Union, but it pledged to keep them in perspective. The "inordinate fear of communism" that had been the hallmark of past policy was to be replaced by a tolerance for ideological diversity and a heightened concern for human rights.[1]

Such a deemphasis of the Soviet threat was unprecedented among post-war presidencies, and it is not surprising that some officials in the Carter administration, especially the career professionals in the national security bureaucracies, took a somewhat jaundiced view of the new policy. Even some of Carter's key appointees, including National Security Adviser Zbigniew Brzezinski, did not embrace it. Apart from the President himself, whose approach to foreign policy was founded in deeply held moral principles, perhaps no one in the administration embodied the new approach better than United Nations Ambassador Andrew Young. At least while Young was in office, the Carter administration's policy in southern Africa best exemplified the new approach in practice.

In Latin America, this new vision of U.S. policy drew its intellectual inspiration from the findings of the Commission on U.S.–Latin American Relations—a bipartisan group of prominent U.S. citizens convened under the chairmanship of Ambassador Sol Linowitz.[2] The commission argued that the emergence of detente, the decline of U.S. global hegemony in the post-Vietnam period, and the growing assertiveness, economically and diplomatically, of Latin America required fundamental changes in U.S. policy toward the hemisphere. Military and security issues should no longer dominate the agenda; intervention, whether overt or covert, was no longer appropriate. Instead, the commission held that economic issues were the key to the future of hemispheric relations.

The Linowitz commission offered three political recommendations that ultimately defined the Carter administration's initial agenda for Latin America: negotiation of a Canal treaty with Panama; normalization of relations with Cuba; and active promotion of human rights.

If the United States was to build a more equal partnership with Latin America, settlement of the Canal issue was the necessary first step. The colonial status of the Canal Zone had become an irritant in U.S. relations, not only with Panama but with Latin America as a whole. By negotiating an agreement to turn the Canal over to the left-leaning populist government of Omar Torrijos, the Carter administration hoped to prove in practice that a policy based on cooperation and tolerance could be a more effective way of safeguarding U.S. interests than a policy of hemispheric dominance. To negotiate a new Canal treaty, Carter appointed Sol Linowitz.

If the Canal was the most important substantive issue for Carter's Latin American policy to address, Cuba was the most important symbolically. A decade and a half of U.S. hostility had neither dispensed with Fidel Castro nor cowed him, and nothing spoke more pointedly about the hegemonic presumption of the United States in Latin America than its stubborn refusal to reconcile itself to Castro's revolution.[3] By moving to normalize relations with Cuba, the Carter administration sought to bring to a close one of the least laudatory and least successful chapters in the history of U.S.–Latin American relations.

President Carter's decision to make the promotion of human rights a major objective of U.S. foreign policy was at once the most celebrated and excoriated of his international initiatives. From the outset, the policy was presented in moral terms: it was an approach to the world as good and decent as the American people themselves. In the international arena, Carter sought with this policy to repair the damage done to the image of the United States by the ferocity of the war in Vietnam, while simultaneously posing a stark moral contrast between the United States and the Soviet Union. At home, Carter hoped to reconstruct bipartisan domestic support for foreign policy by grounding it in principles to which no one could easily object.

Yet the Carter administration never saw its human rights policy in strictly moral terms. It was also intended to distance the United States from the brutal excesses of decaying autocracies. Right-wing dictatorships bent on preserving anachronistic social orders were regarded as bad security risks; the more they relied upon force to sustain themselves, the more rapidly they mobilized and radicalized their opponents, thus hastening their own demise. For the United States to enlist wholeheartedly in support of such governments would actually endanger national security, for ultimately such regimes would collapse and an angry populace would not soon forget that the United States had sided with the tyrants. Such was the national security doctrine behind Carter's human rights policy.[4]

Despite the complaints of Carter's conservative critics, human rights were never allowed to overshadow immediate national security concerns of a more traditional sort. When key allies such as South Korea, Iran, or the Philippines were involved, the issue of human rights was always muted.

Though global in scope, Carter's human rights policy found its most consistent expression in Latin America. In 1977, there appeared to be no immediate security threats in the hemisphere, so the advocacy of human rights was undiluted by fears of political instability. While there were still a few guerrilla movements fighting against the military regimes of Central America, they appeared to be little more than feeble remnants from the 1960s, incapable of posing a serious challenge to the existing regimes. The Cubans, despite their willingness to dispatch troops to Africa, had long since lost faith in the region's potential for revolution and had not provided arms to guerrillas in the western hemisphere for nearly a decade.

Carter's human rights policy was applied full force in Central America, where the four nations of the northern tier—Nicaragua, El Salvador, Guatemala, and Honduras—were all ruled by military dictatorships, most of them notorious for their systematic and brutal use of repression against all shades of political dissidents. Not coincidentally, Central America was also a region on which the Congressional pioneers of the human rights movement had focused their attention in 1975 and 1976.[5]

The Carter administration encountered deep and powerful resistance to its Latin American program from the Republican right. Negotiating the Canal treaties with Omar Torrijos proved much easier than getting the United States Senate to ratify them. The "giveaway" of the Canal, as presidential aspirant Ronald Reagan referred to it, became a symbol for conservatives of all that was wrong with U.S. foreign policy in the post-Vietnam era. In retrospect it is clear that the treaties strengthened U.S. security by averting conflict with Panama. Yet the treaties were just barely ratified by the Senate, and the battle over ratification cut deeply into the Carter administration's store of political capital in Congress.

Carter's tentative move toward normalizing relations with Cuba proved to be considerably less controversial, perhaps because it was so short-lived. After a cautious but successful beginning, the movement toward normalization was brought to an abrupt halt when Cuba deployed combat troops to Ethiopia in early 1978. From then on, Carter's rhetoric about Cuba was indistinguishable from that of his five predecessors.

If the Canal treaties were narrowly a success, and detente with Cuba an abject failure, the record on Carter's human rights policy in Latin America proved to be more mixed. Specialists agreed that the policy saved the lives of many dissidents, especially in the southern cone. It also reinforced the movement to restore democracy in Brazil, and at a critical moment preserved democracy in the Dominican Republic from a military coup.

In Central America, pressures from the United States led the regimes in Nicaragua, El Salvador, and Guatemala to temporarily relax the reign of official violence unleashed in the early 1970s against their moderate opponents. But when these relaxations produced a resurgence of open opposition from Christian Democratic and Social Democratic parties, the incumbent regimes all reacted by tightening down once again.

Rather than submit to U.S. scrutiny on human rights practices, the governments of Guatemala, El Salvador, and Honduras preempted Washington by refusing to accept military assistance. After 1977 the dictatorships of Central America's northern tier received little or no military aid from the United States.

THE NICARAGUAN INSURRECTION   ▲

The outbreak of revolution in Nicaragua threw the Carter administration's human rights policy into crisis.[6] As Nicaragua's stability slipped away in the months following the assassination of opposition leader Pedro Juaquín Chamorro, the administration's desire to promote human rights was forced to compete with resurgent concerns about national security. At first the administration appeared paralyzed, unable to reconcile its conflicting priorities of order and progress into a clear, coherent policy. Washington could not bring itself to break completely with Somoza, but neither was it willing to reenlist wholeheartedly on the side of his increasingly brutal national guard. To have given Somoza the military means to sustain himself in power would have made a mockery of the human rights policy, and this Carter was unwilling to do.

Yet there was great fear that Somoza's demise would herald victory for the radical Sandinista National Liberation Front (FSLN), the guerrillas who, week by week, were capturing the political initiative while the moderate opposition waited in vain for the United States to oust Somoza for them. This fear of the radical left produced some clarity in U.S. policy during the last eight months of the Somoza dynasty; Washington's unambiguous objective was to prevent the Sandinistas from coming to power.

The means for achieving this remained at issue, however. Should Somoza be forced out in favor of a government of moderates whose capacity to govern was uncertain? Or should Somoza be given the military wherewithal to defend himself, whatever the cost in bloodshed? Officials in the State Department argued for pressure to force Somoza's resignation because of his abysmal human rights record and because his departure was the only way to engineer a moderate succession. The Defense Department and the National Security Council countered that the human rights policy was largely responsible for Somoza's difficulties in the first place, and that the United States ought to reassert support for him, both because he was a loyal ally and because he constituted the best bulwark against the FSLN.[7] This debate was never clearly resolved; the United States vacillated between supporting Somoza in limited ways and trying to ease him out, never fully committing itself to either course of action.[8]

The September 1978 uprisings in Nicaragua's major cities and the indiscriminate violence used by the national guard to suppress them convinced Carter's State Department that Somoza would not be able to restore political stability. From October 1978 to January 1979, the United States presided over a mediation between Somoza and his moderate opponents in the hope of devising a compromise formula for peaceful transition to a new government that would either exclude the FSLN or restrict it to minimal participation.[9]

Despite threats from Washington, Somoza refused to make any real concessions. Those within the administration who thought Somoza should be supported were able to block those who wanted to use the full weight of U.S. pressure to force him to resign. Sensing the Carter administration's lack of resolve, Somoza simply delayed the mediation as long as possible, leaving the moderate opposition so fragmented and demoralized that it played only a minor role in the anti-Somoza struggle after the mediation collapsed in January 1979.[10]

The final battle within the Carter administration over Nicaragua policy took place when the Sandinistas launched their final military offensive against the national guard in June 1979. The United States called for a special meeting of the Organization of American States at which Secretary of State Cyrus Vance presented a plan calling for Somoza's resignation, a broadly based government of national reconciliation, and an OAS peacekeeping force to be sent to Nicaragua in order to enforce a cease-fire.[11]

Latin America's reaction to the U.S. proposal may well have marked the nadir of Washington's influence in the OAS. Only Somoza supported the plan. The call for a peacekeeping force was widely condemned as a transparent effort to justify U.S. intervention to keep the Sandinistas from defeating the national guard. That such a proposal was even advanced was a policy error of significant proportions, and it was closely linked to the ongoing bureaucratic battle within the administration.

When the final offensive began, the escalating crisis in Nicaragua came immediately under the authority of the White House Special Coordinating Committee for crisis management. This committee was composed of senior officials (Deputy Secretary of State Warren Christopher, Secretary of Defense Harold Brown, National Security Adviser Zbigniew Brzezinski, and CIA Director Stansfield Turner) who took over management of U.S. policy from the State Department's Nicaragua Task Force, staffed largely by Latin American specialists. Under Brzezinski's chairmanship, the committee pointedly ignored the recommendations of the State Department specialists, who warned that the peacekeeping proposal would meet with widespread derision in Latin America. The advice of the specialists was scorned because of the basic policy differences over Nicaragua that had divided the State Department from the Defense Department and NSC since the beginning of the insurrection against Somoza in January 1978.[12]

Eventually, Somoza was driven from power by a coalition between the Sandinistas, whom Washington feared, and the moderate opposition, whom Washington had tried to court. In the wake of Somoza's defeat, U.S. policy shifted from an attitude of outright hostility toward the FSLN to an attitude of cautious cordiality toward the new revolutionary government. The change was no less stark for having been forced by circumstances, since it carried with it the implication that even radical social and political change in Nicaragua did not necessarily threaten the vital interests of the United States.

Nevertheless, considerable tension born of mistrust lay below the surface of this peculiar friendship. The long history of U.S. support for Somoza could not be wholly forgiven or forgotten by Nicaragua's new leaders, nor could they shake the fear and suspicion that Washington might yet concoct a counterrevolutionary scheme to rob them of their victory. In Washington, policymakers could not ignore the Marxist origins of many of the Sandinista leaders, even though Somoza's defeat had been engineered by a politically heterogeneous coalition. There was always the possibility that the guerrillas, having won power, would shed their moderate garb, dump their middleclass allies, and steer the revolution sharply leftward, down the road of Cuban-style Marxism-Leninism.

Yet the interests of both Nicaragua and the United States lay in maintaining good relations. Nicaragua was in desperate need of foreign assistance to rebuild an economy shattered by war. The United States pledged to help finance the recovery, but the maintenance of cordial relations was obviously a necessary condition for the fulfillment of Washington's promise. Moreover, other financial assistance—from Latin America, Western Europe, and the international financial institutions—would tend to follow Washington's lead, so a deterioration of U.S.-Nicaraguan relations would have economic ramifications far beyond the aid dollars from Washington alone.

For the United States, maintaining good relations with Nicaragua was a means of salvaging something from the failure to keep the FSLN out of power in the first place. Though, from Washington's perspective, the insurrection had been "lost," perhaps Nicaragua itself need not be. Policymakers in the Carter administration consciously set out to avoid repeating the errors of 1959 and 1960, when U.S. hostility drove the Cuban revolution into the arms of the Soviet Union.

With much at stake on both sides, U.S. and Nicaraguan officials made a major effort to stay on good terms. Some officials within the Carter administration hoped eventually to push Nicaragua toward a Costa Rican model of pluralism; others doubted this was possible but were willing to coexist with the Sandinistas nonetheless. Almost everyone understood that, in the short run at least, the FSLN would have cordial relations with Cuba, that it would provide some aid to the Salvadoran guerrillas who had aided the FSLN in the struggle against Somoza, and that there would inevitably be conflict between the FSLN and the Nicaraguan private sector as they vied with each other to determine the future of their country.

The Carter administration's immediate objectives were modest—to contain the Nicaraguan revolution within the bounds that would not damage the vital interests of the United States. In practice, this meant accepting Nicaraguan friendship with Cuba, but trying to prevent it from becoming a deep military alliance; trying to minimize Nicaraguan aid to the Salvadoran left so that it would not become a major factor in the war there; and trying to moderate the internal policies of the FSLN so that the private sector and its political allies would remain a viable opposition force within a reasonably pluralistic polity. The carrot with which Washington hoped to achieve these objectives was much needed economic aid.

For a year and a half—until Ronald Reagan was elected President and all the actors in Central America began to behave in ways that anticipated what Reagan's new Central American policy would be—the Carter strategy in Nicaragua worked reasonably well. None of the worst fears of either side materialized as both adhered to the implicitly agreed upon rules of the game.

The fall of Somoza conjured up images of Central American dominoes in Washington and prompted a major review of U.S. policy toward the region—a review aimed at devising a more effective strategy for preventing similar guerrilla victories in El Salvador and Guatemala. At issue was the question never adequately addressed during the Nicaraguan crisis: How could the administration reconcile its commitment to human rights with its desire to preserve political stability?

Advocates divided roughly into two camps.[13] Hard-liners concentrated in the Department of Defense and the National Security Council argued that these objectives were inherently contradictory. They pointed out that Washington's criticism of Somoza's human rights record had undermined his rule by encouraging his opponents and depriving him of the military means to maintain order. Central America, so the argument went, was not as stable as it had appeared in 1977, and the spread of insurgency brought the issue of U.S. national security back to the top of the policy agenda. The hard-liners argued for restoring military assistance to the region's anticommunists, even at the expense of human rights—in essence, a return to Kissinger's policy of supporting friendly dictators.

Defenders of the human rights policy in the Department of State replied that military aid could not buy stability. They argued that the ancien regimes of Central America had become obsolete and would not long survive the mounting pressures for social and political change. The old policy of supporting traditional elites was fruitless, for it could neither contain nor resolve the growing crisis. Rather than enlisting on the side of military regimes fated for extinction, the interests of the United States would better be served by trying to manage the inevitable process of change.

Implicitly, such management meant—as it had during the Alliance for Progress—a search for "openings to the center" combined with policies designed to contain the left. Once again, the United States would propose evolutionary change as the antidote to revolution. The unspoken problem in this formulation was the same as the dilemma of the Alliance. By arming existing regimes to enable them to contain insurgency, Washington would end up arming the very elites it sought to displace in favor of the reformist center. Once armed, incumbents would have little incentive to accept even modest change.

Despite this internal contradiction, the reformist option triumphed in the bureaucratic battle, though, like most bureaucratic victories, its triumph was incomplete.[14] The Defense Department continued to press for a resumption of military aid to El Salvador, Honduras, and Guatemala; the State Department resisted. The eventual outcome was a good indicator of the relative strength of the advocates of change and the advocates of order. Military aid was resumed to El Salvador and Honduras, but at low levels, and, in the Salvadoran case, was restricted to nonlethal materials. Throughout the remainder of the Carter administration, the adherents of the reformist strategy searched Central America for a viable center, trying to stave off not only the extreme right in Central America, but an increasingly vociferous conservative opposition within the national security bureaucracy itself.

As the 1980 presidential campaign got underway, Central America increasingly became a focus of partisan politics. The Carter administration's effort to build a constructive relationship with the Sandinistas came under sharp attack by Republicans in Congress, who denounced Carter's aid request for Nicaragua as an example of Democrats befriending communist dictatorship. The opposition was so intense that it nearly scuttled the $75 million aid request for Nicaragua, and did succeed in delaying it for almost a full year.[15]

EL SALVADOR: THE LIMITS OF REFORM   ▲

The clearest test of the Carter administration's policy of promoting reform came in El Salvador.[16] By the summer of 1979, political order in El Salvador was decaying rapidly. Washington began pressuring the government of General Humberto Romero to ease the strictures of military rule and initiate social and political reforms to stem the growth of the revolutionary opposition. Romero refused. Weakened by Washington's overt displeasure with him, he was ousted in October by a group of progressive young military officers who promised the sorts of changes he had resisted. The new junta quickly incorporated civilian leaders from the centrist opposition parties and even suggested its willingness to reach some sort of accord with elements of the radical left. The regime promised to create democratic institutions and to enact social reforms that would break the socioeconomic dominance of the landed oligarchy. This government was, in short, a seemingly perfect vehicle for Washington's new regional policy of reformism and the Carter administration quickly pledged to support it.

Unfortunately, the October junta proved to be incapable of carrying out its promises—a failure due largely to the internal politics of the Salvadoran armed forces and to the reticence of the United States to carry its support for reformism to its logical conclusion. Whenever the progressive officers and their civilian allies proposed reforms of any significance, rightists within the armed forces blocked them as being too extreme. The result was paralysis of the government that could only have been overcome if the progressive officers had been willing to break with their rightist brethren and take full control of the ideologically divided military. This they were unwilling to do—partly because of institutional loyalty and partly because the United States was unwilling to stand behind them. Though Washington favored social reform, it balked at the October junta's willingness to bring the popular organizations into the government and to seek an accord with the guerrillas. The Carter administration's strategy was to isolate the radical left politically, not allow it to share power.

As Chapter 3 recounts, the October junta's paralysis demolished any hope of accord with either the popular organizations or the armed opposition, which proceeded to escalate its insurrectionary activities. The mere suggestion of real socioeconomic change terrified the oligarchy, which escalated the paramilitary terrorism of the death squads. Amidst this spiral of political violence, the moderate civilians within the government sought a showdown with the officers, demanding that reforms be implemented and that the rightist defense minister, General José Guillermo García, be removed. The military refused, the civilians resigned, and the government moved sharply to the right. At this critical juncture, the United States did nothing to preserve the moderate reformist character of the government.

In fact, despite this fundamental shift in the balance of political forces within the government, U.S. policy changed not at all. The Carter administration ignored the new political complexion of the regime and continued to provide both economic and limited military aid, justifying the policy with claims that it was still supporting a moderate centrist reformist government under attack from extremists on both the left and right. The willingness of the Christian Democrats to participate in the new junta, albeit at the insistence of Washington and the sufferance of the Salvadoran armed forces, gave superficial credence to this characterization. But after January 1980, the moderation of the Salvadoran regime was more chimerical than real.

The essential difference between the junta formed in October and its various successors lay in their strategy for resolving the nation's political crisis. The October government had been willing to open a dialogue with the popular organizations and the armed groups on the left, with the goal of eventually ending the country's turmoil by reconciliation. The government of officers and Christian Democrats had as its first priority defeating the left, both politically and militarily. This was much more in line with the Carter administration's strategy of promoting reform in order to preempt the political appeal of the left, and so the new government was welcomed in Washington.

At the insistence of the United States, the new Salvadoran government undertook limited reforms, but this strategy of combining "reform with repression" as Archbishop Oscar Romero characterized it, was always more repressive than reformist. By the end of 1980 it was apparent that the reformist strategy had not worked. The agrarian program, the cornerstone of the reforms, was at a standstill, blocked by the indifference of the government and the resistance of the oligarchy. The level of official violence against civilians had risen dramatically rather than subsiding, as the Christian Democrats had promised, and there was no evidence that the government was making any effort to curtail it, let alone bring its perpetrators to justice.

The progressive officers who ousted Romero were eventually isolated and demoted by their conservative compatriots, until control of the armed forces was once again securely in the hands of the right. The gradual rightward shift of the government was chronicled by a continuous stream of Christian Democratic resignations as various elements within the party reached their threshold of tolerance for cynicism.

By the end of the Carter administration, El Salvador was once again governed by a military dictatorship, now hidden behind the façade of civilian rule. The political center, which Washington had hoped to consolidate and promote, was divided and polarized. The fate of the Christian Democratic Party symbolized the Carter administration's failure. It split into two factions: the conservatives remained in the government but held little power and depended upon the U.S. embassy to physically protect them from their military partners; the more progressive faction allied itself with the guerrillas.

HONDURAS AND GUATEMALA: ▲
CRISES IN THE MAKING

Among the four countries of the northern tier of Central America on which the Carter administration focused its human rights policy, Honduras and Guatemala received the least sustained attention. In part, this was because the crises in Nicaragua and El Salvador monopolized the time and attention of decision makers, but it was also because Honduras and Guatemala represented, respectively, the easiest and the most difficult laboratories for Washington's efforts to promote the political center. In Honduras, crisis seemed avoidable; in Guatemala, it seemed intractable.

As guerrilla insurgencies flourished in Nicaragua, El Salvador, and Guatemala during the latter half of the 1970s, Honduras, as we saw in Chapter 5, remained relatively calm. Because Honduras was the poorest and most backward nation in the region, the pace of economic development and modernization spurred by the Central American Common Market and the Alliance for Progress was much slower there than in neighboring countries. At the same time, the Honduran government reacted to pressures for reform with less intransigence and brutality. Though the military ruled throughout the 1970s, it was willing to tolerate organized dissent from political parties, trade unions, peasant organizations, students, and the press. There were no waves of indiscriminate official violence, no plagues of disappearances, and no death squads. In the early 1970s, the military regime undertook some limited reforms, including land distribution, in order to avert the growth of unrest in the countryside.

For all these reasons, Honduras seemed to offer the brightest prospect for the sort of "centrist solution" envisioned by the Carter administration. At the urging of the United States, the Honduran armed forces held elections for a constituent assembly in 1980 and promised to return the nation to civilian rule after elections in 1981. Though the center-left opposition was effectively barred from the 1980 election, the center-right opposition, the Liberal Party, won an upset victory, and the armed forces accepted the results.

There was, however, another aspect to Carter's policy in Honduras that risked undermining the transition to civilian democracy. Within the broader context of regional policy, Washington considered Honduras to be an island of stability in a sea of turmoil. It was, therefore, the logical locale for the United States to increase its regional military presence. At the same time that Washington was pressing the Honduran armed forces to relinquish power to the civilians, it was increasing military assistance. Some U.S. officials hinted that increased aid was the price the military demanded for returning to the barracks, but it nevertheless had the effect of strengthening the military relative to other institutions in the Honduran polity—exactly the same dilemma encountered in South America during the Alliance for Progress.

Guatemala offered the most severe test of the Carter administration's commitment to reform. When Carter introduced his human rights policy in 1977, the Guatemalan government reacted angrily by refusing to accept further U.S. military aid. Nevertheless, the pressure from Washington did have some initial effect. There was a brief political relaxation in 1978 when the armed forces brought the Christian Democrats into the regime in order to improve its image. The Christian Democrats, more conservative than their Salvadoran brethren, did not noticeably alter the regime's ideological coloration, but even this small opening stimulated other opposition forces. The reaction of the right came swiftly; the political opening disappeared and, in the first three months of 1979, the two most popular leaders of the moderate opposition, Alberto Fuentes Mohr and Manuel Colom Argüeta, were assassinated by death squads. The effect of these murders and the scores more that followed were reminiscent of the effect similar violence had in Nicaragua and El Salvador. The moderate opposition was left demoralized and leaderless, the guerrilla armies of the left gained new adherents, and the prospects for evolutionary change faded even further.

As the Carter administration came to a close, the Lucas García regime in Guatemala was the most corrupt and brutal in Central America. The crisis there was not as acute as in El Salvador because the strength of Guatemala's guerrillas was less than that of their Salvadoran counterparts. Yet the Guatemalan crisis was worse, in a sense, because the prospect for finding a middle course seemed nonexistent. There was no reformist faction in the Guatemalan army to play the role Colonel Aldolfo Majano played in El Salvador in October 1979. Whether by coincidence or design, the Guatemalan right had so systematically killed the leaders of the political center that few were left to carry the mantle of moderate change. In Guatemala, then, Washington seemed to face, in the starkest terms, the choice Carter had hoped to avoid—a choice between the generals and the guerrillas.

THE SEARCH FOR THE CENTER ▲

The vision of Central America developed by the Carter administration after the fall of Somoza was both sophisticated and naïve. It was sophisticated in its recognition that Central American reality had changed in such fundamental ways since World War II that the maintenance of the status quo was no longer a real option. The politicization of the poor, both urban and rural, augured inevitable change in the narrowly based, closed political systems that had historically dominated most of the area. Carter's officials also recognized that change in Central America would inevitably endanger the privileges of existing elites, and that the oligarchs would fiercely resist any diminution of their monopoly of political and economic power.

The naïveté of Carter's policy lay in its belief that it could conjure up a moderate reformist political center to act as the vanguard of evolutionary change—that this center could by itself overcome the intransigence of the right and recapture the political initiative from the radical left. Carter's experience with El Salvador and Guatemala demonstrated the difficulties with this strategy. In both countries, the reformist center reached its zenith in the early 1970s, declining thereafter under the hammer blows of official repression. The defeat of the reformist challenge precipitated the polarization of politics and the growth of insurgency. By 1978, the guerrilla movements in Nicaragua, El Salvador, and Guatemala had grown from small bands isolated in remote rural areas to powerful political movements capable of seriously challenging the existing regimes. Few centrists from the early 1970s remained in the center.

Reversing this polarization of politics proved to be an impossible task, even for Washington. In El Salvador, reformism was forced upon a conservative junta in a desperate attempt to forestall a radical victory, but reformism soon gave way to a new way of repressive violence from the right. In Guatemala, even cosmetic reforms proved impossible to achieve; the Lucas García regime was utterly deaf to Washington's pleas for moderation. Only in Honduras, where the spiral of political violence and polarization had not yet begun, did the Carter administration have any real success in advancing the cause of peaceful change.

The inability of the Carter administration to find a successful strategy for managing the Central American crisis was rooted in the administration's basic objective: not only to keep the radical left out of power, but to keep it from wielding any significant influence in a post-oligarchic order. Thus Washington was forced to rely upon the debilitated political center to carry the mantle of change in the face of oligarchic resistance—a task the center no longer had the strength to accomplish.

Moreover, when Washington confronted the choice between assisting a rightist regime battling insurgency, or risking guerrilla victory, it could not, in the wake of the Sandinista victory in Nicaragua, bring itself to allow a guerrilla triumph. The façade of reform, rather than its substance, became sufficient justification for U.S. support.

The architecture of Carter's whole Central America policy began to collapse as soon as Ronald Reagan was elected President. Throughout the region, political forces on both left and right began to act in anticipation of a drastic shift in U.S. policy once Reagan was inaugurated. Everyone expected the incoming administration to adopt a policy of hostility toward Nicaragua and to sharply increase military assistance to El Salvador.[17]

In El Salvador, the FDR-FMLN tried to preempt Reagan by mounting a "final offensive" designed to depose the regime on the eve of Reagan's inauguration. For the arms to mount such an offensive, the rebels solicited help from Nicaragua, Cuba, and the Eastern bloc. For the Sandinistas, the request posed a difficult dilemma. They had faced a similar supply problem before their final offensive in June 1979, but El Salvador was the most sensitive issue in Managua's relations with Washington. Though the Sandinistas had turned a blind eye to the FDR-FMLN's use of Nicaraguan territory as a way station in their own arms smuggling operations, the Nicaraguans had refrained from making a major commitment to the FDR-FMLN lest they anger the United States.

The expectation that Reagan's policy toward Nicaragua was inevitably going to be hostile, regardless of how the Sandinistas behaved, diminished the incentive for moderation so carefully crafted by the Carter administration. In November and December 1980, U.S. intelligence detected a major increase in the flow of arms into El Salvador from Nicaragua.

In its last few weeks in office, the Carter administration was forced to respond to the unraveling of its Central America policy, even though events had slipped beyond control through no fault of its own. As evidence of Nicaraguan arms transfers to the FDR-FMLN accumulated, Carter came under intense pressure to halt economic aid to Nicaragua. The aid had been approved by Congress in September on condition that Carter certify the Sandinistas were not exporting violence to their neighbors. In January, Carter announced a "suspension" of aid, thereby beginning to dismantle, however unwillingly, his own policy of constructive relations with Nicaragua. By suspending aid rather than canceling it, Carter left open the possibility that aid might be resumed if Nicaragua ceased its support for the Salvadoran guerrillas. But that determination would fall to President Reagan.

In early January, the FDR-FMLN launched its offensive, and its initial successes prompted the Carter administration to resume lethal military assistance to the Salvadoran armed forces—the first such aid since 1977. In order to get the aid to El Salvador quickly, Carter invoked emergency provisions of the foreign aid act that allowed him to provide aid without congressional approval—a provision of law that had not been used since the war in Vietnam.

The final days of the Carter administration set the stage for the entrance of Ronald Reagan. On more than a few occasions, Reagan administration officials would remind their critics, especially congressional Democrats, that it was Jimmy Carter who cut off economic aid to Nicaragua and resumed military aid to El Salvador—doing so in a way that circumvented Congress. But while circumstances finally forced Carter into policy decisions that were, if not alien, at least uncomfortable, the Reagan administration would pursue the policies of hostility toward Nicaragua and military buildup in El Salvador with relish and on a scale that no one in January 1981 could have imagined.

RONALD REAGAN: THE SEARCH FOR VICTORY ▲

Jimmy Carter tried to adapt U.S. foreign policy to a world increasingly beyond the control of the United States. But to many Americans, the "giveaway" of the Panama Canal, the largely symbolic sanctions against the Soviet invasion of Afghanistan, and the image of impotence conveyed by the hostage crisis in Iran appeared to represent a willful retreat by the United States from the summit of world power.

Ronald Reagan was elected in part because he promised to restore the nation's global preeminence, and with it the sense of national pride and security that characterized the "American century" before it was cut short in the jungles of Vietnam.

The Soviet threat loomed as the centerpiece of Reagan's world view and became the cornerstone of his foreign policy. The recurring theme of Reagan's political attack on Carter was that he neglected national security. By pursuing detente singlemindedly, Carter (and other, always unnamed, presidents before him) allegedly allowed U.S. strategic superiority over the Soviet Union to be lost, while at the same time failing to meet the challenge of Soviet expansion in the Third World—e.g., in Ethiopia, South Yemen, Afghanistan, and Nicaragua. By advocating human rights and ideological pluralism, Carter purportedly obscured the distinction between allies and adversaries, criticizing traditional anticommunist friends while improving relations with hostile leftist regimes.

Though Reagan's campaign rhetoric often posed these issues in simplistic terms, his complaints reflected a profound division within the foreign policy community over the status of East-West relations. Carter's foreign policy was premised on detente—the reduction of East-West tensions conceptualized by Kissinger and the Eastern Republican establishment, and supported by Democratic liberals. Reagan's critique, subscribed to by the Republican right and the Cold War Democrats who came to be known as neoconservatives, began from the premise that detente was a fraud. Reagan's supporters did not see themselves as the initiators of a new cold war; for them, the Cold War had never ended. The United States, deluded by its desire for peace, had simply stopped fighting.

The main objective of the new cold warriors was to restore the Soviet threat to its traditional place as the mainspring of U.S. foreign policy. Defense policy, North-South relations, the full gamut of international affairs had to begin with a recognition of the "present danger" posed by the Soviet

Union. This was clearest in the opposition to the SALT II treaty, which was based not so much on the merits of the treaty itself but on the fear that its ratification would lull the American people to sleep, thus setting the stage for another Pearl Harbor.[18]

The Reagan coalition saw the Third World as little more than an arena of East-West struggle, and the U.S. policy toward it had to be defined by the geopolitical logic of the new cold war. During the campaign, Reagan routinely blamed all Third World conflict on Soviet conspiracies, implying that a hard-line toward the Soviet Union would suffice to recapture the global hegemony enjoyed by the United States in the 1950s.[19]

But here, too, the real policy debate was deeper and more complex. The advocates of detente had understood it to encompass certain "rules of the game" in the Third World—that neither superpower would actively seek to expand its influence at the expense of the other. In effect, this meant freezing the international status quo in which most of the Third World was more closely "nonaligned" with the West than with the East.

The Soviet Union, however, never understood detente in these terms. To the Soviets, detente ("peaceful coexistence") meant a reduction of bilateral tensions and increased cooperation on issues of mutual interest. It did not mean acceptance in perpetuity of an international status quo in which the Soviet position was inferior. The death of detente can be traced to this misunderstanding, which materialized first in Angola and later in Ethiopia. To Washington, Soviet policy in these conflicts seemed to violate the rules of the game. In the wake of Ethiopia and later Afghanistan, U.S. relations with the Soviet Union began slipping back into the familiar patterns of the Cold War, and the Carter administration's policy toward the Third World returned to traditional notions of containment.

Carter's disillusionment with Soviet behavior in the Third World was gleefully seized upon by the enemies of detente who proceeded to attack its entire structure. To them, Soviet activism in the Third World was proof that the Cold War was still in progress. Third World governments were little more than soldiers in this war to be enlisted by one side or the other. Consequently, the strategic objective of U.S. policy toward the Third World was to strengthen the global network of U.S. allies while striving to weaken that of the Soviet Union. To this, all other issues were secondary.

The Reaganites' critique of Carter's Latin American policy was particularly sharp. Carter's tolerance for ideological pluralism was, to them, nothing more than a vague justification for embracing anti-American regimes like Torrijos's Panama and Manley's Jamaica, and even pro-Soviet ones like Castro's Cuba. Carter's reduction of military aid to the dictatorships of the Southern cone and Central America on human rights grounds appeared to be nothing less than the willful dismantling of the alliance system of the United States in Latin America. To cast off traditional anticommunist allies for the sake of some vague moral idealism seemed foolish and reckless in the hostile international environment of realpolitik. To contrive such a policy when those allies were beset by leftist insurgency—as they were in Central America—seemed the height of folly, or worse.[20]

Two documents provided the intellectual wellspring of Reagan's Latin American policy: Jeane Kirkpatrick's famous *Commentary* article, "Dictatorships and Double Standards," which offered the critique of Carter's policy; and Committee of Santa Fe's monograph, *A New Inter-American Policy for the Eighties,* which provided the agenda of remedies.

Kirkpatrick's broadside, which first attracted the attention of candidate Reagan to the acerbic professor, rejected Carter's argument that reform and human rights were essential for stability. On the contrary, they had, according to Kirkpatrick, "facilitated the job of insurgents" by causing social disruption while simultaneously restricting the ability of the existing regime to use force to preserve order.[21]

As the basis for a new human rights policy, Kirkpatrick advanced the idea that dictatorial regimes friendly to the United States were "moderately authoritarian," and therefore tolerable because they might eventually evolve into democracies. Communist regimes, on the other hand, were "totalitarian," and never changed. According to Kirkpatrick, this distinction justified a policy that was less harsh on anticommunist torturers who aligned themselves with Washington. The logical conclusion of such a view was that since communism entailed the end of all human rights, anything done to prevent the advent of communism was justifiable on human rights grounds.[22]

The Santa Fe report repeated the critique of Carter's policy, charging that it was one of "indecision and impotence" that had abandoned Latin America to Soviet attack launched by revolutionary proxies. It declared detente to be dead and called not for containment but for the "counterprojection" of U.S. military power in Latin America. This required, inter alia, jettisoning human rights policy, tolerating right-wing authoritarian regimes, revitalizing the Central American Defense Council (CONDECA), mounting a "war of national liberation" against Cuba, and, if need be, intervening directly with U.S. military forces to halt the spread of communism.[23]

Central America became the first test of Reagan's new foreign policy. The Salvadoran guerrillas, anticipating that Reagan would seek massive increases in military aid for the regime in San Salvador, launched a "final offensive" on the eve of Reagan's inauguration, hoping to present the new President with a fait accompli. Though the offensive failed, Reagan entered the Oval Office with Central America dominating the headlines.

Secretary of State Alexander Haig, anxious to establish himself as the "vicar" of foreign policy, announced that El Salvador would be the administration's "test case" in the struggle against international communism. Haig portrayed the Central American crisis in strictly global terms. The test was not merely of the ability of the United States to manage the region, but also —perhaps primarily—a test of Washington's ability to rally Latin America, Europe, and the U.S. Congress behind an aggressive policy of containment in the Third World.[24]

Of equal importance was the administration's desire to send a message to the Soviet Union and Cuba—the countries that the Reagan administration accused of being the real "source" of the turmoil in Central America. In this sense, Haig's "New Monroe Doctrine" (as it was dubbed in the White House) was vintage Cold War logic.[25] By defeating the Soviet challenge in Central America, the United States would demonstrate to the Kremlin that the new President would not tolerate Soviet adventurism in the Third World and would thereby reduce the likelihood of such troublemaking elsewhere. Central America was ideally suited to such a demonstration of force and will, since the United States had an overwhelming geopolitical advantage there. Moreover, since Central America was of marginal importance to the Soviets, the risk of confrontation with the Soviet Union was minimal.

Finally, Reagan's hard-line on Central America had an important domestic political objective—to rebuild the pre-Vietnam foreign policy consensus behind an aggressive containment policy, backed by the willingness to use military force.[26] The Reaganites came to Washington convinced that the United States had been paralyzed by the trauma of Vietnam, and that the security of the nation depended upon overcoming the reluctance to use military force. The prospect of a quick victory in Central America promised to begin purging the national psyche of the Vietnam syndrome. Restoring the nation's willingness to go to war was seen as the path to peace.

Haig's aggressive rhetoric proved to be counterproductive, however. Rather than enlisting the support of Europe, Latin America, and the U.S. public, the hard-line scared people, and Haig's public pronouncements were eventually halted at the insistence of Reagan's political advisers in the White House.[27] But the shifting tides of administration rhetoric did not alter the basic thinking behind its policy. Despite more than the normal quota of bureaucratic in-fighting over tactics, the basic premises and objectives of Reagan's Central American policy remained remarkably consistent throughout his first administration.

The foremost objective was the same as in the Carter administration: to prevent the Salvadoran opposition, the FDR-FMLN, from coming to power. This objective derived from the familiar containment imperative of the past —not to lose any additional countries to communism (or, in its Latin American variant, not to allow "another Cuba").

Many in the Reagan administration, however, were not content with containment; instead, they were eager to try to rollback communism in the Third World.[28] As applied in Central America and the Caribbean, the rollback doctrine was aimed at Nicaragua and Grenada, and perhaps, if fortuitous circumstances arose, at Cuba as well.

The division between the adherents of containment and of rollback closely matched the division between political appointees and foreign policy specialists. Throughout the national security bureaucracy, Reagan's political appointees tended to be committed ideologues of the Republican right, willing and eager to unleash the military power of the United States, both overtly and covertly, against allegedly communist regimes. Foreign policy professionals, on the other hand, generally saw the rollback doctrine as reckless, dangerous, and too costly in both material and political terms.

This division meant that policy toward El Salvador was easier to agree upon than policy toward Nicaragua. The objective of defeating the revolution in El Salvador was universally accepted; disagreements, though often sharp, were merely tactical. Nicaragua proved to be more contentious because it crystallized the administration's internal divisions: Should the "communists" in Managua be overthrown or should they simply be contained? During Reagan's first term, the tension between the adherents of containment and those of the rollback doctrine produced a policy that often appeared schizophrenic and difficult to decipher because the fundamental objective behind it was in dispute. By the beginning of Reagan's second term, however, those intent on ousting the Sandinistas seemed to control the policy agenda.

Even though both the Carter and Reagan administrations shared a common objective at least in El Salvador, there were vast differences between their operational policies. Those differences—which were crucial to the people of Central America—derived from different strategic visions about how to achieve the common objective. Believing that change in Central America was inevitable, Carter sought to prevent an FDR-FMLN victory in El Salvador by political rather than military means. Washington feared that increases in military aid would strengthen the already powerful armed forces at the expense of more reform-minded civilians, thus making change more difficult. Instead, U.S. influence was used to bolster the centrist Christian Democrats in the hope that they could defeat the Salvadoran right and then seek a political solution with the left, or at least with the "democratic" elements of the left.

The primacy of political over military instrumentalities was carried over into Carter's policy toward Nicaragua's revolutionary government. To contain Nicaragua, Carter crafted a policy of coexistence that would give the Sandinistas a large stake in staying on good terms with the United States. Even the covert operations launched by the CIA under Carter were political rather than military—giving money to the Sandinistas' internal opponents rather than to externally based counterrevolutionaries.[29]

Reagan's vision of containment, on the other hand, was primarily military in orientation. In El Salvador, it meant winning the war against the FDR-FMLN, and in Nicaragua, it meant a policy of hostility and military pressure so intense that the Sandinistas would be forced to either turn inward or be destroyed. For those in the administration who were committed to rolling back "communism" in Nicaragua, the policy of pressure was consistent with the ultimate objective of overthrowing the Nicaraguan government.[30]

NICARAGUA: THE MOUNTING PRESSURE   ▲

Initially, the Reagan administration's policy toward Nicaragua was a function of its effort to win the war in El Salvador. Nicaraguan assistance to the FDR-FMLN had expanded during the months prior to the Salvadoran "final offensive," and was seen within the administration as an essential element in the war. Secretary Haig, in particular, firmly believed that the key lesson of Vietnam was the need to "go to the source" to defeat a guerrilla insurgency—i.e., to cut off the guerrillas' logistics.

Thus U.S. policy was framed as to how to halt Nicaragua's aid to the FDR-FMLN. At first, U.S. Ambassador Lawrence Pezzullo was able to persuade the new administration that it could restore the understanding Washington had had with the Sandinistas before Reagan's election—that U.S. economic aid was contingent upon Nicaraguan restraint in El Salvador. Though the Sandinistas responded positively to Pezzullo's efforts, hardliners within the Reagan administration were determined to win Nicaragua's acquiescence not with the carrot of economic aid but with the stick of threatened military action. On April 1, 1981, U.S. economic aid was cut off. Shortly thereafter, Pezzullo left his post as ambassador and retired from the Foreign Service.

Assistant Secretary Thomas O. Enders led a second effort to restore the understanding with Nicaragua in the late summer of 1981, but this too failed, in part because hard-liners in the administration insisted that Washington's proposals be framed in a way certain to offend the nationalism of the Nicaraguan leaders. After a few months of fruitless exchanges, the talks broke down.

This failure, combined with the deteriorating military situation in El Salvador, produced a fullfledged policy of hostility toward Nicaragua—exactly what the hard-liners had sought all along. Secretary Haig went so far as to call for direct military action against both Nicaragua and Cuba as the only effective way to "go to the source." The Pentagon demurred, however, at the prospect of a prolonged and politically unpopular war in Central America.[31]

Instead, Reagan initiated the covert war. At first the covert war was nominally intended to interdict the flow of arms from Nicaragua to the FDR-FMLN. But with the operation being run from Washington by those who sought the Sandinistas' ouster, and with its being conducted on the ground by counterrevolutionary forces who had the same objective, the aim of arms interdiction soon gave way to the goal of eliminating the Sandinista regime. An operation originally slated to include about five hundred commandos ended up by fielding an army of some fifteen thousand.

The creation of the contra army was supplemented by a massive military buildup of the Honduran armed forces financed by the United States, and a series of regional military exercises unprecedented in size and duration. In conjunction with these maneuvers, the United States built in Honduras the basic infrastructure necessary to support direct intervention in Nicaragua by U.S. troops.

The covert war and the military buildup on Nicaragua's borders constituted only one facet of the administration's comprehensive assault on the Sandinista regime. Economic pressures were applied first by halting bilateral aid, then by pressuring multilateral institutions like the World Bank and the Inter-American Development Bank to curtail lending to Nicaragua, and finally by imposing a full trade embargo.

The political rhetoric unleashed against the Sandinistas reached such heights that the Mexicans characterized it as "verbal terrorism."[32] The Sandinistas were alleged to be worse human rights violators than Somoza, "genocidal" in their treatment of the Miskito Indians, anti-Semitic, puppets of Cuba and the Soviet Union, guilty of subversion against all their neighbors, and incompetent to boot.

As Reagan's second term began, however, the administration remained divided between those who insisted that only the elimination of the Sandinistas was enough to secure U.S. interests, and those who were willing to coexist with Nicaragua if the Sandinistas made major concessions, especially in the area of foreign policy. During Reagan's first term, support for the contras was a policy that commanded support from both of these factions. But as it became clear that the contras would not be able to oust the Sandinistas, the question of whether the United States should intervene directly moved to the top of the policy agenda.[33]

EL SALVADOR: LOOKING TO THE RIGHT   ▲

In its efforts to win a military victory in El Salvador, the Reagan administration faced a series of interrelated problems: how to strengthen the combat capacity of the Salvadoran armed forces while simultaneously reducing the capacity of the FMLN; how to politically consolidate the regime in San Salvador; how to manage the resistance of the U.S. Congress and public opinion to the escalating military involvement of the United States in the war; and how to manage international efforts by Europe and Latin America to find a diplomatic solution to the conflict.

Each of these issues produced bureaucratic conflict, since different agencies in the government tended to place different emphasis on them. Yet the general thrust of the administration's strategy remained surprisingly consistent over its first five years in office. Strengthening the armed forces was, from the outset, the first priority; when it came into conflict with the other objectives, it invariably prevailed. Over the years, the Pentagon's assessment of what would be required to win the war expanded exponentially, yet the administration was always prepared to provide whatever resources the Pentagon requested.

The State Department, more than any other agency, saw political consolidation of the regime as essential to long-term stability. When Reagan came to office, the regime in San Salvador was exceptionally weak because it was trying to battle both the left and the far right. Reagan sought to strengthen it by reincorporating the far right. To achieve this, the United States had to deemphasize reforms and human rights, shift its own political investment from the Christian Democrats to the armed forces, and pressure the Christian Democrats to allow greater rightist participation in the government.[34]

This had to be accomplished, however, without producing a regime so dominated by the right that the Christian Democrats would be driven out of it, thereby alienating the U.S. Congress. Within the State Department, at least, some officials also believed that a continuation of agrarian reform and a reduction in the number of political murders were essential to building a viable popular base for the regime. In effect, their strategy was to modernize the Salvadoran oligarchy.

This was the view of Assistant Secretary Enders, who became the principle architect of policy toward Central America after Haig's resignation. Enders had an elaborate strategy in which the regime would be consolidated around a center-right coalition, within which the balance of power would be determined by elections. Washington would use its influence with the military to effect limited reforms sufficient to assure continued congressional support for administration policy.

These efforts would buy time for large-scale U.S. military aid to give the Salvadoran army the upper hand, eventually limiting the guerrillas to isolated pockets of resistance in depopulated northern provinces. Seeing the hopelessness of the war, the center-left politicians of the FDR might be enticed to break with the "Marxist-Leninists" in the FMLN and join an electoral process controlled by the government. The most recalcitrant fighters would remain in the hills, but without domestic or international legitimacy, they would eventually be eradicated. At the State Department, this scenario was dubbed the "Venezuelan solution" because of its superficial similarity to the way in which the insurgency there was defeated in the 1960s.[35]

This solution proved to be untenable. The ideological gulf between the Christian Democrats and the rightists, led by Major Roberto D'Aubuisson, simply could not be bridged. Even when the U.S. embassy forced them both into a coalition government after the March 1982 election, the government was so divided that it remained paralyzed throughout its entire tenure. The situation did not change appreciably even after Duarte was elected president in 1984, because the right maintained its majority in the National Assembly and was able to block most of Duarte's initiatives.

As argued in Chapter 3, the PDC victory in the 1985 National Assembly elections may have solved the problem of governmental paralysis, but it did not resolve the central problems of the war and of the political predominance of the armed forces. By late 1985, Duarte had not yet been unable to gain sufficient control over the army to resume the process of dialogue with the FDR-FMLN.

THE WAR AT HOME   ▲

The inability of the Reagan administration during its first term to produce major advances in human rights practices or in implementation of the agrarian reform made it difficult to persuade Congress that it should keep increasing military aid to El Salvador at the rapid rate demanded by the Pentagon. During the time that Enders was assistant secretary, his strategy for dealing with congressional resistance was a gradualist and conciliatory one. Enders was of the view that Congress could be cajoled into providing the requisite dollars if the administration emphasized its support of human rights, reform, and a "political" rather than "military" solution to the war.[36]

By early 1983, however, events had outrun the gradualist approach. The military situation in El Salvador had deteriorated to the point that massive increases in military aid were needed immediately. Enders and U.S. ambassador to El Salvador Deane Hinton, both of whom argued that efforts to consolidate the regime politically and to manage international and domestic opinion should take priority over strictly military requirements, were fired. Control of the policy shifted to the hard-liners in the administration, led by Jeane Kirkpatrick, CIA Director William Casey, and National Security Advisor William Clark.[37]

The hard-liners' policy was straightforward: do whatever necessary to assure that the Salvadoran armed forces and the contras in Nicaragua would win their respective wars. During the few months that the hard-liners held uncontested sway over policy, the Reagan administration proposed doubling military aid to El Salvador and doubling the size of the contra army trying to overthrow the Sandinistas. They deployed five thousand U.S. combat troops to Honduras and stationed two carrier battle groups off the shores of Nicaragua, under the auspices of never-ending military exercises on a scale unknown in the history of the region.

In short order, the hard-line policy ran into trouble on Capitol Hill. During the first two years of Reagan's presidency, Congress was relatively docile on the issue of Central America. The administration's opponents were vocal and persistent but confined largely to the liberal wing of the Democratic Party; rarely were they able to muster more than a third of the votes in either house. Their only significant victory was achieved in 1981 by passing legislation conditioning U.S. military aid to El Salvador on progress toward human rights, agrarian reform, a political solution to the war, and justice for the murderers of U.S. citizens. But even this action was toothless; it required only that the president certify to Congress every six months that progress was being made toward these goals. This the administration did without apparent qualm or concern for contrary evidence, thus making the whole process a mockery.

By 1983, however, the administration's credibility and support in Congress had begun to erode. The visible failure of Reagan's policy to achieve its stated objectives, its growing price tag, and the president's apparent determination to escalate U.S. involvement rather than reconsider the direction of policy began to frighten moderate Democrats and Republicans who had supported Reagan. The Republicans' poor showing in the 1982 midterm elections reinforced these doubts and shattered the mantle of invincibility Reagan had acquired in 1981. Politicians who had been afraid to criticize the President before the 1982 election felt safer in 1983.

The defection of these moderates, including most of the leadership of the Democratic Party, led to the administration's defeat in a series of important committee votes during March and April. For the first time, it appeared that Congress might repudiate Reagan's Central America policy by crippling it with sharp reductions in military aid to El Salvador and a cutoff of funds for the CIA's secret war against Nicaragua.

The hard-liners replaced Enders's gradualist and conciliatory approach to Congress with a more confrontational style. Rather than trying to persuade Congress of the wisdom of administration policy, they sought to intimidate it with dire predictions of communist victory and an explicit warning that a reluctant Congress would be blamed by Reagan for "losing" Central America. To this familiar political threat was added a new appeal to even baser instincts: If Central America fell to communism, the United States would be inundated with "feet people"—hordes of brown-skinned refugees streaming northward.

President Reagan's extraordinary speech to a Joint Session of Congress on April 27, 1983, exemplified the new approach. He cast the issue of Central America starkly in Cold War terms, railing against the Cuban-Soviet threat, while lavishing praise on the "democratic" government of El Salvador. The threat to blame Congress for losing Central America if it failed to acquiesce to his demands was thinly veiled: "Who among us," he concluded his speech, "would wish to bear the responsibility for failing to meet our shared obligation?"[38] In case there was any doubt as to the import of this closing, Jeane Kirkpatrick was more blunt a few days later when she complained that the problems being encountered by the administration's policy were due to the fact that, "There are some members of Congress who want to see Marxist victories in Central America."[39]

The threat of a McCarthy-style recrimination temporarily silenced Reagan's congressional critics, but it failed to win back the support of the moderates, whose votes were essential to the administration. By year's end, the Congress had cut Reagan's military aid requests for El Salvador and for the Nicaraguan contras by half. The House of Representatives, with the Democratic Party leadership carrying the battle, had twice voted to cut off funding of the covert war entirely; it continued only by virtue of the Republican majority in the Senate.

To cope with continuing congressional opposition, Reagan appointed the National Bipartisan Commission on Central America (the Kissinger Commission) in July 1983. By appointing a putatively bipartisan commission stacked with members certain to support the basic thrust of Reagan's policy, the administration guaranteed a favorable report. The authority of the report could then be used to win back the votes of enough conservative Democrats to guarantee congressional support for Reagan's policy.

Of the twelve members of the Kissinger Commission, only one liberal Democrat, Mayor Henry Cisneros of San Antonio, was intentionally included. Another, Yale Professor Carlos Díaz-Alejandro, was included by mistake because the administration wrongly assumed that his Cuban heritage carried with it an appropriately conservative ideology. All the other Democrats appointed to the commission were hawks with little foreign policy experience and no expertise on Latin America.

The Kissinger Commission presented its report in January 1984 with only a handful of polite dissents. Predictably, it was an endorsement of administration policy, calling for a significant increase in military aid to El Salvador and Honduras. If anything, the report reinforced administration hard-liners on the issue of Nicaragua by rejecting a policy of "static containment." Instead, the report called for efforts to change not just the foreign policy behavior of the Sandinistas but also the character of the regime. If the Sandinistas refused to make the requisite concessions in negotiations, the direct use of U.S. military force would be the "ultimate recourse."[40]

But the commission report did not convince many skeptics that the administration's policy was any wiser or more likely to succeed. On the contrary, the confrontation between Congress and the Reagan administration reached a high-water mark in 1984. In the spring, the House of Representatives came within four votes of repudiating the administration's entire Central American policy. The package of proposals that was narrowly rejected would have banned military aid to Guatemala, limited U.S. military exercises in Honduras, and strictly conditioned aid to El Salvador on a congressionally approved certification.[41]

In June, the House refused to appropriate any additional funds for the covert war against Nicaragua, thereby ending U.S. aid to the contras. Later in the year, the House passed a ban on the introduction of U.S. forces into combat in Central America without prior approval of Congress; the Republican majority in the Senate rejected the prohibition, however, so it was never signed into law.

In 1985, congressional resistance to Reagan's policy began to recede. Congressional Democrats were noticeably more reticent to confront Reagan after the electoral debacle of November 1984. This was especially true in the case of El Salvador, where the 1984 election of José Napoleón Duarte as president and the subsequent Christian Democratic victory in the 1985 legislative elections persuaded many members of Congress that perhaps Reagan's policy was working after all. At a minimum, a broad consensus developed that Duarte should be given a chance to work out his own solution to the Salvadoran conflict. In practical terms, this translated into a willingness to approve Reagan's aid requests with only the slightest reductions and mildest conditions.

When Reagan sought a renewal of military aid for the contras in April, the Democrats held firm against it. But after several weeks of rancorous debate punctuated by an ill-timed trip to Moscow by Nicaraguan President Daniel Ortega, enough conservative Democrats broke ranks to approve Reagan's proposal to provide "humanitarian" aid to the contras. The United States thereby resumed its direct involvement in the covert war against Nicaragua.

The legislative battle over aid to the contras was marked by some of the most inflamatory rhetoric employed in the domestic debate over Central America. Although much of it was directed against Nicaragua, its real target was the Democratic opposition to Reagan's policy. The Secretary of State accused members of Congress of being "self-appointed emissaries" engaged in illegal negotiations with enemy governments.[42] In the Congress, Republicans openly called Democrats "soft on communism" for opposing the restoration of aid to the contras.[43]

The congressional opposition to Reagan's policy had multiple sources. In part it was based upon a sincere belief that his policy was endangering the national interest rather than safeguarding it. By escalating the level of military conflict in the region, the administration risked engulfing the entire region in war and drawing the United States into direct combat involvement. That, in turn would severely damage U.S. relations with Latin American nations like Mexico, Brazil, and Argentina—nations vastly more important to the United States than the ministates of Central America.

But perhaps the most important reason that Congress was willing to confront the President at all on the issue of Central America was existence of widespread public opposition to Reagan's policy, opposition based largely in the religious communities of the United States. The Catholic church, virtually every major Protestant denomination, and many American Jewish organizations were outspoken in their opposition. Across the nation, hundreds of congregations defied the law by offering sanctuary to Central American refugees entering the United States illegally.

Public opinion polls confirmed the reluctance of the general populace to see the United States become more deeply involved in the Central American crisis.[44] Despite its best efforts, the administration was unable to rally public support behind its policy. On the contrary, when the administration's public relations campaigns vaulted Central America into the headlines— as they did in the spring of 1981 and the winter of 1981 and 1982—the effect was usually counterproductive. The administration's incendiary rhetoric frightened people and yielded a sharp increase in public opposition to Reagan's policy. From 1982 onward, public opinion remained remarkably stable. About two out of every three Americans opposed Reagan's handling of the Central American crisis, with large majorities opposed to military aid for El Salvador, the deployment of U.S. advisers there, the military exercises in Honduras, and the covert war against Nicaragua. Within the administration, the consistent opposition of such a large segment of the public was considered a major obstacle to the pursuit of a more aggressive policy in the area.[45]

U.S. ALLIES AND THE SEARCH FOR PEACE   ▲

International opinion was another potential problem for the Reagan administration's policy. Haig's initial hope of rallying the allies around a policy of aggressive containment in Central America never got off the ground. Allied reaction was generally skeptical of Reagan's policy, which conjured up images of Vietnam, even in Europe. Public opinion in Europe was so vehement in its opposition to U.S. policy that the issue of Central America became a symbol around which to organize broader anti-American political appeals. No European government was prepared to actively back Washington in Central America; when the United States imposed a trade embargo on Nicaragua, not only did the Europeans refuse to join it, several of them actually increased economic assistance to Nicaragua to show their displeasure with the U.S. action.[46]

In Latin America, opposition to U.S. policy was almost as universal, especially among the larger nations like Argentina, Brazil, and Mexico. In particular, the four countries bordering Central America—Mexico, Venezuela, Colombia, and Panama—became so fearful of U.S. military intervention in the region that they undertook a series of diplomatic initiatives aimed at reducing the risks of regional war.

Several initiatives undertaken by these countries individually in 1981 and 1982 were ignored in Washington, prompting the four nations to join together in the Contadora group to launch a sustained diplomatic effort to resolve to the Central American crisis peacefully. The Reagan administration reacted coolly to Contadora, fearful that the initiative might move forward in ways inconsistent with U.S. policy. The United States was adamantly opposed to any negotiated solution to the war in El Salvador, except a fanciful one in which the FMLN surrendered in order to partake of elections. Washington was equally adamant in its opposition to any agreement that would require it to accept the continued existence of the Sandinista regime in Nicaragua.

But domestic and international reaction to Contadora was so positive that the administration could not afford to be seen as obstructing its progress. Consequently, Washington offered nominal support for the Contadora effort while at the same time working behind the scenes to assure that it would not take a direction inconsistent with U.S. military objectives in the region. Never did the Reagan administration allow the existence of the Contadora process to interfere with its own actions, even when they weakened Contadora. Perhaps the most flagrant example came in the summer of 1983 when the presidents of the four Contadora nations met and appealed to all the nations involved in Central America to refrain from any action that would heighten military tensions. Almost immediately, the United States announced the first of its massive military maneuvers in Honduras. In September 1984, the Reagan administration worked actively and successfully to block acceptance of a Contadora draft treaty, and in mid-1985, it rejected the Contadora nations' request to resume bilateral talks with Nicaragua.

Washington's close relations with the governments of El Salvador, Honduras, and Costa Rica give the Reagan administration veto power over any agreement drafted by the Contadora nations, since no agreement can take effect until all five of the Central American nations sign it. Washington's apparent lack of interest in achieving an agreement, therefore, left the Contadora process adrift, but it was not likely to die soon, since everyone saw it as the only diplomatic alternative to wider regional war.

THE OTHER CENTRAL AMERICANS: ▲
HONDURAS, COSTA RICA, AND GUATEMALA

As the Reagan administration's military commitment in El Salvador and its covert war against Nicaragua escalated, the role of Honduras became increasingly central to Washington's regional military strategy. As Chapter 5 recounts, Honduras was cast first as a military bulwark to contain Nicaragua and as a rear base for the growing army of counterrevolutionary forces at war with the Sandinistas. As the military situation of the Salvadoran army deteriorated, Honduras also became an important support base for the war against the FDR-FMLN. Initially, this involved coordinated military offensives against guerrilla positions along the Salvadoran-Honduran border. With the creation of the Regional Military Training Center to train Salvadoran forces in Honduras, any pretext of Honduran neutrality in Salvador's civil war was dispelled. By 1984, U.S. intelligence overflights of guerrilla-controlled zones in El Salvador were being flown out of Pamerola Air Base in Honduras.

In 1983, the United States began a major effort to build in Honduras the infrastructure necessary to support direct U.S. intervention in Central America.[47] Massive military exercises carried out by U.S. forces in Honduras served not only to intimidate Nicaragua but also to practice with the Honduran armed forces the military operations that would be used against Nicaragua should the occasion arise. Under the auspices of these exercises, U.S. forces built a number of military airfields and logistics depots without the normal authorization required by Congress.[48]

Washington's policy in Honduras was geared almost entirely to the regional military situation and had very little to do with Honduras per se. But the process of turning Honduras into a forward military base for the United States inevitably had domestic political consequences for Hondurans. As Honduras became increasingly involved in the conflicts of its neighbors, the issue of national security rose to the top of the national political agenda, overshadowing the issues of social and economic reform that the new civilian government had promised to address. As Washington provided ever-larger infusions of military aid to make Honduras a bulwark against Nicaragua (and to compensate the military for its cooperation in

Washington's regional plans), the internal political balance shifted toward the armed forces, which soon established itself as the most powerful institution in the new Honduran polity. General Gustavo Alvarez Martínez, head of the armed forces, emerged as the most powerful figure in the regime—a situation reinforced by the tendency of the U.S. embassy to deal directly with Alvarez rather than going through the president of the country, Roberto Suazo Córdova.

The subordination of civilian politics to General Alvarez met with resistance from several quarters. Opposition elements like the small Christian Democratic Party, the social democratic faction of the ruling Liberal Party (ALIPO), the press, and others criticized the impotence of civilian politicians. Even within the government, there were muted voices of concern.

The military's response to such dissidence was ominous; human rights violations, including disappearances, began to rise. Alvarez also undertook a sophisticated campaign to weaken various civilian political institutions that stood as potential obstacles to his consolidation of power. From trade unions to political parties and even the university, Alvarez promoted rightist challenges to moderate political leaders, dividing whatever institutions he could not gain full control over.

Though the civilians proved unable to halt Alvarez's accumulation of power, his personalistic style of authoritarianism produced sufficient unease among his brother officers that in 1984 he was ousted in a military coup and sent into exile. A number of factors contributed to the military's decision to depose Alvarez, but one of the major ones was resistance to Alvarez's eager willingness to steer Honduras along a course charted by the United States. His successors were a bit less willing to see Honduras used as an instrument of Washington's regional strategy, but the militarization of the economy continued, along with its attendant damage to civilian political authority.

Carter's Central American policy concerned Costa Rica only tangentially. Costa Rica's established democratic political institutions and developed social welfare system made it a model for what the administration hoped to achieve in the rest of the region. But since there was no hint of insurgency in Costa Rica, and its political system retained legitimacy in the eyes of the public despite deepening economic difficulties, Washington saw no need to involve itself.

For the Reagan administration, however, Costa Rica was important because of its strategic location on Nicaragua's southern border. Washington tried hard to enlist Costa Rica in its crusade against the Sandinistas, just as it enlisted Honduras. And just as Honduras became a secure rear area for the contras fighting along Nicaragua's northern border, Washington hoped to make Costa Rica a secure base for contras in the south. Costa Rica's value as an ally against Nicaragua exceeded that of Honduras, though, because the Costa Ricans were so highly respected in Latin America, Europe, and the United States. When democratic Costa Rica, which had no army, declared the Sandinistas to be a threat to the peace of Central

America, it was more likely to be believed than when it was said by Honduran generals.

As we saw in Chapter 6, the Costa Ricans were somewhat reluctant to play the role scripted for them in Washington. While there is a long tradition of animosity between Costa Rican and Nicaraguan governments of whatever ideological bent, most Costa Ricans hoped to stay as distant as possible from the escalating military conflicts in the rest of the region. But the danger that they might be caught up in the battles of their neighbors was not the only threat to Costa Rica's democracy. The other danger was economic. Costa Rica's desperate financial situation necessitated a sharp cutback in the very social welfare programs that had been the foundation of the political system's legitimacy. Costa Ricans began to see unsettling parallels between their plight and what happened to the "Switzerland of South America," Uruguay. Like Costa Rica, Uruguay built its democracy upon the legitimacy provided by an advanced social welfare system atypical for an underdeveloped nation. Like Costa Rica, it was a predominantly middle-class society thought to be immune to the depredations of military intervention in politics. The descent of Uruguay into brutal dictatorship in the 1970s was triggered by an economic crisis that demolished its social welfare system, undermined the legitimacy of its politics, and gave rise to insurgency.

For Costa Ricans, the central political issue became how to best safeguard their democracy against these dual dangers of external turmoil and internal economic austerity. The government of Luis Alberto Monge was divided from the outset about what strategy Costa Rica should pursue. Some argued that close association with the United States and support for U.S. policy in Central America offered the best guarantee of stability because it would assure a continued flow of economic assistance to ease the internal economic problem. Others argued that associating Costa Rica too closely with U.S. policy would lead inevitably to Costa Rica being drawn into the conflicts of its neighbors, and that only a policy of strict neutrality would safeguard the nation. The Reagan administration took advantage of the Costa Ricans' economic fears by making it clear that significant increases in economic assistance were contingent upon Costa Rica's willingness to cooperate with Washington's regional designs. Despite these pressures, the Monge government tried—albeit with only partial success—to maintain Costa Rican neutrality.

Of all the Central American nations, Guatemala remained the one least involved in the regional conflict and the Reagan administration's efforts to resolve it. Reagan came to office determined to restore the traditional U.S. security relationship with Guatemala. Though the guerrilla war there was not nearly as advanced as in El Salvador, the unparalleled brutality and corruption of the Lucas García regime had given the guerrillas new strength, and there was great concern in Washington that without U.S. assistance, the government might gradually lose its ability to contain the guerrillas.

Guatemala's human rights record was so bad that even the Reagan administration, with its disdain for human rights restrictions on military aid, was not prepared to deny that the Lucas García regime was a gross and consistent violator of internationally recognized human rights, and as such was ineligible for assistance. The Reagan administration's strategy, however, was to persuade the Guatemalan military to make at least minimal cosmetic improvements in order to give the administration some grounds for proposing to Congress a resumption of aid. But Lucas García refused, and the human rights situation in Guatemala actually deteriorated. Consequently, Congress rebuffed every administration suggestion that a new relationship with Guatemala be initiated.

After the coup that ousted Lucas García and installed General Efraín Ríos Montt as president in 1982, the administration again tried to convince Congress that aid should be resumed, but the new government's brutal counterinsurgency campaign during the summer of 1982 simply reinforced congressional resistance. When General Humberto Mejía Víctores ousted Ríos Montt in August 1983, the administration once again raised the trial balloon of military aid to Guatemala, but the resumption of death-squad activities in Guatemala's cities led Congress to reduce even economic aid to the new regime.

The scheduling of presidential elections for 1985, however, led Congress to loosen the purse strings slightly in 1984. It seemed likely that if a moderate civilian candidate won the elections and was allowed to take power, the Reagan administration might finally succeed in its perennial effort to restore large-scale military and economic assistance to Guatemala. It seemed less likely, however, that the Guatemalan armed forces would surrender their role as ultimate political authority.

ORDER OR PROGRESS? THE MAINTENANCE OF CONTROL ▲

The differences between Jimmy Carter's and Ronald Reagan's policies in Central America were as sharp as any in the recent history of U.S.–Latin American relations. Yet despite these differences, both policies were designed to achieve the same fundamental objective: to prevent the accession to power of the radical left—i.e., any movement intent on rapid and fundamental social transformation.

Carter was more amenable to change in the region than Reagan. Combining the noninterventionism of Roosevelt's Good Neighbor Policy and the reformism of Kennedy's Alliance for Progress, Carter sought to promote human rights and deal normally with neighboring states, despite their ideological diversity. This approach produced a diplomatic settlement of the Panama Canal issue—an achievement that safeguarded U.S. security in the region far better than any effort to maintain control of the Canal by force would have. Carter also understood that inequality and oppression were the major causes of revolution in Central America, so he sought to build political stability in the region on a foundation of socioeconomic reform and political democratization.

These positive instincts were ultimately undone by the administration's reflexive anathema for radicalism. In Nicaragua, Washington failed in its efforts to replace Somoza with a moderate successor, and then failed to keep the FSLN from coming to power when Somoza finally collapsed. In the wake of the Sandinistas' victory, the Carter administration had some limited success in its efforts to maintain a constructive relationship with the new regime but was hampered in its ability to carry out such a policy by the Republican right in Congress. In El Salvador, Washington found itself allied with a regime that pledged itself to reform and democracy, but in reality was little more than a right-wing military dictatorship hiding behind the façade of civilian politicians who held no real power.

Ronald Reagan came to office proclaiming that the global rivalry between the United States and the Soviet Union would be the keynote of his foreign policy. The administration's early rhetoric and actions in Central America faithfully reflected the East-West optic through which the administration viewed virtually every Third World conflict. Initially, Carter's efforts to promote reformism and human rights were derided as counterproductive—idealistic notions that served only to destabilize U. S. allies locked in mortal combat with Soviet proxies. The new administration quickly embraced old allies with new flows of military aid, regardless of their questionable human rights practices. Where Carter saw poverty and dictatorship as the root causes of revolution, the Reagan administration saw mainly the specter of Cuban subversion. Intervention to stem the perceived spread of communism was restored to its traditional place in the armory of U.S. policy responses —covertly against Nicaragua, overtly against Grenada.

The Reagan administration, like Carter's before it, was forced by circumstances to modify its initial policy instincts regarding Central America. For Reagan, the cause of change was a reluctant Congress and a reluctant population, both of which still remembered the trauma of Vietnam. As U.S. military involvement in Central America deepened during Reagan's first term, the rhetoric of the policy paid greater and greater obeisance to human rights, reform, and a "political solution" to the region's conflicts. Nevertheless, Reagan's commitment to these objectives always appeared only so strong as required to gain continued congressional acquiescence to his military assistance program.

Despite its very different approach to Central America, the Reagan administration did not have much more success managing the crisis than the Carter administration had had. Carter's failures, it turned out, were not a result of his unwillingness to use U.S. power, as the Reaganites charged; rather they were a product of Central American reality—a reality more intransigent than the United States anticipated. The Reagan administration had to learn this the hard way, by seeing their own fond hopes for quick solutions to the regional crisis dashed by events.

Haig's initial hopes for military victory in El Salvador within six months of Reagan's inauguration proved to be wildly overoptimistic. Even the more modest goal of gradually building the Salvadoran army to the point that it could take the initiative from the FMLN was extremely difficult. On the political side, Washington's efforts to promote a stable center-right coalition in San Salvador proved equally hard to manage. The right was more intractable and powerful than Washington anticipated, and the military remained unwilling to surrender its role as the ultimate arbiter of politics.

In Nicaragua, the Sandinistas also proved to be more tenacious and resistant to U.S. destabilization efforts than the administration expected. Covert paramilitary operations grew into a full-scale war with some fifteen thousand contras fighting the Nicaraguan army, but even the Pentagon conceded that the contras had no chance of winning.

The policy of pressures allegedly designed to make the Sandinistas behave as desired by Washington had a wide range of counterproductive effects. Instead of strengthening internal democracy and pluralism, it polarized Nicaraguan politics, thereby endangering the political survival of the internal opposition. Instead of forcing the Sandinistas to reduce their ties to Cuba and the Soviet Union, Washington's hostility led to the rapid expansion of those ties, as the Nicaraguans were forced to find alternative sources for military hardware to fight the war and economic aid to make up for the economic sanctions levied by the United States.

That the policies of Carter and Reagan, so different in conception and in execution, could be so equivalent in their failure to resolve the Central American crisis suggests a deeper similarity below their surface differences. While Carter and Reagan began from nearly opposite visions of the nature of the problem in Central America and how to cope with it, both pursued policies based upon a similar vision of the role of the United States in the region. Carter's openness to ideological pluralism did not extend to welcoming the advent of radical leftist regimes, as his policies in both Nicaragua and El Salvador made eminently clear. Once revolutionary turmoil erupted in Central America, the Carter administration sought, with clarity of purpose, to prevent the radical left from achieving any significant degree of political power.

Keeping the left from power was precisely the goal of the Reagan administration as well. Reagan's method was simply more direct than Carter's —he was prepared to provide the werewithal that existing elites in the region required in order to defeat the leftist challenge. Whereas Carter's containment strategy was essentially political, Reagan's was essential military—but both sought the same result.

The objective of keeping the radical left from attaining power in the Third World—particularly Latin America—is such a time-honored corollary of the containment doctrine that it seemed superfluous to ask where it came from. The doctrine has a mixed parentage—partly a product of the Cold War and the perception that Third World conflicts often or inevitably are an arena in that war, and partly an impetus to protect U.S. economic interests from the depradations of nationalistic regimes.

But in Latin America, and especially the Caribbean Basin, the motives behind containment have another source best exemplified in the phrase that characterizes the region as "our own backyard." That motive is control; the imperative that the United States be in a position to control events in the region, the sovereignty of other states notwithstanding. It is a notion that predates the Cold War—indeed, predates the existence of the Soviet Union —and a notion that has long outlasted the days when the United States had a major economic stake in the area. This motive of control can be traced back at least to the turn of the century, if not earlier, and it forms the basis of what can only be called a uniquely American version of colonialism.

13

THE FAILURE OF THE
HEGEMONIC STRATEGIC VISION

Morris J. Blachman,
Douglas C. Bennett,
William M. LeoGrande,
and Kenneth E. Sharpe

The Central American policies of the Carter and Reagan administrations represent the two ways the United States has confronted revolution. But despite the differences between Carter and Reagan, their policies in Central America produce similar outcomes in terms of U.S. interests in the region. During both administrations, conflict was exacerbated and broadened in scope; there was greater polarization of militants on both the left and the right; refugees from the region increased; U.S. intentions were increasingly questioned by all sides in the dispute as well as by our regional friends and European allies; and national security (the central goal of both) was made less, not more, secure.

That such seemingly different policy orientations led to such similar outcomes reflects that much of what occurs in the region, of course, is a function of internal conditions. But a major factor has been the underlying vision, shared by Carter and Reagan, that presumed U.S. hegemony in the region as both necessary and proper.[1]

At the heart of this hegemonic strategic vision was the unquestioned assumption that it was essential for the United States to maintain veto control over the character of regimes in the region in order to protect American national interests. Indeed the assumption was so deeply rooted that most policymakers came to see the means, the exercise of U.S. hegemony, as the end in and of itself; few analyzed whether such control was really the best means to achieve and protect U.S. national interests. This became particularly serious because during the 1960s and 1970s a second assumption was becoming increasingly unrealistic: that the United States had the power to exercise such control in Central America.

THE HEGEMONIC STRATEGIC VISION IN HISTORICAL PERSPECTIVE ▲

The hegemonic strategic vision had its roots in the early days of the Republic. From Thomas Jefferson to Ronald Reagan, U.S. policymakers have presumed that Latin America was our backyard, what transpired there was critical to U.S. security, and that it naturally fell to us to watch over and control its destiny.

An observation of Jefferson's reflected the first stirrings of this view: "We begin to broach the idea that we consider the whole gulph [sic] stream as our water . . . this is essential to our tranquility and commerce . . . Our strength will permit us to give the law of our own hemisphere."[2] Several years later James Monroe spoke to U.S. concern over European intervention in the hemisphere. He associated the security of the Latin American republics with that of the United States. Any effort on the part of the European powers to "extend their system to any portion of this hemisphere" would be deemed by the United States "as dangerous to our peace and security."[3]

Although the United States took few actions to back up that vision in the ensuing decades, by the turn of the century the Monroe Doctrine had been elevated to an unquestioned first principle of policy in the hemisphere. Referring to the Monroe Doctrine in 1895, Secretary of State Richard Olney declared that "the United States is practically sovereign on this continent, and its fiat is law upon the subjects to which it confines its interpretations."[4]

By the early twentieth century the United States had the power to keep foreign countries out of the hemisphere—especially out of Central America. Success in driving the Spanish out of Cuba in 1898 and the U.S.-backed secession of Panama from Colombia firmly established the United States as the hegemonic military, political, and economic power in the region.

During this age of Roosevelt's "big stick," U.S. policy came to mean more than simply preventing direct foreign intervention. The idea took root that it was incumbent upon the United States to correct any deficiencies in the internal character of Latin American regimes that might encourage foreign intrusion. In 1904, President Roosevelt declared that civilized nations had the responsibility to monitor the character of regimes of those countries that engaged in "chronic wrong doing, or an impotence which results in a general loosening of the ties of civilized society." Building on the foundation of the Monroe Doctrine he declared that,

in the Western Hemisphere the adherence of the United States to the Monroe Doctrine may force the United States, however reluctantly, . . . to the exercise of an international police power.[5]

The Roosevelt Corollary to the Monroe Doctrine guided numerous U.S. interventions in the region as the United States landed troops, took control of external finances (customs receiverships), and made and broke regimes.

The declaration and the interventions that followed solidified in concrete policy terms the hegemonic strategic vision. The policymakers' primary responsibility became to identify the source of any threats that might lead to foreign intervention (and thereby jeopardize U.S. security) and to devise methods for dealing with them. At the time of the Corollary, political turmoil and economic instability were the threats perceived to be of particular concern. These were seen as even more serious to the degree that they seemed to be initiated from abroad. The specific methods for dealing with these threats varied, but a minimum policy sought sufficient control to prevent any situation that might make these countries susceptible to foreign entanglement and intervention. How broadly the United States construed its mission has often been reflected in the comments of key policymakers.[6] In 1927, for example, Undersecretary of State Robert Olds wrote:

> Our ministers accredited to the five little republics, stretching from the Mexican border to Panama . . . have been advisers whose advice has been accepted virtually as law in the capitals where they respectively reside. . . . We do control the destinies of Central America and we do so for the simple reason that the national interest absolutely dictates such a course. . . . Until now Central America has always understood that governments which we recognize and support stay in power, while those we do not recognize and support fall.[7]

Such statements were not mere bluster: the reality was that the United States had the will and the power to enforce its hegemony. The Central American societies were relatively small in population, with simple economies and weak state structures. The governing elites were also small in number and the bulk of the population lived well outside the mainstream of economic and political life. The combination of the penetrability of the Central American nations and the growing military strength of the United States made intervention and control a relatively easy task.

From Direct Intervention to Internal Subversion

In the first part of the twentieth century, the actions of the United States were, as Assistant Secretary of State Adolph Berle, Jr., stated in 1939,

> due more to the fear of European domination than to any desire to increase the area of our territory. Conspicuous among these were the interventions beginning at the time of the Panama Canal incident, the Nicaraguan occupation, and the occupation of Haiti and Santo Domingo.[8]

But, after World War I effectively diminished any threat of direct European aggression, an important shift in U.S. policy began under Hoover and was formalized under Roosevelt as the "Good Neighbor Policy." The new policy was based, said Undersecretary of State Sumner Welles, "on a complete forbearance from interference by any republic in the domestic concerns of any other."[9]

Even so, the specter of Bolshevism spreading south from Mexico had already been used to justify U.S. intervention in Nicaragua. Indeed, President Coolidge's message to Congress in the late 1920s foreshadowed the fears that would preoccupy post–World War II administrations. The United States would be deeply concerned, said Coolidge, with "any serious threat to stability . . . especially if such state of affairs is contributed to or brought about by outside influences or by a foreign power."[10]

With the Truman Doctrine in 1947 a policy of containment was defined and gradually extended to mean not simply stopping the Soviet Union from invading countries on its border but preventing the development of communist influence in any country. Response to the threat of subversion found formal legal expression in hemispheric affairs in a resolution adopted, after considerable U.S. pressure, at the Tenth Inter-American Conference in Caracas in 1954. It stated:

> the combination or control of the political institutions of any American State by the international communist movement, extending to the Hemisphere the political system of an extracontinental power, would constitute a threat to the sovereignty and political independence of the American states, endangering the peace of America, and would call for a Meeting of Consultation to consider the adoption of appropriate action in accordance with existing treaties.[11]

The United States had sought passage of this resolution in an effort to create legal grounds for intervention in Guatemala and similar situations.[12] Ipso facto, communist governments that took power represented expansion of Soviet influence and a threat to the strategic balance between the United States and the Soviet Union. The hegemonic strategic vision thus still defined the direction of U.S. policy in the hemisphere, but the threat to U.S. dominance and control took on a new post–World War II meaning: keeping communism out of the region.

Just as before, few had questioned whether maintaining U.S. hegemony was the best means for serving U.S. interests, so now, few questioned whether keeping out communism was the best means to protect U.S. interests. There was a price to be paid for the lack of debate, however: in the highly charged and rhetorical atmosphere of the Cold War the notion of "keeping out the communists" tended to gloss over important considerations crucial for sound policymaking.[13]

First, it blurred all distinctions on the left. Left was taken necessarily to mean Marxist and Marxist to mean Soviet Communist, and communists, once in power, would inevitably establish a totalitarian system that would tyranize its population and jeopardize U.S. economic, political, and military interests. Few policymakers believed that a leftist government might have normal trade, financial, and investment relationships with the United States and might be less brutal, no worse politically, and perhaps, better economically, than the right-wing regime it replaced.

Communism came to be so broadly defined it included democratic reformers on the left (like Social Democrats); unions whose leaders' rhetoric was anti-American and anticapitalist; aggressive peasant groups seeking land reform; popular organizations in countries like El Salvador and Nicaragua, which used nonelectoral but nonviolent direct action to challenge military regimes and harsh dictatorships; as well as self-declared Marxists, whether they favored nationalist revolutions and nonalignment or whether they were tied to pro-Moscow Communist Parties. Most policymakers assumed a priori that whatever the composition of a leftist (or center-leftist) coalition, the trained and highly committed "communists" were willing to mask their real intentions and engage in whatever devious or heinous actions were necessary to eliminate their opposition and seize control.[14]

Second, it assumed that any leftist regime would threaten U.S. geopolitical interests by providing the Soviet Union with a toehold in the region that would be used to create military allies, topple neighboring states, and establish Soviet bases. The United States might be "encircled," directly threatening its very existence. The possibility of nonaligned governments and nationalist revolutions that would be neither expansionst nor Soviet beachheads was often dismissed out of hand—despite the examples of Yugoslavia, India, and Algeria. Instead, the bipolar world view allowed for only two possibilities in Central and Latin America: nations and movements had to choose between being friends or enemies, part of the solution or part of the problem. Movements that sought to destroy harsh, "anticommunist" militaries or recalcitrant right-wing oligarchies were seen, by definition, as opening the door to communism and thus becoming enemies. Criticism of the United States was seen as tantamount to support for the Soviet Union.

The exclusion of the left from power was seen as a necessary condition for stopping the Soviets from accomplishing their putative aims by means of internal subversion. The fear of communists led to an overexaggeration of their capability, imbuing them with almost superhuman ability to prevail, despite the actual record of dismal failure of such movements, especially the Moscow-oriented ones, in South America.

If few questioned the assumption that leftist meant Marxist meant Communist meant Soviet encirclement, fewer yet questioned either the right or ability of the United States to control the internal character of regimes to keep "the left" out of power. However, the power this would require was often underestimated. It was no longer simply a question of taking control of customs houses or sponsoring coups against often weak chief executives in weak states. It became necessary to limit political turmoil that might provide the basis through which leftist leaders could capture the public imagination, and to contain political movements that might seize power. Whether such social and political disruption would be controlled primarily by military force or by removing the inequities and repression, far more power would have to be exercised than ever before if the United States were to control the character of regimes and social movements.

Breakdown in Consensus: Hard-line versus Moderate Hegemonists

By the early 1960s important differences began to arise in the policymaking community about the best means to keep the left out of power. In the wake of Castro's overthrow of Batista, the failure of U.S. pressure to make him bend to U.S. wishes, his increasingly close relations with the Soviet Union (furthered by U.S. pressure), and the failure of a U.S.-organized Guatemalan-like exile invasion (the Bay of Pigs), the Kennedy administration turned to a somewhat different strategy. U.S. support for the Alliance for Progress grew out of a belief that the best way to prevent revolution—and thus keep out the communists—was by promoting economic and political reforms. Nonetheless, the mailed hand of force was also incorporated in the program to contain those who were seen to be subversives, and to buy time for the reforms to take hold. The local military was to be strengthened through military and economic aid, technical assistance, and training in counter-insurgency. Thus, the Alliance represented a more moderate variant of the hegemonic strategic vision than the traditional big stick approaches of the hard-liners.

These two general conceptions have since dominated the foreign policy debate in Washington. The hard-liners see national security as indivisible. Even events with a low probability of leading to a direct threat to U.S. security are treated as virtually imminent. They see the causes of revolution as primarily external, stimulated and supported by the Soviets or their proxies. In the words of John Foster Dulles (echoed three decades later by the Kissinger Commission) communism was "alien intrigue and treachery," a danger "originating outside the hemisphere."[15] Their policy response relies primarily on the use of force to eliminate the turmoil and establish order. Leftist movements—for the hard-liners, "communism"—are, like cancer, a disease that will spread unless forcibly exorcised.

The moderate hegemonists are more likely to see degrees of threat. They are reluctant to use force as a response to an event they believe has a low probability of threatening U.S. security. They trace the causes of turmoil and revolution primarily to internal reactions to domestic inequality and repression, although these may be exacerbated by external support from the Soviet Union or its allies. Their preferred policy response is to make use of political pressure and economic assistance to achieve reform and end repression, thus cutting the ground from beneath any revolutionary movement that might come to rely on external powers.

Moderate and hard-line hegemonists in Washington both argue that it is the opposition of the other that has frustrated their policies. But the truth is that even at their best, such strategies can only maintain a semblance of control, one that is increasingly costly not only to the region but to U.S. national interests as well.

The moderate hegemonists insist that given time political opposition to right-wing tyranny, support of human rights and economic reform, and economic assistance to aid development will help create more moderate, increasingly democratic governments in Guatemala, Honduras, and El Salvador, and that the reforms these governments sponsor will decompress the internal conditions for turmoil and insurgency. No U.S. policy is sufficient of itself to bring about these results.

They are right in thinking that the internal conditions that breed armed insurgency must be changed. What they often fail to see, however, is that this demands a redistribution of power: the stranglehold of the military and the oligarchy must be broken to bring about reform. Such a strategy requires the participation of key groups seeking major institutional change, and some of these groups are to be found on the left. These groups include unions, peasant and other popular organizations, as well as leftist political parties. Even those who seem to recognize this need for structural change —like Presidents Kennedy and Carter—have still refused to accept its corollary: genuine structural reform in these countries is highly unlikely so long as the left is automatically to be excluded from political participation. If excluding the left is necessary because it is seen as challenging U.S. hegemony, then the policy of these moderates will not work.

The result of such an unrealistic approach is that the moderate hegemonist policy sputters inconsistently and incoherently along, trying to support a weak or nonexistent center as an increasingly violent and revolutionary left takes power, probably in opposition to the United States (as in Nicaragua). These consequences press even those moderates to back the right with U.S. military aid (even though rhetorically they may insist they are supporting the center, as in El Salvador). Increasingly, they come to rely on military force. The "logic" of their unrealistic approach thus leads them eventually to act like hard-liners in order to maintain U.S. hegemony.

Hard hegemonists call for a different strategy, one that is primarily military from the very beginning: first defeat the left so that we can have the order that will then allow reform to begin. When this does not work, they argue for more force and blame their moderate opponents for restricting them from doing what needs to be done.

Such hard-liners are right in recognizing that the United States still has enormous power in the region. We can establish some control by propping up existing militaries or intervening with U.S. troops, if we are willing to pay the increasing moral, economic, and military costs. They point to the success increased military aid to El Salvador has had in preventing the left from taking power. Although that aid has so far failed to defeat the insurgency, enough force and violence could probably restore some kind of "order." It must be remembered, they add, that the Guatemalan military did put down two insurgencies, and in the second instance they did so with little material aid from the United States. But there are two serious problems with such "solutions."

First, they are temporary: the order that might be restored in countries like El Salvador is likely to leave in power the same military oligarchic alliance whose opposition to moderate reform was the cause of the insurgency in the first place. Such policies "work" the way a huge lead cork might work to bottle up a volcano. When a U.S.-backed reformist was finally elected in Guatemala in 1966, he was not only blocked in his reform efforts by the oligarchy and the military, but was forced to sign a pact with the military giving them a free hand to preside over a brutal repression, one that killed not only a few hundred insurgents but thousands of unarmed peasants, labor leaders, and party officials. When the repression ended in the early 1970s, "order" had been restored. Nevertheless, renewed efforts at reform again brought state terror, and this, in turn, spurred more armed insurgency in the late 1970s and early 1980s. This time the military-backed terror reached genocidal proportions.

U.S. interests in long-term regional peace are not served by supporting those who compact the powder in the keg. Force may reduce or contain the successes of insurgency and keep the left out of power longer than the "reform-without-the-left" strategies of the moderate hegemonists, but the solution is no less temporary.

A second problem is that reestablishing such order is increasingly costly and injurious to U.S. national interests. Just to secure this temporary solution the United States must sustain those who engage in massive repression, even genocide. This was, in fact, the policy of Lucas García, Riós Montt, and Mejía Victores in Guatemala. In El Salvador from 1980 to 1985, the regimes the United States supported—and urged not to share power with the left—were themselves responsible for the deaths of over 40,000 noncombatants. Moreover, the U.S.-backed contras in Nicaragua have used terror tactics similar to those many of their leaders used as national guardsmen under Somoza.

Supporting such cemetery methods of control to reestablish order is an unacceptable policy for the United States. It violates all the principles our foreign policy is supposed to protect and promote. Such conduct undermines our moral authority in the region and in the world. We become the friend of the tyrant, not the champion of the oppressed. We eradicate the distinctions we seek to draw between our principles and those of the Soviet Union. In so doing, we allow the Soviets to pose as champions of the downtrodden in this hemisphere where insurgent movements have had little experience with Soviet ill-doings.

The predominant pattern in Central American policy in the Kennedy and Carter administrations was that of moderate hegemony, and strong opposition was faced by hard-liners in Congress and the bureaucracy. With the hard hegemony of the Nixon, Ford, Reagan (and, to some extent, Johnson) administrations the situation was reversed. Clearly not all policymakers fall fully into one category or the other, but these two basic positions have defined much of foreign policy debate since the late 1950s. So different were their diagnoses of the causes of turmoil and their resulting insistence on different policy approaches that each side has often had difficulty understanding its opponents, let alone persuading them that they are wrong.

The lack of consensus on foreign policy frequently constrained the ability of administrations to carry out a coherent and consistent foreign policy along either a hard line or moderate line. Within the foreign-policy-making institutions of the United States, actors who held each of these views have been able to block or derail their opponents' policies. But rarely has either side in this debate raised the question of whether the United States has sufficient power to enforce its hegemonic goals, even more rare is there any questioning of whether attempting such control really serves U.S. interests.

A STATIC VISION OF A CHANGING REALITY   ▲

From the late 1800s through the middle of the twentieth century, U.S. dominance was unchallenged. In the past twenty-five years Central America has changed, however, and many U.S. policymakers seem confounded by these transformations they only dimly understand. This is not surprising. After all, in absolute terms, the United States has much greater power in terms of military force (the United States can deliver far more firepower; transport more people more rapidly to more places; and employ technology that far outstrips that of the late 1940s); economic productive capacity (the United States can produce more sophisticated products more rapidly and distribute them more effectively); and diplomatic capability (the United States has far more people representing it in more places around the globe involved in more activities than ever before).

In Central America, the United States clearly has superior military power, and Central American nations lack adequate defenses to prevent the United States from employing its weapons at will. Engineering social changes, especially installing certain kinds of regimes or undercutting particular social movements has been made much more difficult by profound transformations in the region during the past three decades. Economic growth via light industrialization and agricultural diversification created new classes who want a share in political power to support their economic gains. Peasants organized to redress the grievences thrust upon them by loss of their land to commercialized agriculture, low rural wages, and joblessness. New political parties and popular organizations arose to make demands on traditional elites. The Catholic church was transformed as important segments abandoned their traditional support for the oligarchy and helped organize Christian base communities and popular organizations that joined leftist groups in larger social movements. Militaries, better trained, became more independent from the oligarchies they once served and developed their own interests in politics, business, and corruption. Regional economic ties were strengthened as the countries developed common interests through the Central American Common Market. The oil wealth of Venezuela and, more recently, Mexico, and Panama's acquisition of its Canal gave them new confidence and influence. The agreement of Mexico and Venezuela to provide oil at discounted prices to countries in the region foreshadowed an increasingly important role for these countries. Later they were joined by Panama and Columbia in trying to mediate political settlements to regional problems, often at odds with the policies of the Reagan administration.

Such changes in the region limited the power of the United States to shape events. It was relatively easy for the United States to help create a national guard in Nicaragua and install Somoza as its head in the early 1930s, but the United States could not remove Somoza, save the national guard, and install a moderate, pro-U.S. regime in the late 1970s. To overthrow the Arbenz regime in Guatemala in 1954 required only a small operation in a society in the earliest stages of social mobilization, but the political repression and instability following the 1954 overthrow mobilized even larger segments of the population into national life. This politicization of broader publics, now including the Indians; the growth of a stronger, more autonomous and increasingly vicious military; and the development of a more complex economic and class structure have made U.S. control over the internal character of Guatemala a much more difficult, if not impossible, task. We seem unable to stop human rights abuses, nor can we produce a centrist, reformist government.

In El Salvador we can get the military to hold elections, persuade the government to pass land-reform laws, and keep the economy from collapsing by providing millions in aid, but our best efforts cannot create a strong, moderate government capable of ending the repression and corruption of the military and paramilitary forces and redistributing social and economic power. In Honduras, the United States can induce the government and the military to accept maneuvers, training camps, forward bases, and a staging area for the U.S.-supported contras, but we do not have the capacity to stop the dangerous side effects of the militarization we have promoted: a weakening of the fragile democracy that seemed to be emerging, inflation, disinvestment, and the growth of opposition movements who, seeing reform frustrated, are increasingly angered by the nature of U.S. involvement.

Abraham Lowenthal aptly summed up the challenge this changing regional reality has posed:

> The unmet challenge of United States policy during the past twenty years has been how to respond to the erosion of the brief postwar period of virtually unchallenged dominance in the Western Hemisphere—how to cope with hegemony in decline.[16]

THE HEGEMONIC STRATEGIC VISION ▲
AND U.S. INTERESTS

The altered reality of Central America demands a fresh assessment of U.S. interests. The hegemonic strategic vision that has guided U.S. foreign policy toward the region, however, rests upon an assessment that increasingly harms rather than serves our national interest. It insists that maintaining control over internal events in Central American countries to exclude the left from power is vital to the welfare of the United States. Indeed, exercising such control is confused with the national interest itself: Keeping the left out of power is defined as furthering our national interest. But confusing a means with an end it is supposed to serve is fatal for rational policymaking. As the case studies in this book make clear time and time again, trying to control internal events in Central American countries has yielded policies that are increasingly costly and increasingly counterproductive.

The hegemonic strategic vision focuses almost exclusively on defense and national security, overlooking other important U.S. interests in the region. Worse, many of its claims about security issues are based on misunderstandings of reality or improbable assumptions. These erroneous claims need to be cleared away before we can arrive at a more balanced assessment of U.S. interests in the region.

As described by various spokespersons for the Reagan administration and the National Bipartisan Commission on Central America (the Kissinger Commission), the security threat in Central America has several dimensions.

First, they claim, is the danger that revolutionary regimes such as Nicaragua will act as "platforms" for exporting subversion to their neighbors. This revived domino theory portrays instability as eventually spreading to endanger Panama and Mexico, threatening the Canal and our southern border.

Second is the fear that revolutionary regimes in Central America will constitute a potential military threat. This will occur, it is argued, because it is likely that such regimes will fall under the control of Marxist-Leninists, who are likely to align themselves with the Soviet Union and are then likely to undertake a buildup of miliary forces threatening the security of neighboring states and possibly even that of the United States itself. Nicaragua and Cuba are cited as places where this has already occurred. Regularly mentioned as potential targets of conventional attack are Venezuelan and Mexican oil fields, the Panama Canal, and the sea lanes of the Caribbean.

Third is the concern that the credibility of U.S. security guarantees elsewhere in the world will be undermined by the inability or unwillingness of the United States to prevent the establishment of hostile regimes in its recognized sphere of influence—"our own backyard."

Because any revolutionary regime of the left is considered likely to subvert its neighbors and align with the Soviets to threaten U.S. and regional security, the consistent policy assumption since World War II has been that the United States must prevent leftist movements from becoming leftist governments if we are to protect our national security.

With this approach, if normal diplomatic efforts fail, then abnormal undertakings become necessary: the CIA-sponsored "liberation" of Guatemala in 1954, the Bay of Pigs invasion of 1961, the Dominican intervention of 1965, and the present arming of contras against the Sandinista regime in Nicaragua. So deeply grounded has become the assumption that leftist regimes by their very existence automatically threaten U.S. security, that many policymakers and most citizens rarely examine the arguments behind this premise. For fear of being tarred as "soft" on communism, few raise the question of whether keeping the left out of power is an appropriate means to protect security. Few even bother to distinguish among groups on the left. Such assumptions about potential threats to U.S. interests, however, need to be scrutinized carefully.

The Domino Theory

The domino theory assumes that revolution is a disguised form of external aggression. Success in one country, it argues, provides a platform for the "export of revolution" to the next. There is both a simplistic and a sophisticated version of this theory.

The simplistic version holds that external subversion is the source of internal turmoil: if not for the subversive activities of Moscow, Cuba, and Nicaragua, there would be no political instability in Central America.

Few specialists take this view seriously. Central America's long history of socioeconomic inequality and political dictatorship provide more than sufficient cause for insurgency. The guerrilla movements in Nicaragua, El Salvador, and Guatemala, for example, did not receive significant assistance from abroad in the mid and late 1970s, the period when they expanded rapidly.

The sophisticated version of the domino theory acknowledges that political instability in Central America is caused by internal grievances but that the success of a revolutionary movement in one nation still tends to increase the risk for others. Even indigenous rebellions require outside assistance to succeed. In El Salvador, for example, this view argues the army would be able to contain and eventually defeat the insurgency if it were not for Nicaraguan and Cuban aid.

This subtler version of the domino theory is also seriously flawed—not because the situation it asserts is not possible but because it blurs important distinctions and assumes what it ought to prove.

First, it fails to distinguish among leftist regimes: its proponents tend to assume that revolutionary regimes on the left seek to export revolution. Mexico is a good example of the erroneous nature of that view. In the early years following its revolution many U.S. officials saw the Mexicans as

Bolsheviks, spreading their revolution as far south as Nicaragua. But the reality is that the revolution in Mexico was primarily nationalist, its energies directed internally, not to the export of revolution.

Second, this version of the domino theory still focuses the attention of policymakers away from dealing with the roots of armed insurgency in a repressive system, a situation made worse by our support. While paying lip service to indigenous causes of revolution, those who point to external assistance as responsible for exploiting internal problems often miss the depth of these internal problems. It is not poverty and inequality that suddenly get ignited by outside arms or ideas; it is the brutal suppression of attempts at nonviolent reform by oligarchs and officers that moves numbers of people to pick up the guns and risk their lives to make revolutions. By pointing to insurgents who seek outside arms, policymakers in Washington mistake symptoms for causes and justify aid for the very military and security forces whose opposition to reform generated armed insurgency in the first place.

Finally, the domino theory blinds policymakers to important differences in internal situations. Revolutionaries have been practically nonexistent in Costa Rica and Honduras, where there have been adequate channels for reform. In Panama, whose canal is the geostrategic source of much U.S. concern, it was precisely the success of the late President Torrijos in regaining sovereignty over the Canal and in initiating social and economic reforms that most defused latent revolutionary potential. While it is true that an insurgent victory in one Central American nation reverberates throughout the region, encouraging revolutionaries elsewhere, the spread of such images will not automatically spark revolutions and push over other governments like the mechanical fall of dominoes. Unfortunately, the policy designed to avoid the falling of dominoes may be creating similar outcomes for different reasons. The real threat in those countries is not the domino of neighboring revolution, but the spillover effect of region-wide social disruption that strains social, economic, and political systems. These countries have little margin with which to absorb those stresses.

Military Buildups

The Sandinistas' military buildup, as we saw in Chapter 4, was originally defensive in character—initially responding to the Sandinistas' expectation of hostility from the United States and later to the reality of U.S. hostility and the contra armies it backed. But the buildup led to three overinflated notions of security threat: one involving nuclear capability and two others involving hostile conventional forces.

Administration emphasis on the Soviet arms that are part of the buildup inevitably triggered memories of Soviet attempts to place intermediate-range nuclear missiles in Cuba in 1962. Any such attempt by the Soviet

Union to place offensive strategic weapons in the region would indeed constitute a threat to U.S. security interests.

The Sandinistas have made it clear that they want to avoid such acquisitions for fear of being embroiled in an East-West confrontation. As a signatory to the Treaty of Tlatelolco, Nicaragua pledged to keep the region free of nuclear weapons, and in April 1985, the Sandinistas reaffirmed their commitment to that treaty. Moreover, given the capabilities the Soviets have developed with long-range and submarine-launched missiles and their earlier experience of badly miscalculating the U.S. response in 1962, they are not likely to try again. The U.S.-Soviet accord that ended the missile crisis has prevented the reintroduction into Cuba of weapons that would pose a direct nuclear threat to the United States. But most important, the emplacement of nuclear weapons in any Central American country would be a major issue between the United States and the Soviet Union, not simply one between us and the Central American country. This means that U.S. policymakers must state plainly and clearly to the Soviet Union, so that there can be no miscalculation, that such an action would be as unacceptable now as it was in 1962.

The Reagan administration's most public concern, however, has been not with a nuclear threat but with two other dangers it saw in connection with hostile conventional forces in the region: it has argued that the Sandinistas might launch an attack upon one of their neighbors, and that they might use their conventional forces to threaten the sea lanes of the Caribbean or the Panama Canal.

Neither of these actions is likely, since they would involve Nicaragua in a military confrontation with the United States, a confrontation the Sandinistas could have no hope whatever of winning. An attack upon a neighboring country would, under the Rio Treaty, give the United States and the rest of the Inter-American system sufficient reason for intervening. The Sandinistas are fully aware of this. They have carefully avoided letting border incidents flare into a wider conflict, despite the fact that Honduras shelters a contra exile army of over fifteen thousand.

Arguments alleging dangers to vital sea lanes and the Panama Canal, like the domino theory, come in both simplistic and sophisticated versions.

The simplistic view insists that we keep in mind that some 40 percent of all U.S. trade and substantial amounts of crude oil bound for the East Coast traverse the Caribbean sea lanes, making them a vital link between the U.S. economy and the world. The implied argument is that the U.S. economy could be crippled if the Caribbean sea lanes were threatened by hostile powers in Central America.

In fact this threat is a mirage. Each Central American country, Nicaragua included, depends on the Canal and sea lanes for their economic well-being as much or more than the United States. It would make no sense to cut off their own economic lifelines. Indeed, no Central American country comes close to having the military capability to do so. Further, for any Central American state to try to disrupt U.S. trade by interdicting the sea lanes

would be an act of war to which the United States would surely respond
with overwhelming force. In no more than a few days, the United States
could destroy utterly the ability of any Central American nation to continue
the conflict.

The more serious version of the argument portrays a scenario of conven-
tial war in Europe or the Middle East between NATO and the Warsaw Pact,
during which time a brief interruption of the sea lanes could conceivably
have significant consequences. The ability of the United States to move
reinforcements and supplies quickly across the Atlantic by ship would be
strategically important. If a country in the Caribbean Basin used its conventional forces to interdict U.S. shipping even for a few days, the interruption
could prove critical. This danger was repeatedly cited by the Reagan administration as the basis of its opposition to the construction of the airport
on Grenada, and later as one of the rationales for the U.S. invasion of the
island.

While the interdiction of the sea lanes is a potential security problem for
which contingency plans should be developed, it is nevertheless a very
unlikely event. To even project its occurrence demands making a series of
increasingly improbable assumptions.

First, one must assume that a revolutionary regime in Central America
would adopt a national security stance hostile to the United States and
sympathetic to the Soviet Union. The example of Cuba demonstrates that
this is possible, but it also demonstrates that the outcome depends at least
in part upon the policy the United State adopts towards the regime. A policy
that does not isolate or threaten such a regime makes this assumption less
likely.

Second, one must assume that such a hostile regime would grant the
Soviets military basing facilities, or itself use facilities provided by the
Soviet Union in accordance with Soviet global strategy. Because such an
alliance would effectively close off to a regime all normal economic relations
with the United States and much of the West, the Central Americans would
have to demand an economic quid pro quo of the Soviet Union in order to
survive. Therefore, one must further assume that the Soviet Union would
be prepared to take on the economic burden of "another Cuba." As we saw
in our chapter on the Soviet Union, however, this is highly unlikely, given
the state of the Soviet economy and Soviet commitments in Afghanistan,
Poland, Vietnam, Africa, and Cuba. In exchange for such an investment,
the Soviets would acquire military facilities that offer only a marginal
strategic advantage over what they already have.

Third, one must assume that such a conventional war between the United
States and the Soviet Union does not cross the nuclear threshold, since
otherwise sea lanes would be largely irrelevant.

Finally, any attack on U.S. shipping in international waters would be an
act of war calling forth an appropriate U.S. military response. Because the
United States has the conventional forces needed to destroy quickly whatever ability any Central American country may have to attempt to interdict

the sea lanes, the U.S. could rapidly prevent any aggressor from launching any subsequent attacks. One has to assume, therefore, that a Central American regime would be prepared to suffer devastating U.S. retaliation and be prepared to commit political suicide in order to give the Soviet Union a marginal and fleeting advantage in a global conventional conflict. While it is possible to imagine such a scenario, the probability of its occurrence is immeasurably low and its ultimate threat minimal. It makes no sense to anchor U.S. policy on such a far-fetched scheme.

Those who detail the hypothetical threat to the sea lanes ignore two facts: that Nicaragua has shown no interest in allowing itself to be used as a Soviet forward base, and that the Soviet Union has shown no interest in paying the economic price of obtaining one. The Sandinistas have explicitly ruled out the establishment of any foreign military base on their territory. In September 1984 they offered to sign the regional treaty drafted by the Contadora nations that would have prohibited such installations and provided for the reduction of foreign military advisers. In bilateral negotiations with the United States, Nicaragua proposed an agreement addressing these same issues. The Soviets, for their part, have refused to provide large-scale economic economic aid to the faltering Nicaraguan economy, just as they refused to provide it to Allende's government in Chile or Manley's in Jamaica.

Credibility

The claim that U.S. credibility is at stake in Central America is familiar to those who remember the justifications for continued involvement in Southeast Asia. But unlike the threat of falling dominoes or threatened sea lanes, the threat to credibility is difficult to measure objectively because it is intangible, depending entirely upon the perceptions of others.

The argument often invokes the vital U.S. interest in Western Europe in defense of military involvements in the Third World. The willingness of the United States to use force abroad, even when its own interests are only indirectly involved, is held to be essential to the solidarity of the western alliance. If, it is asserted, the United States shrinks from paying the relatively small cost of using force in the Third World, who will believe the United States would risk nuclear annihilation to defend Europe? The credibility doctrine is thus limitlessly expansive: any local conflict can be seen as a challenge to U.S. credibility, regardless of the intrinsic importance of U.S. interests in the region. And once the United States has made a commitment the doctrine can be used to justify continued involvement even if nonvital interests are at stake. Perhaps the United States should not have committed so much in the first place, policymakers can argue, but since we have made the commitment, "credibility" demands we follow through.

Credibility is a two-edged sword, however; ill-advised interventions in the Third World weaken the credibility of the United States in Europe and among our real friends in the Third World. In the last twenty years, nothing has shaken the European alliance more deeply than the growing perception that the United States lacks wisdom and prudence in its use of military force in the Third World. The post–World War II generation recalls not merely the liberation from Nazism, but the war in Vietnam; it fears not that the United States may be unwilling to defend Europe, but that Washington's recklessness will drag Europe into war. Recently, even European leaders long identified as friends of the United States have begun to share this fear —which is why France, Spain, Greece, Italy, the Scandanavian countries, and others have been unwilling to support U.S. sanctions against Nicaragua and have counseled diplomacy, not the "big stick."

In Latin America, key U.S. allies and friends have staunchly opposed our policies. Mexico, Panama, Colombia, Venezuela, and the new more democratic regimes in Argentina and Brazil have also counselled a path of multilateral diplomacy and coexistence with Cuba and Nicaragua. U.S. credibility in Europe and Latin America, properly understood, is more damaged than preserved by Washington's response to every brushfire war as if it were a global challenge.

We do have Third World allies who would be disheartened by a policy change in Central America, particularly dictators whose survival depends in part upon the support that they receive from the United States. This, however, is a message well worth sending. Dictatorships that believe they can rely on the United States to protect them from the wrath of their own people are less inclined to allow political openings or social changes that are the prerequisites for building stable, legitimate political systems. Stability in such places cannot be guaranteed forever by force of arms, and the process of change will be helped by some healthy worry on the part of those with established privilege.

In the end, the damage that has been done to U.S. crediblity by the crisis in Central America is largely self-inflicted. Credibility is at risk in direct proportion to how much it is wagered. More than anything else, it is the inflated rhetoric of the Reagan administration that has raised the stakes of U.S. credibility in Central America. And in the last analysis, the most important allies of the United States are more disturbed, and with good reason, when the United States fails to exhibit the maturity to recognize error or failure and to change course.

U.S. NATIONAL INTERESTS IN CENTRAL AMERICA ▲

The United States is so extensively involved in Central America that noninvolvement—neo-isolationism of any sort—is not a realistic option. The question is, how are we best to use our power and influence in the region to pursue our national interests? Before we can outline a new policy that answers that question, however, we need a new understanding of what those interests are.

Part of what makes the hegemonic strategic vision a counterproductive approach to national security is that it tends to be concerned only with immediate issues and present crises. It directs our attention only to putting out fires, not to preventing them. It does not take into account the deeper structural problems in the region that engender conflict and chaos. Ironically, it poorly serves national security because the United States sees no other national interests in the region. The United States does have other interests, mutually supporting interests, in encouraging an environment of peace, broadly shared development, and democracy. These other interests are important in themselves, but they are also crucial in building the foundations of a longer-term stability in the region.

Security

The central U.S. security interest in the region is to prevent the Soviet Union from using this area to threaten the United States militarily. The stationing of Soviet nuclear missiles or Soviet combat troops in the region is unacceptable, just as the stationing of Soviet missiles in Cuba was unacceptable in 1962. This concern—an issue involving the United States and the Soviet Union, not the United States and particular Central American countries—is a primary security interest for the United States. So too would be actual attempts to disrupt sea lanes in the region; the United States needs to be prepared to respond with overwhelming force and to make clear that we have the capability and will to do so. But the United States also has other, less threatening, security interests.

It is in our interests to discourage foreign aggression by one country against another in the region and to work multilaterally with other countries to prevent or halt such aggression. It is also in our interest to discourage any country from giving substantial material assistance to insurgent groups that seek to take power by force in other countries and to work with other countries to minimize such assistance. Such security concerns reflect our interest in minimizing risks to our own country by ensuring that a region so close to our border is not militarily hostile to us.

Our national interest must be understood more broadly than such narrow, risk-minimizing, short-term security concerns. We have an interest in establishing an environment that is far more than "not hostile"—an environment that is positively supportive of what we value. Such an environment would be one where there were conditions for long-term peace, where the fruits of development were shared broadly among the vast majority of the people, and where the governments were democratic. While the United States has neither the responsibility nor the power to *impose* such conditions unilaterally, it does have an interest in working to develop them. An intelligent policy that sought to pursue our national interests would work to minimize security threats and maximize peace, broadly shared development, and democracy.

Peace

A peaceful Central America will be one in which these states maintain normal relations with one another and with the United States, are not involved in efforts to subvert one another, and are not involved in a conventional arms race that heightens border tensions and robs precious resources from the tasks of development.

Peace in the region also demands that the causes for violent turmoil within each country be alleviated. This does not mean that each country must adopt U.S. economic and political models, but it does demand a commitment by the United States and other governments in the region to two other goals. First, the wrenching poverty of the region must be alleviated and this demands not simply growth but redistribution so that the majority of the population shares in the fruits of growth: the goal here is broadly shared development. Second, long-term peace demands an end to internal repression and an increase in the legitimacy of governments earned by their promotion of popular participation in the making of national policy: the goal here is to encourage movement toward democracy.

Broadly Shared Development

Direct U.S. economic interests in Central America are relatively modest. While investment and trade flows with the United States are crucial to each country in the region, they represent only a small proportion of U.S. totals. Nor does Central America provide any strategic resources. If the entire region were to be closed to U.S. economic activity—a worst-case scenario —the economic effect on the United States would be negligible.

The United States does, however, have an interest in addressing the problems of poverty in the region. The persistence of hunger, malnutrition, illiteracy, and disease must be of concern to a country that values human life and dignity. Such problems are also a major source of political instability and of pressure for migration out of the region.

To address these problems, the United States needs to support economic growth, but growth alone is not a panacea. Development plans that lack any provision for redistribution or structural change may be naïve in expecting the poor to prosper from what trickles down from private-sector initiative. This is not a theoretical or ideological point, but a historical fact. Case studies show that the growth stimulated in the 1950s, 1960s, and 1970s by new investments (public and private, domestic and foreign), by the Central American Common Market, and by the Alliance for Progress did not foster an improvement for the growing number of poor in the region. Indeed it was precisely growth without redistribution under conditions of political dictatorship that produced instability in Guatemala, El Salvador, and Nicaragua in the 1960s and 1970s. Economic growth is only likely to contribute to broadly shared development and political stability when it takes place in a political environment where governments are committed to improving the conditions of their people, as in Costa Rica and, to a lesser extent, in Panama and Honduras.

It follows that the United States has an interest in regimes that are willing to take serious steps to alleviate poverty. This is a political as much as an economic problem. Its solution requires regimes that are prepared to undertake structural changes in the existing social order: land reform, for example. But the case studies show that such reform efforts, even when relatively modest, engender the resistance of traditional elites who have long benefited from the status quo and may be willing to use electoral fraud, extralegal harassment, and violence to keep down reformers. Under such circumstances, the reformers, on the center and on the left, are likely to turn to extra-electoral actions—demonstrations, sit-ins, land seizures, and even armed insurgency. Since the structural reforms demanded by these reformers are essential for long-term peace and development, the United States must be prepared to live with a certain amount of disruption and conflict in the region.

U.S. interests in broadly shared development should not be confused with U.S. power to guarantee such development. It requires complex internal changes that not even the best U.S. policy can assure. A realistic U.S. policy must thus seek to encourage broadly shared development by concentrating its assistance in countries where governments are truly committed to such a goal. A policy that simply "throws money" at problems of poverty, independent of the character of the regime, is naïve, wasteful, and potentially dangerous. It may support growth that leads only to armed insurrection and strengthen the power of exactly those elites that oppose real development.

Democracy

The United States has an interest in seeing the end of repressive governments and the flowering of democracy in Central America, but at the same time it has an interest and an obligation to coexist with regimes that do not organize their politics in accord with our values.

The interest that the United States has in democracy is both moral and pragmatic. It is moral in that we cannot long maintain a foreign policy rooted in values that are at variance with those upon which we base our own politics. It is pragmatic in that the more regimes respond to the concerns of the majority, the more likely it is that conflict will be resolved in a manner that is orderly, lawful, and widely viewed as legitimate.

Central American nations face awesome difficulties in creating and sustaining genuine democracy. The military regime in Honduras in the late 1970s, for example, allowed a kind of press freedom, and a certain space for political organization and rural protest that distinguished it in important ways from the closed and cruel dictatorships in El Salvador and Guatemala —and that made possible the further political openings that the Carter administration promoted. In Nicaragua, the censorship, the violations of due process of the law, the forced relocations of the Miskito Indians, and so on, created conditions that seriously limited democratization. The relaxation of censorship during the 1984 elections, the elimination of the terror and death squads of the former regime, the toleration of certain limited organized dissent, and the freedom of parties to participate in the elections are positive steps.

On the other hand, we should not assume that a regime is democratic just because it holds elections. If a political community is deeply polarized, if the price of dissent is disappearance or assassination—as was the case during the 1982 and 1984 Salvadoran elections and before the 1985 Guatemalan elections—the procedures of elections cannot in themselves produce conciliation or stability. What is most basic to democracy is the kind of political community that Costa Rica has been able to approximate: one of tolerance and respect in which meaningful dissent and freedom of organization are respected for everyone. Beyond this, countries grow in democracy to the extent that they create channels of response to the legitimate demands of citizens and mechanisms that hold leaders accountable for their use of power.

The United States does not have the wherewithal by itself to create democracy for others. People must build democracies for themselves, and there are some countries where this is a difficult and long-term process. There are real limits on the power of the United States to do good. But if the United States does not confuse democratic forms (like elections) with content (conditions of tolerance and freedom of organization, for example), it can help facilitate those conditions that make democracy possible.

There are fewer limits, however, on the power of the United States to do harm: it does have the power to obstruct democratic efforts or to undermine existing democracies. This is a natural corollary of the economic, political, and military power of the United States, and the difficulties authoritarian regimes face in making transitions to democracy. Since efforts to move toward democracy and reform threaten the privileges of traditional elites, their resistance will often be fierce. If they can count on the moral and material assistance of the United States, as could the Somoza regime, the Salvadoran military, and Guatemalan oligarchs and officers (before 1977), the efforts of democrats will be all the more difficult, and the United States will be identified with the forces of reaction. In cases where a fragile democracy is emerging, U.S. policies can undermine the effort, as in Honduras in the early 1980s where the U.S.-backed military buildup is strengthening antidemocratic forces, especially in the military.

The United States must thus be temperate in pursuing its interest in democracy. At best we can promote the conditions under which democracy has the best chance to emerge and to flourish. The United States can and should make clear its preference for the democratic form of government in our relations with other countries, but we must also be prepared to maintain constructive relations with less democratic regimes that do not threaten our vital interests and are not gross and consistent violators of the human rights of their citizenry.

14

SECURITY THROUGH DIPLOMACY: A POLICY OF PRINCIPLED REALISM

Kenneth E. Sharpe, Douglas C. Bennett, Morris J. Blachman, and William M. LeoGrande

The United States needs a new foreign policy for Central America, one deeply rooted in an accurate assessment of contemporary realities in the region, one that embodies our nation's founding principles and responds to our genuine interests in the region. We must give up past policies guided by a hegemonic strategic vision that has become increasingly costly and counterproductive. What we need is a policy of principled realism, one that pursues not only our security, but peace, democracy, and broadly shared development as well.

A policy of principled realism, based on a nonhegemonic vision, would be guided by the following:

1. The foremost long-term objective of U.S. policy must be to promote broadly shared development and encourage democracy. While not ignoring the East-West dimension of regional conflict, such a policy would recognize that this aspect is secondary. The primary and long-term sources of turmoil in Central America are inequality and authoritarianism.
2. Diplomatic solutions should be a primary objective of U.S. policy. The peaceful settlement of disputes through diplomacy, especially in an area where U.S. political and economic influence is great, minimizes the risk that regional issues will be caught up in the East-West conflict. The escalation and internationalization of regional conflict presents the greatest danger of superpower involvement and confrontation.
3. We should refrain from undertaking any policy that is unable to garner allied support, except in the most extraordinary circumstances where

there is a direct and immediate danger to U.S. security. Our ability to achieve our interests is enhanced if we work together with our allies in the region, rather than acting unilaterally.

4. The United States should work diplomatically, in concert with our allies, to change the behavior of any regime which is a gross and systematic violator of human rights or which enforces deep social inequality by repressive means. The United States should not render assistance, military or economic (except humanitarian or disaster relief), to such a regime. Any regime, leftist or rightist, which engages in these practices plants the seeds of its own destruction. The interests of the United States are not served by befriending authoritarian regimes in Central America, even though they may align themselves with the West against the Soviet Union.

5. The United States should apply the same policy principles to all countries. The key test to determine the response of the United States is how regimes behave in practice, regardless of their location on an ideological spectrum. The interests of the United States are not automatically endangered by revolutionary regimes.

Following these guidelines would better safeguard our national interests than current efforts to maintain hegemony in Central America. But the habit of control, once acquired, is difficult to break. Policy changes similar to these have been suggested in the past, and have invariably been attacked as unworkable. Some opponents of a new approach are honestly unwilling to accept the passing of U.S. dominance in Central America and are prepared to pay the increasingly heavy costs of maintaining it. Others, however, are so accustomed to taking U.S. hegemony for granted that they misconstrue any policy that begins from a different premise as synonymous with neo-isolationist withdrawal.

The policy of principled realism is not a retreat to neo-isolationism. Neo-isolationism is not a feasible alternative for the United States—our economic and political influence in the region is too great. Our weight will be felt whether it is consciously exercised or not. The alternative to hegemony and interventionism is not isolationism but rather a more intelligent involvement. We do not have to control internal events in the region in order to protect our security. Indeed, it is exactly this understanding that frees us to become more intelligently involved in encouraging peace, broadly shared development, and democracy. How, then, are military force, aid, and diplomacy best employed to achieve the objectives of a policy of principled realism? How are problems of external aggression and armed insurgency to be dealt with?

The use of military force is often taken to be the most effective means of securing a desired outcome in the international arena, and the frustrations of diplomacy can easily tempt powerful nations like the United States to simply impose a solution on weaker adversaries. But the effectiveness of military force as an instrument of foreign policy can be easily overestimated, as the United States discovered in Vietnam and the Soviet Union is discovering in Afghanistan.

A policy of principled realism views force as a legitimate but last resort, to be used only in instances where there is a clear and present danger to the security of the United States, or to hemispheric peace as determined by the OAS in accord with the prescriptions of the Rio treaty. The principal instruments for advancing U.S. interests would be multilateral and bilateral diplomacy, and bilateral assistance programs.

Assistance programs should be used to create a structure of incentives for potential recipients to behave in ways consistent with U.S. interests. Except for humanitarian assistance (which should be distributed strictly on the basis of need), economic aid should be withheld from regimes determined to maintain deep social inequality or that are gross and consistent violators of internationally recognized human rights. With such regimes, the United States must guard against the temptation to reward minimum changes that are no more than cosmetic efforts to influence U.S. aid policy.

When governments do show a determination to address the problems of poverty and inequality with policies that promote broadly shared development, the United States should be generous with its assistance. Governments that pursue land reform, literacy, rural health care, and employment opportunities for all deserve to be seriously considered for economic aid. On the other hand, governments that pursue none of these but try to curry favor merely by aligning themselves with the United States against the Soviet Union, do not deserve our assistance.

Military assistance programs to Central America should be strictly limited to governments that enjoy some popular basis of legitimacy so that U.S. aid will not be used for the repression of popular dissent—a more restrictive criterion than the simple absence of gross and consistent human rights violations. There are only two legitimate needs for military equipment that the United States should be prepared to meet: the need for adequate forces to defend a nation against external aggression, and the need to defend democratic institutions against internal violence by a small, well-armed minority.

The provision of military assistance must be part of a broader policy of supporting multilateral agreements limiting the regional arms race, and providing mechanisms for the peaceful settlement of international disputes. In this way, the need for large military establishments in the region can be greatly circumscribed. If, despite these efforts, a government acts in violation of international peace, the policy of the United States should be to set in motion the multilateral security arrangements defined in the OAS Charter, the Rio treaty and the UN Charter. Needless to say, the United States should refrain from providing military or economic assistance to a government engaged in such a violation of the peace, but more active sanctions —except in extraordinary cases—should await multilateral action.

Armed insurgency against an existing government poses a different sort of threat to peace. In Central America, insurgency is most typically a product of social inequality and political repression practiced by right-wing authoritarian regimes. In such circumstances, the United States should seek to promote a negotiated settlement of the conflict. The United States should refrain from allying itself with an existing authoritarian regime merely because of the radicalism of its opponents.

The emphasis a policy of principled realism places on diplomacy to seek peaceful, negotiated settlements of international and internal conflicts better safeguards our national interests than current efforts to maintain hegemony in Central America. But the benefits of diplomacy are often overlooked by those policymakers who erroneously assume that security and diplomacy are somehow antithetical. Diplomacy, they argue, is unrealistic and unreliable. International agreements are hard to achieve and impossible to enforce. The international arena is a jungle in which no agreement is an adequate substitute for the ability to use force. Being "realistic" is taken as synonymous with "being tough," which in turn is taken to mean using force. Indeed, for some, force is no longer simply one means to protect security, it is the only means. Such a narrow view of security is dangerous, for it blinds policymakers to the ways in which diplomacy may be far more effective in serving our national interests— including our security interests.

Though arduous, diplomacy has the great advantage of solving international problems with relatively small expenditures of resources. Its primary instrument is negotiation, and when successful, its results are less costly and more enduring than the use of force because all parties have an interest in abiding by the outcome. When compliance is coerced, the coercion must be constant to maintain the status quo.

To seek security through diplomacy does not mean that tomorrow you begin to "trust" your enemies: that kind of idealism is as naïve and dangerous as a reflexive reliance on force. Trust is something that must be created by small, incremental steps, each of which tests the sincerity of the opponents, each of which is verifiable and enforceable, and each of which convinces opponents that the next step is worth taking. Good diplomacy structures agreements which are grounded in the self-interest of each party, so that each side has good reason to keep their part of the bargain if the other does. Creating such trust does not necessarily mean that each party likes the other's government or goals; it simply means gaining confidence that each can rely on the other to do what they say.

To seek security through diplomacy does not mean rejecting the use of force: it means making intelligent choices about when and where to use it. Force, or the threat of it, may be useful in certain circumstances to back diplomacy, but the preceding chapters have shown that U.S. policy has too often been one of gunboats without diplomacy. The confusion of force with security is tied up with the confusion of hegemony and national interest. Force is necessary if the United States is to control the internal character of regimes in Central America; but such control is not necessary to protect U.S. interests. Indeed, the case studies in this book have shown that the use of force directly, or indirectly through proxies, has usually been counterproductive.

Diplomacy can be an especially effective instrument for the United States in Central America because we have great influence in the region, economically and politically. This influence provides U.S. diplomats with enormous leverage that no other nation or combination of nations can rival. We saw in Chapter 11 how the Reagan administration used that influence to weaken the Contadora process and thus block a regional diplomatic solution to the Central American crisis. It could just as easily have been used to promote one.

Those who are skeptical of the efficacy of diplomacy are ordinarily equally leery of multilateral approaches to international problems since these require diplomacy of a high order. Multilateralism triggers images of weakness, of the United States allowing others to determine or constrain its course of action. In part, the Reagan administration's hostility to the Contadora process reflected such an attitude.

There is no doubt that multilateral action requires a willingness to compromise on the part of individual participants, since each will have different interests and a different notion of how the problem should be addressed. The United States cannot pursue a multilateral approach to the Central American conflict while at the same time being unwilling to restrain its behavior so that it accords with the interests of other participants. The refusal of the Reagan administration to act with such restraint is precisely why its rhetorical assertions of support for Contadora ring hollow in the face of its record of behavior.

The unwillingness of the Reagan administration to cooperate with the Contadora nations is not proof of U.S. strength but of its isolation. That isolation is not the product of any profound difference of national interest between us and the Contadora nations. On the contrary, they are among our best friends in Latin America. They share our basic interests in avoiding the spread of the conflict, preventing an increased Cuban or Soviet presence, and promoting democracy and economic development. They do not, however, share the idea that the United States must maintain its hegemony over the region. If the imperative of control were to be dropped, it would open wide vistas for diplomatic cooperation, allowing us to supplement our own considerable influence with the enormous resources our allies could bring to bear.

Abandoning the imperative of control would also strengthen the moral authority of our leadership in the region. The influence enjoyed by the United States in the international arena is not solely a function of our wealth and military might. To a considerable degree it is rooted in the values upon which the United States was founded: democracy, self-determination and social equality. When we allow the pursuit of short-term advantage to divert our foreign policy from these principles—as we have too often done in Central America—we undermine our claim to moral leadership. Moreover, a democratic society cannot long sustain a foreign policy that contravenes its most basic precepts. Eventually either the policy or the precepts must give way.

The basic precepts of a policy of principled realism laid out above should not be taken as precise policy prescriptions. Rather, they are the general rules that serve to fashion specific policy prescriptions that respond to concrete and difficult historical realities. Political realities are complex and changing; at times, trade-offs must be made between various policy objectives, trade-offs that are impossible to predict and script ahead of time. No set of policy principles is a substitute for practical reason. Perhaps the best way to understand how a policy of principled realism might work in practice is to apply it to the situation in Central America in 1986.

NICARAGUA   ▲

In Nicaragua, the United States confronts a radical revolutionary government that came to power by deposing a right-wing dictatorship that was for decades a close ally of Washington—unfortunately a familiar dilemma in U.S. foreign policy. The United States has a long and unappealing history of backing such dictatorships in Central America and elsewhere in the Third World because they were friendly and maintained stability. In exchange, Washington was willing to overlook the gross social inequality and political repression that often characterized the internal politics of such allies. But with predictable regularity, regimes such as Batista's in Cuba, Somoza's in Nicaragua, and the shah's in Iran have proven incapable of sustaining themselves in the face of the polarization of politics brought about by their own policies.

When regimes such as these succumb to revolution, they are succeeded by governments predisposed to distrust the United States, or even to see it as an enemy because of its support for the old order. In these circumstances, revolutionary governments almost always have some ideological affinity for socialism, which may, in its more radical variants, have little place for pluralist democracy. Such revolutionary governments will look, almost reflexively, to upgrade their relations with the Soviet bloc as a way of diversifying their dependency on the West in general, and the United States in particular. They may also see in the Soviet Union and its allies a source of military aid to defend the revolution against the anticipated hostility of the United States—an anticipation born of historical experience in Latin America.

It is difficult to imagine a less opportune set of circumstances for developing a positive relationship between the United States and a revolutionary government. That our traditional policies toward the Third World so often present us with this nearly intractable dilemma is in itself a major indictment of them. A central objective of the policy of partnership and realism advocated here is to avoid arriving at situations such as these, where the best one can hope for is to minimize the damage to U.S. interests.

But the legacy of the past cannot be wished away. Any policy that asserts the need to establish a new basis for relations between the United States and our closest neighbors must be able to handle the difficult case of a revolution in power—like the revolution in Nicaragua.

The U.S. relationship with Nicaragua could be quite different today if we had taken a different approach to the Somoza regime a decade or two ago, ending our uncritical support for the dictatorship. Our failure to do so narrowed the choices available to policymakers in the Carter administration when Nicaragua exploded in revolution in 1978. Despite the legacy of past policy, the Carter administration tried to formulate a constructive relationship with the new revolutionary government. Despite mistrust and difficulties, Carter's policy achieved some limited success because it was premised on the interest both nations had in avoiding mutual animosity. But Carter's policy came unraveled after Ronald Reagan's 1980 presidential victory, and the new administration replaced it with a policy of thoroughgoing hostility whose highest priority was to overthrow the Sandinistas—a policy that seemed to have scant chance of success and has proved increasingly counterproductive.

What would a policy of principled realism prescribe? Most importantly, it would have a very different set of objectives from those pursued by the Reagan administration. The top priority would be to assure that Nicaragua did not become a strategic asset for the Soviet Union, thereby introducing the East-West conflict into the region in a way that directly endangered the security of the United States.

It is important to recognize at the outset that Nicaragua has shown no interest in becoming a forward base for Soviet strategic weapons, nor has the Soviet Union shown any interest in emplacing such weapons there. This problem is a potential, rather than a clear and present, danger. This danger is first and foremost a problem in relations between the United States and the Soviet Union. The United States should clearly and unequivocally advise the Soviets that it will not tolerate the stationing of strategic weapons in Nicaragua, any more than it was willing to tolerate their placement in Cuba in 1962. Nicaragua should be informed of this position as well. If such weapons were to be introduced, the United States, in consultation with its allies in Latin America and Europe, should take whatever steps are required to achieve their removal.

Regional (as distinct from global) security concerns should be a priority of U.S. policy as well. The United States, along with all the nations of the hemisphere, have an interest in preventing armed aggression, direct or indirect, by one nation against another. All nations in the hemisphere are bound by the OAS Charter and the Rio treaty to abstain from such behavior, including the provision of material assistance to insurgent movements fighting against a neighboring government. That these commitments are often bent and broken does not diminish their importance for the preservation of regional peace.

If, as the Reagan administration has so often claimed, the United States has evidence of Nicaraguan arms shipments to the guerrillas in El Salvador, it should take that evidence to the OAS as required by the Rio treaty and seek multilateral sanctions against Nicaragua in order to halt that aid. A unilateral military response, such as the Reagan administration has pursued, is itself a violation of international law, leaving the United States vulnerable to condemnation before such international forums as the World Court.

A multilateral response is more effective because it strengthens U.S. relations with its allies around the hemisphere, whereas a unilateral response weakens them. And a lawful response that has the support of key U.S. allies is also more likely to command broad bipartisan support at home, making it more sustainable. The first step toward such a policy would be to halt the covert war against Nicaragua. The second step would be to give full and unequivocal support to the efforts of the Contadora nations to address the full range of regional security issues in a multilateral diplomatic context. A successful Contadora accord would address not only the issue of support for cross-border subversion but also the issues of the regional military arms race and the foreign military presence. If Nicaragua, or any state, were to violate a signed Contadora agreement, there would then be a clear basis for multilateral sanctions.

The United States has an interest in promoting democracy and equitable economic development in Nicaragua—interests that should have a higher priority than they have traditionally had in U.S. policy. For decades these interests were subordinated to the desire to maintain Somoza's friendship. But the reality of postrevolutionary Nicaragua is that the United States can no longer impose its will. Even the most skillful policy can do no more than create conditions that tend to favor democracy and development. But current policy is producing a more authoritarian Nicaragua and a poorer one.

Events of the past five years have shown that as the Sandinistas face increasing military pressure, they grow less tolerant of internal opposition, which tends to be identified, rightly or wrongly, with the armed contras. Ending U.S. military pressure provides no guarantee that the Sandinistas would allow pluralism to flourish. But a continuation of it is almost certain to produce deepening authoritarianism. A policy of principled realism would lift U.S. military pressure, seeking instead to improve the prospects for Nicaraguan democracy by providing economic incentives for the observance of democratic rights and values.

An overall policy of principled realism would look to diplomatic means of resolving our conflicts with Nicaragua and multilateral support for our actions. Relations between Nicaragua and the United States have deteriorated so seriously over the past few years that bilateral negotiations are probably an essential adjunct to the regional negotiations occurring under the auspices of Contadora. The United States should not only reopen the bilateral talks with Nicaragua that Washington ended in December 1984, but actively work to redefine bilateral relations along the lines sketched above.

The fundamental difference between these prescriptions and the direction of current policy should be obvious. A policy of principled realism does not begin with the premise that the United States must maintain control over the nature of regimes in Central America in order to protect our interests, so it does not conclude that the United States must reestablish the control that has been lost in Nicaragua. Current U.S. policy seeks the overthrow of the Sandinista government as a way of reasserting that control. A policy of principled realism would not.

Current policy assumes that the radical leftist character of the Sandinista regime makes it incompatible with U.S. interests in the region. A policy of principled realism begins with the premise that revolutionary governments of the left are no more an inherent threat to U.S. interests than reactionary governments of the right. Whether a regime is willing to live in peace with its neighbors is something to be demonstrated in practice—it cannot be assumed. And how amenable to democratic political and social reform an authoritarian government is cannot be simplistically deduced from which end of the ideological spectrum it lies on.

The United States should always use its political, economic, and diplomatic influence to encourage democracy and economic development, and U.S. aid and friendship should depend upon the responsiveness of other nations to our interest in promoting these values. But it should not be the policy of the United States to seek the violent overthrow of governments, on the right or on the left, that organize their politics and their societies differently from ours.

We saw in Chapters 4 and 11 that over the course of the past few years, there have been several opportunities to move toward a diplomatic solution of the legitimate security concerns the United States has regarding Nicaragua. In early 1981, the Reagan administration simply ignored Nicaragua's demonstrated willingness to curtail material support for the Salvadoran guerrillas in exchange for normal relations with the United States. Later that year, Washington severed bilateral talks focused on the same issue. In 1982, the administration agreed only reluctantly to reopen a dialogue with Nicaragua based upon the initiative of Mexican President López-Portillo and halted that dialogue before the year was out. Similarly fruitless negotiations were held in the latter half of 1984, again at the urging of Mexico.

Since 1982, the Nicaraguans have clearly and repeatedly indicated their willingness to reach agreement on the full range of regional security issues raised under the auspices of Contadora. The United States has insisted that this is not enough, that the Sandinistas must be willing to negotiate the internal character of the Nicaraguan government. In 1985, the administration added the demand that the Sandinistas open a dialogue with the contras as a necessary condition for the United States to cease its military pressure on the regime.

The Reagan administration's obsessive focus on the nature of the Nicaraguan government illustrates with particular clarity how the imperative of control actually weakens the ability of the United States to secure its basic interests. The United States does have legitimate security interests in Central America, foremost among them the maintenance of international peace and the restriction of any Soviet military presence sufficient to threaten the United States or its allies. The multilateral efforts of the Contadora nations and the bilateral proposals made by Nicaragua all suggest that the Sandinistas are prepared to make concessions on their foreign policy behavior that would meet U.S. security concerns. But such agreements would leave the Sandinista regime intact, and therefore would require that Washington accepts its loss of control in Nicaragua. Rather than abandon the hegemonic presumption, the United States is instead passing up the opportunity to achieve its basic security interests diplomatically.

The alternative is not difficult to conceive. The United States should relax its military and economic pressures against the Nicaraguan government, reopen bilateral negotiations, and give sincere support to the Contadora process in order to achieve verifiable agreements on the basic issues of strategic and regional security. Then, working in tandem with our allies, we should establish a system of incentives to encourage democracy and reconciliation in Nicaragua.

EL SALVADOR   ▲

When the United States confronts a revolution in progress against a friendly regime, as in El Salvador, there is rarely any equivocation—almost always the United States comes to the aid of the threatened regime, regardless of its character. In those rare instances when Washington withholds support from such a regime, it is usually because policymakers have judged that it cannot survive. Under such circumstances, U.S. support may be curtailed as a way of easing out the existing government so it can be replaced with a government more capable of defeating the revolutionary threat. This was precisely the design of U.S. policy toward Somoza's government in Nicaragua in early 1979, and toward Romero's government in El Salvador in the fall of that year.

But it is hard to find a single contemporary example of a Latin American revolution (as distinct from a military coup in which one faction of the existing elite replaces another) where Washington remained neutral. Such reliably consistent behavior patterns are rare in international affairs. The explanation, as discussed in earlier chapters, is the imperative of keeping leftist political forces from power. In the late twentieth century, most revolutionary movements have a strong leftist, or Marxist, component.

Washington's opposition to revolutions, then, is based upon the a priori assumption that revolutionary victories mean the advent of the radical left to power, that the radical left in power will challenge the traditional control exercised by the United States, and that this loss of control will open the region to increased Soviet influence, if not military presence. Just below the surface is the additional worry that successful revolutions tend to inspire revolutionaries elsewhere, thereby multiplying the basic problem. This is the logic by which the United States has become an antirevolutionary power.

On some occasions, Washington's support for existing regimes is tempered by a desire to promote reform—to change the unstable status quo gradually as a way of warding off revolution. These reformist interludes do not have an impressive record of success, largely because they spring less from principle than from instrumentalism. The interest of the United States in reform tends to diminish proportionally as the revolutionary threat subsides. In truth, the animus for reform has never approached the strength and permanence of the imperative for order.

There is no objective basis in the national interest for the United States to act as a bastion of counterrevolution. The imperative of maintaining control that has led us to this stance is a false interest, as this book has tried to demonstrate. When revolution erupts in a neighboring country, there is no a priori reason for the United States to support either side. The proper policy depends entirely upon the character of the existing regime and its opposition.

But before elaborating this argument, it is important to distinguish between authentic revolutionary movements and terrorist groups. Although some cases may fall in a "gray area" that makes them difficult to define, it is possible to distinguish between a broadly based revolutionary movement, in which people challenge an authoritarian regime that does not serve their interests, and an armed minority that seeks to use violence to destabilize a regime that has broad legitimacy and is responsive to popular demands.

This is a crucial distinction. In the case of a legitimate government under attack, the United States should be prepared to provide security assistance sufficient to allow it to defend itself. But when an authentic revolution erupts against an authoritarian regime, the United States has no compelling interest in defending that regime against its own people, or preventing a revolutionary victory—even if the likely outcome of such a victory is an authoritarian regime of the left. In short, between authoritarianism of the right and left, the United States should be indifferent—willing to conduct normal but not close or friendly relations—and prepared to use its influence to bring about democratic reforms.

It is hard to imagine the United States investing its power and resources to support a left-wing authoritarian regime. It should be equally hard to imagine the United States supporting right-wing authoritarian regimes.

The neutrality in the face of revolution advocated above does not imply noninvolvement. On the contrary, the influence that the United States has in Central America gives it the opportunity to play a uniquely valuable role as mediator, promoting peaceful negotiated solutions to internal armed conflicts. Such solutions hold the best hope of avoiding both variants of authoritarianism and therefore better serve U.S. interests than the traditional role of nemesis to revolutions.

The conflict in El Salvador, we saw in Chapter 3, fits this basic pattern. The revolutionary movement began as a result of legitimate grievances against a repressive military dictatorship, and it secured a significant base of popular support for itself. The reforms the United States has been able to initiate in El Salvador since 1980 have not been unimportant, but they have not fundamentally altered the basic dynamics of the politics that set the revolution in motion.

A policy of principled realism would seek a negotiated settlement of the Salvadoran conflict, rather than seeking military victory for the existing regime. Indeed, several opportunities for a positive resolution of the crisis have been missed over the past six years, opportunities that the United States might have taken advantage of had it not been so determined to prevent the opposition from achieving any share of political power. The resulting years of war have, of course, been costly for El Salvador, but even worse, they have left a legacy that makes the situation more intractable as time goes on.

The first opportunity came after young officers led a coup in October 1979, and set up a civilian-military junta. The announced plans for an end to violence and corruption, free elections, and land reform opened the possibility for a government of national reconciliation. Reform-minded officers seemed to be on the ascendant within the military; the insurgents were few in number, and many of the peasants, workers, students, and professionals organized in radical popular associations were to some degree willing to give the new junta a chance. The civilians on the junta and in the cabinet were respected leaders, including Social Democrats and Christian Democrats. The rightist oligarchy and the reactionary officers within the military were at their weakest.

At this moment, the United States could, and should, have stated clearly and forcefully that it supported the new government and the goal of national reconciliation, that it would actively oppose efforts of the far right to block reform and reconciliation, and that if a government committed to national reconciliation were ousted by a rightist coup, all U.S. military and economic assistance would be terminated.

Instead, because it feared the new government might seek to incorporate the radical left rather than defeat it, the United States stood by as the far right forced the collapse of the October junta. The rightist government that followed maintained the façade of civilian rule, but its main priority was winning the war against the guerrillas.

A second opportunity was lost in the spring of 1981, shortly after Reagan came to office. Sobered by the failure of their January military offensive, and facing reduced aid from Cuba and Nicaragua, the FDR-FMLN signaled its interest in a negotiated settlement. In March and April, Archbishop Rivera y Damas offered to mediate and got agreement from the FDR-FMLN, the Christian Democratic International, the Socialist International, the pope, and, more tentatively, from junta leader José Napoleón Duarte.

Once again, had the United States thrown its support behind this initiative, making clear that continued military assistance was contingent upon the willingness of the Salvadoran military to accept a negotiated solution to the war, a solution might have been achieved. Instead, when the archbishop went to Washington in April to seek U.S. support, Vice-President Bush and the State Department said they were not interested. Without U.S. support, Duarte was powerless to bring the Salvadoran military to the bargaining table.

The third opportunity came in the wake of Duarte's election as president in 1984 and the victory of his Christian Democrats in the legislative elections in 1985. Duarte ran for election on the promise that he would seek a negotiated end to the war, and in October 1984, he initiated unconditional negotiations, as the FDR-FMLN had been calling for since late 1981. Duarte's proposal came at a propitious time. Exhausted by four years of civil war, the public supported the move overwhelmingly. Pragmatic officers in the high command were willing to accept negotiations because the war seemed stalemated. Furthermore, few officers dared openly oppose Duarte because they understood that it was only his presence that convinced the U.S. Congress to back high levels of military aid. The FDR-FMLN, long ready to negotiate, was also weary of the war and anxious to find a political solution.

For the negotiations to move beyond the initial exuberance of the La Palma meeting, however, the Salvadoran military had to accept them. Had the United States vigorously supported the negotiating process, it would have strengthened the pragmatists within the armed forces and given Duarte a much freer hand in the dialogue. Instead, the Reagan administration paid lip service to the idea of dialogue, while denouncing any compromise that would allow the opposition to share power. Washington would accept nothing more than an agreement to allow the rebels to participate in the next round of elections in return for amnesty—in effect only the terms of the FDR-FMLN's surrender were negotiable. The dialogue died forthwith.

In 1986, and for the foreseeable future, the key to finding a negotiated political solution to the war in El Salvador is the willingness of the armed forces to accept such a solution, for it is the officer corps that still retains ultimate control over politics, setting the limits of civilian authority. Only the United States has the influence to bring the Salvadoran military to the bargaining table. Without U.S. support, a negotiated solution is impossible.

That is not to say that a shift in U.S. policy would necessarily suffice to persuade the military to negotiate. The Salvadoran army has a long history of resisting initiatives from the United States—on human rights, agrarian reform, and military tactics to name but a few instances—when Washington's proposals seemed to contravene the military's own interests. But there is evidence that when the United States exercises its full leverage over the Salvadoran army, as it did in late 1983 on the issue of the death squads, it gets results. Further, the risks of trying a new policy would be less than the nearly certain costs of the current alternatives: either increased U.S. military involvement or continued bloody stalemate.

If Washington sought to persuade the military to seek a negotiated solution to the war, it would have to demonstrate the seriousness of its commitment by making such a solution a condition of continued U.S. assistance. Strictly speaking, progress toward a negotiated settlement of the war *was* a condition of military aid in 1982 and 1983 (as written into the foreign aid act), but the Reagan administration simply ignored the law.

The first step in such a policy would be to cut aid from the current levels, which are aimed at achieving military victory. This would send a clear signal that the U.S. was firmly behind a negotiated solution rather than a military one.

The second step would be to clearly lay out conditions for continued aid: an acceptable human rights record free of gross and systematic violations; serious efforts toward a settlement of the conflict; and socioeconomic reforms that encouraged broadly shared development.

Thus far, the United States has not used its leverage to press for negotiations because serious negotiations would have to take into account the political and military power of the FDR-FMLN, and would almost certainly produce some form of institutional political role for the opposition in a transition government—i.e., "power-sharing." But keeping the left out of power has been the central objective of U.S. policy in El Salvador under both Carter and Reagan. It is that objective, rather than any actual U.S. interest, that has prevented Washington from taking advantage of various opportunities to pursue a negotiated end to the war, and which continues to do so, condemning both El Salvador and the United States to a war without end.

GUATEMALA ▲

Guatemala is the nation in Central America where the United States has historically been most involved in maintaining control by the use of military force against revolutionary movements. From the CIA-sponsored coup against Arbenz in 1954 to the counterinsurgency programs of the mid-1970s, no Central American nation received more military aid or advisers. Yet today, the United States has less influence in Guatemala than anywhere else in the region. This alone should serve as a stark indicator of how rapidly Central America has changed in recent decades, and how difficult it is becoming to sustain control of it.

As in Nicaragua and El Salvador, the Guatemalan regime has traditionally been controlled by economic and military elites that systematically blocked efforts at social or political reform, often physically eliminating opponents, moderate and radical alike, with barbarous efficiency. Until 1977, the United States supported and reinforced this regime rather than see it threatened by revolution.

The pivotal failure of U.S. policy in Guatemala came in 1954. The United States should have supported the reformism of Arbenz rather than over-throwing him to regain banana land for United Fruit. Subsequent aid to various Guatemalan military governments compounded this initial error by helping existing elites to resist any pressures for change. Certainly the United States could not have forced reforms on a recalcitrant Guatemalan regime, as President Carter discovered in 1977, but without U.S. support over the past three decades, the Guatemalan elite would not have been so secure, and perhaps might not have been so sure of its ability to repress all dissent.

In a case like Guatemala, where, until early 1986, an authoritarian regime of the right was secure enough that it did not depend on U.S. assistance for its immediate survival, how can Washington assert any effec-tive leverage for change? Because U.S. leverage is limited in such cases, there is a temptation to provide aid to the existing regime in hopes of buying influence that can then be used to promote reform. More often than not, this is a trap that leads us into a relationship with an odious regime without producing any fundamental changes in it. Our interests are damaged to the same degree as when we support authoritarian regimes uncritically.

The policy of the United States toward such a regime should be to maintain proper but distant relations, deny military assistance, and, given the regime's gross violations of human rights, to actively discourage our allies from providing military assistance as well. Economic assistance should also be withheld, except for humanitarian assistance, which should be channeled through nongovernmental organizations.

The policy of the Carter administration toward Guatemala came close to this prescription. It was excoriated by some as unrealistic because it did not produce improvement in the Guatemalan regime's behavior. In fact, it was Carter's critics who lacked realism, for they judged the effectiveness of the sanctions solely by immediate impact. They did not ask whether decades of support for the Guatemalan regime had ever produced superior results. Nor did they look beyond the short term to ask what impact the sanctions might have on the long-term ability of the Guatemalan regime to sustain itself, or the effect they might have on U.S. relations with a future post-oligarchic Guatemalan government.

How a policy of principled realism would handle the situation of Guatemala in the aftermath of the 1985 elections depends on what the real significance of the election proves to be. The United States should make clear that in order to qualify for a resumption of U.S. assistance, Guatemala must embark on an authentic program of democratic reforms, not merely the façade of them.

Unfortunately, the elections are unlikely to alter the basic structure of power in which the military has the last word. It would be a mistake for the United States to rush to resume a close military relationship. Successive Guatemalan regimes have become skillful at trading minor concessions for aid while avoiding serious reform. We should publicly welcome any movement toward broader political participation and increased respect for civil liberties, and we should join with our regional allies to diplomatically encourage progress, but a resumption of assistance should await clear evidence that the character of the government has changed, and that it is willing at long last to make peace with its own people.

COSTA RICA, HONDURAS, PANAMA   ▲

With a constitutional democracy like Costa Rica, or even with struggling civilian governments like Honduras and Panama, U.S. foreign policy faces quite different problems than with revolutionary or right-wing regimes. The difficulties these more moderate regimes face principally are how to over-come existing impediments to reform, development, and the expansion of democracy, and how to maintain stability in the face of these transitions. An adequate U.S. foreign policy must understand the differences between these regimes and the others, and it must look for ways to respond to these countries' definitions of their own problems and needs.

The Panama Canal treaties provide a model for policies toward these regimes. Here the United States gave up the hegemonic presumption: through diplomacy we achieved more security for a strategic asset, we increased the legitimacy of a moderate regime, and we won respect for ourselves throughout Latin America.

In the 1980s, the United States must address itself to two basic policy problems in these nations. The first concerns how we respond to the severe economic problems confronting Panama, Costa Rica, and Honduras. The second concerns how to prevent these essentially stable countries from being caught up in the conflicts of their neighbors.

Economically, the United States needs to be sensitive to the enormous influence exerted by the U.S. economy (business cycles, interest rates, etc.), and by the public and private economic actors based in the United States (transnational corporations and banks, AID, the Export-Import Bank, etc.). Without quite realizing it, our behavior can deal powerful, destabilizing shocks to these economies. Regimes like Costa Rica, which have a commit-ment to broadly shared development, are exactly the ones whose requests for aid—loans, technical assistance—deserve the most serious considera-tion. Moreover our interest in helping such governments solve their own problems should make us more tolerant of economic practices unfamiliar to the United States such as state enterprises, vigorous regulation of foreign investment, or even demands for special tariff consideration from the United States.

Many of these regimes have faced acute economic troubles in recent years. High oil prices, high interest rates, declining exports because of world recession, and regional instability have brought on severe balance-of-payments problems. Costa Rica, for example, has been forced to impose austerity and has had difficulty tightening its belt in ways that do not breach a basic commitment to social justice, thereby threatening the legitimacy of its democratic institutions. The United States should not only be open to requests for aid but also encourage multilateral agencies such as the IMF and the World Bank to take the lead. Moreover, the United States should take its cues from the regime itself, respecting for example, Costa Rica's commitment to a state welfare system. While regimes seeking assistance must show themselves to be fiscally responsible to qualify for aid, this should not be construed narrowly to mean following orthodox monetary policy.

The second kind of policy problem that commonly arises in dealing with regimes like Costa Rica and Honduras involves the spillover of conflicts elsewhere in the region. Recent U.S. policies have wrongly defined the central problems of Costa Rica and Honduras as security problems—containing Nicaragua and preventing future insurgencies in these countries. The resulting U.S. policies, we saw in Chapters 5 and 6, actually exacerbated the situation.

In Honduras, the United States poured in huge amounts of military aid, sought protection for CIA-sponsored contras, and used the country as a staging ground for massive military maneuvers. The result was to exacerbate border tensions with Nicaragua, create serious local disruption in those areas of the country were the contras operated, worsen the climate for investments, limit freedom of dissent for domestic opposition groups, strengthen the hand of the military—in these and other ways encouraging conditions that could breed insurgency.

In Costa Rica, the Reagan administration pressured the government not only to allow the contras a base of operations but also to develop a military to cope with nonexistent internal subversion—a problem the administration believed was sure to arise on the faulty logic of the domino theory. As a result, Costa Rica's 1948 decision to do without a national military—a key to its stability and democracy—has been called into question and tensions have been raised that strain the fabric of its democracy. The problems today are much more difficult as a result of these policies. But a policy of principled realism could still help contain regional conflict rather than spread it. Such a policy would halt contra activity against Nicaragua, encourage Costa Rica to maintain only its small police force, and work with other regional actors to encourage Nicaragua, Honduras, and Costa Rica to create mechanisms, such as the ones suggested by the Contadora countries, for lessening conflicts along their borders. While such a policy would not completely insulate these borders, given the turmoil in the region, it would be far more likely than current policy to lessen border tensions, promote broadly shared development, and strengthen democratic institutions in these countries.

The United States cannot put a quick or easy end to Central America's social and political turmoil. No policy, regardless of the amount of money or force committed, can promise to produce stable, equitable democratic governments. The very changes that swept the region over the past few decades, shaking the oligarchic order to its foundations, have also made the region less amenable to control from Washington. As difficult as it may be for us to adjust to this new reality, it will not go away. We ignore it at our own peril, for efforts to recapture the halcyon days of U.S. hegemony have only deepened the instability, polarization, and violence that have come to dominate Central American politics.

The call to abandon this hegemonic presumption not only is value-based (a democratic society ought not have a foreign policy whose first premise is to keep its closest neighbors under limited sovereignty), but it is also based first and foremost upon a realistic assessment of the limits of the possible. We need to found our policy toward Central America on our real national interests rather than on the false interest of hegemony. We need to be less concerned with controlling how our neighbors organize their own politics and society and more concerned with how they actually behave toward us and the other nations of the region.

The traditional imperative of keeping the left out of power at all costs is proving increasingly difficult to achieve in a region grown as complex and politically active as Central America. Our efforts to enforce this ban have been counterproductive to the real national interests they were originally meant to serve because they have made it more difficult to stabilize the region's domestic conflicts and thereby raised the risk of regional war. Such efforts have also alienated us from our traditional allies in the area, who share our real interests in security, democracy, and development, but who strongly oppose our efforts to control events in a region that is as much their backyard as it is ours.

In short, the United States needs a policy for Central America that is designed to meet the limited security problems posed by the regional conflict, and does so as much as possible by diplomacy rather than the reflexive use of force; that shows a strict preference for democracy rather than for one variety of authoritarianism over another, but does not seek to impose that preference by force; and that works to encourage structural economic and social change that addresses the real roots of the region's political unrest. Whether we can craft such a policy and pursue it consistently in the future will determine how well we get along with our neighbors in a rapidly changing neighborhood.

1: THE ORIGINS OF CRISIS

I want to acknowledge the extraordinary help of the volume editors—Morris Blachman, William LeoGrande, and Kenneth Sharpe—who have contributed in so many ways to this essay that it constitutes a truly collective enterprise. I will, however, accept the blame for overt errors of fact or interpretation.

1. Ralph Lee Woodward, Jr., *Central America, A Nation Divided* (New York: Oxford University Press, 1985), 76–79.
2. Ibid., 169.
3. Ibid., 160.
4. Foreign investors came to play an important part in coffee production in late nineteenth-century Nicaragua, and Germans acquired substantial amounts of coffee-growing land in Guatemala, but many of these outsiders eventually became nationals.
5. Herewith a rarely noted paradox: while enclave situations engender dependency of the host state upon external economic forces, they can also imbue the state with considerable autonomy from internal economic sectors—such as the landed elite. Reliance on one group can mean liberation from another.
6. Woodward, *Central America*, 277.
7. Ibid., 270–83.
8. Between 1950 and 1976, the figures for students trained under the Military Assistance Program and International Military Education and Training Program in Central America were Costa Rica 696, El Salvador 1,925, Guatemala 3,213, Honduras 2,888, Nicaragua 5,167, and Panama 4,389. U.S. Defense Security Assistance Agency, *Foreign Military Sales and Military Assistance Facts*, (Washington, D.C., 1977), 30–31. Most of this training occurred in the 1960s and 1970s.
9. Robert S. Leiken, ed., *Central America: Anatomy of Conflict* (New York: Pergamon Press, 1984), 63.
10. Henry Kissinger et al., *Report of the National Bipartisan Commission on Central America*, (Washington, D.C.: Government Printing Office, 1984), 36.
11. Recent elections in El Salvador and Nicaragua have been the object of much controversy as Chapters 3 and 4 make clear. Participation and competition in both was limited: the left could not run in El Salvador, the right would not run in Nicaragua. U.S. praise for the Salvadoran results and denunciation of the Nicaraguan process has only heightened skepticism in the region about the acceptability and significance of elections in general.
12. William M. LeoGrande, "Through the Looking Glass: The Report of the National Bipartisan Commission on Central America," *World Policy Journal 1* (Winter 1984):281.

2: GUATEMALA

Professor Carol Smith of Duke University participated in early stages of the preparation of this manuscript. Her contributions are gratefully acknowledged.

1. Susanne Jonas, "Guatemala: Land of Eternal Struggle," in *Latin America: The Struggle with Dependency and Beyond*, ed. Ronald G. Chilcote and Joel C. Edel-

stein (New York: Schenkman/John Wiley, 1974), 95–96; Moisés Behar, "Food and Nutrition of the Maya Before the Conquest and at the Present Time," in *Biomedical Challenges Presented by the American Indian*, ed. Pan American Health Organization (Washington, D.C.: Pan American Health Organization, 1968), 114–19.

2. Carlos Tejada Valenzuela, "Nutrición y prácticas alimentarias en Centroamérica: un estudio histórico de la población maya," *Universidad de San Carlos: Publicación Anual*, 2nd series, (1970), 103–8.

3. Jonas, "Guatemala," 130.

4. Jonathan Fried et al., "Indian Rebellions, 1524–1944," in *Guatemala in Rebellion: Unfinished History*, Jonathan Fried, et al., eds., (New York: Grove Press, 1983), 24–25.

5. Max Gordon, "A Case History of U.S. Subversion: Guatemala, 1954," *Science and Society* 35 (Summer 1971); portions reprinted in Fried, *Guatemala in Rebellion*, 50.

6. Rene Poitevín, *El proceso de industrialización en Guatemala* (San José, Costa Rica: Editorial Universitaria Centroamericana, 1977), 51–52; Gabriel Aguilera Peralta, "El proceso de militarización en el estado guatemalteco," *Polémica*, no. 1 (September-October 1981):32–33.

7. For summaries of the reform process begun under Arévalo, see Cole Blasier, *The Hovering Giant: U.S. Responses to Revolutionary Change in Latin America* (Pittsburgh: University of Pittsburgh Press, 1976), 54–65; Richard H. Immerman, *The CIA in Guatemala: The Foreign Policy of Intervention* (Austin, Texas: University of Texas Press, 1982), 44–57; Stephen Schlesinger and Stephen Kinzer, *Bitter Fruit: The Untold Story of the American Coup in Guatemala* (Garden City, N.Y.: Doubleday, 1981), 25–42; Thomas Melville and Marjorie Melville, *Guatemala: The Politics of Land Ownership* (New York: The Free Press, 1971), 27–39; Poitevín, *El proceso de industrialización*, 51–53.

8. Susanne Jonas, "The Democracy Which Gave Way: The Guatemalan Revolution of 1944–54," in *Guatemala*, ed. Susanne Jonas and David Tobis (New York: North American Congress on Latin America, 1974), 47–50. According to Jonas (p. 52): "The economic measures of the revolution did more to spread private property than to abolish it." According to Eduardo Galeano, in *Guatemala: Occupied Country* (New York: Monthly Review Press, 1969), 51: "the agrarian reform law laid down as its basic objective *the development of the peasant capitalist economy and the capitalist agricultural economy in general.*"

9. The 1952 Agrarian Reform Law was designed to expropriate only the *unused* land of large plantations. Owners were to be reimbursed with twenty-five-year bonds paying interest at the rate of 3 percent. *Cultivated* holdings of any size were exempt from seizure. The expropriated land, in turn, was to be distributed to landless peasants. Prior to the enactment of the law, about 2 percent of the population had owned over 70 percent of the nation's farmland. By 1954, when the reform was ended, more than 100,000 campesino families had received titles to agricultural property. For details concerning Decree 900 (the Agrarian Reform Law), its provisions and its implementation, see Jonas, "Guatemala," 158–60; Schlesinger and Kinzer, *Bitter Fruit*, 54–56; Melville and Melville, *Guatemala: The Politics*, 51–58; Walter LaFeber, *Inevitable Revolutions* (New York: Norton, 1983), 115–18.

10. LaFeber, *Inevitable*, 118; similar but slightly different data can be found in Schlesinger and Kinzer, *Bitter Fruit*, 75–77; Melville and Melville, *Guatemala: The Politics*, 61–63.

11. LaFeber, *Inevitable*, 118–19. For more detailed information see Jonas, "Guatemala," 165, especially *n.* 12.

12. Blasier, *The Hovering Giant*, 97, 226–32.

13. Quoted in LaFeber, *Inevitable*, 119.

14. Schlesinger and Kinzer, *Bitter Fruit*, 56–62; Blasier, *The Hovering Giant*, 154–58.

15. The best full-length treatments of this episode are Immerman, *The CIA in*

Guatemala; Schlesinger and Kinzer, *Bitter Fruit.* Shorter versions can be found in Blasier, *The Hovering Giant,* 159–77.

16. Washington Office on Latin America (referred to as WOLA hereafter), *Guatemala: The Roots of Revolution* (Washington, D.C.: Washington Office on Latin America, February 1983), 8; Jonas, "Showcase for Counterrevolution." in *Guatemala,* 74–75; Schlesinger and Kinzer, *Bitter Fruit,* 221.

17. Jonas, "Showcase," 75.

18. Richard Adams, *Crucifixion by Power* (Austin, Texas: University of Texas Press, 1970), 400.

19. LaFeber, *Inevitable,* 125.

20. Adams, *Crucifixion,* 194–95.

21. Ibid., 149–55; Jonas, "Guatemala: Land of Eternal Struggle," 177–84; Jonas, "Showcase," 81.

22. Charles D. Brockett, "The Right to Food and United States Policy in Guatemala," *Human Rights Quarterly* (Summer 1984):372. For a very detailed account of this process, see Susanne Jonas, "Masterminding the Mini-Market: U.S. Aid to the Central American Common Market," in *Guatemala,* 86–103.

23. WOLA, *Roots,* 2; and World Bank, *Guatemala: Economic and Social Position and Prospects* (Washington, D.C.: World Bank, 1978), 27, cited in Charles D. Brockett, "Malnutrition, Public Policy, and Agrarian Change in Guatemala," *Journal of Interamerican Studies and World Affairs;* Vol. 26, (November 1984), 47.

24. For a case study, see Robert H. Trudeau, "The Effects of Malnutrition and Repression on Political Participation in Guatemala," (Paper delivered at the Annual Meeting of the Southern Political Science Association, Memphis, Tenn., 1981), 10–12.

25. Jonas, "The New Hard Line: U.S. Strategy for the 1970s," *Guatemala,* 105–6.

26. Ibid., 106.

27. One source, acknowledging macroeconomic growth and then using systematic analysis to answer this question, says, "[This growth] has not resulted in any substantive increase in the internal market or in the economy's capacity to absorb available labor." Programa Centroamericana de Ciencias Sociales, *Estructura agraria, dinámica de población y desarrollo capitalista en Centroamérica* (San José, Costa Rica: Editorial Universitaria Centroamericana, 1978), 121.

28. Trudeau, "The Effects of Malnutrition," 14.

29. For an excellent case study of the growth of one such commodity, cotton, and its effects on Guatemala's society and ecosystems, see Adams, "The Costs of Growth: Cotton," in *Crucifixion,* 353–79.

30. Brockett, "Malnutrition," 491.

31. WOLA, *Roots,* 3.

32. Brockett, "Malnutrition," 492.

33. Lehman B. Fletcher et al., *Guatemala's Economic Development* (Ames, Iowa: Iowa State University Press, 1970), 196.

34. U.S. Agency for International Development (AID), *Report of the AID Field Mission in Guatemala* (Guatemala City, Guatemala: U.S. Agency for International Development, 1980); cited in WOLA, *Roots,* 6.

35. Hugo Amigo, "Características de la alimentación y nutrición del Guatemalteco," *Alero,* 3rd series (March-April 1978):124.

36. Inter-American Development Bank, "Nutrition and Socio-Economic Development of Latin America" (Proceedings of a symposium held in Washington, D.C., 28 June 1978), 19.

37. George Black, with Milton Jamail and Norma Stoltz Chinchilla, *Garrison Guatemala* (New York: Monthly Review Press, 1984), 19; Adams, *Crucifixion,* 269.

38. Howard Sharckman, "The Vietnamization of Guatemala: U.S. Counterinsurgency Programs," in *Guatemala,* 194.

39. Ibid., 194–95.

40. WOLA, *Roots,* 9.

41. Black, *Garrison,* 21.

42. Danilo Barilas, 1975, cited ibid., 31.
43. Ibid., 52.
44. Ibid., 52–54.
45. Melville and Melville, *Guatemala: The Politics,* 189.
46. Black, *Garrison,* 21.
47. Jonas, "Guatemala," 196.
48. Ibid., 195.
49. Jonas, "The New Hard Line," 104–8.
50. Sharckman, "The Vietnamization of Guatemala," 196. According to *Time,* 26 January 1968, eighty-five of those killed were guerrillas, five hundred were guerrilla sympathizers, and the rest were innocent peasants who happened to be living in the wrong place at the wrong time.
51. Quoted in WOLA, *Roots,* 10; WOLA cites as an important source Normal Gall, "Slaughter in Guatemala," *New York Review of Books* 17, (20 May 1971):12–17.
52. Raul García Granados, chief adviser of former President Lucas, quoted in WOLA, *Roots,* 10.
53. Cited ibid., 9.
54. Normal Gall, "Slaughter in Guatemala," cited in ibid., 9.
55. Ibid., 11.
56. Ibid.
57. An excellent, detailed description of the Church's new approach to social change can be found in Penny Lernoux, *Cry of the People* (New York: Penguin Books, 1982).
58. Data in this and subsequent paragraphs describing political violence since around 1978 were obtained from a variety of published sources, including the daily press in Guatemala and newsletters and bulletins of various academic, educational, and political organizations.
59. For a detailed summary and analysis of this violent reaction by the government and the elite sectors that were affected, see Shelton H. Davis and Julie Hodson, *Witnesses to Political Violence in Guatemala: The Suppression of a Rural Development Movement* (Boston: Oxfam-America, 1982); for details from the perspective of the Indian communities themselves, see Rarihokwats, ed., *Guatemala: The Horror and the Hope* (York, Pa.: Four Arrows, 1982). For a systematic analysis of political violence, especially in rural Guatemala, see Gabriel Aguilera Peralta, et al., *Dialéctica del terror en Guatemala* (San José, Costa Rica: Editorial Universitaria Centroamericana, 1981).
60. Concerned Guatemala Scholars, *Guatemala: Dare to Struggle, Dare to Win* (Brooklyn, N.Y.: Concerned Guatemala Scholars, 1981), 47–54.
61. Caesar D. Sereseres, "The Guatemalan Legacy: Radical Challengers and Military Politics," in *Report on Guatemala: Findings of the Study Group on United States–Guatemalan Relations,* The Johns Hopkins University School of Advanced International Studies Papers in International Affairs, no. 7 (Boulder, Colo.: Westview Press, 1985), 31.
62. For a good summary of this history, see Concerned Guatemala Scholars, *Guatemala: Dare to Struggle,* 13–44; Black, *Garrison,* 66–74.
63. An interesting account of this period is given in Mario Payeras, *Days of the Jungle* (New York: Monthly Review Press, 1983); see also Black, *Garrison,* 72–78.
64. For more details see Black, *Garrison,* 102–7.
65. The full text of the 1982 URNG statement, "The Unity Statement of the Revolutionary Organization—EGP, ORPA, FAR, PGT—To the People of Guatemala," is available from the Network in Solidarity with Guatemala (NISGUA) in Washington, D.C. Excerpts are published as "The Revolution Will End Our People's Repression," in Fried et al., *Guatemala in Rebellion,* 290. The full text of the URNG statement is also found in *Guatemala: The People United* (San Francisco: Solidarity Publication, 1982); Black, *Garrison,* 183–85.
66. The number of orphans was reported by Dr. Thomas Baudillo Navarro, president of Guatemala's Supreme Court; cited in *Guatemalan Church in Exile,* "Orphans and Disappeared, Victims of Government Repression," (15 November 1984):4.

Data on refugees in Mexico is taken from "Haven or Quarantine," *Guatemala!* 5, (July-August 1984):6–7. Information on internal refugees is found in "The New Society Is Already Being Built: Interview with Rigoberta Menchú," *Guatemala!* 5, (September-October 1984):4–5.

67. See the 1982 Amnesty International Report, "Massive Extrajudicial Executions in Rural Areas under the Government of General Efraín Ríos Montt," reprinted in U.S. Congress, House of Representatives, Committee on Banking, Finance and Urban Affairs, Subcommittee on International Development and Finance, *Inter-American Development Bank Loan to Guatemala*, 97th Cong., 2d sess., 1982, 46–76.

68. In addition to the report by the Organization of American States (OAS), in late 1983 the United Nations General Assembly voted to condemn Guatemala because of human rights violations, and Amnesty International published updated reports on government violations. In early 1984, Americas Watch did likewise. For details about some of these violations, see "Rights Abuses Continue under Mejía," *Central America Bulletin*, (January-February 1984):8–9, 12.

69. "Mejía Víctores: No Pretense of Human Rights," *Guatemala*, 5 (January-February, 1984), 4–5.

70. U.S. Congress, House of Representatives, Committee on Foreign Affairs, and Senate, Committee on Foreign Relations, *Country Reports on Human Rights Practices for 1982*, 98th Cong., 1st sess., 1983, 518.

71. Amnesty International, "Massive Extrajudicial," 63.

72. Chris Norton, "Guatemala, Charged with Rights Violations, Searches for Respect," *Christian Science Monitor*, 18 January 1985.

73. Details can be found in various issues of *Update on Guatemala; Enfoprensa: Information on Guatemala; Ceri-Gua: Panorama Informativo; Servicio de Información y Análisis de Guatemala; Boletín; Washington Report on the Hemisphere; Guatemala Network News;* and in reports from various human rights organizations and in statements by the hierarchy of the Guatemalan Catholic Church.

74. For more details, see various 1985 issues of *Update on Guatemala; Enfoprensa: Information on Guatemala; Ceri-Gua: Panorama Informativo;* and "Peace March for the Disappeared," *Guatemala Network News* 3, no. 2 (April-May 1985):3, 13; Stephen Kinzer, "1,000 Marchers in Guatemala Call Attention to Abductions," *New York Times*, 14 April 1985; "Killings Chill Rights Group in Guatemala," *New York Times*, 19 April 1985.

75. James LeMoyne, "Guatemala, Awaiting Vote, Learns Killings Rise," *New York Times*, 2 March 1985.

76. A good account of the civil patrols is found in Americas Watch, *Guatemala: A Nation of Prisoners* (New York: Americas Watch Committee, January 1984). For a good example of how this stated purpose of the patrols can be accepted as real, even in the "responsible" media, see Barbara Wright, "Guatemala's Civilian Patrols Help Quash Leftist Rebels in North," *Christian Science Monitor*, 13 December 1983.

77. See *Ceri-Gua: Panorama Informativo*, no. 51 (7–13 January 1985):5 6.

78. For a thorough analysis and description of this program, its model villages, and its implications for Guatemalans, see *Guatemalan Church in Exile*, "Guatemala, A New Way of Life: The Development Poles," (September-October 1984). For evidence of U.S. fiscal and ideological support for the program, see "Model Villages and the Development Centers," *Guatemala Network News* 3, no. 5 (December 1984-January 1985):7; "AID Funds for the Strategic Hamlets," *Enfoprensa: Information on Guatemala* 2, no. 49 (7 December 1984):4. For documentation of the opposition of the Guatemalan Catholic Church hierarchy to this development-counterinsurgency scheme, see *Ceri-Gua: Panorama Informativo*, (18–24 March 1985):3; and Chris Krueger and Kjell Enge, *Without Security or Development: Guatemala Militarized* (Washington, D.C.: Washington Office on Latin America, June 1985).

79. James LeMoyne, "For Mayans of Guatemala, Calamity Strikes Again," *New York Times*, 10 January 1985.

80. *Ceri-Gua: Panorama Informativo*, (7–13 January 1985):6; "Counterinsurgency, Politics, and Instability," *Central America Bulletin* (April 1985), reprinted in *Guatemalan Network News* 3, (April-May 1985):5, 8.

81. The phrase is taken from the title of Edward S. Herman and Frank Brodhead, *Demonstration Elections: U.S.-Staged Elections in the Dominican Republic, Vietnam, and El Salvador* (Boston: South End Press, 1984). For a more in-depth description of the legitimization—as opposed to democratization—aims of the 1984 and 1985 electoral processes, see Robert H. Trudeau, "Guatemalan Elections: The Illusion of Democracy" (Paper delivered at the National Conference on Guatemala, Washington, D.C., 15 June 1984), especially 13–18.

82. Stephen Kinzer, "Guatemala Rivals Look to Transition," *New York Times*, 21 April 1985.

83. The FY1978 law is PL95–148. On the formal understanding with Congress, which lasted until 1981, see the comments by Rep. Michael Barnes in John M. Goshko, "Guatemala Likely Will Get U.S. Helicopter Spare Parts," *Washington Post*, 6 November 1982.

84. Peralta, "El Proceso," 36; Lars Schoultz, "Guatemala: Social Change and Political Conflict," in U.S. Congress, House of Representatives, Committee on Foreign Affairs, *Human Rights in Guatemala*, 97th Cong., 1st sess., 1981, 114–15.

85. Flora Montealegre and Cynthia Aronson, "Background Information on Guatemala, Human Rights, and U.S. Military Assistance," in *Revolution in Central America*, ed. Stanford Central America Action Network (Boulder, Colo.: Westview, 1983), 306–7; Stephen Kinzer, "Guatemala Spurns Renewed U.S. Military Aid," *New York Times*, 7 July 1984.

86. Stephen W. Bosworth and Stephen E. Palmer, *The Situation in Guatemala*, U.S. Department of State Bulletin 81 (Washington, D.C.: Government Printing Office, October 1981), 80.

87. U.S. Congress, Senate, Committee on Foreign Relations, *Foreign Assistance Authorization for Fiscal Year 1982*, 97th Cong., 1st sess., 1981, 428, 458.

88. Christopher Dickey, "Haig's Emissary in Guatemala Discounts Charges of Rights Abuse," *Washington Post*, 14 May 1981.

89. Inter-American Development Bank Loan to Guatemala, 11–16.

90. Lou Cannon, "Reagan Praises Guatemalan Military Leader," *Washington Post*, 5 December 1982.

91. Ibid., 6 November 1982.

92. (Raleigh, N.C.) *News and Observer*, 27 November 1983.

93. "U.S. Aid Slated for Guatemala," *Guatemala Network News* 3, (April-May 1985): 10.

94. "New U.S. Ambassador," *Guatemala!* 5, (September-October 1984):9–10.

95. U.S. Congress, Senate, Committee on Appropriations, *Foreign Assistance and Related Programs Appropriations, Fiscal Year 1982*, 97th Cong., 1st sess., 1981, pt. 1:269.

96. Development and humanitarian assistance given by the U.S. government to various independent private voluntary organizations (Catholic Relief Services, CARE, and so on) rather than to the Guatemalan government has sometimes encouraged meaningful social and economic reforms. These programs are typically oriented toward local subsistence and self-help rather than toward large-scale development schemes that the elites control. Note, however, that these aid programs encourage local organization, which, as we have seen, the military views as a threat. Indeed, in the past few years Guatemalan elites have effectively destroyed many of the private voluntary organization programs in rural Guatemala. They are clearly capable of doing so again in the future. See Davis and Hodson, *Witnesses to Political Violence*.

97. For an in-depth analysis of Guatemalan political developments reflecting this point of view, see Edelberto Torres-Rivas, "Prólogo: La contrarevolución y el terror," in Peralta, *Dialectica del Terror*, 9–33.

98. Interestingly enough, this analysis is also offered by at least some elements of the nonmilitary economic elite, who blame much of Guatemala's current ills on U.S.

assistance to a corrupt military that keeps Guatemala poor and unstable *and* violates the tenets of market capitalism, while preventing the civilian elite from accomplishing its mission—economic development. (This increasingly acrimonious debate, based on economic arguments, was the main item on the agenda in 1985 in Guatemala, as the national economy sank further into crisis due to military management and international pressures.) For an interesting exposition of this "right-wing dependency" thesis, see Jorge E. Torres Ocampo, *Reflexión, análisis, crítica, y autocrítica de la situación política de Guatemala* (Guatemala City, Guatemala: n.p., 1980). Torres Ocampo, a leader of the extreme right-wing National Liberation Movement (MLN) political party, was assassinated shortly after this booklet was published.

99. Reported in "Vinicio Cerezo, Presidential Candidate," *Enfoprensa: Information on Guatamala* 2, (21 December 1984):3.

100. In fact, given the institutional strength of the military and the intransigence of antireformist sectors of Guatemala's elite, even coups d'état mean little. Even if General Ríos Montt *had* been "getting a bum rap"—as President Reagan asserted—and truly wished to reform Guatemala, his power to do so would have been extremely limited. His fall from power in 1983 is at least partially attributable to opposition engendered in the face of proposed tax reforms requested by the International Monetary Fund. IMF pressures were very much part of the political agenda in 1985 as well, as the Mejía government attempted to chart a course between the civilian elites wanting a "free market" system and the IMF's insistence on economic regulations, new taxes, and restrictions on imports. Changes in personnel in the presidency, whether by election or by coup d'état, do not change the domestic context of inequality and polarization, nor do they significantly increase the polity's capacity for reform, at least in part because of damage done by past U.S. policies. As a U.S. State Department official commented: "If only we had an Arbenz now. . . . We are going to have to invent one, but all the candidates are dead." (Cited in Marlise Simons, "Guatemala: The Coming Danger," in *El Salvador: Central America in the New Cold War,* ed. Marvin Gettleman et al. (New York: Grove Press, 1981), 327.

101. Stephen Kinzer, "Guatemala Rulers Renew Vow on Today's Voting," *New York Times*, 3 November 1985.

3: EL SALVADOR

1. Thomas Anderson, *Matanza: El Salvador's Communist Revolt of 1932* (Lincoln, Neb.: University of Nebraska Press, 1971).

2. Enrique Baloyra, *El Salvador in Transition* (Chapel Hill: University of North Carolina Press, 1982), 7.

3. U.S. attaché to Central America, Major A. R. Harris, wrote in 1931: "About the first thing one observes when he goes to San Salvador is the number of expensive automobiles in the streets. There seems to be nothing between these high priced cars and the ox cart with its barefooted attendant. There is practically no middle class between the very rich and the very poor." Anderson, *Matanza,* 83–84.

4. Quoted in Tommie Sue Montgomery, *Revolution in El Salvador, Origins and Evolution* (Boulder, Colo.: Westview Press, 1982), 47.

5. Baloyra, *El Salvador,* 30.

6. Carmen Deere and Martin Diskin, "Rural Poverty in El Salvador: Dimensions, Causes, and Trends" from research project, *Rural Poverty in Central America: Dimensions and Causes* (Geneva: International Labour Organization, June 1983), 36–40. By 1971, 1.5 percent of all farms accounted for 49 percent of all farmland, and 92 percent of the farms represented only 27 percent of the land, usually inferior in quality. (3rd Agrarian Census, 1971).

7. Baloyra, *El Salvador,* 22–32.

8. James Dunkerley, *The Long War, Dictatorship and Revolution in El Salvador* (London: Junction Books, 1982), 73; and Baloyra, *El Salvador,* 18–22.

9. See for example Montgomery, *Revolution*, 55–95; Balyora, *El Salvador*, 33–52.
10. Quoted in Robert Armstrong and Janet Shenk, *El Salvador: The Face of Revolution* (Boston: South End Press, 1982), 79. See also Tommie Sue Montgomery, "Christianity as a Subversive Activity in Central America" in *Trouble in Our Backyard*, ed. Martin Diskin, (New York: Pantheon, 1984), 75–100.
11. Baloyra, *El Salvador*, 161. See also Dunkerley, *The Long War*, 90–102; and Robert Leiken, "The Salvadoran Left," in *Central America: Anatomy of Conflict*, ed. Robert Leiken (New York: Pergamon Press, 1984), 111–130; and Montgomery, *Revolution*, 119–157.
12. The military and the oligarchy labeled these groups as "subversive" and "terrorist" and identified them as mere arms of the guerrillas. As these popular organizations were violently repressed, many of them did affiliate with armed groups but with one exception (28 February Popular League linked to the ERP) they remained distinct from and not simply fronts for the guerrillas. This definition of such organizations as "subversive" is an example of common manipulation of symbols of legitimacy by the oligarchy, a weapon used with great success (the U.S. embassy has been particularly receptive) to move the center of political discourse to the right. See Baloyra, *El Salvador*, 67–72.
13. Allan Nairn, "Behind the Death Squads," *The Progressive* (May 1984): 20–29. See also James Dunkerley, *The Long War*, 76; and Raymond Bonner, *Weakness and Deceit, U.S. Policy and El Salvador*, (New York: Times Books, 1984), 59–63.
14. Dunkerley, 103–4; Nairn, "Death Squads." By the early 1980s there were a number of other death squads—the Secret Anti-Communist Army; the Maximiliano Hernández Martínez Anti-Communist Brigade—"financed by right-wing Salvadoran businessmen, commanded by military officers, and made up of soldiers, ex-soldiers, and civilians." Bonner, *Weakness and Deceit*, 330.
15. The reduction of military aid was largely symbolic, since aid had already been suspended by President Gerald Ford after Salvadoran Army Chief of Staff Manuel Alfonso Rodríguez was convicted in New York of trying to sell several thousand machine guns to the mafia in the United States. Cynthia Aronson, *El Salvador: A Revolution Confronts the United States* (Washington, D.C.: Institute for Policy Studies, 1982), 35.
16. Bonner, *Weakness and Deceit*, 36, 39–40.
17. Baloyra, *El Salvador*, 83–84; Bonner, *Weakness and Deceit*, 36–39; Alan Riding, "Salvadoran Battle of the Two Romeros," *New York Times*, 26 February 1978; Alan Riding, "El Salvador's Dissidents Disappointed at U.S. Silence," *New York Times*, 8 May 1978.
18. Baloyra, *El Salvador*, 73, 83–85.
19. Ibid., 86. For an excellent discussion of the coup see Montgomery, *Revolution*, 7–20.
20. Baloyra, *El Salvador*, 90.
21. Dennis Volman, "Salvador death squads, a CIA connection?," *Christian Science Monitor*, 8 May 1984; Nairn, "Behind the Death Squads"; Baloyra, *El Salvador*, 92.
22. Aronson, *El Salvador: A Revolution*, 47.
23. Baloyra, *El Salvador*, 96–101.
24. Armstrong and Shenk, *El Salvador*, 141.
25. Joel Brinkley, "Ex-Envoy Accuses 6 Salvador Exiles," *New York Times*, 3 February 1984.
26. Christopher Dickey, "Behind the Death Squads," *New Republic*, 26 December 1984, 18.
27. Craig Pyes, "A Dirty War in the Name of Freedom," and "Right Built Itself in Mirror Image of Left for Civil War," *Albuquerque Journal*, 18 December 1983.
28. Americas Watch, *Report On Human Rights in El Salvador*, January 26, 1982 (New York: Vintage Books, 1982), 43.
29. The FDR leadership, meeting in a Jesuit high school, were surrounded by two hundred uniformed civilians and brutally assassinated. Among them was FDR President Enrique Alvarez, former minister of agriculture in the first junta.

According to Ambassador White, Duarte knew who the killers were but admitted being powerless to bring them to justice. Robert White, "The Problem That Won't Go Away," *New York Times Magazine*, 18 July 1982, 21.

30. "El Salvador 1984," *Report on the Americas* 18, no. 2 (March-April 1984):32. This report was prepared by a team of social scientists who edit *Estudios Centroamericanos* (ECA), a journal of the Central American University (UCA) in San Salvador.

31. The Fuerzas Populares de Liberación (FPL), which by early 1983 constituted about 20 percent of the fighting force, has historically been closest to Cuba and Nicaragua. But with respect to the Soviet Union, it has had two orientations: the original leadership that split from the Salvadoran Communist Party had few criticisms of Moscow since it abandoned its line of "peaceful transition" for Central America; those with Christian activist origins were extremely radical and considered the Soviet Union corrupt and oppressive. A reshuffling of leadership in the FPL in late 1983 (following internal conflicts over strategy and the murder of a top leader and suicide of Salvador Cayetano Carpio) brought the FPL closer to the other groups in the FMLN but also created a splinter group which pledged to follow Carpio's more radical line. This group seems to have been responsible for the killing of civilian politicians in San Salvador in late 1983 and early 1984. It was not under the FDR-FMLN umbrella. The Ejército Revolucionario del Pueblo (ERP), with about 40 percent of the guerrillas, and the Fuerzas Armadas de Resistencia Nacional (FARN), with 15 percent, were nationalistic, favored nonalignment, and were critical of the Cuban presence in Managua. Only the Communist Party's Fuerzas Armadas de Liberación (FAL), with less than 10 percent, remained firmly in the Soviet camp. Leiken, "The Salvadoran Left"; Stephen Kinzer, "Salvador Rebels Revile Late Chief," *New York Times*, 14 November 1983.

32. Craig Pyes, "The New American Right Cooks Up a Hot Potato," *Albuquerque Journal*, 22 December 1983.

33. For detailed discussions of these initiatives see Bonner, *Weakness and Deceit*, 284–89; Wayne S. Smith, "Dateline Havana: Myopic Diplomacy," *Foreign Policy* 48 (Fall 1982):159–62.

34. Secretary of State Alexander Haig, "An Agenda for Cooperation in the Western Hemisphere," before the General Assembly of the Organization of American States in Saint Lucia, 4 December 1981, U.S. Department of State, Bureau of Public Affairs (Washington, D.C., 4 December 1982).

35. Cited in Bonner, *Weakness and Deceit*, 230.

36. Laurence R. Simon, James C. Stephens, and Martin Diskin, *El Salvador Land Reform 1980–1981*, (Boston: Oxfam, 1982), 11.

37. Craig Pyes, "To the Brotherhood, Reds Infect Every Niche of El Salvador," *Albuquerque Journal*, 20 December 1983; and Baloyra, *El Salvador*, 144. See his excellent discussion of the conflicts between the private sector and Duarte, and the failure of the United States to broker collaboration, 143–53.

38. Baloyra, *El Salvador*, 144.

39. For a detailed discussion of the formation of ARENA out of these elements, see Pyes, "Right Built Itself."

40. This assistance and support is detailed by Pyes, "The New American Right."

41. Fear limited freedom of the press. It also limited where the Christian Democrats could campaign and organize and what they could say: they could not campaign for reconciliation with the FDR or against the corruption and repression of the military and paramilitary forces and expect to live. Indeed, the Christian Democrats themselves claimed hundreds of party workers had been killed—the great majority by the extreme right—in the two years before the election. Further, the resources available to the oligarchy's ARENA party were enormous, and the PCN, the old ruling party of the military, still had great organizational strength in rural areas where it had been identified as "the government" by many peasants since 1950.

42. The fourth largest category was "null" and "blank" ballots—almost 12 percent of the total vote. Baloyra, *El Salvador*, 3, 176.

43. "Salvadoran Land Program Is Criticized," *New York Times*, 15 February 1984.
44. Sam Dillon, "García Quits, Averting a Mutiny in Salvador," *Miami Herald*, 19 April 1983. This analysis was first suggested by William LeoGrande.
45. Marlise Simons, "Foes of Rightist Leader in Salvador Take Steps to Weaken His Powers," *New York Times*, 20 November 1982.
46. For an argument that there was conscious deceit, see the examples throughout Bonner, *Weakness and Deceit.*
47. See discussion in Americas Watch, *Report on Human Rights*, xxvii–xxviii, 43–45, 280–89.
48. Dickey, "Behind the Death Squads," 21.
49. Americas Watch Committee and the American Civil Liberties Union, *As Bad As Ever: A Report on Human Rights in El Salvador*, 4th Supp., 31 January 1984, 9.
50. "New Choice in El Salvador Likes Role of Mediator," *New York Times*, 19 April 1983; Raymond Bonner, "Cover-up Charged in Death of Nuns," *New York Times*, 3 March 1984; Larry Rohrer, "Salvador Defense Lawyer Charges Cover-Up in Slaying of U.S. Nuns," *New York Times*, 6 May 1985; Bonner, *Weakness and Deceit*, 78–80.
51. Americas Watch, "As Bad As Ever," 5.
52. Bonner, *Weakness and Deceit*, 358–59.
53. Lydia Chávez, "U.S. Envoy Castigates Salvadorans on Terrorism," *New York Times*, 26 November 1983. A year earlier, Ambassador Hinton had become frustrated with continued death-squad activities and also condemned them. But the White House quickly disassociated itself with Hinton's remarks.
54. *U.S. Aid to El Salvador: An Evaluation of the Past, A Proposal for the Future*, A Report prepared for the Arms Control and Foreign Policy Caucus by Jim Leach, George Miller, and Mark O. Hatfield, February 1985, 28, 37; "El Salvador 1984," 38–39.
55. Lydia Chávez, "U.S. Pilot Program in Salvadoran Area in Danger of Failing," *New York Times*, 19 December 1983.
56. Leonel Gómez, "Behind the Violence in El Salvador," *Boston Globe*, 4 December 1982. Gómez was an adviser to ISTA director Viera before he was assassinated with Hammer and Pearlman in January 1981.
57. Richard Halloran, "U.S. Said to Draw Up Latin Troops Plan," *New York Times*, 8 April 1984; *New York Times*, 10 April 1984.
58. Philip Taubman, "CIA Said to Have Given Money to 2 Salvador Parties," *New York Times*, 12 May 1984. Terry Lynn Karl explains how some of this money may have been channeled through a Venezuelan-sponsored Christian Democratic public relations firm. Karl, "After LaPalma: The Prospects for Democratization in El Salvador," *World Policy Journal*, Vol. 2 (Spring 1985), 317. The U.S. also funneled funds to the PCN candidate in an effort to take votes away from D'Aubuisson in the March elections.
59. "El Salvador 1984," 36–40.
60. Ibid., 40; Americas Watch, *The Continuing Terror:* Seventh Supplement *to the Report on Human Rights in El Salvador*, September 1985, 146.
61. The real per capita GDP of lower-income groups declined about 35 percent between 1978 and 1983. Primary school enrollment declined from 85 percent before the war to 50 percent by 1984. The value added by the manufacturing sector declined by 33 percent between 1978 and 1983. (Leach et al., *U.S. Aid to El Salvador*, 37.) Agricultural production declined by 7.4 percent in 1982 and 8.7 percent in 1983. Consumption levels fell by 27 percent between 1979 and 1981, and by a further 20 percent by 1983. The overall consumer price index rose by 97.7 percent from 1980 to 1983. As a result of Decree 544, outlawing all labor union activity, real minimum wages in both the public and private sectors declined by 65 percent between 1979 and early 1983. Official figures show 38 percent without work in early 1983; unemployment and underemployment together afflict almost 80 percent of the population. "El Salvador 1984," 38–39.
62. Leach et al., *U.S. Aid to El Salvador*, 36. The land reform was already faltering badly when Duarte took office. After two years of ARENA control of land-reform

agencies, a report by AID's inspector general in January 1984 found all three phases of land reform in serious difficulty: Phase I faced economic constraints that made the majority of cooperatives unviable and right-wing violence that forced a number to relinquish titles; Phase II was not implemented; Phase III faced physical intimidation of new and prospective landholders. U.S. AID Inspector General, *Agrarian Reform in El Salvador,* 18 January 1984, cited in Leach et al., *U.S. Aid to El Salvador,* 35.

63. There were a number of social and economic areas in which reformers looked for positive moves: efforts to meet demands by rural workers in coffee, cotton, and sugar to improve wages and working conditions and the demands of urban lower- and middle-class groups for wage and salary increases and price controls on essential goods to counter the drastic drop in real wages since 1980; efforts to begin the critical Phase II of the land-reform program (this phase had effectively been canceled by the right's ability to get a constitutional provision increasing the maximum amount of unexpropriable land from 100 to 250 hectares and other delays preventing implementation); a distribution of credit and technical assistance to cooperatives and individual producers in Phase I and Phase III lands; efforts to reactivate Phase III of the land reform (in June 1984 the rightist-dominated assembly refused to extend deadlines); and efforts to improve benefits in the social security program. For a full discussion of land reform and the demands for reform facing Duarte, see Martin Diskin, *Agrarian Reform in El Salvador: An Evaluation* (San Francisco: Institute for Food and Development Policy, 1985).

64. Duarte aimed to use his power over governmental institutions to give privilege to certain groups that might be won over to support him. In 1984, for example, he gave preferential access to credits and foreign exchange to nontraditional exporters (e.g., cotton growers) and industrialists. But he stood firm against the demands of the coffee growers. However, as Duarte tried to divide them, the rightists called for the same kind of unity meetings they had held in early 1982. See discussion by Ricardo Stein in "El Salvador: Can the Duarte Experiment Work?" *Report on the Americas* 19, no. 1 (January-February 1985):30.

65. For a detailed breakdown of the actual distribution of aid see Leach et al., *U.S. Aid to El Salvador,* 8–38 and 49–60. This report argues that only 15 percent of the total aid (about $1.7 billion) provided from FY1981 through FY1985 went to reform and development. About 30 percent of the total aid program ($523 million) went for military equipment and services. About 11 percent went for commercial food aid. And about 44 percent went for what it calls "indirect war-related aid": cash transfers ($585 million), aid to displaced persons ($92 million), and aid to rebuild infrastructure damaged by the insurgents ($90 million). It points out that cash transfers (the largest single U.S. aid program) help fill the government budget deficit (largely war-caused), indirectly finance the expansion of the armed forces, and allow the private business community to import by replacing sources of foreign exchange. Reports by Arthur Young and Company and the General Accounting Office show that some of the dollars are illegally diverted to bank accounts in Miami and elsewhere. See also William Goodfellow, "U.S. Economic Aid to El Salvador: Where is the Money Going," *International Policy Report* (Washington, D.C.: Center for International Policy, May 1984).

66. U.S. Agency for International Development, "Policy Dialogue Objectives in El Salvador," 1984, Mimeograph. Cited and discussed in Diskin, *Agrarian Reform in El Salvador.*

67. Americas Watch, *"Draining the Sea": A Report on Human Rights in El Salvador,* March 1985; Americas Watch, *The Continuing Terror,* 137–156.

68. Cited in Julia Preston, "What Duarte Won," *New York Review of Books,* 15 August 1985, 30. See also Paul Tsongas, ". . . Needs Reagan's Help," *New York Times,* 15 May 1984.

69. Enrique Baloyra, "Dilemmas of Political Transition in El Salvador," *Journal of International Affairs* 38, (Winter 1985): 231. Carranza was sent to the Salvadoran

embassy in Madrid. Colonel José Ricardo Pozo, former director of the S-2 intelligence unit of the Treasury Police, was sent to Paraguay as military attaché. Lieutenant Colonel Jorge Adalberto Cruz and Colonel Mario Denis Morán were assigned to the Inter-American Defense College in Washington, D.C. Significantly, there was concern in the military that the decision to transfer these officers be made by the high command before Duarte took office, reported the *New York Times,* "so that it would appear the military, and not a civilian President, was cleaning house, according to diplomats." "Salvadoran Army Shifts 2 Rightists," *New York Times,* 25 May 1984. The concern of the officer corps to let Duarte know the limits of his power with the military was made clear by a special commission of officers that at the end of April asked the defense minister to inform the winner of the elections that he would not be able to "change the organic structure of the armed forces." Lydia Chávez, "Salvador Officers Warn Civilians Not to Meddle," *New York Times,* 29 April 1984.

70. Golcher conceded that serious human rights violations may have been committed by this unit—but because he was unable to prove specific crimes against any member he ordered the unit dispanded. He said that members of the S-2 intelligence squad often wore civilian clothes and "acted on" intelligence as well as collecting it. " 'When they wanted to do an operation, they would take some of the uniformed police along, or bring them into the unit to work on intelligence,' Colonel Golcher said, indicating that the unit was a power unto itself that carried out death squad killings." James LeMoyne, "A Salvador Police Chief Vows an End to Abuses," *New York Times,* 1 July 1984.

71. Americas Watch reported 39 such killings recorded by Tutela Legal during the last six months of 1984, a sharp drop from the 185 killings the office recorded in the first six months of the year. This reflects the continuation of a trend. Tutela Legal recorded 449 death-squad killings in the last six months of 1983 and 810 death-squad killings in the first six months of 1983. There were 56 disappearances during the last six months of 1984. This contrasts with 139 in the first six months of 1984; 209 in the last six months of 1983; and 326 in the first six months of 1983. But Americas Watch also reported that it was not aware of any instance in which the three security forces have apprehended anyone involved in the current death-squad killings or diassapearances, or in the thousands that took place since 1979. Americas Watch, *"Draining the Sea,"* 38–40.

72. This strike activity, beginning in early 1984 as the elections approached, was the first stike activity since the repression against the labor movement began in 1980. At least 37,000 workers took part in strikes at the Social Security Institute, the Institute of Agrarian Reform, the Salvadoran Teachers Union, the textile industry, and various financial institutions. When Duarte took office he was able to settle these strikes, granting wage increases. (Karl, "After La Palma," 320; Baloyra, "Dilemmas," 232.) On 1 May 1985, 10,000 to 15,000 workers and peasants were allowed to demonstrate (the biggest demonstration in years) to demand wage increases, price controls, dialogue with the left, and an end to government efforts to try to control the unions. "Formalizando Realidades," *Processo,* 6 May 1985, 1–2. (San Salvador: Centro Universitario de Documentación e Información de la Universidad Centroamericana). Some strike and labor leaders, however, were dealt with harshly. For example, see Americas Watch, *The Continuing Terror,* 144–151.

73. The figures from Tutela Legal, which Americas Watch argues are conservative, show 1,048 killings of civilian noncombatants by the armed forces and paramilitary forces allied to them from July 1984 through December 1984. (Testimony by Aryeh Neier, Vice-Chairman of Americas Watch, U.S. Congress, House Committee on Foreign Affairs, Subcommittee on the Western Hemisphere, 31 January 1985.

74. Americas Watch, *"Draining the Sea,"* 3–27.

75. Cited in Leach et al., *U.S. Aid to El Salvador,* 63.

76. Leach et al., *U.S. Aid to El Salvador,* 14–5, 27–29.

77. Ibid., 5, 28. See also Americas Watch and the Lawyers Committee for Interna-

tional Human Rights, *Free Fire: A Report on Human Rights in El Salvador*, August 1984, 40; "Duarte Issues Rules for Air Attacks," *New York Times*, 13 September 1984; Americas Watch, *The Continuing Terror*, 7–38.

78. Displaced persons registered by the Red Cross in zones of conflict increased from 80,000 to 105,000 between January and July of 1984; and displaced persons in government-controlled areas rose from 262,000 to 342,000 from November 1983 to May 1984. Americas Watch and the Lawyer's Committee, *Free Fire*, 32–34.

79. Ochoa claimed that there were no longer any civilians in these zones but relief officials said otherwise. Chris Hedges, "Salvadoran Army Attempts to Mobilize Civilians," *Dallas Morning News*, 21 January 1985.

80. Testimony of Aryeh Neier before the Subcommittee on the Western Hemisphere, *Developments in El Salvador*. See also the comparison of forced relocation in El Salvador with the case of the Miskito Indians in Nicaragua in Americas Watch, *"Draining the Sea,"* 45–49.

81. Army Major Ricardo Salvador Murcia, quoted in "Salvadorans Say 42 Killed in Hamlets," *Washington Post*, 9 September 1984.

82. Edward Cody, "Duarte: Limited Power Over Military," *Washington Post*, 17 September 1984.

83. Ochoa was just sent out of the country, to Washington again, after an abortive coup attempt against Duarte in late 1985. Lydia Chávez, "Attempts Told to Stop Salvador Killings," *New York Times*, 1 June 1984.

84. A report of the U.S. Senate Select Committee on Intelligence, released in October 1984, found that "numerous Salvadoran military and security forces as well as other official organizations have been involved in encouraging or conducting death-squad activity or other violent abuses. This has included many middle-level officers and a few high-ranking officials; a large number of low-level personnel have also been involved." U.S. Congress, Senate, Select Committee on Intelligence, *"Recent Political Violence in El Salvador,"* 5 October 1984. The four officers transferred abroad clearly represent only a fraction of those involved.

85. Leonel Gómez, "Behind the Violence in El Salvador," *Boston Globe*, 4 December 1982. The role of the Armed Forces Security Council is discussed by Colonel Roberto Santivañez, former director of ANSESAL, in Doyle McManus, "Contra Linked to Slaying of Salvador Bishop," *Los Angeles Times*, 22 March 1985, and in Dennis Volman, "Salvador Death Squads, a CIA Connection?" *Christian Science Monitor*, 8 May 1984. Duarte's lack of power in this crucial area was evident from his inability to carry through even the limited agenda he set for himself. Shortly after his inauguration he created a commission to investigate five key cases: the assassination of Archbishop Romero; the masssacre at La Hojas; the killings in the well at Armenia; the murders of Hammer and Pearlman, the U.S. labor advisers; and the murder of John Sullivan. Depite the existence of detailed evidence in some of these cases, the commission was unable to make headway. The example at La Hojas is the clearest. The colonel who commanded the garrison and the captain who led the troops that committed the massacre are very well known and they remain on active duty. Americas Watch, *"Draining the Sea,"* 67–68; James LeMoyne, "2 Years after Massacre, Salvadoran Seeks Justice," *New York Times*, 25 February 1985. In the case of Hammer and Pearlman, there is evidence from the FBI, from AFL-CIO–sponsored investigations, and testimony from the national guardsman who did the killing, that Lieutenant López Sibrián and Captain Eduardo Alfonso Avila, both in the national guard's intelligence unit, gave the orders. Sibrián was released by the courts—fearful judges refused to prosecute on technical grounds—and Avila was never charged, although Salvadoran officials claimed in March 1985 that they would reopen the case. James LeMoyne, "New Inquiry Into '81 Salvador Killings Predicted," *New York Times*, 24 May 1985. Two national guardsmen have just been convicted (February 1986), yet the crime's "intellectual author's," the two officers mentioned above, remain free.

86. The assembly refused to fund a commission to investigate notorious cases of right-wing terror. The assembly put conservatives in key positions as head of the

supreme court, attorney general, and solicitor general—further restraining Duarte's efforts to investigate corruption and right-wing terror. Baloyra, "Dilemmas of Political Transition," 234–35.

87. The need to destroy the death-squad organizations became even more critical after the right lost the 1985 assembly elections. The gradual decline in death-squad activity that began in 1983 was attributable not simply to the influence of the pragmatists inside the military but to three other factors: the elimination of the direct pressure for democratization and reform by the destruction of the popular organizations through the massive terror of the 1980 to 1982 period; the power to block challenges to oligarchy that resulted from control of the assembly from March 1982 to March 1985; and the hesitancy of Duarte and his supporters to push hard for reform or negotiations before the 1985 elections. The reemergence of popular organizations, the right's loss of majority control of the assembly, and the pressure on Duarte for reform confronted the right with a situation somewhat like it faced in 1980 and 1981, and death squad killings began to increase again in 1985. Americas Watch, *The Continuing Terror,* 89–97.

88. Americas Watch, *"Draining the Sea,"* 17.

89. Americas Watch, *The Continuing Terror,* 137–156.

90. Chris Hedges, "Duarte Denounces Rights Office," *Dallas Morning News,* 30 March 1985.

91. In May 1984, for example, three days after Duarte's election, the House only narrowly backed the more or less unrestricted El Salvador aid package sought by the president when it approved by a four-vote margin the Broomfield-Murtha Amendment. The approval of supplemental aid asked for by the president came only after strong lobbying in Washington by Duarte himself. The "Kasten-Dodd" Amendment to the FY1985 Foreign Aid Appropriation cuts off all U.S. aid in the event of a coup.

92. This was also the conclusion of Americas Watch Vice-Chairman Aryeh Neier, *Developments in El Salvador.*

93. The May 1984 plot was led by Hector Regalado, named by D'Aubuisson as chief of security for the Constituent Assembly. Retired Lieutenant General Vernon Walters was sent to talk to D'Aubuisson. Two weeks after the plot was foiled, the United States granted D'Abuisson a visa to visit the United States. "When asked how they reconciled issuing the visa with their beliefs about D'Aubuisson's role in the May plot, U.S. officials said that the administration decided that the best way to persuade the rightist to behave like a responsible political leader would be to treat him like one," reported the *Los Angeles Times.* After the October attempt, a senior U.S. official was reported in the *Los Angeles Times* as saying: "It's happening again. We do not have any evidence that D'Aubuisson is involved this time, but otherwise it's the same people." Washington Office on Latin America, *President Duarte's "October Surprise" Opens Pandora's Box,* October 1984, 6–7.

94. Another signal was the lack of any strong U.S. reaction to the mysterious death of Lieutenant Colonel Domingo Monterrosa. He and other officers closely associated with Blandon (and thus with the peace talks) were killed when their helicopter was sabotaged, and some Salvadoran military officers reportedly thought this was an action by the extreme right to warn Blandon. Dennis Volman, "Salvador's Military Backs Away from Duarte's Peace Talks; Some Senior Officers Said to Lose Confidence in U.S. Protection," *Christian Science Monitor,* 18 January 1985; James LeMoyne, "Bomb Suspected in Salvadoran Crash," *New York Times,* 28 November 1984; and personal interviews.

95. James LeMoyne, "Duarte Protests Reports that U.S. Favors Rightists," *New York Times,* 10 February 1985.

96. The figures for 1984 were 42,000 (Leach, et al., *U.S. Aid to El Salvador,* 21), and the armed forces were still expanding into 1985.

97. Ibid., 21–24.

98. Ibid., 21.

99. Ibid., 29.

100. "U.S. Bolstering Salvadoran Copters," *New York Times*, 19 September 1984.

101. See U.S. Congress, House Committee on Foreign Affairs, Subcommittee on Western Hemisphere Affairs, *Developments in El Salvador*, testimony by Edward L. King, 31 January 1985.

102. Ibid. The guerrillas, for example, were able to mass assaults during 1984 at the Cerron Grande dam, Suchitoto, and El Salto.

103. James LeMoyne, "Salvadoran Army Improving, but Rebels Adjust," *New York Times*, 29 January 1985; Julia Preston, "What Duarte Won," *New York Review of Books*, 15 August 1985, 33, and Subcommittee on Foreign Affairs, *Developments in El Salvador*. King suggested that the new tactics might encourage the FMLN to seek antiaircraft guns and shoulder-fired rockets, which, if obtained, would result in an escalation of the level and intensity of the fighting.

104. The administration has given little public evidence as to the *significance* or *source* of outside military assistance. Middle-ranking diplomats at U.S. embassies in El Salvador, Nicaragua, and Honduras have expressed doubt that the weapons from Nicaragua represent the majority of arms in rebel hands. Stephen Kinzer, "U.S. and Salvadoran Officials Note Steady Rebel Gains," *New York Times*, 25 April 1983. An experienced intelligence officer in El Salvador reported in March 1983 that military aid from Nicaragua and Cuba is not a key factor in the Salvadoran guerrilla campaign. Many have been captured from the Salvadoran army, the national guard, and the police. Drew Middleton, "Salvador's Army's Troubles," *New York Times*, 5 March 1983. In July 1983 officials in El Salvador and Washington said that the flow of military supplies to Salvadoran rebels from outside the country has been only a trickle for many months. One knowledgeable source said that the major army and air force ammunition dump at Ilopango Air Force Base was "also a guerrilla supply warehouse." Middlemen for the guerrillas were buying 81-millimeter mortar shells for about $5 a round. Charles Mohr, "Salvador Rebels Reported to Get Little Arms Aid," *New York Times*, 31 July 1983. A former CIA analyst, David MacMichael, who left the agency in July 1983, and who had access to the most sensitive intelligence about arms shipments, concluded: "The administration and the CIA have systematically misrepresented Nicaraguan involvement in the supply of arms to Salvadoran guerrillas to justify its efforts to overthrow the Nicaraguan Government." Philip Taubman, "In From the Cold and Hot for Truth," *New York Times*, 11 June 1984. See also the detailed report by Julia Preston, "Proof of Arms Smuggling into Salvador Lacking," *Boston Globe*, 10 June 1984.

105. See for example discussion of these new tactics by rebel commander Joaquin Villalobos. James LeMoyne, "Salvadoran Rebels Draw a Bead on the Economy," *New York Times*, 13 July 1985.

106. The café raid followed a number of other guerrilla attacks, including one on a prison near the capital in which the guerrillas freed scores of people, many of them political prisoners, and a March 27 attack on national police headquarters. What particularly marked the June raid was the indiscriminate killing of civilians by the guerrillas. This followed another episode in April at Santa Cruz Loma where the guerrillas also killed a number of civilians. Such actions, while common among the armed forces, had been previously rare among the guerrillas. Indeed, members of the FDR publically criticized the attack. "What seems wrong to us," said Rubén Zamora, "is attempting a military action in an area full of civilians." Tim Golden, "Salvador Rebel Politicians, Fighters Differ Over Massacre," *Miami Herald*, 27 June 1985. Should such occurrences prove to be a pattern, and not an exception, the urban guerrilla activities and kidnappings may erode support for the guerrillas and will be used to justify the kinds of activities the military has long been involved in. In early 1985, U.S. advisers had already begun training a SWAT-type counterterrorist force made up of members of the treasury policy—the security forces most frequently linked to human rights abuses in recent years. Tim Golden, "Salvador Will Act to Block Urban Terror," *Miami Herald*, 23 June 1985.

107. U.S. Congress, House Committee on Foreign Affairs, Subcommittees on Human

Rights and International Organizations, and on Western Hemisphere Affairs, *The Military Stalemate in El Salvador and Related Matters*, testimony by Edward L. King, Western Hemisphere Affairs, February 2, 1984; and House Subcommittee on Western Hemisphere Affairs, *On the Military Situation*.

108. In early 1984 the FMLN resorted to forced recruitment in zones they controlled but abandoned this practice a few months later. Americas Watch, *"Draining the Sea,"* 59–60. James LeMoyne, "Salvadoran Rebels Say Forced Recruiting is Over," *New York Times*, 7 October 1984.

109. King, *Developments in El Salvador*.

110. King, *The Situation in El Salvador*.

111. Leach et al., *U.S. Aid to El Salvador*, 31.

112. For detailed discussions of the emergence of a negotiations strategy within the FDR-FMLN see Leiken, *Central America;* and "El Salvador 1984," 31–35. Both of these pieces also discuss the relationship between the FDR and the FMLN and the integral role that the FDR—despite the destruction of its mass base and its original nonviolent, democratic character—plays within the coalition. The Salvadoran social scientists writing in *Report on the Americas* conclude: "Nevertheless, the FDR's real weight has to be recognized, not only in setting the alliance's diplomatic agenda but also in working out the broad political lines of FMLN-FDR unity. The FDR, and in particular some of its leaders, can be credited in large measure with the new spirit of compromise visible within the FMLN." "El Salvador 1984," 32.

113. Joaquin Villalobos, interview with Terry Karl and other members of a congressional delegation to El Salvador, 13 April 1985. By 1984, the opening bargaining position of the FDR-FMLN was a three-stage plan. In the first stage, the government would present a formula to guarantee security, end human-rights violations, stop weapons imports, and send U.S. advisers out of the country. In exchange, the FDR-FMLN would freeze arms and terminate economic sabotage. In the second stage there would be a formal cease-fire, with territorial concessions to both rebel and government forces. In the final stage there would be a broad national dialogue, a new government, a new constitution, and the reorganization of the armed forces. Only at this point would national elections be held. From *A Hope for Peace*, (La Palma: FMLN-FDR Political-Diplomatic Commission, November 1984), quoted in Karl, "After La Palma," 326.

114. Karl, "After La Palma," 322. Karl points out that similar views were expressed by Duarte in *Playboy*, October 1984, and by leading party officials she interviewed in San Salvador, October 1983.

115. By mid-1984, for example, there had been meetings between Congressional moderates and Blandon that stressed the importance of negotiations. Blandon privately told some Senators that he was willing to talk with the FMLN. Interviews by authors with Congressional staff, December 1984.

116. Washington Office on Latin America, *President Duarte's "October Surprise,"* 18.

117. James LeMoyne, "Salvador Rebels Offer 3-Step Peace Plan," *New York Times*, 1 December 1984. While the rebel offer was a natural negotiation response to Duarte's proposal, the government position seemed to have hardened by late November 1984. Before the talks Duarte said he expected a formal reply to his peace offer. Julio Adolfo Rey Prendes, a government representative, said his delegation read their proposal line by line, pausing after each sentence to ask the rebels if they agreed or disagreed. He added (not surprisingly) that the rebels protested that they were being treated like schoolchildren. "We said it doesn't matter," he said. "We want an answer." "Salvadorans Report 'Tense' Talks; Rebels' Plan Was Not Discussed," James LeMoyne, *New York Times*, 3 December 1984.

118. James LeMoyne, "Duarte is Faulted on Plan for Talks," *New York Times*, 23 November 1984. Shortly before the withdrawal of the business group, an ultrarightist group issued a statement asking: "Who will be the three Judases [from the Private Enterprise Association] who will lend themselves to betray the fatherland, causing uncountable deaths among our officers and troops?"

119. James LeMoyne, "Duarte Will Not Attend Peace Talks Next Week," *New York Times*, 24 November 1984.
120. The Reagan administration's actions—announcing Ambassador Pickering would be transferred soon after rightist assassination attempts, granting D'Aubuisson a visa after the assassination attempt, and other signals—were discussed above.
121. Cynthia Brown, ed., *With Friends Like These: The Americas Watch Report on Human Rights and U.S. Policy in Latin America*, (New York: Pantheon, 1985), 115.

4: NICARAGUA

I have drawn extensively on the work and advice of William LeoGrande for the international relations aspects of this essay. LeoGrande, Mary Erickson, Joseph Kahl, Jeff Ross, Ken Sharpe, and Rose Spalding read earlier drafts of the manuscript and offered valuable suggestions.

  1. Inter-American Development Bank (referred to as IDB hereafter), *Economic and Social Progress in Latin America: 1978 Report* (Washington, D.C.: Inter-American Development Bank, 1978), 138; Charles Teller, "The Demography of Malnutrition in Latin America," *Intercom* 9 (1981):10.
  2. On agro-export development in Nicaragua see Jaime Wheelock, *Nicaragua imperialismo y dictadura* (Havana: Editorial de ciencias sociales, 1979); Orlando Nuñez Soto, *El Somocismo y el modelo agro-exportador* (Managua, Nicaragua: Universidad Nacional Autónoma, n.d.).
  3. IBD, *Economic and Social Progress*, 141, 333.
  4. Dennis Gilbert, "The Bourgeoisie and the Nicaraguan Revolution," in *Nicaragua Five Years Later*, ed. Thomas W. Walker (New York: Praeger, 1985), 163–182.
  5. Joanne Omang, "Nicaraguan Leader Makes U.S. Tour," *Washington Post*, 9 October 1984.
  6. On the early history of the FSLN see David Nolan, *The Ideology of the Sandinistas and the Nicaraguan Revolution* (Coral Gables, Fla.: University of Miami, Institute of Inter-American Studies, 1984); John Booth, *The End and the Beginning: The Nicaraguan Revolution* (Boulder, Colo.: Westview, 1982).
  7. Chamorro's death was later attributed to Somoza's son, Anastasio Somoza Por tocarrero, and his business partner, who had been subjects of a *La Prensa* exposé.
  8. George Black, *Triumph of the People: The Sandinista Revolution in Nicaragua* (London: Zed Press, 1981), 132.
  9. Booth, *The End and the Beginning*, 129.
 10. William LeoGrande, "The United States and The Nicaraguan Revolution," in *Nicaragua in Revolution*, ed. Thomas W. Walker (New York: Praeger, 1982), 66.
 11. Ibid., 69.
 12. Superior Council of Private Enterprises (COSEP), *Analisis sobre la ejecución del programa de gobierno de reconstrucción nacional* (Managua, Nicaragua: Superior Council of Private Enterprises, 1980).
 13. LeoGrande, "The United States," 73–75.
 14. Alejandro Bendana, "The Foreign Policy of the Nicaragua Revolution," in *Nicaragua in Revolution*, 319–328.
 15. Alan Riding, "Nicaragua Seeking Accord in El Salvador," *New York Times*, 12 February 1981; Juan de Onis, "Haig Says Cuban Weapons Support of Salvadoran Rebels Is at a Peak," *New York Times*, 28 February 1981; John M. Goshko and Don Oberdorfer, "U.S. To Send More Aid, Advisors to El Salvador," *Washington Post*, 3 March 1981; John M. Goshko, "State Department Shifts, Seeks to Cool off Salvador Publicity," *Washington Post*, 13 March 1981.
 16. Joseph Collins, *What Difference Could a Revolution Make?* (San Francisco: Institute for Food and Development Policy, 1985) 44.
 17. *Barricada (Managua)*, 30 July 1981.
 18. *Barricada*, 22 October 1981.
 19. John M. Goshko, "Haig Won't Rule Out Anti-Nicaragua Action," *Washington*

Post, 13 November 1981; Michael Getler and Don Oberdorfer, "U.S. Nearing Decision on Nicaragua," *Washington Post*, 22 November 1981.

20. Bernard Gwertzman, "Haig Is Cautious About Any Accord with Nicaraguans," *New York Times*, 16 March 1982; and "Covert Action Bar in Nicaragua Urged," *Washington Post*, 16 March 1982.

21. "A Secret War for Nicaragua," *Newsweek*, 8 November 1982; Leslie H. Gelb, "Reagan Backing Covert Action, Officials Assert," *New York Times*, 14 March 1982; Leslie H. Gelb, "State Dept. Aides Said To Question Role in Nicaragua," *New York Times*, 7 April 1983; Patrick E. Taylor and Bob Woodward, "U.S. Approves Covert Plan in Nicaragua," *Washington Post*, 10 March 1982.

22. Gordon Mott, "A 'Static' War's Effect on Nicaraguan Village," *New York Times*, 11 November 1984; David Rogers and David Ignatius, "The Contra Fight," *Wall Street Journal*, 6 March 1985; "CIA Internal Report Details U.S. Role in Contra Raids in Nicaragua Last Year," *Wall Street Journal*, 6 March 1985.

23. Guy Gugliotta and Juan O. Tamayo, "Rebels Score Huge Gains in Nicaragua," *Miami Herald*, 27 January 1985; Doyle McManus and Robert C. Toth, "The Contras: How U.S. Got Entangled," *Los Angeles Times*, 4 March 1985.

24. Bernard Weinraub, "Nicaragua Offers Truce If U.S. Halts Aid to Rebels," *New York Times*, 23 April 1985; Steven V. Roberts, "Eight-Hour Talks Fail on Accord to Aid Nicaraguan Rebels," *New York Times*, 23 April 1985; James LeMoyne, "War Is Never Far Away for Nicaraguan Rebels," *New York Times*, 24 March 1985; Larry Rohter, "Tides of War Reach a Remote Town in Nicaragua," *New York Times*, 24 March 1985; Larry Rohter, "Little in Nicaragua Escapes War's Onslaught," *New York Times*, 19 March 1985; Edward Cody and Christopher Dickey, "Ex-Rebel Leader Alleges CIA Vows to Aid Overthrow in Managua," *Washington Post*, 27 November 1984; Juan Tamayo, "Sandinista Policies Made Rebels of Us, Small Farmers Say," *Miami Herald*, 27 January 1985.

25. Americas Watch, *Violations of the Laws of War by Both Sides in Nicaragua, 1981–1985*, (New York: Amnesty International, 1985); Stephen Kinzer, "Sandinista Foes See Travel Bars," *New York Times*, 25 November 1984; Stephen Kinzer, "The High Cost of War in Nicaragua: Two Mothers Pay in Grief," *New York Times*, 15 January 1985; Larry Rohter, "Nicaragua Rebels Accused of Abuses," *New York Times*, 7 March 1985; James LeMoyne, "Anti-Sandinista Indians Reported Quitting Battle," *New York Times*, 9 April 1985; "Vandals Raid Somoza's Tomb," *Washington Post*, 30 September 1984; Jack Anderson, "Atrocities by 'Our' Side in Nicaragua," *Washington Post*, 30 September 1984; Juan O. Tamayo, "Civilians Are Trapped in a Deadly Crossfire," *Miami Herald*, 27 January 1985.

26. Joel Brinkley, "CIA Primer Tells Nicaraguans How to Kill," *New York Times*, 17 October 1984.

27. Americas Watch, *Miskitos in Nicaragua 1981–1984*, (New York: Amnesty International, 1984).

28. Alma Guillermoprieto, "OAS Study Says Miskito Indians Suffered Abuse from Sandinistas," *Washington Post*, 8 June 1984.

29. Don Oberdorfer and Patrick E. Tyler, "U.S.-Backed Nicaraguan Army Swells to 7000 Men," *Washington Post*, 8 May 1983; "A Secret War for Nicaragua," *Newsweek*, 8 November 1982.

30. Cody and Dickey, "Ex-Rebel Leader Alleges"; Robert C. Toth and Doyle McManus, "Contras and CIA: A Plan Gone Awry," *Los Angeles Times*, 3 March 1985.

31. Philip Taubman, "Nicaraguan Exile Limits Role of U.S.," *New York Times*, 9 December 1982; Christopher Dickey, "Well-Armed Units Show Strongholds," *Washington Post*, 3 April 1983.

32. Don Oberdorfer, "Washington's Role Troubles Congress," *Washington Post*, 3 April 1983; Martin Tolchin, "Key House Member Fears U.S. Breaks Law on Nicaragua," *New York Times*, 14 April 1983.

33. Philip Taubman, "Nicaraguans and the United States," *New York Times*, 25 May 1983; Don Oberdorfer, "Shultz Hints at Asylum for Guerrillas," *Washington Post*, 8 August 1983.

34. "A Secret War for Nicaragua," *Newsweek,* 8 November 1982; Philip Taubman, "U.S. Reportedly Sending Millions to Foster Moderates in Nicaragua," *New York Times,* 11 March 1982; Leslie H. Gelb, "State Dept. Aides Said . . ." *New York Times,* 7 April 1983; Leslie H. Gelb, "Argentina Tied to Rise in U.S. Anti-Sandinista Acts," *New York Times,* 8 April 1983.

35. Christopher Dickey, "Political Leader of Nicaraguan Rebels Belittles House Vote on Aid," *Washington Post,* 30 July 1983; Booth, *The End and the Beginning,* 213; *Journal of Commerce,* 9 March 1982; E. V. K. Fitzgerald, "Una evaluación del costo económico de la agresión del gobierno estadounidense contra el pueblo de Nicaragua" (Paper presented before the National Meeting of the Latin American Studies Association, Albuquerque, N.M., 18–20 April 1985).

36. Fitzgerald, "Una evaluación del costo," 27; Stephen Kinzer, "Nicaraguans Gear Up for Embargo," *New York Times,* 12 May 1985; Theodore Shabad, "Nicaragua Triples Its Soviet Imports," *New York Times,* 12 May 1985.

37. Michael Dodson and T. S. Montgomery, "The Churches in the Nicaraguan Revolution," in *Nicaragua in Revolution;* Laura O'Shaughnessy, "The Conflicts of Class and World View: Theology in the Post-Revolutionary Nicaragua" (Paper delivered at the Annual Meeting of the Southeastern Council of Latin American Studies, San Juan, Puerto Rico, April 1983); Michael Dodson and Laura O'Shaughnessy, "Religion and Politics," in *Nicaragua Five Years Later,* 119–144.

38. Stephen Kinzer, "Nicaragua's Combative Archbishop," *New York Times Magazine,* 18 November 1984; Juan Tamayo, "Sandinistas, Catholic Hierarchy Swap Accusations, Escalate War of Words," *Miami Herald,* 1 August 1984; Robert J. McCartney, "Church Leaders Seek Funds, Citing Conflict with Sandinistas," *Washington Post,* 14 August 1984.

39. U.S. Congress, Senate Committee on Intelligence Activities, *Covert Action in Chile, Staff Report of the Senate Committee on Intelligence Activities,* 94th Congress, 2nd Session, (Washington, D.C.: Government Printing Office, 18 December 1975).

40. Amnesty International, *Amnesty International Report, 1981* (New York: Amnesty International, 1982), 170–75; "Prepared Statement of Amnesty International on the Human Rights Situation in Nicaragua," delivered before the Sub-Committee on Human Rights and International organizations, U.S. House of Representatives, Sept. 15, 1983 (mimeograph): Americas Watch, *Human Rights in Nicaragua: November 1982 Update;* Americas Watch, *The Miskitos in Nicaragua;* Americas Watch, *Human Rights in Nicaragua,* April 1984; Americas Watch, *Violations of the Laws of War.*

41. Stephen Kinzer, "Disillusion with Nicaragua Grows in Europe," *New York Times,* 16 November 1983; Bayardo Arce, *Secret Speech before the Nicaraguan Socialist Party (PSN),* (Washington, D.C.: U.S. Department of State), March 1985).

42. This conclusion is based on interviews with Coordinator leaders. See also Stephen Kinzer, "Disillusion with Nicaragua Grows in Europe," *New York Times,* 16 November 1983; Robert J. McCartney, "Sandinista Foes Always Intended to Boycott Vote," *Washington Post,* 30 July 1984; Enrique Bolanos G., *Linea directa: Entrevista radial* (Managua: n.p., 1984).

43. *La Prensa,* 28 December 1983; 24 July, 15 August 1984. At the beginning of October 1984, Cruz and FSLN leader Bayardo Arce, negotiating in Brazil at the meetings of the Socialist International, appeared close to an agreement under which the Coordinator would have participated in elections. But the negotiations collapsed when it suddenly appeared that Cruz did not have the Coordinator behind him. See Dan Williams, "Many Sandinistas See Vote in Nicaragua as Nuisance," *Los Angeles Times,* 9 October 1984; Miguel D'Escoto, "Moment of Truth in Nicaragua: A Reply," *Washington Post,* 1 October 1984; Brian Nicholson, "Sandinistas Stand Firm on Election Date," *Washington Post,* 3 October 1984; John Lantigua, "Collapse of Talks Reflects Polarization of Sides in Nicaragua," *Washington Post,* 4 October 1984; Mimi Whitfield, "Nicaraguan Election Deal Collapses," *Miami Herald,* 3 October 1984.

44. William R. Long, "Nicaragua Assembly Plans Draft Constitution Based on 'Reali-

ties of Revolution,'" *Los Angeles Times*, 10 January 1985; Latin American Studies Association (LASA), *The Electoral Process in Nicaragua: Domestic and International Influences*, Report of the Latin American Studies Association Delegation to Observe the Nicaraguan General Election of 4 November 1984 (Austin, Texas: LASA, 1985); Dennis Volman, "Nicaraguan Opposition Thinks Powerful Ortegas May Edge Closer to Political Pact," *Christian Science Monitor*, 8 November 1984; Clifford Krause, "Nicaraguan Election Offers a Surprise: Opposition at Least Gets to State Its Case," *Wall Street Journal*, 11 October 1984.

45. LASA, *The Electoral Process;* Dennis Volman, "Nicaragua Vote Seen as Better Run than Salvador's," *Christian Science Monitor*, 5 November 1984; Dennis Volman, "Nicaraguan Opposition," *Christian Science Monitor*, 8 November 1984; *Financial Times*, 7 November 1984; *Manchester Guardian/Le Monde*, 8 November 1984; Washington Office on Latin America, *A Political Opening in Nicaragua*, (Washington, D.C.: WOLA, 1984).

46. LASA, *The Electoral Process;* Stephen Kinzer, "Nicaraguans Vow Strong Opposition," *New York Times*, 18 November 1984.

47. Philip Taubman, "U.S. Is Reported to Oppose Electoral Challenge to Sandinistas," *New York Times*, 21 October 1984; David Durenberger, "As Nicaraguans Prepare to Vote," *New York Times*, 2 November 1984; George Black, "Success Undercut," *New York Times*, 2 November 1984; Robert J. McCartney, "Vote Boycott Lamented," *Washington Post*, 9 November 1984.

48. Collins, *What Difference Could a Revolution Make?* 87–88.

49. Ibid., 31; Marlise Simons, "Nicaragua Hastens Land Redistribution as Pressures Mount," *New York Times*, 19 July 1983.

50. Valerie Miller, "The Nicaraguan Literacy Crusade" in *Nicaragua in Revolution*, 241–258.

51. Americas Watch, *Violations of the Laws*.

52. Fitzgerald, "Una evaluación del costo."

53. Gilbert, "The Bourgeoisie."

54. Jaime Wheelock, *El Gran Desafío* (Managua, Nicaragua: Editorial Nueva Nicaragua, 1983).

55. Naciones Unitas, Consejo Economico y Social, *Notas para el estudio económico de America Latina, 1982: Nicaragua*, 11 March 1983 (New York: United Nations, 1983).

56. Americas Watch, *Violations of the Laws*.

57. Fitzgerald, "Una evaluación del costo."

58. Joel Brinkley, "Nicaraguan Army: 'War Machine' or Defender of a Besieged Nation?" *New York Times*, 30 March 1985; Dan Williams, "Managua Jittery About Contras, Seeks U.S. Talks," *Los Angeles Times*, 4 March 1985; U.S. Department of State, *Background Paper: Central America* (Washington, D.C.: Department of State, 1983).

59. Clifford Krause and Robert S. Greenberger, "Despite Fears of U.S., Soviet Aid to Nicaragua Appears to Be Limited," *Wall Street Journal*, 3 April 1985.

60. Eddie Adams, "How Latin American Guerrillas Train on Our Soil," *Parade Magazine*, 15 March 1981; Jo Thomas, "Nicaraguans Train in Florida as Guerrillas," *New York Times*, 17 March 1981; Alan Riding, "Rightist Exiles Plan Invasion of Nicaragua," *New York Times*, 2 April 1981; Christopher Dickey, "Anti-Sandinista Drive Grows, Exiles Say," *Washington Post*, 9 May 1981.

61. Krause and Greenberger, "Despite Fears of U.S."; Williams, "Managua Jittery"; Fred Hiatt, "Nicaraguan Buildup Called Defensive," *Washington Post*, 13 November 1984; U.S. Congress, House Subcommittee on Foreign Affairs, prepared statement delivered by John H. Buchannan, 97th Congress, 2nd Session, 21 September 1982 (mimeographed).

62. Statement by Buchannan.

63. Williams, "Managua Jittery"; Anthony Lewis, "When Reason Flees," *New York Times*, 10 March 1985.

64. Brinkley, "Nicaraguan Army: 'War Machine.'"

65. Krause and Greenberger, "Despite Fears of U.S."; U.S. Departments of State and

Defense, *The Soviet-Cuban Connection in Central America and the Caribbean* (Washington, D.C.: Departments of State and Defense, March 1985) 25.

66. U.S. Departments of State and Defense, *The Soviet-Cuban Connection*, 24–27.

67. Mimi Whitfield, "Nicaragua: Cuban Advisors Are Few," *Miami Herald*, 20 March 1985.

68. Stephen Kinzer, "Nicaragua Sends 100 Cubans Home," *New York Times*, 3 May 1905.

69. Krause and Greenberger, "Despite Fears of U.S."; Fitzgerald, "Una evaluación del costo," 28.

70. Bernard Gwertzman, "Black Clouds in Mideast," *New York Times*, 5 October 1983.

71. Alan Riding, "Nicaragua Seeking Accord," *New York Times*, 12 February 1981; Drew Middleton, "Salvador Army's Troubles," *New York Times*, 5 March 1983; Stephen Kinzer, "U.S. and Salvadoran Officials Note Steady Rebel Gains," *New York Times*, 25 April 1983; Steven V. Roberts, "Vote on Aid Cutoff: A House Divided and Confused," *New York Times*, 30 July 1983; Christopher Dickey, "Nicaraguan Aid Called Not Vital to Salvadorans," *Washington Post*, 21 February 1983.

72. Christopher Dickey, "Nicaraguan Says Country Ready for Peace Talks," *Washington Post*, 19 March 1985; Taubman, "Nicaraguans and the United States"; Alan Riding, "Nicaraguans Sound Gloomy on U.S.," *New York Times*, 8 July 1985.

73. John M. Goshko, "U.S. Stalling on Negotiations with Nicaragua," *Washington Post*, 17 April 1982; Steven R. Weisman, "Latin Peace Plan Stirs U.S. Interest," *New York Times*, 7 October 1982; Philip Taubman, "U.S. Seeks Increase in Covert Activity in Latin America," *New York Times*, 25 July 1983.

74. Lou Cannon, "U.S. Said to Doubt Cuban Bid to End Arms Aid," *Washington Post*, 15 August 1982.

75. This conclusion is supported by a 1982 National Security Council strategy document, later leaked to the press. See Raymond Bonner, "President Approved Policy of Preventing 'Cuba-Model' States," *New York Times*, 7 April 1983.

76. U.S. Embassy, Managua, *State Department Outlines Nicaraguan Proposals* (mimeographed, April 1982).

77. Roy Gutman, "America's Diplomatic Charade," *Foreign Policy*, no. 56 (Fall 1984): 11.

78. Richard J. Meislin, "State Department Aide Visits Nicaragua for Talks," *New York Times*, 14 October 1983.

79. "Nicaraguan Presents State Department with Four Treaties on Latin America," *New York Times*, 21 October 1983.

80. McManus and Toth, "The Contras: How U.S. Got Entangled"; Doyle McManus and Robert C. Toth, "CIA Mining of Harbors 'a Fiasco,'" *Los Angeles Times*, 5 March 1985; Rogers and Ignatius, "The Contra Fight."

81. Rogers and Ignatius, "The Contra Fight"; "CIA Internal Report," *Wall Street Journal*, 6 March 1985.

82. Ibid.; Edward Cody, "Rebels Solicit Private Groups," *Washington Post*, 6 July 1984; Robert J. McCartney, "Rebels Keep Alive Nicaraguan War," *Washington Post*, 10 December 1984; Philip Taubman, "Private Aid to Latin Rebels at Issue," *New York Times*, 13 December 1984; Alfonso Chardy, "Private Aid Fuels Contras in Nicaragua," *Miami Herald*, 9 September 1984.

83. Philip Taubman, "Nicaraguan Talks Are Said to Stall," *New York Times*, 2 November 1984; Philip Taubman, "U.S. Says It Has Halted Talks with Nicaragua," *New York Times*, 19 January 1985; Robert S. Greenberger, "U.S. May Adopt Tougher Stance on Nicaragua," *Wall Street Journal*, 16 November 1984.

84. Alma Guillermoprieto and David Hoffman, "Document Describes How U.S. 'Blocked' a Contadora Treaty," *Washington Post*, 6 November 1984; Philip Taubman, "Nicaragua Talks Are Said to Stall," *New York Times*, 2 November 1984; Norman Kempster and Doyle McManus, "U.S. Move on Latin Pact Backfires," *Los Angeles Times*, 6 October 1984.

85. Philip Taubman, "U.S. . . . Halted Talks."
86. Gerald M. Boyd, "Reagan Terms Nicaraguan Rebels 'Moral Equal of Founding Fathers,' " *New York Times*, 2 March 1985; Hedrick Smith, "President Asserts Goal Is to Remove Sandinista Regime," *New York Times*, 22 February 1985; Bill Keller, "U.S. General Says Nicaraguan Rebels Cannot Win Soon," *New York Times*, 28 February 1985.
87. Stephen Kinzer, "The High Cost of War."
88. Bill Keller, "U.S. General Says."

5: HONDURAS

The author gratefully acknowledges the intellectual aid and encouragement of the other authors of this book, especially that of Morris Blachman, William LeoGrande, Ken Sharpe, Tom Bossert, and Dennis Gilbert. I have also benefited enormously from discussions with Mark Rosenberg and Hondurans both too numerous and involved in events to be named here. Financial support for the field research of this study came from the Tinker Foundation, the Latin American and Caribbean Center, and International Affairs, Florida International University.

1. Steven Volk, "Honduras: On the Border of War," *Report on the Americas* 15, (November-December 1981):6.
2. Mario Posas, "Honduras at the Crossroads," *Latin American Perspectives* 17, (Spring/Summer 1980):47.
3. Beginning in 1911, when the United States diplomatically intervened to topple the Davila government, it repeatedly made and unmade presidents in Honduras, usually on behalf of U.S. banana firms. Normally, pressure from the U.S. embassy was sufficient; but on one occasion in 1924, two hundred marines from the gunship *USS Milwaukee* briefly occupied Tegucigalpa on the pretext of safeguarding American lives and property. See Edgardo Quiñonez and Mario Argueta, *Historia de Honduras*, 2d ed. (Tegucigalpa: ESP Editorial, 1979), 123–24.
4. Charles A. Brand, "The Background of Capitalistic Underdevelopment: Honduras to 1913" (Ph.D dis., University of Pittsburgh, 1972), 108–18.
5. Volk, "Honduras," 14.
6. Villeda Morales, a middle-class Liberal, won the election of 1954 by a plurality though not an absolute majority and was kept from assuming office by the complex political machinations of the conservatives. The new coalition president, Lozano Díaz, was unable to maintain cooperation among various parties and was ousted in late 1956 in the military's first modern coup. When new elections were called in 1957 the Villeda reformists were swept into power. For good summaries of this period see Steve Lewontin, "From Carias to Galvez," *Honduras Update* 2, (August 1984):5–6; Charles W. Anderson, *Politics and Economic Change in Latin America* (Princeton, N.J.: Van Nostrand, 1967), 269–74.
7. The war exposed rampant military corruption and sparked unrest among lower-ranking officers. For example, of the 1,000 troops supposedly stationed in Copán Province, only 463 really existed: the other 537 were found only on payrolls. See "Honduras: Militarization and Denationalization," *Envio* (Managua) 3, no. 35 (May 1984):2.
8. Anderson, *Politics and Economic Change*, 194.
9. Although the economic dimensions of the crisis in Honduras are arguably some of the most important, and certainly underreported, aspects of Honduran reality at present, the emphasis here is on political and military affairs. For an in-depth discussion of Honduran economic policy, the state of the economy, and the U.S. role, see Philip L. Shepherd, *The USS Honduras: United States Foreign Policy and the Destabilization of Honduras* (in preparation).
10. David Ignatius and David Rogers, "Aiding the Contras," *Wall Street Journal*, 5 March 1985; and "The Contra Fight," *Wall Street Journal*, 6 March 1985.
11. The proportion of U.S. aid going to military as opposed to economic development purposes depends heavily on how one classifies Economic Support Funds (ESF),

which in Honduras have gone mainly for balance-of-payments support. Even if one includes ESF assistance as wholly "economic development" aid, U.S. military assistance has increased from 7 percent of all U.S. aid in 1979 to nearly one-third —29 percent—of all aid proposed for the 1984 fiscal year.

12. By 10 April 1984, the *Wall Street Journal* claimed that 3,400 Salvadoran and 2,300 Honduran troops had been trained at CREM. Honduran sources, however, cite a three-to-one ratio of Salvadoran-to-Honduran troops trained, and U.S. plans to train nine Salvadoran and only three Honduran battalions had to be scrapped when the Honduran military objected.

13. Pamela Constable, "Dichotomy in U.S. Role in Honduras," *Boston Globe*, 12 June 1984.

14. "Report on Honduras," *Congressional Record*, 98th Cong., 2nd sess., 1984, 130, pt. 13:S1122–25.

15. James McCartney, "Powerful U.S. General Calls Signals in Central America," *Miami Herald*, 31 May 1984.

16. Philip B. Wheaton, *Inside Honduras: Regional Counterinsurgency Base* (Washington: Ecumenical Program for Interamerican Communication and Action Task Force, 1982), 28.

17. In 1983 APROH, with Alvarez as its president, became a kind of "shadow government," the real center of decision-making behind the civilian regime. For the bizarre and frightening story of APROH, see Centro de Documentacion de Honduras (CEDOH), "APROH: Origen desarrollo y perspectivas," *Boletin Informativo*, special no. 9 (March 1984).

18. Mark B. Rosenberg, "Honduran Scorecard: Democrats and Military in Central America," *Caribbean Review* 12 (Winter 1983):13; also see George Black, "Fortress Honduras: Delivering a Country to the Military," *The Nation*, 28 January 1984, 90–92.

19. Americas Watch, "Human Rights in Honduras: Signs of the 'Argentine Method,' " *An Americas Watch Report* (New York: Americas Watch, 1982).

20. These data are from the Comite para la Defensa de los Derechos Humanos en Honduras, *Boletin Mensual* 3, no. 13 (February-March 1984):2; and press releases of the Committee in *El Tiempo*, 22 February, 23 February, 29 February and 2 March 1984.

21. John D. Negroponte, "Let's Stop Stereotyping Central America," *Los Angeles Times*, 12 August 1983.

22. Americas Watch, the Lawyers' Guild, and the Washington Office on Latin America, *Honduras on the Brink*, (February 1984), 9, jointly issued the report, which details the deterioration in human rights. See *Honduran Update* 2, (April 1984):7.

23. Ernesto Paz Aguilar, "Reflexiones Sobre la Politica Reagan hacia Centroamerica," *El Tiempo*, 18 October 1983.

24. Juan Arancibia, "Honduras, crisis y desarrollo," *Revista Centroamericana de Economia* 4, (January-April 1983):63.

25. J. Mark Ruhl, "The Honduran Agrarian Reform Under Suazo Córdova, 1982–85: An Assessment," *Inter-American Economic Affairs* 39 (Autumn 1985): 63–80.

26. Centro de Documentacion de Honduras (CEDOH), *Los Refugiados Salvadorenos en Honduras* (Tegucigalpa: CEDOH, 1982), 29–32.

27. George Black and Anne Nelson, "The U.S. in Honduras: The Mysterious Death of Fr. Carney," *The Nation*, 4 and 11 August 1984.

28. See for example, Kai Bird and Max Holland, "Capitol Letter: The Aid Game," *The Nation*, 15 February 1986, 169; Juan O. Tamayo, "Sandinistas' Anti-Rebel Offensive Hikes Tension on Borders," *Miami Herald*, 9 June 1985; James LeMoyne, "Anti-Sandinista Indians Reported Quitting Battle," *New York Times*, 9 April 1985.

29. Richard Meislin, "Honduras Hints at Softer Line," *New York Times*, 10 June 1984; Richard Meislin, "Honduran Army Reviewing Ties to U.S.," *New York Times*, 7 June 1984; Juan O. Tamayo, "New Honduran Chiefs Send Mixed Signals to U.S.," *Miami Herald*, 29 April 1984.

30. Examples of Alvarez's dictatorial methods within the armed forces abound: Al-

varez conducted secret inspections of unit commanders and had junior officers followed and their phones tapped; his proposed restructuring of the military would have set up a vast network of internal "inspectors," in effect, spies to detect dissension; he bypassed and snubbed the Superior Council of the Armed Forces (CONSUFA), the collegial decision-making organ of the military; he arrogantly forbade other high-ranking officers from talking with civilian government officials without first submitting an agenda; he decided on his own without consulting other officers to allow the United States to train Salvadoran troops in Honduras; and, having first risen from colonel to general to brigadier general in less than two years at age forty-five (violating military regulations), he then proposed to lengthen the time between promotions and raise the minimum age for general to fifty-five years.

31. Leticia Salomon, "La doctrina de la seguridad nacional en Honduras: Analisis de la caida del General Gustavo Alvarez Martinez," Centro de Documentacion de Honduras (CEDOH), *Boletin Informativo*, special no. 11 (May 1984):16.
32. Marcia McLean, "Suazo Knew Nothing," *Honduran Update* 2, no. 8, (May 1984):4.
33. This felicitous phrase is borrowed, with apologies, from Colin Danby, "Raising the Rent," *Honduran Update* 2, no. 9 (July 1984):3–5.
34. "We Have Lost Everything, Even Our Honor," *El Tiempo*, 28 July 1983.
35. Juan Tamayo, "Internal Splits Wrack Honduras Officers Corps," *Miami Herald*, 3 February 1985. This was apparent almost immediately after the removal of Alvarez. See Colin Danby, "Lopez Seeks a Better Deal," *Honduran Update* 2, (August 1984):1–2.
36. Alfonso Chardy, "U.S. Weighs Major Buildup in Honduras," *Miami Herald*, 8 November 1984. For instance, Honduras was the first Contadora participant to suggest the need for further revisions in the treaty draft accepted by Nicaragua. Juan O. Tamayo, "Contadora's Sponsors Agree to Revise Peace Treaty," *Miami Herald*, 7 October 1984.
37. For more information on the elections and democracy in Honduras, see Philip L. Shepherd, "Missed Opportunities: The Problems of Formal Democracy in Honduras," (forthcoming).
38. It is a measure of both U.S. influence and the benefits the military enjoys under the current façade of "democracy" that no military coup took place during the constitutional crisis of March–May 1985. The serious political stalemate and associated dangers were real; civilians of all political stripes begged the military to intervene and yet there was no coup.

6: COSTA RICA

We would like to thank Kenneth Sharpe for his helpful comments. We also want to extend our appreciation to Wynn Hill, Cheryl Federline, Ken Menkhaus, Theresa Riehle, and Sheila Klee for their assistance. In particular, we want to thank those Costa Ricans who so kindly shared their time and thoughts with us.

1. David Reed, "Central America's Beacon of Hope," *Reader's Digest*, December 1981, 148–52.
2. Oscar Arias Sanchez, "Barriers to Development in Costa Rica," *International Development Review* 15, no. 2 (1973):5.
3. Oscar Arias Sanchez, *Quien gobierna en Costa Rica*, 2d ed. (San José, Costa Rica: Editorial Universitaria Centroamericana, 1978), 241.
4. Quoted in "Costa Rica: Economic Decline Challenges Social Stability," *Update* 3, no. 14 (13 April 1984).
5. See Flora Montealegre, "Costa Rica at the Crossroads," *Development and Change* 14 (1983): 277–96.
6. Ralph Lee Woodward, Jr., *Central America, a Nation Divided* (New York: Oxford University Press, 1985), 225.
7. Walter LaFeber, *Inevitable Revolutions* (New York: W.W. Norton, 1983), 101–3.

8. Tord Hoivik and Solveig Aas, "Demilitarization in Costa Rica: A Farewell to Arms?" *Journal of Peace Research* 18, (1981):333–41.
9. Ibid.; see also Charles D. Ameringer, *Democracy in Costa Rica* (New York: Praeger, 1982); and Howard I. Blutstein et al., *Area Handbook for Costa Rica*, prepared by Foreign Area Studies of the American University, (Washington, D.C.: Government Printing Office, 1970).
10. Woodward, *Central America*, 226.
11. Harold D. Nelson, ed., *Costa Rica: A Country Study*, Area Handbook Series, (Washington, D.C.: Government Printing Office, 1983), 87.
12. Woodward, *Central America*, 227–28.
13. See Blutstein, *Area Handbook;* Charles F. Denton, *Patterns of Costa Rican Politics* (Boston: Allyn and Bacon, 1971); Edgar Mohs, "La Salud: Una Revolucion Silenciosa," *Le Monde Diplomatique*, en español: suplemento Costa Rica, May 1984; Phillip W. Rourk, *Equitable Growth: The Case of Costa Rica*, Case Studies in Development Assistance, no. 6, prepared for the Development Studies Program, (Washington, D.C.: U.S. Agency for International Development, July 1979); and Washington Institute for Values in Public Policy, Task Force Report, *Central America in Crisis* (Washington, D.C.: Washington Institute for Values in Public Policy, 1984).
14. Ameringer, *Democracy*, 40–41.
15. Bruce Herrick and Barclay Hudson, *Urban Poverty and Economic Development: A Case Study of Costa Rica* (New York: St. Martin's Press, 1981), 149.
16. Ibid.
17. Ameringer, *Democracy*, 94.
18. Herrick and Hudson, *Urban Poverty*, 78.
19. Washington Institute, *Central America in Crisis*, contains a wealth of data in numerous tables; see also the Inter-American Development Bank *Annual Report, 1984.*
20. Ameringer, *Democracy*, 98.
21. R. Peter Dewitt, "The Inter-American Development Bank and Policy Making in Costa Rica," *The Journal of Developing Areas* (October 1980):71.
22. Inter-American Development Bank (referred to as IDB hereafter), *Economic and Social Progress in Latin America: 1982 Report*, (Washington, D.C.: Inter-American Development Bank, 1982), 229.
23. Ameringer, *Democracy*, 98. From 1960 to 1978, Ameringer reports employment in industry "rose from 43,000 to 104,000."
24. James Nelson Goodsell, "Record Debt has Blunted Costa Rican Literacy Gains," *Christian Science Monitor*, 14 September 1984.
25. IDB, *Annual Report 1984*, 126.
26. For an excellent and concise discussion of this economic crisis see Richard Feinberg, "Costa Rica: The End of the Fiesta," in *From Gunboats to Diplomacy* (Baltimore: Johns Hopkins University Press, 1984), 103–4. Feinberg also summarizes some of the key structural problems in the economy discussed in this chapter.
27. Rourk, *Equitable Growth*, 65.
28. IDB, *Economic and Social Progress: 1982 Report*, 232.
29. Feinberg, "Costa Rica," 105.
30. IDB, *Economic and Social Progress: 1982 Report*, 231.
31. Feinberg, "Costa Rica," 105.
32. IDB, *Economic and Social Progress: 1982 Report*, 231.
33. Feinberg, "Costa Rica," 103.
34. Ibid.
35. In 1981, total public external debt had climbed to $2.8 billion, and along with the private debt, Costa Rica's total debt reached a figure roughly four times as much as the year's earnings from exports and amounted to about 80 percent of the gross domestic product for the year. Debt service payments alone for 1981

amounted to $577 million, a burgeoning proportion of its exports. Rodolfo Silva, in a speech given in Costa Rica to the National Forum on the Economy, 2 September 1983.

36. Foreign Broadcast Information Service (referred to as FBIS hereafter), *Daily Report, Latin America*, 16 May 1985, 2.

37. IDB, *Economic and Social Progress: 1982 Report*, 229.

38. IDB, *Economic and Social Progress: 1984 Report*, 268.

39. IDB, *Economic and Social Progress: 1983 Report*, 198–99.

40. Mitchell A. Seligson, "Agrarian Reform in Costa Rica: The Impact of the Title Security Program," *Inter-American Economic Affairs* 35, no. 4 (Spring 1982):34.

41. Marc Edelman, "Recent Literature on Costa Rica's Economic Crisis," *Latin American Research Review* 18, no. 2 (1983):166–80; Ameringer, *Democracy*, 100.

42. Rafael Angel Rojas, "Democratizar la Economía Costaricense," *La Nación Internacional*, 11–17 June 1982.

43. Seligson, "Agrarian Reform," 36.

44. Rourk, *Equitable Growth*, 85.

45. Washington Institute, *Central America in Crisis*, 78.

46. Rourk, *Equitable Growth*, 85.

47. Ibid., 59–60. On page 63, Rourk refers to José Luis Vega Carballo's study of the 1960 through 1975 period, which provides some insight in the degree to which Costa Rica's economy has become transnationalized. In each of seven major industrial groupings, foreign investment accounts for more than half of the value of the sector—fertilizer and related products, 94 percent; radios and electronic equipment, 92 percent; office equipment and paper products, 73 percent; furniture and accessories, 71 percent; containers and packaging, 65 percent; food and beverages, 61 percent; and pharmaceuticals, 60 percent—although in only one case do they constitute more than 27 percent of the number of firms in their particular industrial grouping. Rodolfo Cerdas has estimated "that multinational corporations control some 85 percent of new industries." Cited in Montealegre, "Costa Rica at the Crossroads," 294.

48. *Costa Rica, A Dynamic Democracy: Summary of Export and Investment Program* (San José, Costa Rica: The Costa Rican Coalition of Development Initiative, n.d.).

49. Claudia González Vega, "Costa Rica: el Costa Social del Ajuste," *La Nación Internacional*, 4–10 June 1983.

50. Arias Sanchez, "Barriers to Development," 6.

51. Rourk, *Equitable Growth*, 92.

52. Washington Institute, *Central America in Crisis*, 81.

53. Edelman, "Recent Literature," 176.

54. Ibid.

55. Angel Rojas, "Democratizar."

56. Seligson, "Agrarian Reform," 35.

57. James Nelson Goodsell, "Record Debt."

58. The development of a "managerial bourgeoisie" was reflected in the rapid growth of executives employed by others, from 9.6 percent in 1959 to 63.7 percent in 1973. Hoivik and Aas, "Demilitarization," 346.

59. Feinberg, "Costa Rica," 104.

60. Ibid., 106.

61. FBIS, *Daily Report, Latin America*, 16 May 1985, P4.

62. Juan Manuel Villasuso E., "Crisis y Democratizacion Economica de Costa Rica," *Le Monde Diplomatique, en español: suplemento Costa Rica*, May 1984.

63. "Costa Rica: Economic Decline," 1.

64. Steven R. Harper, *U.S. Assistance to Costa Rica: Foreign Aid Facts*, updated 23 April 1985 (Washington, D.C.: Library of Congress, Congressional Research Service), 3.

65. FBIS, *Daily Report, Latin America*, 16 May 1985, P3.

66. IDB, *Economic and Social Progress: 1984 Report*, 271.

67. Juan O. Tamayo, "Costa Rican Vote: Quaintly Uneventful," *Miami Herald*, 4 March 1985; FBIS, *Daily Report, Latin America* 9 May 1985, P1.

68. FBIS, *Daily Report, Latin America*, 17 July 1985, P3.
69. Denis Volman, "U.S. Anti-Sandinista Efforts Begin to Strain Ties with Costa Rica," *Christian Science Monitor*, 3 July 1984; Sam Dillon, "Debt, Rebels Undercut U.S. Relations with Costa Rica," *Miami Herald*, 17 June 1984.
70. Sam Dillon, "Debts, Rebels Undercut."
71. Ibid.
72. Ibid.
73. Edward Cody, "Costa Rican Leaders Irked by 'Lip Service' of U.S. Ambassador," *Washington Post*, 4 February 1984.
74. Ibid.
75. Sam Dillon, "Debts, Rebels Undercut."
76. Ibid.
77. Jean Hopfensperger, " 'Neutral' Costa Rica Is Jittery about U.S. Military Aid," *Christian Science Monitor*, 31 May 1984.
78. Dan Williams, "Costa Rica Struggles to Remain Neutral," *Los Angeles Times*, 27 May 1984.
79. FBIS, *Daily Report, Latin America*, 12 June 1985, P2.
80. Nicaragua was estimated to owe $200 million; Guatemala $50 to $60 million; and buyers in El Salvador and Honduras about $30 million per country.
81. *Central America Report* 2, no. 20 (31 May 1985):154.
82. FBIS, *Daily Report, Latin America*, 13 May 1985, P2.
83. Ibid., P1.
84. Ibid.
85. Tim Coone, "Costa Rica Dismantles Nicaraguan Rebel Camp," *Financial Times*, 28 February 1985.
86. FBIS, *Daily Report, Latin America*, 2 May 1985, P1.
87. Ibid., 29 May 1985, P1.
88. Stephen Kinzer, "In Fearful Costa Rica, the Yanquis Are Welcome," *New York Times*, 11 July 1985.
89. Robert D. Tomasek, *The Deterioration of Relations Between Costa Rica and the Sandinistas*, Occasional Papers Series no. 9 (Washington, D.C.: American Enterprise Institute for Public Policy Research, September 1984), 6.
90. For a fuller discussion of these border incidents, see ibid. and the FBIS reports.
91. FBIS, *Daily Report, Latin America*, 9 May 1985, P1.
92. FBIS, *Daily Report, Latin America*, 12 June 1985, P4; FBIS, *Daily Report, Latin America*, 13 June 1985, P2; and FBIS, *Daily Report, Latin America*, 17 June 1985, P1.
93. Tomasek, *Deterioration of Relations*, 12.
94. Two government agencies, the Office of Judicial Investigation and the Ministry of National Security, have claimed that Costa Ricans have been trained in Nicaragua and Cuba to infiltrate labor and peasant organizations, foment strikes, and carry on terroristic acts. Tomasek, *Deterioration of Relations*, 12. Such claims must be viewed with caution. Travel by labor and peasant leaders to these countries and their participation in legal strikes and demonstrations can be used by conservative elements to discredit legitimate organization and protest. Security officials who made such claims were pressed in interviews to give examples of Costa Ricans who had been trained abroad and had been involved in terrorist activities; they claimed that this was not yet a problem. But the perception that it could be a problem is very real and threatens to make domestic conflict less tractable by perceiving it in international terms.
95. Tomasek, *Deterioration of Relations*, 23.
96. Ibid., 21, 31.
97. "Nicaraguan-Costa Rican Relations Thaw," *Update* 3, (24 January 1984):1.
98. Edward Cody, "Costa Rican Leaders," *Washington Post*, 4 February 1984.
99. "20,000 Demonstrate in Costa Rica to Support Policy of Neutrality," *New York Times*, 16 May 1984.
100. FBIS, *Daily Report, Latin America*, 9 May 1985, P2.
101. Constantino Urcuyo Fournier, "Politicas de Seguridad y Defensa: Esfuerzos por

la Democracia y la Neutralidad," *Le Monde Diplomatique, en español: Suplemento Costa Rica,* May 1984.

102. Tomasek, *Deterioration of Relations,* 20.
103. Richard J. Meislin, "U.S. Said to Seek Costa Rica Shift," *New York Times,* 11 May 1984.
104. FBIS, *Daily Report, Latin America* 12 June 1985, P3–4.
105. Edward Cody, "Costa Rica Struggles to Stay Neutral," *Washington Post,* 21 May 1984.
106. FBIS, *Daily Report, Latin America,* 23 May 1985, P3; Stephen Kinzer, "2 Held in Costa Rica Tell of Trip from U.S. to Join 'Contras,' " *New York Times,* 3 July 1985.
107. FBIS, *Daily Report, Latin America,* 12 June 1985, P1–2.
108. Robert Graham, "Costa Rica Walks Tightrope of Neutrality" *Financial Times,* 27 April 1985; *Miami Herald,* 30 April 1985; Kinzer, "2 Held in Costa Rica Tell of Trip from U.S. to Join 'Contras.' "
109. Marc Edelman and Jayne Hutchcroft, "Costa Rica," *Report on the Americas* 18, (March-April 1984):9.
110. Tomasek, *Deterioration of Relations,* 15.
111. Jean Hopfensperger, "Neutral Costa Rica . . ." *Christian Science Monitor,* 31 May 1984.
112. Ibid.
113. Ibid.
114. Kinzer, "In Fearful Costa Rica," *New York Times.*
115. Tim Coone, "Costa Rica Dismantles Nicaraguan Rebel Camp," *Financial Times,* 28 February 1985.
116. "Green Berets Arrive," *Central America Report,* 31 May 1985, 155.
117. Silvio Dobri, "Costa Rica About to Create a Army?", *Miami Herald,* 12 June 1983.
118. Edelman and Hutchcroft, "Costa Rica," 10.
119. Silvio Dobrin, "Costa Rica . . ." *Miami Herald,* 12 June 1983.
120. "Green Berets Arrive," 155.
121. Kinzer, "In Fearful Costa Rica," *New York Times.*
122. Joel Brinkley, "Costa Ricans at Odds Over Question: Is U.S. Seeking to Militarize Nation?" *New York Times,* 19 May 1985.
123. Arias Sanchez, "Barriers to Development," 9.
124. Ibid.

7: PANAMA

Of the many people who assisted me with this project, special acknowledgement is due Moss Blachman for his role as a challenging editor and to Ken Sharpe for having first interested me in Panama. I am also particularly indebted to Guillermo Castro and Steve Ropp for their penetrating insights into Panamanian politics and their comments on my earlier drafts, and to my two Panamanian students, Ricardo Arango and Adriana Samos, who helped me keep in touch with Panama.

1. Indeed, U.S. troops had put down several earlier independence revolts. See David N. Farnsworth and James W. McKenney, *U.S.-Panama Relations, 1903–1978: A Study in Linkage Politics* (Boulder, Colo.: Westview Press, 1983), 15.
2. The most coherent and readable history of U.S.-Panamanian relations is Walter LaFeber, *The Panama Canal: The Crisis in Historical Perspective* (New York: Oxford University Press, 1979); see also Sheldon B. Liss, *The Canal: Aspects of United States–Panamanian Relations* (Notre Dame, Ind.: University of Notre Dame Press, 1967); Ricaurte Soler, *Formas ideológicas de la nación panameña* (San José, Costa Rica: EDUCA, 1972).
3. For analysis of class structure: Ricaurte Soler, *Panamá: Nación y oligarquía: 1925–1975* (Panamá: Ediciones de la Tareas, 1982); Marco Antonio Gandasequi, "La concentración del poder económica en Panamá," in Ricaurte Soler, ed.,

Panamá: Dependencia y liberación (San José, Costa Rica: EDUCA, 1976). Guillermo Castro disagrees with this analysis, arguing for a greater role for the rural-based oligarchy. Personal communication with author, November 1984.

4. In this chapter, the term *populism* denotes a social movement that combines lower- and middle-class groups with limited sectors of the upper class who support a nationalistic program that challenges both the United States and the traditionally dominant elites. Usually such a movement relies also on charismatic leadership and a strong commitment to the use of the state for reforms that will bring benefits to both lower and middle classes.

5. Steve C. Ropp, *Panamanian Politics: From Guarded Nation to National Guard* (New York: Praeger and Hoover Institution, 1982), 26. Ropp places more emphasis on racism as a central dynamic of Arías's populism. See his "Leadership and Political Transformation in Panama: Two Levels of Regime Crisis," in Steve C. Ropp and James A. Morris, eds., *Central America: Crisis and Adaptation* (Albuquerque, N.M.: University of New Mexico Press, 1984), 227–55.

6. L. D. Langley, "U.S.-Panamanian Relations Since 1941," *Journal of Inter-American Studies* 12, (July 1970):342.

7. Humberto E. Ricord, "El Tratado Remón-Eisenhower," in Boris Blanco et al., *Relaciones entre Panamá y los Estados Unidos* (Panamá: Biblioteca Nuevo Panamá, Ministerio de Educación, 1973), 253–264; LaFeber, *The Panama Canal*, Chapter 4.

8. Langley, "U.S.-Panamanian Relations," 348–61; LaFeber, *The Panama Canal*, 140.

9. Harry G. Johnson, "Panama as a Regional Financial Center: A Preliminary Analysis of Development Contribution," *Economic Development and Cultural Change* 24, (January 1976):261–86; Guillermo Castro Herrera, "Panamá 1977, apuntes para un análisis," *Revista de Relaciones Internacionales* (Mexico), no. 18 (1978):21–25.

10. Gandasequi, "La concentración del poder económica"; Daniel Goldrich, *Sons of the Establishment: Elite Youth in Panama and Costa Rica* (Chicago: Rand McNally, 1966).

11. LaFeber, *The Panama Canal*, 149–56.

12. Renato Pereira, *Panamá: Fuerzas armadas y política* (Panamá: Ediciones Nueva Universidad, 1979), 121–34.

13. Steve C. Ropp, "Military Reformism in Panama: New Directions or Old Inclinations," *Caribbean Studies* 12, (October 1972):45–63.

14. Richard F. Nyrop, ed., *Panama: A Country Study*, Area Studies Series, (Washington, D.C.: Government Printing Office, 1981), 148.

15. Martin C. Needler, "Omar Torrijos, the Panamanian Enigma," *Intellect* 2 (March 5, 1979):15–21; Pereira, *Panamá: Fuerzas*, 121–25; LaFeber, *The Panama Canal*, 163–67; see also Ropp, "Leadership and Political Transformation in Panama."

16. LaFeber, *The Panama Canal*, Chapter 6. For another important critique of the treaties see Xabier Gorostiaga, "Diez tesis sobre los tratados del Canal de Panamá," *Praxis Centroamericana* 1 (July-December 1982):122–54.

17. Interview by author with César Quintero, Director of Electoral Tribunal, July 1983.

18. Nestor Porcell G. "Actitudes y opiniones de los votantes panameños frente al Tratado Torrijos-Carter," *Informativo Centro de Investigaciones y Análisis Administrativa, Universidad de Panamá* 1 (January 1978).

19. Interviews by the author with Humberto Ricord, Dean of School of Law and Political Science, University of Panama, July 1983; Ricardo Mareñgo, Director of Dirreción Ejecutivo para Asunto del Tratado; Oscar Vargas, Director Political Relations, Foreign Ministry; Richard Dotson, Political Officer, U.S. Embassy, January 1984.

20. Farnsworth and McKenney, *U.S.-Panama Relations*, Chapter 8.

21. Emerelda Brown et al., "Panama: For Whom the Canal Tolls?" in NACLA, *Report on the Americas* 13, (September-October 1979):30–35.

22. For a detailed account of this process up to mid-1984 see Thomas John Bossert, "Panama," in Jack Hopkins, ed., *Latin America and Caribbean Contemporary Record*, vol. 3 (New York: Holmes and Meier, 1985).

23. Gonzalo Ramírez, "Crisis Política," *Diálogo Social* 18, (March 1985):11–13.

24. James LeMoyne, "The Opposition Takes Cover in Panama," *New York Times*, 13 October 1985.

25. "Panama Coup," *The Baltimore Sun*, 7 October 1985.

26. Economic Commission on Latin America, "Panama," *Economic Survey of Latin America 1967* and *Economic Survey of Latin America 1970* (Santiago, Chile: ECLA, 1969, 1972).

27. Economic Commission on Latin America, "Panama," *Economic Survey of Latin America 1980* (Santiago, Chile: ECLA, 1982), 413–29; INFOPRESS Centroamerica, "Panama," *Centro América 1982: Análisis economicós y políticos sobre la región* (Guatemala: INFOPRESS, June 1982), 4–35; U.S. Department of Commerce, *Foreign Economic Trends and Their Implications For the United States: Panama* (Washington, D.C.: Government Printing Office, October 1983); U.S. Embassy, Panama, "Economic Statistics from Panama," airgram to Department of State, 12 January 1984; "La economía en 1983," *Diálogo Social* 17, (January 1984):22–26.

28. Estimates from Guillermo Chapman, economic consultant, from an interview with the author in July 1983. For other estimates of Canal's economic importance see Xabier Gorostiaga, *Panamá y la zona del canal* (Buenos Aires, Argentina: Tierra Nueva, 1975); Alfred E. Osborne, Jr., "On the Economic Cost to Panama of Negotiating a Peaceful Solution to the Panama Canal Question," *Journal of Interamerican Studies and World Affairs* 19 (November 1977):509–21.

29. The pipeline, however, is more than offsetting the loss of Canal revenues and is generating additional economic growth in a previously disadvantaged region of the country.

30. U.S. Department of Commerce, *Foreign Economic Trends*, 11.

31. Dirección de Estadísticas y Censo, *Panamá en cifras: años 1977 a 1981* (Panamá: November 1982); interviews with Guillermo Chapman, July 1983, and Ralph Buck, Economic Officer, U.S. Embassy, January 1984.

32. U.S. Department of Commerce, *Foreign Economic Trends*, 5–6.

33. Ibid.; Interview with Peter Becker, Economic Officer, U.S. Embassy, January 1984.

34. Interview with Guillermo Chapman, July 1983.

35. Interviews with Humberto Ricord; Ricardo Arias Calderón, President of Christian Democratic Party, July 1983; Raúl Alberto Leis, Director of Centro de Estudios y Acción Social in July 1983 and January 1984; Guillermo Castro Herrera, independent investigator in July 1983 and January 1984. See also Soler, *Formas ideológicas;* Nestor Porcell, *Returno al principio* (Panamá: Editorial Universitaria, 1976); and Guillermo Castro Herrera, "Panamá en la transición al neocolonialismo: Notas sobre la conjuntura política y sus perspectivas" (Panamá n.d., mimeographed).

36. Interviews in January 1984 with Ricardo Mareñgo, Richard Dotson, Oscar Vargas.

37. Raúl Leis, "Escuela de las Américas," *Diálogo Social* 17, (September 1984):6–13; Roberto Eisenmann, Jr., "La Escuela de las Américas," *La Prensa*, 17 September 1984.

38. "Conjuntura de Panamá," *Diálogo Social* 17, (January 1984):6–9; James Aparicio, "El CONDECA," *Diálogo Social* 17, (February 1984):50–51.

8: THE ECONOMICS OF STRIFE

1. This is a conservative estimate. It multiples U.S. growth times 1.3, the responsiveness of Central American exports to growth in foreign GDP, as calculated by the Inter-American Development Bank for the Central American countries (un-

weighted average). Inter-American Development Bank (referred to as IDB here-after) *External Debt and Economic Development in Latin America: Background and Prospects* (Washington, D.C.: IDB, 1983), 131–36. (The estimate is conservative because the IDB figures refer to growth in all industrialized countries; given the concentration of Central American trade with the United States, the multiplier would probably be much larger. Central American merchandise exports in 1982 amounted to $6,272 million. This figure multiplied by .065 (i.e., 1.3 times 5 percentage points) equals $408 million. Feinberg and Newfarmer estimated the effects of the free trade provisions of the Caribbean Basin Initiative (CBI) to range from $40 million to $90 million in 1980 dollars. See Richard Feinberg and Richard S. Newfarmer, "Caribbean Basin Initiative: Bold Plan or Empty Promise?" in *From Gunboats to Diplomacy: New U.S. Policies for Latin America*, ed. Richard S. Newfarmer (Baltimore: The Johns Hopkins University Press, 1984). Rousslang and Lindsey, in a study for the International Trade Commission, use a different methodology and calculate a slightly lower effect. See Donald Rous-slang and John Lindsay, "The Benefits to Caribbean Basin Countries from the U.S. CBI Tariff Eliminations" (Washington, D.C.: U.S. International Trade Commission, 6 July 1985, mimeographed). Newfarmer presents a systematic consideration of various U.S. economic policies and their consequences for the region. Richard S. Newfarmer, "U.S. Policy Toward the Caribbean Basin: The Balance Sheet," *Journal of Interamerican Studies and World Affairs* 27 (February 1985): 63–90.

2. See Walter LaFeber, *Inevitable Revolutions: The United States and Central America* (New York: W.W. Norton, 1983); Jerome Levinson and Juan de Onis, *The Alliance that Lost Its Way* (Chicago: Quadrangle Books, 1970).

3. The author prepared some background tables with published data taken from official sources, including national and balance-of-payments accounts of the countries involved, the International Monetary Fund, the World Bank, and the Inter-American Development Bank. Statistics cited in the text without footnote originate from these sources.

4. Inter-Press Service, "Studies Find Child Malnutrition Widespread," as reported in Foreign Broadcast Information Service (Referred to as FBIS hereafter), 25 July 1984. See also Carmen Diana Deere and Martin Diskin, "Rural Poverty in El Salvador: Dimensions, Trends, and Causes," (Study prepared for the International Labor Organization, New York, January 1983, mimeographed).

5. Solon Barraclough, "Agrarian Reform: Diversion or Necessity?" (Paper delivered at Johns Hopkins University School for Advanced International Studies Conference on Alternative Economic Strategies for Central America, Washington, D.C., 14–16 May 1984).

6. U.S. Department of State, "Central America: Agriculture, Technology, and Unrest," Bureau of Intelligence and Research, Report 839-AR, 15 May 1984 (unclassified).

7. U.S. Agency for International Development, "Background Papers for the Kissenger Commission Report," (U.S. Department of State, Washington, D.C., September 1983, mimeographed).

8. John Weeks, *The Economies of Central America* (New York: Holmes and Meier, 1984).

9. William R. Cline and Enrique Delgado, Introduction to *Economic Integration in Central America*, ed. William R. Cline and Enrique Delgado (Washington, D.C.: Brookings Institution, 1978).

10. See William R. Cline, "Benefits and Costs of Economic Integration in Central America," ibid., for a full exploration of this problem.

11. The evolution of these relations are presented in LaFeber, *Inevitable Revolutions*, and several of the country studies in Newfarmer, *From Gunboats to Diplomacy*. As a specific example, recall the well-documented political involvement of the United Fruit Company in the CIA-directed overthrow of the Arbenz regime in 1954. Another example is the bribes reportedly paid to the president of Honduras to avoid taxation on banana exports. See most recently Stephen Schlesinger and

Stephen Kinzer, *Bitter Fruit: The Untold Story of United Fruit in Central America* (Garden City, New York: Doubleday, 1983); *New York Times*, 10 April 1974 and 19 July 1978.

12. Clark Reynolds "Employment Problems of Export Economies in a Common Market: The Case of Central America," in *Economic Integration*. Calculated from the data presented in Table 12, p. 214.

13. Ibid.

14. For a description of industrial structure in selected industries and the role of acquisitions in shaping market structure, see Gert Rosenthal, "The Expansion of Transnational Enterprise in Central America: Acquisition of Domestic Firms" (Paper delivered at Centro de Investigación y Documentación Económica Symposium on Transnational Enterprise in Latin America. Queretero, Mexico, 7–14 April 1975).

15. See Weeks, *The Economies.*

16. For an articulate statement of this view, see James Fox, "Financial Needs for Central American Development" (Paper delivered at Johns Hopkins University School for Advanced International Studies Conference on Alternative Economic Strategies for Central America, Washington, D.C., 14–16 May 1984).

17. Two factors made the debt service problem less severe for Central America than for the rest of the hemisphere. First, the region—with the exception of Costa Rica and Panama—had not been a prime market for private commercial banks during the heady days of the massive expansion of overseas lending. The region's debt grew more slowly during the 1970s than the rest of Latin America. Second, many of the new loans came from public sources, which offered lower interest rates and longer maturities. Nearly three-quarters of the region's debt in 1980 was owed to multilateral or bilateral creditors. In contrast, Latin America as a whole owed only 30 percent to official lenders and the rest to private commercial banks. More important, a much smaller share of the debt—only about 30 percent of the $6.5 billion in disbursed medium- and long-term debt—was contracted at variable interest rates pegged to the widely fluctuating international rate. See World Bank, *World Debt Tables* (Washington, D.C.: World Bank, 1983); Jorge Pérez-López, "Central America's External Debt in the 1970s and Prospects for the 1980s," Occasional Paper #6, (Miami, Fla.: Florida International University, fall 1983).

18. For example, in 1983 we visited a lumber mill that had been caught up in the street-to-street battles between insurgents and the Somoza forces and had suffered bomb damage. Both of the main saws were partially destroyed and the owner was in the process of refurbishing the plant, in part by canabalizing one machine to reconstruct the other.

19. World Bank, *World Development Report, 1983* (Washington, D.C.: World Bank, 1983), 198–99.

20. These statistics are understated; expenditures on the armed services are often hidden in the budgets of other ministries, a practice especially common in Honduras.

21. United Nations, Economic Commission for Latin America, *Centroamerica: Apreciaciónes Sobre el Comercio Intraregiónal en 1982*, Report E/CEPAL/MEX /CCE/L.413 (8 October 1982) 7.

22. Gabriel Siri, *El Salvador and Economic Integration in Central America* (Toronto: Lexington Books, 1984), 107.

23. See Inter-American Development Bank, Economic Report: *Costa Rica*, No. GN 1470, July 1983 (Washington, D.C.: Inter-American Development Bank, 1983); other country reports useful in preparing the background work for this paper included: *El Salvador*, No. GN 1474, August 1983; *Honduras* No. GN 1457, January 1983; *Economic Report Guatemala* No. GN 1467, June 1983; Economic Report: *Nicaragua* No. GN 1471, July 1983.

24. Michael Best presents a provocative analysis of the political economy of taxation in Central America (not including Panama). He concludes that the tax composition of Central American countries reflects the interests of the dominant classes, particularly rural landlords, not the interests of the peasants, merchants, and

workers. See "Political Power and Tax Revenues in Central America," *Journal of Development Economics* 3 (1976): 49–82.

25. Forest Colburn, "Rural Labor and State in Postrevolutionary Nicaragua," *Latin American Research Review* 19, no. 3:103–17.

26. Information obtained from interviews with both governmental and nongovernmental sources in Nicaragua.

27. Henry Kissinger et al., *Report of the National Bipartisan Commission on Central America* (Washington, D.C.: Government Printing Office, 1984).

28. See Manuel Sevilla, "Economic Policy in El Salvador," for a thorough discussion of reforms that would facilitate more equitable and more rapid growth in El Salvador; see also Claudio Gonzalez-Vega, "Central America: Foreign Assistance, Policy Reforms, and Domestic Financial Markets in Reconstruction and Growth." (Both papers were delivered at Johns Hopkins University School for Advanced International Studies Conference on Alternative Economic Strategies for Central America, Washington, D.C., 14–16 May 1984.)

29. Siri, *El Salvador,* 107.

30. Kissinger et al., *Report,* 66.

31. Quantitative estimates of the effects of various U.S. economic policies on the Caribbean Basin can be found in Newfarmer, "U.S. Policy Toward the Caribbean Basin." U.S. macroeconomic and trade policies are more important than either the CBI or economic aid.

32. Enlarging the CBI can be anticipated to trigger protectionist objections; initiating reforms in U.S. industrial and labor-market policies could be helpful in reducing these. U.S. Congress, Joint Economic Committee, *Policies for Industrial Growth in a Competitive World* (Washington, D.C.: Government Printing Office, 25 May 1984). This report presents a detailed discussion of industrial and trade policies that would facilitate growth in developing countries. See particularly the discussion of U.S. labor-market policy by Michael Podgursky ("Labor Market Policy and Structural Adjustment").

33. See J. Berhman, "Commodity Stabilization Programs for Less Developing Countries," *Policy Alternatives for a New International Economic Order,* ed. William R. Cline (New York: Praeger, 1979); Siri, *El Salvador,* presents the argument as it applies specifically to Central America.

9: CUBA

1. William Durch, "The Cuban Military in Africa and the Middle East," Professional Paper no. 201 (Arlington, Va.: Center for Naval Analysis, 1977).

2. For a discussion of Cuban foreign policy during this period, see Carla A. Robbins, *The Cuban Threat* (New York: McGraw-Hill, 1983).

3. For a detailed study of Cuban foreign policy during this period, see D. Bruce Jackson, *Castro, the Kremlin, and Communism in Latin America* (Baltimore: Johns Hopkins University Press, 1969).

4. Edward Gonzalez, "Complexities of Cuban Foreign Policy," *Problems of Communism* 26, (November-December 1977):1–36. Even the Reagan administration acknowledges the halt in Cuban material aid during the 1970s; see Kenneth N. Skoug (Director of Cuban Affairs), "The United States and Cuba," *Current Policy* no. 646 (Washington, D.C.: Department of State, 17 December 1984).

5. James Petras, "Socialism in One Island: A Decade of Cuban Revolutionary Government," *Politics and Society* 1, (February 1971):20.

6. Carmelo Mesa-Lago, *Cuba in the 1970s* (Albuquerque, N.M.: University of New Mexico Press, 1978), 116–45.

7. Ibid.

8. William M. LeoGrande, "Cuban-Soviet Relations and Cuban Policy in Africa," *Cuban Studies* 10, (January 1980):35–52.

9. Ibid.

10. Richard Millet, *Guardians of the Dynasty* (Maryknoll, N.Y.: Orbis, 1977), 258.

11. Ibid., 233, 242–43.
12. "Somoza Lashes Back," *Newsweek*, 9 July 1979.
13. U.S. Congress, House of Representatives, Subcommittee on Inter-American Affairs, *Impact of Cuban-Soviet Ties in the Western Hemisphere: Hearings*, Statement of Martin J. Scheira, Defense Intelligence Agency, 96th Cong., 2nd sess. (Washington, D.C.: Government Printing Office, 1980).
14. Smith Hempstone, "It's Logical for Israel to Continue Supplying Weapons to Nicaragua," *Washington Post*, 13 December 1978; Karen DeYoung, "Andean Nations Provide Sandinistas a Diplomatic Opening," *Washington Post*, 18 June 1979; DeYoung, "Somoza Refuses to Quit, Pins Hopes on OAS Split," *Washington Post*, 23 June 1979; DeYoung, "Somoza Reported Meeting with Latin Allies," *Washington Post*, 14 July 1979.
15. William M. LeoGrande, "The Revolution in Nicaragua: Another Cuba?" *Foreign Affairs* 58, (Fall 1979):28–50.
16. This was the gist of a widely disseminated CIA report on Cuban aid to Central American guerrillas dated 2 May 1979.
17. Ibid.
18. "Nicaraguan Leaders Travel to Havana," *Washington Post*, 27 July 1979.
19. Castro's speech of 26 July 1979, *Granma Weekly Review* (Havana), 5 August 1979.
20. "Managua-Havana Ties Set," *New York Times*, 29 July 1979.
21. "Transcript of Statements at State Department on the Military Buildup in Nicaragua," *New York Times*, 10 March 1982; and Fidel Castro's interview with U.S. journalists 28 July 1983 in "Fidel Castro on Central America," *Cuba Update* 4, (August 1983).
22. Charles A. Krause, "Nicaraguan Defense Minister Sets Off on Arms Buying Trip," *Washington Post*, 1 September 1979.
23. "Transcript of Statements"; and "Fidel Castro on Central America."
24. "Transcript of Statements"; and "Fidel Castro on Central America."
25. "Nicaragua, Cuba Announce $130 Million Aid Agreement," *Washington Post*, 7 April 1982.
26. "Ronald Reagan Imposes a Trade Embargo on Nicaragua," *Newsweek*, 13 May 1985.
27. Marlise Simons, "Castro Advises Nicaragua to Avoid His Errors," *Washington Post*, 9 November 1980. Castro has also publicly praised the Sandinistas for their moderation and argued that the preservation of pluralism and the private sector were correct policies for Nicaragua's circumstances; see his speech in Managua on the first anniversary of the Sandinista triumph, 19 July 1980, and his speech on 26 July 1980, reprinted in *Fidel Castro Speeches*, Michael Taber, ed. (New York: Pathfinder, 1981), 310–38.
28. For a discussion of U.S. policy objectives with regard to Nicaragua during the last year and a half of the Carter administration, see William M. LeoGrande, "The United States and the Nicaraguan Revolution," in Thomas W. Walker, ed., *Nicaragua in Revolution* (New York: Praeger, 1981), 63–78.
29. Interview by author with Alfonso Robelo, July 1982. When Edén Pastora announced his decision to take up arms against the Sandinista government, a key reason, he said, was that his former comrades-in-arms had turned the country over to the Cubans; see Christopher Dickey, "Ex-Commander Surfaces, Assails Nicaragua's Rulers," *Washington Post*, 16 April 1982.
30. On 26 July 1980, Castro said that armed struggle was "the only road to liberation" for Latin America, especially in places subject to massive repression like El Salvador and Guatemala. *Fidel Castro Speeches*, 316–38.
31. House Subcommittee on Inter-American Affairs, *Impact of Cuban-Soviet Ties*, Statement of Randolph Pherson, Central Intelligence Agency, 46.
32. On the intensity of the Cubans' commitment to Nicaragua, see Fidel Castro, *Speech: 30th Anniversary of the Attack on the Moncada Garrison, 26 July 1983* (Havana, Cuba: Editora Política, 1983).
33. Fidel Castro commented repeatedly on the reactionary character of the 1980

Republican platform. The fullest discussion of it is in his speech of 26 July 1980, in which he calls Reagan's advisers "lunatics"; see *Fidel Castro Speeches*, 329.

34. Robert White, former U.S. ambassador to El Salvador, said that the evidence of Nicaraguan aid to the Salvadoran guerrillas was "unconvincing" until early November 1980. Karen DeYoung, "Sleuth of the Salvador Papers," *Washington Post*, 14 March 1981.

35. In April 1982, a senior Cuban official met with a group of U.S. foreign policy specialists, including the author, and admitted that Cuba had provided "material support" to the Salvadoran guerrillas prior to the spring of 1980, but he contended that no aid had been provided since that time. For a fuller discussion of the meeting, see Seweryn Bialer and Alfred Stepan, "Cuba, the United States, and the Central American Mess," *New York Review of Books*, 27 May 1982, 17–21.

36. Ibid.

37. The paucity of evidence for any Cuban role outside of El Salvador and Guatemala is demonstrated by how little the Reagan administration was able to find to put in its various white papers designed to demonstrate Cuba's aggressiveness. See, for instance, U.S. Department of State, *Cuba's Renewed Support for Violence in Latin America*, Special Report no. 90, 14 December 1981 (Washington, D.C.: Department of State, 1981); U.S. Departments of State and Defense, *Background Paper: Central America*, 27 May 1983 (Washington, D.C.: Departments of State and Defense, 1983); U.S. Departments of State and Defense, *The Soviet-Cuban Connection in Central America and the Caribbean*, March 1985 (Washington, D.C.: Departments of State and Defense, March 1985).

38. Ibid.

39. U.S. Department of State, *Communist Interference in El Salvador*, Special Report, no. 80, 23 February 1981 (Washington, D.C.: Department of State, 1981).

40. Quoted in Richard Halloran, "Military Aspect of Crisis Underlined by Haig and a Pentagon Study," *New York Times*, 21 February 1981.

41. Quoted in Lee Lescaze "U.S. Actions 'Possible' in Cuba Arms Flow, Reagan Aide Says," *New York Times*, 23 February 1981.

42. On this and other lessons drawn from the Vietnam War by the United States military, see Colonel Harry G. Summers, *On Strategy: A Critical Analysis of the Vietnam War* (New York: Dell, 1982).

43. Reagan first suggested a blockade in January 1980 and reaffirmed it in his debate with George Bush on April 23. Jane Franklin, *Cuban Foreign Relations: A Chronology, 1959–1982* (New York: Center for Cuban Studies, 1984), 31–32.

44. "Campaign '84: The Inside Story" *Newsweek: Election Extra*, (Special Edition), November-December 1984, 32

45. Patrick Tyler, "U.S. Plans for Possible Rise in Cuban Role in Nicaragua," *Washington Post*, 17 April 1983.

46. Wayne S. Smith, "Dateline Havana: Myopic Diplomacy," *Foreign Policy*, 48 (Fall 1982):157–74.

47. Tyler, "U.S. Plans for Possible Rise in Cuban Role in Nicaragua."

48. Quoted in Ronnie Dugger, "Ronald Reagan and the Imperial Presidency," *The Nation*, 1 November 1980, 430–36.

49. Jane Franklin, *Cuban Foreign Relations: A Chronology, 1983* (New York: Center for Cuban Studies, 1984), 13.

50. Henry Kissinger et al., *Report of the National Bipartisan Commission on Central America* (Washington, D.C.: Government Printing Office, 1984), 121.

51. Fidel Castro, "Main Report to the Second Congress," in *Second Congress of the Communist Party of Cuba: Documents and Speeches* (Havana, Cuba: Political Publishers, 1981), 9–123.

52. Kevin Klose, "Brezhnev Voices Faith in Polish Communists," *Washington Post*, 8 April 1981.

53. U.S. Departments of State and Defense, *The Soviet-Cuban Connection*, 9.

54. Castro, *Speech: 30th Anniversary*.

55. For a statement of the logic behind the Reagan administration's policy toward

Cuba, see Thomas O. Enders, "Dealing with Cuba," *Current Policy* no. 443, 14 December 1982 (Washington, D.C.: Department of State, 1982).

56. Cuba's relations with Mexico have been particularly good in recent years. At the conclusion of a meeting between Castro and Mexican President José Lopez-Portillo in August 1980, Mexico endorsed Cuba's demand for an end to the U.S. embargo and the withdrawal of U.S. forces from the naval base at Guantánamo. In February 1981, Mexico and Cuba signed a broad energy agreement, and later that month, right after presidential envoy Vernon Walters traveled to Mexico to convey the new administration's case against Cuban intervention in Central America, Lopez-Portillo called Cuba the Latin American nation "most dear" to Mexico. Alan Riding, "Mexico Stresses Ties with Cuba in Apparent Rebuff to Reagan," *New York Times*, 21 February 1981.

57. Cuba's new standing in the hemisphere is detailed in Joseph B. Treaster, "Cuba, Once Isolated, Forms New Bonds in South America," *New York Times*, 19 May 1985.

58. Reagan, when asked whether it was his intent to overthrow the Nicaraguan government, answered that he wanted to "remove" its "present structure," and that his policy was designed to make the Sandinistas say "uncle." Hedrick Smith, "President Asserts his Goal is to Remove Sandinista Regime," *New York Times*, 22 February 1985. In a speech to the American Bar Association on 23 May, Secretary of State George Shultz warned that if the Congress refused to give aid to the contras, the time might come when the administration would have to use direct U.S. military force against Nicaragua. Bernard Gwertzman, "Shultz in Warning on Combat Troops for Latin Region," *New York Times*, 24 May 1985.

59. Jim Hoagland, "Salvadoran Rebel Leader Vows Major Offensive," *Washington Post*, 8 March 1982.

60. Ibid.

61. Smith, "Dateline Havana," 160–61.

62. Ibid., 162–63.

63. Ibid., 165–66.

64. Martin Schram, "Cuba Pressing for Full-Scale Negotiations, but White House Says No," *Washington Post*, 11 December 1981.

65. Smith, "Dateline Havana," 156.

66. Alan Riding, "Mexicans Pessimistic on Talks Between U.S. and Caribbean Leftists," *New York Times*, 10 May 1982.

67. Smith, "Dateline Havana," 167.

68. Ibid., 167–68; and Leslie Gelb, "Central America Talks: Less Than Meets the Eye," *New York Times*, 26 March 1982.

69. Castro, *Speech: 30th Anniversary.*

70. "Fidel Castro on Central America."

71. Ibid.

72. The State Department's February 1980 white paper on El Salvador, which greatly exaggerated the amount of external aid provided to the FMLN, nevertheless acknowledged that "Before September 1980 . . . the insurgents acquired weapons predominantly through purchases on the international market and from dealers who participated in the supply of arms to the Sandinistas in Nicaragua." U.S. Department of State, *Communist Interference*, 2.

73. U.S. Congress, House of Representatives, Permanent Select Committee on Intelligence, *U.S. Intelligence Performance on Central America*, 97th Cong., 2nd sess. (Washington, D.C.: Government Printing Office, 1982).

74. U.S. Department of State, *Communist Interference.*

75. See the two lengthy critiques of the white paper: Jonathan Kwitny, "Apparent Errors Cloud U.S. 'White Paper' on Reds in El Salvador," *Wall Street Journal*, 8 June 1981, and Robert G. Kaiser, "White Paper on El Salvador is Faulty," *Washington Post*, 9 June 1981.

76. Ibid.

77. Smith, "Dateline Havana," 160–61; and John M. Goshko, "State Department Shifts, Seeks to Cool Off Salvador Publicity," *Washington Post*, 13 March 1981.

78. Richard M. Weinraub, "U.S. Passed Up Overtures By Cuba," *Washington Post*, 5 September, 1982.

79. Philip Taubman, "In from the Cold, Hot for the Truth," *New York Times*, 11 June 1984.

80. U.S. Congress, House of Representatives, Permanent Select Committee on Intelligence, *Amendment to the Intelligence Authorization Act for Fiscal Year 1983: Report*, 98th Cong., 1st sess., Report 98–122, Part 1 (Washington, D.C.: Committee Print, 1983), 2.

81. See for example, Hedrick Smith, "A Former Salvadoran Rebel Chief Tells of Arms from Nicaragua," *New York Times*, 12 July 1984.

82. Robert J. McCartney, "Proof of Salvadoran Arms Supply is Elusive," *Washington Post*, 8 July 1984.

83. For a discussion of Cuban-Soviet relations, see Jacques Levesque, *The USSR and the Cuban Revolution* (New York: Praeger, 1978).

84. Ibid.

85. Jackson, *Castro, the Kremlin*.

86. Gonzalez, "Complexities of Cuban Foreign Policy."

87. William M. LeoGrande, *Cuba's Policy in Africa, 1959–1980* (Berkeley, Calif.: University of California, 1980).

88. Ibid.

89. William M. LeoGrande, "The Evolution of Nonalignment," *Problems of Communism* 29, (January-February 1980):35–52.

90. U.S. Department of State, *Cuban Armed Forces and the Soviet Military Presence*, Special Report no. 103, August 1982 (Washington, D.C.: Department of State, 1982).

91. The largest component of the aid package during the 1960s and early 1970s was balance of payments credits. Cuban-Soviet trade produced a perennial Cuban deficit, which the Soviet Union absorbed by extending credits on concessionary terms. By 1973, such credits totaled nearly $2 billion. Since 1973, the major channel for Soviet economic aid has been through preferential pricing of key commodities traded between the two nations. The Soviet Union pays premium prices for Cuban sugar and nickel while charging below market price for petroleum. This is essentially a new accounting procedure that shifts the financing of the trade imbalance from credits to grants. Lawrence Theriot, *Cuba Faces the Economic Realities of the 1980s*, prepared for the U.S. Congress, Joint Economic Committee, March 1982 (Washington, D.C.: Government Printing Office, 1982).

92. Joseph G. Whelan, *Latin America in Soviet Third World Policy*, Congressional Research Service Report no. 85–40 S (Washington, D.C.: Library of Congress, 1984), 99; and Carmelo Mesa-Lago, *The Economy of Socialist Cuba* (Albuquerque, N.M.: University of New Mexico Press, 1981), 102–7.

93. The Soviets diverted their own naval forces from the vicinity of Nicaragua when the U.S. began large-scale naval manuevers. Dusko Doder, "Castro Faults Soviets on Managua Aid," *Washington Post*, 24 March 1985.

94. Ibid.

95. "Ronald Reagan Imposes a Trade Embargo on Nicaragua," *Newsweek*, 13 May 1985.

96. LeoGrande, *Cuba's Policy in Africa*.

10: THE SOVIET UNION

1. "Excerpts From the President's Speech to Longshoremen on Central America," *New York Times*, 19 July 1983; and "President's News Conference on Foreign and Domestic Matters," *New York Times*, 27 July 1983.

2. Neill Macaulay, *The Sandino Affair* (Chicago: Quadrangle Books, 1967), 74.

3. Rodolfo Cerdas, *Sandino, el Apra y la Internacional Comunista* (San José, Costa Rica: 1979), 70.

4. Ibid., 48.

5. Ibid., 69.
6. Ibid., 77–80.
7. Ibid., 76–77.
8. N. S. Leonov, *Nekotorye Problemy Politicheskoi Istorii Tsentral'noi Ameriki XX Stoletiia* (Moscow: 1972), 137, and Chapter 4 passim.
9. B. I. Koval', *Latinskaia Amerika: Revolutsiia i Sovremennost'* (Moscow, 1981), 146.
10. Rodolfo Cerdas, *Farabundo Martí, la Internacional Comunista, y la Insurrección Salvadoreña de 1932* (San José, Costa Rica: 1982), 56–67.
11. Ibid., 65–67. The Communist International criticized the Salvadoran Party for acting irresponsibly, arguing that since the United States had the capability to crush the revolution, the insurrection had been an "adventure."
12. There is a Soviet commercial representative in Panama to facilitate trade and other contacts. The Soviet Union exports a substantial volume of consumer goods, like watches, to Panama for sale to transit traffic.
13. The Soviet Union does not have a large number of Central America researchers. Most work is in the Institute of Latin America and the Institute of the International Labor Movement in Moscow. In the two years before the Nicaraguan revolution less than 10 percent of the 531 entries in the Soviet bibliography on Latin America (excluding Cuba) dealt with Central America. *Latinskaia Amerika v sovetskoi Pechati, Ukazatel' Literatury 1977–1978 gg*, (Moscow, 1980).
14. Richard F. Staar, ed., *Yearbook of International Communist Affairs, 1984* (Stanford, Calif.: Hoover Institution Press, 1984), xiv, xv.
15. While the USSR provided political and moral support to the Guatemalan revolution of 1944 to 1954, Soviet leaders knew little about it, had little contact with it, and provided no known material assistance except possibly for an arms shipment that arrived late. The Soviet leadership, of course, was otherwise engaged; the political struggle over the succession to Stalin was at a high pitch in 1954.
16. Jesús M. Blandón, *Entre Sandino y Fonseca* (Managua, Nicaragua: 1981), 178–88.
17. Carlos Fonseca, *Un Nicaragüense en Moscú* (Managua, Nicaragua: 1981), 5; David Nolan, *The Ideology of the Sandinistas and the Nicaraguan Revolution* (Coral Gables, Fla.: University of Miami Press, 1984), 144.
18. Blandón, *Entre Sandino*, 204.
19. Nolan, *Ideology of the Sandinistas*, 23.
20. Ibid.
21. "Beseda s Pervym sekretarem Tsk Nikaraguanskoi sotsialisticheskoi partii Luisom Sanchesom Sancho," *Latinskaia Amerika*, no. 4 (1978):107–11.
22. Ibid., 151.
23. Shafik Jorge Handal, "El poder, el carácter y la via de la revolución y la unidad de la izquierda," *Fundamentos y Perspectivas, Revista Teórica del Partido Comunista de El Salvador*, no. 4 (January 1982):27.
24. For a discussion of the role played by Cuba in the Nicaraguan insurrection, see Chapter 8.
25. As a senior Soviet official commented in mid-1983: "We had no contacts with the Sandinistas when they started the revolution and it was not inspired by us; we are in favor of the Nicaraguan Revolution but we can only help here and there." Interview with the author, Moscow, June 1983.
26. *Latinskaia Amerika*, no. 3 (1980), as quoted in C. G. Jacobsen, *Soviet Attitudes Towards, Aid to, and Contacts with Central American Revolutionaries*, (Washington, D.C.: mimeograph, 1984), 9. Boris Koval, writing in the March 1980 issue of *Latinskaia Amerika* praised Guevara even more: "The Nicaraguan experience [has] demolished the previous simplistic interpretation of guerrilla actions, confirmed the justice of many of Che Guevara's strategic principles, and crystallized his idea of creating a powerful popular guerrilla movement." Quoted in Joseph G. Whelan, *Latin America in Soviet Third World Policy*, Congressional Research Service Report No. 85–40 S (Washington, D.C.: Library of Congress, 1984), 120.
27. S. A. Mikoyan, "Ob osobonnostiakh revoliutsii v Nicaragua," *Latinskaia*

Amerika, no. 3 (1980):34–44. See also, Cole Blasier, *The Giant's Rival: The USSR and Latin America* (Pittsburgh: University of Pittsburgh Press, 1983), 95–98.

28. Handal, "El poder, el carácter y la via," 37–41.

29. Mario Menéndez Rodríguez, *El Salvador: una auténtica guerra civil* (San José, Costa Rica: 1980), 29.

30. Roque Dalton, *Miguel Marmol* (San José, Costa Rica: 1972), 11.

31. Koval, *Latinskaia Amerika*, 157.

32. Shafik Jorge Handal, "Consideraciones acerca del viraje del Partido hacia la lucha armada," *Fundamentos y Perspectivas, Revista Teórica del Partido Comunista de El Salvador*, no. 5 (San Salvador April 1983):23 and passim. The author wishes to thank Dr. Tommie Sue Montgomery for providing this material.

33. Handal, "El poder, el carácter y la via," 37, 40, 41.

34. Handal, "El poder, el carácter y la via," 42.

35. Robert G. Kaiser, "White Paper on El Salvador is Faulty," *Washington Post*, 9 June 1981.

36. Cuban leaders have admitted sending supplies to the Salvadoran guerrillas in 1980 and early 1981 (see Chapter 8). It seems unlikely that Cuban shipments could have been made over the opposition of the Soviet government, but in all likelihood, the Cubans provided the aid at their own initiative.

37. Starr, *Yearbook*, 136.

38. Interview with Carlos González, General Secretary of the Guatemalan Labor Party, *Latinskaia Amerika*, no. 2 (1984):45.

39. O. Ignat'ev, "Pobeda naroda Nicaragua," *Kommunist*, no. 13, (September 1979): 101. The next few paragraphs are drawn from Blaiser, *The Giant's Rival*, 44–45.

40. *Pravda*, 23 March 1984.

41. Morris Rothenberg, "The Soviets and Central America," in *Central America: Anatomy of Conflict* (New York: Pergamon Press, 1984), 131–52.

42. Interview by the author with a staff member of the FSLN, Managua, April 1983.

43. *Vneshniaia Torgovlia SSR v. 1983 g. Statisticheskii sbornik*, (Moscow: Finansy I. Statistika, 1984), 269–70.

44. Supplement to *Vneshniaia Torgovlia*, no. 9 (1984):4.

45. Whelan, *Latin America*, 136–38.

46. Jacobsen, *Soviet Attitudes*, 15–16; Clifford Krause and Robert S. Greenberger, "Defense Fears of U.S., Soviet Aid to Nicaragua Appears to be Limited," *Wall Street Journal*, 3 April 1985.

47. Based on U.S., Soviet, and Nicaraguan official sources in Managua, April 1983. At best, these figures represent gross magnitudes since many were preliminary or received in interviews.

48. Jacobsen, *Soviet Attitudes*, 15–16.

49. The International Institute for Strategic Studies, *The Military Balance 1983– 1984* (London: 1983), 11.

50. Letter to Senator William Proxmire from Secretary of Defense Caspar Weinberger, 6 June 1984; Krause and Greenberger, "Despite Fears of U.S."

51. The Soviet Union has not offered Cuba any formal security agreement either, although the agreement between the Soviet Union and the United States that ended the Cuban missile crisis of 1962 did involve a U.S. pledge not to attack Cuba in exchange for the withdrawal of Soviet missiles.

52. Rothenberg, "The Soviets," 140–41. The Soviets' reluctance to aid the Sandinistas both economically and militarily reportedly caused some serious tensions between Moscow and Havana. Fidel Castro's refusal to attend the funeral of Konstantin Chernenko was purportedly a protest against Chernenko's policy toward Nicaragua.

11: MEXICO, VENEZUELA, AND THE CONTADORA INITIATIVE

The author wishes to thank David Collier, Richard Fagen, Robert Keohane, Phillip Oxhorn, Philippe Schmitter, Cathryn Thorup, and the editors of this volume for their comments. Research support for work in Mexico, Venezuela, Costa Rica, Nicaragua, El Salvador, and Washington was generously provided by the Tinker Foundation and the Committee on Latin American and Iberian Studies, Harvard University.

1. On Colombia, see Bruce Bagley, *Regional Powers in the Caribbean Basin: Mexico, Venezuela and Colombia* (Washington, D.C.: Central America and Caribbean Program, School of Advanced International Studies, Johns Hopkins University Press, 1983); Gerhard Drekonja Kornat, *Colombia: En busqueda de una politica exterior* (Miami, Fla.: Occasional Papers Series, Latin American and Caribbean Center, Florida International University, Fall 1982).

2. See Mario Ojeda, "Mexican Policy Towards Central America in the Context of U.S.-Mexican Relations," in *The Future of Central America: Policy Choices for the U.S. and Mexico*, ed. Richard Fagen and Olga Pellicer (Stanford, Calif.: Stanford University Press, 1983), 138. For other discussions of Mexico's strategic goals in Central America, see Olga Pellicer, "Mexico in Central America: The Difficult Exercise of Regional Power," in *Future of Central America*, 119–33; Rene Herrera Zuniga and Mario Ojeda, "Mexican Foreign Policy in Central America," in *Central America: International Dimensions of the Crisis*, ed. Richard Feinberg (New York: Holmes and Meier Publishers, 1982), 160–86; Olga Pellicer, ed., *La política exterior de Mexico: desagios en los ochenta* (Mexico City, Mexico: CIDE, 1983); Peter Smith, "Mexico: The Continuing Quest for a Policy," in *From Gunboats to Diplomacy*, ed. Richard S. Newfarmer (Baltimore: Johns Hopkins University Press, 1984), 37–53; Cathryn Thorup and Robert Ayres, "Central America: The Challenges to U.S. and Mexican Foreign Policy," Working Paper Series 18, (Washington, D.C.: Overseas Development Council, U.S.-Mexico Project, July 1982).

3. Confidential interview by the author with PRI official in charge of foreign affairs, Mexico City, September 1983. Adolfo Aquilar Zinzer, "Mexico and the Guatemalan Crisis," in *Future of Central America*, 161–86.

4. As part of the San José Agreement, Mexico made a long-term commitment to supply 75,000 barrels per day to Managua. It granted a 30 percent credit that could be repaid in five years at interest rates of 4 percent. On aid to Nicaragua, see Olga Pellicer, "The Difficult Exercise of Regional Power," in *Future of Central America*, 121.

5. "San José Terms to be Tightened," *Latin America Weekly Report*, 22 April 1983. Confidential interview by the author with official from PEMEX, Mexico, September 1983.

6. As one former official in foreign policy recalled: "We knew the Sandinistas. We had received hundreds of political refugees from Nicaragua after the 1978 insurrection. The leaders, *"Los Doce,"* people like Sergio Ramirez, Miguel d'Escoto, and Juaquín Quadra had been in our embassy in asylum. We got to know and understand their concerns. Our ties were close. Everyone hated Somoza. We didn't pressure them and we placed no conditions upon them." Interview by the author, Mexico, September 1983.

7. On 30 April 1981, Humberto Ortega, the minister of defense of Nicaragua, stated that there had been thirty-seven air attacks, fifteen infiltrations of armed bands from Honduras, and at least forty-four violations of Nicaraguan air space in a mere three months. Shortly after his announcement, the Mexican president intervened and helped to settle temporarily the 1981 border crisis. See Stella Calloni and Rafael Cribari, *Guerra encubierta contra Contadora* (Panamá City, Panama: Centro de Capacitacion Social, 1983).

8. "Central America: A Key Failure of the President's Latest Grand Tour," *Latin America Political Report*, 18 July 1980.

9. *Washington Post*, 29 August 1981.

10. Jorge Casteñeda, "Caribbean Basin Security," *New York Times*, 10 March 1982.

11. *New York Times*, 18 May 1982.

12. During 1983, there were persistent rumors of direct IMF pressure upon Mexico to cut its aid to the Nicaraguan regime. While several people interviewed by the author in Mexico City repeated these rumors, no official could claim first hand

knowledge of their accuracy. Bruce Bagley, "Mexican Foreign Policy in the 1980s: A New Regional Power," *Current History* (November 1981):353ff, discusses the impact of Mexico's financial crisis on foreign policy.

13. Confidential interview by the author with PEMEX official in Mexico, September 1983. Confidential interview by the author with official from the Foreign Ministry, September 1983.

14. Interview by the author with Adolfo Aguilar Zinser, Mexico, September 1983.

15. See the essays in Robert Bond, ed., *Contemporary Venezuela and Its Role in International Affairs* (New York: Council on Foreign Relations, 1977); see also Charles Ameringer, "The Foreign Policy of Venezuelan Democracy," in *Venezuela: The Democratic Experience,* ed. John D. Martz and David J. Myers (New York: Praeger, 1977), 335–59.

16. See Arturo Borja and Terry Karl, "La Administración Carter y las relaciones Venezuela/Estados Unidos," in *Carter y América Latina,* Centro de Investigación y Docencia Económicas, Cuadernos Semestrales (Mexico City: 1978). For a history of Venezuela's role in the Caribbean, see Demetrio Boersner, *Venezuela y El Caribe* (Caracas, Venezuela: Monte Avila Editores, 1978).

17. President Pérez, like other members of his party, had spent his years of exile in Central America, often in the company of anti-Somocistas like Pedro Juaquín Chamorro. Chamorro's assasination by Somoza forces and the attack of Edén Pastora (another friend) against the National Palace influenced Pérez's subsequent actions in Nicaragua. Interview by the author with former President Carlos Andrés Pérez at Harvard University, March 1984. Confidential interview by the author with high-level U.S. diplomat, September 1983.

18. See Richard Feinberg, "The Recent Rapid Redefinitions of U.S. Interests and Diplomacy in Central America," in Feinberg, *Central America,* 58–84, for an excellent discussion of foreign policy making in the Carter administration.

19. Interview by the author with former President Pérez, March 1984. A high-level U.S. diplomat claimed that President Pérez was furious about the letter sent to Somoza by President Carter. "Pérez considered this a betrayal of his trust. He had been assured that Somoza was on his way out, but the letter—and Somoza's confidence—seemed to contradict that impression. From that point on, he stopped trusting us." Telephone interview by the author with U.S. diplomat, September 1983. Pérez denies that the letter itself was a turning point in his own decisions. He argues that Somoza had no intention of leaving power and that a prolongation of his dynasty would have only lead to increased radicalization and bloodshed. This understanding led him to take the positions he did on Nicaragua.

20. President Pérez states that Somoza's threats to Costa Rica were the final straw for many Latin Americans closely following the regional struggle. "Torrijos called me and said, 'Cuanto vale tu mujer?' In other words, he asked me how much was I willing to risk in Nicaragua." Shortly after the threats against Costa Rica, Pérez sought bipartisan support for his actions from COPEI and the left. Interview by the author with former President Pérez, March 1984.

21. Before the downfall of Somoza, the United States knew that the Pérez administration was deeply involved in aiding the Sandinistas, "but we didn't have any idea of the extent of the commitment." Telephone interview by the author with U.S. diplomat, September 1983. Venezuelan, Panamanian, and Costa Rican arms supplies fell off when Pérez's administration ended. Cuba picked up the slack, landing weapons near the Nicaraguan–Costa Rican border. Officials in the Carazo administration were later implicated in profiteering from arms sales, leading to a congressional investigation in that country. Interview by the author with official from U.S. Department of State, Washington, D.C., September 1983. Interview by the author with cabinet member, San José, Costa Rica, October 1983. Interview by the author with high-level party members of AD and COPEI, Caracas, 1979. A U.S. diplomat who closely followed Venezuelan actions in Nicaragua claimed that the Carter administration was surprised at the strength of feeling against Somoza and the depth of involvement from Caracas. "Their intelligence was better than ours all along. They knew that Somoza was finished before we

did. They wanted to get on the side of the winners and we didn't know just exactly how much they had actually done so." Telephone interview by the author with U.S. diplomat, September, 1983.

22. *Latin America Political Report* (7 July 1979): 274.

23. According to a Caracas newspaper, *El Diario de Caracas,* Herrera Campins informed Robelo, then a representative of the junta, that aid would only be forthcoming if Christian Democratic leader, José Esteban Gonzáles, were included in the new government. "Nicaragua: Strings and Arrows," *Latin America Political Report* (17 August 1979): 252. Although Venezuelan government officials were unwilling to discuss oil supplies to Nicaragua, Venezuelans in their embassy in Washington confirmed that oil shipments had been suspended until Nicaragua paid its bills. They denied any political implications but did reveal that Costa Rica also had not paid its bills and that oil supplies continued to that country. Interview by the author with Venezuelan diplomat, Washington, September 1983. Subsequently, Mexico picked up Venezuela's Nicaraguan quota. Interview by the author with DRI official, Managua, October 1983.

24. Confidential interview by the author with a former Venezuelan ambassador to Nicaragua, Caracas, November 1983. The phrase about "nailing masks" was apparently used often by other Christian Democrats and was first pointed out to the author by a U.S. diplomat.

25. Confidential interview by the author with former Venezuelan ambassador to Central America, Caracas, November 1983.

26. In January 1982, Venezuelan intelligence personnel were caught collaborating with counterrevolutionary forces from a base inside the Venezuelan embassy in Managua. Venezuelan, Honduran, Salvadoran, and Argentine officials collaborated with Nicaraguan rightists to sabotage the country's largest oil refinery and cement plant. When Miguel d'Escoto flew to Caracas to present taped evidence that implicated Venezuelan embassy personnel, Caracas was clearly embarrassed. Although it denied the charges, COPEI officials subsequently admitted the involvement of some Venezuelans but claimed that they were working for the CIA, not working for the Venezuelan government. Interview by the author with former Venezuelan ambassador to Nicaragua and COPEI party-government official in charge of Central America policy, Caracas, November 1983.

27. Interview by the author with José Napoleón Duarte, El Salvador, September 1983. For an acknowledgment of this friendship, see Republica de Venezuela, "Declaración del Presidente Luis Herrera Campins en el National Press Club" (Caracas: Ediciones de la Presidencia de la Republica, 1981). For a more complete discussion of the impact of Venezuelan Christian Democrats on the Salvadoran party, see Terry Karl, "After La Palma: The Prospects for Democracy in El Salvador," *World Policy* (Winter 1985): 305–30.

28. This information was first revealed by then Assistant Secretary of State Thomas O. Enders, to the dismay of the Venezuelans. Enders confirmed that Venezuela had trained two battalions of *cazadores* and had sent advisers to El Salvador. In January 1981, Congressman Eloy Torres of the MAS (Movimiento al Socialismo) claimed that officials of the national guard and the army were being used as advisers in El Salvador. He accused the government of working with the CIA to create a spy network headquartered in the Sheraton Hotel in San Salvador. Reportedly this included at least seven officials of the Venezuelan political police. President Herrera denied the congressional charges and the statement by Thomas Enders, but Venezuelan officials privately admit the veracity of the former assistant secretary's remarks. "Enders Puts Venezuela on the Spot Over El Salvador, *Latin America Weekly Report* (4 February 1983): 1. Interview by the author with COPEI party member in charge of foreign affairs for the party, Caracas, November 1983.

29. Confidential interview by the author with official of IVEPO, San Salvador, September 1983.

30. This policy shift was captured in confusing policy declarations by the Venezuelan government. In mid-1981, Interior Minister Rafael Montes de Oca proclaimed

"an absolute coincidence of views" with U.S. support of the ruling junta in El Salvador. A month earlier President Herrera had issued a joint statement with President López Portillo that favored international mediation to resolve the conflict in El Salvador, a position rejected by the United States. "Coming Down on Both Sides of Diplomatic Fence," *Latin America Weekly Report,* 29 May 1981; "U.S. Lauds Diplomatic Offensive," *Latin America Weekly Report* (27 February 1981): 9; and "U.S. Steps Up Aid to Junta," *Latin American Weekly Report* (6 March 1981)· 5

31. Jackson Diehl, "U.S. to Sell Venezuela F-16s in Shift of Regional Arms Policy," *Washington Post,* 3 October 1981.

32. See the observations by Nestor Mora, "Balance para una herencia: Intactos y aún agravados encontrara el próximo gobierno nuestros problemas internacionales," *El Nacional,* 9 October 1983. This article, highly critical of Venezuela's foreign policy, prompted a response by Foreign Minister José Alberto Zambrano Velasco.

33. By the fall of 1983, members of the Socialist International had begun to criticize Nicaragua for its press censorship and for its delay in holding elections. Four Socialist leaders, Willy Brandt, Felipe Gonzáles, Daniel Oduber, and Carlos Andrés Pérez, sent a letter to the Sandinistas, suggesting an early date for Nicaraguan elections. The letter was intended to be a private message. It stated that these leaders did not wish to interfere in internal matters but warned about Nicaragua's growing isolation in Western Europe and Latin America. The letter was apparently intercepted by an intelligence agency and an inaccurate version was printed in the *International Herald Tribune* on 18 July 1983. The newspaper reported that the letter was an ultimatum to the Nicaraguan regime, a fact that is denied by all parties involved. At one point, however, tensions between AD and the Nicaraguan regime grew so serious that an SI meeting scheduled to be held in Caracas had to be changed to another country. Interviews by the author with an official of the Spanish foreign ministry, Madrid, March 1984; with Costa Rican foreign ministry official, San José, October 1983; with DRI official, Managua, September 1983.

34. "Ideas y criterios para la política exterior de Venezuela" (Confidential AD party memo prepared for the 1983 elections, Caracas) 17. Confidential interview by the author with high-level AD party official, Caracas, November 1983. Interview by the author with a former Venezuelan foreign minister, Caracas, November 1983.

35. Interview by the author with former President Rafael Caldera, Caracas, November 1983. Interview by the author with COPEI official associated with IFEDEC, Caracas, November 1983.

36. The Falklands-Malvinas war touched a responsive historical cord in Venezuela, which holds Britain responsible for its own border dispute with Guyana since Britain originally awarded the contested territory, which is over half of the present-day Guyana, to that country. Furthermore, the disregard for the Monroe Doctrine exhibited by U.S. support of Britain was particularly sensitive in Caracas since the Roosevelt corollary to the Monroe Doctrine, the key doctrinal basis for U.S. policy in the region, actually originated in a dispute between Britain and the United States over Venezuela's external debt. "Venezuela's Ties with U.S. Plummet As It Rallies Behind the Argentines," *New York Times,* 23 May 1982. Interview by the author with COPEI party official in charge of foreign affairs, Caracas, November 1983.

37. Secretaria de Relaciones Exteriores de Mexico, "Documentos relacionados con la gestion del grupo Contadora," compiled for the author by the Subsecretaria de Planeacion y Asuntos Culturales (Mexico: September 1983). The history of Contadora, which is not recounted here due to space limitations, can be found in Stella Calloni and Rafael Cribari, *Guerra Encubierta.*

38. A majority of OAS countries agreed that the Grenada action violated Article 18 of the OAS charter, which says that no country or group of countries has the right to interfere in the internal affairs of another state "for any reason." Article 20 says that national territory is inviolable and cannot be occupied militarily, "even temporarily." In the United Nations, Peru, Chile, Brazil, Mexico, Colombia,

Venezuela, Argentina, Ecuador, Panama, Uruguay, Bolivia, Nicaragua, Costa Rica, and several Caribbean nations voted to censure the United States. El Salvador was the only OAS member that voted against the motion to censure. *Daily Journal* (Caracas), 6 November 1983. For more on the Latin American response to Grenada, see Carlos Andrés Pérez, "Venezuela, La Social Democracia y su Politica hacia Centro America y el Caribe" (Speech at Harvard University, 15 March 1984).

39. For a discussion of the U.S. military buildup in Central America, see Allan Nairn, "Endgame: U.S. Military Strategy in Central America," *Report on the Americas* 18 (May-June 1984):19–55. Also see Hedrick Smith, "U.S. Latin Force in Place If Needed, Officials Report," *New York Times*, 23 April 1984; and Robert Graham, "Reagan's Creeping Commitment," *Financial Times*, 1 May 1984. For an excellent study of militarization, see Jozef Goldblat and Victor Millan, "The Honduras-Nicaraguan Conflict and Prospects for Arms Control in Central America," in *World Armaments and Disarmament, SPIRI Yearbook 1984*, (Stockholm: Stockholm International Peace Research Institute, 21 June 1984).

40. Interview by the author with former high-level official of the López-Portillo administration, Mexico, September 1983. Interview by the author with official of PEMEX, Mexico, September 1983. Olga Pellicer, "Politica Exterior Mexicana: Continuidad e Incertidumbre en Momentos de Crisis" (Unpublished manuscript, August 1983).

41. In Venezuela, the invasion of Grenada provoked an emergency meeting of the Council of Security and Defense. The Herrera Campins administration eventually condemned the invasion, while Acción Democrática and the left critiqued the intervention as, in part, "an attempt to scare the Nicaraguans." Interview by the author with official in charge of AD foreign policy, Caracas, November 1983. *El Nacional,* 8 November 1983.

42. The San José "Enders Forum" caused serious tensions between participants and nonparticipants. Mexico had always declined participation in the Forum for Peace and Democracy. Venezuela had accepted, then declined at the last moment, ostensibly due to previous commitments at the UN on the part of its foreign minister. The Venezuelans supported the meeting's main purpose in a cable, but Venezuela was never active and the initiative eventually died. Interview by the author with official in the Foreign Ministry, San José, Costa Rica, November 1983. See the editorial in *Uno Mas Uno,* 6 February 1983.

43. The secretary general of the United Nations, Pérez de Cuellar, supported the position that the OAS was not an appropriate forum for the problems of Central America: "Since Cuba is not a member of the OAS and Nicaragua has no competence in this organism, obviously the OAS is not the appropriate forum to resolve the situation in Central America." *El Dia,* 19 April 1983. Interview by the author with an official of a working commission of the Contadora group, Panamá, October 1983.

44. For an example of the Reagan administration's rhetorical support of Contadora, see President Reagan's letter to the Latin American group, in Secretariade Relaciones Exteriores de Mexico, "Documentos." In private, however, U.S. officials in Washington and in Central America either expressed derision or dismissed regional peace initiatives as unimportant. Interview by the author in the U.S. Department of State, Latin America section, Washington, D.C., September 1983; with U.S. officials in U.S. embassy, San José and Managua, October 1983.

45. In Costa Rica, for example, officials complained about pressure from the U.S. embassy to block efforts toward the drafting of a meaningful neutrality position in the Central American conflict. Divisions over the appropriate policy toward the ARDE contra army were reflected in public disputes between Foreign Minister Fernando Volio and Angel Solano, who had the responsibility of securing the border with Nicaragua. The United States openly supported Volio and pressed for the removal of Angel Solano. Volio, the spokesperson for the hard-line against Nicaragua and a close associate of the U.S. embassy, was eventually replaced in the face of strong opposition to his policies by other cabinet ministers. Due to

his close association with the U.S. hard-line in Central America, he was unoffi-
cially declared persona non grata by Mexico and by the Socialist International
while he was still foreign minister. Interview by the author with Cabinet member,
San José, Costa Rica, October 1983. Interview by the author with Guido Fer-
nandez, former editor of *La Nación* (San José), October 1983. Gonzalo Fascio,
former foreign minister of Costa Rica, denied any pressure from the United States
on Costa Rica's present policies, but one member of the political section of the
U.S. embassy in San José explained that a strict interpretation of Costa Rican
neutrality, the position of the majority of the cabinet, could violate the U.S.
understanding of the OAS treaty and would not be welcome by the United States.
"We have communicated our feelings about this." Interview by the author with
an official of the U.S. embassy, San José, Costa Rica, October 1983. Some cabinet
members in the Monge government expressed fears that a border agreement
between Nicaragua and Costa Rica could lead to a withdrawal of U.S. aid, which
is essential during the present financial crunch. Interview with two ministers, San
José, Costa Rica, October 1983.

46. *New York Times,* 23 September 1984.
47. The United States claims the timetable for the withdrawal of foreign advisers
favors the Soviet Union and Cuba. It objects to the closing of its military schools
and bases, argues that a verification commission made up of four impartial
countries might favor Nicaragua, worries that Nicaragua will violate an arms
freeze by clandestinely shipping weapons to the FDR-FMLN, and dislikes the
idea of a protocol that would have the Soviet Union and the United States agree
in writing not to interfere with the implementation of the agreement. This protocol, in the State Department's view, admits a political role for the Soviets and
Cubans in Central America, thus the very signature of these countries is not
acceptable. The revised draft, supported by the United States, would take out
provisions against U.S. military exercises in the region, delete the requirement
for the removal of U.S. bases, drop the protocol, and change the composition of
the verification commission. See the *Oakland Tribune,* 9 November 1984; International Policy Report, "Contadora: A Text for Peace," November 1984.
48. *Washington Post,* 6 November 1984.
49. Contadora has received the support of the European community, the Socialist
International, Pope John Paul II, the Soviet Union, the International Labor
Organization and members of the U.S. Congress. Resolution 530 of the United
Nations Security Council stated "its satisfaction with the efforts made by the
Contadora group" and the United Nations General Assembly also adopted Resolution 38/10, which expressed its complete support. On 11 November 1983, the
General Assembly of the OAS also voted to support Contadora. Isidro Morales,
"Contadora: A Hope Beyond Despair" (Statement by the minister of foreign
affairs of Venezuela, Harvard University, 19 April 1984).
50. Spain has been particularly active in mobilizing support for the Contadora group
in Europe. Felipe Gonzales, who has close ties with Latin American leaders, had
previously offered Spain's aid in mediating the Central American dispute, but
later adopted a behind-the-scenes role due to the Latin American reluctance to
involve an extracontinental power. Interview by the author with PSOE official in
charge of Central American policy, Madrid, March 1984. See Nadia Malley,
"Nicaraguan Relations with Western Europe and the Socialist International"
(Paper presented at the 1984 Annual Meeting of the American Political Science
Association, Washington, D.C., 30 August–2 September 1984).
51. The Reagan administration greeted the formation of the "support group" with
its customary dual stance: It stated that it viewed this effort to breathe new life
into Contadora as positive, then simultaneously announced that it would continue
to seek military aid for the rebels fighting against the Nicaraguan government.
In a document leaked from a meeting between Undersecretary of State for Latin
American Affairs Elliot Abrams and U.S. ambassadors in the region, Abrams
reportedly stated that "it is necessary that we develop an active diplomacy in
order to hinder the attempts at Latin American solidarity that could be directed

against the U.S. and its allies, whether these efforts are initiated by the Support Group [composed of Brazil, Argentina, Uruguay, and Peru], Cuba, or Nicaragua." *Excelsior,* 8 September 1985, cited in "Contadora Group Calls for Peace," *Central America Bulletin,* vol. 5, no. 2, 6.

52. These trade-offs can be traced through the Contadora documents themselves. See Secretaria de Relaciones Exteriores, "Documentos relacionados con la gestion."

53. See Viron P. Vaky, "Hemispheric Relations: Everything is Part of Everything Else," *Foreign Affairs* 59, (1981):617–47. Also see his discussion of the meaning of negotiations in "Reagan's Central American Policy: An Isthmus Restored," in *Central America: Anatomy of a Conflict,* ed. Robert Leiken (New York: Pergamon Press, 1984), 233–57.

12: GRAPPLING WITH CENTRAL AMERICA: FROM CARTER TO REAGAN

Chapters 12, 13, and 14 result from a joint effort. The editor who took primary responsibility for each chapter is listed first, the other authors are listed alphabetically. We would like to thank the other contributors for helping us formulate the arguments in this section over the course of many meetings. We would also like to thank the following people, who read chapters 12, 13, and 14 in manuscript and offered many valuable comments and suggestions during two roundtable sessions at the Overseas Development Council: Richard Feinberg, who hosted the roundtables in addition to participating in them, Cynthia Aronson, Peter Bell, Margaret Daly Hayes, Louis Goodman, Peter Hakim, Abraham Lowenthal, Theodore Moran, Richard Nuccio, Scott Palmer, Wayne Smith, and Viron P. Vaky.

1. "The President's Address at Commencement Exercises at the University of Notre Dame, May 22, 1977," *Presidential Documents: Jimmy Carter,* vol. 13, no. 22 (Washington, D.C.: Government Printing Office, 1977), 744.

2. The Commission on United States–Latin American Relations (the Linowitz Commission) produced two reports: *The Americas in a Changing World* (New York: Quadrangle, 1975); and *The United States and Latin America: Next Steps* (New York: Center for Inter-American Relations, 1976).

3. On the notion of hegemonic presumption, see Abraham F. Lowenthal, "The United States and Latin America: Ending the Hegemonic Presumption," *Foreign Affairs* 55, (Fall 1976):199–213.

4. For an excellent description and evaluation of the Carter administration's human rights policy in Latin America, see Richard E. Feinberg, "U.S. Human Rights Policy: Latin America," *International Policy Report* 6, (October 1980).

5. For an excellent history of the human rights issue see Lars Schoultz, *Human Rights and United States Policy Toward Latin America* (Princeton: Princeton University Press, 1981).

6. For a more detailed examination of the Carter administration's response to the insurrection against Somoza, see William M. LeoGrande, "The United States and the Nicaraguan Revolution," in *Nicaragua in Revolution,* ed. Thomas W. Walker (New York: Praeger, 1982), 63–78.

7. "Crisis in Nicaragua," *Washington Post,* 29 August 1978.

8. The administration was also hamstrung by the activities of Congressmen Charles Murphy (D-Texas) and John Murphy (D-New York), close friends of Somoza, who repeatedly held key legislation (including the implementing legislation for the Panama Canal treaties) hostage to Carter's policy toward Nicaragua. William M. LeoGrande, "The United States and the Nicaraguan Revolution," in *Nicaragua in Revolution,* 63–82.

9. Richard E. Feinberg, "The Recent Rapid Redefinitions of U.S. Interests and Diplomacy in Central America," in *Central America: International Dimensions of the Crisis,* ed. Richard E. Feinberg (New York: Holmes and Meier, 1982), 58–84.

10. Karen DeYoung, "Somoza Says U.S. is Pressing His Overthrow," *Washington Post*, 31 January 1979.

11. *Statement of Secretary of State Cyrus Vance at the OAS Meeting of Foreign Ministers, June 21, 1979* (Washington, D.C.: U.S. Department of State, 1979).

12. Bernard Gwertzman, "A Painful Decision for Carter," *New York Times*, 22 June 1979; Graham Horey, "OAS Resists U.S. Viewpoint," *New York Times*, 25 June 1979.

13. For a discussion of this debate, see John M. Goshko, "U.S. Debates Aid to Latin American Rightists to Bar Takeovers," *Washington Post*, 2 August 1979.

14. The best summary statement of the policy is *Statement by Assistant Secretary of State Viron P. Vaky before the Subcommittee on Inter-American Affairs, U.S. House of Representatives, September 11, 1979* (Washington, D.C.: U.S. Department of State, 1979).

15. An account of the Nicaragua aid package's odyssey through Congress appears in LeoGrande, 73–76.

16. For a more detailed discussion of Carter's policy toward El Salvador, see William M. LeoGrande and Carla Anne Robbins, "Oligarchs and Officers: The Crisis in El Salvador," *Foreign Affairs* 58, (Summer 1980).

17. The Republican Party Platform called for halting U.S. aid to "Marxist" Nicaragua and helping the Nicaraguan people "restore democracy." Key Reagan advisers were on record attacking Carter for having "lost" Nicaragua and for blocking the efforts of the "nationalist" far right in El Salvador to regain power; they called for Washington to be more willing to use military force against Cuban-Soviet expansion. Committee of Santa Fe, *A New Inter-American Policy for the Eighties* (Washington, D.C.: The Council, 1980).

18. The most complete account of this view and its institutional expression in the Committee on the Present Danger is Jerry W. Sanders, *Peddlers of Crisis* (Boston: South End Press, 1983).

19. Among Reagan's more outlandish statements was the following: "The Soviet Union underlies all the unrest that is going on. If they weren't engaged in this game of dominoes, there wouldn't be any hot spots in the world." Quoted in Ronnie Dugger, "Ronald Reagan and the Imperial Presidency," *The Nation*, 1 November 1980, 430–36.

20. In an article published just before the 1980 election, several Reagan advisers implied that some of the people responsible for Carter's Latin American policy were under the influence, consciously or not, of the Cuban intelligence service. Roger Fontaine et al., "Castro's Specter," *Washington Quarterly* (Autumn 1980):-3–27.

21. Jeane Kirkpatrick, "Dictatorships and Double Standards," *Commentary* (November 1979):34–45.

22. *Ibid.*

23. Committee of Santa Fe, *A New Inter-American Policy*.

24. Bernard Gwertzman, "El Salvador: A Test Issue," *New York Times*, 14 February 1981; John M. Goshko, "U.S. Prepares to Aid Salvador in First Test of Reagan Policy," *Washington Post*, 14 February 1981.

25. "The Staff Struggle for President's Attention," *Washington Post*, 28 February 1981.

26. Gwertzman, "El Salvador: A Test Issue"; Goshko, "U.S. Prepares to Aid Salvador."

27. John M. Goshko, "State Dept. Shifts, Seeks to Cool Off Salvador Publicity," *Washington Post*, 13 March 1981.

28. By 1985, the administration was more or less publicly providing support to insurgencies against "Communist" regimes in Nicaragua, Cambodia, and Afghanistan, and was pushing Congress to repeal the 1975 prohibition on covert operations in Angola.

29. "A Secret War for Nicaragua," *Newsweek*, 8 November 1982, and Philip Taubman, "Congressman Faults Support by U.S. for Anti-Sandinistas," *New York Times*, 8 April 1983.

30. Perhaps the clearest declarations of the rollback position were given by Undersecretary of Defense Fred C. Iklé, who called for military victory for the forces of democracy in Central America and rejected any solution that would allow for the maintenance of a "Communist" Nicaragua, since that would require a partitioning of Central America on the model of Eastern Europe. See, for example, "Remarks of Fred C. Iklé, 12 September 1983," News Release No. 450–83, U.S. Department of Defense; and "Remarks of Fred C. Iklé, 16 November 1983," News Release No. 566–83, U.S. Department of Defense.

31. Don Oberdorfer, "More U.S. Effort Yields Less Result," *Washington Post*, 4 March 1982.

32. Marlise Simons, "Mexico Warns Against Attack on Nicaragua," *Washington Post*, 25 November 1981.

33. Reagan, when asked whether it was his intent to overthrow the Nicaragua government, answered that he sought to "remove" its "present structure," which he characterized as communist. Hedrick Smith, "President Asserts His Goal is to Remove Sandinista Regime," *New York Times*, 2 February 1985. Secretary of State Shultz in a speech to the American Bar Association warned that if Congress refused to aid the contras, direct U.S. military action might have to be taken against Nicaragua. Bernard Gwertzman, "Shultz in Warning on Combat Troops for Latin Region," *New York Times*, 24 May 1985.

34. See Chapter 3 for a discussion of this approach.

35. Michael Getler, "U.S. Pumps in Arms, Widens Training to Rescue El Salvador," *Washington Post*, 5 March 1982.

36. Hedrick Smith, "Reagan Uses Joint Session in Attempt to Rescue His Central America Policy," *New York Times*, 27 April 1983.

37. Bernard Weinraub, "Friction Reported Over Latin Policy," *New York Times*, 10 March 1983.

38. For the text of this speech, see President Ronald Reagan, "Central America: Defending Our Vital Interests," *Current Policy* no. 482 (Washington, D.C.: U.S. Department of State, 1983).

39. "Congressmen Attacked Over El Salvador Stand," *New York Times*, 5 May 1983.

40. Henry Kissinger et al., *Report of the National Bipartisan Commission on Central America* (Washington, D.C.: Government Printing Office, 1984).

41. This was the gist of the Foreign Assistance Authorization reported to the House floor by the Foreign Affairs Committee. These provisions, however, were deleted on the floor and replaced by a Republican substitute (the "Broomfield Amendment") that gave the administration virtually everything it had asked for in the region. "Congress Primed to Keep Salvador Aid Flowing," *Congressional Quarterly Weekly Report*, 18 August 1984.

42. Don Oberdorfer, "Shultz Backs off Attack on Meddling Congress," *Washington Post*, 24 May 1985.

43. "House, in Dramatic Shift, Backs 'Contra' Aid," *Congressional Quarterly Weekly Report*, 15 June 1985.

44. William M. LeoGrande, *Public Opinion and Central America* (Washington, D.C.: Washington Office on Latin America, 1984).

45. Ibid., 2.

46. On opinion in Europe see Andrew Pierre, ed., *Central America as a European-American Issue* (New York: Council on Foreign Relations, 1985).

47. For a detailed discussion of how the United States created the infrastructure necessary to support an invasion of Nicaragua, see Joel Brinkley, "Nicaragua and U.S. Options: An Invasion is Openly Discussed," *New York Times*, 4, 5 June 1985.

48. This was the conclusion reached by the General Accounting Office in a study of the military construction completed by the Pentagon during military exercises in Honduras. See "Pentagon Erred in Use of Latin Funds, GAO Says," *Washington Post*, 25 June 1984.

13: THE FAILURE OF THE HEGEMONIC STRATEGIC VISION

1. For two important discussions of the hegemonic presumption in U.S. foreign policy see Abraham Lowenthal, "The United States and Latin America: Ending the Hegemonic Presumption," *Foreign Affairs* 55, (October 1979):199–213; and Abraham Lowenthal, "Ronald Reagan and Latin America: Coping with Hegemony in Decline," in *The Eagle Defiant*, ed. Kenneth A. Oye, Robert J. Lieber, and Donald Rothchild, (Boston: Little Brown, 1983), 311–36. For a more detailed historical discussion, see also Walter LaFeber, *Inevitable Revolutions: The United States in Cenral America*, Expanded Ed. (New York: W.W. Norton, 1984).

2. William A. Williams, *Empire as a Way of Life* (Oxford: Oxford University Press, 1980), 61–62.

3. Thomas L. Karnes, ed., *Readings in: The Latin American Policy of the United States* (Tucson, Ariz.: University of Arizona Press, 1972), 38–40.

4. Gaddis Smith, "The Legacy of Monroe's Doctrine," *New York Times Magazine*, 9 September 1984.

5. Karnes, *Latin American Policy*, 190–91.

6. Secretary of State Knox sought to paint U.S. actions with the brush of moral authority when in 1909 he described the United States as having a "moral right to prevent Panama from getting into a controversy with any government which might eventually require the United States to take part in the controversy and support Panama." Cited in J. Llyod Mecham, *A Survey of United States–Latin American Relations* (Boston: Houghton Mifflin, 1965), 314.

7. Cited in Richard Millett, "Central American Paralysis," *Foreign Policy*, no. 39 (Summer 1980):101.

8. Cited in Samuel Flagg Bemis, *The Latin-American Policy of the United States: A Historical Interpretation* (New York: W.W. Norton, 1967), 167.

9. *Christian Science Monitor*, 4 February 1936.

10. Graham H. Stuart and James L. Tigner, *Latin America and the United States*, 6th ed. (Englewood Cliffs, N.J.: Prentice-Hall, 1975), 512.

11. Cited ibid., 805.

12. See *Foreign Relations of the United States (1952–1954)*, vol. 4 of *The American Republics* (Washington, D.C.: Department of State) 264–306.

13. Shortly after leaving office, Nicholas Katzenbach made the comment that the Johnson administration had been successful in achieving its goals in Latin America, especially in the area of development. When asked how he could support that contention in the face of the dramatic increase in authoritarianism and repression between 1963 and 1969, he snapped back, "We kept the commies out, didn't we." Personal discussion, New York University, February 1969.

14. That notion, so strong in John Foster Dulles's thinking, was given renewed emphasis most recently in the Kissinger Commission report.

15. Cited in Richard Immerman, *The CIA and Guatemala: The Foreign Policy of Intervention* (Austin: University of Texas Press, 1982), 147. Dulles's logic, Immerman rightly points out, was that "no country in Latin America could voluntarily embrace communism" as "indigenous Communism did not exist." This position was echoed in the Kissinger Commission Report over three decades later; the commission accepted that indigenous revolution was no threat to the United States, but they ruled out leftist revolutions as indigenous. See William M. LeoGrande, "Through the Looking Glass: The Report of the National Bipartisan Commission on Central America," *World Policy Journal* 1, (Winter 1984): 257–64.

16. Lowenthal, "Ronald Reagan and Latin America," 325.

DOUGLAS C. BENNETT is an associate professor of political science at Temple University. He is coauthor (with Kenneth Sharpe) of *The State Versus Transnational Corporations: The Political Economy of the Mexican Automobile Industry* (Princeton University Press, 1985).

MORRIS J. BLACHMAN is an associate professor of government and international studies at the University of South Carolina. He has written on U.S. foreign policy and Latin America and has consulted on numerous projects with both governmental and nongovernmental agencies. His publications include *Terms of Conflict: Ideology in Latin American Politics.*

COLE BLASIER, a professor of political science at the University of Pittsburgh, is the author of *The Giant's Rival, the USSR and Latin America* and *The Hovering Giant, U.S. Responses to Revolutionary Change in Latin America*. Once a foreign service officer in Belgrade, Bonn, and Moscow, he initiated the U.S./USSR exchange in Latin American studies. Blasier is president-elect of the Latin American Studies Association.

THOMAS JOHN BOSSERT teaches political science at Sarah Lawrence College and at the Harvard School of Public Health. With over ten years of research experience in Central America, he has published on the state and public policy—in particular health policy—in *Comparative Politics, Political Science Quarterly*, and in Thomas W. Walker, ed., *Nicaragua: The First Five Years* (Praeger, 1985).

MARTIN DISKIN is a professor of anthropology at Massachusetts Institute of Technology. He has researched rural populations in Mexico and Central America for the past twenty-five years. His publications have addressed agrarian reform in El Salvador and U.S. foreign policy in Central America. Most recently he edited *Trouble in Our Backyard* (Pantheon, 1984).

DENNIS GILBERT is an associate professor of sociology at Hamilton College and a visiting associate professor at Cornell University. Since 1982, his research and writing have been devoted to Nicaragua. He is currently completing a book on the Sandinista revolution.

RONALD G. HELLMAN is a professor in the Ph.D. program in sociology and director of the Bildner Center for Western Hemisphere Studies at the Graduate School and University Center, City University of New York. Among his publications are *Terms of Conflict: Ideology in Latin American Politics* and *Politics of Compromise: Coalition Government in Colombia.*

TERRY KARL is an assistant professor of government at Harvard University and is currently a visiting scholar in the Department of Political Science at the University of California, Berkeley. She has written numerous articles on Central America, Venezuela, and Cuba and is completing a book on the impact of oil booms on oil-exporting countries.

WILLIAM M. LEOGRANDE is an associate professor of political science in the School of Government and Public Administration at The American University in Washington, D.C. He is the author of *Cuba's Policy in Africa, 1959–1980* and has written widely in the field of Latin American politics and U.S. relations with Latin

America for such journals as *Foreign Affairs, Foreign Policy, World Policy, Problems of Communism,* and *The Latin American Research Review.*

RICHARD S. NEWFARMER was a senior fellow at the Overseas Development Council at the time this chapter was written. He is currently an economist in the Latin American Region of the World Bank. (The views expressed in his chapter do not necessarily reflect official policy of the World Bank). He served on the economics faculty at the University of Notre Dame from 1977 to 1980; he is editor of *From Gunboats to Diplomacy* and *Profits, Progress, and Poverty* and has authored numerous journal articles on Latin American economics.

LARS SCHOULTZ is a professor of political science at the University of North Carolina at Chapel Hill. He is the author of *Human Rights and United States Policy Toward Latin America* and coeditor of *Latin America, the United States and the Inter-American System.*

KENNETH E. SHARPE is an associate professor of political science at Swarthmore College. He has over five years of fieldwork experience in Mexico, Central America, and the Caribbean. He is the author of *Peasant Politics: Struggle in a Dominican Village* and coauthor (with Douglas Bennett) of *Transnational Corporations and the Mexican State: The Political Economy of the Mexican Automobile Industry.*

PHILIP L. SHEPHERD is an assistant professor in the Department of Marketing and Environment at Florida International University, Miami, Florida. In 1981 he served as assistant director of the Peace Corps Training Center in Tegucigalpa, Honduras. He has written several articles on U.S.-Honduran relations.

PETER H. SMITH is a professor of history and political science at the Massachusetts Institute of Technology. He has written extensively on the political dynamics of Argentina and Mexico, and he has recently turned his attention to U.S.-Mexican relations. His latest book is *Modern Latin America,* coauthored with Thomas E. Skidmore. In 1981 Smith served as president of the Latin American Studies Association.

ROBERT TRUDEAU is an associate professor of political science at Providence College. He has over three years field work experience in Central America and was a Fulbright Lecturer in Guatemala in 1980. He has written numerous papers on Guatemala, one of which appears in Richard Newfarmer, ed., *From Gunboats to Diplomacy.*